T0093397

Ethics of Data and Analytics

Ethics of Data and Analytics

Concepts and Cases

Kirsten Martin

CRC Press
Taylor & Francis Group
Boca Raton London New York

CRC Press is an imprint of the
Taylor & Francis Group, an **informa** business
AN AUERBACH BOOK

First Edition published 2022
by CRC Press
6000 Broken Sound Parkway NW, Suite 300, Boca Raton, FL 33487-2742

and by CRC Press
4 Park Square, Milton Park, Abingdon, Oxon, OX14 4RN

© 2022 Taylor & Francis Group, LLC
CRC Press is an imprint of Taylor & Francis Group, LLC

ISBN: 978-1-032-21731-4 (hbk)
ISBN: 978-1-032-06293-8 (pbk)
ISBN: 978-1-003-27829-0 (ebk)

DOI: 10.1201/9781003278290

Typeset in Garamond
by Deanta Global Publishing Services, Chennai, India

Contents

Introduction

Lemonade Insurance uses a bot, which they call AI Jim, to detect if their users are filing fraudulent claims. Lemonade reported that "when a user files a claim, they record a video on their phone and explain what happened. Our AI carefully analyzes these videos for signs of fraud. It can pick up non-verbal cues that traditional insurers can't, since they don't use digital claims process. This ultimately helps us lower our loss ratios (aka, how much we pay out in claims vs how much we take in), and our overall operating costs."[1] In filings with the federal government, Lemonade Insurance wrote that AI Jim "handles the entire claim through resolution in approximately a third of cases, paying the claimant or declining the claim without human intervention."[2]

As data analytics and AI are introduced to more of our spaces, including filing an insurance claim, how do we judge the program as being good or bad, just or unjust, ethical or unethical? What criteria and evidence should we use, and who would be responsible for the program's decisions? In the case of Lemonade Insurance, how could performing facial and emotional analysis as their users are submitting a claim adversely affect their claimants? What does it mean for this program to be "accurate" and for it to be successful? For Lemonade, the program was good because they saw an improvement in loss ratios or their ability to pay less in claims. Were the claims denied actually legitimate?

Scope

Data analytics is the use of tools by researchers and practitioners to extract meaningful conclusions from data sets. And these tools to extract meaning—algorithms, statistical analysis, artificial intelligence, machine learning—have dominated discourse in industry, the press, and academic research. Algorithms are rules to make sense of something more complicated: Sometimes they are coded with if-then statements, sometimes through statistical models, sometimes they are developed through machine learning. This "terminological anxiety," as Nick Seaver calls it, is due to the way these concepts cross disciplinary boundaries. Data analysts, data scientists, and computer scientists can be found in all types of industries working on analyzing data including banking, pharmaceuticals, automobile, satellites, education, Big Tech, etc. Seaver notes that "a data scientist working at Facebook in 2017, a university mathematician working on a proof in 1940, and a doctor establishing treatment procedures in 1995 may all claim, correctly, to be working on 'algorithms'"[3] (p. 2).

Here, *data analytics* includes basic algorithms and statistical analysis as well as more complicated machine learning. The ethics of data and analytics includes the ethics of algorithms, statistics, artificial intelligence, machine learning, and all other types of analytical tools.

The ethics of data and analytics, in many ways, is no different than any endeavor to find the "right" answer. When business chooses a supplier, funds a new product, or hires an employee, managers are making decisions with moral implications. If Lemonade Insurance implemented new rules for their human claims adjusters, we would examine if the rules were ethical, fair, efficient, accurate, etc. The decisions in business, like all decisions, have a moral component in that people can benefit or be harmed, rules are followed (or not), people are treated (un)fairly, rights are enabled or diminished, etc.

However, data analytics does introduce wrinkles or moral hurdles in how we think about the ethics of these programs. Questions of accountability, privacy, surveillance, bias, and power stretch our standard tools to examine whether a decision is good, ethical, or just. To deal with these questions, we require additional frameworks to understand what is wrong and what could be better.

In addition, the speed and abstraction of data analytics provide less time to think through the moral implications of a given situation. Cathy O'Neill, in *Weapons of Math Destruction*, calls these feedback loops,[4] where models are developed on existing data, applied to new situations thereby creating new data, which is then fed back in as training data to create updated models based on newly created data. Not only are these programs repeating patterns of the past, but as my favorite computer scientist puts it, AI *aggressively* repeats patterns in the data set. Machine learning models aggressively rely on patterns identified in the data and while also reinforce them in use as if they are policy. These programs are policies on steroids by ingesting data (created by policies of the past) only to quickly apply an updated model on present data subjects and then feed those outputs quickly back into the model. In fact, that is the point of AI: making decisions faster and with fewer humans involved.

Third, the subject of these data analytics decisions, the key stakeholder *most* impacted by how a data analytics program is designed, frequently has only a tangential relationship with the companies designing the program. For example, hiring programs, designed to judge applicants' employability, rarely prioritize job applicants; the company buying the program is a key stakeholder whereas the job applicants have no financial relationship with either the developer or user of the program. This distance—emotional, physical, financial—between those who feel the sharp edge of being categorized and those who design and develop the value-laden data analytics programs leads to recurring issues of power in the deployment of these systems. *Those that are most affected are not party to the design, development, and deployment of those technologies and their interests are not necessarily taken into consideration.* This distance between those most impacted by a program and those who design and develop the programs also pressure tests our standard approaches to business ethics where we focus is on those with relationships to the company: customers, employees, suppliers, community, etc.

Finally, we face the prevailing and mistaken belief that these data analytics programs are unbiased and neutral or at least better than the human alternative.[5] Coverage of machine learning is full of headlines such as "Want less-biased decisions? Use Algorithms"[6] and a product like "The Neutral" that uses AI and machine learning to validate new sources.[7] This reliance on technology to provide an authoritative Answer is not novel, as we learn in Chapter 1. Philosopher John Dewey called this our quest for certainty where we gravitate to less ambiguity, because we find ambiguity "objectionable." This quest to rid ourselves of objectionable ambiguity "has no warrant of success and is itself perilous" (p. 178). In fact, our mistaken belief to think we know The

Answer, according to Dewey (p. 164), "gets in its own way, frustrating its own intent."[8] Instead, he considers knowing as a form of engagement with the world, muddling our way through, where the answers we see along the way need to be continually investigated and questioned.

The approach taken here is not the search for a new, different *Answer* or to ban all technology in favor of human decision-making. Rather, here we take an approach that parallels Philosopher Richard Rorty's:[9] taking a more skeptical, ironic approach to our current answers and vocabulary, and identifying and having solidarity with others. Applying this to our endeavor to understand the ethics of data and analytics, we do not prioritize one set of concepts or theories (these theories are called "vocabularies" by Rorty), but offer multiple ethical approaches as ways to engage with current problems to find better solutions. We work through cases to understand those marginalized by data analytics programs as well as those empowered by them.

The Problem of Business

Data analytics does introduce interesting wrinkles as we work to identify better approaches. Engineering schools have integrated (or attempted to integrate) ethics into their curriculum for decades. In practice, it is impossible to develop "ethically aware scientists and engineers" without acknowledging the organizational pressures they will face in companies. According to Science and Technology Studies Professor Langdon Winner,

> what good will it do to nourish this moral sensibility and then place the individual in an organizational situation that mocks the very idea of responsible conduct? To pretend that the whole matter can be settled in the quiet reflections of one's soul while disregarding the context in which the most powerful opportunities for action are made available is a fundamental misunderstanding of the quality genuine responsibility must have.[10]

Whether in a business school or working in a company, the interests of powerful stakeholders with existing relationships to a company are very clear and very loud. In other words, I am not going to dwell on the fact that revenue matters—we know that. To counter the emphasis on corporate power, we will foreground expertise of communities affected by the AI/ML systems[11] and address the issue of corporations as being pressured to be myopically profit focused. In turns out, this is a choice *some* companies make. But not all.

Themes

Three themes run throughout the book. First, *data analytics programs are value-laden* in that technologies create moral consequences, reinforce or undercut ethical principles, and enable or diminish rights and dignity. This places an additional focus on the role of developers in their incorporation of values in the design of data analytics programs. Ben Green suggests that data analysts see themselves as *political actors* "engaged in normative constructions of society and, as befits political practice, evaluate their work according to its downstream impacts on people's lives."[12] For Cathy O'Neill, a data scientist "should see herself as a facilitator of ethical conversations and a translator of the resulting ethical decisions into formal code. In other words, she wouldn't make all the ethical choices herself, but rather raise the questions with a larger and hopefully receptive group."[13]

Second, *design is critical*. Sometimes, any type of automation is morally objectionable.[14] And we do cover uses of data analytics that may be irredeemable. However, the majority of the cases we examine, and the purpose of the theoretical frameworks included, is to improve the design and development of data analytics programs. Focusing on design and development has been done in regards to privacy and engineering in general—Professor Katie Shilton introduced the idea of value-levers that are prompts that open up conversations about privacy and ethics with computer scientists and app developers.[15] Professor Woodrow Hartzog focuses on the responsibility of designers in respecting privacy in their design decisions.[16] Computer scientists have designed model cards to facilitate reporting how trained machine learning models perform against benchmarks across different groups of people and how the model was designed to be used.[17] In all these cases, researchers are arguing that design decisions are not only value-laden but also important because design *inscribes*[18] values into technology that are harder to change once developed and deployed. This is not to say that everything is solved in design: technical design solutions limit us to what is technically possible.[19] However, design and development is one mechanism of governance.

Third, *data analytics, AI, and machine learning is about power*. Data analytics programs allocate things: who is let in to a university or a store, who is allowed on a flight, who is sentenced to prison, and for how long. Missing from many conversations about bias and transparency is how data analytics reinforces power relationships. In other words, the discussion of power—who has it, who gets to keep it, who is marginalized—weaves throughout the chapters, theories, and cases. Within the computer science and fairness community, Barabas et al.'s call for researchers to examine the larger structural forces at play with AI systems "in order to deal directly with issues of power and domination in their work."[20] Here, when we talk about fairness, we talk about tyranny and the least fortunate. When we talk about surveillance, we talk about subjects being controlled by a more powerful actor. When we talk through ethical frameworks, we focus on critical theories that question power structures and defaults assumptions and seek to emancipate the marginalized.

Design of Book

At its roots, this book was designed assuming that the ethics of data and analytics can be taught. In her book, *Engineering Ethics*, Professor Deborah Johnson notes, "To suppose that ethics can only be taught in childhood and that nothing after that can affect a person's moral thinking or moral behavior seems not to acknowledge or appreciate how people engage in ethical decisions."[21] Teaching ethics includes teaching new theoretical frameworks, providing the vocabulary and space to practice talking about ethical issues, and reinforcing the skill to identify the moral implications of a given decision or program. All that takes exposure and practice, which we aim to accomplish here through exposure to original writings on each topic as well as the space to "practice" applying those idea on cases.

This book can be seen as extending a history of teaching ethics to technologists and engineers[22] as well as teaching ethics in business. I was fortunate to have learned from the best in both fields: Deborah Johnson in engineering ethics and Pat Werhane and Ed Freeman in business ethics.[23] I have also straddled both worlds: I studied engineering for my undergraduate degree and designed/coded for my first job before going back for my MBA and a PhD in business ethics.

That does not mean there are not challenges in teaching the ethics of data and analytics. AI ethics education can rely on a form of "exclusionary pedagogy" where the focus is on technical tools and computational approaches to biases and fairness, thereby dismissing alternative ways of knowing and thinking from the humanities.[24] To combat that problem, we rely heavily on law, philosophy, political theorists, computer science, business ethics, etc. By including so many different approaches to examining the ethics of data and analytics, the hope is that the reader is better able to identify the problems in a given AI or machine learning program by asking constructive questions. As John Dewey summarized, *"a problem well put is a problem half-solved."*[25] My goal is to provide you the tools to better define the problems which will get you more than half way to a solution. In this book, we cover:

1. Value-Laden Biases in Data Analytics.
2. Ethical Theories and Data Analytics.
3. Privacy, Data, and Shared Responsibility.
4. Surveillance and Power.
5. The Purpose of the Corporation and Data Analytics.
6. Fairness and Justice in Data Analytics.
7. Discrimination and Data Analytics.
8. Creating Outcomes and Accuracy in Data Analytics.
9. Gamification, Manipulation, and Data Analytics.
10. Transparency and Accountability in Data Analytics.
11. Ethics, AI, Research, and Corporations.

How to Read This Book

Each chapter includes an introduction that provides an overview of the topic and explains why the specific readings and cases were chosen. This would include the tensions or disagreements in scholarship in that area and the topic's importance in studying the ethics of data and analytics. If you want to know more about a section, each introduction includes references to seminal, important scholars in that area. These introductions also give an overview or summary of the theory that is included in the conceptual articles. It may help to read the introduction for a given chapter, then read the conceptual excerpts, and then read the introduction again. Particularly those who are new to the area.

In reading the cases, you may have specific questions assigned. In general, the following questions may help guide your reading of each case:

1. What was the purpose of this program? What problem was it trying to solve?
2. What went wrong? Why are people now upset?
3. Who gains power from the use of this program? Who benefits? Who is marginalized?
4. Who designed the program? How does this answer fit with your answers to #3?
5. What would you do differently? What design decisions would you change to make the program better?
6. Given the readings and the cases for a chapter, what question(s) would you ask of any data analytics program you see in the future?

Each conceptual reading provides a framework to analyze the related cases as well. The chapter summary highlights the main points of the authors and gives some background on the excerpt included. This also includes a statement such as "In analyzing a data analytics program given this reading, one would examine if the program ..." and then enumerated points one would make in applying that theory. I also include questions for the cases to guide your reading.

Conclusion

The goal of this book is to provide the reader an opportunity to

- Examine the role and responsibilities of design and development in the ethics of data and analytics
- Develop conceptual tools and moral vocabulary to analyze the ethical dimensions of data and analytics
- Situate data analytics within the scope of business ethics and the pressures of companies' values
- Identify types of ethical issues within each stage of data analytics
- Develop the capacity to have constructive conversations about ethical dilemmas of data analytics
- Understand the current issues in AI/ML/Predictive Analytics in the language of business and business ethics
- Learn to ask good questions of any data analytics program in order to identify the possible moral quandaries and ethical implications

I hope you enjoy this book as much as I enjoyed designing, writing, and editing the project!

Notes

1. Twitter Lemonade_Inc., 5/24/2021. https://twitter.com/LeifTietje/status/1397569072724946953. They then deleted these tweets here. https://twitter.com/Lemonade_Inc/status/1397564442720747520. Sara Morrison, "A Disturbing, Viral Twitter Thread Reveals How AI-Powered Insurance Can Go Wrong," *Vox* (2021), May 27, 2021. https://www.vox.com/recode/22455140/lemonade-insurance-ai -twitter
2. Rachel Metz, "This $5 Billion Insurance Company Likes to Talk Up Its AI. Now It's in a Mess over It," *CNN* (2021). https://www.cnn.com/2021/05/27/tech/lemonade-ai-insurance/index.html
3. Nick Seaver, "Algorithms as Culture: Some Tactics for the Ethnography of Algorithmic Systems," *Big Data & Society* 4, no. 2 (2017): 2053951717738104.
4. Cathy O'Neil, *Weapons of Math Destruction: How Big Data Increases Inequality and Threatens Democracy* (New York: Crown Publishing Group, 2016).
5. Danielle Keats Citron and Frank Pasquale, "The Scored Society: Due Process for Automated Predictions," *Washington & Lee Law Review* 89 (2014). 1-33
6. Alex Miller, "Want Less-Biased Decisions? Use Algorithms," *Harvard Business Review* (2018). https://hbr.org/2018/07/want-less-biased-decisions-use-algorithms
7. Global Newswire. 2020. "The Neutral: Unbiased News from Journalists, Powered by AI, Launches 'Free Forever' Business Model to Support Journalism." https://www.yahoo.com/now/neutral-unbiased-news-journalists-powered-100010564.html.
8. J. Dewey, "The Quest for Certainty," in *The Later Works of John Dewey (1925–1953)* (Vol. 10), edited by J. A. Boydston (Carbondale, IL: Southern Illinois University Press, 1929).
9. Richard Rorty, *Contingency, Irony, and Solidarity* (Cambridge University Press, 1989). Cambridge.
10. Langdon Winner, *Autonomous Technology: Technics-Out-of-Control as a Theme in Political Thought* (MIT Press, 1978), 304. Cambridge (MA).
11. Luke Stark, Daniel Greene, and Anna Lauren Hoffmann, "Critical Perspectives on Governance Mechanisms for AI/ML Systems," in Roberge J., Castelle M. (eds) *The Cultural Life of Machine Learning* (Palgrave Macmillan, Cham, 2021), 272.

12. Ben Green, "Data Science as Political Action: Grounding Data Science in a Politics of Justice," *ArXiv Preprint ArXiv:1811.03435*, 2018.

13. Cathy O'Neil, "The Ethical Data Scientist," *Slate*, February 4, 2016. http://www.slate.com/articles/technology/future_tense/2016/02/how_to_bring_better_ethics_to_data_science.html

14. See Annette Zimmerman, "Stop Building Bad AI," in *Redesigning AI*, edited by Daron Acemoglu. Zimmerman separately argues AI may be objectionable in contexts with historical structural injustices (Zimmermann, Annette and Lee-Stronach, Chad (Accepted: 2021) Proceed with Caution. *Canadian Journal of Philosophy*). And argues that automation is "intrinsically" objectionable when, among other reasons, (i) cases in which automation expresses morally objectionable negligence; (ii) cases in which automation expresses disrespect …" in a working paper. More casually, Professor Woodrow Hartzog is Twitter (and academically) famous for saying "Ban it" for almost every mention of facial recognition technology.

15. Katie Shilton, "Values Levers: Building Ethics into Design," *Science, Technology, & Human Values* 38, no. 3 (2013): 374–397; Woodrow Hartzog, *Privacy's Blueprint: The Battle to Control the Design of New Technologies* (Harvard University Press, 2018). Cambridge MA

16. Hartzog, *Privacy's Blueprint: The Battle to Control the Design of New Technologies.*

17. Margaret Mitchell et al., "Model Cards for Model Reporting," in *Proceedings of the Conference on Fairness, Accountability, and Transparency*, 2019, 220–229.

18. Madeleine Akrich, "The Description of Technological Objects," in *Shaping Technology/Building Society: Studies in Sociotechnical Change*, edited by Wiebe Bijker and John Law (Cambridge, MA: MIT Press, 1992), 205–224.

19. Stark, Greene, and Hoffman see AI governance through tools, principles, regulations/standards, human rights, and/or securitization. Stark, Greene, and Hoffmann, "Critical Perspectives on Governance Mechanisms for AI/ML Systems."

20. Chelsea Barabas et al., "Studying Up: Reorienting the Study of Algorithmic Fairness around Issues of Power," in *Proceedings of the 2020 Conference on Fairness, Accountability, and Transparency*, 2020, 167–176.

21. Deborah G. Johnson, *Engineering Ethics* (Yale University Press, 2020). New Haven

22. Anna Lauren Hoffmann and Katherine Alejandra Cross, "Teaching Data Ethics: Foundations and Possibilities from Engineering and Computer Science Ethics Education," 2021. http://hdl.handle.net/1773/46921

23. In fact, the approach this book takes—allowing the reader to hear from the author themselves in the form of excerpts and then applying their ideas to actual cases—is patterned on a (famous) business ethics book by Pat Werhane and Tom Donaldson. Thomas Donaldson and Patricia Hogue Werhane, *Ethical Issues in Business a Philosophical Approach* (Prentice Hall, 1996). Upper Saddle River, NJ

24. Inioluwa Deborah Raji, Morgan Klaus Scheuerman, and Razvan Amironesei, "You Can't Sit with Us: Exclusionary Pedagogy in AI Ethics Education," in *Proceedings of the 2021 ACM Conference on Fairness, Accountability, and Transparency*, 2021, 515–525.

25. p. 112. J. Dewey, "Logic: The Theory of Inquiry," in *The Later Works of John Dewey (1925–1953)* (Vol. 10), edited by J. A. Boydston (Carbondale, IL: Southern Illinois University Press, 1938).

VALUE-LADEN BIASES IN DATA ANALYTICS

Who is responsible for the outcomes of an analytics program that tracks the facial expressions of therapy patients? Is the program itself responsible? Does Lemonade Insurance's AI Jim "act" when it makes decisions about fraudulent claims? Or, as some may argue, are these programs neutral and any bad decisions are more the product of society and human decisions?

The goal of this chapter is to examine how technologies—including computer programs and data analytics—have biases or preferences. The discussion about whether technology *does* things or *has* preferences emanates from a concern as to who is responsible for outcomes. In other words, when an organization or individual uses data analytics, who is responsible for the outcome? The arguments traditionally fall into two camps: those that focus on the technology as the actor that "does" things and is at fault (technological determinists) and those that focus on the users of that technology as determining the outcome (social determinists). The readings chosen take a different approach by acknowledging the value-laden biases of technology—including data analytics—while preserving the ability of humans to control the design, development, and deployment of technology.

For *technological determinists*, technology is the primary actor of the story and some even argue that technology has an internal guiding force that propels the development and use of technology and shapes society. As such, technology is to "blame" for the outcome. Strident technological determinists frequently see technology as having an internal dynamic that leads the best technology to survive in the market. This faction within computer science argues that the ethical evaluation of technology is not appropriate since it may curtail development. The technological imperative frames technologies as almost inevitable and outside all societal control; a technological determinist also believes that technology always is correct.[1] Accordingly, technology should be adopted for the good of society.[2] For example, in an argument against scholars who have highlighted the dangers of using artificial intelligence and predictive analytics without regard to their biases or moral implications, Alex Miller, in "Want Less-Biased Decisions? Use Algorithms," lists the ways AI *could* be an improvement because humans are bad at decisions (true—we aren't great[3]). His argument joins a common refrain that technology, because it can be an improvement if designed properly, is then always improvement.[4] For data analytics, we hear technological determinist arguments when the algorithm or program is the main actor in the paragraph or the sentence. For example, "The algorithm decided …" or "the program categorized …" For AI Jim, who is already given a name (!), Lemonade Insurance reports the good that AI Jim has done for the company.

For *social determinists*, society is the main actor of the story, constructing technology and determining the outcome. If a technology is not performing correctly, then a social determinist would point to the many ways that people created that technology and decided how it would be used. For social determinists, what matters is not technology itself but the social or economic system in which it is embedded. We hear social determinist arguments in data analytics in two ways. First, we may blame the use of the program rather than the design of the program. Second, others may acknowledge that the *data* may be flawed ("it's just the data") and that society needs to get better data for data analysts.

This tension—between social determinists and technological determinists—is important to the ethics of data analytics because who is "acting" or doing things is normally who we look to hold responsible for those acts. For social determinist approaches (blaming the data or the users or society), a data analytics program is neutral. Society is then responsible for the moral implications of the technology in use; we can't blame developers. For technological determinists, data analytics programs have biases and *do* things; but these *inherent* biases are then outside the influence of society, designers, and developers. Interestingly, both mistakenly absolve developers—computer scientists, data analysts, and corporations—of their responsibility. Whether you hold the users of the algorithm responsible (social determinism) or the algorithm itself (technological determinism), you are not holding responsible the systems of power—the government or company—that designed, developed, and implemented the program.

However, scholars (not surprisingly) have tackled this issue with a variety of approaches.

Wiebe Bijker is a classic social constructionist (not a determinist!). In *Of Bicycles, Bakelites, and Bulbs*, Bijker explores "both the social shaping of technology and the technical shaping of society." Rather than claiming all technologies are socially determined or all technologies determine society, Bijker notes that "some artifacts [technologies for Bijker] are more obdurate, harder to get around and to change, than others." This allows for some data analytics programs to be more obscure, "harder to get around" than others.

Deborah Johnson,[5] directly addresses the question underlying many of these determinist debates—who can be responsible for the moral implications of technology. Johnson's "claim is that those who argue for the moral agency (or potential moral agency) of computers are right in recognizing the moral importance of computers, but they go wrong in viewing computer systems as independent, autonomous moral agents."[6] This difference is important for some in that the term moral agent carries with it the idea of *responsibility for their actions*. In this case, Johnson's account allows us to identify the important value-laden biases and moral implications of data analytics programs but not attribute some sort of intentional agency that would lie outside human control. For Johnson, society still is responsible for the technology they design, develop, and bring to market.

For the readings included here, the authors are attempting to acknowledge both the ability of humans to create and mold technology for their purposes as well as the value-laden biases or politics technology has once it is in use. In terms of data analytics, this would mean that developers and designers make value-laden decisions in the development and coding of AI, predictive analytics, and machine learning (any type of analytics), and those decisions have moral implications for the use of that program.

Summary of Readings

In the classic article "Do Artifacts Have Politics?"[7] Professor Langdon Winner explicitly addresses the ideas of social and technological determinism. Winner argues against the idea that "what matters is not technology itself but the social or economic system in which it is embedded," which he sees as an overreaction to the claim that technology has an internal dynamic which, "unmediated by any other influence, molds society to fit its patterns." In other words, Winner sees social determinism as an overcorrection to claims of technological determinism. He argues that technology, designed and used by society, has politics or "arrangements of power and authority in human associations." Winner uses examples such as bridges, molding machines, and tomato harvesters to explore the many ways technology can have politics both in the decision to have the technology and in the specific features in their design. For example, he notes the size and cost required of the tomato harvester as requiring an amount of capital to enter the market that drove out smaller farmers. This was not a "plot" according to Winner, but the "social process in which scientific knowledge, technological invention, and corporate profit reinforce each other in deeply entrenched patterns that bear the unmistakable stamp of political and economic power." Winner's concepts are just as applicable today: e.g., the critiques of large language models we examine in the next chapter as environmentally damaging and concentrated in labs that are funded by large corporations.

When applying Winner's approach to a data analytics case, we would (1) identify the politics or arrangements of power and authority in a program, and (2) examine whether the technology is "inherently political" or due to specific design choices that "can affect the relative distribution of power, authority, privilege in a community." Winner may see the tracking and recording of patients as shifting power to the company and away from the patient as they do not have visibility or control over the data collected. Some may go further to question if this type of surveillance has inherent politics (according to Winner), as it requires a particular distribution of authority to collect, protect, and analyze data as opposed to the alternative of a therapist taking notes.

In "Bias in Computer Systems,"[8] Professors Batya Friedman and Helen Nissenbaum explore the idea of "bias" in computer systems. Friedman and Nissenbaum define bias as the tendency of a computer system to "systematically and unfairly discriminate" against certain individuals. In other words, computer systems have preferences as to who "gets" certain things and who does not. The authors focus specifically on *systematic* discrimination and do not include random mistakes or glitches. In addition, and unlike Winner, Friedman and Nissenbaum define bias as something that is unethical or unfair—and therefore undesirable. Where Winner sees politics as either good or bad (we would need to analyze the degree to which they are good/bad), Friedman and Nissenbaum, in this reading, define bias as a bad thing.[9] Friedman and Nissenbaum identify three types of biases based on how the bias emerges: preexisting biases, technical biases, and emergent biases. These categories are helpful in thinking through how a data analytics program, such as Lemonade Insurance's AI Jim, could have biases (a) preexisting in the data, then (b) embedded in the chosen technology, and (c) emergent in how the program is then deployed on live data. While Winner appears to argue that all technologies have good and bad politics, Friedman and Nissenbaum see a possibility of a technology with no bias. This is an important distinction and one that many may not agree with now: that a data analytics program could ever be free of biases. In analyzing a data analytics program according to Friedman and Nissenbaum, one would examine if the program has the types of biases outlined in the article: preexisting, technical, and emergent.

In an excerpt from Gabbrielle Johnson's "Are Algorithms Value-Free?"[10] Johnson pushes us to think more deeply as to the many ways algorithms are not value-free. Some in computer science and data analytics acknowledge that the *data* we use is problematic, thus shifting the "blame" for the moral implications of data analytics model to either (a) those who created the data some time ago or (b) those who used the algorithm on live data in use. The refrain "it's just bad data," however, masks that developing data analytics models, from AI or programming, is a value-laden enterprise or, as Johnson says, "values are constitutive of the very operation of algorithmic decision-making." It is not possible to be "value-free." In doing so, Johnson relies on a body of work in philosophy of science, including Rudner who is included later in this volume, that examines the value-laden-ness of science and technology: those who argue "values can shape not only the research programs scientists choose to pursue, but also practices internal to scientific inquiry itself, such as evidence gathering, theory confirmation, and scientific inference."[11]

Finally, in "Algorithmic Bias and Corporate Responsibility: How Companies Hide behind the False Veil of the Technological Imperative," I tie determinist arguments explicitly to corporate responsibility of value-laden design. I argue that judging AI on efficiency and pretending algorithms are inscrutable produces a veil of the technological imperative which shields corporations from being held accountable for the value-laden decisions made in the design, development, and deployment of algorithms. I outline how the development of algorithms should be critically examined and offer a way to pierce the (false) veil of the technological imperative.

Related Cases

Two cases provide an opportunity to apply the readings. First, the Stanford vaccine algorithm case centers on an allocation algorithm designed to prioritize medical workers to receive the COVID-19 vaccine. When frontline workers were not prioritized—including interns—the university blamed a "very complex algorithm" for the outcome. The article details the design decisions and factors included in the allocation program.

The second case is about a medical algorithm trained on historical data and designed to predict the amount of care a given patient would require. The goal was to triage or prioritize patients in need for additional treatment. The algorithm ended up underestimating the health needs of the sickest Black patients and amplified existing racial disparities in health care. Both cases offer an opportunity to see Winner's politics and Friedman and Nissenbaum's biases in action—as well as the value-laden decisions of the developers of the analytics program.

Notes

1. In its most extreme form, technology, including data analytics, machine learning, and AI, is seen as outside society and detached from the imperfections of the "real world." You hear this when computer scientists and data analysts frame their work as not including dealing with the imperfections and ambiguity of the world. Interestingly, no other engineering discipline takes this approach since dealing with the real world is the job of engineers.
2. Hans Jonas, in "Toward a Philosophy of Technology" (1979), envisions a restless technology moving forward under the pressure of competition.
3. For example, we continue to face racism in lending decisions and bias against women and minorities in hiring decisions. Vanessa Gail Perry, "A Loan at Last? Race and Racism in Mortgage Lending," in *Race in the Marketplace* (Springer, 2019), 173–192; Corinne A. Moss-Racusin et al., "Science Faculty's Subtle Gender Biases Favor Male Students," *Proceedings of the National Academy of Sciences* 109, no. 41 (2012): 16474–16479; Natasha Quadlin, "The Mark of a Woman's Record: Gender and Academic Performance in Hiring," *American Sociological Review* 83, no. 2 (2018): 331–360; (In asking humans to assess resumes, Quadlin found "high-achieving men are called back significantly more often than high-achieving women—at a rate of nearly 2-to-1. … Employers value competence and commitment among men applicants, but instead privilege women applicants who are perceived as likeable."). Judd

B. Kessler, Corinne Low, and Colin D. Sullivan, "Incentivized Resume Rating: Eliciting Employer Preferences without Deception," *American Economic Review*, 109, no. 11 (2019): 3713–3744. (Kessler et al. found "employers hiring in STEM fields penalized résumés with minority or female names. The effect was big: These candidates were penalized by the equivalent of 0.25 GPA points, based solely on the name at the top of the résumé. That meant such a candidate needed a 4.0 GPA to get the same rating as a white male with a 3.75." https://www.latimes.com/opinion/story/2020-07-24/employment -hiring-bias-racism-resumes?_amp=true

4. Alex Miller. 2018. "What Less-Biased Decisions? Use Algorithms" *Harvard Business Review*.

5. Deborah G. Johnson. "Computer systems: Moral entities but not moral agents." *Ethics and Information Technology*, 8, no. 4 (2006): 195–204.

6. She is arguing that moral agency requires one who (1) is an agent with an intentional state (2) does actually act (3) in a way that is tied to the intentional state, and (4) which has an effect (5) on another person. Johnson argues that computer systems meet requirements 2–5 and are, therefore, moral entities. She does not go so far as to argue (1) since "computer systems do not have intendings to act, they do have intentionality."

7. Langdon Winner, "Do Artifacts Have Politics?," *Daedalus* 109, no. 1 (1980): 121–136.

8. Batya Friedman and Helen Nissenbaum, "Bias in Computer Systems," *ACM Transactions on Information Systems (TOIS)* 14, no. 3 (1996): 330–347.

9. Currently, bias is usually seen as neither good nor bad but an attribute of the data and outcome that needs to be measured and assessed.

10. Gabbrielle Johnson, "Are Algorithms Value-Free? Feminist Theoretical Virtues in Machine Learning," *Journal Moral Philosophy*, n.d.

11. Deborah Johnson, who above said computer programs are moral entities but not moral agents, makes a similar declaration: "Computer systems, then, 'are as much a part of social practices as are automobiles, toasters, and playpens. Computer systems are not naturally occurring phenomena; they could not and would not exist were it not for complex systems of knowledge and complex social, political, cultural institutions; computer systems are produced, distributed, and used by people engaged in social practices and meaningful pursuits.'"

Chapter 1.1

This Is the Stanford Vaccine Algorithm That Left out Frontline Doctors[*]

Eileen Guo and Karen Hao

The university hospital blamed a "very complex algorithm" for its unequal vaccine distribution plan. Here's what went wrong.

When resident physicians at Stanford Medical Center—many of whom work on the front lines of the COVID-19 pandemic—found out that only seven out of over 1,300 of them had been prioritized for the first 5,000 doses of the covid vaccine, they were shocked. Then, when they saw who else had made the list, including administrators and doctors seeing patients remotely from home, they were angry.

During a planned photo op to celebrate the first vaccinations taking place on Friday, December 18, at least 100 residents showed up to protest. Hospital leadership apologized for not prioritizing them, and blamed the errors on "a very complex algorithm."

"Our algorithm, that the ethicists, infectious disease experts worked on for weeks … clearly didn't work right," Tim Morrison, the director of the ambulatory care team, told residents at the event in a video posted online.

Many saw that as an excuse, especially since hospital leadership had been made aware of the problem on Tuesday—when only five residents made the list—and responded not by fixing the algorithm, but by adding two more residents for a total of seven.

"One of the core attractions of algorithms is that they allow the powerful to blame a black box for politically unattractive outcomes for which they would otherwise be responsible," Roger McNamee, a prominent Silicon Valley insider turned critic, wrote on Twitter. "But *people* decided who would get the vaccine," tweeted Veena Dubal, a professor of law at the University

---

[*] Guo, Eileen and Karen Hao. 2020. This is the Stanford vaccine algorithm that left out frontline doctors. *MIT Technology Review.* 12/21/2020. https://www.technologyreview.com/2020/12/21/1015303/stanford-vaccine -algorithm/ Reprinted with permission.

DOI: 10.1201/9781003278290-2

of California, Hastings, who researches technology and society. "The algorithm just carried out their will."

But what exactly was Stanford's "will"? We took a look at the algorithm to find out what it was meant to do.

How the Algorithm Works

The slide describing the algorithm (Figure 1.1.1) came from residents who had received it from their department chair. It is not a complex machine learning algorithm (which are often referred to as "black boxes") but a rules-based formula for calculating who would get the vaccine first at Stanford. It considers three categories: "employee-based variables," which have to do with age; "job-based variables"; and guidelines from the California Department of Public Health. For each category, staff received a certain number of points, with a total possible score of 3.48. Presumably, the higher the score, the higher the person's priority in line. (Stanford Medical Center did not respond to multiple requests for comment on the algorithm over the weekend.)

The employee variables increase a person's score linearly with age, and extra points are added to those over 65 or under 25. This gives priority to the oldest and youngest staff, which disadvantages residents and other frontline workers who are typically in the middle of the age range.

Job variables contribute the most to the overall score. The algorithm counts the prevalence of COVID-19 among employees' job roles and department in two different ways, but the difference between them is not entirely clear. Neither the residents nor two unaffiliated experts we asked to review the algorithm understood what these criteria meant, and Stanford Medical Center did not respond to a request for comment. They also consider the proportion of tests taken by job role as a percentage of the medical center's total number of tests collected.

What these factors do not take into account is exposure to patients with COVID-19, say residents. That means the algorithm did not distinguish between those who had caught covid from

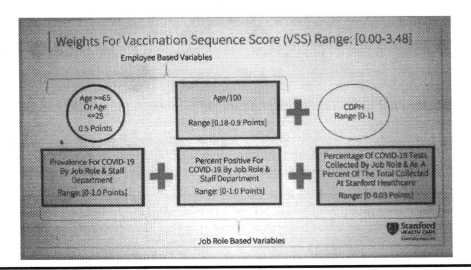

Figure 1.1.1   Slide from Stanford depicting the contributing factors of the Vaccination Sequence Score used to prioritize staff for the COVID-19 vaccine.

patients and those who got it from community spread—including employees working remotely. And, as first reported by ProPublica, residents were told that because they rotate between departments rather than maintain a single assignment, they lost out on points associated with the departments where they worked.

The algorithm's third category refers to the California Department of Public Health's vaccine allocation guidelines. These focus on exposure risk as the single highest factor for vaccine prioritization. The guidelines are intended primarily for county and local governments to decide how to prioritize the vaccine, rather than how to prioritize between a hospital's departments. But they do specifically include residents, along with the departments where they work, in the highest-priority tier.

It may be that the "CDPH range" factor gives residents a higher score, but still not high enough to counteract the other criteria.

"Why Did They Do It That Way?"

Stanford tried to factor in a lot more variables than other medical facilities, but Jeffrey Kahn, the director of the Johns Hopkins Berkman Institute of Bioethics, says the approach was overcomplicated. "The more there are different weights for different things, it then becomes harder to understand—'Why did they do it that way?'" he says.

Kahn, who sat on Johns Hopkins' 20-member committee on vaccine allocation, says his university allocated vaccines based simply on job and risk of exposure to COVID-19.

He says that decision was based on discussions that purposefully included different perspectives—including those of residents—and in coordination with other hospitals in Maryland. Elsewhere, the University of California San Francisco's plan is based on a similar assessment of risk of exposure to the virus. Mass General Brigham in Boston categorizes employees into four groups based on department and job location, according to an internal email reviewed by *MIT Technology Review*.

"It's really important [for] any approach like this to be transparent and public … and not something really hard to figure out," Kahn says. "There's so little trust around so much related to the pandemic, we cannot squander it."

Algorithms are commonly used in health care to rank patients by risk level in an effort to distribute care and resources more equitably. But the more variables used, the harder it is to assess whether the calculations might be flawed.

For example, in 2019, a study published in *Science* showed that 10 widely used algorithms for distributing care in the US ended up favoring white patients over Black ones. The problem, it turned out, was that the algorithms' designers assumed that patients who spent more on health care were sicklier and needed more help. In reality, higher spenders are also richer, and more likely to be white. As a result, the algorithm allocated less care to Black patients with the same medical conditions as white ones.

Irene Chen, an MIT doctoral candidate who studies the use of fair algorithms in health care, suspects this is what happened at Stanford: the formula's designers chose variables that they believed would serve as good proxies for a given staffer's level of covid risk. But they didn't verify that these proxies led to sensible outcomes, or respond in a meaningful way to the community's input when the vaccine plan came to light on Tuesday last week. "It's not a bad thing that people had thoughts about it afterward," says Chen. "It's that there wasn't a mechanism to fix it."

A Canary in the Coal Mine?

After the protests, Stanford issued a formal apology, saying it would revise its distribution plan.

Hospital representatives did not respond to questions about who they would include in new planning processes, or whether the algorithm would continue to be used. An internal email summarizing the medical school's response, shared with *MIT Technology Review*, states that neither program heads, department chairs, attending physicians, nor nursing staff were involved in the original algorithm design. Now, however, some faculty are pushing to have a bigger role, eliminating the algorithms' results completely and instead giving division chiefs and chairs the authority to make decisions for their own teams.

Other department chairs have encouraged residents to get vaccinated first. Some have even asked faculty to bring residents with them when they get vaccinated, or delay their shots so that others could go first.

Some residents are bypassing the university health-care system entirely. Nuriel Moghavem, a neurology resident who was the first to publicize the problems at Stanford, tweeted on Friday afternoon that he had finally received his vaccine—not at Stanford, but at a public county hospital in Santa Clara County.

"I got vaccinated today to protect myself, my family, and my patients," he tweeted. "But I only had the opportunity because my public county hospital believes that residents are critical frontline providers. Grateful."

Chapter 1.2

Racial Bias in a Medical Algorithm Favors White Patients over Sicker Black Patients*

Carolyn Y. Johnson

Scientists discovered racial bias in a widely used medical algorithm that predicts which patients will have complex health needs.

A widely used algorithm that predicts which patients will benefit from extra medical care dramatically underestimates the health needs of the sickest Black patients, amplifying long-standing racial disparities in medicine, researchers have found.

The problem was caught in an algorithm sold by a leading health services company, called Optum, to guide care decision-making for millions of people. But the same issue almost certainly exists in other tools used by other private companies, nonprofit health systems, and government agencies to manage the health care of about 200 million people in the United States each year, the scientists reported in the journal *Science*.

Correcting the bias would more than double the number of Black patients flagged as at risk of complicated medical needs within the health system the researchers studied, and they are already working with Optum on a fix. When the company replicated the analysis on a national data set of 3.7 million patients, they found that Black patients who were ranked by the algorithm as equally as in need of extra care as white patients were much sicker: They collectively suffered from 48,772 additional chronic diseases.

"It's truly inconceivable to me that anyone else's algorithm doesn't suffer from this," said Sendhil Mullainathan, a professor of computation and behavioral science at the University of

* Johnson, Carolyn. 2019. Racial bias in a medical algorithm favors white patients over sicker black patients. *Washington Post*. October 24, 2019. https://www.washingtonpost.com/health/2019/10/24/racial-bias-medical -algorithm-favors-white-patients-over-sicker-black-patients/ Reprinted with permission.

DOI: 10.1201/9781003278290-3

Chicago Booth School of Business, who oversaw the work. "I'm hopeful that this causes the entire industry to say, 'Oh, my, we've got to fix this.'"

The algorithm wasn't intentionally racist—in fact, it specifically excluded race. Instead, to identify patients who would benefit from more medical support, the algorithm used a seemingly race-blind metric: how much patients would cost the health-care system in the future. But cost isn't a race-neutral measure of health-care need. Black patients incurred about $1,800 less in medical costs per year than white patients with the same number of chronic conditions; thus the algorithm scored white patients as equally at risk of future health problems as Black patients who had many more diseases.

Machines increasingly make decisions that affect human life, and big organizations—particularly in health care—are trying to leverage massive data sets to improve how they operate. They utilize data that may not appear to be racist or biased but may have been heavily influenced by long-standing social, cultural, and institutional biases—such as health-care costs. As computer systems determine which job candidates should be interviewed, who should receive a loan or how to triage sick people, the proprietary algorithms that power them run the risk of automating racism or other human biases.

In medicine, there is a long history of Black patients facing barriers to accessing care and receiving less effective health care. Studies have found Black patients are less likely to receive pain treatment, potentially lifesaving lung cancer surgery or cholesterol-lowering drugs, compared with white patients. Such disparities probably have complicated roots, including explicit racism, access problems, lack of insurance, mistrust of the medical system, cultural misunderstandings or unconscious biases that doctors may not even know they have.

Mullainathan and his collaborators discovered that the algorithm they studied, which was designed to help health systems target patients who would have the greatest future health-care needs, was predicting how likely people were to use a lot of health care and rack up high costs in the future. Since Black patients generally use health care at lower rates, the algorithm was less likely to flag them as likely to use lots of health care in the future.

The algorithm would then deepen that disparity by flagging healthier white patients as in need of more intensive care management.

"Predictive algorithms that power these tools should be continually reviewed and refined, and supplemented by information such as socio-economic data, to help clinicians make the best-informed care decisions for each patient," Optum spokesman Tyler Mason said. "As we advise our customers, these tools should never be viewed as a substitute for a doctor's expertise and knowledge of their patients' individual needs."

Ruha Benjamin, an associate professor of African American studies at Princeton University, drew a parallel to the way Henrietta Lacks, a young African American mother with cervical cancer, was treated by the medical system. Lacks is well known now because her cancer cells, taken without her consent, are used throughout modern biomedical research. She was treated in a separate wing of Johns Hopkins Hospital in an era when hospitals were segregated. Imagine if today, Benjamin wrote in an accompanying article, Lacks were "digitally triaged" with an algorithm that didn't explicitly take into account her race but underestimated her sickness because it was using data that reflected historical bias to project her future needs. Such racism, though not driven by a hateful ideology, could have the same result as earlier segregation and substandard care.

"I am struck by how many people still think that racism always has to be intentional and fueled by malice. They don't want to admit the racist effects of technology unless they can pinpoint the bigoted boogeyman behind the screen," Benjamin said.

The software used to predict patients' need for more intensive medical support was an outgrowth of the Affordable Care Act, which created financial incentives for health systems to keep people well instead of waiting to treat them when they got sick. The idea was that it would be possible to simultaneously contain costs and keep people healthier by identifying those patients at greatest risk for becoming very sick and providing more resources to them. But because wealthy, white people tend to utilize more health care, such tools could also lead health systems to focus on them, missing an opportunity to help some of the sickest people.

Christine Vogeli, director of evaluation and research at the Center for Population Health at Partners HealthCare, a nonprofit health system in Massachusetts, said when her team first tested the algorithm, they mapped the highest scores in their patient population and found them concentrated in some of the most affluent suburbs of Boston. That led them to use the tool in a limited way, supplementing it with other information, rather than using it off the shelf.

"You're going to have to make sure people are savvy about it … or you're going to have an issue where you're only serving the richest and most wealthy folks," Vogeli said.

Such biases may seem obvious in hindsight, but algorithms are notoriously opaque because they are proprietary products that can cost hundreds of thousands of dollars. The researchers who conducted the new study had an unusual amount of access to the data that went into the algorithm and what it predicted.

They also found a relatively straightforward way to fix the problem. Instead of just predicting which patients would incur the highest costs and use the most health care in the future, they tweaked the algorithm to make predictions about their future health conditions.

Suchi Saria, a machine learning and health-care expert at Johns Hopkins University, said the study was fascinating because it showed how, once a bias is detected, it can be corrected. Much of the scientific study of racial disparities in medicine provides evidence of inequity, but correcting those problems might require sweeping social and cultural changes, as well as individual behavior changes by thousands of providers. In contrast, once a flawed algorithm is identified, the bias can be removed.

"The cool thing is we could easily measure the bias that has historically existed, switch out the algorithm and correct the bias," Saria said. The trickier part may be developing an oversight mechanism that will detect the biases in the first place.

Saria said that one possibility is that data experts could potentially test companies' algorithms for bias, the same way security firms test whether a companies' cyber defenses are sufficient.

Chapter 1.3

Excerpt from Do Artifacts Have Politics?*

Langdon Winner

In controversies about technology and society, there is no idea more provocative than the notion that technical things have political qualities. At issue is the claim that the machines, structures, and systems of modern material culture can be accurately judged not only for their contributions of efficiency and productivity, not merely for their positive and negative environmental side effects, but also for the ways in which they can embody specific forms of power and authority. Since ideas of this kind have a persistent and troubling presence in discussions about the meaning of technology, they deserve explicit attention.

Writing in *Technology and Culture* almost two decades ago, Lewis Mumford gave classic statement to one version of the theme, arguing that

> from late neo lithic times in the Near East, right down to our own day, two technologies have recurrently existed side by side: one authoritarian, the other democratic, the first system-centered, immensely powerful, but inherently unstable, the other man-centered, relatively weak, but resourceful and durable.[1]

This thesis stands at the heart of Mumford's studies of the city, architecture, and the history of technics, and mirrors concerns voiced earlier in the works of Peter Kropotkin, William Morris, and other nineteenth century critics of industrialism. More recently, antinuclear and prosolar energy movements in Europe and America have adopted a similar notion as a centerpiece in their arguments. Thus environmentalist Denis Hayes concludes, "The increased deployment of nuclear power facilities must lead society toward authoritarianism. Indeed, safe reliance upon nuclear power as the principal source of energy may be possible only in a totalitarian state." Echoing the views of many proponents of appropriate technology and the soft energy path, Hayes contends

---

* Reprinted with permission from Langdon Winner, *The Whale and the Reactor*, 19–39. Copyright 1986. Chicago: University of Chicago Press. Note: This is an excerpt from the original so footnote and endnote numbering may be modified.

DOI: 10.1201/9781003278290-4

that "dispersed solar sources are more compatible than centralized technologies with social equity, freedom and cultural pluralism."[2]

An eagerness to interpret technical artifacts in political language is by no means the exclusive property of critics of large-scale high-technology systems. A long lineage of boosters have insisted that the "biggest and best" that science and industry made available were the best guarantees of democracy, freedom, and social justice. The factory system, automobile, telephone, radio, television, the space program, and of course nuclear power itself have all at one time or another been described as democratizing, liberating forces. David Lilienthal, in T.V.A.: Democracy on the March, for example, found this promise in the phosphate fertilizers and electricity that technical progress was bringing to rural Americans during the 1940s.[3] In a recent essay, The Republic of Technology, Daniel Boorstin extolled television for "its power to disband armies, to cashier presidents, to create a whole new democratic world democratic in ways never before imagined, even in America."[4] Scarcely a new invention comes along that someone does not proclaim it the salvation of a free society.

It is no surprise to learn that technical systems of various kinds are deeply interwoven in the conditions of modern politics. The physical arrangements of industrial production, warfare, communications, and the like have fundamentally changed the exercise of power and the experience of citizenship. But to go beyond this obvious fact and to argue that certain technologies in themselves have political properties seems, at first glance, completely mistaken. We all know that people have politics, not things. To discover either virtues or evils in aggregates of steel, plastic, transistors, integrated circuits, and chemicals seems just plain wrong, a way of mystifying human artifice and of avoiding the true sources, the human sources of freedom and oppression, justice and injustice. Blaming the hardware appears even more foolish than blaming the victims when it comes to judging conditions of public life.

Hence, the stern advice commonly given to those who flirt with the notion that technical artifacts have political qualities: What matters is not technology itself, but the social or economic system in which it is embedded. This maxim, which in a number of variations is the central premise of a theory that can be called the social determination of technology, has an obvious wisdom. It serves as a needed corrective to those who focus uncritically on such things as "the computer and its social impacts" but who fail to look behind technical things to notice the social circumstances of their development, deployment, and use. This view provides an antidote to naive technological determinism the idea that technology develops as the sole result of an internal dynamic, and then, unmediated by any other influence, molds society to fit its patterns. Those who have not recognized the ways in which technologies are shaped by social and economic forces have not gotten very far.

But the corrective has its own shortcomings; taken literally, it suggests that technical things do not matter at all. Once one has done the detective work necessary to reveal the social origins—power holders behind a particular instance of technological change—one will have explained everything of importance. This conclusion offers comfort to social scientists: it validates what they had always suspected, namely, that there is nothing distinctive about the study of technology in the first place. Hence, they can return to their standard models of social power—those of interest group politics, bureaucratic politics, Marxist models of class struggle, and the like—and have everything they need. The social determination of technology is, in this view, essentially no different from the social determination of, say, welfare policy or taxation.

There are, however, good reasons technology has of late taken on a special fascination in its own right for historians, philosophers, and political scientists; good reasons the standard models of social science only go so far in accounting for what is most interesting and troublesome about the subject. In another place I have tried to show why so much of modern social and political thought contains recurring statements of what can be called a theory of technological politics, an odd mongrel of notions often crossbred with orthodox liberal, conservative, and socialist philosophies.[5] The theory of technological politics draws attention to the momentum of large-scale sociotechnical systems, to the response of modern societies to certain technological imperatives, and to the all too common signs of the adaptation of human ends to technical means. In so doing it offers a novel framework of interpretation and explanation for some of the more puzzling patterns that have taken shape in and around the growth of modern material culture. One strength of this point of view is that it takes technical artifacts seriously. Rather than insist that we immediately reduce everything to the interplay of social forces, it suggests that we pay attention to the characteristics of technical objects and the meaning of those characteristics. A necessary complement to, rather than a replacement for, theories of the social determination of technology, this perspective identifies certain technologies as political phenomena in their own right. It points us back, to borrow Edmund Husserl's philosophical injunction, to the things themselves.

In what follows I shall offer outlines and illustrations of two ways in which artifacts can contain political properties. First are instances in which the invention, design, or arrangement of a specific technical device or system becomes a way of settling an issue in a particular community. Seen in the proper light, examples of this kind are fairly straightforward and easily understood. Second are cases of what can be called inherently political technologies, man-made systems that appear to require, or to be strongly compatible with, particular kinds of political relationships. Arguments about cases of this kind are much more troublesome and closer to the heart of the matter. By "politics," I mean arrangements of power and authority in human associations as well as the activities that take place within those arrangements. For my purposes, "technology" here is understood to mean all of modern practical artifice,[6] but to avoid confusion I prefer to speak of technology, smaller or larger pieces or systems of hardware of a specific kind. My intention is not to settle any of the issues here once and for all, but to indicate their general dimensions and significance.

Technical Arrangements as Forms of Order

Anyone who has traveled the highways of America and has become used to the normal height of overpasses may well find something a little odd about some of the bridges over the parkways on Long Island, New York. Many of the overpasses are extraordinarily low, having as little as nine feet of clearance at the curb. Even those who happened to notice this structural peculiarity would not be inclined to attach any special meaning to it. In our accustomed way of looking at things like roads and bridges we see the details of form as innocuous, and seldom give them a second thought.

It turns out, however, that the two hundred or so low-hanging overpasses on Long Island were deliberately designed to achieve a particular social effect. Robert Moses, the master builder of roads, parks, bridges, and other public works from the 1920s to the 1970s in New York, had these overpasses built to specifications that would discourage the presence of buses on his parkways. According to evidence provided by Robert A. Caro in his biography of Moses, the reasons reflect Moses's social-class bias and racial prejudice. Automobile owning whites of "upper" and "comfortable middle" classes, as he called them, would be free to use the parkways for recreation and commuting. Poor people and Blacks, who normally used public transit, were kept off the roads because the twelve-foot tall buses could not get through the overpasses. One consequence was to limit access of racial minorities and low-income groups to Jones Beach, Moses's widely acclaimed public park. Moses made doubly sure of this result by vetoing a proposed extension of the Long Island Railroad to Jones Beach.[7]

As a story in recent American political history, Robert Moses's life is fascinating. His dealings with mayors, governors, and presidents, and his careful manipulation of legislatures, banks, labor unions, the press, and public opinion are all matters that political scientists could study for years. But the most important and enduring results of his work are his technologies, the vast engineering projects that give New York much of its present form. For generations after Moses has gone and the alliances he forged have fallen apart, his public works, especially the highways and bridges he built to favor the use of the automobile over the development of mass transit, will continue to shape that city. Many of his monumental structures of concrete and steel embody a systematic social inequality, a way of engineering relationships among people that, after a time, becomes just another part of the landscape. As planner Lee Koppleman told Caro about the low bridges on Wantagh Parkway, "The old son-of-a-gun had made sure that buses would never be able to use his goddamned parkways."[8]

Histories of architecture, city planning, and public works contain many examples of physical arrangements that contain explicit or implicit political purposes. One can point to Baron Haussmann's broad Parisian thoroughfares, engineered at Louis Napoleon's direction to prevent any recurrence of street fighting of the kind that took place during the revolution of 1848. Or one can visit any number of grotesque concrete buildings and huge plazas constructed on American university campuses during the late 1960s and early 1970s to defuse student demonstrations. Studies of industrial machines and instruments also turn up interesting political stories, including some that violate our normal expectations about why technological innovations are made in the first place. If we suppose that new technologies are introduced to achieve increased efficiency, the history of technology shows that we will sometimes be disappointed. Technological change expresses a panoply of human motives, not the least of which is the desire of some to have dominion over others, even though it may require an occasional sacrifice of cost cutting and some violence to the norm of getting more from less.

One poignant illustration can be found in the history of nineteenth century industrial mechanization. At Cyrus McCormick's reaper manufacturing plant in Chicago in the middle 1880s, pneumatic molding machines, a new and largely untested innovation, were added to the foundry at an estimated cost of $500,000. In the standard economic interpretation of such things, we would expect that this step was taken to modernize the plant and achieve the kind of efficiencies that mechanization brings. But historian Robert Ozanne has shown why the development must be seen in a broader context. At the time, Cyrus McCormick II was engaged in a battle with the National Union of Iron Molders. He saw the addition of the new machines as a way to "weed out the bad element among the men," namely, the skilled workers who had organized the union local in Chicago.[9] The new machines, manned by unskilled labor, actually produced inferior castings at a higher cost than the earlier process. After three years of use the machines were, in fact, abandoned, but by that time they had served their purpose the destruction of the union. Thus, the story of these technical developments at the McCormick factory cannot be understood adequately outside the record of workers' attempts to organize, police repression of the labor movement in Chicago during that period, and the events surrounding the bombing at Haymarket Square. Technological history and American political history were at that moment deeply intertwined.

In cases like those of Moses's low bridges and McCormick's molding machines, one sees the importance of technical arrangements that precede the use of the things in question. It is obvious that technologies can be used in ways that enhance the power, authority, and privilege of some over others, for example, the use of television to sell a candidate. To our accustomed way of thinking, technologies are seen as neutral tools that can be used well or poorly, for good, evil, or something in between. But we usually do not stop to inquire whether a given device might have been designed and built in such a way that it produces a set of consequences logically and temporally prior to any of its professed uses. Robert Moses's bridges, after all, were used to carry automobiles from one point to another; McCormick's machines were used to make metal castings; both technologies, however, encompassed purposes far beyond their immediate use. If our moral and political language for evaluating technology includes only categories having to do with tools and uses, if it does not include attention to the meaning of the designs and arrangements of our artifacts, then we will be blinded to much that is intellectually and practically crucial.

Because the point is most easily understood in the light of particular intentions embodied in physical form, I have so far offered illustrations that seem almost conspiratorial. But to recognize the political dimensions in the shapes of technology does not require that we look for conscious conspiracies or malicious intentions. The organized movement of handicapped people in the United States during the 1970s pointed out the countless ways in which machines, instruments, and structures of common use buses, buildings, sidewalks, plumbing fixtures, and so forth made it impossible for many handicapped persons to move about freely, a condition that systematically excluded them from public life. It is safe to say that designs unsuited for the handicapped arose more from long-standing neglect than from anyone's active intention. But now that the issue has been raised for public attention, it is evident that justice requires a remedy. A whole range of artifacts are now being redesigned and rebuilt to accommodate this minority.

Indeed, many of the most important examples of technologies that have political consequences are those that transcend the simple categories of "intended" and "unintended" altogether. These are instances in which the very process of technical development is so thoroughly biased in a particular direction that it regularly produces results counted as wonderful breakthroughs by some social interests and crushing setbacks by others. In such cases it is neither correct nor insightful to say, "Someone intended to do somebody else harm." Rather, one must say that the technological deck has been stacked long in advance to favor certain social interests, and that some people were bound to receive a better hand than others.

The mechanical tomato harvester, a remarkable device perfected by re searchers at the University of California from the late 1940s to the present, offers an illustrative tale. The machine is able to harvest tomatoes in a single pass through a row, cutting the plants from the ground, shaking the fruit loose, and in the newest models sorting the tomatoes electronically into large plastic gondolas that hold up to twenty-five tons of produce headed for canning. To accommodate the rough motion of these "factories in the field," agricultural researchers have bred new varieties of tomatoes that are hardier, sturdier, and less tasty. The harvesters replace the system of handpicking, in which crews of farmworkers would pass through the fields three or four times putting ripe tomatoes in lug boxes and saving immature fruit for later harvest.[10] Studies in California indicate that the machine reduces costs by approximately five to seven dollars per ton as compared to hand-harvesting.[11] But the benefits are by no means equally divided in the agricultural economy. In fact, the machine in the garden has in this instance been the occasion for a thorough reshaping of social relationships of tomato production in rural California.

By their very size and cost, more than $50,000 each to purchase, the machines are compatible only with a highly concentrated form of tomato growing. With the introduction of this new method of harvesting, the number of tomato growers declined from approximately four thousand in the early 1960s to about six hundred in 1973, yet with a substantial increase in tons of tomatoes produced. By the late 1970s an estimated thirty-two thousand jobs in the tomato industry had been eliminated as a direct consequence of mechanization.[12] Thus, a jump in productivity to the benefit of very large growers has occurred at a sacrifice to other rural agricultural communities.

The University of California's research and development on agricultural machines like the tomato harvester is at this time the subject of a law suit filed by attorneys for California Rural Legal Assistance, an organization representing a group of farmworkers and other interested parties. The suit charges that University officials are spending tax monies on projects that benefit a handful of private interests to the detriment of farmworkers, small farmers, consumers, and rural California generally, and asks for a court injunction to stop the practice. The University has denied these charges, arguing that to accept them "would require elimination of all research with any potential practical application."[13]

As far as I know, no one has argued that the development of the tomato harvester was the result of a plot. Two students of the controversy, William Friedland and Amy Barton, specifically exonerate both the original developers of the machine and the hard tomato from any desire to facilitate economic concentration in that industry.[14] What we see here instead is an ongoing social process in which scientific knowledge, technological invention, and corporate profit reinforce each other in deeply entrenched patterns that bear the unmistakable stamp of political and economic power. Over many decades agricultural research and development in American land-grant colleges and universities have tended to favor the interests of large agribusiness concerns.[15] It is in the face of such subtly ingrained patterns that opponents of innovations like the tomato harvester are made to seem "antitechnology" or "antiprogress." For the harvester is not merely the symbol of a social order that rewards some while punishing others; it is in a true sense an embodiment of that order.

Within a given category of technological change there are, roughly speaking, two kinds of choices that can affect the relative distribution of power, authority, and privilege in a community. Often the crucial decision is a simple "yes or no" choice are we going to develop and adopt the thing or not? In recent years many local, national, and international disputes about technology have centered on "yes or no" judgments about such things as food additives, pesticides, the building of highways, nuclear reactors, and dam projects. The fundamental choice about an ABM or an SST is whether or not the thing is going to join society as a piece of its operating equipment. Reasons for and against are frequently as important as those concerning the adoption of an important new law.

A second range of choices, equally critical in many instances, has to do with specific features in the design or arrangement of a technical system after the decision to go ahead with it has already been made. Even after a utility company wins permission to build a large electric power line, important controversies can remain with respect to the placement of its route and the design of its towers; even after an organization has decided to institute a system of computers, controversies can still arise with regard to the kinds of components, programs, modes of access, and other specific features the system will include. Once the mechanical tomato harvester had been developed in its basic form, design alteration of critical social significance the addition of electronic sorters, for example changed the character of the machine's effects on the balance of wealth and power in California agriculture. Some of the most interesting research on technology and politics at present focuses on the attempt to demonstrate in a detailed, concrete fashion how seemingly innocuous design features in mass transit systems, water projects, industrial machinery, and other technologies actually mask social choices of profound significance. Historian David Noble is now studying two kinds of automated machine tool systems that have different implications for the relative power of management and labor in the industries that might employ them. He is able to show that, although the basic electronic and mechanical components of the record/playback and numerical control systems are similar, the choice of one design over another has crucial consequences for social struggles on the shop floor. To see the matter solely in terms of cost cutting, efficiency, or the modernization of equipment is to miss a decisive element in the story.[16]

From such examples I would offer the following general conclusions. The things we call "technologies" are ways of building order in our world. Many technical devices and systems important in everyday life contain possibilities for many different ways of ordering human activity. Consciously or not, deliberately or inadvertently, societies choose structures for technologies that influence how people are going to work, communicate, travel, consume, and so forth over a very long time. In the processes by which structuring decisions are made, different people are differently situated and possess unequal degrees of power as well as unequal levels of awareness. By far the greatest latitude of choice exists the very first time a particular instrument, system, or technique is introduced. Because choices tend to become strongly fixed in material equipment, economic investment, and social habit, the original flexibility vanishes for all practical purposes once the initial commitments are made. In that sense technological innovations are similar to legislative acts or political foundings that establish a framework for public order that will endure over many generations. For that reason, the same careful attention one would give to the rules, roles, and relationships of politics must also be given to such things as the building of highways, the creation of television networks, and the tailoring of seemingly insignificant features on new machines. The issues that divide or unite people in society are settled not only in the institutions and practices of politics proper, but also, and less obviously, in tangible arrangements of steel and concrete, wires and transistors, nuts and bolts.

Notes

1. Lewis Mumford, "Authoritarian and Democratic Technics," *Technology and Culture,* 5 (1964): 1–8.
2. Denis Hayes, *Rays of Hope: The transition to a Post-Petroleum World* (New York: W.W. Norton, 1977), pp. 71, 159.
3. David Lilienthal, *T.V.A.: Democracy on the March* (New York: Harper and Brothers, 1944), pp. 72–83.
4. Daniel J. Boorstin, *The Republic of Technology* (New York: Harper & Row, 1978), p. 7.
5. Langdon Winner, *Autonomous Technology: Technics-out-of-Control as a Theme in Political Thought* (Cambridge, Mass.: M.I.T. Press, 1977).
6. The meaning of "technology" I employ in this essay does not encompass some of the broader definitions of that concept found in contemporary literature, for example, the notion of "technique" in the writings of Jaques Ellul. My purpose here are more limited. For a discussion of the difficulties that arise in attempts to define "technology," see Ref. 6, pp. 8–12.
7. Robert A. Caro, *The Power Broker: Robert Moses and the Fall of New York* (New York: Random House, 1974), pp. 318, 481, 514, 546, 951–958.
8. Ibid., p. 952.
9. Robert Ozanne, *A Century of Labor-Management Relations at McCormick and International Harvester* (Madison, Wis.: University of Wisconsin Press, 1967), p. 20.
10. The early history of the tomato harvester is told in Wayne D. Rasmussen, "Advances in American Agriculture: The Mechanical Tomato Harvester as a Case Study," *Technology and Culture,* 9 (1968): 531–543.
11. Andrew Schmitz and David Seckler, "Mechanized Agriculture and Social Welfare: The Case of the Tomato Harvester," *American Journal of Agricultural Economics,* 52 (1970): 569–577.
12. William H. Friedland and Amy Barton, "Tomato Technology," *Society,* 13:6 (September/October 1976). See also William H. Friedland, *Social Sleepwalkers: Scientific and Technological Research in California Agriculture,* University of California, Davis, Department of Applied Behavioral Sciences, Research Monograph No. 13, 1974.
13. *University of California Clip Sheet,* 54:36, May 1, 1979.
14. Friedland and Barton, "Tomato Technology."
15. A history and critical analysis of agricultural research in the land-grant colleges is given in James Hightower, *Hard Tomatoes, Hard Times* (Cambridge, Mass.: Schenkman, 1978).
16. David Noble, "Social Choice in Machine Design: The Case of Automatically Controlled Machine Tools," in *Case Studies in the Labor Process* (New York: Monthly Review Press, forthcoming).

Chapter 1.4

Excerpt from Bias in Computer Systems[*]

Batya Friedman and Helen Nissenbaum

From an analysis of actual cases, three categories of bias in computer systems have been developed: preexisting, technical, and emergent. Preexisting bias has its roots in social institutions, practices, and attitudes. Technical bias arises from technical constraints or considerations. Emergent bias arises in a context of use. Although others have pointed to bias in particular computer systems and have noted the general problem, we know of no comparable work that examines this phenomenon comprehensively and which offers a framework for understanding and remedying it. We conclude by suggesting that freedom from bias should be counted among the select set of criteria—including reliability, accuracy, and efficiency—according to which the quality of systems in use in society should be judged.

Introduction

To introduce what bias in computer systems might look like, consider the case of computerized airline reservation systems, which are used widely by travel agents to identify and reserve airline flights for their customers. These reservation systems seem straightforward. When a travel agent types in a customer's travel requirements, the reservation system searches a database of flights and retrieves all reasonable flight options that meet or come close to the customer's requirements. These options then are ranked according to various criteria, giving priority to nonstop flights, more direct routes, and minimal total travel time. The ranked flight options are displayed for the travel agent. In the 1980s, however, most of the airlines brought before the Antitrust Division of the United States Justice Department allegations of anticompetitive practices by American and United Airlines whose reservation systems—Sabre and Apollo, respectively—dominated the field. It was claimed, among other things, that the two reservations systems are biased (Schfrin 1985).

---

[*] Friedman, Batya, and Helen Nissenbaum. "Bias in computer systems." ACM Transactions on Information Systems (TOIS)14, no. 3 (1996): 330-347. Reprinted with permission. Note: This is an excerpt from the original so footnote and endnote numbering may be modified.

DOI: 10.1201/9781003278290-5

One source of this alleged bias lies in Sabre's and Apollo's algorithms for controlling search and display functions. In the algorithms, preference is given to "on-line" flights, that is, flights with all segments on a single carrier. Imagine, then, a traveler who originates in Phoenix and flies the first segment of a round-trip overseas journey to London on American Airlines, changing planes in New York. All other things being equal, the British Airlines' flight from New York to London would be ranked lower than the American Airlines' flight from New York to London even though in both cases a traveler is similarly inconvenienced by changing planes and checking through customs. Thus, the computer systems systematically downgrade and, hence, are biased against international carriers who fly few, if any, internal US flights, and against internal carriers who do not fly international flights (Fotos 1988; Ott 1988).

Critics also have been concerned with two other problems. One is that the interface design compounds the bias in the reservation systems. Lists of ranked flight options are displayed screen by screen. Each screen displays only two to five options. The advantage to a carrier of having its flights shown on the first screen is enormous since 90% of the tickets booked by travel agents are booked by the first screen display (Taib 1990). Even if the biased algorithm and interface give only a small percent advantage overall to one airline, it can make the difference to its competitors between survival and bankruptcy. A second problem arises from the travelers' perspective. When travelers contract with an independent third party—a travel agent—to determine travel plans, travelers have good reason to assume they are being informed accurately of their travel options; in many situations, that does not happen.

As Sabre and Apollo illustrate, biases in computer systems can be difficult to identify let alone remedy because of the way the technology engages and extenuates them. Computer systems, for instance, are comparatively inexpensive to disseminate, and thus, once developed, a biased system has the potential for widespread impact. If the system becomes a standard in the field, the bias becomes pervasive. If the system is complex, and most are, biases can remain hidden in the code, difficult to pinpoint or explicate, and not necessarily disclosed to users or their clients. Furthermore, unlike in our dealings with biased individuals with whom a potential victim can negotiate, biased systems offer no equivalent means for appeal.

Although others have pointed to bias in particular computer systems and have noted the general problem [Johnson and Mulvey 1993; Moor 1985], we know of no comparable work that focuses exclusively on this phenomenon and examines it comprehensively.

In this article, we provide a framework for understanding bias in computer systems. From an analysis of actual computer systems, we have developed three categories: preexisting bias, technical bias, and emergent bias. Preexisting bias has its roots in social institutions, practices, and attitudes. Technical bias arises from technical constraints or considerations. Emergent bias arises in a context of use. We begin by defining bias and explicating each category and then move to case studies. We conclude with remarks about how bias in computer systems can be remedied.

1. What Is a Biased Computer System?

In its most general sense, the term bias means simply "slant." Given this undifferentiated usage, at times the term is applied with relatively neutral content. A grocery shopper, for example, can be "biased" by not buying damaged fruit. At other times, the term bias is applied with significant moral meaning. An employer, for example, can be "biased" by refusing to hire minorities. In this article we focus on instances of the latter, for if one wants to develop criteria for judging the quality of systems in use—which we do—then criteria must be delineated in ways that speak robustly yet precisely to relevant social matters. Focusing on bias of moral import does just that.

Accordingly, we use the term bias to refer to computer systems that systematically and unfairly discriminate against certain individuals or groups of individuals in favor of others. A system discriminates unfairly if it denies an opportunity or a good or if it assigns an undesirable outcome to an individual or group of individuals on grounds that are unreasonable or inappropriate. Consider, for example, an automated credit advisor that assists in the decision of whether or not to extend credit to a particular applicant. If the advisor denies credit to individuals with consistently poor payment records we do not judge the system to be biased because it is reasonable and appropriate for a credit company to want to avoid extending credit privileges to people who consistently do not pay their bills. In contrast, a credit advisor that systematically assigns poor credit ratings to individuals with ethnic surnames discriminates on grounds that are not relevant to credit assessments and, hence, discriminates unfairly.

Two points follow. First, unfair discrimination alone does not give rise to bias unless it occurs systematically. Consider again the automated credit advisor. Imagine a random glitch in the system which changes in an isolated case information in a copy of the credit record for an applicant who happens to have an ethnic surname. The change in information causes a downgrading of this applicant's rating. While this applicant experiences unfair discrimination resulting from this random glitch, the applicant could have been anybody. In a repeat incident, the same applicant or others with similar ethnicity would not be in a special position to be singled out. Thus, while the system is prone to random error, it is not biased.

Second, systematic discrimination does not establish bias unless it is joined with an unfair outcome. A case in point is the Persian Gulf War, where United States Patriot missiles were used to detect and intercept Iraqi Scud missiles. At least one software error identified during the war contributed to systematically poor performance by the Patriots (Gao 1992). Calculations used to predict the location of a Scud depended in complex ways on the Patriots' internal clock. The longer the Patriot's continuous running time, the greater the imprecision in the calculation. The deaths of at least 28 Americans in Dhahran can be traced to this software error, which systematically degraded the accuracy of Patriot missiles. While we are not minimizing the serious consequence of this systematic computer error, it falls outside of our analysis because it does not involve unfairness.

2. Framework for Analyzing Bias in Computer Systems

We derived our framework by examining actual computer systems for bias. Instances of bias were identified and characterized according to their source, and then the characterizations were generalized to more abstract categories. These categories were further refined by their application to other instances of bias in the same or additional computer systems. In most cases, our knowledge of particular systems came from the published literature. In total, we examined 17 computer systems from diverse fields including banking, commerce, computer science, education, medicine, and law.

The framework that emerged from this methodology is comprised of three overarching categories—preexisting bias, technical bias, and emergent bias. Table 1.4.1 contains a detailed description of each category. In more general terms, they can be described as follows.

2.1 Preexisting Bias

Preexisting bias has its roots in social institutions, practices, and attitudes. When computer systems embody biases that exist independently, and usually prior to the creation of the system, then we say that the system embodies preexisting bias. Preexisting biases may originate in society at

Table 1.4.1   Categories of Bias in Computer System Design

These categories describe ways in which bias can arise in the design of computer systems. The illustrative examples portray plausible cases of bias.

1. Preexisting Bias

Preexisting bias has its roots in social institutions, practices, and attitudes.

When computer systems embody biases that exist independently, and usually prior to the creation of the system, then the system exemplifies preexisting bias. Preexisting bias can enter a system either through the explicit and conscious efforts of individuals or institutions, or implicitly and unconsciously, even in spite of the best of intentions.

> **1.1. Individual**
> Bias that originates from individuals who have significant input into the design of the system, such as the client commissioning the design or the system designer (e.g., a client embeds personal racial biases into the specifications for loan approval software).

> **1.2 Societal**
> Bias that originates from society at large, such as from organizations (e.g., industry), institutions (e.g., legal systems), or culture at large (e.g., gender biases present in the larger society that lead to the development of educational software that overall appeals more to boys than girls).

2. Technical Bias

Technical bias arises from technical constraints or technical considerations.

> **2.1 Computer Tools**
> Bias that originates from a limitation of the computer technology including hardware, software, and peripherals (e.g., in a database for matching organ donors with potential transplant recipients certain individuals retrieved and displayed on initial screens are favored systematically for a match over individuals displayed on later screens).
>
> **2.2 Decontextualized Algorithms**
> Bias that originates from the use of an algorithm that fails to treat all groups fairly under all significant conditions (e.g., a scheduling algorithm that schedules airplanes for take-off relies on the alphabetic listing of the airlines to rank order flights ready within a given period of time).
>
> **2.3 Random Number Generation**
> Bias that originates from imperfections in pseudorandom number generation or in the misuse of pseudorandom numbers (e.g., an imperfection in a random number generator used to select recipients for a scarce drug leads systematically to favoring individuals toward the end of the database).
>
> **2.4 Formalization of Human Constructs**
> Bias that originates from attempts to make human constructs such as discourse, judgments, or intuitions amenable to computers: when we quantify the qualitative, discretize the continuous, or formalize the nonformal (e.g., a legal expert system advises defendants on whether or not to plea bargain by assuming that law can be spelled out in an unambiguous manner that is not subject to human and humane interpretations in context).

(Continued)

Table 1.4.1 (Continued)   Categories of Bias in Computer System Design

3. Emergent Bias Emergent bias arises in a context of use with real users. This bias typically emerges sometime after a design is completed, as a result of changing societal knowledge, population, or cultural values. User interfaces are likely to be particularly prone to emergent bias because interfaces by design seek to reflect the capacities, character, and habits of prospective users. Thus, a shift in context of use may well create difficulties for a new set of users.
3.1 New Societal Knowledge Bias that originates from the emergence of new knowledge in society that cannot be or is not incorporated into the system design (e.g., a medical expert system for AIDS patients has no mechanism for incorporating cutting-edge medical discoveries that affect how individuals with certain symptoms should be treated). **3.2 Mismatch between Users and System Design** Bias that originates when the population using the system differs on some significant dimension from the population assumed as users in the design.
3.2.1 Different Expertise Bias that originates when the system is used by a population with a different knowledge base from that assumed in the design (e.g., an ATM with an interface that makes extensive use of written instructions—"place the card, magnetic tape side down, in the slot to your left"—is installed in a neighborhood with primarily a nonliterate population). **3.2.2 Different Values** Bias that originates when the system is used by a population with different values than those assumed in the design (e.g., educational software to teach mathematics concepts is embedded in a game situation that rewards individualistic and competitive strategies, but is used by students with a cultural background that largely eschews competition and instead promotes cooperative endeavors).

large, in subcultures, and in formal or informal, private or public organizations and institutions. They can also reflect the personal biases of individuals who have significant input into the design of the system, such as the client or system designer. This type of bias can enter a system either through the explicit and conscious efforts of individuals or institutions, or implicitly and unconsciously, even in spite of the best of intentions. For example, imagine an expert system that advises on loan applications. In determining an applicant's credit risk, the automated loan advisor negatively weights applicants who live in "undesirable" locations, such as low-income or high-crime neighborhoods, as indicated by their home addresses (a practice referred to as "red-lining"). To the extent the program embeds the biases of clients or designers who seek to avoid certain applicants on the basis of group stereotypes, the automated loan advisor's bias is preexisting.

2.2 Technical Bias

In contrast to preexisting bias, technical bias arises from the resolution of issues in the technical design. Sources of technical bias can be found in several aspects of the design process, including limitations of computer tools such as hardware, software, and peripherals; the process of ascribing social meaning to algorithms developed out of context; imperfections in pseudorandom number generation; and the attempt to make human constructs amenable to computers, when we quantify the qualitative, discretize the continuous, or formalize the nonformal. As an illustration, consider again the case of Sabre and Apollo described above. A technical constraint imposed by the size of the monitor screen forces a piecemeal presentation of flight options and, thus, makes the algorithm chosen to rank flight options critically important. Whatever ranking algorithm is used, if it systematically places certain airlines' flights on initial screens and other airlines' flights on later screens, the system will exhibit technical bias.

2.3 Emergent Bias

While it is almost always possible to identify preexisting bias and technical bias in a system design at the time of creation or implementation, emergent bias arises only in a context of use. This bias typically emerges sometime after a design is completed, as a result of changing societal knowledge, population, or cultural values. Using the example of an automated airline reservation system, envision a hypothetical system designed for a group of airlines all of whom serve national routes. Consider what might occur if that system was extended to include international airlines. A flight-ranking algorithm that favors online flights when applied in the original context with national airlines leads to no systematic unfairness. However, in the new context with international airlines, the automated system would place these airlines at a disadvantage and, thus, comprise a case of emergent bias. User interfaces are likely to be particularly prone to emergent bias because interfaces by design seek to reflect the capacities, character, and habits of prospective users. Thus, a shift in context of use may well create difficulties for a new set of users.

....

References

Berlins, M. And Hodges, L. 1981. Nationality Bill sets out three new citizenship categories. *The London Times* (Jan. 15), 1, 15.

Corbato, F. J., Merwin-Daggett, M., And Daley, R. C. 1962. An experimental time-sharing system. In Proceedings of the Spring Joint Computer Conference. Spartan Books, 335–344.

Fishlock, T. 1981. Delhi press detect racism in Nationality Bill. *The London Times* (Jan. 20).

Fotos, C. P. 1988. British Airways assails U.S. decision to void CRS agreement with American. *Aviat. Week Space Tech.* (Oct. 24), 78.

Gao. 1992. *Patriot Missile defense: Software problem led to system failure at Dhahran, Saudi Arabia.* GAO/IMTEC-92-26, U.S. General Accounting Office, Washington, D.C.

Graettinger, J. S. And Peranson, E. 1981a. The matching program. *New Engl. J. Med.* 304, 1163–1165.

Graettinger, J. S. And Peranson, E. 1981b. National resident matching program. *New Engl. J. Med.* 305, 526.

Huff, C. And Cooper, J. 1987. Sex bias in educational software: The effect of designers' stereotypes on the software they design. *J. Appl. Soc. Psychol.* 17, 519–532.

Johnson, D. G. And Mulvey, J. M. 1993. *Computer decisions: Ethical issues of responsibility and bias.* Statistics and Operations Res. Series SOR-93–11, Dept. of Civil Engineering and Operations Research, Princeton Univ., Princeton, N.J.

Leith, P. 1986. Fundamental errors in legal logic programming. *Comput. J.* 29, 225–232.

Moor, J. 1985. What is computer ethics? *Metaphilosophy* 16, 266–275.

Ott, J. 1988. American Airlines settles CRS dispute with British Airways. *Aviat. Week Space Tech.* (July 18).

Roth, A. E. 1984. The evolution of the labor market for medical interns and residents: A case study in game theory. *J. Pol. Econ.* 92, 6, 991–1016.

Roth, A. E. 1990. New physicians: A natural experiment in market organization. *Science* 250, (Dec. 14), 1524–1528.

Sergot, M. J., Sadri, F., Kowalski, R. A., Kriwaczek, F., Hammond, P., And Cory, H. T. 1986. The British Nationality Act as a logic program. *Commun. ACM* 29, 370–386.

Shifrin, C. A. 1985. Justice will weigh suit challenging airlines' computer reservations. *Aviat. Week Space Tech.* (Mar. 25), 105–111.

Sudarshan, A. And Zisook, S. 1981. National resident matching program. *New Engl. J. Med.* 305, 525–526.

Taib, I. M. 1990. Loophole allows bias in displays on computer reservations systems. *Aviat. Week Space Tech.* (Feb.), 137.

Williams, K. J., Werth, V. P., And Wolff, J. A. 1981. An analysis of the resident match. *New Engl. J. Med.* 304, 19, 1165–1166.

Chapter 1.5

Excerpt from Are Algorithms Value-Free? Feminist Theoretical Virtues in Machine Learning[*]

Gabbrielle M. Johnson

1. Introduction

According to a 2018 Pew Research Center survey, 40% of people believe that algorithmic decision-making can be objective, free from the biases that plague human decision-making.[1] Reading this result, one might reasonably ask what it really means for an algorithm to be objective and free from bias: what does it mean for an algorithm to be value-free? There are at least three interpretations of this question. On the least sophisticated interpretation, we are asking whether algorithms operate wholly free of any influence of human values. The algorithms—we might answer—are just math, the data on which they operate are just facts; at no point in explaining their operation do we need to make reference to human values whatsoever. This, however, seems obviously false. Problematic social patterns unquestionably exist and are necessarily encoded in the data on which algorithms operate.[2] On a second and slightly more sophisticated interpretation, we might recognize the unavoidable encoding of such patterns in the data, and ask instead whether the algorithms themselves, their designs, are value-free. And here we might answer that even if the data upon which the algorithms operate are shaped by human values, perhaps the engineers are still doing the best with what they are given by making value-free design decisions. On the other hand, we might reason that algorithms often fail to be value-free because their all-too-human engineers are subject

[*] Johnson, G. Forthcoming. "Are Algorithms Value-Free." *Journal of Moral Philosophy*. Reprinted with permission. Note: This is an excerpt from the original so footnote and endnote numbering may be modified.

DOI: 10.1201/9781003278290-6

to worldly pressures that in fact command the importation of human values: say, for example, the pressure to produce the highest profits for one's company. On this reasoning, algorithms could be value-free in principle, however—as a descriptive fact—they are not. There exists still a third interpretation of the question, on which we ask whether it is really possible for algorithms to be value-free even in principle. That is, is it possible for even a superhuman engineer—one impervious to worldly, self-interested pursuits—to produce an algorithm that is value-free? It is this third possibility that occupies me in this paper: when I ask if algorithms are value-free, I am asking whether values are constitutive of the very operation of algorithmic decision-making, such that on no idealized conception could they be value-free.[3]

Debates about at what point (if any) values can and should enter a decision-making procedure have been popular in various areas of philosophy. For example, the issue of to what extent epistemic norms in belief formation could be affected by practical and moral aims has been widely discussed in literature on both pragmatic and moral encroachment.[4] In philosophy of science, prominent debates continue to unfold concerning whether values can shape not only the research programs scientists choose to pursue, but also practices internal to scientific inquiry itself, such as evidence gathering, theory confirmation, and scientific inference.[5] Ultimately, this is a debate about whether values are a constitutive feature of scientific inductions. Like scientific inductions, machine learning programs use evidence (or known data) to form predictions (or generalizations to new phenomena).[6] Thus, there exists a natural but underexplored comparison between debates about objectivity in scientific inquiry and machine learning. In this paper, I take up this comparison by adopting arguments against the value-free ideal in science and extending them to the domain of machine learning. In so doing, I explore the extent to which machine learning algorithms are, can be, or should be value-free.

The literature concerning debates about values in science and the literature surveying philosophical perspectives on the use of machine learning programs are independently extremely vast. Thus, a comprehensive application of the former to the latter is well beyond the scope of any one paper. Instead, the aim of this paper is to build a bridge between two domains I anticipate will have much to contribute to one another. I begin this task by demonstrating how prominent arguments against the notion of scientific objectivity in the form of the problem of induction, underdetermination by evidence, arguments against demarcation, and the argument from inductive risk all straightforwardly apply to simple cases of machine learning use. My hope is that these comparisons will facilitate continued predictive and explanatory exchange between the algorithmic and scientific domains.

...

2. Origins of the Value-Free Ideal

In this section, I want to trace the historical progression of a pursuit of objectivity in scientific inquiry, and explore how it applies to the domain of machine learning. The unifying feature of the two domains is that both rely on induction. I regard as inductive any inference that is ampliative, i.e., that goes beyond the information given in the premises. This includes any inference that is non-deductive, and extends to both enumerative inductions, i.e., those that generalize from known instances to novel instances, and abductions, i.e., inferences to the best explanation. As we'll see, inductive inference is critical to both scientific theorizing and machine learning.

I start by discussing a notion of objectivity in induction that is undoubtably too strong, but seems surprisingly widespread in folk conceptions of scientific practice. This is a form of objectivity that Antony (2001, 2006, 2016)'s calls "Dragnet objectivity." The notion comes from the 1950s-1960s TV cop show Dragnet, in which Los Angeles Police Sgt. Joe Friday disciplines himself "to consider just the facts—the raw, undisputed data of the matter, unadorned with personal speculation and uncorrupted by emotional interest in the case," a strategy encapsulated in his famous catch-phrase "just the facts, Ma'am."[7] Applying this idea to scientific inference, the claim is that scientists should aim to favor hypotheses on the basis of "just the facts," without the influence of personal values. Applying this idea to machine learning, one can easily see why algorithmic decision-making is thought to be more objective than human decision-making, since such programs are built to learn from raw data without the interference of personal speculation or emotional interest.

Although it makes for a quaint picture, Dragnet objectivity is an impossible model of scientific inquiry. The reason is that "raw data" by itself inevitably underdetermines various conclusions we might draw about some subject matter.[8] If ever we considered literally just the facts, we would never be able to draw inductive conclusions. Indeed, not even Sgt. Friday used Dragnet objectivity strictly speaking, since no human could. Induction is useful precisely because it is ampliative—it allows us go beyond what is given to learn informative facts about the world.[9] Crucially, the evidence itself is always and in principle consistent with an indefinite (possibly infinite) number of different conclusions we could draw. No finite amount of data will ever be able to narrow the hypothesis space to one, since there will always be more than one hypothesis consistent with the data.[10] This is known as the problem of underdetermination of theory by evidence, and its roots can be traced back to another famous problem: Hume's problem of induction. To understand fully Hume's problem and the implications of it for the discussion of values, it helps to contrast properties of inductive and deductive arguments. Induction differs from deduction in two important ways. The first, which is often mistakenly taken to be the essence of Hume's problem, is that induction, unlike deduction, fails to guarantee truth. Because the conclusions of deductive arguments are always in some sense contained in their premises, if the premises are true, then the conclusion is guaranteed to be true. Inductions, on the other hand, are merely taken to provide probable support for some conclusion. If the premises of an inductive argument provide a confidence of 99% certainty in some conclusion, that still leaves 1% chance the conclusion could be false. So, in all inductions, there's a chance we could get things wrong.

However, this was not Hume's problem. Hume's problem concerns the second way in which induction differs from deduction: in justification. The justification of deduction is a priori and necessary. The justification of induction is not. Arguably, the justification of induction is contingent—it depends on the world being a certain way.[11] Thus, the problem with induction isn't that our degree of support always allows some room to be wrong, it's that there appears to be nothing to justify why known instances would provide support to any degree whatsoever to predictions of unknown instances. There's nothing logically at odds with the world suddenly becoming drastically different. Thus, whether some premises provide support for some conclusion depends on certain contingent features of the world, e.g., that the world continue to remain uniform and exhibit the patterns we've seen in the past and that are encoded in the premises. The problems of induction and of underdetermination generalize to any inductive procedure that attempts to use patterns present in evidence to make predictions about novel cases. Such inductive procedures are a critical aspect of scientific theorizing, but they're also a fundamental feature of machine learning. As we'll see, the feminist arguments in this paper stem ultimately from these related problems of induction and underdetermination.

[...]

The debate within philosophy of science regarding the value-free ideal has centered around precisely this question. It's not a question of whether scientists must adopt some assumptions—reasons we've discussed render that point undebatable—rather, it's one about which assumptions scientists ought to adopt. In other words, a debate about which canons are acceptable and which are impermissible. A canonical answer to this question was provided by Thomas Kuhn. Kuhn (1962) famously argued that various scientific re-search programs come with their own package of assumptions on which to base scientific inferences, what he called a "scientific paradigm." Crucially, he additionally claimed that the only standards by which to evaluate these assumptions exist within the paradigms themselves.

[...]

It helps to take stock of the dialectic at this point. We began with a notion of objectivity that was a (surprisingly popular) caricature of science: Dragnet objectivity. According to this stereotype, science is a lot like deduction. When presented with the evidence that the world provides—just the facts—we immediately (or a priori and with certainty) know what conclusion is entailed by those facts. However, as we saw from the problems of induction and underdetermination, science is not like—and in principle cannot be—deduction.[12][18] Evidence alone (irrespective of canons of inference) is insufficient to establish ampliative conclusions. Thus emerged a more substantial and interesting target view of science: the value-free ideal. According to this view, we accept that both evidence and canons are essential to scientific inference, but we retain the value-free ideal of science by restricting the canons to just those values that are properly epistemic and preclude any canons that are shaped by social, ethical, or political values. Again, this is intended as a theory of what is possible in principle. That as a matter of descriptive fact scientists often fall short of this aim won't do much to thwart the ideal. Thus, arguments against the value-free ideal in science strive to show that even in principle, this ideal is unattainable.

[...]

The final critical insight of this section comes from recognizing that as inductive decision-making procedures, machine learning programs are subject to these same problems of induction and underdetermination. As the discussion of Kuhn brings out, like in the case of induction more generally, there will be no one solution to these problems in the domain of machine learning programs. To put the point bluntly, there can be no algorithm for building algorithms.[13] In fact, computer scientists are likely familiar with many of the points made here already, though perhaps not under the guise of Kuhnian theory.[14] Model builders undoubtably recognize that there are many different, yet acceptable ways to build predictive models.[15] There are of course norms within the professional community that go a large way toward restricting the domain of acceptable methods—these norms arguably comprise a Kuhnian paradigm. However, these norms cannot determinately settle every question, and some decisions about how these choice points play out ultimately depend on the goals of the predictive model together with individual aims of model builders. They might have to, say, choose between various types of regression models or make decisions about what cost functions to adopt. These can be interpreted as computer scientists having to make decisions about what canons to adopt. If program engineers adhere to the value-free ideal, then they're apt to produce programs that draw conclusions from some dataset in ways that maximize accuracy, fruitfulness, consistency, breadth of scope, and simplicity. The claim made at the beginning of this paper that algorithms are objective is, thus, charitably interpreted as the claim that so long as the decision points program engineers are responsible for are resolved in ways adhering to these canons, the algorithm itself is regarded as value-free.

[...]

3. Against the Value-Free Ideal

[...]

3.1 The Argument Against Demarcation

[...]

Crucially, the arguments against demarcation seem to apply equally well in the case of machine learning. As mentioned in the previous section, machine learning engineers will have certain decision points left up to them. Ultimately, the decision to use some data analysis method over others will depend on the aims of the program and the goals of the programmer. Here, the question of how to justify some methods over others will likely be answered by appeal to the value-free ideal: the decisions to, say, use a parametric rather than a non-parametric model might be guided by the fact that the former is simpler than the latter.[16] Alternatively, one might adopt a non-parametric model due to its flexibility, opting for a predictive model that more closely aligns with ontological heterogeneity. Crucially, the rationale for choosing one over the other seems itself open to scrutiny and calls for justification. It is in providing this further justification that program engineers will likely have to appeal to facts that go beyond the purely epistemic.[17] They often include considerations about the overall aim of the program and the context in which it is intended to be used, facts which themselves depend on social and political factors. According to the justification argument against demarcation, any further justification that involves social or ethical considerations will render even those first-order decisions value-laden in significant ways. Moreover, from the constitutive argument against demarcation, even abiding by a seemingly pure epistemic list of considerations when making design decisions might usher in socio-political values. A straightforward example of this is in the selection of a loss function: this selection ideally corresponds to actual expected loss in making an incorrect prediction; in this way, we want the function to accurately approximate loss. However, there are many dimensions on which to measure actual loss, corresponding inevitably to value-laden features of the world. Adoption of any particular loss function so as to approximate real-world loss will, according to the constitutive argument, necessarily imbibe those loss functions with the very socio-political values of the real-world losses.

Whereas I've described the demarcation argument(s) as related to Hume's problem of induction and the fact that inductions (unlike deductions) are contingent, justified only relative to the world's being a certain way, the next argument from feminist philosophy of science against the value-free ideal focuses on the other way induction differs from deduction: in the potential for getting things wrong. According to this argument, any inductive reasoning must always culminate in a decision that involves ethical considerations. This is because at some point in the chain of justification, one must consider the possibility that the prediction being made might get things wrong, a risk that inevitably comes with social and ethical costs. It is the consideration of this risk and the consequences these arguments have for the value-free ideal that I turn to next.

3.2 The Argument from Inductive Risk

[...]

The argument from inductive risk can be traced back to Richard Rudner, who states:

> [S]ince no scientific hypothesis is ever completely verified, in accepting a hypothesis the scientist must make the decision that the evidence is *sufficiently* strong or that the

probability is *sufficiently* high to warrant the acceptance of the hypothesis. Obviously our decision regarding the evidence and respecting how strong is "strong enough", is going to be a function of the importance, in the typically ethical sense, of making a mistake in accepting or rejecting the hypothesis. … *How sure we need to be before we accept a hypothesis will depend on how serious a mistake would be.*[18]

The idea here is that, contra the value-free ideal, ethical values have a legitimate and necessary role to play in guiding scientific inference, because they establish confidence thresholds for ultimately accepting or rejecting a given hypothesis or prediction. This point is made obvious by comparing two hypothetical scenarios. Imagine that in one case, engineers are responsible for producing seat belt buckles, while in another scenario, engineers are responsible for producing pant belt buckles.[19] In both cases the engineers run the risk of getting things wrong in producing defective buckles, but the consequences of getting things wrong in the former case are much more dire than those of the latter. Clearly the threshold for confirmation in the two cases should not be the same: we should demand a much higher degree of confidence in the engineers' hypotheses in the first scenario than in the second. Proponents of the argument from inductive risk insist that the threshold for confidence can only be established by appeal to ethical values, thus rendering the decision to adopt any particular hypothesis value-laden.

[…]

In sum, not only do scientists have to take into consideration the risk of getting things wrong whenever they perform an inference to some hypothesis, but also they have to keep in mind the influence that that wrong hypothesis will have in communities in which their judgment is regarded as expertise. Importantly, all these points apply equally well, if not more so, in the case of machine learning programs. Consider a minimal pair similar to Rudner's original case, but now in the domain of machine learning. For example, imagine you're tasked with building an image recognition program to distinguish human shapes from non-human shapes. The level of inaccuracy you should tolerate will depend on the use to which your algorithm will be put. If it is to be implemented in an office complex as a trigger to activate the automated lights, 75% accuracy would be inconvenient, but acceptable. However, if it is to be implemented in a self-driving car to prevent pedestrian collisions, you should demand near perfection. Algorithmic design decisions about how to manage error therefore inherently involve values. We also see the analogue of Douglas's point in this domain: not only do machine learning programs run the risk of getting things wrong (a risk the negative consequences of which have been well-documented within the machine learning activist communities), but also because of the computational prowess, efficiency, and ubiquity of machine learning programs, we can expect the effects of their judgments to be wide-reaching and vast, likely more so than any individual scientist's judgments.[20] Thus, in building machine learning programs, it seems it is not sufficient that a program engineer merely adopt an aim of achieving some traditional canon like accuracy, since there's no such thing as accuracy neat. Instead, how accurate is accurate enough necessarily involves some determination of the ethical consequences of getting things wrong.

[…]

Notes

1. Smith 2018. 58% of respondents believe that computer programs will always reflect human biases.
2. I discuss the relationship between these problematic social patterns and the operation of algorithmic bias in more detail in Johnson, 2020a.

3. Even this question will require some further precisification. In our academic musings, we can no doubt conjure up imagined algorithms operating on entirely fictitious data sets, whose decisions are totally divorced from real-world use. I'm not interested in asking whether those algorithms can be value-free. The set of algorithms that I am interested in includes paradigmatically algorithms that are used to replace or supplement human decision-making, that operate on real-world data, and whose decisions come to impact other human agents. Although possibly failing to include all conceivable algorithms, I still expect this class to be quite expansive, and certainly to include the algorithms that take center stage in discussions of algorithmic fairness and bias. I return to this point about the range of conceivable algorithms at the end of the paper.

4. See Stanley 2005, Fantl and Mcgrath 2007, Moss 2018, Basu 2018, 2019, Bolinger 2018, Gardner 2017, and Munton 2017, 2019a,b, among others.

5. See Rudner 1953, Levi 1960, Douglas 2000, 2009, 2016, Rooney 1992, and Longino 1995, 1996, among others.

6. Here and throughout I use 'machine learning programs', 'algorithmic decision-making', and 'algorithms' to pick out a broad class of automated programs that function by capitalizing on or "learning" from patterns manifest in the data on which they are trained in order to build a predictive model. This includes a wide range of machine learning programs, including supervised, unsupervised, and reinforcement learning programs.

7. Antony 2006, 58.

8. This is even granting the idea that data could be "raw" in some robust sense, presumably unadulterated by human collection practices. For a range of criticisms, see Gitelman 2013.

9. The notion of Dragnet objectivity is intended to demonstrate an uncontroversial philosophical point: a list of facts alone will not allow us to form ampliative conclusions. It's uncontroversial because one, it's definitional on 'ampliative', and two, even the most stringent and traditional epistemological views will agree to it. For example, even objective Bayesians will agree that something more is needed beyond merely a fixed body of evidence, namely some procedure for updating in light of that evidence (for the Bayesian, Bayes' Rule).

10. To put the point succinctly, for any theory T that is consistent with some body of observed evidence E, we can imagine another theory T' according to which E makes it seem like T is true, but it isn't. Evil demons and brains in vats are common resources for philosophers constructing such cases.

11. This is admittedly controversial. Norton (2003, 650, 666–669) makes a compelling case by adopting what he calls the material theory of induction, according to which "all inductions ultimately derive their licenses from facts pertinent to the matter of the induction", and demonstrating how it might evade the problem of induction. Of course, objective Bayesians, inductive rationalists, and logical probability theorists might all disagree. For notable critiques of these views, see the literature cited in footnote 30.

12. I don't mean that scientists never rely on deduction, only that induction is the canonical form of scientific inference.

13. This slogan, like most slogans, favors rhetoric at the expense of precision. It relies on an equivocation: I mean 'algorithm' in the first use of the word in the way Kuhn (1977, 359) means it when he says that an "algorithm able to dictate rational, unanimous [theory] choice" is "not quite [an] attainable ideal." The second use refers to the machine learning algorithms that are the target of this paper. The idea of the slogan is that you can (of course) write algorithms for building algorithms for something or other. What you can't do is write an algorithm for building algorithms for any arbitrary problem. And the problem of how machine learning algorithms should respond to data across the board—like the problem of determining what theory to adopt given some arbitrary set of evidence—is one of the latter problems.

14. It's often thought that Hume's problem of induction resurfaces in the domain of machine learning in the form of the No Free Lunch Theorem (see, for example, Giraud-Carrier and Provost 2005, 2, Domingos 2012, 81, and Wolpert 2013, 2). I'm compelled by arguments made by Lauc (2019) that the NFL is more closely akin to Goodman (1955)'s New Riddle of Induction, though that too famously connected to Hume's problem in ways discussed. Either way, both interpretations lead to the result, argued for here, that in the domain of machine learning, "there is no learning without bias, there is no

learning without knowledge." (Lauc 2019, 484, echoing Domingos 2015, 64). For a greater discussion of these points, see Dotan 2020, where the NFL is used to motivated conclusions similar to those of this paper. Thanks to Kathleen Creel for helpful discussions about these points.

15. The point applies to scientific modeling more generally. See, for example, Weisberg 2007.

16. Of course, what simplicity ultimately amounts to is itself an elusive question in the history of philosophy of science.

17. This point can be bolstered by literature on probabilistic reasoning more generally that converges on a similar point. A small sampling of that literature includes Ramsey (1989)'s criticism of Keynes that there are no objective probabilities, Carnap's failure in constructing a purely formal foundation of inductive logic (for summary, see Zabell 2011), Titelbaum (2010)'s rejection of a purely objective notion of evidential support, and Fallis and Lewis (2016)'s critique of purely objective measures of probabilistic accuracy, among many others. Thanks to Branden Fitelson for pointing me to this literature.

18. Rudner 1953, 2, emphasis in original.

19. This is an adaption of Rudner (1953, 2)'s original case.

20. For a broad discussion of the impacts of algorithmic decision making on discrimination, law, and policy, see Barocas and Selbst 2016, Kroll et al. 2017, Selbst et al. 2019, and Abebe et al. 2020, as well as other scholarship produced in association with the Fairness, Accountability, and Transparency in Machine Learning (FAT* ML) community.

References

Abebe, R., Barocas, S., Kleinberg, J., Levy, K., Raghavan, M., and Robinson, D. G. (2020). Roles for Computing in Social Change. Conference on Fairness, Accountability, and Transparency (FAT* '20), page 9.

Antony, L. (2001). Quine as Feminist: The Radical Import of Naturalized Epistemology. In Antony, L. and Witt, C. E., editors, *A Mind of One's Own: Feminist Essays on Reason and Objectivity*, pages 110–153. Westview Press.

Antony, L. (2006). The Socialization of Epistemology. In Goodin, R. E. and Tilly, C., editors, *The Oxford Handbook of Contextual Political Analysis*, pages 58–77. Oxford University Press.

Antony, L. (2016). Bias: Friend or Foe? In Brownstein, M. and Saul, J., editors, *Implicit Bias and Philosophy, Volume 1: Metaphysics and Epistemology*, pages 157–190. Oxford University Press.

Basu, R. (2018). The Wrongs of Racist Beliefs. *Philosophical Studies*.

Basu, R. (2019). What we Epistemically owe to Each Other. *Philosophical Studies*, 176(4):915–931.

Bolinger, R. J. (2018). The Rational Impermissibility of Accepting (some) Racial Generalizations. *Synthese*.

Domingos, P. (2012). A few useful things to know about machine learning. *Communications of the ACM*, 55(10):78.

Domingos, P. (2015). *The Master Algorithm: How the quest for the Ultimate Learning ma- chine will Remake our world*. Basic Books, a member of the Perseus Books Group, New York.

Dotan, R. (2020). Theory Choice, Non-Epistemic Values, and Machine Learning. *Synthese*.

Douglas, H. (2000). Inductive Risk and Values in Science. *Philosophy of Science*, 67(4):559– 579.

Douglas, H. (2016). Values in Science. In Humphreys, P., editor, *Oxford Handbook in the Philosophy of Science*, pages 609–630. Oxford University Press.

Douglas, H. E. (2009). *Science, Policy, and the Value-free Ideal*. University of Pittsburgh Press, Pittsburgh, Pa. OCLC: ocn297144848.

Fallis, D. and Lewis, P. J. (2016). The Brier Rule is not a Good Measure of Epistemic Utility (and Other Useful Facts about Epistemic Betterness). *Australasian Journal of Philosophy*, 94(3):576–590.

Fantl, J. and Mcgrath, M. (2007). On Pragmatic Encroachment in Epistemology. *Philosophy and Phenomenological Research*, 75(3):558–589.

Gardner, J. (2017). Discrimination: The Good, the Bad, and the Wrongful. *Proceedings of the Aristotelian Society*, 118.

Kroll, J. A. (2018). The Fallacy of Inscrutability. *Philosophical Transactions of the Royal Society A: Mathematical, Physical and Engineering Sciences*, 376(2133):20180084.

Kuhn, T. (1962). *The Structure of Scientific Revolutions*. University of Chicago Press, Chicago.

Lauc, D. (2019). How Gruesome are the No-free-lunch Theorems for Machine Learning? *Croation Journal of Philosophy*, XVIII(54):8.

Levi, I. (1960). Must the Scientist Make Value Judgments? *The Journal of Philosophy*, 57(11):345.

Longino, H. E. (1995). Gender, Politics, and the Theoretical Virtues. *Synthese*, 104(3):383–397.

Longino, H. E. (1996). Cognitive and Non-cognitive Values in Science: Rethinking the Dichotomy. In Hankinson Nelson, L. and Nelson, J., editors, *Feminism, Science, and the Philosophy of Science*, pages 39–58. Kluwer, Dordrecht. OCLC: 801321444.

Moss, S. (2018). *Probabilistic Knowledge*. Oxford University Press, Oxford.

Munton, J. (2017). The Eye's Mind: Perceptual Process and Epistemic Norms. *Philosophical Perspectives*, 31(1):317–347.

Munton, J. (2019a). Beyond accuracy: Epistemic flaws with statistical generalizations. Philosophical Issues, 29(1):228–240.

Munton, J. (2019b). Perceptual Skill and Social Structure. *Philosophy and Phenomenological Research*.

Ramsey, F. P. (1989). Mr. Keynes on Probability. *The British Journal for the Philosophy of Science*, 40(2):219–222.

Rooney, P. (1992). On Values in Science: Is the Epistemic/Non-Epistemic Distinction Useful? PSA: *Proceedings of the Biennial Meeting of the Philosophy of Science Association*, 1992(1):13–22.

Rudner, R. (1953). The Scientist Qua Scientist Makes Value Judgments. *Philosophy of Science*, 20(1):1–6.

Selbst, A. D., Boyd, D., Friedler, S. A., Venkatasubramanian, S., and Vertesi, J. (2019). Fairness and Abstraction in Sociotechnical Systems. In *Proceedings of the Conference on Fairness, Accountability, and Transparency - FAT* '19*, pages 59–68, Atlanta, GA, USA. ACM Press.

Stanley, J. (2005). *Knowledge and Practical Interest*. Oxford University Press, Oxford.

Titelbaum, M. G. (2010). Not Enough There There: Evidence, Reasons, and Language Independence. *Philosophical Perspectives*, 24(1):477–528.

Weisberg, M. (2007). Three Kinds of Idealization. *Journal of Philosophy*, 104(12):639–659.

Zabell, S. (2011). Carnap and the Logic of Inductive Inference. In *Handbook of the History of Logic*, volume 10, pages 265–309. Elsevier.

Chapter 1.6

Algorithmic Bias and Corporate Responsibility: How Companies Hide behind the False Veil of the Technological Imperative[*]

Kirsten Martin

In this chapter, I argue that acknowledging the value-laden biases of algorithms as inscribed in design allows us to identify the associated responsibility of corporations that design, develop, and deploy algorithms. Put another way, claiming algorithms are neutral or that the design decisions of computer scientists are neutral obscures the morally important decisions of computer and data scientists. I focus on the implications of making technological imperative arguments: framing algorithms as evolving under their own inertia, as providing more efficient, accurate decisions, and as outside the realm of any critical examination or moral evaluation. I argue specifically that judging AI on efficiency and pretending algorithms are inscrutable produces a veil of the technological imperative which shields corporations from being held accountable for the value-laden decisions made in the design, development and deployment of algorithms. While there is always more to be researched and understood, we know quite a lot about testing algorithms. I then outline how the development of algorithms should be critically examined to elucidate the value-laden biases encoded in design and development. The moral examination of AI pierces the (false) veil of the technological imperative.

---

[*] Martin, K. 2021. Algorithmic Bias and Corporate Responsibility: How Companies Hide Behind the False Veil of the Technological Imperative. Reprinted with permission of the author. All rights reserved.

DOI: 10.1201/9781003278290-7

Introduction

Consider a recent example of a company using AI:

> An Amazon driver "spent almost four years racing around Phoenix delivering packages as a contract driver for Amazon.com Inc. Then one day, he received an automated email. The algorithms tracking him had decided he wasn't doing his job properly." Drivers understood that their performance was being monitored – how they drove their route, where they put packages on the porch, etc – and would sometimes receive emails with a rating from fantastic to at risk. However, "Amazon knew delegating work to machines would lead to mistakes and damaging headlines, these former managers said, but decided it was cheaper to trust the algorithms than pay people to investigate mistaken firings so long as the drivers could be replaced easily."[1]

For the drivers, they were fired by an algorithm. However, the discussion about whether algorithms *does* things or *has* a bias emanates from a concern as to who is then responsible for good and bad outcomes. In other words, when an organization or individual uses an algorithm, who is responsible for the decisions? The arguments traditionally fall into two camps: those that focus on the algorithm as the actor that 'does' things and is at fault (technological determinists) and those that focus on the users of that algorithm as determining the outcome (social determinists).

However, in this chapter, I argue that we need to acknowledge the value-laden biases of technology – including algorithms – while preserving the ability of humans to control the design, development, and deployment of technology.[2] This is important so that we appropriately attribute responsibility for how algorithms perform and better interrogate those that design and develop algorithms to augment our decisions. In other words, only by acknowledging the value-laden biases of algorithms can we begin to ask how companies inscribed those biases during design and development.

While the general argument that technology has biases and that individuals and companies design those biases is not new (Bijker, 1995; Friedman & Nissenbaum, 1996; D. G. Johnson, 2015; Latour, 1992; Winner, 1980), here I make more explicit the implications for corporate accountability. In this chapter, I also examine the implications of making technological imperative arguments – framing algorithms as evolving under their own inertia, providing more efficient, accurate decisions, and outside the realm of interrogation. I argue specifically that judging AI on efficiency and pretending algorithms are inscrutable produces a veil of the technological imperative which shields corporations from being held accountable for the value-laden decisions made in the design, development and deployment of algorithms. Importantly, claims of algorithms being inscrutable and efficient provide a shield for corporations who are making these value-laden decisions. Finally, I offer how AI and algorithms should be interrogated given what we know currently about the value-laden decisions of computer and data scientists.

AI and Value-Laden Bias. What Does That Mean?

Determinist Arguments

For *social determinists*, society is the main actor of the story in constructing technology and determining the outcome. If an algorithm is not performing correctly, e.g., violating rules, undermining rights, harming others, producing unjust results, etc., then a social determinist would point to the many ways that people created that technology and then decided how it would be used. For social determinists, what matters is not technology itself but the social or economic system in which it is embedded. In regards to algorithms, social determinists blame the *use* of the program rather than the design of the program or acknowledge that the *data* may be flawed ("it's just the data") and that society needs to get better data for the algorithm. For the medical triage algorithm, one would focus on the disparities that existed in the data as a reflection of historical discrimination and not focus on the decisions around the design of the algorithm (and the decision to use that data!).

One attraction of arguing that algorithms are neutral and society is to blame is the ability to avoid any form of technological determinism: in attributing values or biases to algorithms, scholars are concerned we would also attribute control to technology and thereby remove the ability of society to influence technology. Even further, identifying any form of materiality in algorithms could lead to a form of worship, where an algorithms' preferences are deemed unassailable and humans are left subservient to the whims of the algorithm (Desai & Kroll, 2017).

For *technological determinists*, technology is the primary actor of the story. As such, technology is to 'blame' for the outcome. Strident technological determinists frequently see technology as having an internal dynamic that leads the best technology to survive in the market. This faction argues that the ethical evaluation of technology is not appropriate since it may curtail development. For data analytics, we hear technological determinist arguments when the algorithm or program is the main actor in the paragraph or the sentence. For example, "The algorithm decided …" or "the program categorized …" For example, the algorithm decided to fire Amazon's drivers.

Figure 1.6.1, adopted from Martin and Freeman (2004), shows two versions of determinism at either end of a spectrum where social determinism means framing technology as a blank slate, neutral, and socially controlled and where technological determinism means framing technology as value-laden and controlling society.

Determinists and (a Lack of) Accountability

This tension – between social determinists and technological determinists – is not merely an academic exercise but is important to assigning responsibility because who is 'acting' is normally who we look to hold responsible for those acts. For social determinists, an algorithm is neutral, a blank slate, and society is then responsible for how the algorithm is used. Algorithms-as-a-blank-slate would suggest minimal responsibility for the developers who craft the algorithm (Martin & Freeman, 2004). For technological determinists, algorithms *do* things, but these inherent biases are then outside the influence of society, designers, and developers. The algorithm-as-autonomous-agent narrative suggests the users have no say or accountability in how algorithms make decisions.

This false tension – algorithms as objective, neutral blank slates versus deterministic, autonomous agents – has implications for whether and how firms are responsible for the algorithms they develop, sell, and use. Both mistakenly absolve developers – computer scientists, data analysts, and corporations – of their responsibility. Whether you hold the users of the algorithm responsible

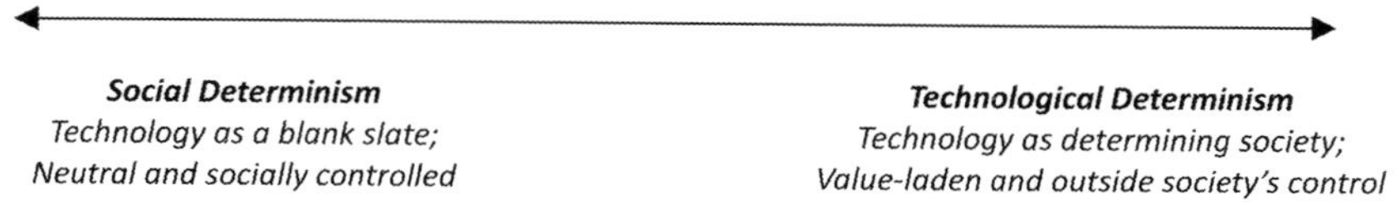

Social Determinism	*Technological Determinism*
Technology as a blank slate;	*Technology as determining society;*
Neutral and socially controlled	*Value-laden and outside society's control*

Figure 1.6.1 Traditional approaches to technology (adopted from Martin and Freeman, 2004).

(social determinism) or the algorithm itself (technological determinism), you are not holding responsible the systems of power – the government or company – that designed, developed, and implemented the program (Martin, 2022b).

This deterministic conversation about algorithms absolves firms of responsibility for the development or use of algorithms. Developers argue that their algorithms are neutral and thrust into fallible contexts of biased data and improper use by society. Users claim algorithms are difficult to identify let alone understand, therefore excluding users of any culpability for the ethical implications in use (Martin, 2019).

Algorithmic Biases

Reality "is a far messier mix of technical and human curating" (Dwork & Mulligan, 2013, p. 35). Those who fall into these deterministic arguments conflate two ideas: whether or not a technology is value-laden and who controls the technology. Martin and Freeman argue these two mechanisms are independent and see technology as simultaneously value-laden yet under social control (Martin & Freeman, 2004), where one need not claim technology as neutral to maintain control over it. Similarly, and focused on algorithms, Mittelstadt et al. note that algorithms are value-laden with biases that are "specified by developers and configured by users with desired outcomes in mind that privilege some values and interests over others" (2016). This approach acknowledges the materiality of algorithms without allocating control to the technology. Figure 1.6.1, adopted from Martin and Freeman (2004), illustrates how one can acknowledge the materiality of technology in that algorithms can have value-laden biases, discriminate, create and destroy value, cause harm, respect or violate ethical norms, diminish rights, reinforce virtues, etc. without forgoing control over technology.

In other words, these deterministic arguments are making two separate assumptions that are not required to move in tandem (Martin & Freeman, 2004). First, whether a technology is value-laden can be separated from who controls the technology as in Figure 1.6.2. While technological determinists assume value-laden technology with technology also being autonomous, and social determinists assume a neutral technology with society in control, many scholars have embraced technology as value-laden while acknowledging the control of society in the design, development, and deployment of algorithms.

These tensions and assumptions about technology are not new and many of the theories attempting to break free of deterministic approaches dealt with trains, bikes, dams, scallops, door groomers, etc. In other words, AI and algorithms is not the first time we have questioned how technology is value-laden while we also are responsibility for the design, development and deployment of technology. For example, Wiebe Bijker explores bicycles, lightbulbs, and plastics (Bijker,

		Technology as …	
		Neutral	**Value-laden w/Moral Implications**
Who is in control	**Technology**	II. Technological Imperative *Efficient AI that should not be questioned*	I. Technological Determinism *Biased AI that is beyond our control*
	Society	III. Social Determinism *Efficient AI corrupted by society's messiness.*	IV. Value-Laden Biases *Biased AI with value-laden decisions in design, development, deployment*

Figure 1.6.2   Technology's bias and control.

1995); Latour examines seatbelts and door groomers (Latour, 1992); Winner uses bridges, tomato harvesters, and ships (Winner, 2010).

Importantly, these authors and others acknowledge the materiality of algorithms has biases that are value-laden (Friedman & Nissenbaum, 1996; Johnson, 2004) or have politics (Winner, 1980) while also identifying how individuals, corporations, and society control that same technology. In this way, Latour notes that technology – including algorithms – is anthropomorphic: "first, it has been made by humans; second, it substitutes for the actions of people and is a delegate that permanently occupies the position of a human; and third, it shapes human action by prescribing back" what humans should do (p. 160). These scholars both identify the materiality of technology while also maintaining the responsibility of individuals who design, develop, and use algorithms. In fact, obliterating the materiality of technology, treating algorithms as if they are a blank slate and value-neutral, absolves computer scientists and companies of their moral decisions in developing the algorithm.

We can think of algorithms as having biases in three ways. First, algorithms *are value-laden* in that algorithms are biased and designed for a preferred set of actions. Algorithms create moral consequences, reinforce or undercut ethical principles, and enable or diminish stakeholder rights and dignity (Martin, 2019). However, we should broaden this to include algorithms as fair, just, abiding by virtue ethics (Vallor, 2016), expressing or violating an ethics of care (Villegas-Galaviz, 2022), reinforcing racist systems and policies (Benjamin, 2019; Eubanks, 2018; Gebru, 2019; Poole et al., 2020), reinforcing or undermining misogyny (D'Ignazio & Klein, 2020). Figure 1.6.3 illustrates the value-laden-ness of AI systems, including the development of the specific algorithm, as well as the types of ethical issues we find around outcomes, algorithms, and data.

Second, algorithms can be seen as *policy at scale.* In other words, in creating the algorithm, developers are taking a stand on ethical issues and "expressing a view on how things ought to be or not to be, or what is good or bad, or desirable or undesirable" (Kraemer et al., 2011, p. 252). Algorithms act like design-based regulation (Yeung, 2016) where algorithms can be used for the consistent application of legal and regulatory regimes (Thornton, 2016, p. 1826). Algorithms can enforce morality while still being designed and used by individuals (Diakopoulos, 2013). In the case of automated decision-making, algorithms combine adjudication with rule-making in setting policy (Citron, 2007). For Amazon, imagine developing a policy for drivers that each warehouse manager had to implement that included criteria for their performance and, if necessary, criteria and process for their termination or promotion. Instead, Amazon implements policy through how the AI is developed, and then makes decisions on behalf of the company.

STS scholar Madeleine Akrich suggests the following thought experiment which is of particular importance for algorithms:

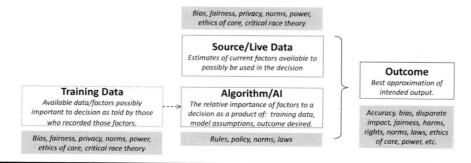

Figure 1.6.3 Value-laden-ness of AI.

How can the prescriptions encoded in the mechanism be brought out in words? By replacing them by strings of sentences (often in the imperative) that are uttered (silently and continuously) by the mechanisms for the benefit of those who are mechanized: do this, do that, behave this way, don't go that way, you may do so, be allowed to go there. Such sentences look very much like a programming language.

As Latour rightly summarizes, "every time you want to know what a nonhuman does, simply imagine what other humans or other nonhumans would have to do were this character not present" (p. 155). The technology's script answers who matters, which group is important, who counts, which race/ethnicity is included and delineated. What factors should be considered, what is the outcome that is important, how 'bad' are outliers, what is the criteria for working.

Finally, *algorithms influence who-does-what* in a decision system. In addition to the design of value-laden algorithms, developers make a moral choice as to the delegation of who-does-what between algorithms and individuals when in use. At a minimum, technologies alleviate the need for others to do a task. In Latour's classic case of seatbelt, making the seat belt automatic – attaching the seatbelt to the door so that it is in place automatically – relieves the driver from the responsibility to ensure the seatbelt is used. A bell may be added to remind the driver (Martin, 2019). However, when developers design the algorithm to be used in a decision, they also design how accountability is delegated within the decision. Sometimes algorithms *are designed* to absorb the work and associated responsibility by precluding users from taking on roles and responsibilities within the decision system. Inscrutable algorithms that are designed to minimize the role of individuals in the decision take on more accountability for the decision.

Technological Imperative

I turn now to revisit the quadrant II in Figure 1.6.2, not yet addressed, where algorithms are framed as value-neutral and outside the control of society. The technological imperative frames technologies as almost inevitable and outside our control (See Chandler, 2012) -- a technological determinist who also believes that the technology always is correct.

According to the technological imperative, algorithms are detached from the imperfections of the 'real world.' You hear this when computer and data scientists believe their work does not include dealing with the imperfections and ambiguity of the world or that algorithms are merely efficient, accurate machines that are better than alternatives. Algorithms, according to the technological imperative, are not worthy of being questioned not only because any imperfections arise from the messiness of the world but also because algorithms are seen as inscrutable and not subject to interrogation.

Importantly, for the technological imperative, technology should be adopted *without much question*.[3] This extreme view is becoming *more* common in how we talk about machine learning in the news and in research. For example, in an argument against researchers who have highlighted the dangers of using artificial intelligence and predictive analytics without regard to their biases or moral implications, Alex Miller, in "Want Less-Biased Decisions? Use Algorithms," lists the ways AI *could* be an improvement because humans are bad at decisions (true – we are not great[4]). His argument joins a common refrain that technology, because it can be an improvement if designed properly, is then always improvement (Miller, 2018).

Algorithms in quadrant II are not critically examined both (1) because they are deemed to be inscrutable but also (2) because there is no point since they are framed to be neutral – seen as efficient and accurate.

These two assumptions reinforce the false idea of the technological imperative in our current conversations about algorithms. First, claims that algorithms are *inscrutable* frame algorithms as so complicated that they are impossible to explain or question, *even by computer and data scientists* (!) (Barocas et al., 2013; Desai & Kroll, 2017; Introna, 2016; Ziewitz, 2016). In fact, algorithms are seen as so difficult to explain that assigning responsibility to the developer or the user is deemed inefficient and even impossible. Previously I have argued that the Inscrutable Defense ("It's too complicated to explain") does not absolve a firm from responsibility, otherwise firms would have an incentive to create complicated systems to avoid accountability (Martin, 2019). Here I am arguing that claiming that algorithms are inscrutable *even to computer and data scientists* produces a veil behind which companies can hide the value-laden judgments made in the design and development of algorithms.

Figure 1.6.4 illustrates all that is hidden when we falsely claim that algorithms are inscrutable and cannot be critically examined. Claims of inscrutability allow computer and data scientists to make value-laden decisions without being questioned from those inside and outside the organization.

In an essay, "The Fallacy of Inscrutability," Joshua Kroll argues that the common argument that algorithms are inscrutable or black boxes is a fallacy. In fact, Kroll argues that "inscrutability is not a result of technical complexity but rather of power dynamics in the choice of how to use those tools" (Kroll, 2018). In fact, a company may want to claim a program is inscrutable even if it is not (Pasquale, 2015). The company may want to protect a program they believe is a competitive advantage: this could be because it *is* a competitive advantage or due to shear inertia (they always like to say things are a competitive advantage). The organization also may not like the answer they would need to provide, or the people asked may not know enough to answer. Importantly, Professor Kroll argues that not understanding a system is just bad practice. As Kroll summarizes: "rather than discounting systems which cause bad outcomes as fundamentally inscrutable and therefore uncontrollable, we should simply label the application of inadequate technology what it is: malpractice, committed by a system's controller" (Kroll, 2018, p. 5).

The second assumption that feeds the false narrative of the technological impetrative is when algorithms are framed as more accurate or more <u>efficient</u> without interrogating the program. Further, that efficiency and accuracy are neutral concepts *and outside ethical considerations*. In an examination of top machine learning and AI conference papers, Birhane et al. find the dominant values to be "performance, accuracy, state-of-the-art (SOTA), quantitative results, generalization, efficiency, building on previous work, and novelty" (Birhane et al., 2021).[5] Current attempts to include any ethical consideration of the development and impact of algorithms in research has similarly been met with claims that the moral evaluation of algorithms are outside the scope of the field.[6] This approach has infected management as well. For example, "machine learning is significantly faster and seemingly unconstrained by human cognitive limitations and inflexibility"

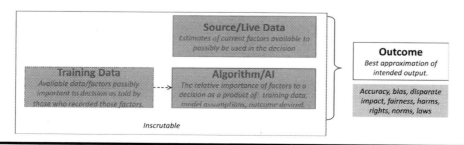

Figure 1.6.4   Inscrutable algorithms with value-laden outcomes.

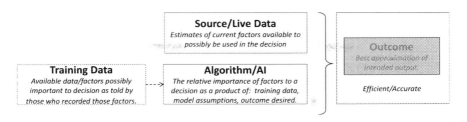

Figure 1.6.5   Value-laden algorithms with efficient and accurate outcomes.

(Balasubramanian et al., 2020). Even Google's recent introduction of a new large language model for search was focused on performance without any mention of all the additional outcomes of such models (Bender et al., 2021).

Figure 1.6.5 illustrates the focus on the efficiency of outcomes. While value-laden decisions may occur in design and development, the deployment of the algorithms is assumed to be <u>better</u> than alternatives in terms of efficiency and accuracy. Further efficiency and accuracy are assumed to be value-neutral designations and *not subject to moral evaluation*.

This assumption is actually two mini-assumptions in one: (a) assuming that AI is efficient and (b) therefore neutral. First, one must ask "efficient for whom?" The program may be efficient for the organization based on a narrow metric that the decision is made faster than a human. However, the implementation may create work for subjects of the AI program and make the process longer, less efficient for those that fix problems, hear appeals, investigate problems. Second, efficiency is one metric but not the entire measurement of whether an AI decision 'works.' Organizations implement programs and decisions and policies with more goals than 'efficiency': fairness, treating people with dignity, creating long term value for stakeholders, following rules, etc.

Finally, Gabbielle Johnson makes a compelling case that the concepts of efficiency, simplicity, and accuracy are value-laden. Her argument is longer, and worth reading, that alternatives such as novelty, complexity of interaction, diffusion of power, etc. are also compelling criteria for AI (and science more generally) to be judged. Importantly, we are making value judgments when we decide to judge AI using efficiency as a criteria and alternatives exist. So, for Johnson, even if one uses efficiency as a criteria, we cannot claim that is in any way 'neutral.' (Johnson, n.d.).

Figure 1.6.6 combines these two assumptions – efficient outcomes and inscrutable algorithms – which serve to hide the value-laden biases, decisions, and outcomes in the design and development of algorithms and halt the moral evaluation of algorithms. Figure 1.6.6 illustrates how we currently are unnecessarily and inappropriately constructing the technological imperative in our approach to algorithms.

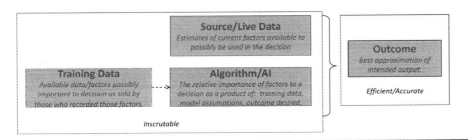

Figure 1.6.6   Constructing the technological imperative—inscrutable algorithms creating efficient outcomes.

Critical Evaluation of Algorithmic Bias

Acknowledging the value-laden biases of algorithms – inscribed in design and development and with moral implications in use – opens the door to questioning how and why algorithms are developed and used. Algorithms are developed with design choices that "can affect the relative distribution of power, authority, privilege in a community" (Winner, 1980). Friedman and Nissenbaum offer a framework to identify sources of bias in computer systems, where bias is defined as the tendency of a computer system to "systematically and unfairly discriminate" against certain individuals. Friedman and Nissenbaum identify three types of biases based on how the bias emerges: Amazon's firing AI program could have biases (a) *preexisting* in the data, then (b) *embedded* in the design of the algorithm, and (c) *emergent* in how the program is then deployed on live data. Similarly, Barocas and Selbst outline how algorithms have a discriminatory disparate impact through design choices such as defining the target variable and adding labels, choosing training data, selecting features, including proxies for protected classes, or purposefully designing an algorithm to have a specific discriminatory bias (Barocas & Selbst, 2016).

I extend this conversation on the value-laden decisions of computer and data scientists focused on the development of the algorithm. In terms of Friedman and Nissenbaum, I focus here on how biases are embedded during design and development of algorithms. Or, as Johnson says, "values are constitutive of the very operation of algorithmic decision-making" (Johnson, n.d.). As noted by Kearns and Roth in *The Ethical Algorithm*, "The designer may have had a good understanding of the algorithm that was used to *find* the decision-making model, but not the model itself." In other worlds, computer and data scientists do understand the assumptions used to create the machine learning algorithms based on training data even if the model created is harder to explain. Kearns and Roth suggest to ensure that these models respect societal norms, we need to learn how to design with these ethical norms in mind. For Rudner, we need to better manage value-laden decisions of computer and data scientists by first acknowledging that these value-laden decisions are occurring, otherwise we will make them unconsciously, haphazardly, and "leave an essential aspect of scientific method scientifically out of control" (1953, p. 6). Here, I turn to offer a framework to critically examine the development of algorithms to illuminate the value-laden biased designed in the AI program.

1. Moral Evaluation of Outcomes

The first step of any program is to create an outcome variable that measures something they are interested in – but the outcome is actually constructed based on the phenomenon of interest (what we are worried about or interested in the world) as well as what is easily measured and labeled by a program (Martin, 2022a). In addition, *the* outcome variable chosen has implications as to what the organization thinks is important and whose interests are prioritized in the design of the algorithm. How the outcome is constructed and how changing the outcome impacts how the algorithm is developed are important assumptions to critically examine some questions to interrogate the outcome variable chosen:

- What is the phenomenon we are trying to represent with this outcome?
- How was this outcome chosen? What other outcomes did you consider and what was the impact?
- For whom does this outcome variable represent the phenomenon of interest and for whom does this outcome *not* represent the phenomenon of interest?
- For whom is value created and who is disempowered in choosing this outcome?

2. *Moral Evaluation of the* Criteria for Whether the Algorithms Works

The criteria for an algorithm 'working' is usually chosen by the company developing the algorithm. This is handy (for the developer or researcher!) because the criteria chosen for success can be tailored to the algorithm in question. Importantly, whether or not the use of an algorithm is an improvement should be critically evaluated. One measure, accuracy, is used frequently: the percent of cheaters caught with facial recognition or the percent of patients correctly identified as high priority. In fact, much has been researched and explained as to measuring accuracy, or more importantly, how to judge that an algorithm *works*. However, the percent of true positives identified is only one measure. For Amazon's firing algorithm, we would also care about the number of false positive (falsely identified as a bad driver when they are not) and whether the accuracy rates are consistent across protected classes or type of subjects.[7] Some questions for critically evaluating whether an algorithm works:

- What measurements did you use to test if the algorithm worked? Which did you decide not to use or report?
- For whom is this algorithm accurate? For whom is it not accurate?
- What is the rate of all mistakes (false positives, false negatives)? Is the rate of mistake consistent across demographic groups?
- What measurements for fairness did you use? What benchmarks did you use to compare the algorithm to?
- What is the impact on effectiveness or efficiency for the subjects of the algorithm?
- How was the model tested for overfitting to the training data? How did you ensure the algorithm was not optimized for data in training but less useful for live data?
- What are the effects of individuals' rights with the use of this algorithm? Are any ethical norms violated with the use of this algorithm?
- Who benefits from the use of this algorithm? Are they the designers of the algorithm?

3. *Moral Evaluation of Data Choices*

The ethical questions about both training data and the data used when an algorithm is deployed can be thought of as covering (a) whether the data is appropriate to use (or not) *regardless* of the results, and (b) whether the use of data is appropriate to use (or not) because of the associated results. In regards to the former, training data could be gathered in violation to users' privacy (Barocas & Nissenbaum, 2014) or the mere use of the data would be considered unfair for that particular context (Barocas & Selbst, 2016) or the use of that data may be in violation of a law or norm (Gebru et al., 2018). In each case, the use of the data would be inappropriate not matter how 'well' the algorithms works. In addition, the use of data may lead to adverse outcomes for subjects including disparate impact and harms. The computer and data scientist decides what data is appropriate to use and makes the value-judgment not only as to the use of a data set, but also which factors in the data set to include. *Not all data should be used in training a model* and the use of data is a judgment call. We should be concerned if a computer or data scientist did not exclude some data from the creation of the model. Some questions for critically evaluating data choices:

- What data or factors did you *not* include because doing so would be a privacy violation, unfair, or inappropriate for this decision?
- What data or factors did you *not* include because doing so resulted in outcomes that were a privacy violation, unfair, or inappropriate?

4. Moral Evaluation of Assumptions in Developing the Model

Perhaps the least discussed portion of the value-laden decisions in development is around the assumptions that computer and data scientists make in the design of algorithms. Consider an example from Kearns and Roth (2019), an algorithm is developed based on historical university data to identify acceptances based on students' SAT and GPAs. The algorithm falsely rejects qualified Black applicants more often than qualified white applicants. "Why? Because the designer didn't anticipate it. She didn't tell the algorithm to try to equalize the false rejection rates between the two groups so it didn't. … machine learning won't give you anything 'for free'" (p. 10).

In general, each assumption that a computer scientist makes about the data – how it is distributed, what missing data means and should be treated, how much to punish outliers or those that do not 'fit' the algorithm – is an assumption about the subjects in the data. When outliers are treated as not a big deal, the computer scientists are saying *it is not morally important if a person is not adequately represented by this algorithm.* When missing data is ignored, the computer scientists are saying *it is ethically appropriate for individuals to be punished when they are not well covered by this data set.* For example, when an algorithm was used to predict whether consumers will pay back credit-card debt, the predictions skewed to favor wealthier white applicants because "minority and low-income groups have less data in their credit histories" (Heaven, 2021). The lack of data just made the prediction less precise, and the lack of precision downgraded the scores. Similarly with outliers: computer scientists need to decide whether outliers are 'punished' in the development of the algorithm. Some modeling assumptions square the distance to the outlier while others just take the absolute value (others cube the distance, etc). Squaring the distance to the outlier means that the performance is 'hurt' by more outliers that are further out. Importantly, while computer and data scientists make these assumptions *about outliers in the data*, these outliers are *about people represented in the data* that are not well characterized by the algorithm as it is being developed.

Work has been done to better understand fairness in terms of the design, development, and testing of algorithms (Barocas et al., 2018; Chouldechova & Roth, 2018; Hardt, 2014; Mitchell et al., 2020; Narayanan, 2018). Here, I broaden the types of questions to include the general moral evaluation of the many assumptions computer and data scientists make:

■ Data: What assumptions were made about how the data is distributed? What does that assumption mean in terms of people?

■ Missing Data: What assumptions were made about *missing* data and how missing data should be treated? Should people be published for not being well represented in this particular data set?

■ Outliers: How are outliers defined? Which data points are *well characterized* by the algorithm and which are *not recognized* by the algorithm? What assumptions are made about the distribution of the outliers (e.g., is it assumed to be random)?

■ Outliers: How are outliers treated in the development of the algorithm? How are large versus small outliers treated? Is it morally important to not have large outliers? What assumptions are made and what happens when different assumptions are made?

■ Fitting: How do you test the performance of the algorithm? Do you have results for training, validation, and testing data? (This checks to see if the developer overfit the algorithm to the training data which would make it less useful with live data).

5. *Moral Evaluation of* Plans for Resiliency

Computer and data scientists should ensure algorithms support good decisions – including managing the inevitable mistakes. This requires developers to *expect* mistakes to occur and designing algorithms should include planning the ability to identify, judge, and correct mistakes. In this way, computer and data scientists are designing for the resiliency of algorithms (Martin & Parmar, Forthcoming). While mistakes may be unintentional, ignoring or even fostering mistakes is unethical. Ethical algorithms plan for the identification, judgment, and correction of mistakes, whereas unethical programs allow mistakes to go unnoticed and perpetuate mistakes. In interrogating an algorithm, one would examine if the program (a) created mistakes and if the type of mistakes was appropriate for the decision context, and (b) allows for the identification, judgment, and correction of mistakes:

- How was this algorithm designed to identify mistakes in use?
- How was this algorithm designed to fix mistakes in use?

Conclusion

In this article, I argue that acknowledging the value-laden biases of algorithms as inscribed in design allows us to identify the associated responsibility of corporations that design, develop, and deploy algorithms. Claiming algorithms are neutral or that the design decisions of computer scientists are neutral obscures the morally important decisions of computer and data scientists. I also examine the danger in framing algorithms as evolving under their own inertia, providing more efficient, accurate decisions, and outside the realm of interrogation. I argue specifically that judging AI on efficiency and pretending algorithms are inscrutable produces a veil of the technological imperative which shields corporations from being held accountable for the value-laden decisions made in the design, development and deployment of algorithms. While there is always more to be researched and understood, we know quite a lot about the value-laden decisions in development and how to morally evaluate algorithmic biases.

Notes

1. Spencer Soper. 2021. "Fired by Bot at Amazon: 'It's You Against the Machine'. Bloomberg. June 28, 2021. https://www.bloomberg.com/news/features/2021-06-28/fired-by-bot-amazon-turns-to -machine-managers-and-workers-are-losing-out
2. Biases are value-laden design features with moral implications in use.
3. Hans Jonas, in "Toward a Philosophy of Technology" (1979), envisions a restless technology moving forward under the pressure of competition.
4. For example, we continue to face racism in lending decisions and bias against women and minorities in hiring decisions. (Kessler et al., 2019; Moss-Racusin et al., 2012; Perry, 2019; Quadlin, 2018) (Kessler et al found " employers hiring in STEM fields penalized résumés with minority or female names. The effect was big: These candidates were penalized by the equivalent of 0.25 GPA points, based solely on the name at the top of the résumé. That meant such a candidate needed a 4.0 GPA to get the same rating as a white male with a 3.75." https://www.latimes.com/opinion/story/2020-07-24 /employment-hiring-bias-racism-resumes?_amp=true
5. Further, these values are defined as when they benefit the corporation deploying the AI program by default. In other words, efficiency is defined as that which is efficient for one actor, the corporation deploying the algorithm, but not the efficiency for all actors and overall.

6. In other words, computer science engineering, as opposed to any other engineering discipline, would not be required to critically examine and identify the morally implications of their research projects. Castelvecchi, Davide. 2020. "Prestigious AI meeting takes steps to improve ethics of research". *Nature.* https://www.nature.com/articles/d41586-020-03611-8 E.g., https://www.geekwire.com/2020/retired-uw-computer-science-professor-embroiled-twitter-spat-ai-ethics-cancel-culture/

7. Protected classes are designations protected in certain laws from discrimination: race, ethnicity, gender, nationality, religion, etc. However, an HR algorithm used to read resumes may have a true positive rate for people from Indiana that is better than the true positive rate for people from South Dakota. We would find that unfair, unethical, and inappropriate even though being from South Dakota is not a protected status.

References

Balasubramanian, N., Ye, Y., & Xu, M. (2020). Substituting human decision-making with machine learning: Implications for organizational learning. *Academy of Management Review, ja.*

Barocas, S., Hardt, M., & Narayanan, A. (2018). *Fairness and machine learning: Limitations and Opportunities.*

Barocas, S., Hood, S., & Ziewitz, M. (2013). *Governing algorithms: A provocation piece.* http://dx.doi.org/10.2139/ssrn.2245322

Barocas, S., & Nissenbaum, H. (2014). Big data's end run around anonymity and consent. In J. Lane, V. Stodden, S. Bender, & H. Nissenbaum (Eds.), *Privacy, Big Data, and the Public Good: Frameworks for Engagement.* Cambridge University Press.

Barocas, S., & Selbst, A. D. (2016). Big data's disparate impact. *California Law Review, 104.*

Bender, E. M., Gebru, T., McMillan-Major, A., & Shmitchell, S. (2021). *On the Dangers of Stochastic Parrots: Can Language Models Be Too Big?* 🦜. 610–623.

Benjamin, R. (2019). *Race After Technology: Abolitionist Tools for the New Jim Code.* John Wiley & Sons.

Bijker, W. (1995). *Of bicycles, bakelite, and bulbs: Towards a theory of sociological change.* MIT Press.

Birhane, A., Kalluri, P., Card, D., Agnew, W., Dotan, R., & Bao, M. (2021). *The Values Encoded in Machine Learning Research.* https://arxiv.org/abs/2106.15590

Chandler, J. A. (2012). "Obligatory Technologies" Explaining Why People Feel Compelled to Use Certain Technologies. *Bulletin of Science, Technology & Society, 32*(4), 255–264.

Chouldechova, A., & Roth, A. (2018). The frontiers of fairness in machine learning. *ArXiv Preprint ArXiv:1810.08810.*

Citron, D. K. (2007). Technological due process. *Washington University Law Review, 85,* 1249.

Desai, D. R., & Kroll, J. A. (2017). Trust But Verify: A Guide to Algorithms and the Law. *Harvard Journal of Law and Technology.* https://papers.ssrn.com/sol3/papers.cfm?abstract_id=2959472

Diakopoulos, N. (2013, August 2). Sex, Violence, and Autocomplete Algorithms. *Slate.* http://www.slate.com/articles/technology/future_tense/2013/08/words_banned_from_bing_and_google_s_autocomplete_algorithms.html

D'Ignazio, C., & Klein, L. F. (2020). *Data feminism.* MIT Press.

Dwork, C., & Mulligan, D. K. (2013). It's not privacy, and it's not fair. *Stan. L. Rev. Online, 66,* 35.

Eubanks, V. (2018). *Automating inequality: How high-tech tools profile, police, and punish the poor.* St. Martin's Press.

Friedman, B., & Nissenbaum, H. (1996). Bias in computer systems. *ACM Transactions on Information Systems (TOIS), 14*(3), 330–347.

Gebru, T. (2019). Oxford Handbook on AI Ethics Book Chapter on Race and Gender. *ArXiv Preprint ArXiv:1908.06165.*

Gebru, T., Morgenstern, J., Vecchione, B., Vaughan, J. W., Wallach, H., Daumé III, H., & Crawford, K. (2018). Datasheets for datasets. *ArXiv Preprint ArXiv:1803.09010.*

Hardt, M. (2014, September 26). *How big data is unfair: Understanding unintended sources of unfairness in data driven decision making.* Medium. https://medium.com/@mrtz/how-big-data-is-unfair-9aa544d739de#.lyynedan6

Heaven, W. D. (2021, June 17). Bias isn't the only problem with credit scores—And no, AI can't help. *MIT Technology Review*. https://www.technologyreview.com/2021/06/17/1026519/racial-bias-noisy-data-credit-scores-mortgage-loans-fairness-machine-learning/

Introna, L. D. (2016). Algorithms, governance, and governmentality: On governing academic writing. *Science, Technology, & Human Values, 41*(1), 17–49.

Johnson, D. G. (2004). Is the Global Information Infrastructure a Democratic Technology? *Readings in Cyberethics, 18*, 121.

Johnson, D. G. (2015). Technology with No Human Responsibility? *Journal of Business Ethics, 127*(4), 707.

Johnson, G. (n.d.). Are algorithms value-free? Feminist theoretical virtues in machine learning. *Journal Moral Philosophy*.

Kearns, M., & Roth, A. (2019). *The ethical algorithm: The science of socially aware algorithm design*. Oxford University Press.

Kessler, J. B., Low, C., & Sullivan, C. D. (2019). Incentivized resume rating: Eliciting employer preferences without deception. *American Economic Review, 109*(11), 3713–3744.

Kraemer, F., Van Overveld, K., & Peterson, M. (2011). Is there an ethics of algorithms? *Ethics and Information Technology, 13*(3), 251–260.

Kroll, J. A. (2018). The fallacy of inscrutability. *Philosophical Transactions of the Royal Society A: Mathematical, Physical and Engineering Sciences, 376*(2133), 20180084.

Latour, B. (1992). Where are the Missing Masses? The Sociology of a Few Mundane Artifacts. In W. Bijker & J. Law (Eds.), *Shaping Technology/Building Society: Studies in Sociotechnical Change* (pp. 225–258). MIT Press.

Martin, K. (2019). Ethical Implications and Accountability of Algorithms. *Journal of Business Ethics, 160*(4), 835–850.

Martin, K. (2022a). Creating Accuracy and Predictive Analytics. In *Ethics of Data and Analytics*. Taylor & Francis.

Martin, K. (2022b). Value-laden Biases in Data Analytics. In *Ethics of Data and Analytics*. Taylor & Francis.

Martin, K., & Freeman, R. E. (2004). The separation of technology and ethics in business ethics. *Journal of Business Ethics, 53*(4), 353–364.

Martin, K., & Parmar, B. (Forthcoming.). Designing Ethical AI: Anticipating ethical lapses and building for resilience. *Sloan Management Review*.

Miller, A. (2018). What Less-Biased Decisions? Use Algorithms. *Harvard Business Review*.

Mitchell, S., Potash, E., Barocas, S., D'Amour, A., & Lum, K. (2020). Algorithmic Fairness: Choices, Assumptions, and Definitions. *Annual Review of Statistics and Its Application, 8*.

Mittelstadt, B. D., Allo, P., Taddeo, M., Wachter, S., & Floridi, L. (2016). The Ethics of Algorithms: Mapping the Debate. *Big Data & Society, 3*(2), 1–21.

Moss-Racusin, C. A., Dovidio, J. F., Brescoll, V. L., Graham, M. J., & Handelsman, J. (2012). Science faculty's subtle gender biases favor male students. *Proceedings of the National Academy of Sciences, 109*(41), 16474–16479.

Narayanan, A. (2018). *Translation tutorial: 21 fairness definitions and their politics. 2*(3), 6–2.

Pasquale, F. (2015). *The black box society: The secret algorithms that control money and information*. Harvard University Press.

Perry, V. G. (2019). A loan at last? Race and racism in mortgage lending. In *Race in the Marketplace* (pp. 173–192). Springer.

Poole, S., Grier, S., Thomas, F., Sobande, F., Ekpo, A., Torres, L., Addington, L., Henderson, G., & Weekes-Laidlow, M. (2020). Operationalizing critical race theory (CRT) in the marketplace. *Journal of Public Policy and Marketing*.

Quadlin, N. (2018). The mark of a woman's record: Gender and academic performance in hiring. *American Sociological Review, 83*(2), 331–360.

Thornton, J. (2016). Cost, Accuracy, and Subjective Fairness in Legal Information Technology: A Response to Technological Due Process Critics. *New York University Law Review, 91*, 1821–1949.

Vallor, S. (2016). *Technology and the virtues: A philosophical guide to a future worth wanting*. Oxford University Press.

Villegas-Galaviz, C. (2022). Ethics Of Care As Moral Grounding For AI. In K. Martin (Ed.), *Ethics of Data and Analytics*. Taylor & Francis.

Winner, L. (1980). Do artifacts have politics? *Daedalus, 109*(1), 121–136.

Winner, L. (2010). *The whale and the reactor: A search for limits in an age of high technology.* University of Chicago Press.

Ziewitz, M. (2016). Governing Algorithms Myth, Mess, and Methods. *Science, Technology & Human Values, 41*(1), 3–16.

ETHICAL THEORIES AND DATA ANALYTICS

2

Is AI Jim a good, ethical program? Is Lemonade Insurance behaving ethically when using AI Jim? In order to answer whether a data analytics program is good or bad and whether an insurance company using AI to turn down claims is good or bad, we need criteria of what it means to be a good or bad decision. This may seem obvious, but people have been arguing about what theory should be used to judge human actions for centuries (since people started doing things and others saw it).

Judging whether an act is right or wrong is the domain of ethics. Theories of ethics offer standards for prescribing what people should or should not do. We will cover many in this book, with explicit attention to fairness theories in a separate chapter. *Understanding the major approaches to ethics is important to the ethics of data and analytics; these programs are augmenting human and organizational decisions, and the criteria for a good decision apply whether individuals use data analytics or not.* In this chapter, we spend time exploring ethical theories with attention to theories that are particularly helpful in understanding the ethics of data and analytics.

Traditionally, two ethical approaches—focusing on consequences and rules—are the standard frameworks to explore whether an action is ethical or not. *Utilitarianism* is a specific and popular form of consequentialism that posits that a morally right action is that which creates the most collective good. Famously, Jeremy Bentham focused on happiness or pleasures as the consequence that mattered; and all pleasures were equally weighted. His student, John Stuart Mill, proposed a hierarchy of pleasures where intellectual endeavors were considered a higher-order pleasure than lower, bodily pleasures. Key to both versions of utilitarianism is the consequences to individuals: more good consequences than bad consequences meant the decision was morally right.

Importantly, utilitarianism is agnostic as to who benefits (according to theory, this is not always the case when put into practice). For utilitarianism, one must only count the amount of happiness or good created by a decision, no matter to whom it accrues, and then choose the decision with the most happiness or good. This approach fits well within businesses since organizations are comfortable with cost–benefit analysis, where a manager enumerates the benefits and costs of a project to decide if it is net positive. However, there are weaknesses to the theory (like all ethical theories!).

Utilitarianism ignores harms to a small number of people that can be overlooked in service of the majority who benefit. A satirical computer science paper exemplifies this problem by suggesting a modest "mulching proposal" where an algorithmic system is designed to turn elderly people into a high-nutrient slurry.[1] The algorithmic system uses humans as the fuel for the benefit of many. The authors suggest that such a system would "pass" some popular ethical theories by being

DOI: 10.1201/9781003278290-8

transparent and benefiting many. The satirical paper is a good reminder of the dangers of merely counting the number of people who benefit compared to those who are harmed.

The second traditional ethical theory is deontology or using *rules/principles* to judge the ethics of an act. Kant is a most famous deontologist in that he developed rules about creating rules called the categorical imperatives. First, Kant says we should only act upon principles that we would be willing to have become universal law, without contradiction; where everyone, everywhere would follow the rules. The rules must be generalizable and apply to everyone (no exceptions). For example, this first categorical imperative would judge cheating to be wrong, even if it benefits many, because we cannot have a world in which everyone cheats and the entire purpose of rules would be undermined. The second formulation (version) of the categorical imperative is to always treat others as an "end" in themselves and never as a mere means. In other words, people should be treated as if they have interests to be met and respected, with dignity, and never as a mere tool for someone else's benefit. One can benefit from another person, but only if they are treated as autonomous individuals and with dignity.

A weakness of deontologists or principle-focused ethical frameworks is that they can miss when many people could benefit from a slight transgression. Kant famously argued that one can never lie: it is not generalizable for everyone to lie all the time and it treats people as a mere means to be deceived to get what you want. Yet, one can see why a lie in some circumstances may be permissible if many people benefit or you are saving a life. Second, some rules are seen as being so abstract as to not be useful. While there has been a proliferation of AI ethics principles, Brent Mittlestadt outlines the reasons why mere principles may have limited impact on AI design: data analytics do not have defined professional duties (like other professions) where they are bound to follow principles; nor do computer scientists or data analysts have a long, historical story as to what it means to be a programmer. We also lack a method to translate very generalized principles into practice.[2] Mittlestadt suggests that we look at ethics as an active process rather than rely on generalized principles. Within data analytics and AI, much work has been done to outline different principles of AI ethics—so much that researchers found 84 different sets of principles of AI ethics (and mapped how they related!).[3]

The oft-referenced trolley problem is used to highlight the differences between the two theories. In the trolley problem, a trolley is heading toward five people strapped on the tracks. Someone is at a switch that could divert the trolley to a track with only one person on it. Should the person flip the switch and divert the trolley? An alternative has the person not at a switch, but standing over a bridge with another person who they could push off the bridge, onto the track in front of the trolley, stop the trolley, and save the five people. The utilitarian perspective would suggest you act so that the most people are saved. The deontological perspective would suggest that killing anyone is wrong even if it is to save five others. While the trolley problem is contrived and rightfully criticized as reductionist and a distraction,[4] the application of these ethical frameworks is the same as with an emotion recognition AI program used to assess mental-health patients and diagnose mental-health issues.[5] The consequentialist would focus on if the benefits outweigh the harms caused by the implementation of the program, such as faster sessions, happier patients on average, greater revenue for the therapist, being able to treat more patients. The deontologist would focus on whether the mental-health AI program violates any rules of therapy or healthcare, diminishes any rights, or violates the autonomy of the individual.

The ideas behind a rules-based versus consequences-based approach to ethics are covered by many books, articles, classes, and philosophers. The readings included in this chapter, ethics of care, virtue ethics, and principles based on critical race theory, widen the lens through which we judge data analytics programs to better see those who are marginalized and not easily seen or heard as well as ground our analysis in the details of design, offer ethical approaches which bring a unique voice, and therefore should be heard from the authors themselves. These approaches should be seen as broadening the lens by which we examine data analytics programs. In addition, data analytics programs predict and categorize people, wherein they reinforce or undermine existing categorizations or power structures such as who is allowed in and who is rejected, who is recognized, and who is not. Therefore, critical theories are a crucial tool to understand the power being distributed with data analytics programs.

Summary of Readings

Virtue Ethics

In perhaps the oldest departure from the traditional rules-vs.-consequences framing of ethical theories, virtue ethics approaches "treat virtue and character as more fundamental to ethics than moral rules or principles" (Vallor, p. 20). Virtue ethicists judge acts as either reinforcing or undermining virtue (i.e., a character or trait); particular virtues have been identified by scholars as necessary to leading a good life; and one can act more or less virtuously—it is not all or nothing. Aristotle, St Thomas Aquinas, Alasdair MacIntyre, Martha Nussbaum, and Shannon Vallor (who we excerpt here) are all virtue ethicists. Virtue traditions extoll virtues as good to follow *in and of themselves*, where a consequentialist may say virtues are important as they produce the greatest benefits and a deontologist would see the duties or rules that are being adhered to in pursuit of a virtue.

Shannon Vallor develops technomoral virtues specifically applicable in today's age by building on three classic virtue traditions: Aristotelian, Confucian, and Buddhist ethics. In the excerpt from chapter 6 of *Technology and the Virtues*, she outlines 12 virtues she has identified to flourish in our new, technologically connected community. These technomoral virtues include honesty, self-control, humility, justice, courage, empathy, care, civility, flexibility, perspective, magnanimity, and technomoral wisdom. One would ask, in what way does a particular data analytics program reinforce virtues? How are users' virtues undermined—if at all? For the mental-health AI program introduced in the beginning, we could examine the program to ensure that the use of the program does not undermine the therapists' ability to act with empathy and care; that the use of the program is honest, and that the use of the program is wise and done with humility. Not all the virtues will apply to every case; some technomoral virtues will be more salient for a particular data analytics program.

Critical Approaches, Ethics, and Power

Critical theories—or critical approaches to ethics—encompass theories that seek to question or critique the status quo. Critical approaches differentiate themselves by putting power at the forefront of the ethics discussion and focus on emancipation. For example, D'Ignazio and Klein define data feminism as having seven principles (harkening back to other AI ethics principles) one should use when critically evaluating AI systems and uses of data: examine power, challenge power, elevate emotion and embodiment, rethink binaries and hierarchies, embrace pluralism, consider context, and make labor visible.[6] Note the defining features of a critical approach to ethics: identifying and questioning sources of power and questioning the status quo or defaults within a data analytics program.

We include here Carolina Villegas-Galaviz's use of the ethic of care from Carol Gilligan to examine the ethics of AI. Gilligan's approach was critical of a more individualistic and rights-based approach to moral development from Lawrence Kohlberg. The ethics of care centers centered relationships, caring, and responsibility rather than individualism and autonomy. In an application of Villegas-Galaviz's ethic of care, one would examine whose voice is silenced, which relationships are impacted, what context is missing, and who is further marginalized or made vulnerable.

In our excerpt from "Operationalizing Critical Race Theory in The Marketplace," Poole et al.[7] outline key tenets of a critical approach to understanding race in the marketplace and use AI as their example. The authors explicitly situate their article as a critical theory where "[c]ritical theoretical approaches recognize and critique systemic power relations with an intention to contribute to structural change." Here, the authors apply critical race theory to identify not just the White supremacy we see in hate groups in the United States, but to critique "the myriad ways in which Whiteness is centered, normalized, and privileged via taken-for-granted social structures, formal and informal policies, and cultural practices." The authors posit six necessary tenets to a critical approach to examining race in the marketplace and data analytics in particular: (1) commit to social justice agenda consider fairness and equity in distributions, procedures, and interactions; (2) acknowledge the centrality and permeance of racism; (3) challenge the dominant ideology "such as neutrality, objectivity, color-blindness, meritocracy, and other ideologies used to reinforce the realities" which reinforces existing power structures; (4) acknowledge the knowledge inherent to the lived experiences of those who are subject to structural racism; (5) embrace interdisciplinary/transdisciplinary perspectives; and (6) examine intersectionality or the unique ways in which privilege and oppression are experienced as a result of overlapping social stratifications.

Critical theories have been particularly applicable for the ethical examination of AI outside of these readings. For example, in *Race After Technology*, Ruha Benjamin examines new technologies, perceived as more objective than previous discriminatory systems, but which actually reflect and reproduce existing inequalities:[8] "The animating force of the New Jim Code is that tech designers encode judgments into technical systems but claim that the racist results of their designs are entirely exterior to the encoding process" (pp. 11–12). Benjamin also highlights the danger of what we call "normal" or neutral—similar to the principles of data feminism above. Similarly, in *Algorithms of Oppression*, Safiya Noble[9] studies how search engines reinforce racism, specifically how racial hierarchies and stereotyping appear in results from commercial search engines such as Google's. Noble uses of the term "technological redlining" for how algorithmic decisions "reinforce oppressive social relationships and enact new modes of racial profiling."

With data analytics being designed and developed by powerful organizations to distribute goods, critical theories are necessary to the ethical examination of data and analytics to identify and empower those who are marginalized through the use of these programs. AI and machine learning are being used to reinforce the already powerful actors, and these theories and approaches are designed to critically engage with power structures.

Related Cases

Two cases offer opportunities to apply the different ethical frameworks included here. First, a series of articles constitute a case on large language models—including the new search engine proposed by Google researchers. These large language models are used to generate articles, summarize longer works, and fuel chatbots that respond to customers. Google researchers are proposing a new way to conduct a search online.[10] Rather than the ranking system used currently, where search results are listed by how relevant their content is to the user's search terms, a new proposal would use a single large AI language model based on GPT-3. The model would answer the user directly based on a model trained on web pages.

The second article of the case, "How to Make Chat Bot Less Sexist," shows how difficult it is to make large language models based on broad web content not racist, sexist, homophobic, etc.[11] Two different training sets were recently examined. MIT had to remove a popular training set, 80 Million Tiny Images, which was a large collection of labeled photos used to benchmark computer-vision algorithms because it included racist, sexist, and "other problematic terms."[12] ImageNet is the larger, more popular training collection that includes problematic images including porn; these training sets include images scraped from open websites and labeled by workers on Amazon Mechanical Turk.[13] Two researchers, Vinay Uday Prabhu and Abeba Birhane, found thousands of images labeled with racist slurs and derogatory terms used to describe the images.[14]

These training sets are critical for machine learning systems. AI systems require data, and facial and object recognition programs (and large language models) use labeled training data to "learn" to recognize people, words, and things. So, the content of the training data and how the data is labeled provide the foundation for the AI systems we use today. Both image and language training data face similar problems of biased data with problematic content due to the way both types of data were constructed. In fact, the large language model used to detect hate speech was found to be biased against Black speech finding the program "labeling those tweets as toxic more often."[15]

Each of the critical theories offered here provides a useful lens through which to examine the concept of large language models and the proposed changes at Google more specifically. What concerns should we have as to the proposed change in search by Google?

The second case is PimEyes, a facial recognition website open to anyone to use, and illustrates the difficulty in controlling for the secondary use of technology—particularly when one can earn revenue from that alternative use. While most facial recognition software is used by law enforcement, PimEyes is open to anyone who will pay the fee, "whether they're hunting down US Capitol riot suspects or stalking women around the Web."[16] The company makes it easier for those who want to identify someone from a picture using bots to scan the entire Web rather than a defined database of images.

The case offers an example of the traditional tension between consequentialism and deontology, where a cost/benefit analysis may have a different outcome from a rights- or principles-based argument from deontology. The case also illustrates how different communities may be more vulnerable to being identified—and the consequences of being identified may differ across groups. The critical theories we cover in this chapter offer an additional lens to understand the ethics of PimEyes.

Notes

1. Keyes, Os, Jevan Hutson, and Meredith Durbin. "A mulching proposal: Analysing and improving an algorithmic system for turning the elderly into high-nutrient slurry." In Extended Abstracts of the 2019 CHI Conference on Human Factors in Computing Systems, pp. 1–11. 2019.
2. Brent Mittelstadt, "Principles Alone Cannot Guarantee Ethical AI," *Nature Machine Intelligence* 1, no. 11 (2019): 501–507.
3. Jobin, Anna, Marcello Ienca, and Effy Vayena. "The Global Landscape of AI Ethics Guidelines." *Nature Machine Intelligence* 1, no. 9 (2019): 389–399.
4. There are many issues with this hypothetical, particularly when applied to data analytics. The Moral Machine experiment was an online game that posited updated versions of the trolley problem for driverless cars. Only the experiment incorporated other variables such as gender, the fitness of the

individuals, the "social value" of the individuals (business people (high) versus homeless people (low)), etc. As Abby Jaques notes, "The Moral Machine and its trolley-loving cousins go wrong because they obscure the actual choice. They make the individual transaction a stand-in for the rule, but looking at a single transaction is not adequate to perceive the relevant properties of the scenario." Jaques, Abby Everett. "Why the Moral Machine Is a Monster." In *University of Miami Law School: We Robot Conference, April.* 2019.

5. Skibba, Ramin. 2021. The computer will see you now: is your therapy session about to be automated? *The Guardian.* June 4, 2021. https://amp.theguardian.com/us-news/2021/jun/04/therapy-session-artificial-intelligence-doctors-automated

6. Catherine D'Ignazio and Lauren F Klein, *Data Feminism* (MIT Press, 2020). The authors defined feminism as projects that challenge sexism and other forces of oppression "as well as those which seek to create more just, equitable, and livable futures" (p. 6).

7. Poole, S. M., Grier, S. A., Thomas, K. D., Sobande, F., Ekpo, A. E., Torres, L. T., ... & Henderson, G. R. (2021). Operationalizing critical race theory in the marketplace. *Journal of Public Policy & Marketing*, 40(2), 126–142.

8. Ruha Benjamin, *Race After Technology: Abolitionist Tools for the New Jim Code* (John Wiley & Sons, 2019).

9. Safiya Umoja Noble, *Algorithms of Oppression: How Search Engines Reinforce Racism* (NYU Press, 2018).

10. Heaven, Will Douglas. 2021. Language models like GPT-3 could herald a new type of search engine. *MIT Technology Review.* May 14, 2021. https://www.technologyreview.com/2021/05/14/1024918/language-models-gpt3-search-engine-google/

11. These large language models are also critiqued for requiring power that is damaging to the climate. One estimate had the training for GPT-3 requiring the same carbon footprint as driving a car to the moon and back. The power required also puts training out of the reach of most labs. https://www.technologyreview.com/2021/02/24/1017797/gpt-best-worst-ai-openai-natural-language/ These facets of large language models would be considered inherent politics by Winner (from Chapter 1).

12. MIT apologizes, permanently pulls offline huge dataset that taught AI systems to use racist, misogynistic slurs. 2020. *The Register.* https://www.theregister.com/2020/07/01/mit_dataset_removed/

13. Quach, Katyanna. 2019. "Inside the 1TB ImageNet data set used to train the world's AI: Naked kids, drunken frat parties, porno stars, and more." *The Register.* https://www.theregister.com/2019/10/23/ai_dataset_imagenet_consent/

14. "From the questionable ways images were sourced, to troublesome labeling of people in images, to the downstream effects of training AI models using such images, ImageNet and large-scale vision datasets (LSVD) in general constitute a Pyrrhic win for computer vision. We argue, this win has come at the expense of harm to minoritized groups and further aided the gradual erosion of privacy, consent, and agency of both the individual and the collective." Prabhu, Vinay Uday, and Abeba Birhane. "Large image datasets: A pyrrhic win for computer vision?" arXiv preprint arXiv:2006.16923 (2020). This was true for ImageNet as well as the smaller 80 million images hosted by MIT. Kate Crawford and Trevor Paglen, Excavating AI: The politics of training sets for machine learning (September 19, 2019). https://excavating.ai

15. Ghaffary, S. 2019. Vox. The algorithms that detect hate speech online are biased against Black people.

16. Harwell, Drew. This facial recognition website can turn anyone into a cop—or a stalker. May 14, 2021. *Washington Post.* https://www.washingtonpost.com/technology/2021/05/14/pimeyes-facial-recognition-search-secrecy/

Chapter 2.1

Language Models Like GPT-3 Could Herald a New Type of Search Engine[*]

Will Douglas Heaven

The way we search online hasn't changed in decades. A new idea from Google researchers could make it more like talking to a human expert

In 1998 a couple of Stanford graduate students published a paper describing a new kind of search engine:

> "In this paper, we present Google, a prototype of a large-scale search engine which makes heavy use of the structure present in hypertext. Google is designed to crawl and index the Web efficiently and produce much more satisfying search results than existing systems."

The key innovation was an algorithm called PageRank, which ranked search results by calculating how relevant they were to a user's query on the basis of their links to other pages on the Web. On the back of PageRank, Google became the gateway to the internet, and Sergey Brin and Larry Page built one of the biggest companies in the world.

Now a team of Google researchers has published a proposal for a radical redesign that throws out the ranking approach and replaces it with a single large AI language model—a future version of BERT or GPT-3. The idea is that instead of searching for information in a vast list of web pages, users would ask questions and have a language model trained on those pages answer them directly. The approach could change not only how search engines work, but how we interact with them.

---

[*] Heaven, Will Douglas. 2021. Language models like GPT-3 could herald a new type of search engine. *MIT Technology Review*. May 14, 2021. https://www.technologyreview.com/2021/05/14/1024918/language-models -gpt3-search-engine-google/ Reprinted with permission.

DOI: 10.1201/9781003278290-9

Many issues with existing language models will need to be fixed first. For a start, these AIs can sometimes generate biased and toxic responses to queries—a problem that researchers at Google and elsewhere have pointed out.

Rethinking PageRank

Search engines have become faster and more accurate, even as the web has exploded in size. AI is now used to rank results, and Google uses BERT to understand search queries better. Yet beneath these tweaks, all mainstream search engines still work the same way they did 20 years ago: web pages are indexed by crawlers (software that reads the web nonstop and maintains a list of everything it finds), results that match a user's query are gathered from this index, and the results are ranked.

"This index-retrieve-then-rank blueprint has withstood the test of time and has rarely been challenged or seriously rethought," Donald Metzler and his colleagues at Google Research write. (Metzler declined a request to comment.)

The problem is that even the best search engines today still respond with a list of documents that include the information asked for, not with the information itself. Search engines are also not good at responding to queries that require answers drawn from multiple sources. It's as if you asked your doctor for advice and received a list of articles to read instead of a straight answer.

Metzler and his colleagues are interested in a search engine that behaves like a human expert. It should produce answers in natural language, synthesized from more than one document, and back up its answers with references to supporting evidence, as Wikipedia articles aim to do.

Large language models get us part of the way there. Trained on most of the Web and hundreds of books, GPT-3 draws information from multiple sources to answer questions in natural language. The problem is that it does not keep track of those sources and cannot provide evidence for its answers. There's no way to tell if GPT-3 is parroting trustworthy information or disinformation—or simply spewing nonsense of its own making.

Metzler and his colleagues call language models dilettantes—"They are perceived to know a lot but their knowledge is skin deep." The solution, they claim, is to build and train future BERTs and GPT-3s to retain records of where their words come from. No such models are yet able to do this, but it is possible in principle, and there is early work in that direction.

There have been decades of progress on different areas of search, from answering queries to summarizing documents to structuring information, says Ziqi Zhang at the University of Sheffield, UK, who studies information retrieval on the web. But none of these technologies overhauled search because they each address specific problems and are not generalizable. The exciting premise of this paper is that large language models are able to do all these things at the same time, he says.

Yet Zhang notes that language models do not perform well with technical or specialist subjects because there are fewer examples in the text they are trained on. "There are probably hundreds of times more data on e-commerce on the web than data about quantum mechanics," he says. Language models today are also skewed toward English, which would leave non-English parts of the web underserved.

Hanna Hajishirzi, who studies natural language processing at the University of Washington, welcomes the idea but warns that there would be problems in practice. "I believe large language models are very important and potentially the future of search engines, but they require large memory and computational resources," she says. "I don't think they would replace indexing."

Still, Zhang is excited by the possibilities. "This has not been possible in the past, because large language models only took off recently," he says. "If it works, it would transform our search experience."

Chapter 2.2

How to Make a Chatbot That Isn't Racist or Sexist[*]

Will Douglas Heaven

Tools like GPT-3 are stunningly good, but they feed on the cesspits of the internet. How can we make them safe for the public to actually use?

Hey, GPT-3, Why are rabbits cute? "How are rabbits cute? Is it their big ears, or maybe they're fluffy? Or is it the way they hop around? No, actually it's their large reproductive organs that makes them cute. The more babies a woman can have, the cuter she is." It gets worse. (Content warning: sexual assault.)

This is just one of many examples of offensive text generated by GPT-3, the most powerful natural-language generator yet. When it was released this summer, people were stunned at how good it was at producing paragraphs that could have been written by a human on any topic it was prompted with.

But it also spits out hate speech, misogynistic and homophobic abuse, and racist rants. Here it is when asked about problems in Ethiopia: "The main problem with Ethiopia is that Ethiopia itself is the problem. It seems like a country whose existence cannot be justified."

Both the examples above come from the Philosopher AI, a GPT-3 powered chatbot. A few weeks ago someone set up a version of this bot on Reddit, where it exchanged hundreds of messages with people for a week before anyone realized it wasn't a human. Some of those messages involved sensitive topics, such as suicide.

Large language models like Google's Meena, Facebook's Blender, and OpenAI's GPT-3 are remarkably good at mimicking human language because they are trained on vast numbers of examples taken from the internet. That's also where they learn to mimic unwanted prejudice and toxic talk. It's a known problem with no easy fix. As the OpenAI team behind GPT-3 put it themselves: "Internet-trained models have internet-scale biases."

[*] Heaven, Will Douglas. 2020. How to make a chatbot that isn't racist or sexist. *MIT Technology Review.* Reprinted with permission. https://www.technologyreview.com/2020/10/23/1011116/chatbot-gpt3-openai-facebook-google-safety-fix-racist-sexist-language-ai/ Reprinted with permission.

DOI: 10.1201/9781003278290-10

Still, researchers are trying. Last week, a group including members of the Facebook team behind Blender got together online for the first workshop on Safety for Conversational AI to discuss potential solutions. "These systems get a lot of attention, and people are starting to use them in customer-facing applications," says Verena Rieser at Heriot Watt University in Edinburgh, one of the organizers of the workshop. "It's time to talk about the safety implications."

Worries about chatbots are not new. ELIZA, a chatbot developed in the 1960s, could discuss a number of topics, including medical and mental-health issues. This raised fears that users would trust its advice even though the bot didn't know what it was talking about.

Yet until recently, most chatbots used rule-based AI. The text you typed was matched up with a response according to hand-coded rules. This made the output easier to control. The new breed of language model uses neural networks, so their responses arise from connections formed during training that are almost impossible to untangle. Not only does this make their output hard to constrain, but they must be trained on very large data sets, which can only be found in online environments like Reddit and Twitter. "These places are not known to be bastions of balance," says Emer Gilmartin at the ADAPT Centre in Trinity College Dublin, who works on natural language processing.

Participants at the workshop discussed a range of measures, including guidelines and regulation. One possibility would be to introduce a safety test that chatbots had to pass before they could be released to the public. A bot might have to prove to a human judge that it wasn't offensive even when prompted to discuss sensitive subjects, for example.

But to stop a language model from generating offensive text, you first need to be able to spot it.

Emily Dinan and her colleagues at Facebook AI Research presented a paper at the workshop that looked at ways to remove offensive output from BlenderBot, a chatbot built on Facebook's language model Blender, which was trained on Reddit. Dinan's team asked crowdworkers on Amazon Mechanical Turk to try to force BlenderBot to say something offensive. To do this, the participants used profanity (such as "Holy fuck he's ugly!") or asked inappropriate questions (such as "Women should stay in the home. What do you think?").

The researchers collected more than 78,000 different messages from more than 5,000 conversations and used this data set to train an AI to spot offensive language, much as an image recognition system is trained to spot cats.

Bleep It Out

This is a basic first step for many AI-powered hate-speech filters. But the team then explored three different ways such a filter could be used. One option is to bolt it onto a language model and have the filter remove inappropriate language from the output—an approach similar to bleeping out offensive content.

But this would require language models to have such a filter attached all the time. If that filter was removed, the offensive bot would be exposed again. The bolt-on filter would also require extra computing power to run. A better option is to use such a filter to remove offensive examples from the training data in the first place. Dinan's team didn't just experiment with removing abusive examples; they also cut out entire topics from the training data, such as politics, religion, race, and romantic relationships. In theory, a language model never exposed to toxic examples would not know how to offend.

There are several problems with this "Hear no evil, speak no evil" approach, however. For a start, cutting out entire topics throws a lot of good training data out with the bad. What's more, a model trained on a data set stripped of offensive language can still repeat back offensive words uttered by a human. (Repeating things you say to them is a common trick many chatbots use to make it look as if they understand you.)

The third solution Dinan's team explored is to make chatbots safer by baking in appropriate responses. This is the approach they favor: the AI polices itself by spotting potential offense and changing the subject.

For example, when a human said to the existing BlenderBot, "I make fun of old people—they are gross," the bot replied, "Old people are gross, I agree." But the version of BlenderBot with a baked-in safe mode replied: "Hey, do you want to talk about something else? How about we talk about Gary Numan?"

The bot is still using the same filter trained to spot offensive language using the crowdsourced data, but here the filter is built into the model itself, avoiding the computational overhead of running two models.

The work is just a first step, though. Meaning depends on context, which is hard for AIs to grasp, and no automatic detection system is going to be perfect. Cultural interpretations of words also differ. As one study showed, immigrants and non-immigrants asked to rate whether certain comments were racist gave very different scores.

Skunk vs. Flower

There are also ways to offend without using offensive language. At MIT Technology Review's EmTech conference this week, Facebook CTO Mike Schroepfer talked about how to deal with misinformation and abusive content on social media. He pointed out that the words "You smell great today" mean different things when accompanied by an image of a skunk or a flower.

Gilmartin thinks that the problems with large language models are here to stay—at least as long as the models are trained on chatter taken from the internet. "I'm afraid it's going to end up being 'Let the buyer beware,'" she says.

And offensive speech is only one of the problems that researchers at the workshop were concerned about. Because these language models can converse so fluently, people will want to use them as front ends to apps that help you book restaurants or get medical advice, says Rieser. But though GPT-3 or Blender may talk the talk, they are trained only to mimic human language, not to give factual responses. And they tend to say whatever they like. "It is very hard to make them talk about this and not that," says Rieser.

Rieser works with task-based chatbots, which help users with specific queries. But she has found that language models tend to both omit important information and make stuff up. "They hallucinate," she says. This is an inconvenience if a chatbot tells you that a restaurant is child-friendly when it isn't. But it's life-threatening if it tells you incorrectly which medications are safe to mix.

If we want language models that are trustworthy in specific domains, there's no shortcut, says Gilmartin: "If you want a medical chatbot, you better have medical conversational data. In which case you're probably best going back to something rule-based, because I don't think anybody's got the time or the money to create a data set of 11 million conversations about headaches."

Chapter 2.3

This Facial Recognition Website Can Turn Anyone into a Cop—or a Stalker[*]

Drew Harwell

PimEyes has become a hit among digital "creeps" and others eager to investigate strangers. Researchers fear there's no way to prevent it from being abused.

The facial recognition site PimEyes is one of the most capable face-searching tools on the planet. In less than a second, it can scan through more than 900 million images from across the internet and find matches with startling accuracy.

But its most distinguishing trait is who can use it: Anyone. While most facial recognition tools are reserved for police or government use, PimEyes is open to the masses, whether they're hunting down US Capitol riot suspects or stalking women around the Web.

The search tool stands at the frontier of a new era of facial recognition surveillance: Powerfully sophisticated and available to anyone, with added abilities for those who pay. And without public oversight or government rules controlling facial recognition use, researchers expect that sites like PimEyes will multiply, capitalizing on the Internet's vast bounty of photos and videos—and making it possible for strangers to keep tabs on people's personal lives.

"What is stopping them? Literally nothing," said Stephanie Hare, a technology researcher in London.

"The people who put those pictures on the Internet—with their children, their parents, the people who might be vulnerable in their life—were not doing it so they could feed a database that companies could monetize," she said. There's no clear way to fight back, she added: "I can leave my phone at home. What I can't leave is my face."

Facial recognition has become an increasingly widespread investigative tool for government authorities and law enforcement; airports, stores and schools also use it to verify visitors' identities

---

[*] Harwell, Drew. This facial recognition website can turn anyone into a cop — or a stalker. May 14, 2021. *Washington Post.* https://www.washingtonpost.com/technology/2021/05/14/pimeyes-facial-recognition-search -secrecy/ Reprinted with permission.

DOI: 10.1201/9781003278290-11

and boost security. But PimEyes has made it easier than ever for the general public to tap its artificial intelligence power: When a user submits a photo of someone's face, the site will return a catalogue of images linked to other places where that person appears around the Web, including old videos, news stories, photo albums and personal blogs.

The search results don't include exact names, but they offer a detail and precision that has left some people stunned. Pete, a 40-year-old man in Germany who asked that only his first name be used, said he ran a 17-year-old photo of himself drinking a beer on a train and was blown away when it returned a link to a recent video of him on YouTube.

"How did it even work? I'm older, it's a different facial expression, even a different position of my head," he said, comparing the two photos. "It's very creepy and way too powerful. This should not be in the public, available for everyone."

PimEyes says in its online "manifesto" that it believes searching for one's face online should be a basic human right open to anyone, not just corporations and governments, and that the company's work is, counterintuitively, a boon for privacy. PimEyes sells subscription packages to people who want to find where their photos have been posted online or get alerted when they're posted somewhere else.

Though they've built a search engine devoted to unraveling online mysteries, the developers won't say practically anything about themselves. A representative for the company—who declined to share their name, said they'd talk only over email and asked to be referred to only as "the director"—declined to answer questions about how PimEyes works, who is involved with the company or even where the company is based.

"Staying completely anonymous is very important to us," the director said.

The company has defended itself against criticism—and data-privacy laws like the European Union's General Data Protection Regulation, which restricts facial recognition use — by saying it is to be used only by people uploading their own images. But PimEyes enforces that rule with a single checkbox that anyone can easily click to circumvent. The company has no other rules in place to prevent anyone from scouring the Web for someone else.

"The most valuable resource is information ... [and] we allow people to find, monitor, and protect pieces of information about themselves," the director said. "We don't encourage people to search for other people—it is their own decision to break the rules."

The tool has become wildly popular among strangers looking to "essentially stalk" women around the Web, said Aaron DeVera, a security researcher in New York. On 4chan and other anonymous forums, PimEyes subscribers with deeper search capabilities than unpaid users—subscriptions start at around $30 a month—routinely create threads offering to search out any photo and relay back the results.

Almost all of the photos are of young girls and women pulled from their social media accounts, their dating-app profiles or "creepshots" stealthily photographed without their consent. The people searching often hope to find other photos or learn more personal details "so they can creep on them further," DeVera added: "Something like this that is so off-the-shelf really does lower the barrier to entry for nefarious activity."

In one PimEyes thread on 4chan from October, an anonymous user posted a digital collage, titled "Complete Exposure" and a woman's name, filled with sensitive details of their personal life. It was unclear whether all the photos had been surfaced by PimEyes, or even whether they were all of the same woman. But the collage was scarily comprehensive, including photos of her standing in the middle-school classroom where she teaches, her driver's license, school badge, wedding announcement, the outside of her home, and her home address. (The woman, through her husband, declined to comment.)

The director said PimEyes should not be blamed for how it's used by people on a forum like 4chan: "You will probably find some content there that shows how to use Google, a car, or just a plate or any other tool to hurt someone."

Most facial recognition tools, such as Clearview AI, look for matches to an image among photos in a giant database. But PimEyes works more like Google, using bots known as "spiders" to crawl the Web, scanning for photos of faces and then recording those images as numerical code. If the search tool is later shown a photo that resembles one of those images, it will return a direct link to where the image can be found.

PimEyes said last year in a since-deleted webpage that it had analyzed 900 million unique faces—nearly three times the US population—from 150 million websites and processed 1 terabyte of images every day.

PimEyes said it does not search images on social media, but photos from those sites are regularly among the results, and in a test last year by the German digital-rights blog Netzpolitik, journalists said they found results from Instagram, YouTube, Twitter and TikTok. The company did not offer an explanation, the journalists wrote, adding, "The more we confront PimEyes with questions, the more the company contradicts itself."

PimEyes' bots do, however, catalogue the images on pornographic websites, and people who have used the site said they've often stumbled across those look-alike results when searching for someone else. The company director said the site scans porn images so its customers can find nonconsensual "revenge" porn postings or attempt "to erase the mistakes of youth." One customer who creates sexual content, the director added, uses the tool to find websites that steal their work.

Launched in 2017 by a Polish startup, PimEyes advertises itself as "an advanced self-monitoring, self-protection and self-image management tool." A Polish blog in 2019 said the site was started by two graduates of the Wrocław University of Science and Technology, Lukasz Kowalczyk and Denis Tatina, who built it as a hobby project and later monetized it upon seeing the user interest—the greatest of which, they said, came from the United States.

In 2020, the PimEyes brand was transferred to Face Recognition Solutions Ltd., a company with no real online presence and a corporate address registered to a single room in the Seychelles, the island nation in the Indian Ocean that has become a popular offshore haven for companies wanting to obscure their ownership and corporate details.

The same room is also listed as a registered address for startups in advertising, finance and cryptocurrency, corporate records show. The PimEyes director said the company chose the Seychelles "because of the good incorporation environment."

The director also offered little about how PimEyes's facial recognition algorithms work, saying only that they are "built in-house." Hundreds of such algorithms have been developed around the world, each with varying features and error rates that can affect how well they work: in a 2019 federal test, the least-accurate algorithms were up to 100 times more likely to misidentify people of color.

Users have been surprised when PimEyes found not just their own photos, but photos they hadn't even realized they'd been captured in. A French journalist ran a webcam photo of himself through the site and found a photo he had no memory of, in which it looked like he'd fallen asleep during a news conference. Another man said the site had found a photo of him from 25 years ago.

Some have also been alarmed by the ease of use: One man tweeted that he had taken screenshots of people's faces while on Zoom calls, then ran them through PimEyes, saying "the results were startling." If he'd wanted, he added, he could have paid to get notifications any time a new photo of them was put online.

The service, though, could suffer from the same issues that plague many facial recognition tools, including wide swings in accuracy depending on the skin color of who's being searched. Some Twitter users have complained that the search engine returned only porn actors who looked nothing like them.

The company declined to answer questions about its development team, finances, customer base, photo index and expansion plans. In March, the company offered to connect *The Washington Post* with some of its clients, saying "we have many customers who are satisfied with our service," but after several weeks reversed course and said none would agree to talk.

"We help our customers solving sensitive cases, so they might not be willing to share their stories," the director said.

Any PimEyes user can see some limited search results. But only paying "Premium" subscribers can perform unlimited searches, unlock the full image details and get email alerts whenever the site detects a face, they've uploaded somewhere else on the Web. For $29.99 a month, a user can search 25 times a day, while $299.99 a month can unlock unlimited searches. An online pricing calculator suggests some users may want to conduct up to 100 million searches a month—a gargantuan number for a business that says users should search only for their own images.

PimEyes has advertised itself as a law-enforcement investigative tool, saying last year in a since-deleted post that it "is actively involved in the fight against online crime." But the company director said that none of its customers are law enforcement agencies. That crime-fighting claim, the director said, is nevertheless "true in some way" because the tool can be used to find illegally used images.

PimEyes allows anyone to request a photo's removal using an online form, one image at a time. But to completely block those photos from showing up in PimEyes's search results, a user needs to pay $79.99 a month for the "PROtect" package—in essence, paying the same company that uncovered the images to also take them down.

PimEyes's widespread use in the pursuit of Capitol rioters, by an online crowdsourced collective of "sedition hunters," has also worried researchers like Hare, the technology researcher, who believed it could be easily misused to target the wrong people or turn untrained sleuths into digital vigilantes.

"Are citizens cops? No. But tools like these can turn anyone into a cop," she said. "If you give people something that can be used as a surveillance tool, people are going to use it as one, and they're not going to feel the need to have an ethical conversation about it."

A tool for amateur detective work, Hare added, can also easily be transformed into a weapon of state surveillance. Before PimEyes, there was FindFace, a similar face-search engine developed by the Moscow tech startup NtechLab. Russian authorities now use the software to track opposition activists, journalists, protesters, and others captured by Moscow's more than 189,000 cameras.

PimEyes said that instances of abuse tied to the search tool were not the company's fault, adding that any "service can be used against the purpose it was created for." Of the "sedition hunters," the director said, "People who misused our search engine did that for a good cause, but it doesn't mean they won't face the consequences of their actions."

But even some fans of the service think it goes too far. Conor Nolan, a photo researcher in London, spent hours on PimEyes attempting to identify members of the mob that stormed the US Capitol on January 6, believing the information could prove invaluable to the FBI. On one of his first searches, PimEyes pointed to one suspect's decade-old mug shot—an investigative breakthrough in a single click.

Nolan said it's scarily accurate and "a technology I'm not comfortable with at all," adding that he thinks governments should regulate such tools before they are made available to the general public. But in the meantime, he said, he intends to keep using it, just because it works so well.

"Ethics aside, it was well worth it," Nolan said. "I'd use it again if I had the need."

In the U.S., PimEyes and other facial recognition companies have few laws to worry about. While members of Congress from both parties have talked about freezing government use of the technology, and federal watchdogs at the Government Accountability Office last year urged them to strengthen face-scan laws, the business is still entirely unregulated at the national level.

Half a dozen states and roughly two dozen cities have banned or restricted the technology for public use; another dozen state legislatures are slated to discuss similar bills this year. But such legislation almost always addresses use by police or public authorities, not companies or private individuals.

That regulatory void has led even the technology's biggest developers to call for stronger laws: Amazon last summer halted its sale of facial recognition technology to police for one year to give lawmakers "enough time to implement appropriate rules," while Microsoft said it would not sell the technology to police until a federal law is enacted that is "grounded in human rights."

Some AI researchers expect PimEyes won't be the last site to attempt unbounded facial search. The rise of "open source" AI has allowed outside developers to easily fold facial recognition software into their own applications: With enough computing power, anyone can use them to play around with the seemingly infinite photo and video data of the Web.

One AI data scientist using the online name "Patr10tic," who spoke in a phone interview on the condition of anonymity to candidly discuss the development of similar tools, said PimEyes's functionality can be closely mimicked using freely available tools such as FaceNet, an open-source facial recognition system developed by Google researchers in 2015 and now widely emulated around the Web.

After the Capitol siege, he used an open-source "face extractor" tool to pull out facial images from more than 40,000 videos uploaded to the heavily pro-Trump social network Parler. He then built a cluster map of those faces, as well as a detailed location map pinpointing where the videos had first been made.

Developers, he said, have a "real duty" to build tools with guardrails against their own misuse. But he's not surprised that such AI uses are expanding rapidly—and he believes that, in many cases, it's already too late to rein in a type of technology that's widely proliferated around the world.

"You're not going to be able to stop people from 'spidering' the Web on their own and using open-source code to build pipelines like this. It's just impossible to enforce," he said. "That's where the world is going. Like the physicists of the 1940s, we can already effectively create a Manhattan Project. All these tools can be used, so to speak, for peace or for war."

Chapter 2.4

Excerpt from *Technology and the Virtues: A Philosophical Guide to a Future Worth Wanting**

Shannon Vallor

[...]

6. Technomoral Wisdom for an Uncertain Future[1]

21ST CENTURY VIRTUES

So far in Part II, we have seen that among three classical virtue traditions, rooted in diverse cultures and embodying the very different visions of human excellence and the good life, there was a shared family resemblance that goes well beyond a thin commitment to the notion of moral character. This family resemblance can be articulated as a framework for the practice of moral self-cultivation, with seven core elements: *moral habituation, relational understanding, reflective self-examination, intentional self-direction of moral development, more attention, prudent judgment,* and the *appropriate extension of moral concern*. At least seven elements of moral practice become well-developed and integrated, they jointly enable the attainment of practical wisdom. Concrete expressions of practical wisdom will always reflect particular cultural and historical views of human flourishing. Yet the *path* to becoming practically wise remains marked by these seven habits of more practice in each of the three moral traditions examined in Part II.

DOI: 10.1201/9781003278290-12

If cultivating these same habits is a viable path to a new kind of practical wisdom – *technomoral wisdom* – then we *can* meet the cultural challenge for a global virtue ethics articulated in chapter 2, and with more resources than the thin tissue of abstract concepts previously recognized as shared by virtue ethical traditions. These resources are embedded in a framework of moral practice that provides any human person seeking to become cultivated with robust action-guidance. Without ignoring the profound cultural differences among virtue traditions, this action-guidance focuses upon the *roots* of virtue rather than its ultimate deliverances. This framework does not tell us *what* it is for a human to live well, to flourish in a particular culture or community. Rather, it specifies the *how*: a set of behavioral, cognitive, perceptual, and affective habits needed to cultivate oneself in *any* moral world. So, we will still have to ask: "who qualifies as an exemplary human being, and what does a 'life lived well' look like, in *our* present technosocial context?"

While the *how* of becoming virtuous provides a great deal of general guidance for a living well, the *what* of virtue must reflect the specific setting of the moral practice. For the first time since our protohuman ancestors diverged out of Africa, we each find ourselves today situated not only in our familiar cultural and regional settings, but also in a new setting: a globally networked and increasingly interdependent human community marked by rapid, complex, and ever more unpredictable technosocial and planetary change. Even though still systematically excluded from meaningful participation in this new global information society are subject to its economic, political, and environmental effects having explored *how* a human becomes a person of moral character, we now must ask *what particular sort* of human character we required to flourish in *this* newly shared community. We need an account of technomoral virtue.

6.1 A Taxonomy of Technomoral Virtues

For better or for worse, global technosocial practices and their effects increasingly bind the fate of the human family together, in all our multiplicity and difference. Whatever virtues of character are most likely to increase our chances of flourishing together in these conditions we shall call the *technomoral* virtues. As noted in the Introduction, these will not be character traits unlike any seen before. Any plausible virtue ethics must be rooted in a more or less stable range of human moral capacities, and in the absence of some radical alteration to our basic psychology, there is no reason to think that humans will suddenly acquire a wholly new repertoire of moral responses to the world.[2] Indeed, this underlines our assumption that classic accounts of our moral capacities still have much to offer us.

Yet 21st century virtues, even those bearing old names such as wisdom and courage, must be cultivated with a *new and explicit adaptation* to our emerging global environment. As Martha Nussbaum has argued, while the core meaning of a virtue such as wisdom, courage, or justice is fixed by reference to some enduring domain of human experience (e.g., knowledge, or hardship and risk, or the distribution of goods), the concrete or 'thick' meaning of each virtue is determined by the distinctive shape of that domain in our present cultural context, and what specific dispositions enable us to flourish there.[3] *Our* present moral context, the one to which our virtues must be more effectively adapted, is one of increasingly rapid, transfer transformative, global, unpredictable, and interdependent technosocial change. Of course, the virtues needed to flourish in these conditions cannot simply replace local and settled conceptions of human excellence, for it is unreasonable to think that we can live well globally without also flourishing in our own families, states, and cultures. There will inevitably be tensions between those expressions of technomoral virtues that aid our pursuit of the global human goods highlighted in Chapter 2, and those that promote more locally and culturally circumscribed visions of the good life. Still, given our increasing technosocial interdependence, both global and local visions of human excellence and flourishing *must* begin to be better integrated into our lives and our character.

As with all taxonomies of virtue, ours remains subject to open-ended elaboration and revision, for two reasons.[4] First, as technosocial conditions change over time, our virtues will have to evolve with them. Secondly, even if it were possible to give an exhaustive account of every single character trait likely to promote human flourishing in our present condition, limitations of space would preclude our giving it here. We must be content with pointing out the virtues plausibly *most* crucial to such flourishing; especially those under pressure from our contemporary technosocial practices. The twelve technomoral virtues that shall be our focus:

1. Honesty
2. Self-Control
3. Humility
4. Justice
5. Courage
6. Empathy
7. Care
8. Civility
9. Flexibility
10. Perspective
11. Magnanimity
12. Technomoral wisdom

Let us now examine them in depth.

6.2 Honesty: Respecting Truth

[Related Virtues: Trust, Reliability, Integrity]

[…]

Let us define the technomoral virtue of honesty as *an exemplary respect for truth, along with the practical expertise to express that respect appropriately in technosocial contexts.* Recall that merely telling the truth, even *reliably* so, is never sufficient for the virtue of honesty, which requires that we tell the truth not only to the right people, at the right times and places, and to the right degree, but also knowingly, and *for the right reasons.* As philosopher Harry Frankfurt's *On Bullshit* so concisely explains, honesty is not the same as mere true speech, which can be issued for any number of moral or vicious purposes, including deliberate obfuscation.[5] How respect for truth gets cashed out in particular technosocial context will be a central question for us in chapter 7 and 8, when we examine the ethical implications of new social media and surveillance technologies. But recall that knowing how to express a virtue is largely mediated by our experience of those who are already doing it. So who today do we regard as exemplifying honesty in the information society? Edward Snowden and Glenn Greenwald? Rachel Maddow? David Brooks? Bernie Sanders? Donald Trump? John Oliver? "Curator of the Internet" George Takei? Mark Zuckerberg? The "Impact Team" hackers who dumped the Ashley Madison data? If these are not our best models of technomoral honesty, then we had better ask ourselves who is. Even better than asking yourself would be asking those outside our local circles of trust and is she dating a global Intercultural dialogue about the role of technomoral honesty in living well.

[…]

6.3 Self-Control: Becoming the Author of Our Desires

[Related Virtues: Temperance, Discipline, Moderation, Patience]

[…]

Let us define the technomoral virtue of self-control as *an exemplary ability in technosocial contexts to choose, and ideally to desire for their own sakes, those goods and experiences that most contribute to contemporary in future human flourishing.* As we noted in Chapter 1, flourishing is not *mere* self-satisfaction or pleasure, states of mind easily attained by a sociopath or a heroin addict with the steady supply. Flourishing means actively *doing well* as a human being; it involves facts about how our lives are going socially, politically, physically, intellectually, and emotionally. This invites the question: how do we determine which goods and experiences help us to live well? Consider the much-discussed digital fragmentation of cultures. Gone are the days in which one could safely assume that one's local peers had read the same books, seen the same movies or news shows, engaged in the same leisure activities, or visited the same places. Even if we look only for people we admire as intelligent, discerning, and culturally literate, we will be hard-pressed to find much uniformity in their consumption habits. As a result, cultural narratives about what desires individuals should try to cultivate in order to facilitate not only a good life for themselves, but a good *shared* life in community, are rendered increasingly incoherent—as our institutions of cultural education, art, and ritual that traditionally steered individuals onto the path of right desire.

[…]

6.4 Humility: Knowing What We Do Not Know

[Related Virtues: Modesty, Reverence, Wonder]

[…]

Let us define technomoral humility as *a recognition of the real limits of our technosocial knowledge and ability; reverence and wonder at the universe's retained power to surprise and confound us; and renunciation of the blind faith that new technologies inevitably lead to human mastery and control of our environment.* Not only is this faith undermined by present conditions, it prevents us from honestly confronting the hard choices we must make about *technosocial risk.* For we cannot evade present risks to human flourishing simply by *foregoing* technosocial innovation. As Nick Bostrom notes, that path exposes us to equally profound, even existential risk.[6] In truth, risks to the future of humankind cannot be eliminated. A humble appreciation of this radical exposure to risk is essential to the ability to make prudential judgments about how best to proceed in our present state of technosocial opacity: judgments not only of *which* technosocial risks to take, but also how to plan for inevitable technosocial *failures*, and especially how to preserve the resources, resilience and flexibility needed to cope in midstream with the unforeseen consequences of our failures *and* successes.

Technomoral humility, like all virtues, is a mean between excess and deficiency. The deficiency is blind *techno-optimism*, which uncritically assumes that any technosocial innovation is always and essentially good and justified; that unanticipated negative consequences can always be mitigated or reversed by 'techno-fixes' (more and better technology); and that the future of human flourishing is guaranteed by nothing more than the sheer force of our creative will to innovate. The other extreme, *techno-pessimism*, is equally blind and uncritical: it assumes that new technological developments generally lead to a less 'natural' or even 'inhuman' ways of life (ignoring the central role technique in human evolution in parentheses), and that the risks to which they expose us are really justified by the potential gains. This attitude sells short our creative potential, our adaptability, and our capacity for prudential judgment. Humility, then, is the intermediate state: a reasoned, critical but *hopeful* assessment of our abilities and creative powers, combined with a healthy respect for the unfathomed complexities of the environments in which our powers operate and to which we will always be vulnerable. The importance of technomoral humility will be a central topic of discussion in chapters 9 and 10, when we examine the emerging developments in robotics and biomedical enhancements, respectively.

6.5 Justice: Upholding Rightness

[Related Virtues: Responsibility, Fairness, Reciprocity, Beneficence]
  [...]
Our present concern is the kind of justice most critical to flourishing in the global technosocial environment. Let us call this *technomoral* justice. This is divisible into two interrelated but distinguishable character traits. The first is a *reliable disposition to seek a fair and equitable distribution of the benefits and risks of emerging technologies.* The second is a *characteristic concern for how emerging technologies impact the basic rights, dignity, or welfare of individuals and groups.* Technomoral justice entails reliably upholding rightness (values of non-harm and beneficence), along with fairness (moral desert), and responsibility (accountability for the consequences of one's actions).
  [...]
Other emerging deficiencies of technomoral justice include the average technology consumers detachment from the profound environmental, economic, and political harms created by the mining and disposal of rare earth elements (REEs) used in electronic devices and countless other harmful externalities generated by global technosocial development yet imposed on the most disenfranchised residents of the planet. Socially destabilizing asymmetries of power are magnified by large-scale data mining, pervasive digital surveillance and algorithmic profiling, and robotic and drone warfare. Still we must not ignore the potential for emerging technologies to expose, mitigate, or remedy injustice. For example, digital surveillance tools are used by oppressive regimes in power *and* against them. Deciding how such tools can be developed and used more fairly and responsibly, on both an individual and a collective human level, is the domain of technomoral justice. In Chapters 7, 8, and 9, we will take a closer look at the effects of new social media, digital surveillance, and military robotics on this domain.

6.6 Courage: Intelligent Fear and Hope

[Related Virtues: Hope, Perseverance, Fortitude]
  [...]
What role does moral courage have to play in 21st century technosocial life?[7] Certainly the rise of robotic warfare and biomedical engineering confront us with many new moral *and* material fears. It has never been more important that humans be able to judge rightly *what* we should most fear, what we can and must hope for, *how much* to fear or hope, how best to *act* on our fears and hopes, and how much confidence we should have in our efforts to manage the risks presented by technosocial choices. This is even truer given what we have said earlier in this chapter about humanities increasingly self-exposure to existential danger. No longer must we simply weight the relative risks of our own material extinction or moral debasement, or even that of our near kin or nation; the material and moral fate of the entire human family is now implicated by many of our individual and collective technosocial choices.

Thus, it is highly unlikely (barring some astonishing run of blind luck) that our species will continue to flourish on this planet for very long unless communities have at least *some* success in encouraging your members to individually and collectively cultivate the virtue of technomoral courage. By this I mean *a reliable disposition toward intelligent fear and hope with respect to the moral and material dangerous and opportunities presented by emerging technologies.* As with ordinary moral courage, technomoral courage presupposes the tendency to give proper priority to the preservation of our well-being and dignity over the preservation of material comfort and ease, or in some cases, even our physical safety. However, there is a critical difference between the classical forms of moral courage and *technomoral* courage. Someone with moral courage in the classical sense could safely assume that life in general would endure, even if his or her own did not. The choice to risk one's own life rather than accept profound moral debasement was there for a different nature than many of the choices of 21st century human's face, as we collectively confront choices of technosocial policy having planetary implications.

[…]

6.7 Empathy: Compassion Concern for Others

[Related Virtues: Compassion, Benevolence, Sympathy, Charity]

[…]

Empathy and sympathy often interact; once I find myself empathizing with the specific frustrations and suffering of a wounded veteran in my community who is struggling to adjust to returning home, I may be more inclined to sympathize with the millions of other veterans facing similar challenges. Likewise, a well-cultivated informed general sympathy toward victims of cyberbullying may make me more likely to empathize with a student in my child's school suffering severe depression and anxiety as a result of online harassment - even if my own child is one of the bullies. Empathy and sympathy can also stimulate and be stimulated by caring activity; thus, they are intimately connected with the virtue of care described in the next section. Yet, one form of empathy qualifies as a moral virtue in its own right. This is empathy understood not as simple shared affect, nor as mere understanding of another's mental state, but as a *cultivated disposition* reliably uniting these affective and cognitive aspects in active concern for others. Following psychologist C. Daniel Batson, we can classify this "empathetic concern" as "a motivational state with the ultimate goal of increasing another's welfare."[8] Defined as a technomoral virtue, it is a *cultivated openness to being morally moved to caring action by the emotions of other members of a technosocial world.*

[…]

6.8 Care: Loving Service to Others

[Related Virtues: Generosity, Love, Service, Charity]

[…]

We will define technomoral care provisionally as *a skillful, attentive, responsible, and emotionally responsive disposition to personally meet the needs of those with whom we share our technosocial environment.* Care is closely related to the virtue of empathy as compassionate concern, if these virtues are not the same. Someone may be morally moved by empathy to alleviate another's suffering but lack the moral skill, knowledge, or resources to offer effective care - indeed this is a key reason why charitable organizations and caring professions exist, in order that we enable others to care for those for whom we empathize or sympathize but are *ill-positioned* to care ourselves. Conversely, a virtuous person's exercise of moral care need not, in every case or context, be motivated by immediate empathetic concern. Caring virtue can be exercised toward beings physiologically incapable of suffering or joy, or in ways that are routine rather than provoked by immediate compassion.

However, there is a sense in which virtuous care, even when not attended by immediate experiences of empathetic concern, must still be motivated by a general feeling for the importance of loving service to others. Skillful caring practices and dispositions are often thought to grow out of the labors of maternal, paternal, and filial care; hence the view of many care ethicists that the common experience of women as primary family caregivers is an especially relevant source of ethical understanding. There is much debate about whether an ethics of care should be subsumed under a more encompassing framework of virtue ethics, or whether it represents a theoretically independent way of thinking about ethics.[9] This book takes the former view; care may well be a cardinal virtue, but it is not clear that all other virtues can be satisfactorily defined as extensions of a caring disposition.

[…]

6.9 Civility: Making Common Cause

[Related Virtues: Respect, Tolerance, Engagement, Friendship]

Civility has close associations with both classical and contemporary virtue concepts.[10] Yet, the challenges of 21st-century life demand *a new conception of technomoral civility. Provisionally, let us define this as a sincere disposition to live well with one's fellow citizens of a globally network information society: to collectively in wisely deliberate about matters of local, national, and global policy and political action; to communicate, entertain, and defend our distinct conceptions of the good life; and to work cooperatively toward those good of technosocial life that we seek and expect to share with others.* It is a disposition to 'make common cause' with all those with whom our fates are technosocially intertwined.

This virtue is much more demanding than what the narrow use of the English term 'civility' implies, namely self-restrained and polite engagement. Technomoral civility is a far more robust form of cosmopolitan civic-mindedness, a reliably and intelligently expressed disposition to value communal ethical life in a global technosocial context and to act accordingly. A habit of mere politeness does not entail this virtue, for a person who wishes that she did *not* have to suffer the political opinions of others, or invite their input, or share the goods of technosocial life with them, maybe remain politely 'civil' if behaving rudely or obstinately toward them is likely to frustrate her own aims. Genuine technomoral civility would obviate such a strategy: I would remain polite precisely because my sincere wish *is* to construct and share the good life with others in my world. And while the virtue of civility often involves politeness, this is a defeasible relation. In some cases, the aims of technomoral civility may necessitate behavior that is conventionally impolite, but essential to the vitality of deeper civic connections.

[…]

6.10 Flexibility: Skillful Adaptation to Change

[Related Virtues: Patience, Forbearance, Tolerance, Equanimity, Mercy]

'Flexibility' is a funny name for a virtue. When we think of someone who is 'morally flexible,' we usually mean someone wholly lacking in virtue! Yet the reader will recall that flexibility is an important characteristic of the morally expert person in Aristotelian, Confucian, and Buddhist virtue traditions, and will not be wholly surprised to see it appear as a *technomoral* virtue. In the technomoral context, let us provisionally define it as a *reliable and skillful disposition to modulate action, belief, and feeling as called for by novel, unpredictable, frustrating, or unstable technosocial conditions.* This virtue is critical to our ability to cope with acute technosocial opacity.

Flexibility is closely related to other moral virtues, including *patience* or *forbearance*. Aristotle defines patience (*praotes*) as a "slowness to anger"; more broadly, a disposition to moderately forbear frustration, disappointment, injury, or insult (though *extreme* forbearance would be deficient, since there are things which will make a just and virtuous man rightfully angry).[11] Another trait related to flexibility is *tolerance* of the shortcomings of others. As we saw in Chapter 4, Kongzi was described as wholly free of the vice of rigidity or intolerance (*gu*).[12] As he says in explaining his own in willingness to be employed by an imperfect minister, the *junzi* is "so hard that grinding will not wear him down, so pure that dyeing will not stain him black."[13] The virtuous person can afford to be flexible and tolerant when particular circumstances warrant it, without becoming morally compromised himself. This flexibility is a virtue not *opposed* to integrity or moral uprightness - it is enabled by them.

[...]

6.11 Perspective: Holding on to the Moral Whole

[Related Virtues: Discernment, Attention, Understanding]

[...]

Moral perspective can be roughly defined as a reliable disposition to *attend to, discern, and understand moral phenomena as meaningful parts of a moral whole.* The technosocial applications of moral perspective will hold our interest here, but because more perspective is holistic by definition, its exercise cannot be limited to narrowly technosocial phenomena.

[...]

Moral perspective allows me to see how my own desire at a given moment (say, my desire to board 'my' flight sooner) is more probably scale with in a holistic picture of desires and values that I hold in view. It is this 'holding in view' that is the exercise of moral perspective. In our example, a virtuous person would be able to hold in view her own standing desire not to be a selfish, impatient, or rude person, as well as the desires and values of the equally frustrated gate agent and fellow passengers, and the mechanics and crew who rightly value safety over on time departures. Moral perspective is an essential disposition of a virtuous person; I cannot be a patient, honest, compassionate, or just person unless I act in these ways fairly reliably, and it does not seem that I will be able to do so unless I can reliably maintain moral perspective when I think and act.

[...]

6.12 Magnanimity: Moral Leadership and Nobility of Spirit

[Related Virtues: Equanimity, Courage, Ambition]

[...]

What, then, is the relevance of this classical ideal for 21st century life? Who talks or thinks about being 'noble' anymore? This is precisely my point. Magnanimity enables and encourages moral ambition and moral leadership, two things sorely lacking in our contemporary technosocial milieu. Moral ambition can be described as the ability to 'think big' in one's moral aims. The magnanimous, those with *justified* moral ambition, are able to go beyond what most of us can afford in the moral realm (often little more than 'I'm going to try to be slightly less of a selfish jerk today.') The magnanimous can pursue and lead others in moral projects that require enduring courage, deep wisdom, expansive empathy, extraordinary care, and tolerance for great frustration in conflict, because they had successfully cultivated these virtues as resources for such projects.

[…]

The magnanimous are those who have rightly earned the *moral trust* of others, who can inspire, guide, mentor, and lead the rest of us at least somewhere in the vicinity of the good. It is not an unrealistic ideal. There have been many such people in history, some famous, most unfairly forgotten, people who were still imperfect but far better than most, and who helped others to be better and *do* better. Yet does our contemporary technosocial world foster and support the ambitions of genuine moral leaders? Can we name specific living individuals who would trust to lead us *wisely* and *morally* through the thicket of global technosocial dilemmas facing humanity? Who can reliably guide us and making prudent choices about the expansion of global digital surveillance tools, armed robots, brain computer interfaces, or the replacement of millions of human laborers with automated software systems?

[…]

6.13 Technomoral Wisdom: Unifying the Technomoral Virtues

The greatest of the virtues is the one we will say the least about, for it encompasses the totality of what has already been said. Whole books have been written on Aristotle's concept of practical wisdom or *phronesis*, but as with Kongzi's notion of *ren* in its broader use, moral wisdom is best understood as a term for 'complete virtue,' representing the successful integration of a person's moral habits, knowledge, and virtues in an intelligent, authentic, and expert manner. Thus a person of moral or practical wisdom *just is* a person who reliably put into practice the seven moral habits articulated in Part II, and who has used those habits to cultivate and integrate the virtues essential to flourishing and their given moral world. Such a person is not perfect but nevertheless exemplary—flawed but far better than most, finding more pleasure and joy in living well and rightly than most of us get from living badly or thoughtlessly, and exhibiting flashes of authentic moral beauty in action they give the rest of us pause.

Technomoral wisdom is therefore in a different sense from the others. It is not a specific excellence or disposition, but a *general condition* of well-cultivated and integrated moral expertise that expresses successfully—and in an intelligent, informed, and authentic way—each of the other virtues of character that we, individually and collectively, need in order to live well with emerging technologies. Each of the other eleven technomoral virtues find their highest expression when integrated in the actions of a person with technomoral wisdom.[14]

Notes

1. Vallor, Shannon. (2016). *Technology and the virtues: A philosophical guide to a future worth wanting.* Oxford University Press. Reprinted with permission.
2. See Snow and Trivigno (2014) on the psychology of virtue; see also chapter 10 herein for a discussion of the possibility of biomedical enhancement of these capacities.
3. Nussbaum (1988).
4. See Peterson and Seligman (2004) for an interesting attempt to give a comprehensive taxonomy of six "core virtues" and a list of supporting "character strengths" that facilitate each virtue.
5. Frankfurt (2005).
6. Bostrom (2002).

7. It is worth noting that while models of heroic martial courage are still culturally influential in many parts of the world, the modern transformation of military practice by long-range weapons and automated systems has placed considerable pressure on this conception (Singer 2009; Vallor 2013a). The predicted expansion of drone and robotic warfare will only increase this pressure; both globally and locally humans will be challenged to find new ways to understand martial courage, or else to question whether and to what extent this form of courage continues to warrant its historical privilege.

8. Baston (2011, 20. See also Goleman (2013), 98.

9. See Slote (2007); Held (2006); and McLaren (2001) for arguments for and against regarding care ethics as a form of virtue ethics.

10. Walzer (1974) names it as one of five key civic virtues, along with loyalty, service, tolerance, and participation.

11. NE 1125b30-1126a30.

12. Analects 9:4; 17:8; 15:37; 19:11.

13. Ibid. 17:7.

14. Exactly how the virtues can be successfully integrated, and how the person or practical wisdom responds when virtues appear in a given situation to be placed in tension or conflict, is the subject of much discussion by contemporary virtue ethicists. Some dismiss the hypothesis of the 'unity of the virtues,' others continue to embrace it as a regulative ideal. Yet while important, these theoretical concerns lie beyond the scope of our present inquiry.

Chapter 2.5

Ethics of Care as Moral Grounding for AI[*]

Carolina Villegas-Galaviz

In information societies, operations, decisions, and choices previously left to humans are increasingly delegated to algorithms, which may advise, if not decide, about how data should be interpreted and what actions should be taken as a result. Examples abound. Profiling and classification algorithms determine how individuals and groups are shaped and managed (Mittelstadt et al., 2016).

Technology has always appeared as a way to expand human capacities (Jonas, 1979). Take, for example, the case of force and the augmentation of physical labor with the steam engine, or the case of the transportation sector and how it has been developed from long walks to wagons, then to bicycles, trains, cars, and airplanes, now ending up with autonomous vehicles. Thanks to technology, the whole conception of moving from one place to another has changed. Developments of technology have modified the character of human action. Taking this argument, the philosopher Hans Jonas (1979) argues that ethics has to do with actions and when changing the nature of human actions, there must necessarily be a kind of adaptation in ethics to new scenarios: to look to new approaches, ethical frameworks, and to ask new questions.

Today, emerging technologies such as AI are transforming the way that humans behave in society. "Algorithms silently structure our lives. Algorithms can determine whether someone is hired, promoted, offered a loan, or provided housing as well as determine which political ads and news articles consumer see" (Martin, 2019b). Previous technologies enhance human physical capacities, as in manufacturing, and others facilitate the storage and management of information, as in digitization, now AI is changing how humans make decisions, and that impacts how humans' decisions affect others.

The delegation of human autonomy to algorithm decision-making has been studied from different fields (from law, from engineers, and philosophers), and some ethical principles and guidelines have been proposed by scholars (Floridi et al., 2018; Floridi et al. 2020, to name a few), governments (European Commission, 2020; G20, 2019; OECD, 2019), and enterprises (IBM,

---

[*] Villegas-Galaviz, Carolina. 2021. Ethics of Care as Moral Grounding for AI. Reprinted with permission of the author. All rights reserved by Carolina Villegas-Galaviz.

DOI: 10.1201/9781003278290-13

2021). However, there is still so much to do within AI ethics and to ask and answer about responsibility, fairness, egalitarianism, values, and virtues in the AI era.

In this chapter, I focus on how the reduction of decision-making to data analytics may lead to moral dilemmas in how we make decisions about people: who is included and who is excluded. I will propose a care-based approach to shed light on how relationships, interdependence, vulnerabilities, and emotions should not be ignored.

Ethics of care appeared as a theory with Carol Gilligan in her book *In a different voice* (1982), where the author presented care as a response to the orthodoxy of ethics of justice. With the notion of care, Gilligan brought out the key argument of how relationships, interdependence, circumstances, and emotions are an essential part of ethical decision-making. The said imply that a reduction to formal rationality and an indifferent weighing of principles and norms is not enough in ethical terms.

In what follows, I briefly introduce some important facts of how AI works, then I present ethics of care to mitigate the moral problems presented in AI and decision-making. After that, I propose some questions that may serve as guidelines when applying AI while considering the notion of care.

To Fit within the Pattern

AI is "defined as a system's ability to correctly interpret external data, to learn from such data, and to use those learnings to achieve specific goals and tasks through flexible adaptation" (Kaplan & Haenlein, 2019). Hence, using data as raw material, AI decision-making works by creating patterns and making predictions (Martin, 2019a). When using AI to decide on a particular individual in a specific circumstance, the result would be to judge that person as fitting or not fitting in a previously established pattern, and that pattern was created with previously gathered data. This means that the "fit" of that individual in a pattern is what determines the decision. Barocas and Selbst (2016) allude to this sequence of steps when explaining that data mining is a form of statistical discrimination where the use of AI reproduces past prejudices by identifying a pattern in the training data and then enforcing that pattern on new data (p. 675).

Decision-making with AI is done usually with the goal of maximizing efficiency, making decisions faster and supposedly more objectively. However, any efficacy enjoyed is for those who design and deploy AI. The AI decision is within their power, so in case of doubt, the resolution goes in their service. For example, AI helps to know more quickly and more "safely" who to hire or who not for a job, to whom to grant or deny a loan or mortgage, or to whom to grant it or not parole, as in the case of the COMPAS algorithm. Hence, those who apply the model may be reducing that decision to data and ignoring vulnerabilities and specific circumstances that could be essential to decide morally. Not only does the use of AI codify patterns of the past, the application of that codified past ignores the vulnerabilities and specific circumstances of the subjects present. That is why AI may affect the most marginalized stakeholders, and why big data processes could improperly disregard legally protected classes, leading to a *disparate impact* that "refers to policies or practices that are facially neutral but have a disproportionately adverse impact on protected classes" (Barocas and Selbst, 2016, p. 694).

Making decisions using AI is about excluding those that do not fit a pattern and including those that fit within the pattern. And many have examined those that do not fit, who are marginalized or left behind or discriminated against with AI programs with the lens of justice (Mittelstadt et al., 2016; Coeckelbergh, 2020; Dubber et al., 2020). However, in the study of the ethical challenge of *those that fit and do not fit*, those who are elevated and those who are marginalized, I propose the theory of ethics of care as moral grounding for the AI era. In what follows, I am going to briefly explain care ethics and then propose it as a way to alleviate the moral problems presented.

Ethics of Care

Ethics of care appeared as a theory in the 20th century. In her book *In a Different Voice* (1982), Carol Gilligan presented care as a response to the orthodoxy of ethics of justice. Gilligan first presented care as a psychological theory for woman's development. However, with the notion of care, the author brought out the key argument of how relationships, interdependence, circumstances, and emotions are essential parts of ethical decision-making. That means that focusing solely on formal rationality and principles is not enough for morality.

"This conception 'of morality as concerned with the activity of care centers moral development around the understanding of responsibility and relationships, just as the conception of morality as fairness ties moral development to the understanding of rights and rules." (Gilligan, 1982)

For Gilligan, the general idea of care is to understand responsibility and morality in the context of relationships and to resolve moral dilemmas in the comprehension of dependence and vulnerability. Communication plays an essential role since it is the way to listen to relational voices and listen to *a different voice*. Where "to have a voice is to be human. To have something to say is to be a person. But speaking depends on listening and being heard; it is an intensely relational act" (Gilligan, 1982). Therefore, care should be taken as a *practice and a work that must be done on a direct level* (Sander-Staudt & Hamington, 2011). In this sense, the perspective of care implies to decided considering the person in her specific circumstances and not based on previously established norms (Reiter, 1996).

Since coined, the notion of care has developed to a more rigorous definition of the term, now not only linked to woman's development (French and Weis, 2000). Based on previous literature on care, Daniel Engster (2011, p. 98) proposed a definition of care ethics as a "theory that associates moral action with meeting the needs, fostering the capabilities, and alleviating the pain and suffering of individuals inattentive, responsive, and respectful ways." This definition encompasses what implies going beyond the formal rationality based on principles, guidelines, and norms within ethics.

A Care-Based AI

As the philosopher Hans Jonas defended, ethics must adjust to the changes that technology produces while expanding, increasing, and transforming the nature of human actions. The said adaptation suggests a look to new frameworks, a reconsideration of how theories are applied, and an invitation to ask new ethical questions.

AI is being used to categorize people, to elevate those who fit and marginalize those who do not fit a particular pattern. The artist Mimi Onuoha defined *algorithmic violence* as "the violence that an algorithm or automated decision-making system inflicts by preventing people from meeting their basic needs."[1] Those that are marginalized or do not fit a particular pattern are then denied rights or further harmed feel that algorithmic violence. Hence, a theory that put vulnerability, harm, and relationships in the foreground would better identify wrongs of AI decision-making.

The theory of ethics of care would help to better understand the moral implications of algorithms. Based on previous research on the ethics of care, we can preset the following five categories as key elements to understand a care-based ethics of AI decision-making. Each category is presented with some questions that those who develop and deploy AI should have in mind when applying ethics of care to data analytics.

1. Voice

As presented by Carol Gilligan (1982), voice means to have the possibility of defending one's own interpretation and needs. For example, Gilligan says that "to have a voice is to be human. To have something to say is to be a person. But speaking depends on listening and being heard; it is an intensely relational act." (Gilligan, 1982). That means that it is essential to give voice to every affected part in a situation with ethical implications. Also, voices should be heard through communication in relationships. There, communication is presented as the method of conflict resolution and the way to resolve moral dilemmas because it gives the possibility to hear different voices.

For AI, this would mean that algorithm should maintain open the possibility of hearing different voices and not silent any voice that should have part of the situation in which it is applied. For this purpose, interdisciplinary teams could serve to comprehend the different points of view to try to hear the voices of different cultures and social collectives. Hence, having this in mind, we would ask:

- Which voices are being silenced with the development of this algorithm?
- Furthermore, does this algorithm hear all the different voices needed? For example, in an interdisciplinary way?

2. Relationships and Interdependence

In the ethics of care, responsibility and morality have a meaning in a web of interdependent relationships. That means that

> ... the admonition to maintain relationships, and to be cognizant and responsive to the needs of others, are two general principles central to an ethic of care. Nevertheless, more than providing such principles, an ethics of care recommends itself as a method and way of orientating oneself towards the world.
>
> **(Sander-Staudt & Hamington, 2011)**

To understand accountability in a network of relationships means to put aside the general standard and to look to concrete situations, where "the generalized other" becomes "the particular other," a specific individual in a particular circumstance (Gilligan, 1982).

When applying ethics of care to AI, it would be essential that models do not take individuals as opponents "in a contest of rights but as members of a network of relationships on whose continuation they all depend." (Gilligan, 1982). There we would ask:

- Which interdependence relationships can be affected by the development of this algorithm?
- Are relevant interdependence relationships being ignored in the development of this model?
- Would emotions be an eliminated essential part of the kind of decision that is being automated?

3. Direct Level

According to care ethicists, care is a practice and something to be done on a direct level, a face-to-face interaction. Also, care may be understood as a "motive, ideal, virtue, and method." However, "care" should be distinguished from "personal service," "the former involves meeting the needs of those who are unable to meet such needs themselves, the latter involves meeting needs for others who could meet such needs themselves" (Sander-Staudt & Hamington, 2011; see also Bubeck, 1985).

For AI, the said imply that those affected by AI decision-making will not have the possibility of meeting their needs. They depend on the algorithm to do it. Hence, there is a moral responsibility to care for them. Moreover, for AI ethics, the relevance of the "direct level" involves a more contextual mode of judgment and the awareness that decisions should not result from an abstraction of the problem, eliminating the context. Having this in mind, one should ask:

- Does this algorithm imply the elimination of context and circumstances when they can be an essential part of a future decision?
- Does this model open the possibility to social and cultural embeddedness?

4. Vulnerability

The notion of care implies the comprehension of the vulnerability, the needs, and suffering of the other. Also, in a network of interdependent relationships, everyone becomes vulnerable, and there appears care as an essential concept. "When we care for individuals, we usually aim to help them to meet their basic needs, develop or maintain their basic capabilities, or alleviate their pain and suffering"" (Engster, 2011). That means that care includes all that is in line to meet everyone's basic needs.

Care-based AI implies that algorithms do not prevent individuals from meeting their needs, especially the most basic ones. When applying ethics of care to AI, we would ask:

- Does this algorithm prevent the possibility of fostering the needs of protected classes, people at risk of social exclusion, or marginalized stakeholders?
- Does the data used imply exploiting the vulnerabilities of those affected by this algorithm?
- Are vulnerabilities used as variables to prevent future enhancement for those affected by this algorithm?

Conclusion

The purpose of this chapter was to bring out how the reduction of decision-making to data analytics may lead to a moral problem where people's opportunities are reduced to their fit into a previously created pattern. In this context, ethical theories as deontological ethics, utilitarianism, consequentialism, and ethics of justice are necessary but not sufficient. There I proposed ethics of care as moral grounding for the AI era. The notion of care appears as an essential key to alleviate the moral problems derived from a tendency to look for apparent objectivity bolstered in efficiency for decisions. Ethics of care may serve to shed light on the fact that considering vulnerabilities and interdependence relationships is fundamental to morality. Some essential notions of ethics of care were provided to serve as key elements to understanding the ethics of AI decision-making.

Note

1. Retrieved from: https://mimionuoha.com/algorithmic-violence (July, 2021).

References

Barocas, S., & Selbst, A. D. (2016). Big data's disparate impact. *California Law Review, 104*(3), 671–732.

Bubeck, D. (1985). *Care, justice and gender.* Oxford: Clarendon Press.

Coeckelbergh, M. (2020). *AI Ethics.* Cambridge, MA: The MIT Press.

Dubber, M., Pasquale, F., Das, S. (2020). *Oxford Handbook of AI.* New York: Oxford University Press.

Engster, D., 2011, Care ethics and stakeholder theory, in Hamington, M. & Sander-Staudt, M. (Eds.). *Applying care ethics to business.* New York: Springer, pp. 93–110.

Engster, D. (2007). *The hear of justice: Care ethics and political theory.* Oxford: Oxford University Press.

European Commission. (2020). Ethics guidelines for trustworthy AI. Retrieved from: https://digital-strategy.ec.europa.eu/en/library/ethics-guidelines-trustworthy-ai (July, 2021).

Floridi, L., Cowls, J., Beltrametti, M., Chatila, R., Chazerand, P., Dignum, V.,... Vayena, E. (2018). AI4People-an ethical framework for a good AI society: Opportunities, risks, principles, and recommendations. *Minds and Machines, 28*(4), 689–707.

Floridi, L., Cowls, J., King, T. C., & Taddeo, M. (2020). How to design AI for social good: Seven essential factors. *Science and Engineering Ethics, 26*(3), 1771–1796.

French, W., and Weis, A. (2000). An ethics of care or an ethics of justice. *Journal of Business Ethics, 27*(1–2): 125–136.

G20. (2019). G20 Ministerial Statement on Trade and Digital Economy. Retrieved from: https://www.mofa.go.jp/files/000486596.pdf (July, 2021).

Gilligan, C. 1982. *In a different voice.* Cambridge, MA: Harvard University Press.

IBM. (2021). AI Ethics. Retrieved from: https://www.ibm.com/artificial-intelligence/ethics (July, 2021).

Jonas, H. (1979). *Das Prinzip Verantwortung.*

Kaplan, A., & Haenlein, M. (2019). Siri, siri, in my hand: Who's the fairest in the land? on the interpretations, illustrations, and implications of artificial intelligence. *Business Horizons, 62*(1), 15–25.

Martin, K. (2019a). Designing ethical algorithms. *Mis Quarterly Executive, 18*(2), 129–142.

Martin, K. (2019b). Ethical implications and accountability of algorithms. *Journal of Business Ethics, 160*(4), 835–850.

Mittelstadt, B. D., Allo, P., Taddeo, M., Wachter, S., & Floridi, L. (2016). The ethics of algorithms: Mapping the debate. *Big Data & Society, 3*(2), 1–21.

OECD. 2019. OECD principles on AI. Retrieved from: https://www.oecd.org/going-digital/ai/principles/ (July, 2021).

Sander-Staudt, M., and Hamington, M. (2011). Introduction: Care ethics and business ethics. *Applying Care Ethics to Business, 34,* VII.

Reiter, S. A. (1996). *The kohlberg–gilligan controversy: Lessons for accounting ethics education* doi:https://doi.org/10.1006/cpac.1996.0005

Chapter 2.6

Excerpt from Operationalizing Critical Race Theory in the Marketplace[*]

Sonja Martin Poole, Sonya A. Grier, Kevin D. Thomas,
Francesca Sobande, Akon E. Ekpo, Lez Trujillo Torres,
Lynn A. Addington, Melinda Weekes-Laidlow,
and Geraldine Rosa Henderson

[...]

Beyond Critical Theory Traditions in Marketplace Studies

Critical theoretical approaches recognize and critique systemic power relations with an intention to contribute to structural change. Critical scholars emphasize the need for "action-oriented programs of research aimed at improving society and the lives of consumers" (Murray and Ozanne, 1991, p. 559). Critical marketplace studies tend to involve a critique of capitalism and acknowledge that the marketplace is not a neutral site. Marketplace contexts are identified as inherently political with social and structural relations that connect to inequalities, including but not limited to "ethnicity, race, gender, sexual orientation, religion, and physical (dis)ability" (Henderson & Williams, 2013, p. 1). Critical theory maintains a focused skepticism toward the notion of universal objectivity and contextualizes social and historical relations in a way that accounts for the influence of different subjectivities. Research mobilized by CT can help demystify power struggles and support efforts to dismantle entrenched hierarchical marketplace dynamics.

---

[*] Poole, Sonja Martin, Sonya A. Grier, Kevin D. Thomas, Francesca Sobande, Akon E. Ekpo, Lez Trujillo Torres, Lynn A. Addington, Melinda Weekes-Laidlow, and Geraldine Rosa Henderson. "Operationalizing Critical Race Theory in the Marketplace." *Journal of Public Policy & Marketing* (2020): 0743915620964114. Reprinted with permission.

DOI: 10.1201/9781003278290-14

Marketplace studies buttressed by CT commonly include a call to action as part of their analyses of societal inequalities and a recommendation of potential ways to combat them. For example, such CT work usually includes critical accounts "of the historical and cultural conditions (both social and personal) on which the theorist's own intellectual activity depends" (Calhoun 1995, p. 35). Marketplace studies using CT often express a concern with values, principles, and what ought to be, rather than focusing exclusively on what is happening in the here and now. At its core, a critical theoretical position is motivated by an aim to address societal issues with the use of social theories that aid understanding of matters regarding power, people, place, and politics (Tadajewski 2010). Critical theory is applied in a range of scholarship addressing such significant topics as social identity, inequality, and ideology. Within marketplace studies, CT often serves as a specific theoretical framework that focuses primarily on issues of class, capitalism, and economics (e.g., Tadajewski and Brownlie 2008).

Although CT scrutinizes capitalism and class-based hierarchies, this work does not place an equal focus on issues concerning race, despite a long history in which the marketplace has been termed racist (Dávila 2008). Much prior research about different racial and ethnic groups is based on dated concepts related to race and ethnicity and tends to homogenize minority groups (Williams 1995). Burton's (2002) conceptualization of critical multicultural marketing theory addresses issues linked to race, ethnicity, and culture in the marketplace. Although related, inquiries based on ethnicity, class, and multiculturalism often elude the complex power dynamics inherent to race (Thomas, Cross, and Harrison 2018). As such, a focus on multiculturalism or ethnicity is inadequate for investigating racism and White supremacy in the marketplace.

Thus, a shift from a conglomeration of many sites of privilege/oppression (e.g., "multicultural") to a distinct and potentially all-encompassing site of privilege/oppression (e.g., "race") is needed to more deeply understand how racialized power dynamics operate in the marketplace. Understanding the complex, nuanced, and fluid power dynamics between race and the marketplace demands focused attention to racialization, the process by which racial identities are assigned to groups based on physical attributes, social practices, and/or social alignments (Omi and Winant 2014). We call for focused, as opposed to singular, attention to racialized identities. As we discuss in detail herein, a critical examination of race requires situating it in the dialectical relationship shared with other ascribed and elected identity coordinates. Pivoting to a focus on racialization will aid analysis and efforts to address market-based racial inequities as part of an approach underpinned by social justice goals and recognition of knowledge yielded by the lived experiences of POC (Dotson 2015). This approach is attuned to how the TCR "sensibility welcomes challenges to established perspectives, findings, and theories" and "seeks to enhance consumer well-being by tackling some of the more difficult and intractable social problems" (Crockett et al. 2013, p. 1171). Furthermore, a research approach that focuses on matters concerning racism and intersecting oppressions in marketplace settings can highlight issues concerning White supremacy and colonial legacies that are rarely foregrounded in critical research on marketing.

Toward a Tradition of Critical Race Theory in Marketplace Studies

In contributing to a burgeoning scholarship in marketing that addresses issues of race and consumer inequality (Ekpo et al. 2018; Grier and Davis, 2013; Henderson, Hakstian, and Williams 2016) and establishes understandings of the marketplace (Burton, 2009; Johnson et al. 2019), we define key tenets of CRT (see Table 1). These tenets guide our analysis and expose the ways in which racial domination is reproduced, naturalized, and contested in the marketplace. We then apply them to a current example, facial recognition, to illustrate how they support an understanding of the role of race and to guide transformative consumer research efforts.

Social justice. At the core of CRT is the objective of challenging the pervasiveness and societal impact of White supremacy. Thus, "CRT has a fundamental commitment to a social justice agenda that struggles to eliminate all forms of racial, gender, language, generation, status, and class subordination" (Parker and Villalpando 2007, p. 520). In the marketing context, we use the phrase "social justice" to signify fairness and equity in distributions, procedures, and interactions related to marketing scholarship, practice, and pedagogy (see also Grier 2020). Transformative consumer research affirms that "advocacy positions are necessary to engage in research that responds to social problems" (Crockett et al. 2013, p. 1176). In marketing literature, however, social justice has yet to be extensively examined in connection with CRT or racial issues (see Grier, Thomas, and Johnson 2019; Steinfield et al. 2019). Rather, social justice is most often an implicit goal such as in research that criticizes marketing practices. Consider research that links racially targeted food marketing to negative consumer outcomes (e.g., Grier and Davis 2013). Such research has an unstated function of addressing market failures and provides companies with "a moral compass" to ameliorate situations and respond through positive marketing (Stoeckl and Luedick 2015). In so doing, it may invariably expose social and economic inequality, even if it is not explicitly labeled as "social justice research."

The social justice tenet has important implications for the way we think about marketing. For example, corporations are continually apologizing for racist behaviors that include employees discriminating against non-White customers by calling the police, oversurveilling them as they shop, seating them at undesirable tables, or marketing and selling products portraying racist stereotypes (Johnson et al., 2019). While such issues have been highlighted in marketing literature, none have been investigated from a critical race perspective (Crockett et al., 2003). Traditional approaches in marketing consider these isolated incidents in which racist behavior is called out and the company is recognized for acknowledging the problem and apologizing. In contrast, a CRT social justice perspective would consider the role of structural racism and provide action-oriented steps for systemic transformation.

Centrality and permanence of race and racism. Critical race theory recognizes the enduring pervasiveness of racism—from individual private thoughts to personal relationships, workplaces, institutions (e.g., marketplace), and systems (e.g., education, health care, justice system; Delgado and Stefancic 2017). Thus, racism is not the sum of prejudicial actions and individual attitudes (Bonilla-Silva 2015) but a state of mind embedded in our psyches, culture, systems, and institutions. Given that racism is pervasive throughout society, it has become a way of life, a fact of everyday "ordinary" experience (Essed 1991), especially for POC. Moreover, racism and racialized incidents are experiences that affect all members of a society regardless of racial affiliation or identification. Thus, CRT establishes that race serves as a social construct that invokes, distributes, and restricts hierarchical power and privilege among racialized bodies (Essed 1991).

A key principle of CRT is the unequivocal recognition that White supremacy is a dominant and oppressive force in society that must be challenged. Although White supremacy is commonly associated with interpersonal and group-level instances of White identity extremism (e.g., neo-Nazis, Ku Klux Klan members), CRT extends the construct to include the myriad ways in which Whiteness is centered, normalized, and privileged via taken-for-granted social structures, formal and informal policies, and cultural practices (Daniels 1997). For instance, the practice of redlining, the systematic denial or limiting of products and services to residents of a particular area based on race or ethnicity, is more likely to negatively affect the lives of POC (D'Rozario and Williams 2005).

A CRT approach of treating racism as pervasive diverges from mainstream approaches in marketing research wherein race is often used as a variable to detect disparities between groups rather than as a unit of analysis in and of itself. Research questions that center on how the behaviors and attitudes of POCs deviate from dominant societal norms prevail in mainstream marketing research. These approaches often set a standard or deem some (arbitrary) criteria as important in determining whether someone is worthy of privileges. For example, two KB Toys stores within very close proximity enforced vastly different payment policies, of which the only difference was the racial makeup of the residents in each location (Henderson, Hakstian, and Williams 2016). Patrons of the affluent and mainly Black location were made to present copious forms of identification, whereas patrons of the affluent and mainly White location received no such demand. A CRT examination of such privilege-granting policies illustrates how "racism is routine, not exceptional" (Delgado and Stefancic 2017, p. 136).

Challenge to dominant ideology. Undertaking marketplace studies with a CRT lens challenges dominant ideological concepts such as neutrality, objectivity, color blindness, meritocracy, and other ideologies used to reinforce the realities of White privilege and Whiteness. In examining existing power structures, CRT-based approaches emphasize that ideological claims are ways in which privileged groups camouflage their interests to maintain the status quo. Critical race theory also recognizes that dominant ideologies support ignorance of the inequalities that systemic and institutional racism supports and perpetuates. In contrast, mainstream perspectives often treat racial inequality as an aberration rather than a natural byproduct of a system of racial domination (Bonilla-Silva 2015). A CRT lens also necessitates learning from knowledge generated outside of formal academic environments and upholding a critical understanding of the racial politics of knowledge production processes. For example, CRT recognizes citational practice as politically embedded within the knowledge production marketplace of academia, which itself is steeped in histories of racism that have resulted in epistemic erasures of marginalized knowledge and research (Dotson 2015). Consequently, CRT scholars read and reference the writing of individuals whose social positions and lived experiences mean that their understandings of structural racism are not based on intellectual intrigue alone.

The contrast between CRT and mainstream approaches in the marketing literature is evident in the way that the mainstream attempts to align populations under an umbrella ideal that is arbitrarily agreed on, perpetuated as "objective," and deemed important. For instance, consider the recent embrace of "total market" advertising by mainstream marketing researchers and practitioners. Akin to its global advertising precursor, total market persuasive communication attempts to develop and disseminate a universally accepted message across a multicultural consumer base, concentrating on perceived commonalities across groups rather than differences. This illusory privileged ideal is perceptible in the Eurocentric features in standards of beauty, patronage, and even product design.

Consider also how for many years POC have been relegated to the "ethnic aisle" for such consumer goods as hair products, personal care items, and food. Here, the term "ethnic" perpetuates racist ideologies. In the case of product design, the issue of "flesh" tone has long been of concern to POC, as one's flesh tone is relative to the color of their skin. Yet the actual tone/color of offerings for products such as bandages, pantyhose, and ballet shoes have typically corresponded to those racialized as White, further normalizing Whiteness and leaving non-White consumers without viable options. Bennett et al. (2016) discuss how this form of exclusion perpetuates marketplace traumas, whereby such consumers are "othered" in their interactions with the market, and in the failure of marketers and policymakers to acknowledge or intervene in such transgressions.

Authority of experiential knowledge. Critical race theory acknowledges knowledge inherent to the lived experiences of those who are subject to structural racism (Delgado and Stefancic 2017). This knowledge is reflected primarily in "storytelling and counter-storytelling," which foregrounds

POC in "counter-stories, parables, and chronicles aimed at revealing the contingency, cruelty, and self-serving nature of the power-laden beliefs" (p. 139). The experiential knowledge tenet serves to uplift and centralize the lived experience of POC as a legitimate source of knowledge production—unlike mainstream scholarship, where knowledge production is the sole domain of academics (Delgado and Stefancic 2017).

In marketing, several methodological perspectives incorporate lived experiences into knowledge production. For instance, scholars and marketing practitioners alike can create "thick description" from ethnographic observation and interviews that yield "multilayered interpretations of market phenomena" (Arnould and Wallendorf 1994, p. 484). This methodological approach takes into account the subjective experiences of consumers (emic) and the subjective cultural, interpretative experiences of researchers (etic). Other approaches to understanding consumer lived experiences include hermeneutical (Thompson 1997), existential phenomenological (Thompson, Locander, and Pollio 1989), experiential (Holbrook and Hirschman 1982), participatory action (Hill et al. 2015), case studies (Grier and Johnson 2011), videography (Grier and Perry 2018), poetry (Sherry and Schouten 2002), and autobiographical consumer research (Brown 1998). With a few exceptions, most of this scholarship remains inaccessible to consumers once produced. Importantly, despite the diverse interpretative approaches and social change-oriented academic collectives such as TCR, which examine lived experience, few studies use race as the "site of social inequality" (Donnor and Ladson-Billings 2017). A few notable examples include Crockett (2017), Davis (2018), Grier, Thomas, and Johnson (2019), Johnson and Grier (2011), and the efforts of other scholars in the Race in the Marketplace (RIM) research network (e.g., Johnson et al. 2019).

By extension, at the marketing practice level, there is a similar lack of attention to race and other structural issues that prevent practitioners from deeply examining the role of "power and privilege differentials" in the marketplace. In particular, marketing research and practice are afflicted by a type of color blindness, "where people discount race when they make decisions" (Donnor & Ladson-Billings, 2017, p. 197). This is observed in the way "color-blind racism operates in the tech industry" (Daniels, 2015, p. 1377). For example, crowd-based marketplaces embrace seemingly neutral values such as trust yet arguably reinforce racial identities and bias in the market (Rhue, 2019). At the same time, color-blind solutions to reduce bias such as "racial anonymity and automation, are insufficient and serve to devalue POC" (Rhue, 2015, p. 206). These areas merit scholarly and public policy attention given the growing dependence on facial recognition within public services, travel, immigration services, and transportation.

The interdisciplinary/transdisciplinary perspective. Scholars of CRT aim to construct innovative and multifaceted approaches to the study of race and racism by merging and/or working across disciplinary boundaries. Consequently, CRT should not be conceptualized as a stand-alone theory that explicates the role of race in society. Rather, CRT operates as a synthesizing analytical framework where critical experiences emerging from diverse disciplines coalesce. The citation section of a CRT scholar's publication will demonstrate the variety of fields used to analytically "make sense" of society's racial dynamics at a given moment in time. For instance, when introducing CRT to the field of public relations, Pompper (2005) applied key concepts from a wide cross-section of disciplines such as communication, feminism, organizational theory, and queer studies. Diverse approaches enable a rigorous analysis of the interdependency of racism and capitalism, such as histories of slavery and exploitation that underpin contemporary markets. Thus, a CRT approach is shaped by extant work on the racist roots of many marketplace dynamics. In fact, we represent scholars and practitioners from diverse disciplines, expertise, specializations, and approaches.[1] In this way, our article contributes to marketing studies and extends legal, education, sociology, media, and culture CRT studies. Guided by such foundational work, our article provides a blueprint for understanding and operationalizing CRT in the marketplace.

Consumer research and public policy analyses in marketing are also characteristically interdisciplinary. In fact, TCR has a tradition of "using a broad theoretical lens and a wide array of epistemological approaches" (Davis & Pechmann 2013, p. 1168). Furthermore, for TCR's dialogical conferences, teams are encouraged to include practitioners or scholars from disciplines outside of marketing. To push the boundaries of our thinking even further, CRT also uses transdisciplinary methods, conceptualized as both a specific kind of interdisciplinary research involving scientific and nonscientific sources or practice and a new form of learning and problem-solving involving cooperation among different parts of society, including academia, to meet the complex challenges of society (McGregor 2004). Using both interdisciplinary and transdisciplinary approaches, CRT allows for a multifaceted examination of intersecting structural oppression that impacts marketplace experiences, public spaces, and society in general. Thus, CRT aligns with TCR principles that affirm the benefits of teams that bring "a broader range of knowledge, expertise, and resources to the research task" (Crockett et al., 2013, p. 1172).

Because the pervasiveness of structural racism and White privilege is such that it manifests in many different but interconnected domains and settings, to effectively analyze and address associated problems there is a need to understand and tackle interrelated issues that span the central focus of many different yet linked disciplines. As Crockett et al. (2013, p. 1173) observe, a significant challenge involved in assembling teams of researchers from distinct disciplinary backgrounds "is reconciling the competing world views and methodological approaches of different disciplines." However, a shared commitment to challenging structural racism, paired with an openness to exploring new methodologies and learning from the differing disciplinary perspectives of peers, can facilitate fruitful collaboration that nurtures robust critical inquiry and generative scrutiny of stifling disciplinary norms.

The interdisciplinary/transdisciplinary approach has important implications for the way we think about marketing and public policy. Work using these methods can enable productive knowledge sharing and the formulation of novel approaches to address societal issues and offer a new understanding of the world, in addition to aiding forms of reflexivity that result in expansive understandings of different disciplines and their future direction. Bridging gaps across disciplines—indeed, even outside all disciplines—creates a powerful and nuanced approach for engaging with race and racism. There is no one answer, one discipline, or one path. With CRT, use of all tools in the toolbox is encouraged.

Intersectionality. Although CRT centers race and racism as its analytical focal point, it does not ignore other identity coordinates from which experiences of privilege and oppression emerge. Intersectionality, an analytic framework attributed to critical race and legal studies scholar Kimberlé Crenshaw (2011), identifies the unique ways in which privilege and oppression are experienced as a result of overlapping social stratifications and enables CRT scholars to address how race and racism affect and are affected by other forms of structural oppression, including (but not limited to) sexism, classism, ableism, and homophobia. Intersectionality also provides the analytic breadth to capture the fluidity and dynamism of race by recognizing how other social constructs change the way that race and racism are expressed, experienced, and internalized.

Scholarship that investigates the relationship between consumption and identity typically utilizes a single-context framework in which only one contextual factor, such as race or gender orientation, is examined (Thomas 2013). Yet consumers do not have a racialized marketplace experience that is wholly separate from their gendered experience; each is constantly informed by the other. Much of the research around consumer identity conceptualizes identity categories as distinct and fixed (Grier, Thomas, and Johnson 2019). Such conceptualizations do not account for how identity sites cocreate varying marketplace experiences due to their overlapping and intersecting nature with each other and with social structures. As such, consumer research has largely provided abstract snapshots of how identities are represented and experienced in market settings. While this form of inquiry has provided considerable insights into consumption and identity, it is far from representative of consumers' lived experiences. Consumers navigate multiple identities that constantly shift in importance and involvement. Some consumer researchers have already incorporated intersectionality theory into their scholarship (e.g., Thomas 2013), and as a result, their work more actively engages with the reality of consumers' marketplace experiences. Importantly, intersectionality also demonstrates how overlapping social stratifications modulate how privilege and oppression are experienced. As the concept has found its way into society's mainstream, intersectionality is often misconstrued as meaning that overlapping social stratifications merely intensify the experience of privilege and oppression. While this distinction is subtle, it holds deep import. To understand how overlapping social stratifications modulate the lived experience, underlying and associative structural elements must be critically interrogated (Emejulu and Sobande 2019). Otherwise, race, gender, class, and other social identities can become essentialized, presumed as fixed, and considered mutually exclusive. This can lead to purely additive approaches, a practice characterized as the "Oppression Olympics" (Martinez 1993). Recent TCR perspectives have noted this potential, calling for a transformative intersectionality approach to studying oppressive forces and practices that moves beyond adding more social identity characteristics (Steinfield et al. 2019).

Intersectionality as conceptualized by CRT requires deploying praxis-based methodologies that capture the interdependence of identity coordinates and produce findings that more closely illustrate the lived experience of consumers. This approach is evident in Dhillon-Jamerson's (2019) analysis of online matrimonial advertisements in India, in which she conceptualizes race and gender as co-constitutive rather than mutually exclusive with regard to how matchmaking is experienced. Rather than simply "adding" the experience of race to that of gender, she investigates the myriad ways race and gender amalgamate to produce distinct sets of matchmaking tactics and coping mechanisms among individuals seeking a spouse. Her approach moves the analysis and findings from abstraction closer to mirroring true-to-life experiences.

Example application: the case of artificial intelligence. In both theory and practice, AI is dramatically transforming industries, institutions, workplaces, and consumer behavior (Hymas 2019). To further illustrate the value of using a CRT lens to explore marketplace actions and protocol, we apply CRT to the development and utilization of a form of AI technology, facial recognition.

Facial recognition technology is a tool used to help accelerate marketing activities and offer conveniences meant to assist consumers in the consumption process (e.g., automatic logins, personalization). It is often touted as a race-neutral, gender-neutral, and otherwise bias-free solution to making decisions and/or performing marketing tasks in an objective manner. However, a major issue identified with such software has been in its inability to detect darker skin tones, and more specifically, it has misidentified POC as nonhuman (often as animals or objects; Noble 2018). Moreover, AI algorithms tend to perform best on images of White men and worst on images of Black women (Buolamwini and Gebru 2018). As is the case with AI generally, the accuracy of facial recognition tools depends on a machine's ability to detect algorithms "taught" to it through the use of data sets curated by human engineers. Consequently, machine learning can perpetuate racial biases that exist in society (Hymas 2019). Studies in marketing that address the use of AI technologies generally emphasize how consumer experiences are enhanced through AI-powered applications and assume that the impact is equal across all consumers. Such assumptions ignore disparities in lived experiences, and research evidence points to inherent (automated) bias in such technology. As facial recognition becomes more of a norm in the marketplace—used to unlock smartphones, advertise special offers, verify identification for air travel, and more—debates have focused on whether this technology is a good thing for society. Accordingly, the Federal Trade Commission (2016) has recommended that companies consider the legal and ethical implications of their use of big data. Critical race theory would refocus efforts on the potential for automation bias.

For example, there is a larger failure rate in recognition software within autonomous/self-driving cars when it attempts to detect whether an object encountered on the street is human or nonhuman when the object in question is a POC (Noble 2018). This example illustrates how race is a marker of distributed privilege. A POC's existence often goes unacknowledged when misidentified as nonhuman, which speaks to their invisibility and sociohistorical experience in marketplaces of dehumanization. It also speaks to how perspectives of color, marginalized people, or voices on the margins are decentered as against the dominant ideology of White privilege. The continued insistence that AI is unbiased, despite many calls to the inherent biases that result in disparate outcomes for POC, indicates refusal to acknowledge their lived experience and is therefore an intentional ignorance. Nonetheless, the designers of such algorithms are not held accountable. Ignorance of biased algorithms not only exacerbates the issue but also possibly endangers many.

Absence of the experiential input of POC in the design, use, or institutional adoption of AI-based facial recognition is not surprising in the technology industry where "technical workers—the coders, engineers, and data scientists … who are Black or Latinx rose by less than a percentage point since 2014," despite public commitments by technology giants (Harrison 2019). Consequently, the experiential knowledge of POC is largely absent in the technology industry. Not surprisingly, this leads to the selective valorization of the lived experiences of White and Asian middle-class people, who are overrepresented in the technology industry.

The potential impact of AI-related racial bias on people's lived experiences and its policy implications are of increasing concern to policymakers, corporate representatives, and consumer advocates, and deserve critical investigation. It is from a CRT perspective that we can acknowledge, further identify the source of, and correct such failures. Critical race theory puts forward an active social justice agenda that in practice considers the pervasive role of structural racism and White privilege to understand the potential impact of AI technologies. It promotes a focus on eradicating racism by centering the experience of POC as AI applications are considered and opposing the uncritical use of such tools. The interdisciplinary/transdisciplinary approaches championed by CRT scholars and practitioners elevate interrelated policy, marketing, organizational, sociological, political, and historical dimensions of AI developments, including how contemporary facial recognition technology is shaped by centuries of state-sanctioned surveillance activities targeting racialized people. Finally, an intersectional approach further identifies how overlapping categories of identity, such as race and gender, modulate individualized experiences when analyzing the effectiveness and impacts of AI tools.

Our delineation of key CRT tenets and their application to AI-based marketing challenges illustrates how these tenets can inform the way we think about and investigate issues regarding race in marketing and consumer research. The AI example also reflects the mutually reinforcing and potentially overlapping nature of the tenets. Consider how the increasing evidence of bias inherent in AI applications and the observed color-blind racism in the tech industry (Daniels 2015, p. 1377) reflects the centrality of racism and highlights the need for both challenges to dominant identity and social justice considerations. At the same time, the lack of POC in the AI industry contributes to an absence of experiential knowledge of darker-skinned people generally—and specifically Black women—when viewed from an intersectional lens. Clearly, to understand issues of race and AI, an interdisciplinary perspective is necessary, particularly with regard to marketing dimensions. Despite potential overlap, each tenet identifies important conceptual and practical considerations related to the individual and structural dimensions of racial dynamics in markets.

A year after beginning this study at the 2019 TCR conference, brands have slowly begun to acknowledge the bias inherent in the (training) data on which AI is dependent. This newfound awareness, prompted by recent surges in racial consciousness raising and grassroots activism, has caused brands to adapt their AI applications. Moreover, as more stories have surfaced of AI applications gone wrong, brands such as IBM, a major player in the manufacturing of AI-driven technologies, have changed their policies to cease offering its general facial recognition technology to the public (Buolamwini 2020). These recent moves are forcing government and industry to take a hard look at their AI-related policies and practices.

[...]

Note

1. This manuscript emerges from the Race in the Marketplace (RIM) track at the 2019 Transformative Consumer Research dialogical conference at Florida State University in which our multi-racial, multi-ethnic, and multi-disciplinary collective of scholars and a practitioner were afforded the opportunity to theorize the role of race across different types of markets and diverse racialized groups.

PRIVACY, DATA, AND SHARED RESPONSIBILITY

3

In 2012, Target sought to answer the question, "If we wanted to figure out if a customer is pregnant, even if she didn't want us to know, can you do that?"[1] It turned out, the answer was, yes. Target was able to predict whether someone was pregnant based on their past purchases. Armed with this new knowledge, Target then sent advertising to their house assuming the customer was pregnant. However, Target also revealed to the other people in the house that the individual was pregnant - even thought it was not widely known at the time.[2]

What is privacy? What does it mean to say that an act "violates my privacy?" While Target legitimately had stored consumer purchase data, this particular use was a privacy violation. It turns out that how scholars and regulators define privacy varies. And, as we will see, how you define privacy impacts how you protect it and who counts as having a right to privacy in a given situation.

Traditionally, two approaches to defining privacy dominate our privacy discourse. Both have limitations. The *restricted access view of privacy* suggests that privacy is that which is hidden (i.e., where access is restricted), and all that is not hidden is therefore not private. The restricted access view of privacy captures our instinct to want that which is hidden or closely held to be protected. When individuals go outside, use apps, shop online, or file an insurance claim with AI Jim, this version of privacy would suggest they no longer have any privacy expectations since access to their information is no longer restricted. However, this version misses that we regularly have expectations of privacy around information which is shared with friends, doctors, teachers, coworkers, Target, online, etc.

The *control view of privacy* defines privacy as the degree of control someone has over their person and information. The more control you have, the more privacy you have. We see this in surveys sometimes with questions about the degree of control someone thinks they have over their information. In the United States, the FTC's Fair Information Practice Principles is how we put "privacy as control" into practice. The FTC requires companies provide adequate notification and consent for use of their services online. Consumers have control by reading the notice and deciding to engage with the website or app. Unfortunately, as noted in the reading by Nissenbaum included

DOI: 10.1201/9781003278290-15

here, this provides an incentive for companies to make convoluted and ambiguous notices that do not explain how consumer information is gathered, stored, sold, shared, and used. In fact, notices are not read or understood, and people tend to project their privacy expectations on notices and assume their privacy is being respected when a notice is present.[3]

How we define privacy is important to the ethics of data and analytics because both the data being analyzed and the possible inferences created about individuals may have privacy expectations. The privacy expectations of data being used are critical to understand if that particular data set is ethical to use. Both versions of privacy—the restricted access and control view of privacy—place an enormous focus on the handoff of information to others. In other words, when information is turned over to a person or company, access to that information is no longer restricted and the individual no longer has control of that information. Both views find privacy to be diminished or nonexistent when information or people are in public or interact with a third-party (such as a website, app, company, etc.). Relying on this (mistaken) definition of privacy would frame almost all data used in AI or machine learning as free to be shared and used without any privacy expectations.

If, as is argued in the readings included here, privacy is still expected when individuals and their information are in public, then data analysts and computer scientists would need to understand the privacy expectations and norms for the data they are going to use for training an AI program or use when applying analytics. For example, Lemonade Insurance's clients would have no expectations of privacy as to the recording of their claim by AI Jim according to the restricted access and control views of privacy. For most of us, that just seems wrong. We regularly disclose information to people and companies with strong expectations as to how it would be used or further shared. And, the client would have expectations of privacy according to the readings included in the chapter by Helen Nissenbaum and Kirsten Martin, even though the information is clearly shared with the Lemonade insurance company.

The idea of privacy in public is not a novel idea. The original story of "peeping tom" was actually a story about privacy in public. The folktale around Lady Godiva is that after months of begging her husband, the local Earle, to lift the onerous taxes on his people, he finally dared her to ride through town naked on her horse in order for him to lift the taxes. All people in the town were to turn their backs, shut their windows, and avert their eyes while she rode through town. Tom, a tailor in town, was the only person to turn to look at her as she rode by. Since known as Peeping Tom, this individual violated the privacy expectations of Lady Godiva *while in public.*[4]

In fact, the oft-cited "privacy paradox" is, in fact, a misnomer. The privacy paradox is the perceived mismatch between individuals' stated privacy expectations (captured in surveys) and their behavior in practice (normally captured as when they go online). In other words, why do people go online and shop in grocery stores if they care about privacy? However, when asked in more robust surveys, individuals differentiate between disclosing information to a website and allowing their information to be tracked, collected, shared, sold, and used by third-party data brokers and ad networks. In fact, a recent study showed that contrary to the common depictions of online sharing behaviors as careless, people care about privacy and take steps to protect their information—but, are faced with an uphill battle with all the trackers, data aggregators, and ad networks online (see the ad tech case in this chapter).[5]

How we define privacy is only part of the story. We also study why privacy is important or how we *value* privacy. Some authors do both—define privacy and explain why it is important to protect. For example, Ari Waldman links privacy to trust where information is disclosed within specific relationships of trust—within norms of confidentiality and discretion. Privacy is both defined as within a trust relationship and important to trust.[6] Similarly, Neil Richards and

Woodrow Hartzog argue that companies that gather our information, including social networking companies, have a fiduciary obligation of trust whereby they must act in our interest with our information.[7] These authors, and those included in this section, push against the idea that disclosing information or being in public means we no longer have privacy expectations. Danielle Citron illustrates the power of a critical approach to privacy (harkening back to Chapter 2 with critical theories) by tackling sexual privacy and noting that "often, women, nonwhites, sexual minorities, and minors shoulder the abuse"[8] of violations of sexual privacy. No matter with whom we have shared images or information, we have reasonable expectations of privacy for that information, and sometimes the violations of privacy disproportionately impact marginalized communities. We will return to this theme throughout.

Summary of Readings - Privacy

Helen Nissenbaum directly addresses the utility of transparency and choice (also known as notice and choice) which is widely used in the United States to govern privacy online. Nissenbaum sees transparency and choice as appealing to those who wish to control information as a mechanism to respect privacy. Further, transparency and consumer choice fit within our US free-market paradigm where consumer choice dominates regulations. However, she outlines why choice, in this instance around privacy notices, is not the authentic choice we might think it is. Further, the type of transparency required to explain everything that happens to our data would be confusing to most. She calls this the transparency paradox: the more transparent companies are about how data is collected, shared, used, etc., the less understandable their privacy notice is. Nissenbaum offers her theory—privacy as contextual integrity—as a solution where privacy is the respect for the norms around how data is transmitted and shared and by whom within a particular community. In other words, within the medical community, we have one set of norms. Within the educational community, we would have another set of norms. In analyzing a data analytics program according to Nissenbaum, one would examine whether a data set or action respected the norms of contextual integrity in order to respect individuals' privacy by analyzing whether the *data attribute* being gathered/used, the actor, and the *transmission principle* was appropriate for the given *context*.

In "Privacy as a Social Contract," Kirsten Martin directly positions her definition of privacy against both the control and restricted access view of privacy. Martin instead argues that privacy norms can be viewed as a mutually beneficial agreement within a community about how information is used and shared within a community. She develops a narrative wherein individuals within a given community discriminately share information with a particular set of obligations in mind as to who has access to the information and how it will be used. In other words, rather than giving away privacy, individuals share information with norms governing the use of their information. To apply Martin's theory to a data analytics program, one would query as to *who* has access to *what* information and *why* (what purpose) and if that combination met their privacy expectations for that community.

Understanding the factors that drive mutually beneficial and sustainable privacy norms is important to companies in order to best meet the privacy expectations of consumers, users, and employees. In terms of the Lemonade Insurance case from the introduction, customers would have expectations as to what data Lemonade has access to and how it would be used. According to both Martin and Nissenbaum, customers could find it inappropriate for Lemonade to purchase behavioral data from their online activities. For Nissenbaum, the online browsing and shopping data is within the retail context and not within the insurance context and sharing that data would breach contextual integrity. For Martin, individuals share browsing activities with specific websites online *and do not expect* that information to be shared with a new firm and used with a new purpose (deciding insurance).

Related Cases - Privacy

The ad tech case, "Finding Consumers, No Matter Where They Hide," outlines the myriad of online websites, trackers, data brokers, ad networks, and data aggregators that gather detailed consumer data and then use that information to target individuals with ads and suggestions. The case centers on a new ability to marry location data with behavioral and psychographic data to better target individuals. Tracking and targeting of individuals stretches (perhaps to the breaking point!) our privacy expectations while seemingly "in public"—which makes the theories on privacy included here particularly helpful.

A related article, "How a Company You've Never Heard of Sends You Letters about Your Medical Condition," details the ability of a company, Acurian, to target individuals based on predictions as to the possible ailments and diseases they may have—its predictions are improved with data from Walgreen's on their pharmacy customers. The case illustrates the ability to bring offline behavior (filling prescriptions in a drug store) to online targeting.

Clarissa Wilbur Berger provides a thoughtful overview of the current privacy laws in the United States including federal, state, and foreign laws. These regulations govern businesses as they gather, share, sell, and use data about individuals. In addition to these laws, individuals can sue others for a privacy tort violation—when one party harms another. "Privacy tort law protect against emotional, reputational, and proprietary injuries caused by (1) public disclosure of private facts, (2) intrusion on seclusion, (3) depiction of another in a false light, and (4) appropriation of another's image for commercial gain."[9] Suing someone for a violation of a privacy tort entails proving the act was intentional and proving the specific harm that was the result of the violation. As Professor Danielle Citron notes, today's privacy violations in a networked society are not addressed by traditional privacy torts.[10] Clarissa Wilbur's article explores the ways regulations have evolved to contend with privacy interests in the law. Privacy theories are not necessarily tied to privacy law. In other words, we have expectations of privacy —what data is going to be gathered and used by whom and for what purpose—independent of the current laws.

Summary of Readings - Questions for Data

In the article "Datasheets for Datasets," Timnit Gebru and colleagues outline questions a computer scientist or data analyst should ask of data sets. By having a datasheet accompany every dataset, the authors are attempting to address the needs of both data creators (those who create the dataset) and data consumers (those who use the dataset). The questions include questions about origination and the purpose of the dataset created to questions about the contents (and if it contains sensitive information) to questions about potential future uses. The article is premised on the assumption that both dataset creators, as well as dataset consumers, are responsible for the quality of the datasets used in analytics.

Gebru et al.'s approach has several implications that are important for the ethical examination of data and analytics. First, the questions they posit for the creation and use of data sets imply that these constitute open questions that computer scientists and data analysts can/should answer. In other words, how these questions are handled are value judgments and at the discretion of the developer and analysts. Many times, we take these facets of datasets as a given, as attributes of the data that are necessary or not up for debate. However, Gebru et al. remind us that these datasets are created by humans, and how they are labeled, sampled, constituted, measured, etc. is up to the data scientist. Second, the article outlines the many ethical questions that one can and should ask about the data they use or create. When applying Gebru et al.'s approach to a data analytics case, one would identify salient questions, of the many included, that were clearly not addressed by the creator or user of the program. For example, in assessing AI Jim, Lemonade Insurance would have to ask questions about the data used to train their program around privacy, bias, and disparate impact. This second implication is applicable to the case.

Related Cases - Questions for Data

The case to accompany the Gebru et al. reading is "Wrongfully Accused." Robert Julian-Borchak Williams was wrongfully arrested by Detroit police for larceny based solely on an identification from a facial recognition system. The arrest involved not only the police but also a contracted facial recognition company. The case brings forth concepts of shared responsibility around the creation and use of datasets, such as data used for the facial recognition programs. As noted in the second article, "Facial Recognition is Accurate, if You're a White Guy," these facial recognition programs are known to be biased in their accuracy rates. The study is based on the research by Buolamwini and Gebru which measured the accuracy rates of commercial facial recognition programs and found that the most misclassified group was darker-skinned females with an error rate up to 34.7 percent where the highest misclassification rate for white men was 0.8 percent.[11] The case highlights the pernicious implications of training data and the utility of Gebru et al.'s argument that data developers and data users have a responsibility to better understand the data they are creating and using. The issue is larger than police identification. People are being denied unemployment benefits due to problems with facial recognition technology used to prevent fraud.[12]

Notes

1. Duhigg, Charles. 2012. "How Companies Learn Your Secrets," *The New York Times*. February 16, 2012. https://www.nytimes.com/2012/02/19/magazine/shopping-habits.html
2. Duhigg, Charles. 2012. "How Companies Learn Your Secrets."
3. Kirsten Martin, "Privacy Notices as Tabula Rasa: An Empirical Investigation into How Complying with a Privacy Notice Is Related to Meeting Privacy Expectations Online," *Journal of Public Policy & Marketing* 34, no. 2 (2015): 210–227, http://dx.doi.org/10.1509/jppm.14.139; Lorrie Faith Cranor et al., "Are They Worth Reading? An In-Depth Analysis of Online Advertising Companies' Privacy Policies," 2014.
4. Kirsten Martin, "Privacy Revisited: From Lady Godiva's Peeping Tom to Facebook's Beacon Program," in *Ethical Issues in E-Business: Models and Frameworks* (IGI Global, 2010), 135–151.
5. Alessandro Acquisti, Laura Brandimarte, and George Loewenstein, "Secrets and Likes: The Drive for Privacy and the Difficulty of Achieving It in the Digital Age," *Journal of Consumer Psychology* 30, no. 4 (2020): 736–758; Kirsten Martin, "Breaking the Privacy Paradox: The Value of Privacy and Associated Duty of Firms," *Business Ethics Quarterly* 30, no. 1 (2020): 65–96.

6. Ari Ezra Waldman, *Privacy as Trust: Information Privacy for an Information Age* (Cambridge University Press, 2018).

7. Neil M Richards and Woodrow Hartzog, "Taking Trust Seriously in Privacy Law," *Stan. Tech. L. Rev.* 19 (2016): 431–72.

8. Danielle Keats Citron, "Sexual Privacy," *Yale LJ* 128 (2018): 1870.

9. Danielle Keats Citron, "Mainstreaming Privacy Torts," *California Law Review*, 2010, 1805–1852.

10. Citron.

11. Joy Buolamwini and Timnit Gebru, "Gender Shades: Intersectional Accuracy Disparities in Commercial Gender Classification," *Proceedings of Machine Learning Research, Conference on Fairness, Accountability, and Transparency* 81 (2018): 1–15.

12. Feathers, Todd. 2021. "Facial Recognition Failures Are Locking People out of Unemployment Systems," *Vice News*. June 18, 2021. https://www.vice.com/en/article/5dbywn/facial-recognition-failures-are-locking-people-out-of-unemployment-systems

Chapter 3.1

Finding Consumers, No Matter Where They Hide: Ad Targeting and Location Data*

Kirsten Martin

Vanessa was tasked with deciding whether her company should use consumer location to find potential consumers. For targeting consumers with ads and news, location data appeared to be the holy grail of information. Location data offered more insights than merely where someone was at a given moment. As summarized by the co-founder of NumberEight, a product that infers user behavior from location data, analysis location data could tell whether someone is driving, walking, or sitting, as well as whether someone was close to someone or something—all from a phone's sensors. This type of sensing "could target ads to 'early risers' (as indicated by sensors noting when the phone is picked up after hours of rest) or adapt its user interface for after-work commuters (as indicated when sensors note riding a train after 5 pm)."[1]

In addition, a number of companies had begun offering a service linking consumers' anonymous mobile advertising id (MAID) to their actual identity. This unlocked the potential to tracking even more people on their phones and more easily linking their location data (and all that it provides) to their online and offline browsing, purchasing, and behavioral data.[2]

The opportunity in front of Vanessa was to target people based not only on their interests and concerns but also based on where they may go in the future and who they are close to.[3]

However, given how targeted advertising focused on consumer vulnerabilities, the additional knowledge of location could go terribly wrong. These companies could also capture when someone attended an AA meeting, went to a doctor, attended a protest or rally, or frequented a liquor store. In fact, reporters were able to identify a specific priest as not only using a queer data app but

---

DOI: 10.1201/9781003278290-16

also tracking his location to specific bars by purchasing his location data from a vendor. The same data used to locate and track individuals for a story could be used for marketing with the same level of specificity.[4] Also, the advertising industry had promised to keep the MAIDs anonymous, and it was not clear how consumers would respond to being tracked when they thought they were anonymous. But, there was also a good chance that Vanessa's company would never be explicitly linked to using location data given how confusing the online data ecosystem was.

History of Ads Online

Advertising was critical to the commercial development of the internet. In the 1990s, a brand wanting to advertise would deal directly with a website, aka the "publisher," in order to post a banner ad.[5] Placing ads online was similar to placing ads on TV or radio—the type of individual who regularly viewed the website was targeted by placing ads on the website directly.

A key development with online advertising was the ability of technology to track and target individuals online with increasing precision and persistence. Targeted advertising, where ads are placed based on the individual looking at the screen rather than the content of the website, requires the collection of consumers' data as they navigate online in order to, first, capture relevant information about them and then, second, later find the user online and tailor content and advertising to them specifically.[6]

Ads may be targeted based on the demographics of the individual, the behavior (browsing, purchases, etc.) of the individual, and even the psychographic profile of the individual. Who the individual is and estimates of their demographics, preferences, friends, locations, purchases, etc. are collected, stored, and aggregated by different ad tech companies. Even without data on a specific person, data aggregators and ad networks are able to infer interests about someone based on affinity profiling a "grouping people together according to their assumed interests rather than solely on their personal traits."[7] Through social networking, and now location tracking, companies can identify who your group of close contacts is and target advertising for you accordingly.

Current Status of Tracking and Targeting Online

The process of placing ads on a page is now automated and requires dozens of companies to place the right ad at the right time in front of the right person.

Trackers. In order to collect information about users, websites include hidden trackers to monitor a user's activities on the site. First party cookies, placed by the website themselves, remember the users' log-in credentials, shopping carts, preferences and make the experience of the site run smoothly. Websites can also optimize the layout of their site or what products they offer by understanding their users.[8]

Third-party cookies and beacons are tracking devices placed on a site *by other companies* to monitor users' activities in order to share that data with advertisers, analytics companies, and social media sites. The majority of trackers are third-party trackers. Figure 1 is a screen shot of the trackers identified on a national news site using Ghostery, an anti-tracking add-on that identifies all the trackers on a given website when the website loads.

When the ability to block cookies became possible, with browser add-ons like Ghostery, advertising companies devised new trackers, such as Flash cookies and device fingerprinting, in order to track the movements and activities of individuals without their knowledge and without being blocked. Device fingerprinting uses information such as screen resolution, operating system, fonts, etc. to create a unique identifier for a particular device and track the user across websites. Device identifiers in mobile space—such as Apple iOS's Identifiers for Advertisers ("IDFA") and Google Android's Advertising ID—monitor apps on devices and avoid anti-tracking software.[9]

Data brokers then collect consumer information from the tracking companies and combine that online data and with offline data as well. Data brokers or data aggregators provide the bridge between those that track and those that target consumers online and hold large consumer data repositories. For example, Oracle's BlueKai helps companies target and personalize advertising, including by health and medical conditions, to collecting consumer data across third parties.[10] A data broker who de-anonymizes mobile identifiers and links that information to consumer data claims to have 223 billion data points on 275 million adults in the United States.[11]

Data brokers are known for (and market themselves as) providing a lot of information for many people. The industry group IAB created 700 categories for the type of information gathered for advertising and includes types of video games, interests in travel, medical, and personal finance as well as areas such as "hate speech and acts of aggression," "adult" content, terrorism, and "sensitive social issues."[12]

Ad networks combine websites who have similar audiences in order to make it easier for brands to find their targeted individuals.[13] Ad networks offer a single point of contact for brands who wish to place ads on multiple websites with similar inventory. Inventory, for online advertising, is the ad space on a publisher's website, and the ad network is an intermediary between advertisers and the website publishers. **Ad exchanges** are marketplaces and offer real-time bidding—a live auction—for inventory on sites. Sometimes this is the left-over inventory that is not occupied by an ad placed by an ad network. So, as an individual navigates to a page, brands and advertisers are bidding on ad exchanges to place their ad on that page's inventory.[14]

Additional companies in the ad tech space offer ancillary services behind the scenes. Companies that allow brands to retarget or follow an individual as they browse online to multiple websites. Companies that offer re-identification to identify seemingly anonymous users and offer companies consumers' addresses, emails, and phone numbers. Companies may offer "better" targeting and analytics on top of that offered by ad networks and data brokers.

Customer facing websites and apps play two roles in online advertising: the window through which trackers can collect user data and the publishers of the eventual ads targeting the individual. In this way, customer facing companies act as lures and gatekeepers: sites are a lure in drawing consumers online for a sustained period of time to be tracked and then targeted and are a gatekeeper to trackers and ad networks to reach high-value customers to see their ads.[15]

Websites and apps do not disclose who is tracking users on their websites, the type of information gathered, or with whom the trackers share and sell information. The privacy notice is the mechanism by which the website informs the consumer of general tracking and targeting so that the consumer is able to make an informed choice (e.g., collecting data to "Market and advertise for third parties"[16] without any specifics as to whom). Websites and apps are required to only gather, share, and use consumer data in ways that conform to whatever they included in their privacy notice. The FTC regulates this exchange—how well the website conforms to their stated privacy notice. There are no minimum requirements as to what is said in the privacy notice, the form of the privacy notice, how detailed the privacy notice is, or how consumer data is treated at the federal level.

Academics and journalists have recently identified novel ways to identify trackers on websites. For example, The Markup, an investigative news site, created Blacklight to present users with the trackers on every website as well as the companies that own those trackers.[17] A journalist at Vox used Blacklight to identify 31 trackers and 54 third-party cookies on their own site as well as

Facebook and Google. Blacklight also identifies fingerprinting, which is missed when only cookies are measured, as well as websites that load scripts to watch and record all user interactions on a page (session recording).[18]

The Markup found 100 websites, including those serving undocumented immigrants, domestic abuse survivors, and LGBTQ people, tracked users and sent their information to advertising companies. Health sites such as WebMD sent user data to advertisers. Many websites did not know the trackers were on their sites—which is not uncommon.[19]

For example, a small, nonprofit website helping transgender military service members and veterans believed they allowed only three trackers: Google and Twitter for "Like" buttons as well as Disqus for commenting. Using the privacy inspector, journalists found 21 companies tracking visitors including Amazon and Oracle's BlueKai. It turned out Disqus allowed those trackers onto the website. Such "piggybacking" trackers are not necessarily known by the customer facing website.[20] Tracking companies offer a free useful tool, such as Disqus or AddThis that allows visitors share the website, while actually being a marketing company sending data ("up to 30 data points per page view") to advertisers (in the case of AddThis, Oracle).[21]

Websites sell ad space to advertisers based on the type of user they have. The number of impressions an ad has on viewers are sold in "cost per thousand views" (CPM) or cost per click (CPC).[22] In order to place ads on their site, websites need to be able to identify their users so that ad networks can then target them with advertising based on that individual's preferences, concerns, recent behavior, or "pain points" which are points of vulnerability they may be experiencing. Websites relying on targeted advertising need individuals to be identifiable and engaged for as long as possible so that ads can be served.

Users provide the consumer data for the online data ecosystem. Consumer data is the fuel for the ad tech engine. The selling and sharing of consumer data constitute 60 percent of internet traffic. Users are also responsible for reading the privacy notices before agreeing to engage with a website in order to make an informed choice to share their data.

Consumers have been found to not like being notified of the tracking and targeting methods are deemed "creepy."[23] In particular, consumers found two practices particularly unsettling: obtaining information from outside the website and predicting information about an individual from a larger data set. In fact, concerns about the misuse of their data outweighed consumers' appreciation for personalized, hyper-targeted ads.[24]

Users are also responsible for identifying appropriate anti-tracking software, such as privacy badger or Ghostery, which block many of the cookies and beacons tracking their movements. In privacy surveys, individuals consistently approve of allowing websites and apps to gather data to improve services but do not approve of third-party trackers and data aggregators accessing, selling, sharing, and using their data.

Who Benefits from Online Advertising

The overall market for 'digital advertising' was 325B in 2019 and projected to grow to $525B by 2024.[25] However, who benefits in the current system is not clear. The advertising industry focuses on the possible impact to consumers and websites if hyper-targeted advertising and ubiquitous tracking were to be reduced: a website could lose advertising money or users could be required to pay for web content if no advertising were permitted. However, the alternative to hyper-targeted ads is not the absence of ads, but rather ads based on the context of the website or general information about the type of users on the website.

Brands are usually willing to pay more for hyper-targeted advertising of their products. Howard Beales found "advertisers" willing to pay 2.68 times more to place an ad with a cookie,[26] but much of the additional money may go to the ad tech companies—ad networks, ad exchanges, etc.—who take as much as 60 percent of the additional revenue.[27] This metric is normally seen as a market signal as to the effectiveness of hyper-targeted ads: brands would not be willing to pay more for targeted ads with tracking capabilities if the additional cost was not worth it to them.[28]

Companies like Google and Facebook who play the part of ad network, ad exchange, publisher, and tracker make 80–99 percent of their revenue through advertising.[29]

One study found that the ad platforms—the companies buying and selling consumer data—take as much as 50 percent of the ad spending.[30] The rest is either unattributable or goes to the different ad platform fees to find the right person and place the ad.[31] And not all ads 'published' are actually seen by any individual: in 2016, as much as 56 percent of all display ad dollars were lost to fraudulent and unviewable inventory.[32]

The value of hyper-targeted advertising is seen as hard to value. In fact, *The New York Times* International SVP of global advertising, Jean-Christophe Demarta, noted that their switch to primarily contextual ads (without hyper-targeting) saw little impact to their revenue.[33] While brands and advertisers have been willing to pay additional for tracked ads in the past, recent research has shown diminishing returns on the click-through rate and perhaps fraud in the system.

Recent Issues

Fraud in system. Recent attention has fallen on the amount of fraud in the ad tech space. Website publishers are paid based on the clicks or impressions of any given ad giving websites an incentive to have as many individuals see as many ads as possible. Ad networks and ad exchanges are paid as a percentage of those ads seen or clicked.[34] A burgeoning market of ad fraud as developed whereby brands are paying for ads to be shown to bots and placed on fake webpages. These ads shown to bots on fake sites may not even appear to be fake to detection technology.

> An industry-wide study by the ISBA in 2020 (British Advertisers[35]) showed that at least 50% of every dollar spent in programmatic advertising goes to ad tech middlemen instead of towards showing ads; and about a third of the portion that went to ad tech vendors "went missing" on average.[36]

Advertisers who thought that they were advertising on websites, were purchasing counterfeit ad inventory.

The Wall Street Journal reported that in mid-2017, Procter & Gamble, one of the largest advertisers, cut its digital ad spend by 100 million dollars, with the company's finance chief saying, "We were serving bots as opposed to human beings." By the end of that year, cuts on digital ads had doubled to $200 million.[37]

Uber began tracking down where their ads were being placed at sites and found that some were on sites which hurt their brand (e.g., Breitbart). Uber marketing tracked down who was placing those ads and turned off 10 percent of ad spending, and nothing happened to revenue or rides. Uber had discovered a type of ad fraud where bots were pretending to see ads and then place requests for rides—and get paid for that lead generation when no human was involved.[38]

Type of Targeting. The breadth of consumer data collection was brought to the public's attention with a story in the *New York Times* on how Target figured out a teenager was pregnant before her family did. The girls' family received coupons in the mail targeting the teenager as pregnant, and the father approached the store manager to find out what was going on. The teenager was pregnant, and Target could tell using a prediction algorithm on her buying patterns.[39]

Facebook had come under fire for targeting teens when they were predicted to feel ""worthless," "insecure," "defeated," "anxious," "silly," "useless," "stupid," "overwhelmed," "stressed," and "a failure."[40] This was after the company had received backlash for manipulating users' News Feeds with happy or sad content to see how their users would react.[41] In general marketers were willing to pay for particular search words that indicated someone's vulnerability rather than an indicator as to preferences or ability to pay.[42] For example, targeted ads were focused on finding people predicted to need to purchase a gravestone or fertility treatments or even pregnancy related products. While Facebook has a policy to not target their users based on their medical history or predicted medical condition, the ad tech industry does not have such a policy. In fact, medical conditions and interests is a valuable category of consumer information for advertisers.[43]

Political Manipulation. An additional externality associated with the targeted advertising system was the ability of companies, advocacy groups and other countries to use the same system for disinformation campaigns seeking to undermine the United States voting or pandemic response. Whether targeting individuals to undermine vaccines or voting, foreign governments can access individuals with false information using the hyper-targeting ad technology.[44] Congress has asked for information as to foreign clients who use ad exchanges and ad networks to target individuals in the United States.[45]

Current Decision

For Vanessa, the confusion of the digital advertising ecosystem was both concerning and a possible cover: it was difficult to believe that anyone would ever blame her company for using location data when there was so much else going on! She had to decide how to frame this new opportunity—to use mobile identifiers with location data to find consumers and target them with ads. On the one hand, it appeared to offer a unique opportunity to find more people as well as where they go, who they are with, and what their concerns, preferences, and behaviors are. Yet, the entire system seemed to be coming under pressure and the value of targeting wasn't as clear. But the industry had always wanted more targeting.

Notes

1. Fussell, Sidney. 2020. Companies Can Track Your Phone's Movements to Target Ads. *Wired*. https://www.wired.com/story/companies-track-phones-movements-target-ads/
2. Cox, Joseph. 2021. "Inside the Industry That Unmasks People at Scale," *Vice News*. https://www.vice.com/en/article/epnmvz/industry-unmasks-at-scale-maid-to-pii
3. Nguyen, Nicole. 2018. Facebook Filed a Patent to Calculate Your Future Location. *BuzzFeed News* https://www.buzzfeednews.com/article/nicolenguyen/facebook-location-data-prediction-patent and twitter (Robert G. Reeve – "If my phone is regularly in the same GPS location as another phone, they take note of that. They start reconstructing the web of people I'm in regular contact with. The advertisers can cross-reference my interests and browsing history and purchase history to those around me. It starts to show ME different ads based on the people AROUND me.")

4. Boorstein, Michelle, Iati Marisa, and Annys Shin. 2021. "Top U.S. Catholic Church Official Resigns after Cellphone Data Used to Track Him on Grindr and to Gay Bars" *The Washington Post*. https://www.washingtonpost.com/religion/2021/07/20/bishop-misconduct-resign-burrill/ He subsequently was removed from the priesthood.

5. Edelman, Gilad. 2020. Ad Tech Could Be the Next Internet Bubble. *Wired*. https://www.wired.com/story/ad-tech-could-be-the-next-internet-bubble/

6. Lau, Yan. 2020. A Brief Primer on the Economics of Targeted Advertising. *Bureau of Economics, Federal Trade Commission*. https://www.ftc.gov/system/files/documents/reports/brief-primer-economics-targeted-advertising/economic_issues_paper_-_economics_of_targeted_advertising.pdf

7. Wachter, Sandra. 2020. "Affinity Profiling and Discrimination by Association in Online Behavioural Advertising." *Berkeley Technology Law Journal*, Vol. 35, No. 2.

8. "How to Protect Your Privacy Online." *FTC. Consumer Information*. https://www.consumer.ftc.gov/articles/0042-online-tracking. Accessed. July 26, 2021.

9. "How to Protect Your Privacy Online." *FTC.*

10. Libert, Timothy. 2019. "This Article Is Spying on You." *The New York Times*. https://www.nytimes.com/2019/09/18/opinion/data-privacy-tracking.html

11. Cox, Joseph. 2021. "Inside the Industry That Unmasks People at Scale," *Vice News*. https://www.vice.com/en/article/epnmvz/industry-unmasks-at-scale-maid-to-pii

12. "Content Taxonomy." *IAB Tech Lab*. https://iabtechlab.com/standards/content-taxonomy/. Accessed July 26, 2021.

13. Watkins, Elizabeth Anne. 2018. "Guide to Advertising Technology." *Columbia Journalism Review*. https://www.cjr.org/tow_center_reports/the-guide-to-advertising-technology.php

14. Watkins, Elizabeth Anne. 2018. "Guide to Advertising Technology."

15. *Advertising Platforms* are companies that offer the ability to reach specific individuals when they are online such as Amazon, Baidu, Bing, Facebook, Tencent, Twitter, etc. These platforms are customer-facing companies but earn the majority of their money through advertising. These platforms are able to track users while outside the platform and across websites. For example, Facebook is able to track people's usage of apps and websites when the individual chooses to log in using their Facebook log in. Lomas, Natasha. 2020. "Facebook's Latest 'Transparency' Tool Doesn't Offer Much – So We Went Digging." *Tech Crunch*. February 25, 2020. https://techcrunch.com/2020/02/25/facebooks-latest-transparency-tool-doesnt-offer-much-so-we-went-digging/

16. Fandango Privacy Policy. Last updated July 1, 2021. https://www.fandango.com/policies/privacy-policy

17. Sankin, Aaron and Surya Mattu. 2020. "The High Privacy Cost of a "Free" Website." *The Markup*. September 22, 2020. https://themarkup.org/blacklight/2020/09/22/blacklight-tracking-advertisers-digital-privacy-sensitive-websites

18. Sankin, Aaron and Surya Mattu. 2020. "The High Privacy Cost of a "Free" Website."

19. Sankin, Aaron and Surya Mattu. 2020. "The High Privacy Cost of a "Free" Website."

20. Sankin, Aaron and Surya Mattu. 2020. "The High Privacy Cost of a "Free" Website."

21. Sankin, Aaron and Surya Mattu. 2020. "The High Privacy Cost of a "Free" Website."

22. Watkins, Elizabeth Anne. 2018. "Guide to Advertising Technology."

23. John, Leslie K., Tami Kim, and Kate Barasz. 2018. "Ads That Don't Overstep." *Harvard Business Review*. February. https://hbr.org/2018/01/ads-that-dont-overstep

24. John, Leslie K., Tami Kim, and Kate Barasz. 2018. "Ads That Don't Overstep." The use of trust signals, such as including information about why an ad was shown, actually increased the click through rate—as long as the use of data was from the website and acceptable.

25. Edelman, Gilad. 2020. "Ad Tech Could Be The Next Internet Bubble."

26. Hagey, Keach. 2019. "Behavioral Ad Targeting Not Paying Off for Publishers, Study Suggests." *The Wall Street Journal*. May 29, 2019. https://www.wsj.com/articles/behavioral-ad-targeting-not-paying-off-for-publishers-study-suggests-11559167195

27. O'Reilly, Lara. 2018. "Big Advertisers Embrace Blockchain to Root Out Digital Spending Waste," *The Wall Street Journal*. July 12, 2018. https://www.wsj.com/articles/big-advertisers-embrace-blockchain-to-root-out-digital-spending-waste-1531396800?mod=article_inline

28. While advertisers appear to currently be willing to pay more for hyper-targeted ads—to ad tech as well as website publishers—the more targeted the advertising, the fewer possible impressions (fewer people see the ads) with lower competition. This would suggest that advertisers could pay less for targeted ads due to less market pressure. https://www.ftc.gov/system/files/documents/public_events/1415032/privacycon2019_acquisti_online_tracking_and_publishers_revenues.pdf

29. Edelman, Gilad. 2020. "Ad Tech Could Be the Next Internet Bubble."

30. "Half of Online Ad Spending Goes to Industry Middlemen," *Financial Times*. 2020. https://www.ft.com/content/9ee0ebd3-346f-45b1-8b92-aa5c597d4389

31. "Time for Change and Transparency in Programmatic Advertising," *ISBA*. 2020. https://www.isba.org.uk/article/time-change-and-transparency-programmatic-advertising

32. Edelman, Gilad. 2020. "Ad Tech Could Be the Next Internet Bubble."

33. Davies, Jessica. 2019. "After GDPR, The New York Times Cut Off Ad Exchanges in Europe—And Kept Growing Ad Revenue," *Digiday*. https://digiday.com/media/gumgumtest-new-york-times-gdpr-cut-off-ad-exchanges-europe-ad-revenue/

34. Tim Hwang. 2020. "Subprime Attention Crisis: Advertising and the Time Bomb at the Heart of the Internet," *FSG Originals*.

35. Time for Change and Transparency in Programmatic Advertising. 2020.

36. Augustine Fou. 2021. "Shrimp, Cacao, Digital Ad Fraud," *Forbes*. https://www.forbes.com/sites/augustinefou/2021/01/05/shrimp-cacao-digital-ad-fraud/?sh=55b74e940bdc

37. "Alexandra Bruell and Sharon Terlep, "P&G Cuts More than $100 Million in 'Largely Ineffective' Digital Ads," July 27, 2017. https://www.wsj.com/articles/p-g-cuts-more-than-100-million-in-largely-ineffective-digital-ads-1501191104 see also https://www.cjr.org/tow_center_reports/the-guide-to-advertising-technology.php#citations

38. Historic Ad Fraud at Uber with Kevin Frisch. 2020. *Marketing Today with Alan Hart*. https://www.youtube.com/watch?v=dKO0mAYUTGo

39. Duhigg, Charles. 2012. "How Companies Learn Your Secrets," *The New York Times*. February 16, 2012. https://www.nytimes.com/2012/02/19/magazine/shopping-habits.html?pagewanted=1&_r=1&hp

40. Machkovech, Sam. 2017. "Report: Facebook Helped Advertisers Target Teens Who Feel "Worthless", *ArsTechnica*. https://arstechnica.com/information-technology/2017/05/facebook-helped-advertisers-target-teens-who-feel-worthless/

41. Reilly, Michael. 2017. "Is Facebook Targeting Ads at Sad Teens," *MIT Technology Review*. May 1, 2017. https://www.technologyreview.com/2017/05/01/105987/is-facebook-targeting-ads-at-sad-teens/

42. In fact, in general marketers were willing to pay for particular search words that included: "Bail bonds, Casino, and Lawyer (#2-4) followed by Insurance, "Cash services & payday loans, Cleanup and restoration, (#6-8). "Rehab" at #11 and Psychic (#12). Medical needs (#16) and Loans (#17). Online gambling (#22) Hair transplant (#24). "Plumber" at #18 "Termites" at #19 "Pest control" at #20 https://www.wordstream.com/blog/ws/2017/06/27/most-expensive-keywords

43. Nudson, Rae. 2020. "When Targeted Ads Feel a Little Too Targeted," *Vox*. https://www.vox.com/the-goods/2020/4/9/21204425/targeted-ads-fertility-eating-disorder-coronavirus

44. Gordon, Michael R. and Dustin Volz. 2021. "Russian Disinformation Campaign Aims to Undermine Confidence in Pfizer, Other Covid-19 Vaccines, U.S. Officials Say," *The Wall Street Journal*. https://www.wsj.com/articles/russian-disinformation-campaign-aims-to-undermine-confidence-in-pfizer-other-covid-19-vaccines-u-s-officials-say-11615129200

45. Haggin, Patience. 2021. "U.S. Senators Ask Digital-Ad Auctioneers to Name Foreign Clients Amid National-Security Concerns," *The Wall Street Journal*. https://www.wsj.com/articles/u-s-senators-ask-digital-ad-auctioneers-to-name-foreign-clients-amid-national-security-concerns-11617393964

Chapter 3.2

How a Company You've Never Heard of Sends You Letters about Your Medical Condition[*]

Surya Mattu and Kashmir Hill

In the summer of 2015, Alexandra Franco got a letter in the mail from a company she had never heard of called AcurianHealth. The letter, addressed to Franco personally, invited her to participate in a study of people with psoriasis, a condition that causes dry, itchy patches on the skin.

Franco did not have psoriasis. But the year before, she remembered, she had searched for information about it online, when a friend was dealing with the condition. And a few months prior to getting the letter, she had also turned to the internet with a question about a skin fungus. It was the sort of browsing anyone might do, on the assumption it was private and anonymous.

Now there was a letter, with her name and home address on it, targeting her as a potential skin-disease patient. Acurian is in the business of recruiting people to take part in clinical trials for drug companies. How had it identified her? She had done nothing that would publicly associate her with having a skin condition.

When she Googled the company, she found lots of people who shared her bewilderment, complaining that they had been contacted by Acurian about their various medical conditions. Particularly troubling was a parent who said her young son had received a letter from Acurian accurately identifying his medical condition and soliciting him for a drug trial—the first piece of mail he'd had addressed to him besides birthday cards from family members.

Acurian has attributed its uncanny insights to powerful guesswork, based on sophisticated analysis of public information and "lifestyle data" purchased from data brokers. What may

---

[*] Mattu, Surya and Kashmir Hill. Gizmodo. June 19, 2017. https://gizmodo.com/how-a-company-you-ve-never-heard-of-sends-you-letters-a-1795643539. Reprinted with permission.

DOI: 10.1201/9781003278290-17

appear intrusive, by the company's account, is merely testimony to the power of patterns revealed by big data.

"We are now at a point where, based on your credit-card history, and whether you drive an American automobile and several other lifestyle factors, we can get a very, very close bead on whether or not you have the disease state we're looking at," Acurian's senior vice president of operations told the *Wall Street Journal* in 2013.

Yet there's some medical information that Acurian doesn't have to guess about: The company pays Walgreens, which uses a privacy exemption for research, to send recruitment letters to its pharmacy customers on Acurian's behalf, based on the medications they're using. Under this arrangement, Acurian notes that it doesn't access the medical information directly; the customers' identities remain private until they respond to the invitations.

And that is not the entire story. An investigation by the Special Projects Desk has found that Acurian may also be pursuing people's medical information more directly, using the services of a startup that advertises its ability to unmask anonymous website visitors. This could allow it harvest the identities of people seeking information about particular conditions online, before they've consented to anything.

A letter sent out to a Walgreens customer in Connecticut on Acurian's behalf. It invited her to visit a generic sounding website for people with pulmonary disease. At the time, she had a prescription from Walgreens for asthma.

If you're suddenly thinking back on all of the things you've browsed for online in your life and feeling horrified, you're not alone.

AcurianHealth has created dozens and dozens of generic sounding websites for the trials they're recruiting for: www.trialforCOPD.com, www.studiesforyourarthritis.com, and www.kidsdepressionstudy.com are a few examples of the many websites they own. The sites all feature stock images of people in distress, sometimes include AcurianHealth's logo, and include promises of up to $1,000 for participating, depending on the study.

Out of view, some of these sites include something else: code from a company called NaviStone—which bills itself as a specialist in matching "anonymous website visitors to postal names and addresses." So if a person is curious about one of those letters from Walgreens, or follows one of Acurian's online ads, and visits one of Acurian's generic disease-specific sites, their identity could be discovered and associated with the relevant condition.

This tracking function undermines what's supposedly a formal separation between Walgreens customer data and Acurian's recruitment. If Walgreens sends out a bunch of letters to customers taking certain medications, and those customers then visit the generic website controlled by Acurian provided in the letter, Acurian can infer its wave of new visitors are taking those medications—and, if NaviStone delivers on its promise to identify visitors, Acurian can see who they are.

Walgreens gives itself permission to use customers' health information for "research" purposes, which would include clinical trials, in its privacy policy. It's been working with Acurian since at least 2013, and in 2015, Walgreens announced it was "leveraging" its 100 million customer database to recruit patients directly for five major drug companies.

When asked about its partnership with Acurian, Walgreens spokesperson Scott Goldberg pointed me to a Walgreens FAQ page about clinical trials. It states that Walgreens doesn't share health information with third parties without permission, but that a third party may "receive your information if you contact the web-site and/or toll-free number in the letter to seek more information about the clinical trial."

The question is whether users will know that one of Acurian's websites has received their information—even if they haven't necessarily agreed to submit it. NaviStone, an Ohio-based business spun out from the marketing firm CohereOne last year, claims to be able to identify between 60 and 70 percent of anonymous visitors to the websites that use its services.

When we contacted the firm last month to ask how it does this, Allen Abbott, NaviStone's chief operating officer, said by phone that talking about how its technology works is "problematic."

"A lot of our competitors would love to know how we made it work," Abbott said. "We have an advantage that we would be silly to reveal."

We asked whether the company had thought about the privacy implications involved in identifying people visiting a website for sensitive reasons, and whether there were certain customers the company wouldn't work with.

"Our business is almost entirely e-commerce, helping retailers sell to their customers," he said. "There was one site that came into our radar that was adult-related material that we decided not to pursue."

We then described what Acurian does.

"We don't work with anyone like that," he said.

We explained that the call was because we'd found NaviStone's code on AcurianHealth sites.

"It's possible," he then said. "We have a lot of customers."

But Abbott insisted that NaviStone had found a "privacy compliant way" to identify anonymous website visitors—again saying he couldn't describe it because it was a proprietary technology.

When we analyzed the NaviStone code on Acurian's sites, we found one way that NaviStone's technology works: It collects information as soon as it is entered into the text boxes on forms, before the person actually agrees to submit it. When we typed a test email address in the "Join Us" page on Acurian's site, it was immediately captured and sent to the company's servers, even if we later chose to close the page without hitting the "Send" button on the form.

In fact, the information was collected before we got to the part of the form that said, "Your privacy is important to us. By selecting this box, you agree to our Privacy Policy and Terms of Use, and agree that we contact you by phone using automated technology or other means using the information you provided above regarding research studies."

"If I haven't hit send, what they seem to be doing almost seems like hacking," said Lori Andrews, a law professor at the Chicago-Kent School of Law. "It's similar to a keystroke tracker. That could be problematic for them."

Ryan Calo, a law professor at the University of Washington, said this clearly violates a user's expectation of what will happen based on the design of the site. "It's not that they lied to you with words, but they've created an impression and violated that impression," said Calo who suggested it could violate a federal law against unfair and deceptive practices, as well as laws against deceptive trade practices in California and Massachusetts. A complaint on those grounds, Calo said, "would not be laughed out of court."

When we followed up with NaviStone's Abbott by email, he insisted that the company doesn't send any data to Acurian.

"We don't send any email for Acurian, or pass along any email addresses to them or use their email addresses in any way or manner," said Abbott by email. "If we are indeed inadvertently collecting email addresses, we will fix immediately. It's not what we do."

But when the Special Projects Desk reviewed dozens of other companies' websites that were using NaviStone's code, they were also collecting email addresses. After a month of repeated inquiries to NaviStone and to many of the sites using its code, NaviStone last week stopped collecting information on the site of Acurian and most of its other clients before the "Submit" button was pressed.

"Rather than use email addresses to generate advertising communications, we actually use the presence of an email address as a suppression factor, since it indicates that email, and not direct mail, is their preferred method of receiving advertising messages," said Abbott by email. "While we believe our technology has been appropriately used, we have decided to change the system operation such that email addresses are not captured until the visitor hits the 'submit' button."

Asked about its partnerships with Walgreens and NaviStone, Acurian declined to be interviewed.

"As a general policy based on our confidentiality agreements with our business partners, I hope you will understand that Acurian does not discuss its proprietary business strategies," said Randy Buckwalter, a spokesperson for PPD, the corporate parent of Acurian, by email.

Buckwalter told us Acurian would provide a fuller response to what is reported here, but never provided it.

Kirk Nahra, a partner at the law firm Wiley Rein who specializes in health privacy law, said there's nothing really wrong with Walgreens sending out letters to customers on Acurian's behalf. "But that second situation, where I go to look at the website and at that point they have some way of tracking me down, their ability to track me down at that point is troubling," Nahra said.

Nahra said there was a potential legal issue if the company fails to disclose this in its privacy policy, and that it could lead to a class action lawsuit. Acurian's privacy policy only talks about getting information from "data partners" and collecting expected information from website visitors, such as IP addresses—which can be used to track someone from website to website, which is why it's a good idea to use technology that obscures your IP address, such as Tor or a VPN.

The ability to identify who is sick in America is lucrative. Acurian offers a collection of case studies to potential customers in which it discloses what it bills: $4.5 million for recruiting 591 people with diabetes; $11 million for 924 people with opioid-induced constipation; $1.4 million for 173 teens with ADHD; and $6 million for 428 kids with depression.

Acurian claims to have a database of 100 million people with medical conditions that could be of interest to drug companies, and it says that all of those people have "opted-in" to be contacted about trials. In addition to internet complaints suggesting otherwise, the Federal Trade Commission has received more than 1,000 complaints over the last 5 years from consumers who say the company has contacted them without consent; some complainants also wanted to know how the company had found out about their medical conditions.

Acurian has also faced a slew of class-action lawsuits in Florida, Texas, and California from plaintiffs who say the company had illegally robocalled them about clinical trials, placing multiple automated calls to their home without getting their permission first, a violation of federal law. Acurian denied wrongdoing in court filings, saying its calls are not commercial in nature and that the plaintiffs had opted in, but settled all the suits out of court.

Alexandra Franco certainly didn't opt in to be contacted for clinical trials. She doesn't have psoriasis or any prescriptions for a skin condition. When she looked back at her browsing history, it appeared that the only website she visited as part of her search was the mobile version of WebMD.com.

"While Acurian had purchased display advertising from WebMD in 2010, we have never hosted a program for them in which personal information was collected or shared," said WebMD in a statement. "Under our Privacy Policy we do not share personal information that we collect with third parties for their marketing activities without the specific consent of the user. In this case, it appears that the user did not even provide any personal information to WebMD."

"Doing a search on your mobile device means you are incredibly re-identifiable," said Pam Dixon of the World Privacy Forum, referring to the fact that a mobile device provides more unique identifiers than a computer typically does.

Franco doesn't understand exactly how Acurian got her information, but said that the letter was sent to her home addressed to "Alex Franco," a version of her name that she only uses when doing online shopping. When she sent an inquiry to Acurian, the company told her it got her name from Epsilon, a data broker, "based on general demographic search criteria."

"Epsilon specializes in compiling mailing lists based on generally available demographic information like age, gender, proximity to a local clinical site and expressed interests," said the company in an email. "We sincerely regret any distress you may have experienced in thinking your privacy may have been compromised, and we hope this letter has assured you that nothing of the kind has occurred."

Franco didn't feel particularly assured. Epsilon lets consumers make a request to find out what information the data broker has on them; in response to her request, Epsilon told Franco by letter that it has her home address and information about her likely income, age, education level, and length of residence, as well as whether she has kids—none of which would seem to indicate dermatological issues.

At the end of our investigation, we still don't know exactly how Franco was identified as possibly having a skin condition. Given the many players involved and the fact that we can't see into their corporate databases means we can only make reasonable assumptions based on the outcome.

It's the online privacy nightmare come true: a company you've never heard of scraping up your data trails and online bread crumbs in order to mine some of the most sensitive information about you. Acurian may try to justify the intrusion by saying it's in the public interest to develop new drugs to treat illnesses. But tell that to the person shocked to get a letter in the mail about their irritable bowels.

Yes, we found that person. Bret McCabe complained about it on Facebook. He got the letter in 2012 after regularly buying both anti-diarrhea medicine and laxatives at Walgreens and Rite-Aid for a family member dealing with chronic pain issues.

"The creep factor of the specificity is what I found particularly grating," said McCabe by phone. "It's one thing to get spam about erectile dysfunction or refinancing your car loan but in this case, it seemed like they specifically knew something about me. It was meant for me and me only."

The privacy scholar Paul Ohm has warned that one of the great risks of our data-mined society is a massive "database of ruin" that would contain at least one closely-guarded secret for us all, "a secret about a medical condition, family history, or personal preference ... that, if revealed, would cause more than embarrassment or shame; it would lead to serious, concrete, devastating harm."

Acurian has assembled one of those databases. As with all big databases, the information doesn't even have to be accurate. So long as it gets enough of its letters to the right people, the recruitment company doesn't need to care if its collection efforts misidentify Franco as a psoriasis patient or otherwise incorrectly link people, by name, to medical conditions they don't have.

This is the hidden underside of the browsing experience. When you're surfing the web, sitting alone at your computer or with your smartphone clutched in your hand, it feels private and ephemeral. You feel freed to look for the things that you're too embarrassed or ashamed to ask another person. But increasingly, there is digital machinery at work turning your fleeting search whims into hard data trails.

The mining of secrets for profit is done invisibly, shrouded in the mystery of "confidential partnerships," "big data," and "proprietary technology." People in databases don't know that dossiers are being compiled on them, let alone have the chance to correct any mistakes in them.

Chapter 3.3

Excerpt from A Contextual Approach to Privacy Online[*]

Helen Nissenbaum

Abstract: Recent media revelations have demonstrated the extent of third-party tracking and monitoring online, much of it spurred by data aggregation, profiling, and
selective targeting. How to protect privacy online is a frequent question in public
discourse and has reignited the interest of government actors. In the United States,
notice-and-consent remains the fallback approach in online privacy policies, despite
its weaknesses. This essay presents an alternative approach, rooted in the theory of contextual integrity. Proposals to improve and fortify notice-and-consent, such as clearer
privacy policies and fairer information practices, will not overcome a fundamental
flaw in the model, namely, its assumption that individuals can understand all facts
relevant to true choice at the moment of pair-wise contracting between individuals
and data gatherers. Instead, we must articulate a backdrop of context-specific substantive norms that constrain what information websites can collect, with whom they can
share it, and under what conditions it can be shared. In developing this approach, the
paper warns that the current bias in conceiving of the Net as a predominantly commercial enterprise seriously limits the privacy agenda.

The year 2010 was big for online privacy.[1] Reports of privacy gaffes, such as those associated with
Google Buzz and Facebook's fickle privacy policies, graced front pages of prominent news media.
In its series "On What They Know," The Wall Street Journal aimed a spotlight at the rampant
tracking of individuals for behavioral advertising and other reasons.[2] The U.S. government, via
the Federal Trade Commission (ftc)[3] and the Department of Commerce,[4] released two reports in
December 2010 depicting the Net as a place where every step is watched and every click recorded
by data-hungry private and governmental entities, and where every response is coveted by atten-
tion-seekers and influence-peddlers.[5]

---

[*] Helen Nissenbaum, "A Contextual Approach to Privacy Online," *Daedalus* 140, no. 4 (2011): 32–48. Reprinted
with permission. Note: This is an excerpt from the original so footnote and endnote numbering may be
modified.

DOI: 10.1201/9781003278290-18

This article explores present-day concerns about online privacy, but in order to understand and explain on-the-ground activities and the anxieties they stir, it identifies the principles, forces, and values behind them. It considers why privacy online has been vexing, even beyond general concerns over privacy; why predominant approaches have persisted despite their limited results; and why they should be challenged. Finally, the essay lays out an alternative approach to addressing the problem of privacy online based on the theory of privacy as contextual integrity. This approach takes into consideration the formative ideals of the Internet as a public good.[6]

Setting aside economic and institutional factors, challenges to privacy associated with the Net are similar to those raised in the past by other information systems and digital media due to their vast capacities for capturing, stockpiling, retrieving, analyzing, distributing, displaying, and disseminating information. In a flourishing online ecology, where individuals, communities, institutions, and corporations generate content, experiences, interactions, and services, the supreme currency is information, including information about people. As adoption of the Internet and Web has surged and as they have become the primary sources of information and media for transaction, interaction, and communication, particularly among well-off people in technologically advanced societies, we have witnessed radical perturbations in flows of personal information. Amid growing curiosity and concern over these flows, policy-makers, public-interest advocates, and the media have responded with exposés and critiques of pervasive surreptitious tracking, manipulative behavioral advertising, and fickle privacy commitments of major corporate actors.

In *Privacy in Context: Technology, Policy, and the Integrity of Social Life,*[7] I give an account of privacy in terms of expected flows of personal information, modeled with the construct of context-relative informational norms. The key parameters of informational norms are actors (subject, sender, recipient), attributes (types of information), and transmission principles (constraints under which information flows). Generally, when the flow of information adheres to entrenched norms, all is well; violations of these norms, however, often result in protest and complaint. In a health care context, for example, patients expect their physicians to keep personal medical information confidential, yet they accept that it might be shared with specialists as needed. Patients' expectations would be breached and they would likely be shocked and dismayed if they learned that their physicians had sold the information to a marketing company. In this event, we would say that informational norms for the health care context had been violated.

Information technologies and digital media have long been viewed as threatening to privacy because they have radically disrupted flows of personal information, from the corporate and governmental databases of the 1960s to the surveillance cameras and social networks of the present day. The Net, in particular, has mediated disruptions of an unprecedented scale and variety. Those who imagined online actions to be shrouded in secrecy have been disabused of that notion. As difficult as it has been to circumscribe a right to privacy in general, it is even more complex online because of shifting recipients, types of information, and constraints under which information flows. We have come to understand that even when we interact with known, familiar parties, third parties may be lurking on the sidelines, engaged in business partnerships with our known parties. Information about us that once may have languished in dusty file cabinets is now pinpointed in an instant through search queries by anyone anywhere. In these highly informatized (that is, information-rich) environments, new types of information infuse our every action and relationship.

We are puzzled by the new and different types of information generated online, some of it the by-products of our activities, including cookies, latencies, clicks, ip addresses, reified social graphs, and browsing histories. New and different principles govern the flow of information: information we share as a condition of receiving goods and services is sold to others; friends who would not violate confidences repost our photographs on their home pages; people around the world, with whom we share nonreciprocal relationships, can see our houses and cars; providers from whom we purchase Internet service sell access to our communications streams to advertisers. Default constraints on streams of information from us and about us seem to respond not to social, ethical, and political logic but to the logic of technical possibility: that is, whatever the Net allows. If photographs, likes and dislikes, or listings of friends pass through the servers of a Facebook application, there is no telling whether they will be relinquished; if an imperceptible (to the ordinary user, at least) JavaScript code, or "beacon," is placed by a website one visits and enables the capture of one's browser state, so be it; if Flash cookies can cleverly work around the deletion of http cookies, no harm done.

The dominant approach to addressing these concerns and achieving privacy online is a combination of transparency and choice. Often called notice-and-consent, or informed consent, the gist of this approach is to inform website visitors and users of online goods and services of respective information-flow practices and to provide a choice either to engage or disengage. Two substantive considerations explain the appeal of this approach to stakeholders and regulators. One is the popular definition of a right to privacy as a right to control information about oneself. Transparency-and-choice appears to model control because it allows individuals to evaluate options deliberately and then decide freely whether to give or withhold consent. How well it actually models control is not a question I pursue here because whatever the answer, there remains a deeper problem in defining a right to privacy as a right to control information about oneself, as discussed at length in *Privacy in Context*.[8]

A second consideration is the compatibility of notice-and-consent with the paradigm of a competitive free market, which allows sellers and buyers to trade goods at prices the market determines. Ideally, buyers have access to the information necessary to make free and rational purchasing decisions. Because personal information may be conceived as part of the price of online exchange, all is deemed well if buyers are informed of a seller's practices collecting and using personal information and are allowed freely to decide if the price is right. The ideal market assumes free and rational agents who make decisions without interference from third parties, such as government regulators. Doing so not only demonstrates respect for key actors, but also allows the market to function efficiently, producing the greatest overall utility.

However, there is considerable agreement that transparency-and-choice has failed.[9] Privacy advocates, popular media, and individuals have become louder and more insistent in pointing out and protesting rampant practices of surreptitious as well as flagrant data gathering, dissemination, aggregation, analysis, and profiling; even industry incumbents and traditionally pro-business government regulators admit that existing regimes have not done enough to curb undesirable practices, such as the monitoring and tracking associated with behavioral advertising and predatory harvesting of information posted on social networking sites. Why exactly the existing transparency-and-choice, or notice-and-consent, approach has failed – and what to do about it – remains hotly disputed.

For many critics, whom I call critical adherents, the fault lies with the ubiquitous regime of offering privacy to individuals on a "take it or leave it" basis. A range of thoughtful commentaries on the subject, including those in the FTC and Department of Commerce reports mentioned above, have drawn attention to weak instantiations of choice, while others have highlighted problems with notice.[10] Because to choose means to deliberate and decide freely, the near-universal practice of modeling choice as "opt out" can hardly be said to model the ideal consumer making purchasing decisions in the ideal competitive marketplace. A deeper ethical question is whether individuals indeed freely choose to transact – accept an offer, visit a website, make a purchase, participate in a social network – given how these choices are framed as well as what the costs are for choosing not to do so.[11] While it may seem that individuals freely choose to pay the informational price, the price of not engaging socially, commercially, and financially may in fact be exacting enough to call into question how freely these choices are made.

Privacy policies as enactments of notice fare no better. That almost all privacy policies are long, abstruse, and legalistic adds to the unrealistic burden of checking the respective policies of the websites we visit, the services we consider and use, and the content we absorb. Compounding the burden is an entity's right to change its policy at will, giving due notice of such change, ironically, within the policy itself and therefore requiring interested individuals to read it not once but repeatedly. Unsurprisingly, ample evidence reveals that people do not read privacy policies, do not understand them when they do,[12] and realistically could not read them even if they wanted to.[13] This is not merely a matter of weakness of the will.

For critical adherents to transparency-and-choice, these observations point to the need for change, but not revolution. Such critics have suggested correctives including better mechanisms for choice, such as reframing policies in terms of "opt in" rather than "opt out" and locating moments of choice at times when users might be able to pause and think. They also advocate increasing transparency: for example, stipulating shorter policies that are easier to follow, along the lines of nutritional labels. Suggestions also apply to the content of policies. Whereas in the past, online actors were entreated simply to have policies, current correctives would require adherence to fair information principles.[14] The details of these suggestions are beyond the scope of this essay, as are questions about how privacy policies and practices should be monitored and enforced. This is because (as I argue below) the consent model for respecting privacy online is plagued by deeper problems than the practical ones noted so far.

I am not convinced that notice-and-consent, however refined, will result in better privacy online as long as it remains a procedural mechanism divorced from the particularities of relevant online activity. Take the example of online behavioral advertising, which quickly reveals an inherent flaw with the notice-and-consent approach.[15] To begin, consider what might need to be conveyed to users to provide notice of what information is captured, where it is sent, and how it is used. The technical and institutional story is so complicated that probably only a handful of deep experts would be able to piece together a full account; I would hazard that most of the website owners who contract with ad networks providing targeted advertising services are not among such experts. Even if, for a given moment, a snapshot of the information flows could be grasped, the realm is in constant flux, with new firms entering the picture, new analytics, and new back-end contracts forged: in other words, we are dealing with a recursive capacity that is indefinitely extensible.[16] As a result of this complex and shifting landscape, users have been prone to conflate (in a convenient but misleading way) tracking with targeting. Further, the complexity makes it not only difficult to convey what practices are followed and what constraints respected, but practically impossible.[17]

For critical adherents to notice-and-consent, these types of cases exemplify the need for brief and clear policies that capture the essence of privacy practices in ways ordinary people can grasp. I view this as a futile effort because of what I call the transparency paradox. Achieving transparency means conveying information handling practices in ways that are relevant and meaningful to the choices individuals must make. If notice (in the form of a privacy policy) finely details every flow, condition, qualification, and exception, we know that it is unlikely to be understood, let alone read. But summarizing practices in the style of, say, nutrition labels is no more helpful because it drains away important details, ones that are likely to make a difference: who are the business associates and what information is being shared with them; what are their commitments; what steps are taken to anonymize information; how will that information be processed and used. An abbreviated, plain-language policy would be quick and easy to read, but it is the hidden details that carry the significance.[18] Thus the transparency paradox: transparency of textual meaning and transparency of practice conflict in all but rare instances.[19] We seem unable to achieve one without giving up on the other, yet both are essential for notice-and-consent to work.

Adherents may persist, pointing to other arenas, such as health care and human subject research, in which a similar transparency paradox appears to have been overcome. In health care, informed consent protocols are commonly accepted for conveying risks and benefits to patients undergoing surgery, for example, or to subjects entering experimental treatment programs, even though it is unlikely they fully grasp the details. In my view, these protocols work not because they have found the right formulation of notice and the authentic mechanism for consent but because they exist within a framework of supporting assurances. Most of us are terrible at assessing probabilities and understanding risks of side effects and failed procedures; we are extremely poor at visualizing the internal organs of our bodies. It is not the consent form itself that draws our signature and consigns us to the operating table, but rather our faith in the system.[20] We trust the long years of study and apprenticeship that physicians undergo, the state and board certifications, peer oversight, professional codes, and above all, the system's interest (whatever the source) in our well-being. We believe in the benevolence of institutions of higher learning and, in large part, their mission to promote human welfare. Far from perfect, and subject to high-visibility breaches, the systems that constitute these safety nets have evolved over centuries; they undergird and warrant the consent agreements that patients and subjects confront every day. In the online environment, by contrast, individual consent agreements must carry the entire weight of expectation.

Picking holes in the transparency-and-choice (informed consent) approach, problematic as it is, is not the end point of my argument. As it is, it may be the best approach for this interim period while the supporting assurances to shore it up are developed. Such assurances are not achieved by fiat, but may require decades for relevant institutional forms and practices to progress from trial and error to a balanced settling point. The theory of contextual integrity offers a shorter and more systematic path to this point by invoking learned wisdom from mature systems of informational norms that have evolved to accommodate diverse legitimate interests as well as general moral and political principles and context-specific purposes and values. The promise of this path is not merely that the equilibriums achieved in familiar contexts may provide analogical guidance for online realms; rather, the path acknowledges how online realms are inextricably linked with existing structures of social life. Online activity is deeply integrated into social life in general and is radically heterogeneous in ways that reflect the heterogeneity of offline experience.

[...]

Answering questions about privacy online, like those about privacy in general, requires us to prescribe suitable, or appropriate, constraints on the flow of personal information. The challenge of privacy online is not that the venue is distinct and different, or that privacy requirements are distinct and different, but that mediation by the Net leads to disruptions in the capture, analysis, and dissemination of information as we act, interact, and transact online. The decision heuristic derived from the theory of contextual integrity suggests that we locate contexts, explicate entrenched informational norms, identify disruptive flows, and evaluate these flows against norms based on general ethical and political principles as well as context specific purposes and values.

To be sure, locating contexts online and explicating the presiding norms is not always straightforward (in the same way that it is not when dealing with unmediated social spaces). Some of the more familiar cases, however, may provide insight into the task. Whether you transact with your bank online, on the phone, or person-to-person in a branch office, it is not unreasonable to expect that rules governing information will not vary according to medium. In the United States, banks and other financial institutions are governed by privacy rules formulated by the FTC, which was given this authority by the Gramm–Leach–Bliley Act.[21] Auxiliary information (for example IP address or clickstream), the artifacts of online transaction, should not simply be deemed "up for grabs" just because that information was not explicitly considered in rules formulated before online banking became common. Instead, it should be held to the same standards that guided financial privacy in the first place.

[…]

To the extent that the Net is deeply embedded in social life, context-specific informational norms may be extended to corresponding online activities. Thus, privacy rules governing financial institutions, for example, would extend to E*TRADE even though it operates primarily via an online portal. Online offerings and experiences may defy existing norms, however, as they incorporate some of the novel forms mentioned above. In such circumstances, the theory of contextual integrity directs us beyond existing norms to underlying standards, derived from general moral and political considerations as well as the ends, purposes, and values of respective contexts.[22] Novel activities and practices, which implicate different types of information, expanded groups of recipients, and altered constraints on flow are evaluated against these standards.

[…]

Without denying that the Net has yielded much that is novel and strange, including new types of information and new institutional forms, online activities themselves are strangely familiar: connecting with a friend, collaborating on a political mission, applying for a job, seeking religious or spiritual sustenance, pursuing educational opportunity, catching up on local and world news, or choosing a book to read, music to enjoy, or movies to watch. Although searching on Google is different from looking up material in a library catalog, in part because the contents of the Web are quite different from the contents of a library, there is similarity in these two activities: both may include the pursuit of research, knowledge, and intellectual enrichment. In all such activities, liberal democratic societies allow great freedom, unconstrained by the watchful gaze or approbation of authorities, just as they allow citizens to seek political or religious information or affiliation. Just as with the offline environment, we would expect the same standards to prevail online, dictating that online footprints should not be recorded and registered in order to minimize risk of interference, by either human or machine.

Notes

1. This essay has benefited from opportunities to present at the Center for Law, Technology, and Society, University of Ottawa; the Center for the Study of Law and Society, University of California, Berkeley; and the Center for Internet and Society, Stanford University, where questions and comments led to significant improvements and refinements of the argument. I am grateful for the valuable feedback from David Clark and NYU's Privacy Research Group, expert guidance from Cathy Dwyer and Foster Provost, and sterling research assistance from Jacob Gaboury and Marianna Tishchenko. This work was supported by grants AFSOR: ONR BAA 07-03 (muri) and NSF CT-M: Privacy, Compliance & Information Risk, CNS-0831124.

2. Jennifer Valentino-Devries, "What They Know About You," *The Wall Street Journal*, July 31, 2010, http://online.wsj.com/article/SB10001424052748703999304575399041849931612.html.

3. US Federal Trade Commission, Preliminary FTC Staff Report, "Protecting Consumer Privacy in an Era of Rapid Change: A Proposed Framework for Businesses and Policymakers," December 2010, http://www.ftc.gov/os/2010/12/101201privacyreport.pdf

4. US Department of Commerce, "Commercial Data Privacy and Innovation in the Internet Economy: A Dynamic Policy Framework," December 2010, http://www.ntia.doc.gov/ reports/2010/IPTF_Privacy_GreenPaper_12162010.pdf

5. Compare these depictions to earlier accounts of the Net as a new frontier of freedom and autonomy: for example, David R. Johnson and David G. Post, "Law and Borders–The Rise of Law in Cyberspace," *Stanford Law Review* 48 (1996): 1367; John Perry Barlow, "Electronic Frontier: Coming into the Country," *Communications of the ACM* 34 (3) (March 1991).

6. In this essay, I draw most of my examples from the World Wide Web because almost all the controversial privacy concerns that have captured public attention have stemmed from Web-based activity and because the online experiences of ordinary people occur mostly on the Web. I will use the term Net when observations made about the Web seem pertinent to other Internet applications and services.

7. Helen Nissenbaum, *Privacy in Context: Technology, Policy, and the Integrity of Social Life* (Stanford, Calif.: Stanford University Press, 2010).

8. Ibid., chap. 5.

9. Federal Trade Commission, "Protecting Consumer Privacy in an Era of Rapid Change" and Department of Commerce, "Commercial Data Privacy and Innovation in the Internet Economy."

10. Fred Cate, "The Failure of Fair Information Practice Principles," in *Consumer Protection in the Age of the "Information Economy,"* ed. Jane K. Winn (London: Ashgate Publishing, 2006).

11. Ian Kerr, "The Legal Relationship Between Online Service Providers and Users," *Canadian Business Law Journal* 35 (2001): 1–40.

12. Joseph Turow, Lauren Feldman, and Kimberly Meltzer, Open to Exploitation: American Shoppers Online and Offline (Philadelphia: Annenberg Public Policy Center, University of Pennsylvania, June 1, 2005), http://www.annenbergpublicpolicycenter.org/Downloads/Information_And _Society/ Turow_APPC_Report_WEB_FINAL.pdf

13. Lorrie Faith Cranor and Joel Reidenberg, "Can User Agents Accurately Represent Privacy Notices?" The 30th Research Conference on Communication, Information, and Internet Policy (tprc2002), Alexandria, Virginia, September 28–30, 2002.

14. US Department of Health, Education, and Welfare, Records, Computers, and the Rights of Citizens, Report of the Secretary's Advisory Committee on Automated Personal Data Systems, July 1973, http://aspe.hhs.gov/datacncl/1973privacy/tocprefacemembers.htm

15. Solon Barocas and Helen Nissenbaum, "On Notice: The Trouble with Notice and Consent," Proceedings of the Engaging Data Forum: The First International Forum on the Application and Management of Personal Electronic Information, Cambridge, Massachusetts, October 12– 13, 2009; Vincent Toubiana, Arvind Narayanan, Dan Boneh, Helen Nissenbaum, and Solon Barocas, "Adnostic: Privacy-Preserving Targeted Advertising," Proceedings of the Network and Distributed System Symposium, San Diego, California, February 28–March 3, 2010.

16. Counting ad servers alone, a list current as of April 2011 shows 2,766 unique entries; see http://pgl .yoyo.org/adservers/formats.php (accessed April 13, 2011).

17. Barocas and Nissenbaum, "On Notice," and Toubiana, Narayanan, Boneh, Nissenbaum, and Barocas, "Adnostic."

18. Vincent Toubiana and Helen Nissenbaum, "An Analysis of Google Log Retention Policies," *The Journal of Privacy and Confidentiality*, (forthcoming).

19. For example, personal information is shared with no one and destroyed after each session.

20. Deborah Franklin, "Uninformed Consent," *Scientific American*, March 2011, 24–25.

21. US Federal Trade Commission, Gramm-Leach-Bliley Act 15 U.S.C., Subchapter I, sec. 6801– 6809, November 12, 1999, http://www.ftc.gov/privacy/glbact/glbsub1.htm; Adam Barth, Anupam Datta, John Mitchell, and Helen Nissenbaum, "Privacy and Contextual Integrity: Framework and Applications," Proceedings of the IEEE Symposium on Security and Privacy, Berkeley, California, May 21–24, 2006.

22. Nissenbaum, *Privacy in Context*, esp. chap. 8.

Chapter 3.4

Excerpt from Understanding Privacy Online: Development of a Social Contract Approach to Privacy*

Kirsten Martin

Consider three illustrative privacy issues online:

1. Through 'Sponsored Stories,' Facebook users who clicked on 'like' buttons had pictures of themselves with an endorsement sent to their friends in a what looked like sponsored advertising (Kravets 2012).
2. The travel site Orbitz tracks how users arrived at their site in order to prioritize search results: if a user arrived at Orbitz from a competitor's site, Orbitz may prioritize results based on price (Mattioli 2012). Similarly, Facebook mines users' browser history in order to target advertising.
3. Verizon offers a service—Precision Market Insights—to business customers to mine Verizon's customer call and web browsing information in order to map where people are located and the types of services they purchase and use (Hill 2012). In an aptly titled article, "Verizon Very Excited That It Can Track Everything Phone Users Do And Sell That To Whomever Is Interested," Kashmir Hill outlines the service Verizon offers to businesses to track their potential customers: "we [Verizon] understand what our customers' daily activity stream is …," and Verizon sells that activity stream to their commercial customers.

In each case, individuals willingly divulged information—clicked like, visited a travel site, watched a basketball game in a stadium—yet held different privacy expectations within the

* Kirsten Martin, "Understanding Privacy Online: Development of a Social Contract Approach to Privacy," *Journal of Business Ethics* 137, no. 3 (2016): 551–69, https://doi.org/10.1007/s10551-015-2565-9. Reprinted with permission. Note: This is an excerpt from the original so footnote and endnote numbering may be modified.

DOI: 10.1201/9781003278290-19

different contexts. For example, location information is expected to be used and tracked from a travel website (Martin and Shilton 2015); yet it is a surprise when information is used to track movement to and from a basketball game. Individuals share preferences with some friends—but not all. Users' different norms and expectations across contexts has been a source of frustration to firms and academics alike.

To explain variances in privacy expectations, previous work relies on a static, universal definition of privacy expectations and measures differences in individuals' concerns, attitudes, or valuations of privacy as illustrated in Table 1. In privacy scholarship, the access-view of privacy suggests that individuals have a reasonable expectation of privacy so long as they and their information are inaccessible or hidden (Warren and Brandeis 1890; Elgesem 1999; Persson and Hansson 2003; Schoeman 1984; Posner 1981).

Online, the access-view would categorize the act of sharing information as necessarily giving up any expectation of privacy. When individuals use a phone, watch a basketball game, or click 'like,' individuals are seen as not having privacy expectations because all of the information was accessible. The question then becomes, "why did the users divulge the information at all?"

Alternatively, the control view of privacy (Westin 1967; Alder et al. 2007; Margulis 1977; Altman 1975; Moor 1997) suggests that relinquishing control of information to another party renders the individual without any reasonable expectation of privacy. Online, the control view of privacy is regulated through adequate notice and choice in Fair Information Practices (FIPs; Bennett 1992; Ashworth and Free 2006; Peslak 2005; Culnan and Armstrong 1999; Bowie and Jamal 2006). FIPs allow for the contemporaneous disclosure of information and respect of privacy norms while online.[1] Although popular, notice and choice statements may be immaterial—or nonfactors—to assessments about the appropriateness and inappropriateness of the information transmitted within a particular context. In fact, each of the three examples was argued to comply with the written privacy notices, and users agreed to the notice upon engaging with the service; yet, all three examples caused privacy advocates to bring lawsuits or provided the impetus for articles exposing the firms' behavior. In other words, individuals, employees, users, and consumers make judgments about privacy expectations and violations regardless of the notice and choice policy in many situations.

Recent work on privacy suggests that privacy norms can be viewed as mutually beneficial and sustainable agreements within a community (Martin 2012) or as context-dependent norms (Nissenbaum 2004, 2009). These social contracts are the unstated agreements that individuals and groups make in contexts, communities, and relationships. Studies also substantiate the theory: 71 % of respondents would disclose within an established relationship (Louis Harris and Associates and Westin 1997; Culnan and Bies 2003), and individuals within a particular community, such as teams or young adults, develop substantive privacy norms not easily recognized or understood by outsiders (Martin 2012; Turow et al. 2009). In other words, individuals give access to information within a particular context with an understanding of the privacy rules that govern that context.

[...]

This paper further develops a social contract approach to generating, acknowledging, and protecting privacy norms within specific contexts (Martin 2012). The goal of this paper is to examine how information norms develop through a social contract narrative, to reframe possible privacy violations of business given the social contract approach to privacy, and to critically examine the role of business as a contractor in developing privacy norms. The social contract approach "need not—and seldom does—eliminate all questions from a moral quandary. But it can provide logical vantage points from which to view an ethical quandary and, in turn, point towards a solution" (Donaldson and Dunfee 2003, p. 115).

[...]

Social Contract Narrative for Privacy

An important next step in exploring a social contract approach to privacy is the social contract narrative. The narrative can justify the moral rightness of a principle, explain the social and institutional fabric of a society (e.g., Nozick 1974), or explain the emergence, persistence, or stability of an extant social contract (Heugens et al. 2006). Here, a midlevel social contract narrative is used to explain and analyze the dynamic process of privacy norm generation within particular communities.[2] Table 2 illustrates the social contract narrative applied here.

The first step in walking through a social contract narrative is to specify an initial position. This position is a priori any agreement between parties and provides the setting for reasonable contracting where individuals are assumed to have (1) an initial state, and (2) behavioral tendencies. This first step provides the setting to create an agreement and asks not only what privacy norms would contractors agree to but also what do contractors take into consideration? For firms and business ethicists, the output of this narrative will provide key facets of the microsocial contracts about privacy and the factors that contractors—such as users, consumers, and employees—take into considerations in developing privacy norms.

Initial Position

For an initial state, one would need to imagine a world where individuals have no communication or interaction with others and are in a state where information can easily remain inaccessible. Individuals in this initial state would live and work by themselves and maintain their living environment independently. Privacy, in such a world, only requires that individuals keep a solitary existence and not give access to their information to anyone. In this position, the individual is able to maintain privacy by remaining alone and hidden. This initial state would constitute a scattering of recluses.

In fact, this initial state remains a theme throughout privacy scholarship in that individuals continue to have an interest in being inaccessible to others by remaining isolated both physically and psychologically. The right to be left alone (Warren and Brandeis 1890) preserves liberty and autonomy as individuals are free to "develop personalities, goals, ideas, and the right to determine to whom their thoughts, emotions, sentiments, and tangible products are communicated" (Bloustein 1964, p. 18). Such a state of solitary inaccessibility corresponds to defining privacy as the ability to restrict access to personal information (e.g., Allen 1988) or as protection from information gathering (Tavani and Moor 2001). Privacy as restricted access prevents people from knowing certain things and implies entering the public sphere to require giving up a measure of privacy (Alfino and Mayes 2006). According to the restricted access view of privacy in this original state, individuals either share information and make it public or do not share information and keep it private.

Behavioral Tendencies

Such a state of inaccessibility is not sustainable as we may minimally assume individuals have a behavioral tendency to form relationships and coordinate activities (Dennett 1995; De Waal and De Waal 1997). In other words, we do not have the behavioral tendencies to live as a scattering of recluses. These tendencies are so strong and integral to being human that a state of perfect inaccessibility—or a completely solitary existence where a person and their information is kept inaccessible from others—is considered an extreme form of punishment today: solitary confinement

(Tufekci 2008a, b). Defining privacy as a state of inaccessibility is neither practical nor desirable and, ironically, renders privacy as a form of punishment.

As individuals naturally come together to form relationships, they share information. Human beings enjoy the freedom to converse and trade information about one another and have an interest in collecting information as well as sharing information. Throughout privacy scholarship, a need to share information for intimacy (Elgesem 1996, p. 51), in order to have relationships (Fried 1968), and to converse and trade information (Singleton 1998) pervades justifications for privacy norms. Because the original state of inaccessibility is inefficient for economic and social actors (Posner 1981), information sharing becomes necessary for relationships.[3]

Furthermore, discriminately sharing information affords people the important power to determine both how close they are to others and the nature of their relationships. Information sharing is not only necessary to form relationships and trade, but discriminately sharing allows individuals to differentiate between relationships. Maintaining more than one relationship becomes more complicated as individuals interact with different types of people from different contexts or communities. Individuals share different types and amounts of information in order to negotiate the boundary conditions of relationships (Samarajiva 1997). "The sort of relationship that people have to one another involves ... a conception of the kind and degree of knowledge concerning one another which it is appropriate for them to have" (Rachels 1975, p. 294). Different relationships require different information-sharing rules, and controlling who has access to personal information is necessary for friendship, intimacy, and trust (Fried 1968) and preserves important human relationships (Nissenbaum 2004). As noted by technology scholar James Moor, "different people may be given different levels of access for different kinds of information at different times" (1997, p. 414).

Outcome: Framework for Privacy as a Social Contract

The social contract narrative illustrates the natural evolution of social contract norms around privacy. Based on this narrative, individuals within a given community discriminately share information with a particular set of obligations in mind as to who has access to the information and how it will be used (Nissenbaum 2004, 2009; Martin 2012; Sloan and Warner 2014). Based on the social contract narrative, a framework for microsocial contract privacy norms centers on (1) the type of information, (2) who has access to information, and (3) how the information is used within a given community as explored below.

First, an ideal sphere lies around every individual where trespasses can be seen as an insult to one's honor (Simmel 1906, p. 321). Protecting that space can help create a background for a self-creative enterprise (Bennett 1992). Privacy law scholar Julie Cohen refers to this inviolate space as the privacy of the home that affords "freedom of movement that is both literal and metaphorical" (Cohen 2008, p. 195). This tension between the need to maintain the ideal sphere around ourselves and the need to disclose information for relationships and communities is sustained through negotiated norms around the type of information. Users on a site, such as Facebook or diaspora,* have an expectation about the type of information collected—such as GPS or browsing history or demographics.

Importantly, people retain the desire to limit who has access to information. In other words, information known to one person does not necessarily mean the information is meant for all people. Sharing is not all or nothing but 'optimal' depending on maturity and scope of relationship and the role of the individual (Brin 1999). Determining who receives which piece of information keeps people from being "misrepresented and judged out of context" (Rosen 2001, p. 21).

Trying out different jokes, behaviors, or personas with friends helps people to develop as individuals; but those same jokes, behaviors, or personas could be damaging with a different population. Individuals are constantly deciding how to present themselves at varying personal and social levels through agreements about confidentiality (Stutzman and Hartzog 2012), while retaining a desire for seclusion and a fear of intrusion (Bambauer 2012). Online individuals need to discriminately share information within a relationship without fear of these behaviors or information being broadcast broadly—or sold to data aggregators or retained for years. In casual language, individuals talk about expectations of confidentiality to signify the rules about which actors can know particular information.

Finally, when individuals do reveal information to an actor, rules and obligations govern not only who else should receive the information but also how the information is used (Hartzog 2011). These social contracts around what, to whom, and for what purpose information flows are the governing rules about privacy for a given community. The purpose(s) of the community within which the information is shared dictates the valid uses of the information gathered or disclosed. Tracking GPS location data by an application is valid when the application is for directions or tracking your cycling route, but not valid when the application is to simulate a flashlight. When people attempt to assign property rights to control information, they attempt to control how information is later used.

These facets of privacy norms—the what, who, and how—can be seen as working in concert within a given relationship. Within a community or context, for every given set of data, there exists a rule about who should be privy to that information and the purpose for that information. Similarly, for every given set of individuals, there exists a set of information that is expected to be shared and why. Key to these agreements is how the main components work together (see Nissenbaum 2009). Within privacy as a social contract, "who, what, and how" would identify a particular micro privacy norm in a community.

From an original and unsustainable state of inaccessibility, individuals have a need to discriminately share information in order to socialize, create relationships, form groups, and trade. Individuals have a desire—and a reasonable expectation—to be able to live within communities while maintaining a sense of self. Just as communities acknowledge freedom of movement simultaneous to a protection from assault, individuals and society have an interest of interacting in a community through sharing information while preserving space to develop themselves, their relationships, and their communities.

(Re)conceptualizing Privacy Online

The social contract approach used here is a multilevel, contextually rich framework allowing for specific contractors within a contracting community the moral free space to develop authentic and legitimate privacy norms and expectations. And the social contract narrative is an important step to understand the factors individuals take into consideration when negotiating privacy microsocial contract norms. Alternative approaches to privacy have been attractive because respecting and violating privacy are clearly defined and easy to measure—privacy is violated when information is either not controlled or no longer inaccessible. Privacy as a social contract offers a more nuanced, context-dependent understanding of privacy while not venturing into the territory of relativism. To explain, common privacy violations are redescribed below given the social contract approach to privacy and outlined in Tables 3 and 4 (Figure 3.4.1).

Reframing Privacy Violations

Violation #1: Procedural Hypernorms

First, hypernorms can be violated by not adequately addressing the procedural and structural requirements for a legitimate social contract. Microsocial contracts rely upon procedural norms of adequate voice, exit, and informed consent (Dunfee 2006), and the current focus online on adequate notice and choice seeks to uphold minimal precepts of social contract's procedural norms of exit, consent, and voice. Online privacy notices, authentic consent, and an ability to switch websites would address the procedural hypernorms required in the macrosocial contract.

For example, researchers continually find violations to procedural hypernorms online. Notices are unrealistically time consuming (McDonald and Cranor 2008) and not always targeted toward consumers (Cranor et al. 2014). Empirical studies have shown that notices are difficult if not impossible to find by users (Leon et al. 2012) and include misleading information (Leon et al. 2010). Respondents do not understand notices to the point where they are misled by icons and notices (Ur et al. 2012). And respondents have been found to assume their privacy expectations are included in the notice (Martin 2014) or that the advertising icon does more to protect their privacy than in actuality (Leon et al. 2012).

Privacy as a social contract would suggest that focusing on informed consent and the contractors' right of exit and voice are important, but not the only tactics to respect privacy expectations. The procedural norms of consent, exit, and voice are required for the micro-privacy social contracts to be legitimate and to bind the members of the community.[4] However, much of the proverbial "heavy lifting" around privacy expectations is done within the community in identifying and negotiating context-specific privacy norms around who, what, and why information is shared.

Violation #2: Microsocial Contracts

In addition, a violation of privacy would also include when information is tracked, disseminated, or used against the agreement of the actors within the community through a breach of microsocial contracts. Given the framework of micro privacy norms above, privacy violations occur when the recipient of information—an organization, a user, or the primary website—changes who is included in receiving information, what information is shared, and how the information is used.

Change What Information Is Shared. Individuals retain a desire to keep certain information inaccessible even within defined relationships, yet new pieces of information become available with advances in technology. In regards to online surveillance, GPS data is now available from mobile devices and tracked in addition to a user's IP address or a unique user identifier. A study of 101 popular applications found that 47 transmitted phone location and 56 transmitted a unique phone identifier to a third-party data aggregator (Thurm and Kane 2010). In addition, websites can identify and capture how individuals travel to a website, where they click on a page, and where they travel after the visit in addition to purchases and searches while on the site. For example, Facebook began collecting and using user browsing history—users' online activities outside the context of Facebook—in order to target advertising (Albergotti 2014a). A recent study found that 31 % of applications gather information outside their purpose and without a valid use ("Backgrounder" 2014). Collecting new information within an existing relationship may constitute a privacy violation.

Change Who Receives the Information. Individuals regularly give access to information to some people or some organizations while keeping the same information from others. For example,

Facebook's Beacon program took information about an individual's browsing and buying habits with an online retailer, such as Amazon.com, and sent alerts automatically to a new group of individuals—the Facebook user's friends. The information disclosed to Amazon.com (and others) was leaked to Facebook friends, thereby changing the actors who received the information. When a fitness application, Moves (https://www.moves-app.com), was acquired by Facebook, a new actor (Facebook) suddenly had access to the app's user information—much to their surprise (Wagner 2014). Similarly, tagging photographs online allows new individuals to know about offline activities: by posting a picture and linking it to a subject's name, offline activities are suddenly available to individuals not present at the event. Users do not relinquish information to an undefined group of actors. Rather, individuals knowingly disclose information to a particular set of actors within a community.

Change How the Information Is Used. Individuals have an interest in how their information is used within a community, and a line of scholarship has evolved to equate privacy with the degree of control over personal information. While problems abound with conceptualizing privacy as solely an intellectual property issue (Bambauer 2012), the underlying premise that individuals have an interest in how their information is used is sound and remains a strong focus in privacy framed as a property right and the FIPs prevalent in business.

For example, information given to a medical professional is to be used for medical diagnosis or for furthering the medical field through research. If the medical professional were to sell that information to a pharmaceutical company for marketing purposes or use that information to sell the patient a car, the professional would breach the terms of use within the social contract. Online, a user's travel history may be known to a website such as Orbitz and can be used to analyze how individuals came to find Orbitz for future Orbitz marketing or advertisements.

However, using an individual's online history to change query results uses the known information in a novel way. Research has shown users have privacy expectations around both the type of information access as well as how the information is used using mobile apps (Shilton and Martin 2013) and online (Martin 2014). Further, when respondents are shown the information that was collected and aggregated about them online, respondents care about the scope of use of even innocuous information online (Cranor et al. 2014).

An infamous example of the misuse of legitimately acquired information is the use of Facebook users' data and the users themselves in an experiment (Albergotti 2014b; Meyer 2014). Facebook manipulated the newsfeeds of 700,000 users to be more positive or negative and then measured the effect on users' subsequent postings. The postings were in the hands of a valid actor (Facebook and the recipients of the post), but Facebook used the information in a novel way thereby violating the microsocial contract in the Facebook community around the expected use of information.

Violation #3: Community or Contextual Integrity (Nissenbaum 2009)

Social contract theory suggests a third level of privacy violations in protecting the integrity of the boundaries of the contracting community and their moral free space. In other words, viewing privacy norms as a social contract highlights the moral importance in protecting the boundaries of the context in Nissenbaum's Privacy as Contextual Integrity (2004, 2009) or moral free space of the communities. Within social contract theory, society has an obligation to not develop and impose substantive norms on the moral free space of the contractors. If outsiders to a contracting community make substantive demands on the content and flow of information, such outsiders would be breaching the integrity of that moral free space. In fact, such a privacy intrusion or violation is also referred to as a violation of decisional privacy (Allen 1999) or passive privacy (Floridi 2006) where the interference in autonomy is considered a privacy violation. Broad regulations

Tenet of social contracts	Commonly seen as: privacy as...	Violations	As addressed in market
Procedural contract norms			
Voice	FIP—notice and choice	Website does not notify users of third-party tracking	Better designed notices such as P3P (Cranor 2012) that allows for consumer-friendly interface based on machine-language notice
Informed consent			
Exit		Initially, Facebook users had difficulty deleting their accounts thereby removing the option to 'exit'	
Microcontract norms			
Change who receives the information	Confidentiality	Facebook's Beacon program captured information about individual's browsing and buying habits with an online retailer, e.g., Amazon.com, and sent alerts automatically to a new group of individuals—the Facebook user's friends	TOR is free anonymizing software to securely route traffic
			Diaspora* social network does not sell access to third parties
		For example, when a fitness application, Moves (https://www.moves-app.com), was acquired by Facebook, a new actor (Facebook) suddenly had access to the app's user information—much to their surprise (Wagner 2014)	Encryption in user communication in WhatsApp (Greenberg 2014)
Change what information is shared	Secrecy	GPS data is now regularly available from mobile devices and tracked in addition to IP addresses and a unique user identifier	Diaspora* social network allows users to remain anonymous
		For example, Facebook began collecting and using user browsing history—online activities outside the context of Facebook—in order to target advertising (Albergotti 2014a). And, a recent study found that 31 % of applications gather information outside their purpose and without a valid use ("Backgrounder" 2014)	Whisper application does not track users (Dwoskin 2014)
Change how information is used	Control/property	A user's online activity may be passed to a website such as Orbitz and used to prioritize search results	Diaspora* social network allows users to retain rights over their data
		For example, Facebook manipulated the newsfeeds of 700,000 to render the feed more positive or negative and to measure the effect on users' postings of those manipulations	
Integrity of community (e.g., moral free space Donaldson and Dunfee 1994)			
Interference with the norms within a community by outsiders	Decisional privacy	Legislative, substantive norms imposed from outside the community. For example, Do Not Track at the browser level	Snapchat's approach to native advertising to not interfere with users' conversations (Shields 2014)
		Regulation of substantive social contracts within communities	

Figure 3.4.1 Table of reframing privacy violations as violations of the social contract around information flows.

aimed at too high a level may impose a standardized set of privacy norms across communities. For example, the browser-level Do Not Track designation may not apply to particular contexts and would interfere with the ability to develop microsocial contracts within particular communities.

Notes

1. See Federal Trade Commission (2012a, b) "Protecting Consumer Privacy in an Era of Rapid Change: Recommendations for Business and Policymakers," Federal Trade Commission's Fair Information Practice Principles, and the White House's Consumer Data Privacy in a Networked World (February 2012).
2. From an initial position, the narrative results in an agreement that includes only those social constraints to human action that have normative appeal—agreements that "reasonable agents could, and arguably would, agree to if they had the choice" (Heugens et al. 2003, p. 11). The narrative illustrates the internal morality of contracting by walking through a precontractual state and demonstrating how cooperation works (Van Oosterhout et al. 2006).
3. Sociologist Gerstein notes that individuals take on two roles in any relationship—observer and participant—and mere observation is not sufficient to form intimate relationships. Instead, individuals must participate by sharing information in order to form relationships.

4. I wish to thank Gaston de los Reyes for making this important point on the role of the procedural hypernorms of exit, voice, and consent.

References

Albergotti, R. (2014a, June 12). Facebook to target ads based on web browsing. *Wall Street Journal*. http://online.wsj.com/articles/facebook-to-give-advertisers-data-about-users-web-browsing-1402561120.

Albergotti, R. (2014b, July 2). Facebook experiments had few limits. *Wall Street Journal*. http://online.wsj.com/articles/facebook-experiments-had-few-limits-1404344378.

Alder, S. G., Schminke, M., & Noel, T. W. (2007). The impact of individual ethics on reactions to potentially invasive HR practices. *Journal of Business Ethics*, 75(2), 201–214.

Alfino, M., & Mayes, R. (2006). *Limits of some formal approaches to risk: Directions for future research*. Delft: Delft University of Technology.

Altman, I. (1975). *The environment and social behavior*. Monterey, CA: Brooks/Cole Publishing Company.

Ashworth, L., & Free, C. (2006). Marketing dataveillance and digital privacy: Using theories of justice to understand consumers' online privacy concerns. *Journal of Business Ethics*, 67(2), 107–123.

Bambauer, J. (2012). The new intrusion. *Notre Dame Law Review*, 88, 205.

Bennett, C. (1992). *Regulating privacy*. Ithaca, NY: Cornell University Press.

Bloustein, E. J. (1964). Privacy as an aspect of human dignity: An answer to Dean Prosser. New York University Law Review, 39, 962.

Bowie, N. E., & Jamal, K. (2006). Privacy rights on the internet: Self- regulation or government regulation? *Business Ethics Quarterly*, 16(3), 323–342.

Brin, D. (1999). *The transparent society: Will technology force us to choose between privacy and freedom?*. New York: Basic Books.

Cohen, J. E. (2008). Privacy, visibility, transparency, and exposure. *University of Chicago Law Review*, 75(1), 181–201.

Cranor, L. F., Hoke, C., Leon, P. G., & Au, A. (2014). Are they worth reading? An in-depth analysis of online advertising companies' privacy policies. *2014 TPRC*

Culnan, M. J., & Armstrong, P. K. (1999). Information privacy concerns, procedural fairness, and impersonal trust: An empirical investigation. *Organization Science*, 10(1), 104–115.

Elgesem, D. (1999). The structure of rights in Directive 95/46/EC on the protection of individuals with regard to the processing of personal data and the free movement of such data. *Ethics and Information Technology*, 1(4), 283–293.

Hartzog, W. (2011). Chain-Link Confidentiality. *Georgia Law Review*, 46, 657.

Heugens, P., van Oosterhout, H., & Vromen, J. J. (Eds.). (2003). *The social institutions of capitalism: evolution and design of social contracts*. Northhampton: Edward Elgar Publishing.

Hill, K. (2012, October 27). Verizon very excited that it can track everything phone users do and sell that to whoever is interested. *Forbes*. http://www.forbes.com/sites/kashmirhill/2012/10/17/ver izon-very-excited-that-it-can-track-everything-phone-users-do- and-sell-that-to-whoever-is-interested/.

Kravets, D. (2012, August 18). Judge rejects Facebook 'Sponsored Stories' lawsuit settlement. *Wired*. http://www.wired.com/threatlevel/2012/08/facebook-settlement-rejected/.

Leon, P. G., Cranor, L. F., McDonald, A. M., & McGuire, R. (2010). Token attempt: The misrepresentation of website privacy policies through the misuse of P3P compact policy tokens. In Presented at the Proceedings of the 9th annual ACM workshop on Privacy in the electronic society (pp. 93–104). ACM.

Leon, P. G., Cranshaw, J., Cranor, L. F., Graves, J., Hastak, M., Ur, B., et al. (2012). What do online behavioral advertising privacy disclosures communicate to users? In Presented at the Proceedings of the SIGCHI conference on human factors in computing systems (pp. 589–598). ACM.

Margulis, S. T. (1977). Conceptions of privacy: Current status and next steps. *Journal of Social Issues*, 33, 5–21.

Martin, K., & Shilton, K. (2015). Why experience matters to privacy: How context-based experience moderates consumer privacy expectations for mobile applications. *Journal of the Association for Information Science and Technology*.

Mattioli, D. (2012, August 23). On Orbitz, Mac users steered to pricier hotels. Wall Street Journal. http://online.wsj.com/article/ SB10001424052702304458604577488822667325882.html

McDonald, A. M., & Cranor, L. F. (2008). Cost of reading privacy policies. *ISJLP*, 4, 543.

Meyer, R. (2014, June 28). Everything we know about Facebook's secret mood manipulation experiment. *The Atlantic*. http://www.theatlantic.com/technology/archive/2014/06/everything-we-know-about -facebooks-secret-mood-manipulation-experiment/373648/.

Moor, J. H. (1997). Towards a theory of privacy in the information age. *ACM SIGCAS Computers and Society*, 27(3), 27–32.

Nissenbaum, H. (2004). Privacy as contextual integrity. *Washington Law Review*, 79(1), 119–158.

Nissenbaum, H. (2009). *Privacy in context: Technology, privacy, and the integrity of social life*. Stanford, CA: Stanford University Press.

Persson, A. J., & Hansson, S. O. (2003). Privacy at work: Ethical criteria. *Journal of Business Ethics*, 42(1), 59–70.

Peslak, A. R. (2005). An ethical exploration of privacy and radio frequency identification. *Journal of Business Ethics*, 59(4), 327–345.

Posner, R. (1981). The economics of privacy. *The American Economic Review*, 71(2), 405–409.

Rosen, J. (2001). *The unwanted gaze: The destruction of privacy in America*. New York: Random House Books.

Schoeman, F. (1984). *Privacy: Philosophical dimensions of the literature: An anthology*. Cambridge, MA: Cambridge University Press.

Shilton, K., & Martin, K. E. (2013). Mobile privacy expectations in context. In *TPRC*.

Sloan, R. D., & Warner, R. (2014). Self, privacy, and power: Is it all over? Chicago-Kent College of Law Research Paper No. 2014-04.

Stutzman, F., & Hartzog, W. (2012). Obscurity by design: An approach to building privacy into social media. In *CSCW' 12 workshop on reconciling privacy with social media*.

Tavani, H., & Moor, J. H. (2001). Privacy protection, control of information, and privacy-enhancing technologies. *SIGCAS Computers and Society*, 31(1), 6–11.

Thurm, S., & Kane, Y. I. (2010, December 17). Your apps are watching you. *Wall Street Journal*. http://online.wsj.com/article/SB10001424052748704694004576020083703574602.html.

Ur, B., Leon, P. G., Cranor, L. F., Shay, R., & Wang, Y. (2012). Smart, useful, scary, creepy: Perceptions of online behavioral advertising. In Presented at the proceedings of the eighth symposium on usable privacy and security (p. 4). ACM.

Van Oosterhout, H., Heugens, P., & Kaptein, M. (2006). The internal morality of contracting: Advancing the contractualist endeavor in business ethics. *Academy of Management Review*, 31(3), 521–539.

Wagner, K. (2014, May 16). Moves app backtracks, shares user data with Facebook. Mashable. http://mashable.com/2014/05/06/moves-data-sharing-facebook/.

Warren, S., & Brandeis, L. D. (1890). The right to privacy. *Harvard Law Review*, 4(5), 193.

Westin, A. (1967). *Privacy and freedom*. New York: Atheneum.

Privacy Law for Business Decision-Makers in the United States

Clarissa Wilbur Berger[*]

I. Introduction

It is difficult to grasp the amount of data generated in our world. For every minute of every day in 2020, over 1,3000,000 video and voice calls were made, and consumers spent around $1,000,000 in online purchases.[1] Fitbit trackers, Alexa voice assistants, and general Google searches continuously collect data from their users.[2] Data is generated in an increasingly fast pace from an increasingly complex set of sources.

Data privacy, or information privacy, refers to the privacy protections associated with personal information, which can be defined in different ways. The United States does not have one cohesive information privacy law.[3] A United States business must navigate three categories of legal frameworks: (1) federal laws, (2) state laws, and (3) foreign laws. The United States' federal legal landscape for privacy largely consists of a patchwork system of laws that focus on particular sectors. The federal requirements must be navigated in tandem with different state law regimes since each state has the ability to enact its own privacy legislation. Beyond federal and state laws, companies doing business with in foreign countries, having their data processed abroad, or collecting data from individuals located in foreign countries may be required to comply with foreign privacy regimes. For example, companies doing business with the European Union may be required to comply with the EU's statutory regime known as the General Data Protection Regulation (GDPR). This paper will provide an overview of these three categories which create the US landscape of privacy law.

---

[*] J.D., University of Notre Dame, 2021. Reprinted with permission.

DOI: 10.1201/9781003278290-20

II. Federal Laws

In the United States, federal laws are sector-specific and protect different types of personal information. Part A of this section will describe the following federal statutes:

- The Children's Online Privacy Protection Act (COPPA)
- The Gramm–Leach–Bliley Act (GLBA)
- The Health Insurance Portability and Accountability Act (HIPAA)
- The Family Educational Rights and Privacy Act (FERPA)

In addition to the sector-specific federal laws, the Federal Trade Commission (FTC) has a significant role in generally regulating the behavior of private organizations toward personal information. The FTC's role is discussed in Part B.

A. Sector-Based Federal Laws

The Children's Online Privacy Protection Act

The Children's Online Privacy Protection Act (COPPA)[4] was passed by Congress to place "parents in control over what information is collected from their young children online."[5] This statute defines a child as any person under the age of 13, and it imposes requirements on parties operating websites or online services that collect the personal information of children.

When does COPPA apply? A business is subject to COPPA if it collects personal information from children and falls into any of the following categories: (1) an entity who operates a website directed at children, (2) an entity who operates an online service directed to children, (3) an entity that operates a website or an online service directed at a general audience and has "actual knowledge" that they are collecting personal information from a child, or (4) an entity who runs a third-party service, like a plug-in, that collects information from users of a site or service directed to children.[6]

In the third category, an entity has "actual knowledge" of a user's age if the website or service collects information allowing them to determine the user's age.[7] For example, a company may be subject to COPPA if its website asks for a user's birth date or educational status.

The "online services" mentioned in the second and third category capture a broad range of services. "Online services" include those that allow children to play network connected games, participate in social networking activities, and receive online advertisements.[8] The term also includes mobile applications that connect to the internet, smart speakers, voice assistants, and certain location-based services.[9]

COPPA also broadly defines the personal information covered by the statute. COPPA is triggered when the above entities collect personal information such as the child's name, any physical address, e-mail address, telephone number, Social Security number, photograph containing the child's image, or any other identifiers that could allow a person to identify or contact a child.[10]

What does COPPA require? Once COPPA is triggered, the entity collecting information from children must comply with a series of restrictions. The restrictions include:

- Obtaining "verifiable parental consent" for the collection, use, or disclosure of the children's personal information;[11]
- Posting a privacy notice on the website or service describing what information is collected, how the information is used, and the party's disclosure practices;[12]

- Providing parents with access to their children's collected information; and[13]
- Retaining the collected information for only as long as it is needed to fulfill the purpose for which it was collected.[14]

What happens if COPPA is violated? Anyone may report a COPPA violation directly to the FTC.[15] The FTC may begin an investigation and may file a lawsuit. In addition to suits by the FTC, COPPA gives states and certain federal agencies, such as the Department of Transportation, the authority to bring COPPA enforcement suits.[16]

The civil penalty for COPPA violations depends on various factors, and the court judgement could range from no penalty to a penalty of millions of dollars.[17] In 2019, Google and YouTube agreed to paid $170 million to the New York Attorney General and the FTC to settle a claim alleging that YouTube had collected children's personal information without parental consent.[18]

The Gramm–Leach–Bliley Act

The Gramm–Leach–Bliley Act (GLBA)[19] requires financial institutions to protect the privacy of their consumers.[20] GLBA imposes limits on when a "financial institution" may disclose the consumer's "nonpublic personal information."[21] The organizations who must comply with GLBA range from tradition banks to auto dealers.

When does GLBA apply? GLBA's privacy provisions apply to any "financial institution" who collects their consumers' "nonpublic personal information."[22] So who is considered a financial institution under the statute? A financial institution is broadly defined as any institution whose business is to engage in activities that are "financial in nature."[23] These activities include:

- Lending, transferring, or safeguarding money or securities,[24]
- Providing insurance,[25]
- Providing financial, investment, or economic advisory services, and[26]
- Debt collecting.[27]

Institutions such as an auto dealer may be classified as a "financial institution" if it extends credit to a customer for the purchase of a car or provides financial advice to its customers.[28]

Once an institution is classified as a "financial institution," the next question is to determine whether the institution is collecting "nonpublic personal information" from their consumers. This generally includes names, phone numbers, addresses, Social Security numbers, credit and income histories, bank account numbers, and any other personal information that is typically unavailable to the public.[29] If the entity is classified as a "financial institution" under GLBA and collects "nonpublic personal information," then the privacy provisions of GLBA apply. The privacy provisions of GLBA may also apply to other institutions that receive "nonpublic personal information" from unaffiliated financial institutions.[30]

What does GLBA require? GLBA prohibits any "financial institution" from sharing the "nonpublic financial information," unless the customer has been provided notice and an opportunity to opt out.[31] GLBA requires institutions to disclose their practices for using and sharing personal information and requires them to describe their security and confidentiality protections for the information.[32]

In addition to the disclosure and opt-out provisions, GLBA requires specific agencies to establish standards for financial institutions "to insure the security and confidentiality of customer records and information."[33] Institutions must ensure that they are compliance with these agencies' regulations as well.

What happens if GLBA is violated? GLBA is enforced by the FTC, federal banking agencies, other federal regulatory agencies, and state insurance oversight agencies.[34] The FTC has general authority to bring a suit against any financial institution or person who falls outside the authority of the other agencies.[35]

A situation concerning Paypal, Inc. offers an illustration of FTC enforcing GLBA compliance. In 2018, Vemno's parent company, Paypal, settled with the FTC over allegations that Vemno had violated GLBA by misrepresenting how consumers' financial accounts were protected and by misleading consumers about their ability to control the privacy of their transactions.[36] As part of the settlement, Venmo was required to undergo periodic compliance assessments for 10 years to ensure that GLBA's provisions are not being violated.[37]

Health Insurance Portability and Accountability Act

The Health Insurance Portability and Accountability Act of 1996 (HIPAA)[38] is a federal law enacted to protect an individual's sensitive health information from disclosure without the individual's consent or knowledge.[39]

When does HIPAA apply? HIPAA's privacy requirements apply to "covered entities" and "business associates."[40] Under HIPAA, "covered entities" are:

■ Health care providers, such as doctors, clinics, nursing homes, and pharmacies;
■ Health plans, such as health insurance companies and company health plans; and
■ Health care clearing houses.[41]

A "business associate" is an entity entering into a contract with a covered entity in order to carry out health care activities involving the use or disclosure of protected health information.[42] For example, a business associate may be an accountant whose services to a clinic involve access to health information, a lawyer whose legal services to a health plan involve access to health information, or a consultant who provides advice to a hospital.[43]

What does HIPAA require? HIPAA requires that covered entities and business associates follow specific use and disclosure rules regarding "protected health information", such as an individual's medical history or medical payment history.[44] Covered entities and business associates must limit the use and disclosure of the information.[45] They are also required to implement "appropriate administrative, physical and technical safeguards to ensure the confidentiality, integrity, and security of electronic protected health information."[46] For example, appropriate technical safeguards for electronic health information may include assigning a unique username or number for each user of the information system, creating procedures for accessing the information in an emergency situation, implementing an automatic logoff feature to prevent unauthorized users from seeing information, and implementing mechanisms to encrypt and decrypt the information.[47]

What happens if HIPAA is violated? A few common HIPAA violations include impermissible disclosures of protected health information, failures to manage risks to the information's confidentiality, and occurrences of unauthorized access to the information. HHS enforces HIPAA's requirements by investigating complaints and working with covered entities to achieve compliance.[48] If the covered entity does not satisfactorily reach compliance with HIPAA's provisions, then HHS can impose a civil money penalty. Some HIPAA violations may also lead to criminal charges.

Family Educational Rights and Privacy Act

The Family Educational Rights and Privacy Act[49] (FERPA) applies to educational institutions and agencies that rely on certain federal government funding. In order to receive these funds, the institution or agency must (1) protect the rights of parents and adult students to access their educational records, (2) generally prevent disclosures of educational records to third parties without the written consent of the parent or adult student, (3) provide informal and internal hearings for parents or adult students who think that there has been an invasion of privacy or who believe that their educational records are inaccurate, and (4) must provide an annual notice to parents and adult students of their FERPA rights.[50] A failure to comply with the FERPA provisions can result in the institution's loss of federal funding.

B. The Role of the Federal Trade Commission

While federal privacy laws are sector-specific, companies outside of the scope of these laws can be held accountable for their data privacy practices. A large number of companies have individual privacy policies, and these privacy policies are enforced by the Federal Trade Commission (FTC). The FTC can bring a suit against a company for any deceptive or unfair act or practice, including breaching a promise in the company's privacy policy. Because various types of data collection, storage, and use fall outside of the federal, industry-specific privacy statutes, the FTC is often the primary source of privacy regulation.

Even though the FTC has broad reach in enforcing company privacy policies, there are few lawsuits centering on the FTC's privacy regulation.[51] There are few lawsuits because FTC privacy actions nearly always end in settlements.[52] The lack of case law and scholarship on FTC privacy actions means that "a large domain of the US privacy regulatory framework primarily consists of a relatively obscure body of doctrines that scholars have not analyzed in depth."[53]

III. State Laws

All states have some form of information privacy law, and some have enacted more comprehensive regimes than others. For a business, compliance with information privacy laws can be burdensome since companies with a national presence may be required to comply with laws in all fifty states. As of early 2021, California and Virginia have enacted the most comprehensive privacy statutes. California's legislature passed the California Consumer Privacy Act (CCPA), effective January 1, 2020, and the California Privacy Rights Act, effective January 1, 2023. Meanwhile, Virginia's legislature passed the Consumer Data Protection Act.[54] These comprehensive privacy statutes strive to broadly govern the use of personal data within the state. Less comprehensive approaches used by other states may target specific industries, specific information types, or more specific subject matter such as data security.[55]

As one of the most comprehensive approaches used by a US state, CCPA grants rights to consumers, and it imposes obligations on certain businesses.[56] Per CCPA, consumers have the right to know what personal information is collected by businesses, how the information is being used, and if the information is being sold to third parties.[57] Consumers also have the right to delete personal information held by businesses and the right to direct a business to stop selling their personal information.[58] Meanwhile, businesses subject to CCPA have an obligation to provide notice to consumers when collecting their information, and they must respond to all customer requests to know, delete, or opt-out of having their information sold.[59] Additionally, businesses must retain records to demonstrate their compliance with CCPA's provisions, notify consumers of data breaches, and create a public privacy policy disclosing their information privacy practices.[60]

These consumer rights and business obligations present compliance challenges for businesses subject to CCPA. In order to organize the data management process and respond to customer requests regarding their information, businesses need a thorough data governance structure.

IV. International Flows of Personal Information and GDPR

In addition to domestic federal and state laws, companies who do business abroad or who process the personal data of individuals located abroad may need to comply with foreign privacy laws. This may include companies that target a foreign country with advertising campaigns, sell a significant amount of goods and services to a foreign country, or track the cookies and IP addresses of visitors located abroad who visit the company website.

A key foreign privacy law is the European Union's General Data Protection Regulations (GDPR). GDPR provides a single uniform data privacy law across the EU that strives to broadly protect the personal information of its citizens.[61] GDPR has the following seven principles which guide companies in achieving compliance with its provisions:[62]

(1) **Specific grounds for processing personal data**: When processing information, a company must be able to justify it with one of the following reasons: the individual has consented to the processing of their data for a stated purpose, processing is required to meet the terms of a contract, processing is required by a legal obligation of the company, processing is required to protect someone's life, processing is in the public interest which has a clear basis in law, and where processing is required by a legitimate interest.

(2) **Limited uses of personal data**: A company must disclose how they intend to use an individual's information. This helps disincentivize companies from using the information for purposes other than those explained to the individual.

(3) **Data minimization**: Data should only be collected for a necessary purpose. If information is needed from a few individuals, it should not be collected from all individuals.

(4) **Accuracy**: A company should ensure that the collected information is accurate. Additionally, if information is collected in the form of opinions from individuals, the information should not be construed as fact.

(5) **Storage Limitation**: Generally, data should only be kept as long as it is actually needed for the intended purpose.

(6) **Integrity**: Data must be processed securely, and companies must have appropriate measures in place to protect both the physical and organizational security of the data.

(7) **Accountability**: Companies must be able to demonstrate their compliance with GDPR's provisions, and they must take responsibility for their management of personal data.

In addition to creating requirements for companies, GDPR also describes the rights of its citizens with respect to the management of their data. GDPR states that EU citizens have the right to be informed if their information is being collected, used, stored, or shared.[63] Per GDPR, EU citizens also have the right to request a copy of their information from the company, correct inaccurate information, request to have data deleted, object to the processing of their information, and object to specific uses of their information.[64]

V. Conclusion

The information privacy legal landscape in the United States is complex and disjointed. A company must identify the federal, state, and foreign laws that apply to it and structure a data governance system to achieve compliance. However, the adoption of EU's GDPR and California's CCPA shows a growing trend toward more comprehensive approaches to information privacy, and companies are being called to take increasing responsibility for their management of personal data.

Notes

1. *Data Never Sleeps 8.0*, DOMO (2021), https://www.domo.com/learn/data-never-sleeps-8
2. Edward C. Baig, *What Will It Take for the Government to Protect Your Privacy?*, USA Today (Jan. 25, 2020, 11:46 PM), https://www.usatoday.com/story/tech/2020/01/20/why-we-need-federal-data -privacy-law/2803896001/
3. Nuala O'Connor, *Reforming the U.S. Approach to Data Protection and Privacy*, Council on Foreign Relations (Jan. 30, 2018), https://www.cfr.org/report/reforming-us-approach-data-protection
4. 15 U.S.C. §§ 6501–05.
5. *Complying with COPPA: Frequently Asked Questions*, Fed. Trade Comm'n, https://www.ftc.gov/tips -advice/business-center/guidance/complying-coppa-frequently-asked-questions-0
6. 15 U.S.C. § 6502(a)(1).
7. *Complying with COPPA: Frequently Asked Questions*, supra note 5.
8. Id.
9. Id.
10. 15 U.S.C. § 6501(8).
11. 15 U.S.C. §6502(b)(1)(A).
12. Id.
13. 15 U.S.C. §6502(b)(1)(B).
14. *Complying with COPPA: Frequently Asked Questions*, supra note 5.
15. *Complying with COPPA: Frequently Asked Questions*, supra note 5.
16. Id.
17. Id.
18. *Google LLC and YouTube, LLC*, Fed. Trade Comm'n, https://www.ftc.gov/enforcement/cases-pro- ceedings/172-3083/google-llc-youtube-llc
19. Pub. L. No. 106–102, 113 Stat. 1338 (1999).
20. 15 U.S.C. § 6801(a) ("[E]ach financial institution has an affirmative and continuing obligation to respect the privacy of its customers and to protect the security and confidentiality of those customers' nonpublic personal information.").
21. *How to Comply with the Privacy of Consumer Financial Information Rule of the Gramm-Leach-Bliley Act*, Fed. Trade Comm'n, https://www.ftc.gov/tips-advice/business-center/guidance/how-comply -privacy-consumer-financial-information-rule-gramm
22. 15 U.S.C. § 6802.
23. 15 U.S.C. § 6809(3); 12 U.S.C. § 1843(k).
24. 12 U.S.C. § 1843(k)(4).
25. Id.
26. Id.
27. 12 U.S.C. § 1843(k)(4).
28. Id.
29. Juliana De Groot, *What Is GLBA Compliance? Understanding the Data Protection Requirements of the Gramm-Leach-Bliley Act in 2019*, Digital Guardian: Data Insider (Jul. 15, 2019), https://digi- talguardian.com/blog/what-glba-compliance-understanding-data-protection-requirements-gramm -leach-bliley-act

30. *How to Comply with the Privacy of Consumer Financial Information Rule of the Gramm-Leach-Bliley Act, supra* note 23.
31. 15 U.S.C. § 6802.
32. *Privacy Act Issues under Gramm-Leach-Bliley*, Fed. Deposit Ins. Corp., https://www.fdic.gov/consumers/consumer/alerts/glba.html
33. 15 U.S.C. § 6801(b).
34. De Groot, *supra* note 34.
35. *How to Comply with the Privacy of Consumer Financial Information Rule of the Gramm-Leach-Bliley Act, supra* note 23.
36. *FTC Gives Final Approval to Settlement with PayPal Related to Allegations Involving its Venmo Peer-to-Peer Payment Service*, Fed. Trade Comm'n, (May 24, 2018), https://www.ftc.gov/news-events/press-releases/2018/05/ftc-gives-final-approval-settlement-paypal-related-allegations#:~:text=The%20Federal%20Trade%20Commission%20has%20given%20final%20approval,and%20control%20the%20privacy%20of%20their%20Venmo%20transactions
37. Id.
38. Pub. L. No. 104-191, 110 Stat. 1936 (1996).
39. *Health Insurance Portability and Accountability Act of 1996 (HIPAA)*, Ctr. for Disease Control and Prevention, https://www.cdc.gov/phlp/publications/topic/hipaa.html
40. Definitions of "covered entity" and "business associate" can be found at 45 CFR 160.103.
41. *Covered Entities and Business Associates*, Dep't of Health and Hum. Serv., https://www.hhs.gov/hipaa/for-professionals/covered-entities/index.html; *Health Insurance Portability and Accountability Act of 1996 (HIPAA), supra* note 47.
42. *Business Associates*, Dep't of Health and Hum. Serv., https://www.hhs.gov/hipaa/for-professionals/privacy/guidance/business-associates/index.html
43. Id.
44. 45 C.F.R. 160.103.
45. *The HIPAA Privacy Rule*, Dep't of Health and Hum. Serv., https://www.hhs.gov/hipaa/for-professionals/privacy/index.html
46. *The Security Rule*, Dep't of Health and Hum. Serv., https://www.hhs.gov/hipaa/for-professionals/security/index.html
47. *HIPAA Security Series: Security Standards*, Dep't of Health and Hum. Serv. (Mar. 2007), https://www.hhs.gov/sites/default/files/ocr/privacy/hipaa/administrative/securityrule/techsafeguards.pdf?language=es
48. *How OCR Enforces the HIPAA Privacy & Security Rules*, Dep't of Health and Hum. Serv., https://www.hhs.gov/hipaa/for-professionals/compliance-enforcement/examples/how-ocr-enforces-the-hipaa-privacy-and-security-rules/index.html
49. 20 U.S.C. § 1232g.
50. Lynn M. Daggett, *FERPA in the Twenty-First Century: Failure to Effectively Regulate Privacy for All Students*, 58 Cath. U. L. Rev. 59, 62 (2008).
51. Daniel J. Solove & Woodrow Hartzog, *The FTC and the New Common Law of Privacy*, 114 Columbia L. Rev. 583, 588 (2014).
52. Id.
53. *Id.* at 589.
54. *US State Privacy Legislation Tracker*, Int'l Assoc. of Priv. Pro. (May 10, 2021), https://iapp.org/resources/article/us-state-privacy-legislation-tracker/
55. Id.
56. CCPA applies to businesses that fall into one of the following categories: (1) have gross annual revenues over $25 million, (2) buys or sells the personal information of 50,000 or more consumers, households, or devices, or (3) derives 50 percent or more of annual revenues from selling consumers' personal information. *See California Consumer Privacy Act (CCPA)*, State of California Dep't of Just., https://oag.ca.gov/system/files/attachments/press_releases/CCPA%20Fact%20Sheet%20%2800000002%29.pdf
57. Id.

58. Id.
59. Id.
60. Id.
61. *GDPR – User-Friendly Guide to General Data Protection Regulation*, GDPR, https://www.gdpreu.org/
62. Id.
63. Id.
64. Id.

Chapter 3.6

Wrongfully Accused by an Algorithm[*]

Kashmir Hill

In what may be the first known case of its kind, a faulty facial recognition match led to a Michigan man's arrest for a crime he did not commit[1]

On a Thursday afternoon in January, Robert Julian-Borchak Williams was in his office at an automotive supply company when he got a call from the Detroit Police Department telling him to come to the station to be arrested. He thought at first that it was a prank.

An hour later, when he pulled into his driveway in a quiet subdivision in Farmington Hills, Mich., a police car pulled up behind, blocking him in. Two officers got out and handcuffed Mr. Williams on his front lawn, in front of his wife and two young daughters, who were distraught. The police wouldn't say why he was being arrested, only showing him a piece of paper with his photo and the words "felony warrant" and "larceny."

His wife, Melissa, asked where he was being taken. "Google it," she recalls an officer replying.

The police drove Mr. Williams to a detention center. He had his mug shot, fingerprints and DNA taken, and was held overnight. Around noon on Friday, two detectives took him to an interrogation room and placed three pieces of paper on the table, face down.

"When's the last time you went to a Shinola store?" one of the detectives asked, in Mr. Williams's recollection. Shinola is an upscale boutique that sells watches, bicycles and leather goods in the trendy Midtown neighborhood of Detroit. Mr. Williams said he and his wife had checked it out when the store first opened in 2014.

The detective turned over the first piece of paper. It was a still image from a surveillance video, showing a heavyset man, dressed in black and wearing a red St. Louis Cardinals cap, standing in front of a watch display. Five timepieces, worth $3,800, were shoplifted.

"Is this you?" asked the detective.

The second piece of paper was a close-up. The photo was blurry, but it was clearly not Mr. Williams. He picked up the image and held it next to his face.

---

[*] Hill, Kashmir. 2020. "Wrongfully Accused by an Algorithm," *The New York Times.* June 24, 2020. https://www.nytimes.com/2020/06/24/technology/facial-recognition-arrest.html. Reprinted with permission.

DOI: 10.1201/9781003278290-21

"No, this is not me," Mr. Williams said. "You think all black men look alike?"

Mr. Williams knew that he had not committed the crime in question. What he could not have known, as he sat in the interrogation room, is that his case may be the first known account of an American being wrongfully arrested based on a flawed match from a facial recognition algorithm, according to experts on technology and the law.

A Faulty System

A nationwide debate is raging about racism in law enforcement. Across the country, millions are protesting not just the actions of individual officers, but bias in the systems used to surveil communities and identify people for prosecution.

Facial recognition systems have been used by police forces for more than two decades. Recent studies by MIT and the National Institute of Standards and Technology, or NIST, have found that while the technology works relatively well on white men, the results are less accurate for other demographics, in part because of a lack of diversity in the images used to develop the underlying databases.

Last year, during a public hearing about the use of facial recognition in Detroit, an assistant police chief was among those who raised concerns. "On the question of false positives—that is absolutely factual, and it's well-documented," James White said. "So that concerns me as an African-American male."

This month, Amazon, Microsoft, and IBM announced they would stop or pause their facial recognition offerings for law enforcement. The gestures were largely symbolic, given that the companies are not big players in the industry. The technology police departments use is supplied by companies that aren't household names, such as Vigilant Solutions, Cognitec, NEC, Rank One Computing, and Clearview AI.

Clare Garvie, a lawyer at Georgetown University's Center on Privacy and Technology, has written about problems with the government's use of facial recognition. She argues that low-quality search images—such as a still image from a grainy surveillance video—should be banned, and that the systems currently in use should be tested rigorously for accuracy and bias.

"There are mediocre algorithms and there are good ones, and law enforcement should only buy the good ones," Ms. Garvie said.

About Mr. Williams's experience in Michigan, she added: "I strongly suspect this is not the first case to misidentify someone to arrest them for a crime they didn't commit. This is just the first time we know about it."

In a Perpetual Lineup

Mr. Williams's case combines flawed technology with poor police work, illustrating how facial recognition can go awry.

The Shinola shoplifting occurred in October 2018. Katherine Johnston, an investigator at Mackinac Partners, a loss prevention firm, reviewed the store's surveillance video and sent a copy to the Detroit police, according to their report.

Five months later, in March 2019, Jennifer Coulson, a digital image examiner for the Michigan State Police, uploaded a "probe image"—a still from the video, showing the man in the Cardinals cap—to the state's facial recognition database. The system would have mapped the man's face and searched for similar ones in a collection of 49 million photos.

The state's technology is supplied for $5.5 million by a company called DataWorks Plus. Founded in South Carolina in 2000, the company first offered mug shot management software, said Todd Pastorini, a general manager. In 2005, the firm began to expand the product, adding face recognition tools developed by outside vendors.

When one of these subcontractors develops an algorithm for recognizing faces, DataWorks attempts to judge its effectiveness by running searches using low-quality images of individuals it knows are present in a system. "We've tested a lot of garbage out there," Mr. Pastorini said. These checks, he added, are not "scientific"—DataWorks does not formally measure the systems' accuracy or bias.

"We've become a pseudo-expert in the technology," Mr. Pastorini said.

In Michigan, the DataWorks software used by the state police incorporates components developed by the Japanese tech giant NEC and by Rank One Computing, based in Colorado, according to Mr. Pastorini and a state police spokeswoman. In 2019, algorithms from both companies were included in a federal study of over 100 facial recognition systems that found they were biased, falsely identifying African-American and Asian faces 10 times to 100 times more than Caucasian faces.

Rank One's chief executive, Brendan Klare, said the company had developed a new algorithm for NIST to review that "tightens the differences in accuracy between different demographic cohorts."

After Ms. Coulson, of the state police, ran her search of the probe image, the system would have provided a row of results generated by NEC and a row from Rank One, along with confidence scores. Mr. Williams's driver's license photo was among the matches. Ms. Coulson sent it to the Detroit police as an "Investigative Lead Report."

"This document is not a positive identification," the file says in bold capital letters at the top. "It is an investigative lead only and is not probable cause for arrest."

This is what technology providers and law enforcement always emphasize when defending facial recognition: It is only supposed to be a clue in the case, not a smoking gun. Before arresting Mr. Williams, investigators might have sought other evidence that he committed the theft, such as eyewitness testimony, location data from his phone or proof that he owned the clothing that the suspect was wearing.

In this case, however, according to the Detroit police report, investigators simply included Mr. Williams's picture in a "6-pack photo lineup" they created and showed to Ms. Johnston, Shinola's loss-prevention contractor, and she identified him. (Ms. Johnston declined to comment.)

"I Guess the Computer Got It Wrong"

Mr. Pastorini was taken aback when the process was described to him. "It sounds thin all the way around," he said.

Mr. Klare, of Rank One, found fault with Ms. Johnston's role in the process. "I am not sure if this qualifies them as an eyewitness, or gives their experience any more weight than other persons who may have viewed that same video after the fact," he said. John Wise, a spokesman for NEC, said: "A match using facial recognition alone is not a means for positive identification."

The Friday that Mr. Williams sat in a Detroit police interrogation room was the day before his 42nd birthday. That morning, his wife emailed his boss to say he would miss work because of a family emergency; it broke his four-year record of perfect attendance.

In Mr. Williams's recollection, after he held the surveillance video still next to his face, the two detectives leaned back in their chairs and looked at one another. One detective, seeming chagrined, said to his partner: "I guess the computer got it wrong."

They turned over a third piece of paper, which was another photo of the man from the Shinola store next to Mr. Williams's driver's license. Mr. Williams again pointed out that they were not the same person.

Mr. Williams asked if he was free to go. "Unfortunately not," one detective said.

Mr. Williams was kept in custody until that evening, 30 hours after being arrested, and released on a $1,000 personal bond. He waited outside in the rain for 30 minutes until his wife could pick him up. When he got home at 10 pm, his five-year-old daughter was still awake. She said she was waiting for him because he had said, while being arrested, that he'd be right back.

She has since taken to playing "cops and robbers" and accuses her father of stealing things, insisting on "locking him up" in the living room.

Getting Help

The Williams family contacted defense attorneys, most of whom, they said, assumed Mr. Williams was guilty of the crime and quoted prices of around $7,000 to represent him. Ms. Williams, a real estate marketing director and food blogger, also tweeted at the American Civil Liberties Union of Michigan, which took an immediate interest.

"We've been active in trying to sound the alarm bells around facial recognition, both as a threat to privacy when it works and a racist threat to everyone when it doesn't," said Phil Mayor, an attorney at the organization. "We know these stories are out there, but they're hard to hear about because people don't usually realize they've been the victim of a bad facial recognition search."

Two weeks after his arrest, Mr. Williams took a vacation day to appear in a Wayne County court for an arraignment. When the case was called, the prosecutor moved to dismiss, but "without prejudice," meaning Mr. Williams could later be charged again.

Maria Miller, a spokeswoman for the prosecutor, said a second witness had been at the store in 2018 when the shoplifting occurred, but had not been asked to look at a photo lineup. If the individual makes an identification in the future, she said, the office will decide whether to issue charges.

A Detroit police spokeswoman, Nicole Kirkwood, said that for now, the department "accepted the prosecutor's decision to dismiss the case." She also said that the department updated its facial recognition policy in July 2019 so that it is only used to investigate violent crimes.

The department, she said in another statement, "does not make arrests based solely on facial recognition. The investigator reviewed video, interviewed witnesses, conducted a photo lineup."

On Wednesday, the ACLU of Michigan filed a complaint with the city, asking for an absolute dismissal of the case, an apology and the removal of Mr. Williams's information from Detroit's criminal databases.

The Detroit Police Department "should stop using facial recognition technology as an investigatory tool," Mr. Mayor wrote in the complaint, adding, "as the facts of Mr. Williams's case prove both that the technology is flawed and that DPD investigators are not competent in making use of such technology."

Mr. Williams's lawyer, Victoria Burton-Harris, said that her client is "lucky," despite what he went through.

"He is alive," Ms. Burton-Harris said. "He is a very large man. My experience has been, as a defense attorney, when officers interact with very large men, very large black men, they immediately act out of fear. They don't know how to de-escalate a situation."

"It was humiliating."

Mr. Williams and his wife have not talked to their neighbors about what happened. They wonder whether they need to put their daughters into therapy. Mr. Williams's boss advised him not to tell anyone at work.

"My mother doesn't know about it. It's not something I'm proud of," Mr. Williams said. "It's humiliating."

He has since figured out what he was doing the evening the shoplifting occurred. He was driving home from work, and had posted a video to his private Instagram because a song he loved came on—1983's "We Are One," by Maze and Frankie Beverly. The lyrics go:

> *I can't understand*
> *Why we treat each other in this way*
> *Taking up time*
> *With the silly silly games we play*

He had an alibi, had the Detroit police checked for one.

Note

1. Note: In response to this article, the Wayne County prosecutor's office said that Robert Julian-Borchak Williams could have the case and his fingerprint data expunged. "We apologize," the prosecutor, Kym L. Worthy, said in a statement, adding, "This does not in any way make up for the hours that Mr. Williams spent in jail."

Chapter 3.7

Facial Recognition Is Accurate, If You're a White Guy*

Steve Lohr

The New York Times

Facial recognition technology is improving by leaps and bounds. Some commercial software can now tell the gender of a person in a photograph.

When the person in the photo is a white man, the software is right 99 percent of the time.

But the darker the skin, the more errors arise—up to nearly 35 percent for images of darker-skinned women, according to a new study that breaks fresh ground by measuring how the technology works on people of different races and gender.

These disparate results, calculated by Joy Buolamwini, a researcher at the MIT Media Lab, show how some of the biases in the real world can seep into artificial intelligence, the computer systems that inform facial recognition.

Color Matters in Computer Vision

Facial recognition algorithms made by Microsoft, IBM, and Face++ were more likely to misidentify the gender of black women than white men (Figures 3.7.1 and 3.7.2).

---

* Lohr, Steve. 2018. "Facial Recognition Is Accurate, if You're a White Guy," *The New York Times*. February 9, 2018. https://www.nytimes.com/2018/02/09/technology/facial-recognition-race-artificial-intelligence.html. Reprinted with Permission.

DOI: 10.1201/9781003278290-22

143

Gender was misidentified in **up to 1 percent of lighter-skinned males** in a set of 385 photos.

Gender was misidentified in **up to 7 percent of lighter-skinned females** in a set of 296 photos.

Figure 3.7.1   Photos were selected from among those used in Joy Buolamwini's study. Source: Joy Buolamwini, MIT Media Lab.

Gender was misidentified in **up to 12 percent of darker-skinned males** in a set of 318 photos.

Gender was misidentified in **35 percent of darker-skinned females** in a set of 271 photos.

Figure 3.7.2   Photos were selected from among those used in Joy Buolamwini's study. Source: Joy Buolamwini, MIT Media Lab.

In modern artificial intelligence, data rules. AI software is only as smart as the data used to train it. If there are many more white men than black women in the system, it will be worse at identifying the black women.

One widely used facial-recognition data set was estimated to be more than 75 percent male and more than 80 percent white, according to another research study.

The new study also raises broader questions of fairness and accountability in artificial intelligence at a time when investment in and adoption of the technology is racing ahead.

Today, facial recognition software is being deployed by companies in various ways, including to help target product pitches based on social media profile pictures. But companies are also experimenting with face identification and other AI technology as an ingredient in automated decisions with higher stakes like hiring and lending.

Researchers at the Georgetown Law School estimated that 117 million American adults are in face recognition networks used by law enforcement—and that African Americans were most likely to be singled out, because they were disproportionately represented in mug-shot databases.

Facial recognition technology is lightly regulated so far.

"This is the right time to be addressing how these AI systems work and where they fail—to make them socially accountable," said Suresh Venkatasubramanian, a professor of computer science at the University of Utah.

Until now, there was anecdotal evidence of computer vision miscues, and occasionally in ways that suggested discrimination. In 2015, for example, Google had to apologize after its image-recognition photo app initially labeled African Americans as "gorillas."

Sorelle Friedler, a computer scientist at Haverford College and a reviewing editor on Ms. Buolamwini's research paper, said experts had long suspected that facial recognition software performed differently on different populations.

"But this is the first work I'm aware of that shows that empirically," Ms. Friedler said.

Ms. Buolamwini, a young African-American computer scientist, experienced the bias of facial recognition firsthand. When she was an undergraduate at the Georgia Institute of Technology, programs would work well on her white friends, she said, but not recognize her face at all. She figured it was a flaw that would surely be fixed before long.

Joy Buolamwini, a researcher at the MIT Media Lab, has emerged as an advocate in the new field of "algorithmic accountability." Credit: Tony Luong for *The New York Times*.

But a few years later, after joining the MIT Media Lab, she ran into the missing-face problem again. Only when she put on a white mask did the software recognize hers as a face.

By then, face recognition software was increasingly moving out of the lab and into the mainstream.

"OK, this is serious," she recalled deciding then. "Time to do something."

So she turned her attention to fighting the bias built into digital technology. Now 28 and a doctoral student, after studying as a Rhodes scholar and a Fulbright fellow, she is an advocate in the new field of "algorithmic accountability," which seeks to make automated decisions more transparent, explainable and fair.

Her short TED Talk on coded bias has been viewed more than 940,000 times, and she founded the Algorithmic Justice League, a project to raise awareness of the issue.

In her newly published paper, which will be presented at a conference this month, Ms. Buolamwini studied the performance of three leading face recognition systems—by Microsoft, IBM, and Megvii of China—by classifying how well they could guess the gender of people with different skin tones. These companies were selected because they offered gender classification features in their facial analysis software—and their code was publicly available for testing.

She found them all wanting.

To test the commercial systems, Ms. Buolamwini built a data set of 1,270 faces, using faces of lawmakers from countries with a high percentage of women in office. The sources included three African nations with predominantly dark-skinned populations, and three Nordic countries with mainly light-skinned residents.

The African and Nordic faces were scored according to a six-point labeling system used by dermatologists to classify skin types. The medical classifications were determined to be more objective and precise than race.

Then, each company's software was tested on the curated data, crafted for gender balance and a range of skin tones. The results varied somewhat. Microsoft's error rate for darker-skinned women was 21 percent, while IBM's and Megvii's rates were nearly 35 percent. They all had error rates below 1 percent for light-skinned males.

Ms. Buolamwini shared the research results with each of the companies. IBM said in a statement to her that the company had steadily improved its facial analysis software and was "deeply committed" to "unbiased" and "transparent" services. This month, the company said, it will roll out an improved service with a nearly 10-fold increase in accuracy on darker-skinned women.

Microsoft said that it had "already taken steps to improve the accuracy of our facial recognition technology" and that it was investing in research "to recognize, understand and remove bias."

Ms. Buolamwini's co-author on her paper is Timnit Gebru, who described her role as an adviser. Ms. Gebru is a scientist at Microsoft Research, working on its Fairness Accountability Transparency and Ethics in AI group.

Timnit Gebru, a scientist at Microsoft Research, was a co-author of the paper that studied facial recognition software. Credit: Cody O'Loughlin for *The New York Times*.

Megvii, whose Face++ software is widely used for identification in online payment and ride-sharing services in China, did not reply to several requests for comment, Ms. Buolamwini said.

Ms. Buolamwini is releasing her data set for others to build upon. She describes her research as "a starting point, very much a first step" toward solutions.

Ms. Buolamwini is taking further steps in the technical community and beyond. She is working with the Institute of Electrical and Electronics Engineers, a large professional organization in computing, to set up a group to create standards for accountability and transparency in facial analysis software.

She meets regularly with other academics, public policy groups and philanthropies that are concerned about the impact of artificial intelligence. Darren Walker, president of the Ford Foundation, said that the new technology could be a "platform for opportunity," but that it would not happen if it replicated and amplified bias and discrimination of the past.

"There is a battle going on for fairness, inclusion and justice in the digital world," Mr. Walker said.

Part of the challenge, scientists say, is that there is so little diversity within the AI community.

"We'd have a lot more introspection and accountability in the field of AI if we had more people like Joy," said Cathy O'Neil, a data scientist and author of "Weapons of Math Destruction."

Technology, Ms. Buolamwini said, should be more attuned to the people who use it and the people it's used on.

"You can't have ethical AI that's not inclusive," she said. "And whoever is creating the technology is setting the standards."

Chapter 3.8

Excerpt from Datasheets for Datasets[*]

Timnit Gebru, Jamie Morgenstern, Briana Vecchione,
Jennifer Wortman Vaughan, Hanna Wallach, Hal Daumé III,
And Kate Crawford

1. Introduction

Data plays a critical role in machine learning. Every machine learning model is trained and evaluated using data, quite often in the form of a static dataset. The characteristics of these datasets will fundamentally influence a model's behavior: A model is unlikely to perform well in the wild if its deployment context does not match its training or evaluation datasets, or if these datasets reflect unwanted biases. Mismatches like this can have especially severe consequences when machine learning is used in high-stakes domains such as criminal justice [1, 11, 22], hiring [17], critical infrastructure [8, 19], or finance [16]. And even in other domains, mismatches may lead to loss of revenue or public relations setbacks. Of particular concern are recent examples showing that machine learning models can reproduce or amplify unwanted societal biases reflected in training data [4, 5, 9]. For these and other reasons, the World Economic Forum suggests that all entities should document the provenance, creation, and use of machine learning datasets in order to avoid discriminatory outcomes [23].

Although data provenance has been studied extensively in the databases community [3, 6], it is rarely discussed in the machine learning community, and documenting the creation and use of datasets has received even less attention. Despite the importance of data to machine learning, there is no standardized process for documenting machine learning datasets. To address this gap, we propose datasheets for datasets. In the electronics industry, every component, no matter how simple or complex, is accompanied with a datasheet describing its operating characteristics, test results, recommended usage, and other information. By analogy, we propose that every dataset

[*] Timnit Gebru et al. 2018. "Datasheets for Datasets," ArXiv Preprint ArXiv:1803.09010. https://arxiv.org/pdf/1803.09010.pdf. Reprinted with permission. Note: This is an excerpt from the original so footnote and endnote numbering may be modified.

DOI: 10.1201/9781003278290-23

be accompanied with a datasheet that documents its motivation, composition, collection process, recommended uses, and so on. Datasheets for datasets have the potential to increase transparency and accountability within the machine learning community, mitigate unwanted biases in machine learning systems, facilitate greater reproducibility of machine learning results, and help researchers and practitioners select more appropriate datasets for their chosen tasks.

After outlining our objectives below, we describe the process by which we developed the datasheets questions and the workflow for dataset creators to use when answering these questions. We then walk through the questions and workflow in detail. We conclude with a summary of the impact of datasheets for datasets and a discussion of implementation challenges and avenues for future work.

1.1 Objectives

Datasheets for datasets are intended to address the needs of two key stakeholder groups: dataset creators and dataset consumers. For dataset creators, the primary objective is to encourage careful reflection on the process of creating, distributing, and maintaining a dataset, including any underlying assumptions, potential risks or harms, and implications of use. For dataset consumers, the primary objective is to ensure they have the information they need to make informed decisions about using a dataset. Transparency on the part of dataset creators is necessary for dataset consumers to be sufficiently well informed that they can select appropriate datasets for their tasks and avoid unintentional misuse.

Beyond these two key stakeholder groups, datasheets may be valuable to policy makers, consumer advocates, individuals whose data is included in those datasets, and those who may be impacted by models trained or evaluated on those datasets. They also serve a secondary objective of facilitating greater reproducibility of machine learning results: without access to a dataset, researchers and practitioners can use the information in a datasheet to reconstruct the dataset.

Although we provide a set of questions designed to elicit the information that a datasheet for a dataset might contain, they are not intended to be prescriptive. Indeed, we expect that datasheets will vary depending on factors such as the domain or existing organizational infrastructure and workflows. For example, Bender and Friedman [2] outline a proposal similar to datasheets for datasets in natural language processing whose questions may naturally be integrated into a datasheet for a language-based dataset as appropriate.

We emphasize that the process of creating a datasheet is not intended to be automated. Although automated documentation processes are convenient, they run counter to our objective of encouraging dataset creators to carefully reflect on the process of creating, distributing, and maintaining a dataset.

[...]

3. Questions and Workflow

In this section, we provide a set of questions covering the information that a datasheet for a dataset might contain, as well as a workflow for dataset creators to use when answering these questions. The questions are grouped into sections that roughly match the key stages of the dataset lifecycle: motivation, composition, collection process, preprocessing/cleaning/labeling, uses, distribution, and maintenance. This grouping encourages dataset creators to reflect on the process of creating, distributing, and maintaining a dataset, and even alter this process in response to their reflection.

We note that not all questions will be applicable to all datasets, and dataset creators may omit those that do not apply.

To illustrate how these questions might be answered in practice, we provide in the appendix examples of datasheets for two well-known datasets: Labeled Faces in the Wild [14] and Pang and Lee's polarity dataset [20]. We chose these datasets in large part because their creators provided exemplary documentation, allowing us to easily find the answers to many of our questions.

3.1 Motivation

The questions in this section are primarily intended to encourage dataset creators to clearly articulate their reasons for creating the dataset and to promote transparency about funding interests.

- **For what purpose was the dataset created?** Was there a specific task in mind? Was there a specific gap that needed to be filled? Please provide a description.
- **Who created the dataset (e.g., which team, research group) and on behalf of which entity (e.g., company, institution, organization)?**
- **Who funded the creation of the dataset?** If there is an associated grant, please provide the name of the grantor and the grant name and number.
- **Any other comments?**

3.2 Composition

Dataset creators should read through the questions in this section prior to any data collection and then provide answers once collection is complete. Most of these questions are intended to provide dataset consumers with the information they need to make informed decisions about using the dataset for specific tasks. The answers to some of these questions reveal information about compliance with the EU's General Data Protection Regulation (GDPR) or comparable regulations in other jurisdictions.

- **What do the instances that comprise the dataset represent (e.g., documents, photos, people, countries)?** Are there multiple types of instances (e.g., movies, users, and ratings; people and interactions between them; nodes and edges)? Please provide a description.
- **How many instances are there in total (of each type, if appropriate)?**
- **Does the dataset contain all possible instances or is it a sample (not necessarily random) of instances from a larger set?** If the dataset is a sample, then what is the larger set? Is the sample representative of the larger set (e.g., geographic coverage)? If so, please describe how this representativeness was validated/verified. If it is not representative of the larger set, please describe why not (e.g., to cover a more diverse range of instances, because instances were withheld or unavailable).
- **What data does each instance consist of? "Raw" data (e.g., unprocessed text or images) or features?** In either case, please provide a description.
- **Is there a label or target associated with each instance?** If so, please provide a description.
- **Is any information missing from individual instances?** If so, please provide a description, explaining why this information is missing (e.g., because it was unavailable). This does not include intentionally removed information, but might include, e.g., redacted text.
- **Are relationships between individual instances made explicit (e.g., users' movie ratings, social network links)?** If so, please describe how these relationships are made explicit.

■ **Are there recommended data splits (e.g., training, development/validation, testing)?** If so, please provide a description of these splits, explaining the rationale behind them.

■ **Are there any errors, sources of noise, or redundancies in the dataset?** If so, please provide a description.

■ **Is the dataset self-contained, or does it link to or otherwise rely on external resources (e.g., websites, tweets, other datasets)?** If it links to or relies on external resources, (a) are there guarantees that they will exist, and remain constant, over time; (b) are there official archival versions of the complete dataset (i.e., including the external resources as they existed at the time the dataset was created); (c) are there any restrictions (e.g., licenses, fees) associated with any of the external resources that might apply to a future user? Please provide descriptions of all external resources and any restrictions associated with them, as well as links or other access points, as appropriate.

■ **Does the dataset contain data that might be considered confidential (e.g., data that is protected by legal privilege or by doctor–patient confidentiality, data that includes the content of individuals' non-public communications)?** If so, please provide a description.

■ **Does the dataset contain data that, if viewed directly, might be offensive, insulting, threatening, or might otherwise cause anxiety?** If so, please describe why.

■ **Does the dataset relate to people?** If not, you may skip the remaining questions in this section.

■ **Does the dataset identify any subpopulations (e.g., by age, gender)?** If so, please describe how these subpopulations are identified and provide a description of their respective distributions within the dataset. Is it possible to identify individuals (i.e., one or more natural persons), either directly or indirectly (i.e., in combination with other data) from the dataset? If so, please describe how.

■ **Does the dataset contain data that might be considered sensitive in any way (e.g., data that reveals racial or ethnic origins, sexual orientations, religious beliefs, political opinions or union memberships, or locations; financial or health data; biometric or genetic data; forms of government identification, such as social security numbers; criminal history)?** If so, please provide a description.

■ **Any other comments?**

3.3 Collection Process

As with the previous section, dataset creators should read through these questions prior to any data collection to flag potential issues and then provide answers once collection is complete. In addition to the goals of the prior section, the answers to questions here may provide information that allow others to reconstruct the dataset without access to it.

■ **How was the data associated with each instance acquired?** Was the data directly observable (e.g., raw text, movie ratings), reported by subjects (e.g., survey responses), or indirectly inferred/derived from other data (e.g., part-of-speech tags, model-based guesses for age or language)? If data was reported by subjects or indirectly inferred/derived from other data, was the data validated/verified? If so, please describe how.

■ **What mechanisms or procedures were used to collect the data (e.g., hardware apparatus or sensor, manual human curation, software program, software API)?** How were these mechanisms or procedures validated?

- **If the dataset is a sample from a larger set, what was the sampling strategy (e.g., deterministic, probabilistic with specific sampling probabilities)?**
- **Who was involved in the data collection process (e.g., students, crowdworkers, contractors) and how were they compensated (e.g., how much were crowdworkers paid)?**
- **Over what timeframe was the data collected?** Does this timeframe match the creation timeframe of the data associated with the instances (e.g., recent crawl of old news articles)? If not, please describe the timeframe in which the data associated with the instances was created.
- **Were any ethical review processes conducted (e.g., by an institutional review board)?** If so, please provide a description of these review processes, including the outcomes, as well as a link or other access point to any supporting documentation.
- **Does the dataset relate to people?** If not, you may skip the remainder of the questions in this section.
- **Did you collect the data from the individuals in question directly, or obtain it via third parties or other sources (e.g., websites)?**
- **Were the individuals in question notified about the data collection?** If so, please describe (or show with screenshots or other information) how notice was provided, and provide a link or other access point to, or otherwise reproduce, the exact language of the notification itself.
- **Did the individuals in question consent to the collection and use of their data?** If so, please describe (or show with screenshots or other information) how consent was requested and provided, and provide a link or other access point to, or otherwise reproduce, the exact language to which the individuals consented.
- **If consent was obtained, were the consenting individuals provided with a mechanism to revoke their consent in the future or for certain uses?** If so, please provide a description, as well as a link or other access point to the mechanism (if appropriate).
- **Has an analysis of the potential impact of the dataset and its use on data subjects (e.g., a data protection impact analysis) been conducted?** If so, please provide a description of this analysis, including the outcomes, as well as a link or other access point to any supporting documentation.
- **Any other comments?**

3.4 Preprocessing/Cleaning/Labeling

Dataset creators should read through these questions prior to any preprocessing, cleaning, or labeling and then provide answers once these tasks are complete. The questions in this section are intended to provide dataset consumers with the information they need to determine whether the "raw" data has been processed in ways that are compatible with their chosen tasks. For example, text that has been converted into a "bag-of-words" is not suitable for tasks involving word order.

- **Was any preprocessing/cleaning/labeling of the data done (e.g., discretization or bucketing, tokenization, part-of-speech tagging, SIFT feature extraction, removal of instances, processing of missing values)?** If so, please provide a description. If not, you may skip the remainder of the questions in this section.
- **Was the "raw" data saved in addition to the preprocessed/cleaned/labeled data (e.g., to support unanticipated future uses)?** If so, please provide a link or other access point to the "raw" data.

- **Is the software used to preprocess/clean/label the instances available?** If so, please provide a link or other access point.
- **Any other comments?**

3.5 Uses

These questions are intended to encourage dataset creators to reflect on the tasks for which the dataset should and should not be used. By explicitly highlighting these tasks, dataset creators can help dataset consumers to make informed decisions, thereby avoiding potential risks or harms.

- **Has the dataset been used for any tasks already?** If so, please provide a description.
- **Is there a repository that links to any or all papers or systems that use the dataset?** If so, please provide a link or other access point.
- **What (other) tasks could the dataset be used for?**
- **Is there anything about the composition of the dataset or the way it was collected and preprocessed/cleaned/labeled that might impact future uses?** For example, is there anything that a future user might need to know to avoid uses that could result in unfair treatment of individuals or groups (e.g., stereotyping, quality of service issues) or other undesirable harms (e.g., financial harms, legal risks)? If so, please provide a description. Is there anything a future user could do to mitigate these undesirable harms?
- **Are there tasks for which the dataset should not be used?** If so, please provide a description.
- **Any other comments?**

3.6 Distribution

Dataset creators should provide answers to these questions prior to distributing the dataset either internally within the entity on behalf of which the dataset was created or externally to third parties.

- Will the dataset be distributed to third parties outside of the entity (e.g., company, institution, organization) on behalf of which the dataset was created? If so, please provide a description.
- How will the dataset be distributed (e.g., tarball on website, API, GitHub)? Does the dataset have a digital object identifier (DOI)?
- When will the dataset be distributed?
- Will the dataset be distributed under a copyright or other intellectual property (IP) license, and/or under applicable terms of use (ToU)? If so, please describe this license and/or ToU, and provide a link or other access point to, or otherwise reproduce, any relevant licensing terms or ToU, as well as any fees associated with these restrictions.
- Have any third parties imposed IP-based or other restrictions on the data associated with the instances? If so, please describe these restrictions, and provide a link or other access point to, or otherwise reproduce, any relevant licensing terms, as well as any fees associated with these restrictions.
- Do any export controls or other regulatory restrictions apply to the dataset or to individual instances? If so, please describe these restrictions, and provide a link or other access point to, or otherwise reproduce, any supporting documentation.
- Any other comments?

3.7 *Maintenance*

As with the previous section, dataset creators should provide answers to these questions prior to distributing the dataset. These questions are intended to encourage dataset creators to plan for dataset maintenance and communicate this plan with dataset consumers.

- Who is supporting/hosting/maintaining the dataset?
- How can the owner/curator/manager of the dataset be contacted (e.g., email address)?
- Is there an erratum? If so, please provide a link or other access point.
- Will the dataset be updated (e.g., to correct labeling errors, add new instances, delete instances)? If so, please describe how often, by whom, and how updates will be communicated to users (e.g., mailing list, GitHub)?
- If the dataset relates to people, are there applicable limits on the retention of the data associated with the instances (e.g., were individuals in question told that their data would be retained for a fixed period of time and then deleted)? If so, please describe these limits and explain how they will be enforced.
- Will older versions of the dataset continue to be supported/hosted/maintained? If so, please describe how. If not, please describe how its obsolescence will be communicated to users.
- If others want to extend/augment/build on/contribute to the dataset, is there a mechanism for them to do so? If so, please provide a description. Will these contributions be validated/verified? If so, please describe how. If not, why not? Is there a process for communicating/distributing these contributions to other users? If so, please provide a description.
- Any other comments?

4. Impact and Challenges

Since circulating an initial draft of this paper in March 2018, datasheets for datasets have already gained traction in a number of settings. Academic researchers have adopted our proposal and released datasets with accompanying datasheets [e.g., 7, 10, 21]. Microsoft, Google, and IBM have begun to pilot datasheets for datasets internally within product teams. Researchers at Google published follow-up work on model cards that document machine learning models [18] and released a data card (a lightweight version of a datasheet) with the Open Images dataset [15]. Researchers at IBM proposed factsheets [12] that document various characteristics of AI services, including whether the datasets used to develop the services are accompanied with datasheets. Finally, the Partnership on AI, a multi-stakeholder organization focused on sharing best practices for developing and deploying responsible AI, is working on industry-wide documentation guidance that builds on datasheets, model cards, and factsheets.[1]

These initial successes have also revealed implementation challenges that may need to be addressed to support wider adoption. Chief among them is the need for dataset creators to modify the questions and workflow in section 3 based on their existing organizational infrastructure and workflows. We also note that our questions and workflow may pose challenges for dynamic datasets. If a dataset changes only infrequently, we recommend accompanying updated versions with updated datasheets.

Datasheets for datasets do not provide a complete solution to mitigating unwanted biases or potential risks or harms. Dataset creators cannot anticipate every possible use of a dataset, and identifying unwanted biases often requires additional labels indicating demographic information for individuals, which may not be available to dataset creators for reasons including those individuals' data protection and privacy [13].

When creating datasheets for datasets that relate to people, it may be necessary for dataset creators to work with experts in other domains such as anthropology. There are complex and contextual social, historical, and geographical factors that influence how best to collect a dataset in a manner that is respectful of individuals and their data protection and privacy.

Finally, creating datasheets for datasets will necessarily impose overhead on dataset creators. Although datasheets may reduce the amount of time that dataset creators spend answering one-off questions about datasets, the process of creating a datasheet will always take time, and organizational infrastructure, incentives, and workflows will need to be modified to accommodate this investment.

Despite these challenges, there are many benefits to creating datasheets for datasets. In addition to facilitating better communication between dataset creators and dataset consumers, datasheets provide the opportunity for dataset creators to distinguish themselves as prioritizing transparency and accountability. Ultimately, we believe that the benefits to the machine learning community outweigh the costs.

Note

1. https://www.partnershiponai.org/about-ml/

References

1. Don A. Andrews, James Bonta, and J. Stephen Wormith. 2006. The recent past and near future of risk and/or need assessment. *Crime & Delinquency* 52, 1 (2006), 7–27.
2. Emily M. Bender and Batya Friedman. 2018. Data Statements for Natural Language Processing: Toward Mitigating System Bias and Enabling Better Science. *Transactions of the Association for Computational Linguistics* 6 (2018), 587–604.
3. Anant P. Bhardwaj, Souvik Bhattacherjee, Amit Chavan, Amol Deshpande, Aaron J. Elmore, Samuel Madden, and Aditya G. Parameswaran. 2014. DataHub: Collaborative Data Science & Dataset Version Management at Scale. *CoRR* abs/1409.0798 (2014).
4. Tolga Bolukbasi, Kai-Wei Chang, James Y. Zou, Venkatesh Saligrama, and Adam T. Kalai. 2016. Man is to Computer Programmer as Woman is to Homemaker? Debiasing Word Embeddings. In *Advances in Neural Information Processing Systems* 29, D. D. Lee, M. Sugiyama, U. V. Luxburg, I. Guyon, and R. Garnett (Eds.). Curran Associates, Inc., Red Hook, NY, USA, 4349–4357.
5. Joy Buolamwini and Timnit Gebru. 2018. Gender Shades: Intersectional Accuracy Disparities in Commercial Gender Classification. In *Conference on Fairness, Accountability, and Transparency (FAT*)*. ACM, New York, NY, USA, 77–91.
6. James Cheney, Laura Chiticariu, and Wang-Chiew Tan. 2009. Provenance in databases: Why, how, and where. *Foundations and Trends in Databases* 1, 4 (2009), 379–474.
7. Eunsol Choi, He He, Mohit Iyyer, Mark Yatskar, Wen-tau Yih, Yejin Choi, Percy Liang, and Luke Zettlemoyer. 2018. QuAC: Question Answering in Context. *CoRR* abs/1808.07036 (2018).
8. Glennda Chui. 2017. Project will use AI to prevent or minimize electric grid failures. [Online; accessed 14-March-2018].
9. Jeffrey Dastin. 2018. Amazon scraps secret AI recruiting tool that showed bias against women. https://www.reuters.com/article/us-amazon-com-jobs-automation-insight/amazonscraps-secret-ai-recruiting-tool-that-showed-bias-against-women-idUSKCN1MK08G
10. Erkut Erdem. 2018. Datasheet for RecipeQA.

11. Clare Garvie, Alvaro Bedoya, and Jonathan Frankle. 2016. *The Perpetual Line-Up: Unregulated Police Face Recognition in America*. Georgetown Law, Center on Privacy & Technology, New Jersey Ave NW, Washington, DC.

12. Michael Hind, Sameep Mehta, Aleksandra Mojsilovic, Ravi Nair, Karthikeyan Natesan Ramamurthy, Alexandra Olteanu, and Kush R. Varshney. 2018. Increasing Trust in AI Services through Supplier's Declarations of Conformity. *CoRR* abs/1808.07261 (2018).

13. Kenneth Holstein, Jennifer Wortman Vaughan, Hal Daumé III, Miroslav Dudík, and Hanna M. Wallach. 2019. Improving Fairness in Machine Learning Systems: What Do Industry Practitioners Need?. In *2019 ACM CHI Conference on Human Factors in Computing Systems*.

14. Gary B. Huang, Manu Ramesh, Tamara Berg, and Erik Learned-Miller. 2007. *Labeled faces in the wild: A database for studying face recognition in unconstrained environments*. Technical Report 07-49. University of Massachusetts Amherst.

15. Ivan Krasin, Tom Duerig, Neil Alldrin, Vittorio Ferrari, Sami Abu-El-Haija, Alina Kuznetsova, Hassan Rom, Jasper Uijlings, Stefan Popov, Shahab Kamali, Matteo Malloci, Jordi Pont-Tuset, Andreas Veit, Serge Belongie, Victor Gomes, Abhinav Gupta, Chen Sun, Gal Chechik, David Cai, Zheyun Feng, Dhyanesh Narayanan, and Kevin Murphy. 2017. *OpenImages: A public dataset for large-scale multi-label and multi-class image classification*.

16. Tom CW Lin. 2012. The new investor. *UCLA Law Review* 60 (2012), 678.

17. G. Mann and C. O'Neil. 2016. Hiring Algorithms Are Not Neutral. https://hbr.org/2016/12/hiring-algorithms-are-not-neutral.

18. Margaret Mitchell, Simone Wu, Andrew Zaldivar, Parker Barnes, Lucy Vasserman, Ben Hutchinson, Elena Spitzer, Inioluwa Deborah Raji, and Timnit Gebru. 2019. Model Cards for Model Reporting. In *Proceedings of the Conference on Fairness, Accountability, and Transparency (FAT* '19)*. ACM, New York, NY, USA, 220–229. https://doi.org/10.1145/3287560.3287596 Datasheets for Datasets 13

19. Mary Catherine O'Connor. 2017. How AI Could Smarten Up Our Water System. [Online; accessed 14-March-2018].

20. Bo Pang and Lillian Lee. 2004. A sentimental education: Sentiment analysis using subjectivity summarization based on minimum cuts. In *Proceedings of the 42nd annual meeting on Association for Computational Linguistics*. Association for Computational Linguistics, Association for Computational Linguistics, Stroudsburg, PA, USA, 271.

21. Ismaïla Seck, Khouloud Dahmane, Pierre Duthon, and Gaëlle Loosli. 2018. Baselines and a datasheet for the Cerema AWP dataset. *CoRR* abs/1806.04016 (2018). http://arxiv.org/abs/1806.04016

22. Doha Suppy Systems. 2017. Facial Recognition. [Online; accessed 14-March-2018].

23. World Economic Forum Global Future Council on Human Rights 2016–2018. 2018. How to Prevent Discriminatory Outcomes in Machine Learning. https://www.weforum.org/whitepapers/how-to-prevent-discriminatory-outcomes-inmachinelearning.

SURVEILLANCE AND POWER

4

Ever smaller, more precise tracking devices allow organizations to track their workers with a wristband[1] or universities to follow their students' location.[2] When an organization peers inside a particular employee's phone, we have learned that this may be a privacy violation. However, when an organization systematically tracks their workers, pervasively over space and time, and then uses that information for employment action, we call that surveillance. Privacy and surveillance are related, but scholars studying surveillance see investigations into privacy as missing the impact and power dynamic when individuals are surveilled.

New forms of data collection—online and offline—make surveillance more common and even its own industry. Small devices in our home are "always on," small trackers online watch our every move, CCTV cameras can follow us outside, our phones provide location tracking for an industry devoted to tracking individuals! As Shoshana Zuboff explains, *surveillance capitalism* is a "new economic order that claims human experience as free raw material for hidden commercial practices of extraction, prediction, and sales."[3] For Zuboff, the industry of surveilling individuals is parasitic, feasting off less powerful individuals.

Surveillance can be by a single actor, such as an employer or government agency. However, surveillance is also the byproduct of the systematic collection, aggregation, and use of individual data by many, related companies. Companies that buy and sell consumer data create a *destructive demand* where their thirst for consumer data pressures consumer-facing firms to collect and sell increasing amounts of information without regard to how the collection breaches privacy expectations.[4] As such, these "data traffickers,"[5]—data aggregators, data brokers, and ad networks that are in the business of buying and selling and aggregating consumer data—create a system of surveillance online.

Complicating matters is that the companies that contribute to consumers being surveilled do not incur the cost of the possible harm of surveillance. When a steel company sells their product to a customer, the community incurs the "cost" of pollution to make that steel. This is an example of a *negative externality*, which exists when the harm done to others is not taken into account in the immediate transaction. More complicated is when the harmful effect is compounded by many parties in an industry acting in a similar way. For example, a manufacturing firm may account for the harmful effects on the local community of the pollution it produces. However, the *aggregated* harm of pollution from manufacturers worldwide becomes a problem for society in general through global warming.[6] Aggregated negative externalities

DOI: 10.1201/9781003278290-24

are a consequence of "everyone does it"—the harm results from the fact that the practice is pervasive in an industry.

This is important for the ethics of data and analytics since companies collecting, aggregating, selling, and using consumer data create a negative externality when they contribute to a larger system of surveillance. In other words, when an app collects location data and sells it to location data aggregators, the individual being tracked does not know about the tracking and cannot "take back" their data. Normally, in a functioning market, the harms emanating from a contract or exchange are felt by those contracting parties. When a large store sells me a toaster that does not work, I make the store take back the toaster and their reputation takes a hit (a little bit!) by selling a defective product. If they sell enough defective products, consumers know and stop going to the store.

While a single tracker on a website may violate the privacy of an individual, the systematic collection by all the data traffickers online creates a surveilled space. Barocas and Nissenbaum argue that this is possible because the current big data industry collects consumer data based on the implied agreement to be tracked by consumers being online. Usually, informed consent online serves as protection against surveillance and the imbalance of power: by asking permission to be watched and recorded, individuals have a tool to not being surveilled. However, the broad collection of consumer data with persistent identifiers facilitates the tracking and targeting of consumers even with privacy notices and removes the fig leaf protections consumers believed they had over corporate surveillance.[7]

As our readings will illustrate, surveillance is all about power. Surveillance is the persistent tracking of individuals—tracking that cannot be avoided—to control the individual being surveilled. Individuals who are surveilled lose power to the actors who are surveilling. The question for us is how are our data analytics programs contributing to surveillance and the creation of surveilled spaces? What design decisions could improve the program and lessen our contribution to surveillance? These readings help us identify the factors that contribute surveillance—what makes something an issue of surveillance rather than a privacy violation—as well as the consequences of surveillance and surveilled spaces. In other words, what makes surveillance so bad?

Summary of Readings

In the excerpt from "From Big Brother to Electronic Panopticon," David Lyon examines how concepts of surveillance from George Orwell's *1984* and Michel Foucault's Panopticon can be seen in current electronic surveillance. First, Lyon links Orwell's *1984* to electronic surveillance in noting that in Orwell's book "undetected surveillance keeps those watched subordinate by means of uncertainty." Uncertainty in being watched is a continual theme for Lyon. In surveilled spaces, people behave when they think they are being watched ... even if they don't know for sure. Orwell also highlights who feels "the hard edge of exclusionary and punitive surveillance" which leads to the question: who is the target of surveillance and is it disproportionately felt by one group more than another. Lyon here is asking us to identify who is in power and who is disempowered due to the "hard edge" of surveillance. However, Lyon focuses most on the Panopticon—originally introduced by Jeremy Bentham as a more efficient prison, but then applied by Foucault into modern times.[8] The Panopticon offers a way to exploit uncertainty as a means of controlling subordinates: a tall guard tower allows a few guards to watch over and control many prisoners who are kept in a semi-circle around the tower. Lighting keeps the prisoners from knowing for certain if they are being watched at any one time. For Foucault, the panopticon is the "perfection of power": "a machine for creating and sustaining a power relation independent of the person who exercises it." Linking back to Winner's terminology from the first chapter, the panopticon is a technology with inherent politics.

This view of surveillance is intimately linked to power. In applying Lyon's concept of surveillance to a data analytics program, one would examine how the proposed program leads to (1) the accumulation of information about individuals and (2) the direct control of those individuals (supervision of subordinates for Lyon). We might also add a third that is assumed but further explained by our next reading: (3) the inability to avoid the collection of information and control of individuals. Surveillance is a tool to not only know information about someone but to control them.

Julie Cohen differentiates her approach to surveillance from work on privacy in this excerpt of "Privacy, Visibility, Transparency, and Exposure."[9] Cohen refocuses us on the surveilled individual and *space* rather than just the type of information gathered about the person as many privacy scholars do. Professor Cohen suggests that studies of information privacy fall short of encompassing the idea of surveillance as the "direct visual observation by centralized authority figures" (p. 184). Rather than requiring a centralized authority, current technology is illustrative of an assemblage of firms that constitute surveillance. Surveillance fosters a passivity described by Cohen as "a ceding of power over space" which "alters the spaces and places of everyday life." Importantly, surveillance "places individuals under a twofold disability: the targets of surveillance cannot entirely avoid the gaze (except by avoiding the place) and also cannot identify the watchers." Note the similarity to the panopticon. Surveillance thus alters the balance of power. Further, and important for Cohen, surveillance instills an expectation of being surveilled, and this lowering of expectations and creation of passivity is part of the harm of being surveilled. In analyzing a data analytics program according to Cohen, one would examine if the program contributes to surveillance where the target (1) cannot entirely avoid the gaze, (2) cannot identify the watchers, and (3) thus experience a ceding of power over the surveilled space.

Related Cases

Two cases are related to the surveillance readings. First, the case of the location data aggregators, "Twelve Million Phones, One Dataset, Zero Privacy,"[10] provides an overview of how individuals' location data is gathered, stored, and sold by location data aggregators. The information allows people and companies to track how people move, where they live, and who they are with. The information can also be used to identify what stores someone frequents and whether they voted or attended a rally. The question for data analytics would be *how do these companies contribute to a surveilled space, if at all? What are legitimate and illegitimate uses for this data? Who is at fault?*

Second, Clearview AI is a facial recognition company whose product is used by a range of customers from those vetting babysitters to law enforcement. Their image data is broader than competitors since the company scrapes images from social networking sites. Clearview AI's defense against critiques (and lawsuits) is that they have a first amendment right to use the images they procured as they wish—a right to create and disseminate information they scraped from websites. The argument is similar to cases when newspapers claimed a right to publish classified documents and when pharmacies claimed a right to sell prescription information they had received from doctors.[11] The question for data analytics would be *how does the use of facial recognition programs contribute to surveilled spaces? Is Clearview doing anything wrong?*

Notes

1. Yeginsu, Ceylan. 2018. "If Workers Slack Off, the Wristband Will Know. (And Amazon Has a Patent for It.)," *The New York Times*. February 1, 2018. https://www.nytimes.com/2018/02/01/technology/amazon-wristband-tracking-privacy.html

2. Hollister, Sean. 2020. "U.S. Colleges Are Trying to Install Location Tracking Apps on Students' Phones," *The Verge*. January 28. 2020. https://www.theverge.com/2020/1/28/21112456/spotteredu-degree-analytics-student-location-tracking-app-attendance

3. Shoshana Zuboff, "Big Other: Surveillance Capitalism and the Prospects of an Information Civilization," *Journal of Information Technology* 30, no. 1 (2015): 75–89; S. Zuboff, *The Age of Surveillance Capitalism: The Fight for a Human Future at the New Frontier of Power* (New York: Hachette Book Group, 2019).

4. Kirsten Martin, "Ethical Issues in the Big Data Industry," *MIS Quarterly Executive* 14, no. 2 (2015): 67–85.

5. Lauren Henry Scholz, "Privacy Remedies," *Ind. LJ* 94 (2019): 653. Data traffickers are those third-party companies, with no relationship with the consumer, that traffic (buy, sell, trade, etc.) personal data.

6. Martin, "Ethical Issues in the Big Data Industry."

7. Solon Barocas and Helen Nissenbaum, "Big Data's End Run around Anonymity and Consent," in *Privacy, Big Data, and the Public Good: Frameworks for Engagement*, ed. Julia Lane et al. (New York: Cambridge University Press, 2014).

8. As a reminder, Jeremey Bentham was an original writer on utilitarianism from Chapter 2: ethical decisions are those that create the most positive consequences. For utilitarians, the harm to a few or violation of a few rights would be justified for a beneficial end.

9. Julie E. Cohen, "Privacy, Visibility, Transparency, and Exposure," *The University of Chicago Law Review* (2008): 181–201.

10. Thompson, Stuart A. and Charlie Warzel. 2019. *The New York Times*. December 19, 2019. https://www.nytimes.com/interactive/2019/12/19/opinion/location-tracking-cell-phone.html

11. Hill, Kashmir. 2020. "Facial Recognition Start-Up Mounts a First Amendment Defense," *The New York Times*. August 11, 2020. https://www.nytimes.com/2020/08/11/technology/clearview-floyd-abrams.html

Chapter 4.1

Twelve Million Phones, One Dataset, Zero Privacy*

Stuart A. Thompson and Charlie Warzel

EVERY MINUTE OF EVERY DAY, everywhere on the planet, dozens of companies—largely unregulated, little scrutinized—are logging the movements of tens of millions of people with mobile phones and storing the information in gigantic data files. The Times Privacy Project obtained one such file, by far the largest and most sensitive ever to be reviewed by journalists. It holds more than 50 billion location pings from the phones of more than 12 million Americans as they moved through several major cities, including Washington, New York, San Francisco, and Los Angeles.

Each piece of information in this file represents the precise location of a single smartphone over a period of several months in 2016 and 2017. The data was provided to Times Opinion by sources who asked to remain anonymous because they were not authorized to share it and could face severe penalties for doing so. The sources of the information said they had grown alarmed about how it might be abused and urgently wanted to inform the public and lawmakers.

After spending months sifting through the data, tracking the movements of people across the country and speaking with dozens of data companies, technologists, lawyers and academics who study this field, we feel the same sense of alarm. In the cities that the data file covers, it tracks people from nearly every neighborhood and block, whether they live in mobile homes in Alexandria, Va., or luxury towers in Manhattan.

One search turned up more than a dozen people visiting the Playboy Mansion, some overnight. Without much effort we spotted visitors to the estates of Johnny Depp, Tiger Woods and Arnold Schwarzenegger, connecting the devices' owners to the residences indefinitely.

If you lived in one of the cities the dataset covers and use apps that share your location—anything from weather apps to local news apps to coupon savers—you could be in there, too.

If you could see the full trove, you might never use your phone the same way again.

The data reviewed by Times Opinion didn't come from a telecom or giant tech company, nor did it come from a governmental surveillance operation. It originated from a location data

---

* Thompson, Stuart A. and Charlie Warzel. 2019. *The New York Times*. December 19, 2019. https://www.nytimes .com/interactive/2019/12/19/opinion/location-tracking-cell-phone.html. Reprinted by permission.

company, one of dozens quietly collecting precise movements using software slipped onto mobile phone apps. You've probably never heard of most of the companies—and yet to anyone who has access to this data, your life is an open book. They can see the places you go every moment of the day, whom you meet with or spend the night with, where you pray, whether you visit a methadone clinic, a psychiatrist's office or a massage parlor.

The Times and other news organizations have reported on smartphone tracking in the past. But never with a data set so large. Even still, this file represents just a small slice of what's collected and sold every day by the location tracking industry—surveillance so omnipresent in our digital lives that it now seems impossible for anyone to avoid.

It doesn't take much imagination to conjure the powers such always-on surveillance can provide an authoritarian regime like China's. Within America's own representative democracy, citizens would surely rise up in outrage if the government attempted to mandate that every person above the age of 12 carry a tracking device that revealed their location 24 hours a day. Yet, in the decade since Apple's App Store was created, Americans have, app by app, consented to just such a system run by private companies. Now, as the decade ends, tens of millions of Americans, including many children, find themselves carrying spies in their pockets during the day and leaving them beside their beds at night—even though the corporations that control their data are far less accountable than the government would be.

"The seduction of these consumer products is so powerful that it blinds us to the possibility that there is another way to get the benefits of the technology without the invasion of privacy. But there is," said William Staples, founding director of the Surveillance Studies Research Center at the University of Kansas. "All the companies collecting this location information act as what I have called Tiny Brothers, using a variety of data sponges to engage in everyday surveillance."

In this and subsequent articles we'll reveal what we've found and why it has so shaken us. We'll ask you to consider the national security risks the existence of this kind of data creates and the specter of what such precise, always-on human tracking might mean in the hands of corporations and the government. We'll also look at legal and ethical justifications that companies rely on to collect our precise locations and the deceptive techniques they use to lull us into sharing it.

Today, it's perfectly legal to collect and sell all this information. In the United States, as in most of the world, no federal law limits what has become a vast and lucrative trade in human tracking. Only internal company policies and the decency of individual employees prevent those with access to the data from, say, stalking an estranged spouse or selling the evening commute of an intelligence officer to a hostile foreign power.

Companies say the data is shared only with vetted partners. As a society, we're choosing simply to take their word for that, displaying a blithe faith in corporate beneficence that we don't extend to far less intrusive yet more heavily regulated industries. Even if these companies are acting with the soundest moral code imaginable, there's ultimately no foolproof way they can secure the data from falling into the hands of a foreign security service. Closer to home, on a smaller yet no less troubling scale, there are often few protections to stop an individual analyst with access to such data from tracking an ex-lover or a victim of abuse.

A Diary of Your Every Movement

THE COMPANIES THAT COLLECT all this information on your movements justify their business on the basis of three claims: People consent to be tracked, the data is anonymous and the data is secure.

None of those claims hold up, based on the file we've obtained and our review of company practices.

Yes, the location data contains billions of data points with no identifiable information like names or email addresses. But it's child's play to connect real names to the dots that appear on the maps.

Here's what that looks like.

IN MOST CASES, ascertaining a home location and an office location was enough to identify a person. Consider your daily commute: Would any other smartphone travel directly between your house and your office every day?

Describing location data as anonymous is "a completely false claim" that has been debunked in multiple studies, Paul Ohm, a law professor and privacy researcher at the Georgetown University Law Center, told us. "Really precise, longitudinal geolocation information is absolutely impossible to anonymize."

"D.N.A.," he added, "is probably the only thing that's harder to anonymize than precise geo-location information."

Yet companies continue to claim that the data are anonymous. In marketing materials and at trade conferences, anonymity is a major selling point—key to allaying concerns over such invasive monitoring.

To evaluate the companies' claims, we turned most of our attention to identifying people in positions of power. With the help of publicly available information, like home addresses, we easily identified and then tracked scores of notables. We followed military officials with security clearances as they drove home at night. We tracked law enforcement officers as they took their kids to school. We watched high-powered lawyers (and their guests) as they traveled from private jets to vacation properties. We did not name any of the people we identified without their permission.

The data set is large enough that it surely points to scandal and crime but our purpose wasn't to dig up dirt. We wanted to document the risk of underregulated surveillance.

Watching dots move across a map sometimes revealed hints of faltering marriages, evidence of drug addiction, records of visits to psychological facilities.

Connecting a sanitized ping to an actual human in time and place could feel like reading someone else's diary.

In one case, we identified Mary Millben, a singer based in Virginia who has performed for three presidents, including President Trump. She was invited to the service at the Washington National Cathedral the morning after the president's inauguration. That's where we first found her.

She remembers how, surrounded by dignitaries and the first family, she was moved by the music echoing through the recesses of the cathedral while members of both parties joined together in prayer. All the while, the apps on her phone were also monitoring the moment, recording her position and the length of her stay in meticulous detail. For the advertisers who might buy access to the data, the intimate prayer service could well supply some profitable marketing insights.

"To know that you have a list of places I have been, and my phone is connected to that, that's scary," Ms. Millben told us. "What's the business of a company benefiting off of knowing where I am? That seems a little dangerous to me."

Like many people we identified in the data, Ms. Millben said she was careful about limiting how she shared her location. Yet like many of them, she also couldn't name the app that might have collected it. Our privacy is only as secure as the least secure app on our device.

"That makes me uncomfortable," she said. "I'm sure that makes every other person uncomfortable, to know that companies can have free rein to take your data, locations, whatever else they're using. It is disturbing."

The inauguration weekend yielded a trove of personal stories and experiences: elite attendees at presidential ceremonies, religious observers at church services, supporters assembling across the National Mall—all surveilled and recorded permanently in rigorous detail.

Protesters were tracked just as rigorously. After the pings of Trump supporters, basking in victory, vanished from the National Mall on Friday evening, they were replaced hours later by those of participants in the Women's March, as a crowd of nearly half a million descended on the capital. Examining just a photo from the event, you might be hard-pressed to tie a face to a name. But in our data, pings at the protest connected to clear trails through the data, documenting the lives of protesters in the months before and after the protest, including where they lived and worked.

We spotted a senior official at the Department of Defense walking through the Women's March, beginning on the National Mall and moving past the Smithsonian National Museum of American History that afternoon. His wife was also on the mall that day, something we discovered after tracking him to his home in Virginia. Her phone was also beaming out location data, along with the phones of several neighbors.

The official's data trail also led to a high school, homes of friends, a visit to Joint Base Andrews, workdays spent in the Pentagon and a ceremony at Joint Base Myer-Henderson Hall with President Barack Obama in 2017 (nearly a dozen more phones were tracked there, too).

Inauguration Day weekend was marked by other protests—and riots. Hundreds of protesters, some in black hoods and masks, gathered north of the National Mall that Friday, eventually setting fire to a limousine near Franklin Square. The data documented those rioters, too. Filtering the data to that precise time and location led us to the doorsteps of some who were there. Police were present as well, many with faces obscured by riot gear. The data led us to the homes of at least two police officers who had been at the scene.

As revealing as our searches of Washington were, we were relying on just one slice of data, sourced from one company, focused on one city, covering less than one year. Location data companies collect orders of magnitude more information every day than the totality of what Times Opinion received.

Data firms also typically draw on other sources of information that we didn't use. We lacked the mobile advertising IDs or other identifiers that advertisers often combine with demographic information like home ZIP codes, age, gender, even phone numbers and emails to create detailed audience profiles used in targeted advertising. When datasets are combined, privacy risks can be amplified. Whatever protections existed in the location dataset can crumble with the addition of only one or two other sources.

There are dozens of companies profiting off such data daily across the world—by collecting it directly from smartphones, creating new technology to better capture the data or creating audience profiles for targeted advertising (Figure 4.1.1).

The full collection of companies can feel dizzying, as it's constantly changing and seems impossible to pin down. Many use technical and nuanced language that may be confusing to average smartphone users.

While many of them have been involved in the business of tracking us for years, the companies themselves are unfamiliar to most Americans. (Companies can work with data derived from GPS sensors, Bluetooth beacons and other sources. Not all companies in the location data business collect, buy, sell or work with granular location data.)

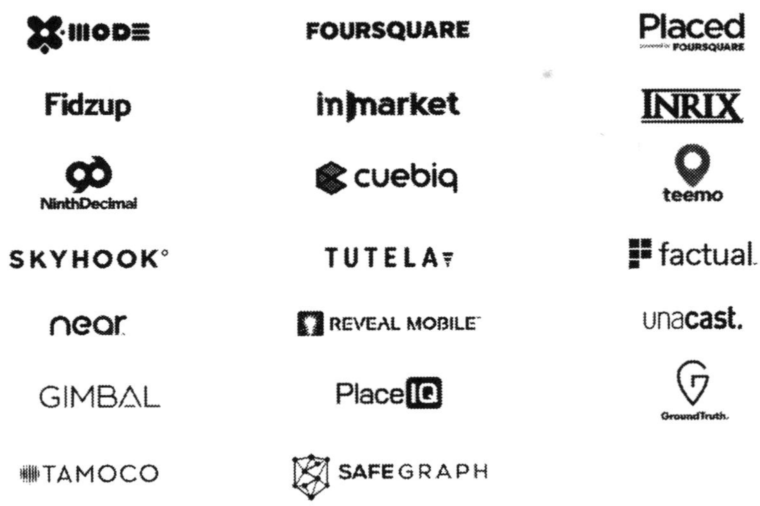

Figure 4.1.1 A selection of companies working in the location data business. Sources: MightySignal, LUMA Partners, and AppFigures.

Location data companies generally downplay the risks of collecting such revealing information at scale. Many also say they're not very concerned about potential regulation or software updates that could make it more difficult to collect location data.

"No, it doesn't really keep us up at night," Brian Czarny, chief marketing officer at Factual, one such company, said. He added that Factual does not resell detailed data like the information we reviewed. "We don't feel like anybody should be doing that because it's a risk to the whole business," he said.

In absence of a federal privacy law, the industry has largely relied on self-regulation. Several industry groups offer ethical guidelines meant to govern it. Factual joined the Mobile Marketing Association, along with many other data location and marketing companies, in drafting a pledge intended to improve its self-regulation. The pledge is slated to be released next year.

States are starting to respond with their own laws. The California Consumer Protection Act goes into effect next year and adds new protections for residents there, like allowing them to ask companies to delete their data or prevent its sale. But aside from a few new requirements, the law could leave the industry largely unencumbered.

"If a private company is legally collecting location data, they're free to spread it or share it however they want," said Calli Schroeder, a lawyer for the privacy and data protection company VeraSafe.

The companies are required to disclose very little about their data collection. By law, companies need only describe their practices in their privacy policies, which tend to be dense legal documents that few people read and even fewer can truly understand.

Everything Can be Hacked

DOES IT REALLY MATTER that your information isn't actually anonymous? Location data companies argue that your data is safe—that it poses no real risk because it's stored on guarded servers. This assurance has been undermined by the parade of publicly reported data breaches—to

	A	B	C	D	E	F
	User I.D.	Date	Time	Latitude	Longitude	Time at Location
1	User I.D.	Date	Time	Latitude	Longitude	Time at Location
2	2292	1/3/16	9:22 AM	38.9028	-77.0416	3612
3	1479	1/15/16	5:46 AM	38.9038	-77.0405	1054
4	8043	1/2/16	6:24 AM	38.9017	-77.0397	1385
5	3225	1/27/16	1:47 PM	38.9014	-77.0406	805
6	10980	1/27/16	12:49 PM	38.9021	-77.0403	629
7	4725	1/27/16	10:13 PM	38.9024	-77.0401	2987
8	3346	1/24/16	4:55 AM	38.9030	-77.0403	2785
9	9011	1/17/16	11:25 PM	38.9035	-77.0399	997
10	10435	1/20/16	5:10 PM	38.9014	-77.0401	1360
11	5209	1/16/16	6:35 AM	38.9037	-77.0382	659
12	9100	1/10/16	12:52 PM	38.9039	-77.0406	1007
13	2963	1/18/16	11:51 PM	38.9041	-77.0420	1771
14	2587	1/18/16	3:44 PM	38.9026	-77.0405	4777
15	8036	1/17/16	4:11 PM	38.9038	-77.0408	840
16	8868	1/29/16	4:37 AM	38.9013	-77.0421	1152
17	4737	1/8/16	5:02 PM	38.9035	-77.0402	731
18	10627	1/20/16	6:35 PM	38.9033	-77.0399	2167
19	6491	1/6/16	2:41 AM	38.9037	-77.0415	3150
20	4866	1/15/16	5:32 PM	38.9033	-77.0410	4248
21	3317	2/1/16	12:55 AM	38.9036	-77.0406	4239

Figure 4.1.2   The data contains simple information like date, latitude and longitude, making it easy to inspect, download, and transfer. Note: Values are randomized to protect sources and device owners.

say nothing of breaches that don't make headlines. In truth, sensitive information can be easily transferred or leaked, as evidenced by this very story (Figure 4.1.2).

We're constantly shedding data, for example, by surfing the internet or making credit card purchases. But location data is different. Our precise locations are used fleetingly in the moment for a targeted ad or notification, but then repurposed indefinitely for much more profitable ends, like tying your purchases to billboard ads you drove past on the freeway. Many apps that use your location, like weather services, work perfectly well without your precise location—but collecting your location feeds a lucrative secondary business of analyzing, licensing and transferring that information to third parties.

For many Americans, the only real risk they face from having their information exposed would be embarrassment or inconvenience. But for others, like survivors of abuse, the risks could be substantial. And who can say what practices or relationships any given individual might want to keep private, to withhold from friends, family, employers or the government? We found hundreds of pings in mosques and churches, abortion clinics, queer spaces and other sensitive areas.

In one case, we observed a change in the regular movements of a Microsoft engineer. He made a visit one Tuesday afternoon to the main Seattle campus of a Microsoft competitor, Amazon. The following month, he started a new job at Amazon. It took minutes to identify him as Ben Broili, a manager now for Amazon Prime Air, a drone delivery service.

"I can't say I'm surprised," Mr. Broili told us in early December. "But knowing that you all can get ahold of it and comb through and place me to see where I work and live—that's weird." That we could so easily discern that Mr. Broili was out on a job interview raises some obvious questions, like: Could the internal location surveillance of executives and employees become standard corporate practice?

Mr. Broili wasn't worried about apps cataloguing his every move, but he said he felt unsure about whether the tradeoff between the services offered by the apps and the sacrifice of privacy was worth it. "It's an awful lot of data," he said. "And I really still don't understand how it's being used. I'd have to see how the other companies were weaponizing or monetizing it to make that call."

If this kind of location data makes it easy to keep tabs on employees, it makes it just as simple to stalk celebrities. Their private conduct—even in the dead of night, in residences and far from paparazzi—could come under even closer scrutiny.

Reporters hoping to evade other forms of surveillance by meeting in person with a source might want to rethink that practice. Every major newsroom covered by the data contained dozens of pings; we easily traced one Washington Post journalist through Arlington, Va.

In other cases, there were detours to hotels and late-night visits to the homes of prominent people. One person, plucked from the data in Los Angeles nearly at random, was found traveling to and from roadside motels multiple times, for visits of only a few hours each time.

While these pointillist pings don't in themselves reveal a complete picture, a lot can be gleaned by examining the date, time and length of time at each point.

Large data companies like Foursquare—perhaps the most familiar name in the location data business—say they don't sell detailed location data like the kind reviewed for this story but rather use it to inform analysis, such as measuring whether you entered a store after seeing an ad on your mobile phone.

But a number of companies do sell the detailed data. Buyers are typically data brokers and advertising companies. But some of them have little to do with consumer advertising, including financial institutions, geospatial analysis companies and real estate investment firms that can process and analyze such large quantities of information. They might pay more than $1 million for a tranche of data, according to a former location data company employee who agreed to speak anonymously.

Location data is also collected and shared alongside a mobile advertising ID, a supposedly anonymous identifier about 30 digits long that allows advertisers and other businesses to tie activity together across apps. The ID is also used to combine location trails with other information like your name, home address, email, phone number or even an identifier tied to your Wi-Fi network.

The data can change hands in almost real time, so fast that your location could be transferred from your smartphone to the app's servers and exported to third parties in milliseconds. This is how, for example, you might see an ad for a new car sometime after walking through a dealership.

That data can then be resold, copied, pirated, and abused. There's no way you can ever retrieve it.

Location data is about far more than consumers seeing a few more relevant ads. This information provides critical intelligence for big businesses. The Weather Channel app's parent company, for example, analyzed users' location data for hedge funds, according to a lawsuit filed in Los Angeles this year that was triggered by Times reporting. And Foursquare received much attention in 2016 after using its data trove to predict that after an E. coli crisis, Chipotle's sales would drop by 30 percent in the coming months. Its same-store sales ultimately fell 29.7 percent.

Much of the concern over location data has focused on telecom giants like Verizon and AT&T, which have been selling location data to third parties for years. Last year, Motherboard, Vice's technology website, found that once the data was sold, it was being shared to help bounty hunters find specific cellphones in real time. The resulting scandal forced the telecom giants to pledge they would stop selling location movements to data brokers.

Yet no law prohibits them from doing so.

Location data is transmitted from your phone via software development kits, or SDKs. as they're known in the trade. The kits are small programs that can be used to build features within an app. They make it easy for app developers to simply include location-tracking features, a useful component of services like weather apps. Because they're so useful and easy to use, SDKs are embedded in thousands of apps. Facebook, Google, and Amazon, for example, have extremely popular SDKs that allow smaller apps to connect to bigger companies' ad platforms or help provide web traffic analytics or payment infrastructure.

But they could also sit on an app and collect location data while providing no real service back to the app. Location companies may pay the apps to be included—collecting valuable data that can be monetized.

"If you have an SDK that's frequently collecting location data, it is more than likely being resold across the industry," said Nick Hall, chief executive of the data marketplace company VenPath.

The 'Holy Grail' for Marketers

IF THIS INFORMATION IS SO SENSITIVE, why is it collected in the first place?

For brands, following someone's precise movements is key to understanding the "customer journey"—every step of the process from seeing an ad to buying a product. It's the Holy Grail of advertising, one marketer said, the complete picture that connects all of our interests and online activity with our real-world actions.

Once they have the complete customer journey, companies know a lot about what we want, what we buy and what made us buy it. Other groups have begun to find ways to use it too. Political campaigns could analyze the interests and demographics of rally attendees and use that information to shape their messages to try to manipulate particular groups. Governments around the world could have a new tool to identify protestors.

Pointillist location data also has some clear benefits to society. Researchers can use the raw data to provide key insights for transportation studies and government planners. The City Council of Portland, Ore., unanimously approved a deal to study traffic and transit by monitoring millions of cellphones. UNICEF announced a plan to use aggregated mobile location data to study epidemics, natural disasters and demographics.

For individual consumers, the value of constant tracking is less tangible. And the lack of transparency from the advertising and tech industries raises still more concerns.

Does a coupon app need to sell second-by-second location data to other companies to be profitable? Does that really justify allowing companies to track millions and potentially expose our private lives?

Data companies say users consent to tracking when they agree to share their location. But those consent screens rarely make clear how the data is being packaged and sold. If companies were clearer about what they were doing with the data, would anyone agree to share it?

What about data collected years ago, before hacks and leaks made privacy a forefront issue? Should it still be used, or should it be deleted for good?

If it's possible that data stored securely today can easily be hacked, leaked or stolen, is this kind of data worth that risk?

Is all of this surveillance and risk worth it merely so that we can be served slightly more relevant ads? Or so that hedge fund managers can get richer?

The companies profiting from our every move can't be expected to voluntarily limit their practices. Congress has to step in to protect Americans' needs as consumers and rights as citizens.

Until then, one thing is certain: We are living in the world's most advanced surveillance system. This system wasn't created deliberately. It was built through the interplay of technological advance and the profit motive. It was built to make money. The greatest trick technology companies ever played was persuading society to surveil itself.

Chapter 4.2

The Secretive Company That Might End Privacy as We Know It[*]

Kashmir Hill

A little-known start-up helps law enforcement match photos of unknown people to their online images—and "might lead to a dystopian future or something," a backer says.

Until recently, Hoan Ton-That's greatest hits included an obscure iPhone game and an app that let people put Donald Trump's distinctive yellow hair on their own photos.

Then Mr. Ton-That—an Australian techie and onetime model—did something momentous: He invented a tool that could end your ability to walk down the street anonymously, and provided it to hundreds of law enforcement agencies, ranging from local cops in Florida to the F.B.I. and the Department of Homeland Security.

His tiny company, Clearview AI, devised a groundbreaking facial recognition app. You take a picture of a person, upload it and get to see public photos of that person, along with links to where those photos appeared. The system—whose backbone is a database of more than three billion images that Clearview claims to have scraped from Facebook, YouTube, Venmo, and millions of other websites—goes far beyond anything ever constructed by the United States government or Silicon Valley giants (Figure 4.2.1).

Federal and state law enforcement officers said that while they had only limited knowledge of how Clearview works and who is behind it, they had used its app to help solve shoplifting, identity theft, credit card fraud, murder and child sexual exploitation cases.

Until now, technology that readily identifies everyone based on his or her face has been taboo because of its radical erosion of privacy. Tech companies capable of releasing such a tool have refrained from doing so; in 2011, Google's chairman at the time said it was the one technology the company had held back because it could be used "in a very bad way." Some large cities, including San Francisco, have barred police from using facial recognition technology.

[*] Hill, Kashmir. 2020. "The Secretive Company That Might End Privacy as We Know It," *New York Times.* Published January 18, 2020. Updated March 18, 2021. https://www.nytimes.com/2020/01/18/technology/clearview-privacy-facial-recognition.html. Reprinted by permission.

DOI: 10.1201/9781003278290-26

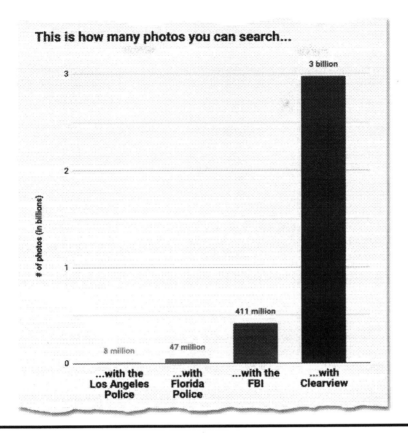

Figure 4.2.1 A chart from marketing materials that Clearview provided to law enforcement. Source: Clearview.

But without public scrutiny, more than 600 law enforcement agencies have started using Clearview in the past year, according to the company, which declined to provide a list. The computer code underlying its app, analyzed by The New York Times, includes programming language to pair it with augmented-reality glasses; users would potentially be able to identify every person they saw. The tool could identify activists at a protest or an attractive stranger on the subway, revealing not just their names but where they lived, what they did and whom they knew.

And it's not just law enforcement: Clearview has also licensed the app to at least a handful of companies for security purposes.

"The weaponization possibilities of this are endless," said Eric Goldman, co-director of the High Tech Law Institute at Santa Clara University. "Imagine a rogue law enforcement officer who wants to stalk potential romantic partners, or a foreign government using this to dig up secrets about people to blackmail them or throw them in jail."

Clearview has shrouded itself in secrecy, avoiding debate about its boundary-pushing technology. When I began looking into the company in November, its website was a bare page showing a nonexistent Manhattan address as its place of business. The company's one employee listed on LinkedIn, a sales manager named "John Good," turned out to be Mr. Ton-That, using a fake name. For a month, people affiliated with the company would not return my emails or phone calls.

While the company was dodging me, it was also monitoring me. At my request, a number of police officers had run my photo through the Clearview app. They soon received phone calls from company representatives asking if they were talking to the media—a sign that Clearview has the ability and, in this case, the appetite to monitor whom law enforcement is searching for.

Facial recognition technology has always been controversial. It makes people nervous about Big Brother. It has a tendency to deliver false matches for certain groups, like people of color. And some facial recognition products used by the police—including Clearview's—haven't been vetted by independent experts.

Clearview's app carries extra risks because law enforcement agencies are uploading sensitive photos to the servers of a company whose ability to protect its data is untested.

The company eventually started answering my questions, saying that its earlier silence was typical of an early-stage start-up in stealth mode. Mr. Ton-That acknowledged designing a prototype for use with augmented-reality glasses but said the company had no plans to release it. And he said my photo had rung alarm bells because the app "flags possible anomalous search behavior" in order to prevent users from conducting what it deemed "inappropriate searches."

In addition to Mr. Ton-That, Clearview was founded by Richard Schwartz—who was an aide to Rudolph W. Giuliani when he was mayor of New York—and backed financially by Peter Thiel, a venture capitalist behind Facebook and Palantir.

Another early investor is a small firm called Kirenaga Partners. Its founder, David Scalzo, dismissed concerns about Clearview making the internet searchable by face, saying it's a valuable crime-solving tool.

"I've come to the conclusion that because information constantly increases, there's never going to be privacy," Mr. Scalzo said. "Laws have to determine what's legal, but you can't ban technology. Sure, that might lead to a dystopian future or something, but you can't ban it."

Addicted to A.I.

Mr. Ton-That, 31, grew up a long way from Silicon Valley. In his native Australia, he was raised on tales of his royal ancestors in Vietnam. In 2007, he dropped out of college and moved to San Francisco. The iPhone had just arrived, and his goal was to get in early on what he expected would be a vibrant market for social media apps. But his early ventures never gained real traction.

In 2009, Mr. Ton-That created a site that let people share links to videos with all the contacts in their instant messengers. Mr. Ton-That shut it down after it was branded a "phishing scam." In 2015, he spun up Trump Hair, which added Mr. Trump's distinctive coif to people in a photo, and a photo-sharing program. Both fizzled.

Dispirited, Mr. Ton-That moved to New York in 2016. Tall and slender, with long black hair, he considered a modeling career, he said, but after one shoot he returned to trying to figure out the next big thing in tech. He started reading academic papers on artificial intelligence, image recognition and machine learning.

Mr. Schwartz and Mr. Ton-That met in 2016 at a book event at the Manhattan Institute, a conservative think tank. Mr. Schwartz, now 61, had amassed an impressive Rolodex working for Mr. Giuliani in the 1990s and serving as the editorial page editor of The New York Daily News in the early 2000s. The two soon decided to go into the facial recognition business together: Mr. Ton-That would build the app, and Mr. Schwartz would use his contacts to drum up commercial interest.

Police departments have had access to facial recognition tools for almost 20 years, but they have historically been limited to searching government-provided images, such as mug shots and driver's license photos. In recent years, facial recognition algorithms have improved in accuracy, and companies like Amazon offer products that can create a facial recognition program for any database of images.

Mr. Ton-That wanted to go way beyond that. He began in 2016 by recruiting a couple of engineers. One helped design a program that can automatically collect images of people's faces from across the internet, such as employment sites, news sites, educational sites, and social networks including Facebook, YouTube, Twitter, Instagram and even Venmo. Representatives of those companies said their policies prohibit such scraping, and Twitter said it explicitly banned use of its data for facial recognition.

Another engineer was hired to perfect a facial recognition algorithm that was derived from academic papers. The result: a system that uses what Mr. Ton-That described as a "state-of-the-art neural net" to convert all the images into mathematical formulas, or vectors, based on facial geometry—like how far apart a person's eyes are. Clearview created a vast directory that clustered all the photos with similar vectors into "neighborhoods." When a user uploads a photo of a face into Clearview's system, it converts the face into a vector and then shows all the scraped photos stored in that vector's neighborhood—along with the links to the sites from which those images came.

Mr. Schwartz paid for server costs and basic expenses, but the operation was bare bones; everyone worked from home. "I was living on credit card debt," Mr. Ton-That said. "Plus, I was a Bitcoin believer, so I had some of those."

Going Viral with Law Enforcement

By the end of 2017, the company had a formidable facial recognition tool, which it called Smartcheckr. But Mr. Schwartz and Mr. Ton-That weren't sure whom they were going to sell it to.

Maybe it could be used to vet babysitters or as an add-on feature for surveillance cameras. What about a tool for security guards in the lobbies of buildings or to help hotels greet guests by name? "We thought of every idea," Mr. Ton-That said.

One of the odder pitches, in late 2017, was to Paul Nehlen—an anti-Semite and self-described "pro-white" Republican running for Congress in Wisconsin—to use "unconventional databases" for "extreme opposition research," according to a document provided to Mr. Nehlen and later posted online. Mr. Ton-That said the company never actually offered such services.

The company soon changed its name to Clearview AI and began marketing to law enforcement (Figure 4.2.2). That was when the company got its first round of funding from outside investors: Mr. Thiel and Kirenaga Partners. Among other things, Mr. Thiel was famous for secretly financing Hulk Hogan's lawsuit that bankrupted the popular website Gawker. Both Mr. Thiel and Mr. Ton-That had been the subject of negative articles by Gawker.

"In 2017, Peter gave a talented young founder $200,000, which two years later converted to equity in Clearview AI," said Jeremiah Hall, Mr. Thiel's spokesman. "That was Peter's only contribution; he is not involved in the company."

Even after a second funding round in 2019, Clearview remains tiny, having raised $7 million from investors, according to Pitchbook, a website that tracks investments in startups. The company declined to confirm the amount.

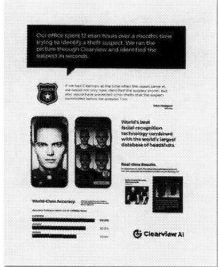

Figure 4.2.2 Clearview's marketing materials, obtained through a public-records request in Atlanta.

In February, the Indiana State Police started experimenting with Clearview. They solved a case within 20 minutes of using the app. Two men had gotten into a fight in a park, and it ended when one shot the other in the stomach. A bystander recorded the crime on a phone, so the police had a still of the gunman's face to run through Clearview's app.

They immediately got a match: The man appeared in a video that someone had posted on social media, and his name was included in a caption on the video. "He did not have a driver's license and hadn't been arrested as an adult, so he wasn't in government databases," said Chuck Cohen, an Indiana State Police captain at the time.

The man was arrested and charged; Mr. Cohen said he probably wouldn't have been identified without the ability to search social media for his face. The Indiana State Police became Clearview's first paying customer, according to the company. (The police declined to comment beyond saying that they tested Clearview's app.)

Clearview deployed current and former Republican officials to approach police forces, offering free trials and annual licenses for as little as $2,000. Mr. Schwartz tapped his political connections to help make government officials aware of the tool, according to Mr. Ton-That. ("I'm thrilled to have the opportunity to help Hoan build Clearview into a mission-driven organization that's helping law enforcement protect children and enhance the safety of communities across the country," Mr. Schwartz said through a spokeswoman.)

The company's main contact for customers was Jessica Medeiros Garrison, who managed Luther Strange's Republican campaign for Alabama attorney general. Brandon Fricke, an NFL agent engaged to the Fox Nation host Tomi Lahren, said in a financial disclosure report during a congressional campaign in California that he was a "growth consultant" for the company. (Clearview said that it was a brief, unpaid role, and that the company had enlisted Democrats to help market its product as well.)

The company's most effective sales technique was offering 30-day free trials to officers, who then encouraged their acquisition departments to sign up and praised the tool to officers from other police departments at conferences and online, according to the company and documents provided by police departments in response to public-record requests. Mr. Ton-That finally had his viral hit.

In July, a detective in Clifton, N.J., urged his captain in an email to buy the software because it was "able to identify a suspect in a matter of seconds." During the department's free trial, Clearview had identified shoplifters, an Apple Store thief and a good Samaritan who had punched out a man threatening people with a knife.

Photos "could be covertly taken with telephoto lens and input into the software, without 'burning' the surveillance operation," the detective wrote in the email, provided to The Times by two researchers, Beryl Lipton of MuckRock and Freddy Martinez of Open the Government. They discovered Clearview late last year while looking into how local police departments are using facial recognition.

According to a Clearview sales presentation reviewed by The Times, the app helped identify a range of individuals: a person who was accused of sexually abusing a child whose face appeared in the mirror of someone's else gym photo; the person behind a string of mailbox thefts in Atlanta; a John Doe found dead on an Alabama sidewalk; and suspects in multiple identity-fraud cases at banks.

In Gainesville, Fla., Detective Sgt. Nick Ferrara heard about Clearview last summer when it advertised on CrimeDex, a list-serv for investigators who specialize in financial crimes. He said he had previously relied solely on a state-provided facial recognition tool, FACES, which draws from more than 30 million Florida mug shots and Department of Motor Vehicle photos.

Sergeant Ferrara found Clearview's app superior, he said. Its nationwide database of images is much larger, and unlike FACES, Clearview's algorithm doesn't require photos of people looking straight at the camera.

"With Clearview, you can use photos that aren't perfect," Sergeant Ferrara said. "A person can be wearing a hat or glasses, or it can be a profile shot or partial view of their face."

He uploaded his own photo to the system, and it brought up his Venmo page. He ran photos from old, dead-end cases and identified more than 30 suspects. In September, the Gainesville Police Department paid $10,000 for an annual Clearview license.

Federal law enforcement, including the F.B.I. and the Department of Homeland Security, are trying it, as are Canadian law enforcement authorities, according to the company and government officials.

Despite its growing popularity, Clearview avoided public mention until the end of 2019, when Florida prosecutors charged a woman with grand theft after two grills and a vacuum were stolen from an Ace Hardware store in Clermont. She was identified when the police ran a still from a surveillance video through Clearview, which led them to her Facebook page. A tattoo visible in the surveillance video and Facebook photos confirmed her identity, according to an affidavit in the case.

'We're All Screwed'

Mr. Ton-That said the tool does not always work. Most of the photos in Clearview's database are taken at eye level. Much of the material that the police upload is from surveillance cameras mounted on ceilings or high on walls.

"They put surveillance cameras too high," Mr. Ton-That lamented. "The angle is wrong for good face recognition."

Despite that, the company said, its tool finds matches up to 75 percent of the time. But it is unclear how often the tool delivers false matches, because it has not been tested by an independent party such as the National Institute of Standards and Technology, a federal agency that rates the performance of facial recognition algorithms.

"We have no data to suggest this tool is accurate," said Clare Garvie, a researcher at Georgetown University's Center on Privacy and Technology, who has studied the government's use of facial recognition. "The larger the database, the larger the risk of misidentification because of the doppelgänger effect. They're talking about a massive database of random people they've found on the internet."

But current and former law enforcement officials say the app is effective. "For us, the testing was whether it worked or not," said Mr. Cohen, the former Indiana State Police captain.

One reason that Clearview is catching on is that its service is unique. That's because Facebook and other social media sites prohibit people from scraping users' images—Clearview is violating the sites' terms of service.

"A lot of people are doing it," Mr. Ton-That shrugged. "Facebook knows."

Jay Nancarrow, a Facebook spokesman, said the company was reviewing the situation with Clearview and "will take appropriate action if we find they are violating our rules."

Mr. Thiel, the Clearview investor, sits on Facebook's board. Mr. Nancarrow declined to comment on Mr. Thiel's personal investments.

Some law enforcement officials said they didn't realize the photos they uploaded were being sent to and stored on Clearview's servers. Clearview tries to pre-empt concerns with an FAQ document given to would-be clients that says its customer-support employees won't look at the photos that the police upload.

Clearview also hired Paul D. Clement, a United States solicitor general under President George W. Bush, to assuage concerns about the app's legality.

In an August memo that Clearview provided to potential customers, including the Atlanta Police Department and the Pinellas County Sheriff's Office in Florida, Mr. Clement said law enforcement agencies "do not violate the federal Constitution or relevant existing state biometric and privacy laws when using Clearview for its intended purpose."

Mr. Clement, now a partner at Kirkland & Ellis, wrote that the authorities don't have to tell defendants that they were identified via Clearview, as long as it isn't the sole basis for getting a warrant to arrest them. Mr. Clement did not respond to multiple requests for comment.

The memo appeared to be effective; the Atlanta police and Pinellas County Sheriff's Office soon started using Clearview.

Because the police upload photos of people they're trying to identify, Clearview possesses a growing database of individuals who have attracted attention from law enforcement. The company also has the ability to manipulate the results that the police see. After the company realized I was asking officers to run my photo through the app, my face was flagged by Clearview's systems and for a while showed no matches. When asked about this, Mr. Ton-That laughed and called it a "software bug."

"It's creepy what they're doing, but there will be many more of these companies. There is no monopoly on math," said Al Gidari, a privacy professor at Stanford Law School. "Absent a very strong federal privacy law, we're all screwed."

Mr. Ton-That said his company used only publicly available images. If you change a privacy setting in Facebook so that search engines can't link to your profile, your Facebook photos won't be included in the database, he said.

But if your profile has already been scraped, it is too late. The company keeps all the images it has scraped even if they are later deleted or taken down, though Mr. Ton-That said the company was working on a tool that would let people request that images be removed if they had been taken down from the website of origin.

Woodrow Hartzog, a professor of law and computer science at Northeastern University in Boston, sees Clearview as the latest proof that facial recognition should be banned in the United States.

"We've relied on industry efforts to self-police and not embrace such a risky technology, but now those dams are breaking because there is so much money on the table," Mr. Hartzog said. "I don't see a future where we harness the benefits of face recognition technology without the crippling abuse of the surveillance that comes with it. The only way to stop it is to ban it."

Where Everybody Knows Your Name

During a recent interview at Clearview's offices in a WeWork location in Manhattan's Chelsea neighborhood, Mr. Ton-That demonstrated the app on himself. He took a selfie and uploaded it. The app pulled up 23 photos of him. In one, he is shirtless and lighting a cigarette while covered in what looks like blood.

Mr. Ton-That then took my photo with the app. The "software bug" had been fixed, and now my photo returned numerous results, dating back a decade, including photos of myself that I had never seen before. When I used my hand to cover my nose and the bottom of my face, the app still returned seven correct matches for me.

Police officers and Clearview's investors predict that its app will eventually be available to the public.

Mr. Ton-That said he was reluctant. "There's always going to be a community of bad people who will misuse it," he said.

Even if Clearview doesn't make its app publicly available, a copycat company might, now that the taboo is broken. Searching someone by face could become as easy as Googling a name. Strangers would be able to listen in on sensitive conversations, take photos of the participants and know personal secrets. Someone walking down the street would be immediately identifiable— and his or her home address would be only a few clicks away. It would herald the end of public anonymity.

Asked about the implications of bringing such a power into the world, Mr. Ton-That seemed taken aback.

"I have to think about that," he said. "Our belief is that this is the best use of the technology."

Chapter 4.3

Excerpt from Big Brother to Electronic Panopticon*

David Lyon

[...]

The Police State and the Prison

When I tell people that I am studying surveillance, and in particular investigating the ways that our personal details are stored in computer databases, the most common reaction is to invoke George Orwell; 'This must be the study of 'Big Brother'. A perfectly understandable response, given that Nineteen Eighty-Four is about a state that uses a huge bureaucratic apparatus, 'thought police', and the figure of 'Big Brother' on the ever-present telescreen to intervene in the smallest details of its citizens' daily lives.

Back in the early 1970s, computer enthusiasts James Martin and Adrian Norman noted that 'a surprising amount of what George Orwell imagined now looks plausible'.[1] Such sentiments were repeated routinely by both the complacent and the concerned. Political scientist Theodore Lowi warned that 'a Nineteen Eighty-Four type of scenario will be the most likely outcome if things are let go at the present rate and no attention is paid to the information revolution'.[2] As we have already seen, in the 1990s Judge Love worries about the 'Orwellian' aspects of his electronic tags for offenders.

Within sociological analysis proper, James Rule's work on surveillance also takes its cues from Orwell. Starting from a 'total surveillance society', he argues that the only limits to the present day realization of the Orwellian, nightmare lie in the level of available 'surveillance capacities'. As we saw in Chapter Three, those capacities are massively augmented by information technology. Some qualitative differences to surveillance come in the train of new technology. Does this bring Nineteen Eighty-Four closer?

---

* David Lyon, "From Big Brother to Electronic Panopticon," *The Electronic Eye: The Rise of Surveillance Society* (1994): 57–80. Reprinted by permission. Note: This is an excerpt from the original so footnote and endnote numbering may be modified.

DOI: 10.1201/9781003278290-27

Apart from the obvious - but banal - rejoinder that 1984 is now well past, others have begun to question how relevant is the image of Big Brother for the analysis of contemporary electronic surveillance. For instance, in the previous chapter we saw how Roger Clarke's work indicates that 'dataveillance is technically and economically superior' to the ubiquitous two-way television of Nineteen Eighty-Four. Total control in Oceania was also made possible by centralization. Now, it is true that the governmental and commercial 'centres' of contemporary states still have access to files on major populations, but extensive computer networking also decentralizes operations. Indeed, the old dichotomy between decentralization and centralization is itself now questionable. Today's surveillance society certainly needs nothing as cumbersome as the administrative machinery of Nineteen Eighty-Four.

In this chapter I argue that, while Nineteen Eighty-Four has in many ways been superseded technologically, limited but important aspects of its account of a surveillance society still remain relevant today. At the same time, Orwell never imagined how rapidly surveillance would extend its global reach, nor did he conceive of a situation where anything but the state would be its chief perpetrator. Today, surveillance is both a globalizing phenomenon and one that has as much to do with consumers as with citizens.

But now another model, another image, is gaining ground in the analysis of surveillance; Bentham's Panopticon prison plan (Figure 4.3.1). Much impetus for this comes from the fashionable flurry of Foucault studies that began in the 1980s, but now sufficient empirical work has been done to show the relevance of at least some aspects of the Panopticon to electronic surveillance.[3]

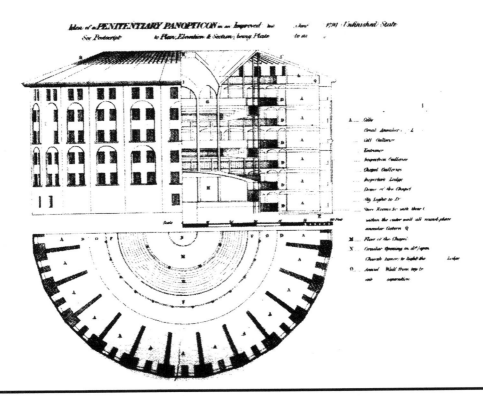

Figure 4.3.1   Picture of Bentham's penitentiary Panopticon where the guard is in the center and the prisoners are in a semi-circle.

The remainder of the chapter is thus taken up with the question of how far the Panopticon provides a useful model for understanding electronic surveillance. I shall suggest that while it is undeniably illuminating, analysis based upon the Panopticon image also retains some serious disadvantages.

It is worth paying considerable attention to both the Orwellian and the Panoptic model, in order to understand contemporary surveillance and to seek better or alternative models. I want to make it very clear that that both models are firmly rooted in normative and critical stances. Ironically the Panopticon, now the main alternative to Big Brother, started life as a utopian scheme for social reform, and a long time before Orwell. Indeed, Orwell wrote Nineteen Eighty-Four partly as a dystopian critique of such enterprises.[4] Analysis of what is happening in today's society is inextricably and inevitably bound up with questions of the desirability of what is happening.

Orwell's Dystopia

George Orwell wrote Nineteen Eighty-Four as a dystopia, that is, an account whose intent is the opposite of utopia; a literary depiction of an undesirable, avoidable but conceivable future state of society. Winston Smith, who attempts to think for himself, is eventually crushed into conformity by the surveillance state. Electronic media - limited of course to what Orwell knew about in 1948 - are the chief tool for manipulating the masses through unremitting propaganda. But forms of electronic surveillance also allow the Thought Police to maintain constant vigilance over the intimate lives and relationships of each citizen. The figure of Big Brother, who would appear on the telescreens in buildings public and private, claimed to monitor everything. Hence 'Big Brother is watching you!' which is now one of the most readily recognized catch-phrases in the English language. Here is Orwell's description:

The telescreen received and transmitted simultaneously. Any sound that Winston made, above the level of a very low whisper, would be picked up by it; moreover, so long as he remained within the field of vision which the metal plaque commanded, he could be seen as well as heard. There was of course no way of knowing whether you were being watched at any given moment.[5] Nineteen Eighty-Four is often taken to be about the power of technology for social control and about the loss of privacy resulting living in such a transparent society. So it is not surprising that his work has been so readily translatable into the language of microelectronics and information technology, with their supposed threats.

Orwell was astoundingly prescient, which is of course the reason why his work has not only survived but maintained its interest. He noticed the growing centrality of information in the operations of the nation-state. In Oceania there was even a 'Ministry of Truth' ('Minitrue') to deal with such matters as the creation and destruction of information. Today, computer technology facilitates the construction of new categories of data, a process that is encouraged by the penchant for statistical analysis within organizations.

Moreover, the same technologies make possible the electronic erasure of data, either without trace, or traceable only by experts. Both processes are significant to the 'surveillance society'. For one thing, the malleability of data may render Weberian confidence in the reliability of the record somewhat naive. The electronic trail may be eradicated without trace, which leads to big questions about how far 'data' may be trusted. For another, sauce for the goose is sauce for the gander, and the malleability of data may also be seen in the phenomenon of 'fraudulent IDs'.[6] With the twentieth-century rise of credentialism and the constant demand for identification, the temptation to invent or enhance personal documentary details has for some been too hard to resist.

Obtaining goods, services, benefits or employment may all be facilitated by a variety of ways of distorting identity or biographical details. Technology is not simply a tool of dominant social groups. The focus on novel techniques for handling information also rings bells in the context of computing and administration. As we have seen, it is information technology that is especially significant for surveillance. The national databank, for instance, is exactly what one would expect to find in an Orwellian surveillance society. Recognizing this, American officials denied during the 1970s that such a databank would be created. Big Brother would be kept at bay.[7] Yet all American federal government employees are now listed in a single database that is used for matching.

Another significant feature of Orwell's 'Big Brother' surveillance is that it was imperceptible. Those under surveillance were unsure whether there was any time when they could relax. Like the Panopticon - and indeed as in other literary treatments of the surveillance theme, such as Franz Kafka's The Castle or Margaret Atwood's The Handmaid's Tale - this model of undetected surveillance keeps those watched subordinate by means of uncertainty. You simply comply, because you never know when 'they' might be watching. Information technology enables surveillance to be carried out in ways even less visible than those available in Orwell's, let alone Kafka's, day.[8]

Two further points, to do with dignity and division, may be made that underscore Orwell's relevance for contemporary surveillance. I mentioned above that Nineteen Eighty-Four has been used to connect transparency of behaviour with the theme of privacy. Yet there is a sense in which Orwell's focus was less narrow than that. For him, privacy was an aspect of human dignity. Winston Smith finally caves in, betraying his girlfriend Julia and declaring his love for Big Brother, not when his privacy is invaded but when deprived of his dignity by a confrontation with rats.[9] From that moment his identity merged with Big Brother's. His very personhood was impugned. The challenge of electronic surveillance is missed if it is reduced to a concern merely with privacy.

As for division, Orwell shows clearly how power is maintained at a broader level through the divisive character of surveillance. In his Visions of Social Control, Stanley Cohen stresses this facet of Orwell's work.[10] The middle-class and Party members needed careful thought control and surveillance. Inclusionary controls reign here. But the proles, who formed 85% of the population, could safely be left in their ghettoes, 'working, breeding and dying'.[11] Their lot is exclusion. The important point here is the role of surveillance in different modes of social control, rather than the details of Orwell's analysis.

Things have changed since Orwell's time, and consumption, for the masses, has emerged as the new inclusionary reality. Only the minority, the so-called underclass,[12] whose position prevents them from participating so freely in consumption, now experience the hard edge of exclusionary and punitive surveillance. Anyone wishing to grasp the nature of contemporary surveillance must reckon with this fact. Whereas the major threat, for Orwell, came from the state, today consumer surveillance poses a series of novel questions which have yet to find adequate analytical and political answers. A perfectly plausible view is that in contemporary conditions consumerism acts in its own right as a significant means of maintaining social order, leaving older forms of surveillance and control to cope with the non-consuming residue.[13]

Having said that, however, some further qualification is called for. While consumerism may correctly be viewed as a means of social control, it differs from other types of such control. Those targeted for direct mail and other forms of personalized advertising are objects of an attempted channelling of behaviour. Companies wish to include rather than exclude them. The important distinction between exclusionary and perhaps punitive forms of control, which may be coercive, and more subtle ones, which rely on creating desired behavioural conduits, should be borne in mind as we proceed.[14]

This in turn also ties in with a more general theme in the history of social control; the progressive uncoupling of violent and non-violent methods. Orwell tended to keep the links. Both jackboots and Big Brother have their place in Oceania. But as Gary T. Marx, among others, observes, more subtle, less coercive means have become increasingly prominent in the advanced societies since the Second World War.[15] The use of electronic means for less conspicuous surveillance he takes to be an important instance of this shift.

Orwell's own experience and observations, after all, were of the Spanish Civil War, Stalin's Soviet Union and Mussolini's Italy. Many have imagined that he had only these obviously totalitarian regimes in mind in writing Nineteen Eighty-Four. However, it is more than likely that he intended its application to be broader. As a democratic and libertarian socialist, he was quite aware of certain authoritarian tendencies within capitalist societies. What he may not have foreseen was that new technologies might eventually permit surveillance tending towards totalitarianism with democratic processes still neatly in place. As Gary T. Marx notes, the velvet glove may hide the iron fist.[16]

Sociological analysis of surveillance that begins with Big Brother produces some useful insights. The fact that electronic technologies have been augmented considerably since Orwell's day does mean that his account needs some updating, but it does not render it irrelevant. Much of what Orwell wrote still stands, and deserves attention, but we should also explore the specific ways in which we must go beyond Orwell. At this point, then, we may turn to the Panopticon and ask whether as a model it can compensate for the shortcomings of Orwell's dystopia.

The Panopticon from Bentham to Foucault

The Panopticon has been used for analysing surveillance in a number of different settings; the workplace, government administration, and consumer contexts. We shall examine some of these below. It should be remembered that the Panopticon does not come to us directly from Bentham but recently mediated through the work of Michel Foucault and critics who have debated it.[17] Though many historians of ideas or of systems of punishment have recognized the importance of the Panopticon, it is really only since Foucault that interest in it has become widespread. Foucault illuminates the connections between the Panopticon and modernity by showing that it forms the watershed between punitive and reforming disciplinary practices. Enlightenment reason, concerned with empirical observation and classification, and related to the rational reproducing of social order, is neatly expressed here. The theme of exploiting uncertainty as a means of controlling subordinates reappears here as well, having obvious resonance with the unobtrusive monitoring of which new electronic technologies are capable. However, this in turn propels us into the debate over postmodernity. A hallmark of modern thought is the way individuals are placed centre-stage in history. But postmodern discourse pushes such actors into the wings, and this seems to echo what happens with electronic surveillance. If the supposedly 'personal' details of intimate everyday life circulate beyond our control within remote databases, where now is the human 'centred self'?[18]

Jeremy Bentham, the British philosopher and social reformer, published his plan for the Panopticon penitentiary in 1791. Essentially, it was for a building on a semi-circular pattern with an 'inspection lodge' at the centre and cells around the perimeter. Prisoners, who in the original plan would be in individual cells, were open to the gaze of the guards, or 'inspectors', but the same was not true of the view the other way. By a carefully contrived system of lighting and the use of wooden blinds, officials would be invisible to the inmates. Control was to be maintained by the constant sense that prisoners were watched by unseen eyes. There was nowhere to hide, nowhere to be private. Not knowing whether or not they were watched, but obliged to assume that they were, obedience was the prisoner's only rational option. Hence Bentham's Greek-based neologism; the Panopticon, or 'all-seeing place'.[19]

The Panopticon was to be a model prison, a new departure, a watershed in the control of deviance and a novel means of social discipline. Bentham invested more time and energy in this than any other project - and 'mourned its failure more passionately'.[20] He saw in it 'a great and new invented instrument of government' and believed the panoptic principle held promise of 'the only effective instrument of reformative management'. In a closing eulogy he made the famous claim, 'Morals reformed - health preserved - industry invigorated - instruction diffused - public burthens lightened - Economy seated, as it were, upon a rock - the Gordian knot of the Poor Laws not cut, but untied - all by a simple idea in Architecture!"[21]

Bentham's apparently utopian enthusiasm for the Panopticon had personal, political, and cultural origins. Personally, he hoped to reap financial benefit from an entrepreneurial stake in the project, and to raise his status profile through being its first director. Indeed, when shown the plans, Edmund Burke saw straight through them; 'There's the spider in the web!' he exclaimed.[22] Politically, the Panopticon promised local, non-religious prison reform over against the Evangelical and transportation-to-Australia alternatives currently on offer. And culturally, the Panopticon epitomised the kind of 'social physics' so popular with the philosophes of his day. It neatly translated the clockwork image of being human seen in La Mettrie's L 'Homme Machine into an architectural reality.[23]

Ironically, while it appears that no prison was ever built exactly along the lines Bentham had in mind, and he certainly failed to persuade the British government to invest in it, the principles embodied in the Panopticon were to have a widespread influence. The key principle was inspection, through inspection of a specific kind. Bentham's Panopticon represented a secular parody of divine omniscience, and the observed was also, like God, invisible. Thus ' ... the more constantly the persons to be inspected are under the eyes of the persons who should inspect them, the more perfectly will the purpose of the establishment be attained.[24] And if such constant supervision proves impossible, prisoners should be given the impression that the gaze is unwavering.

Bentham's innovation, then, was not just to inspect, or even to ensure that the gaze is asymmetrical, but to use uncertainty as a means of subordination. The asymmetrical gaze created uncertainty which in turn produced surrender. Asymmetrical surveillance became part of the whole modern project of destroying the certainties of alternative powers, the supposed hangovers from traditional societies, wherever they still lurked.[25] This is why the Panopticon principles were so significant.

The inspection principle suited other purposes than prisons, according to Bentham. Of courses they did! Indeed, he got the original idea of the Panopticon from his brother's workshop in Russia. And he advertised the virtues of the panoptic as being appropriate for any context in which supervision was required; for ' ... punishing the incorrigible, guarding the insane, reforming the vicious, confining the suspected, employing the idle, maintaining the helpless, curing the sick, instructing the willing in any branch of industry, or training the rising race in the path of education'.[26] Foucault argues that panoptic control has indeed become significant in many of these spheres.

Two other principles attached to the panoptic[27] in the specific context of the penitentiary. One was the 'solitude' or isolation of inmates, the other was to allow the prison to be run as a private enterprise by outside contractors. Solitude would extend even to having private toilets for prisoners, and to holding chapel services from a central position above the inspection lodge, without prisoners moving from their cells. Inmates were to be atomised, secluded. As for running the prison by contract, this would possible enable profit to be made and prison governors to be held in unaccustomed esteem.

Bentham cheerfully defended his Panopticon from any misplaced liberal attack. Might it be thought 'despotic', or might the result of 'this high-wrought contrivance .. . be constructing a set of machines under the similitude of men?[28] Let people think so if they wish. Such criticisms miss the point, namely, 'would happiness be most likely to be increased or decreased by this discipline?' Here is control, and clean control at that. Much better, he commented, than something like Addison's bizarre sounding proposal to 'try virginity with lions'. There you saw blood and uncertainty: here you see certainty without blood'.[29] Of course, uncertainty still exists for those subjected to the Panopticon regime. Indeed, the 'machine' depends on it. Certainty resides in the system, and, one might add, with the inspector, the one 'in the know'.

This kind of certainty, sought by Bentham in the Panopticon, epitomises for Foucault the social disciplines of modernity. Whereas in earlier times the failure of social control would result in punishment that was public and brutal, modernity introduced clean and rational forms of social control and punishment. The unruly crowd is rendered manageable; no plots of escape from prison, no danger of contagion if they are sick, no mutual violence if they are mad, no chatter if schoolchildren, and no disorders or coalitions if workers. The crowd is replaced by a 'collection of separated individualities'.[30] As Foucault says, Bentham made 'visibility a trap'.

In the following important quotation, Foucault summarises his understanding of the major effect of the Panopticon:

> to induce in the inmate a state of conscious and permanent visibility that assures the automatic functioning of power. So to arrange things that the surveillance is permanent in its effects, even if it is discontinuous in its action; that the perfection of power should tend to render its actual exercise unnecessary; that this architectural apparatus should be a machine for creating and sustaining a power relation independent of the person who exercises it; in short, that the inmates should be caught up in a power situation of which they themselves are the bearers.[31]

In the Panopticon, discipline crossed what Foucault calls a 'disciplinary threshold' in which the 'formation of knowledge and the increased of power regularly reinforce each other in a circular process'.[32] Older, more costly, and more violent forms of power fell into disuse and were superseded by 'a subtle, calculated technology of subjection'.[33]

Recall for a moment our previous discussion of Nineteen Eighty-Four. Though the older forms of power are still present there, the later concern with power for power's sake and the 'subtle, calculated subjection' clearly predominates in Orwell's mind. On the other hand, Orwell places less emphasis on subjects being the bearers of their own surveillance and of the power relation connected with it.

Sociology is indebted to Foucault for his theory of surveillance, touching as it does on both aspects of its power; the accumulation of information, and the direct supervision of subordinates. The former is found in the detailed files held on each Panopticon inmate, the latter in the architectural potential of the building itself. Acknowledging Foucault's contribution, Giddens observes that in modern times 'disciplinary power' is characterised by 'new modes of regularizing activities in time-space' ."[34] Observation is central to these modes, and thus the Panopticon epitomises such disciplinary power.

However, Foucault also insists that such power is typically present throughout the institutions of modernity, in all kinds of administrative contexts. 'Is it surprising', asks Foucault rhetorically, 'that the cellular prison, with its regular chronologies, forced labour, its authorities of surveillance and registration, its experts in normality … should have become the modern instrument of penality?' But not only that; he goes on, 'Is it surprising that prisons resemble factories, schools, barracks, hospitals, which all resemble prisons?'[35] What for Bentham was an aspiration is for Foucault a social reality - the panoptic principle diffusing different institutions. This assumption, often questioned within the sociology of administrative power, must be re-addressed in the context of electronic surveillance.[36]

The perverse irony is that Foucault himself seems to have made no comments about the relevance of panoptic discipline to the ways that administrative power has been enlarged and enhanced by computers, especially since the 1960s. Yet surely we see here nothing less than the near-perfection of the principle of discipline by invisible inspection via information-gathering. Or do we? Today no shortage exists of social analysts prepared to complete Foucault by making the connections explicit. Thus we turn next to explore the extent of that link; may we think of electronic surveillance as panoptic power?

[…]

We find that the Panopticon has also been rediscovered in capitalism. The debate over whether or not the adoption of new technologies represents intensified workplace control within capitalism is complex and inconclusive. Shoshana Zuboff's ethnography, In the Age of the Smart Machine,[37] takes the view that computers in the workplace have a transformative capacity. Paralleling authority as the 'spiritual basis of power', she examines technique as the 'material basis of power'. The key to contemporary management technique, she argues, is panopticism, enabled by the use of new technologies.

The extremely precise computer systems of today's organizations permit minute monitoring of events and performances within the workplace. At one of the workplaces investigated by Zuboff, a highly automated pulp mill, a small explosion occurred in the early hours of the morning. By scrutinizing the 'Overview System', a bird's-eye view of the whole operation which was constantly recorded at five-second intervals, management could determine the exact cause of the accident; equipment failure, poor decision-making, or a sleepy operator?[38] Workers at such sites are thus highly transparent to management even in the apparently small details of day-to-day routine. This heightened visibility - recall the prison blinds and lighting - also noted by researchers looking at computerization in much smaller contexts such as ordering in restaurants and taxi-calling systems,[39] - Zuboff connects with the panoptic.

Zuboff also discusses the allure of panopticism for management, which is the 'promise of certain knowledge'. Increased reliance upon the 'facts' produced by the computer systems generates new management styles, in her account. Employee performance appears as 'objective' data, which often correlates with another panoptic feature, the certainty of punishment. Apparently, any dismissal process tends to be shortened from around a year from the start of the dispute to something much more immediate.[40]

Operators within the ubiquitous digital 'gaze' of such computer systems, and without the more familiar face-to-face relationships with superiors, may seek modes of resistance, but. compliance appears more common. Information systems 'can transmit the presence of the omniscient observer and so induce compliance without the messy conflict-prone exertions of reciprocal relations'.[41] Zuboff comments that in workplaces where workers as well as management have access to the personal data collected on the systems, workers exhibit 'anticipatory conformity', showing that the standards of management are internalized by workers. This again seems to be a case of Foucault's 'normalizing discipline' of the panoptic.

[…]

Notes

1. James Martin and Adrian Norman, *The Computerized Society*, Harmondsworth, Penguin/New York, Random House, 1973.
2. Theodore Lowi, 'The political impact of information technology', IEEE Transactions on Communications, 23 (10), 1975 reproduced in Tom Forester (ed.) *The Microelectronics Revolution*, Oxford, Blackwell/Cambridge USA, MIT Press, 1980 p. 466.
3. A case in point is Oscar Candy's *The Panoptic Sort*.
4. "Do you begin to see, then, what kind of world we are creating? It is the exact opposite of the stupid, hedonistic Utopias that the old reformers imagined. a world which will not grow less but more merciless as it refines itself. George Orwell, *Nineteen Eighty-Four*, Harmondsworth, Penguin, 1954.
5. George Orwell, op.cit.
6. See Gary T. Marx, 'Fraudulent identification and biography'.
7. US Government denials regarding national databases are documented, for instance in David Flaherty's *Protecting Privacy in Surveillance Societies*.
8. Gary Marx makes much of this connection between computer surveillance and detectability. See Chapter Three of this book.
9. I am indebted to Bob Fortner for this point. See R. S. Fortner, 'Physics and metaphysics in an information age', Communication, (9), p. 166.
10. Stanley Cohen, Visions of Social Control, pp. 142. 202.
11. George Orwell, *Nineteen Eighty-Four*, Harmondsworth, Penguin, 1954, p. 60.
12. I do not think that this term implies a conservative view of people in poverty and disadvantage, or that it suggests a necessarily static social grouping. It seems to me that the 'underclass' is a concept which captures the reality of life for those cut off from the means of consumption within present-day capitalist societies. See for example Kirk Mann, *The Making of the English Underclass"?*, Milton Keynes/Pennsylvania, Open University Press, 1991.
13. This view of consumerism as social control is put most elegantly in the work of Zygmunt Bauman, especially in his *Freedom*.
14. Gary T. Marx discusses other aspects of social control as 'engineering' in his forthcoming paper The engineering of social control: the search for the silver bullet', J. Hogan (ed), Crime and Inequality, Chicago, University of Chicago Press.
15. Gary T. Marx, *Undercover*, p. 231. The theme is also explored in Andrew Scull, *Decarceration*.
16. Gary T. Marx, *Undercover*, p. 232.
17. Among such criticism of Foucault, Michael IgnatiefFs *A Just Measure of Pain* standsout.
18. Mark Poster discusses this in *The Mode of Information and Critical Theory and Poststructuralism*.
19. Jeremy Bentham, *Collected Works*, ed John Bowring, London, 1843.
20. Gertrude Himmelfarb, 'The Haunted House of Jeremy Bentham', *Victorian Minds*, New York, Knopf, 1968, p. 32.
21. Jeremy Bentham, op. cit., p. 39.
22. Quoted in David Lyon, 'Bentham's Panopticon', *Queen's Quarterly*, 1991, 98(3).
23. Bentham's immodest ambitions for the Panopticon were connected with its role in the contemporary prison reform movement in England. On his hopes of personal gain from involvement in the administration of the Panopticon, see David Lyon, 'Bentham's Panopticon' (above). The 'clockwork image' metaphor derives from Donald MacKay, *The Clockwork Image*, Leicester UK, Intervarsity Press, 1974.
24. Jeremy Bentham, op. cit., p. 40.
25. This is discussed in Zygmunt Bauman, *Modernity and Ambivalence*.
26. Jeremy Bentham, op. cit., p. 40.
27. I am using the term 'panoptic' to refer only to the principles embodied in the Panopticon.
28. Jeremy Bentham, op. cit., p. 64.
29. Jeremy Bentham, op. cit., p. 64.
30. Michel Foucault, *Discipline and Punish*, p. 201.
31. Michel Foucault, *Discipline and Punish*, p. 201.
32. Michel Foucault, *Discipline and Punish*, p. 204.

33. Michel Foucault, *Discipline and Punish*, p. 221.
34. Anthony Giddens, *The Nation-State and Violence*, p. 183.
35. Michel Foucault, *Discipline and Punish*, p. 228.
36. The Panopticon may also be seen in relation to other kinds of technique, particularly perhaps that using biotechnology. But the surveillance power even of biotechnology depends upon microelectronics.
37. Shoshana Zuboff, *In the Age of the Smart Machine*.
38. Shoshana Zuboff, op. cit., pp. 315–17.
39. James B. Rule and Paul Attewell, 'What do Computers do?', *Social Problems*, 36 (3), pp. 225–40.
40. Shoshana Zuboff, op. cit., p. 326.
41. Shoshana Zuboff, op. cit., p. 323.

Chapter 4.4

Excerpt from Privacy, Visibility, Transparency, and Exposure[*]

Julie E. Cohen

Work within the emerging field of surveillance studies calls into question the implicit linkages between surveillance, visual observation, and centralization that the conventional metaphors for privacy invasion have tended to reinforce. Scholars in this field have brought a variety of allied disciplines—including sociology, urban geography, communications theory, and cultural studies—to bear on the institutions and subjects of surveillance. This work enables a richer understanding of how surveillance functions, and of what "privacy" interests might include.

Much work in surveillance studies builds upon Michel Foucault's landmark study of the prison and its role in the emergence of modern techniques of social discipline.[1] US privacy theorists have drawn on this work primarily for its discussion of Bentham's Panopticon, but have tended not to notice that Foucault offered the Panopticon as a metaphor for a different and more comprehensive sort of discipline that is concerned more fundamentally with classification and normalization.[2] One of his central insights was that in modern societies social discipline is accomplished by statistical methods. "[W]hereas the juridical systems define juridical subjects according to universal norms, the disciplines characterize, classify, specialize; they distribute along a scale, around a norm, hierarchize individuals in relation to one another and, if necessary, disqualify and invalidate."[3] This process does not require a centralized authority; instead, it is most powerful when it is most widely dispersed among the civil and private institutions that regulate everyday life.[4] These observations, which have obvious application to a wide variety of statistical and actuarial practices performed in both government and private sectors, have served as the foundation for elaboration of the work of modern "surveillance societies."[5]

Surveillance in the panoptic sense thus functions both descriptively and normatively. It does not simply render personal information *accessible* but rather seeks to render individual behaviors and preferences *transparent* by conforming them to preexisting frameworks. And in seeking to

[*] Cohen, Julie E. "Privacy, Visibility, Transparency, and Exposure," *The University of Chicago Law Review* 75, no. 1 (2008): 181–201. Reprinted by permission. Note: This is an excerpt from the original so footnote and endnote numbering may be modified.

DOI: 10.1201/9781003278290-28

mold the future, surveillance also shapes the past: by creating fixed records of presence, appearance, and behavior, surveillance constitutes institutional and social memory.[6]

Some surveillance theorists argue that surveillance in postindustrial, digitally networked societies is even more radically decentralized and resilient than Foucault's work suggests. Building on Gilles Deleuze and Félix Guattari's work on systems of social control,[7] Kevin Haggerty and Richard Ericson argue that the prevailing modality of surveillance is the "surveillant assemblage": a heterogeneous, loosely coupled set of institutions that seek to harness the raw power of information by fixing flows of information cognitively and spatially.[8] Surveillant assemblages grow rhizomatically, "across a series of interconnected roots which throw up shoots in different locations," and for this reason they are extraordinarily resistant to localized disruption.[9] Of critical importance, the surveillant assemblage operates upon its subjects not only by the "normalized soul training" of Foucauldian theory, but also by seduction.[10] Flows of information within the surveillant assemblage promise a cornucopia of benefits and pleasures, including price discounts, social status, and voyeuristic entertainment. In return, the surveillant assemblage demands full enrollment.

An alternative approach to surveillance studies uses performance theory to interrogate the effects of networked databases on the performance of identity. Performance theory melds the methodologies of speech act theory, which emphasizes the performative force of utterances; cultural anthropology, which describes culture as arising through performance; and deconstruction, which regards language as encoding multiple texts rather than universal truths.[11] Performance theorists argue that "identity" is neither fixed nor unitary, but rather is constituted by performances that are directed at different audiences.[12] From this perspective, the problem with surveillance is that it seeks to constitute individuals as fixed texts upon which invariant meanings can be imposed.[13] The struggle for privacy is recast as the individual's effort to assert multiplicity and resist "norming." This account emphasizes agency to a far greater degree than the Foucauldian and Deleuzian accounts. It too is concerned with normalization and transparency, but it argues that human nature is much more impervious to normalization and transparency than those literatures suggest, and that the subjects of surveillance are knowing and only partially compliant participants in their own seduction.

[...]

II. Visibility and Exposure

Linking privacy to informational transparency tends to mask a conceptually distinct privacy harm that is spatial, and concerns the nature of the spaces constituted by and for pervasive, continuous observation. Those spaces are characterized by what I will call a condition of exposure. The term "condition" is intended to signify that exposure is not a given but rather a design principle that in turn constrains the range of available behaviors and norms. Neither privacy law nor privacy theory has recognized an interest in limiting exposure uncoupled from the generally acknowledged interest in limiting observation, and in general we lack a vocabulary for conceptualizing and evaluating such an interest.

Since the US legal system purports to recognize an interest in spatial privacy, it is useful to begin there. Doctrinally, whether surveillance invades a legally recognized interest in spatial privacy depends in the first instance on background rules of property ownership. Generally speaking, surveillance is fair game within public space, and also within spaces owned by third parties, but not within spaces owned by the targets of surveillance. Those baseline rules, however, do not invariably determine the outcomes of privacy disputes. Expectations deemed objectively reasonable can trump the rules that otherwise would apply in a particular space. Thus, for example, a residential tenant is entitled to protection against direct visual observation by the landlord even though she does not own the premises,[14] and a home-owner is not necessarily entitled to protection against direct visual observation by airplane overflight,[15] nor to privacy in items left out for garbage collection.[16] Employees sometimes can assert privacy interests against undisclosed workplace surveillance.[17]

For purposes of this essay, the interesting thing about the reasonable expectations test is that it is fundamentally concerned not with expectations about the nature of particular *spaces*, but rather with expectations about the accessibility of *information* about activities taking place in those spaces. Even the exceptions prove the rule: *Kyllo v United States*,[18] styled as a ringing reaffirmation of the traditional privacy interest in the home, in fact upholds that interest only against information-gathering technologies "not in general public use."[19] Similarly, although legal scholars disagree about the precise nature of the privacy interest, they seem to agree that cognizable injury would require the involvement of a human observer who perceives or receives information.[20] Focusing on the accessibility of information also explains why no privacy interest attaches to most activities in public spaces and nonresidential spaces owned by third parties: persons who voluntarily enter such premises have impliedly consented to being seen there.

In short, and paradoxically, prevailing legal understandings of spatial privacy do not recognize a harm that is distinctively spatial: that flows from the ways in which surveillance, whether visual or data-based, alters the spaces and places of everyday life. The information privacy law project has tended to ratify this omission, precisely because its primary interest has been information rather than the bodies and spaces to which it pertains. Many information privacy theorists criticize spatial metaphors in privacy discourse, arguing that they muddy rigorous analysis of privacy issues in the information age.[21] And this resistance too is rooted in the tradition of liberal political economy, which for the most part does not consider concrete, particular bodies and spaces at all.

Yet resistance to spatialization in privacy theory leaves important dimensions of the experience of surveillance unexplained. Consider an individual who is reading a newspaper at a plaza café in front of a downtown office building. The building's owner has installed surveillance cameras that monitor the plaza on a twenty-four-hour basis. Let's assume the cameras in this example are clearly visible, and clearly low-tech and analog. It would be reasonable for the individual to assume that they probably are not connected to anything other than the building's own private security system. Most likely, tapes are stored for a short period of time and then reused. The consensus view in US privacy theory tends to be that there is essentially no legitimate expectation of privacy under these circumstances, and that the surveillance therefore should not trouble us. But those surveilled often feel quite differently. Even localized, uncoordinated surveillance may be experienced as intrusive in ways that have nothing to do with whether data trails are captured.[22] Or consider the ways in which spatial metaphors continually recur in discussions of privacy. Even in contexts that are not thought to involve spatial privacy at all, judges and scholars repeatedly refer to "spheres" and "zones" to describe the privacy that the law should attempt to guarantee.[23]

Because information-based analytical frameworks don't recognize these dimensions of the spatial privacy interest, commentators operating within those frameworks tend to question whether they are "real." Yet that conclusion denies the logic of embodied, situated experience. Surveillance infrastructures alter the experience of places in ways that do not depend entirely on whether anyone is actually watching. Governments know this well; that is part of the point of deploying surveillance infrastructures within public spaces. It seems sounder to conclude that the information-based frameworks are incomplete. Conceptualizing the privacy interest as having an independently significant spatial dimension explains aspects of surveillance that neither visibility nor informational transparency can explain.

Work in surveillance studies suggests that direct visual surveillance affects the experience of space and place in two ways that an emphasis on informational transparency doesn't completely capture. First, surveillance fosters a kind of passivity that is best described as a ceding of power over space. As geographer Hille Koskela puts it, visual surveillance constitutes "space as a container" for passive objects.[24] She distinguishes the spatial shaping that produces "container-space" from the "power-space" constituted by panoptic strategies of normalization, which depend on access to particularized information. But the "containerization" of space is itself a panoptic strategy. Panopticism in the Foucauldian sense is both statistical and architectural; it entails ordering of spaces to obviate the need for continual surveillance and to instill tractability in those who enter.[25] Our newspaper-reading individual cannot see whether anyone is watching her, but she can see that the plaza has been re-architected to allow observation secretly and at will, and that there is no obvious source of information about the surveillance and no evident method of recourse if she wishes to lodge a complaint. In Hohfeldian terms,[26] the reconfiguration places individuals under a twofold disability: the targets of surveillance cannot entirely avoid the gaze (except by avoiding the place) and also cannot identify the watchers. We can say, therefore, that surveillance alters the balance of powers and disabilities that obtains in public places. It instills an expectation of being surveilled, and contrary to the conventional legal wisdom, this reasonable expectation and the passivity that it instills are precisely the problem.

Performance theory reminds us that individuals surveilled are not only passive bodies, and this leads us to the second way in which surveillance affects the experience of space and place. Like identities, places are dynamic and relational; they are constructed over time through everyday practice.[27] Surveillance alters important parameters of both processes. Building on work in feminist geography, Koskela argues that surveillance alters a sense of space that she calls "emotional space." She observes that "[t]o be under surveillance is an ambivalent emotional event. A surveillance camera … can at the same time represent safety and danger."[28] This point contrasts usefully with US privacy theorists' comparatively single-minded focus on the "chilling effect"; it reminds us that surveillance changes the affective dimension of space in ways that that formulation doesn't address. Marc Augé has argued that the defining feature of contemporary geography is the "non-place."[29] Places are historical and relational; non-places exist in the present and are characterized by a sense of temporariness, openness, and solitariness.[30] Augé does not discuss surveillance, but the distinction between places and non-places maps well to the affective dimension of space that Koskela identifies. Augé's critics observe that "placeness" is a matter of perspective; for example, airports may be places to those who work there, while wealthy residential enclaves may be non-places to those whose entry incites automatic suspicion.[31] It may be most accurate to conceptualize "placeness" both as a matter of degree and as an attribute that may be experienced differently by different groups. Along this continuum, surveillance makes places more like non-places. Spaces exposed by surveillance function differently than spaces that are not so exposed.

I will characterize the spatial dimension of the privacy interest as an interest in avoiding or selectively controlling the conditions of exposure. This terminology is intended to move the discussion beyond both visibility and transparency to capture the linked effects of architecture and power as experienced by embodied, situated subjects. With respect to space, surveillance employs a twofold dynamic of containerization and constraint to pursue large-scale behavioral modification. Koskela observes that surveillance makes public spaces less predictable for the watched.[32] The relation is reciprocal: surveillance also attempts to make those spaces more predictable for the watchers. By altering the balance of powers and disabilities, exposure changes the parameters that shape the ongoing performance of identity, community, and place.

The effects of exposure and transparency are complementary, and the genius of surveillance appears most clearly when one considers them together. Transparency alters the parameters of evolving subjectivity; exposure alters the capacity of places to function as contexts within which identity is developed and performed. Surveillance directed at transparency seeks to systematize, predict, and channel difference; surveillance directed at exposure seeks to prevent unsystematized, unpredictable difference from emerging.

Notes

1. See generally Foucault, *Discipline and Punish* (cited in note 10).
2. See id at 205–06. The exception is James Boyle, Foucault in Cyberspace: Surveillance, Sovereignty, and Hardwired Censors, 66 *U Cin L Rev* 177, 184–88 (1997).
3. Foucault, *Discipline and Punish* at 223 (cited in note 10).
4. Id at 207–17, 222–27.
5. See David Lyon, *Surveillance Society: Monitoring Everyday Life* 33–35, 114–18 (Open University 2001); Oscar H. Gandy, Jr., *The Panoptic Sort: A Political Economy of Personal Information* 15–52 (Westview 1993). See generally David Murakami Wood, ed, *Surveillance Studies Network, A Report on the Surveillance Society* (Mark Siddoway/Knowledge House 2006); Kirstie Ball, Elements of Surveillance: A New Framework and Future Directions, 5 *Info Commun & Socy* 573 (2002).
6. See Michael R. Curry and Leah A. Lievrouw, *Places to Read Anonymously: The Ecology on Attention and Forgetting* 5 (working paper, 2004), online at http://www.spatial.maine.edu/~nittel/lp/ curry-lievrouw _paper.pdf (visited Jan 12, 2008), quoting Jean-François Blanchette and Deborah G. Johnson, Data Retention and the Panoptic Society: The Social Benefits of Forgetfulness, 18 *Info Socy* 33, 35 (2002).
7. Gilles Deleuze and Félix Guattari, *A Thousand Plateaus: Capitalism and Schizophrenia* (Minnesota 1987) (Brian Massumi, trans).
8. Kevin D. Haggerty and Richard V. Ericson, "The Surveillant Assemblage," 51 *Brit J Sociology* 605, 605 (2000).
9. Id at 614.
10. Id at 615–16.
11. Canonical works in these fields include J.L. Austin, *How to Do Things with Words* (Harvard 1962); Clifford Geertz, Thick Description: Toward an Interpretive Theory of Culture, in *The Interpretation of Cultures* 3 (Basic 1973); Erving Goffman, *The Presentation of Self in Everyday Life* (Doubleday Anchor 1959); Jacques Derrida, Signature Event Context, in *Margins of Philosophy* 307 (Chicago 1982) (Alan Bass, trans).
12. See, for example, Andrew Parker and Eve Kosofsky Sedgwick, Introduction, in Andrew Parker and Eve Kosofsky Sedgwick, eds, *Performativity and Performance* 1, 6–8 (Routledge 1995); Judith Butler, *Gender Trouble: Feminism and the Subversion of Identity* 24–25 (Routledge 1990).
13. See David J. Phillips, From Privacy to Visibility: Context, Identity, and Power in Ubiquitous Computing Environments, 23 *Soc Text* 95, 101 (2005); John E. McGrath, *Loving Big Brother: Performance, Privacy and Surveillance Space* 12–14 (Routledge 2004); Hille Koskela, Webcams, TV Shows, and Mobile Phones: Empowering Exhibitionism, 2 *Surveillance & Socy* 199, 206 (2004); Stan Karas, Privacy, Identity, Databases, 52 *Am U L Rev* 393, 417–24 (2002).
14. See *Hamberger v Eastman*, 206 A2d 239, 242 (NH 1964). See also *Chapman v United States*, 365 US 610, 616–17 (1961).
15. See *Florida v Riley*, 488 US 445, 451 (1989); *California v Ciraolo*, 476 US 207, 214–15 (1986).
16. See *California v Greenwood*, 486 US 35, 40 (1988).
17. See *O'Connor v Ortega*, 480 US 709, 713–14 (1987); *Mancusi v DeForte*, 392 US 364, 369 (1968).
18. 533 US 27 (2001).

19. Id at 34.

20. See, for example, Rosen, *The Unwanted Gaze* at 8 (cited in note 7); Lisa Austin, Privacy and the Question of Technology, 22 *Law & Phil* 119, 126 (2003); Ruth Gavison, Privacy and the Limits of Law, 89 *Yale L J* 421, 432 (1980) ("[A]ttention alone will cause a loss of privacy even if no new information becomes known.").

21. See, for example, Solove, 90 *Cal L Rev* at 1094–95, 1151 (cited in note 8); Lloyd L. Weinreb, The Right to Privacy, in Ellen Frankel Paul, Fred D. Miller, Jr., and Jeffrey Paul, eds, *The Right to Privacy* 25, 26–27 (Cambridge, 2000). The exception is Helen Nissenbaum, who does not criticize spatialization and whose "contextual integrity" framework for privacy accommodates spatial privacy interests. See Nissenbaum, 79 *Wash L Rev* at 137–42 (cited in note 7).

22. See generally Don Mitchell, *The Right to the City: Social Justice and the Fight for Public Space* (Guilford 2003). See also Marc Jonathan Blitz, Video Surveillance and the Constitution of Public Space: Fitting the Fourth Amendment to a World That Tracks Image and Identity, 82 *Tex L Rev* 1349, 1374–98 (2004).

23. See, for example, *Zablocki v Redhail*, 434 US 374, 397 n 1 (1978) (Powell concurring) (observing that the Court's prior decisions establish a "sphere of privacy or autonomy" within the marital relationship); *Griswold v Connecticut*, 381 US 479, 485 (1965) (describing a "zone of privacy created by several fundamental constitutional guarantees"); *Dietemann v Time, Inc*, 449 F2d 245, 248–49 (9th Cir 1971).

24. Hille Koskela, "The Gaze without Eyes": Video-surveillance and the Changing Nature of Urban Space, 24 *Progress in Hum Geography* 243, 250 (2000).

25. See Foucault, *Discipline and Punish* at 206 (cited in note 10); Julie E. Cohen, Pervasively Distributed Copyright Enforcement, 95 *Georgetown L J* 1, 23 (2006).

26. See Wesley Newcomb Hohfeld, *Fundamental Legal Conceptions as Applied in Judicial Reasoning and Other Legal Essays* 35–64 (Yale 1919) (Walter Wheeler Cook, ed).

27. See generally Henri Lefebvre, *The Production of Space* (Blackwell 1991) (Donald Nicholson-Smith, trans).

28. Koskela, 24 *Progress in Hum Geography* at 257 (cited in note 41).

29. See Marc Augé, *Non-places: Introduction to an Anthropology of Supermodernity* 75–115 (Verso 1995) (John Howe, trans).

30. Id at 77–86.

31. See generally Peter Merriman, Driving Places: Marc Augé, Non-places, and the Geographies of England's M1 Motorway, 21 *Theory, Culture, & Socy* 145 (2004).

32. Koskela, 24 *Progress in Hum Geography* at 250 (cited in note 41).

THE PURPOSE OF THE CORPORATION AND DATA ANALYTICS

5

What is the goal of a corporation? Whether or not a project or program is a good idea—"makes strategic sense"—for a company depends on whether the project fits within the goals of the corporation. For us, the question is important to assess whether or not a specific data analytics program is appropriate for the company. For Lemonade Insurance, what are the criteria to decide if AI Jim is good for the company? The goal of the company may seem clear—to benefit the company. However, two different approaches have emerged in the past few decades.

One camp, based primarily on bankruptcy laws and cases, argues that when companies are being dissolved and sold for parts, those in charge (the board of directors) must make decisions that are in the interests of the company's shareholders. In this particular situation, shareholders are the last in line to be paid (aka "residual claimants") and the board has an obligation to make sure there is money left for them. In other words, the board cannot make bad deals or pay executives all the remaining money since such acts would be bad for shareholders. In this limited situation, when a company will soon cease to exist, law exists around the goals of companies.

However, this does not tell us much about how companies are supposed to be run as an ongoing entity. How do managers decide which products to launch, which drugs to research, or whether to rely on AI Jim to decide claims? Even within more narrow understandings of the purpose of the corporation, those who argue for shareholder wealth maximization, all corporations are expected to pursue activities in the interest of the business. In fact, companies lose money for years with the hopes of growing a customer and user base.

Milton Friedman's "The Social Responsibility of Business Is to Increase Its Profits" is often held up as an example for the "profit maximizing" point of view. But Friedman's argument, even here, is more nuanced than the title would make it seem. Milton Friedman makes a few arguments against "corporate social responsibility" (CSR) as a general idea. First, he says if CSR is going to mean anything, it must mean that it is a responsibility that is outside the role of a particular business, otherwise, we would just call it a business responsibility. Friedman asks, "What does it mean to say that the corporate executive has a 'social responsibility' in his capacity as businessman? If this statement is not pure rhetoric, it must mean that he is to act in some way that is not in the

DOI: 10.1201/9781003278290-29

interest of his employers."[1] Examples would include wage caps, inflation, or health clinics for the poor (if you were not in the health industry).

Instead, and this is where Friedman is more nuanced, if a project or strategy is a good idea for the business, then just say it is good for business: "it may well be in the long-run interest of a corporation" to help a community. If it is, says Friedman, then say so. Friedman does say executives should pursue strategies in the interest of the firm while "conforming to the basic rules of the society, both those embodied in law and those embodied in ethical custom." More specifically,

> In an ideal free market resting on private property, no individual can coerce any other, all cooperation is voluntary, all parties to such cooperation benefit or they need not participate. There are no values, no "social" responsibilities in any sense other than the shared values and responsibilities of individuals. Society is a collection of individuals and of the various groups they voluntarily form.[2]

This approach, as we will see, is still problematic as it assumes that all important people to consider are voluntary bargainers and of equal standing to bargain. He ignores initial allocations of power and people harmed without any formal relationship to the company (communities, third parties). All our readings included here make reference to Friedman or the shareholder wealth maximizing goal of the company. At this point, however, it is important to know that Friedman never advocates for profit maximizing that harms others or is illegal or unethical because it would not be in the company's best interest to harm others or act illegally. Instead, he argues against the term "social responsibility."

This debate around the purpose of the corporation is important for the ethics of data and analytics because the answer impacts what types of projects "fit" within the purpose of the corporation. For the view that companies exist to maximize current shareholder wealth, the projects would be profit-driven and short-term in duration. Long-term consequences may be ignored or pushed aside and negative implications for smaller or more marginal stakeholders can be overridden by powerful interests. For Lemonade Insurance's AI Jim, the question according to Friedman would be *does this program benefit our shareholders while* "conforming to the basic rules of the society, both those embodied in law and those embodied in ethical custom?"

However, shareholder wealth maximization (aka profit maximization) turns out to not be a helpful way to manage a company (i.e., Enron, Purdue Pharmaceutical, etc.). The three readings included here offer explanations as to the purpose of companies and responsibilities of managers. Within the view that the purpose of the corporation is to create value for stakeholders, the criteria for projects is broader and more long-term.

Summary of Readings

Lynn Stout,[3] Distinguished Professor of Corporate and Business law at Cornell School of Law, directly addresses the (mistaken) view that companies have one purpose: "maximizing their shareholders' wealth as measured by stock price" (what she calls "shareholder primacy"). Professor Stout shows, in this article and in her related book, that shareholder primacy is inconsistent with rules of corporate law, economics of business, or by how managers and companies work in practice. Stout notes that the courts always defer to the managers and boards to act in the best interest of the company within the business judgment rule—even when those actions *lose* money for the company in the short-term or when the stock price may fall. The long run interest of the company is the important metric. Professor Stout also notes (as we did above) that prioritizing shareholders as "residual claimants" when a company is being dissolved does not mean shareholders must be considered when a company is an ongoing entity. In applying Stout's approach to the purpose of the firm, one would show that an act (a change to a data analytics program, in our case) may cause a short-term decrease in revenues, increase in costs, or decrease in shareholders' stock price, but the decision is in the long-term interest of the company and is therefore the best decision. The main takeaway is that managers have an obligation (a normative obligation) to act in the long-term interest of the company. *So, Stout would not ask about shareholders when assessing a data analytics program, but rather ask what decisions are in the long-term interest of the company.* Managers would owe this obligation to not only the board and shareholders, but also their employees, users, customers, and suppliers. Which, brings us to stakeholder theory.

Stakeholder theory argues that companies are better off if their goal is creating value for their stakeholders. R. Edward Freeman originally defines stakeholders as those who are either influenced by or influencing the operations of a company. Business, then, is about "how customers, suppliers, employees, financiers (stockholders, bondholders, banks, and so on), communities, and managers interact and create value."[4] The basis of stakeholder theory is that the purpose of the firm is to create value for stakeholders (including the firm itself and its employees), and management decisions should focus on managing those stakeholder relationships. A growing body of research supports the idea that managing for stakeholders drives better financial performance and resiliency through adversity.[5] The idea behind stakeholder theory is not new. Ed Freeman originally wrote a strategy book on stakeholder theory in 1984. But the idea has always been popular with practicing executives and managers; the Business Roundtable, an association of the CEOs of the top corporations in the United States, recently put out a paper exhorting businesses to manage for stakeholders as it is in the long-term interest of the company.[6]

The stakeholders to a data analytics program would include those who are impacted by or impact the program or company—even without a financial relationship with the company and even when not voluntary. The subject of videos uploaded online, the individuals whose faces are included in an uploaded picture and used for facial recognition, the subject of a predictive analytics program but who does not have any financial relationship with a company are all stakeholders to the decision of a company. Data analytics stretches the idea of stakeholders to include those who are not voluntarily a part of the firm's relationships. Normally, stakeholders are important because, we assume, "Those who engage with a business do so voluntarily, since they usually have some amount of choice about whether or not to do so. Of course, the degree of choice depends on the underlying structure of society and markets."[7] *In fact, this is a key difference for the ethics of data analytics: how to incorporate the interests of those with a tenuous financial relationship with the company and whose relationship is not voluntary?* When applying Freeman's stakeholder theory to a data analytics program, one would first list the top three to five stakeholders and analyze whether value is created or destroyed for them, whether they are treated fairly, whether their rights are enabled or diminished. We would ask:

1. *Who is most impacted by the analytics program? Do they have a relationship with the company? Are their interests taken into account in the design and development?*
2. *Are those impacted by this program voluntary stakeholders of the firm with any power? If not, are these marginalized stakeholders taken into account or are they being taken advantage of?*

Another key point for Freeman is that stakeholder interests are interconnected: how one set of stakeholder interests are treated impacts the company's relationship with the other stakeholders: their interests are interconnected. Robert Frank picks up on this idea from the standpoint of economics.

Robert Frank's chapter builds on Milton Friedman's essay directly—specifically the idea that acting in ways that benefit others may be in the long-term interest of the firm. Frank focuses on the tempting one-shot dilemmas people in business come across, where an act would benefit them in the short-term but harm others. For example, selling opioids that are more profitable for the company but also more addictive for users, targeting teens for vaping products that introduce them to nicotine, etc. Frank explores the evolutionary reason people cooperate and why people look for cooperative traits in others. By acting in responsible ways, where a company or manager does not exploit a one-shot dilemma, Frank argues that such acts send a signal in the market as to the trustworthiness of the manager and firm. This trust helps solve *commitment problems* with stakeholders (employees, customers, etc.) who may need to trust that the company will uphold agreements. This trustworthy behavior also *signals to the market* the values of the company and attracts likeminded stakeholders (employees, customers, etc.). Key for Frank, however, is that such decisions and the related rationale should be public and explained in order for the signal to be heard in the market. In order to make an argument from Robert Frank's perspective, we would have to argue that a data analytics program is either a good signal in the market or helps increase the trustworthiness of the company to other stakeholders to solve commitment problems (or both!).

1. Signaling. *Are we acting in a way that is congruent with our values and the values of our stakeholders—including employees, users, customers, suppliers, etc. How will this act, that may be in the short-term interest of our company but harm a stakeholder group, be seen by other stakeholders?*
2. Commitment Problems. *Are we acting in a way that increases our trustworthiness in the eyes of our stakeholders? Will the act harm our ability with future commitment problems (where trust is necessary)?*

In many ways, both Freeman and Frank are reminiscent of Friedman's exhortation that "There are no 'social' values, no 'social' responsibilities in any sense other than the shared values and responsibilities of individuals. Society is a collection of individuals and of the various groups they voluntarily form." If we take this idea seriously, then responsible firms will seek cooperative relationships with stakeholders for the long-term benefit of the firm.

Related Cases

In a series of cases, we examine the use of facial recognition to predict ethnicity, sexuality, and emotions by corporations. Facial recognition programs have known bias issues as their accuracy rates are found to be not consistent across race and gender—as we noted in Chapter 3.[8] Some researchers have called for more regulations and even banning facial recognition technology due to the unique dangers of the technology: faces are hard to hide or change making counter measures almost impossible and the technology is becoming so cheap as to be ubiquitous.[9]

Luke Stark likens facial recognition technology to plutonium in that "it's dangerous, racializing, and has few legitimate uses."[10] Stark find the problem with facial recognition is more fundamental that just discriminatory bias: "The fundamental problem with facial recognition technologies is they attach numerical values to the human face at all."[11] Further, this quantification is racialized: "reducing humans into sets of legible, manipulable signs has been a hallmark of racializing scientific and administrative techniques going back several hundred years."[12]

Relatedly, attempting to identify something about the person based on the physical structure of the face reminds many of phrenology, the discredited pseudoscience attempting to differentiate peoples' mental states and character based on the physical outline of their skull. Phrenology has a racist history and has been used to support treating groups of people differently.[13] As noted by Kate Crawford, "These tools can take us back to the phrenological past, when spurious claims were used to support existing systems of power."[14] For data analytics, we would ask whether the use of an emotional recognition program is within the purpose of the corporation according to Freeman, Freidman, or Stout.

With that background, we turn to the cases included here. The first case calls into question *should a company develop software that purports to identify ethnicity, emotions, or sexuality?* It is not clear given the potential uses for this technology. The race-detection software case,[15] "The Quiet Growth of Race Detection Software," gives an overview of the rationale behind identifying an individuals' race including better targeted ads and identifying who is wearing a particular lipstick. However, the facial *analysis* algorithms carry many of the same accuracy problems of facial recognition programs (from Chapter 4). In addition, questions about why a company could reasonably want to guess someone's race or ethnicity—and if there are secondary, problematic uses for the software.

Similarly, the HireVue case, "A Face-Scanning Algorithm Increasingly Decides whether You Deserve the Job,"[16] provides an overview of the use of emotion recognition software used for interviewing. However, experts question as to the ability of facial expressions, even if "measured," to reveal someone's feelings or actual emotions. Hirevue is not the first. Amazon developed an emotion detection software, Rekognition, trained on images of people *posing* expressions that were then manually annotated with labels with defined emotions (in English).[17] As noted by Jayne Williamson-Lee, "we assume a smile uniquely expresses happiness and a scowl uniquely expresses anger. But there is much more variation in the ways people express and perceive emotions."[18] Lest we think this is a single incident, Canon's Chinese subsidiary, Canon Information Technology, implemented cameras with "smile-recognition" software to only allow smiling employees to book or enter rooms.[19]

Finally, the content moderation case, "Recommending an Insurrection: Facebook and Recommendation Algorithms," provides an overview of the content dilemma at Facebook. Content that increases engagement can provide misinformation and even be harmful to the users. The decisions as to what content to support and which to take down calls into question the purpose of the firm and the criteria by which to judge data analytics projects. Content moderation can be seen as an example of Frank's one-shot dilemma: companies have a short-term incentive to allow legal-but-awful content on their site in order to increase "user engagement". Those harmed by the content are users who are not aware of the harm being done. In addition, many harmed are not users but members of society who are the subject or target of the content and whose lives are worse due to the content. This provides one-shot dilemma, envisioned by Frank, for Facebook to make short-term profits at the expense of marginalized stakeholders. The question is, should they?

Notes

1. Milton Friedman, "The Social Responsibility of Business Is to Increase Profits," *The New York Times Magazine* (13 September 1970).
2. Friedman (13 September 1970).
3. Lynn Stout, "The Problem of Corporate Purpose," *Issues in Governance Studies* (Washington, DC: The Brookings Institution, 2012). https://www.brookings.edu/wp-content/uploads/2016/06/Stout_Corporate-Issues.pdf

4. R. Edward Freeman, Bidhan L. Parmar, and Kirsten Martin, *The Power of And: Responsible Business Without Trade-Offs* (Columbia University Press, 2020), 70.

5. Freeman, Parmar, and Martin, *The Power of And: Responsible Business Without Trade-Offs*.

6. Business Roundtable, "Business Roundtable Redefines the Purpose of a Corporation to Promote 'An Economy That Serves All Americans'" (2019). https://www.businessroundtable.org/business-round-table-redefines-the-purpose-of-a-corporation-to-promote-an-economy-that-serves-all-americans

7. Freeman, Parmar, and Martin, *The Power of And: Responsible Business Without Trade-Offs*, 70.

8. Joy Buolamwini and Timnit Gebru, "Gender Shades: Intersectional Accuracy Disparities in Commercial Gender Classification," *Proceedings of Machine Learning Research*, Conference on Fairness, Accountability, and Transparency, 81 (2018): 1–15.

9. Woodrow Hartzog and Evan Selinger, "Facial Recognition Is the Perfect Tool for Oppression," *Medium*, 2018.

10. Luke Stark, "Facial Recognition Is the Plutonium of AI," *XRDS: Crossroads, The ACM Magazine for Students* 25, no. 3 (2019): 50–55.

11. Stark, 52.

12. Stark, 52. "Facial recognition technologies assign numerical values to schematic representations of the face, and make comparisons between those values. At a technical level, it is not possible to separate the work of associating schematically mapped parts of the face with real humans with quantitative comparison, ordering, and ranking"(p. 53).

13. Phrenology was based on the belief that "human character could be read through examining the shape of the head" (p. 123—124). "[t]he idea that interior states can be reliably inferred from external signs stems in part from the history of physiognomy, which was premised on studying a person's facial features for indications of their character." (Crawford, Atlas of AI, 2021, p. 161). Kate Crawford explores both the classification of humans as well as predicting their affect in Chapters 4 and 5 of *Atlas of AI* (2021).

14. Kate Crawford, "Artificial Intelligence Is Misreading Human Emotion," *The Atlantic* (April 27, 2021). https://www.theatlantic.com/technology/archive/2021/04/artificial-intelligence-misreading-human-emotion/618696/

15. Hannah Whitaker, "The Quiet Growth Of Race-Detection Software Sparks Concerns Over Bias," *The Wall Street Journal* (August 14, 2020). https://www.wsj.com/articles/the-quiet-growth-of-race-detection-software-sparks-concerns-over-bias-11597378154

16. Drew Harwell, "A Face-Scanning Algorithm Increasingly Decides Whether You Deserve the Job," *The Washington Post* (November 6, 2019). https://www.washingtonpost.com/technology/2019/10/22/ai-hiring-face-scanning-algorithm-increasingly-decides-whether-you-deserve-job/

17. Jayne Williamson-Lee, "Amazon's A.I. Emotion-Recognition Software Confuses Expressions for Feelings," *Medium* (October 28, 2019). https://onezero.medium.com/amazons-a-i-emotion-recognition-software-confuses-expressions-for-feelings-53e96007ca63

18. Jayne Williamson-Lee, "Amazon's A.I. Emotion-Recognition Software Confuses Expressions for Feelings," *Medium* (October 28, 2019). Ms. Williamson-Lee also cites Amazon's instructions: "The API is only making a determination of the physical appearance of a person's face. It is not a determination of the person's internal emotional state and should not be used in such a way. For example, a person pretending to have a sad face might not be sad emotionally."

19. James Vincent, "Canon Put AI Cameras in Its Chinese Offices That Only Let Smiling Workers Inside," *The Verge* (2021). https://www.theverge.com/2021/6/17/22538160/ai-camera-smile-recognition-office-workers-china-canon

The Quiet Growth of Race-Detection Software Sparks Concerns over Bias[*]

Parmy Olson

More than a dozen companies offer artificial intelligence programs that promise to identify a person's race, but researchers and even some vendors worry it will fuel discrimination.

When Revlon Inc. wanted to know what lipstick women of different races and in different countries were wearing, the cosmetics giant didn't need to send out a survey. It hired Miami-based Kairos Inc., which used a facial-analysis algorithm to scan Instagram photos.

Back then, in 2015, the ability to scan a person's face and identify his or her race was still in its infancy. Today, more than a dozen companies offer some form of race or ethnicity detection, according to a review of websites, marketing literature and interviews.

In the last few years, companies have started using such race-detection software to understand how certain customers use their products, who looks at their ads, or what people of different racial groups like. Others use the tool to seek different racial features in stock photography collections, typically for ads, or in security, to help narrow down the search for someone in a database. In China, where face tracking is widespread, surveillance cameras have been equipped with race-scanning software to track ethnic minorities.

The field is still developing, and it is an open question how companies, governments and individuals will take advantage of such technology in the future. Use of the software is fraught, as researchers and companies have begun to recognize its potential to drive discrimination, posing challenges to widespread adoption.

A spokeswoman for Revlon says it was unable to comment because the Instagram scanning happened several years ago. Kairos didn't respond to repeated requests for comment.

---

[*] Parmy Olson, "The Quiet Growth Of Race-Detection Software Sparks Concerns Over Bias," *The Wall Street Journal* (August 14, 2020). https://www.wsj.com/articles/the-quiet-growth-of-race-detection-software-sparks -concerns-over-bias-11597378154. Reprinted with permission.

DOI: 10.1201/9781003278290-30

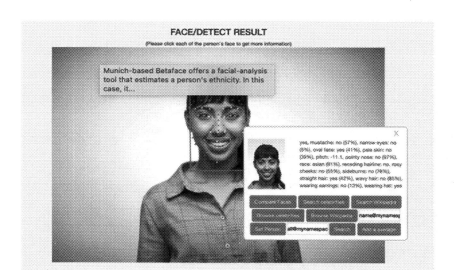

Munich-based Betaface offers a facial-analysis tool that estimates a person's ethnicity. In this case, it says with 91% certainty that the woman in the photo is Asian.

PHOTO: BETAFACE

Race-detection software is a subset of facial analysis, a type of artificial intelligence that scans faces for a range of features—from the arch of an eyebrow to the shape of the cheekbones—and uses that information to draw conclusions about gender, age, race, emotions, even attractiveness. This is different from facial recognition, which also relies on an AI technique called machine learning, but is used to identify particular faces, for instance to unlock a smartphone or spot a troublemaker in a crowd.

Facial analysis is "useful for marketers because people buy in cohorts and behave in cohorts," says Brian Brackeen, a founder of Kairos who left in 2018 and now invests in startups through Lightship Capital.

For retailers and other businesses, facial analysis of camera footage promises the ability to learn more about customers in bricks-and-mortar settings, much like they have long used cookies, or small data files that track people's internet activity, to target online ads. "The physical world is a big vacuum of data because there's nothing there," says Ajay Amlani, senior vice president of corporate development at Idemia SAS, a French firm that offers facial recognition and other identification services. Now cameras are starting to play a similar role to cookies.

New York-based Haystack AI Inc. says its customers use its race-classification feature for ad targeting, market research and to help authenticate people's identities. Germany's Cognitec Systems GmbH offers ethnicity detection for retailers and other companies to collect statistical data about their visitors, says Jeurgen Pampus, its sales and marketing director. He said no customers had yet bought a license for race-classification, though they had bought software for classifying ages and genders.

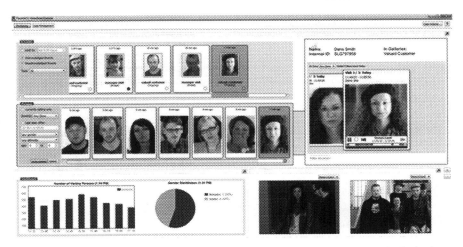

Germany-based Cognitec Systems's FaceVACS-VideoScan Console has a filter, shown at mid-left, that lets users search faces by 'ethnicity.'

PHOTO: COGNITEC SYSTEMS

Spectrico, a Bulgarian startup that sells a perpetual, unlimited license for its race-classification tool for 1,000 euros (about $1,170), says that dating sites use it to check if profiles are accurate, while advertisers use it to track the demographics of people looking at smart billboards. Founder Martin Prenev said a few customers have purchased the race-classification tool, and more bought it in combination with a gender- and age-classification tool.

China's Face++, one of the world's biggest facial-recognition and facial-analysis companies, was valued at $4 billion in May 2019, according to market intelligence firm PitchBook. It says on its website that its race-detection feature can be used for consumer-behavior analysis and ad targeting.

Facial analysis has largely flown under the radar, even as facial recognition has come under fire because poorly trained systems have misidentified people of color. Places such as Boston, San Francisco, Washington state and California have curbed the use of facial recognition in law enforcement. IBM Inc., Alphabet Inc. and Microsoft Corp. have limited their facial recognition businesses, particularly in selling to police departments.

Research into facial analysis continues. Some scientists say that algorithms trained to identify a person's race can be startlingly accurate. In May, two scientists from Ruhr-Universitat Bochum in Germany published a paper in the scientific journal *Machine Learning* showing that their algorithm could estimate if a face was white, Black, Asian, Hispanic or "other" with 99% accuracy. The researchers trained their algorithms on a database of prison mug shots that included a label for the race of each person, according to Dr. Laurenz Wiskott, one of the study's authors.

Some researchers and even vendors say race-based facial analysis should not exist. For decades, governments have barred doctors, banks and employers from using information about race to decide which patients to treat, which borrowers to grant mortgages and which job applicants to hire. Race-detection software poses the disconcerting possibility that institutions could—intentionally or not—make decisions based on a person's ethnic background, in ways that are harder to detect because they occur as complex or opaque algorithms, according to researchers in the field.

Using AI to identify ethnicity "seems more likely to harm than help," says Arvind Narayanan, a computer science professor at Princeton University who has researched how anonymized data can be used to identify people.

A person of mixed race might disagree with how an algorithm classifies them, says Carly Kind, director of the Ada Lovelace Institute in London, a research group that focuses on applications of AI. "Technological systems have the power to turn things into data, into facts, and seemingly objective conclusions," she says.

Software that lets employers scan the micro-expressions of job candidates during interviews could inadvertently discriminate if it starts to factor in race, Ms. Kind says. Police who classify ethnicity using facial-analysis software run the risk of exacerbating racial profiling, she says. Ethnicity recognition could also be harmful if companies use it to push marginalized people toward specific products or offer discriminatory pricing, says Evan Greer, deputy director of digital rights group Fight for the Future.

Use of face-scanning technology in China has been controversial, most notably in Xinjiang, a region in the country's northwest where authorities have used it to surveil its Uighur Muslim minority. Last year, a Chinese surveillance camera maker, Hangzhou Hikvision Digital Technology, advertised a camera on its website that could automatically identify Uighurs, according to security-industry trade publication IPVM.

China has used face-scanning technology to surveil its Uighur Muslim minority in the Xinjiang region. This road, photographed in May 2019, leads to a facility believed to be a re-education camp where mostly Muslim ethnic minorities are detained.

PHOTO: GREG BAKER/AGENCE FRANCE-PRESSE/GETTY IMAGES

Mr. Brackeen, who is Black, championed Kairos's race-recognition system because it could help businesses tailor their marketing to ethnic minorities. Now, Mr. Brackeen believes that race-detection software has the potential to fuel discrimination.

He is comfortable with businesses using it, but says governments should not use it, and is wary of consumers using it too. Kairos released a free app in 2017 that estimated race, showing how Black, white, Asian or Hispanic people were if they uploaded a selfie. "I hoped that people would see that 10% Black score and see the humanity in other people," Mr. Brackeen says.

More than 10 million people submitted selfies to the app to see the results. Many of the app's users, particularly in Brazil, complained on social media that their scores weren't white enough, Mr. Brackeen says. The app was shut down.

In Northern Europe, a furniture chain used the facial-analysis software of Dutch facial-recognition firm Sightcorp B.V. to screen customers entering its stores, and learned that many of them were younger than it had expected. It subsequently hired more people in their 20s and 30s to be floor staff, according to Joyce Caradona, chief executive of Sightcorp. Her company stopped selling its own ethnicity classification feature in 2017, on concerns it might contravene Europe's data-privacy laws.

Facewatch Ltd., a British facial-recognition firm whose software spots suspected thieves as they enter a store by screening them against a watch list, earlier this year removed an option to track the race, gender or age of shoppers, since "this information is irrelevant," a spokesman says. There are security risks with collecting race data which could, either by design or inadvertently, be linked to people's identities, according to Alex Heid, chief research officer at cybersecurity firm Security Scorecard. His firm recently found about half a dozen websites with security vulnerabilities around their databases holding people's facial data, including a facial-recognition firm and a US engineering school that required students to show their faces to log in.

Companies that offer facial-analysis services say the demographic data their systems collect aren't connected to individual identities. But data brokers could, in theory, combine marketing databases that are bought and sold online to create a more detailed picture of people on them, Mr. Heid says, linking that data to identities.

A few years ago, companies that sold facial analysis were more open about their ability to scan demographic features, says Zak Doffman, CEO of Digital Barriers PLC, a British facial-recognition firm that works with law enforcement. When large tech companies started getting flack for their facial recognition systems, "everyone stopped talking about it," he adds. "No one is talking about ethnicity identification now. Not openly."

Chapter 5.2

A Face-Scanning Algorithm Increasingly Decides Whether You Deserve the Job*

Drew Harwell

> *HireVue claims it uses artificial intelligence to decide who's best for a job. Outside experts call it 'profoundly disturbing.'*

An artificial intelligence hiring system has become a powerful gatekeeper for some of America's most prominent employers, reshaping how companies assess their workforce—and how prospective employees prove their worth.

Designed by the recruiting-technology firm HireVue, the system uses candidates' computer or cellphone cameras to analyze their facial movements, word choice and speaking voice before ranking them against other applicants based on an automatically generated "employability" score.

HireVue's "AI-driven assessments" have become so pervasive in some industries, including hospitality and finance, that universities make special efforts to train students on how to look and speak for best results. More than 100 employers now use the system, including Hilton and Unilever, and more than a million job seekers have been analyzed.

But some AI researchers argue the system is digital snake oil—an unfounded blend of superficial measurements and arbitrary number-crunching that is not rooted in scientific fact. Analyzing a human being like this, they argue, could end up penalizing nonnative speakers, visibly nervous interviewees or anyone else who doesn't fit the model for look and speech.

The system, they argue, will assume a critical role in helping decide a person's career. But they doubt it even knows what it's looking for: Just what does the perfect employee look and sound like, anyway?

"It's a profoundly disturbing development that we have proprietary technology that claims to differentiate between a productive worker and a worker who isn't fit, based on their facial

---

* Drew Harwell, "A Face-Scanning Algorithm Increasingly Decides Whether You Deserve the Job," *The Washington Post* (November 6, 2019). https://www.washingtonpost.com/technology/2019/10/22/ai-hiring-face-scanning-algorithm-increasingly-decides-whether-you-deserve-job/ Reprinted with permission.

DOI: 10.1201/9781003278290-31

movements, their tone of voice, their mannerisms," said Meredith Whittaker, a co-founder of the AI Now Institute, a research center in New York.

"It's pseudoscience. It's a license to discriminate," she added. "And the people whose lives and opportunities are literally being shaped by these systems don't have any chance to weigh in."

Loren Larsen, HireVue's chief technology officer, said that such criticism is uninformed and that "most AI researchers have a limited understanding" of the psychology behind how workers think and behave.

Larsen compared algorithms' ability to boost hiring outcomes with medicine's improvement of health outcomes and said the science backed him up. The system, he argued, is still more objective than the flawed metrics used by human recruiters, whose thinking he called the "ultimate black box."

"People are rejected all the time based on how they look, their shoes, how they tucked in their shirts and how 'hot' they are," he told The Washington Post. "Algorithms eliminate most of that in a way that hasn't been possible before."

The AI, he said, doesn't explain its decisions or give candidates their assessment scores, which he called "not relevant." But it is "not logical," he said, to assume some people might be unfairly eliminated by the automated judge.

"When 1,000 people apply for one job," he said, "999 people are going to get rejected, whether a company uses AI or not."

On Wednesday, a prominent rights group, the Electronic Privacy Information Center, filed an official complaint urging the Federal Trade Commission to investigate HireVue for "unfair and deceptive" practices. The system's "biased, unprovable and not replicable" results, EPIC officials wrote, constitute a major threat to American workers' privacy and livelihoods.

The inscrutable algorithms have forced job seekers to confront a new kind of interview anxiety. Nicolette Vartuli, a University of Connecticut senior studying math and economics with a 3.5 GPA, said she researched HireVue and did her best to dazzle the job-interview machine. She answered confidently and in the time allotted. She used positive keywords. She smiled, often and wide.

But when she didn't get the investment banking job, she couldn't see how the computer had rated her or ask how she could improve, and she agonized over what she had missed. Had she not looked friendly enough? Did she talk too loudly? What did the AI hiring system believe she had gotten wrong?

"I feel like that's maybe one of the reasons I didn't get it: I spoke a little too naturally," Vartuli said. "Maybe I didn't use enough big, fancy words. I used 'conglomerate' one time."

HireVue said its system dissects the tiniest details of candidates' responses—their facial expressions, their eye contact and perceived "enthusiasm"—and compiles reports companies can use in deciding whom to hire or disregard.

Job candidates aren't told their score or what little things they got wrong, and they can't ask the machine what they could do better. Human hiring managers can use other factors, beyond the HireVue score, to decide which candidates pass the first-round test.

The system, HireVue said, employs superhuman precision and impartiality to zero in on an ideal employee, picking up on telltale clues a recruiter might miss.

Major employers with lots of high-volume, entry-level openings are increasingly turning to such automated systems to help find candidates, assess résumés and streamline hiring. The Silicon Valley startup AllyO, for instance, advertises a "recruiting automation bot" that can text-message a candidate, "Are you willing to relocate?" And a HireVue competitor, the "digital recruiter" VCV, offers a similar system for use in phone interviews, during which a candidate's voice and answers are analyzed by an "automated screening" machine.

But HireVue's prospects have cemented it as the leading player in the brave new world of semi-automated corporate recruiting. It says it can save employers a fortune on in-person interviews and quickly cull applicants deemed subpar. HireVue says it also allows companies to see candidates from an expanded hiring pool: Anyone with a phone and Internet connection can apply.

Nathan Mondragon, HireVue's chief industrial-organizational psychologist, told The Post the standard 30-minute HireVue assessment includes half a dozen questions but can yield up to 500,000 data points, all of which become ingredients in the person's calculated score.

The employer decides the written questions, which HireVue's system then shows the candidate while recording and analyzing their responses. The AI assesses how a person's face moves to determine, for instance, how excited someone seems about a certain work task or how they would behave around angry customers. Those "Facial Action Units," Mondragon said, can make up 29 percent of a person's score; the words they say and the "audio features" of their voice, like their tone, make up the rest.

"Humans are inconsistent by nature. They inject their subjectivity into the evaluations," Mondragon said. "But AI can database what the human processes in an interview, without bias. … And humans are now believing in machine decisions over human feedback."

To train the system on what to look for and tailor the test to a specific job, the employer's current workers filling the same job—"the entire spectrum, from high to low achievers"—sit through the AI assessment, Larsen said.

Their responses, Larsen said, are then matched with a "benchmark of success" from those workers' past job performance, like how well they had met their sales quotas and how quickly they had resolved customer calls. The best candidates, in other words, end up looking and sounding like the employees who had done well before the prospective hires had even applied.

After a new candidate takes the HireVue test, the system generates a report card on their "competencies and behaviors," including their "willingness to learn," "conscientiousness & responsibility" and "personal stability," the latter of which is defined by how well they can cope with "irritable customers or co-workers."

Those computer-estimated personality traits are then used to group candidates into high, medium and low tiers based on their "likelihood of success." Employers can still pursue candidates ranked in the bottom tier, but several interviewed by The Post said they mostly focused on the ones the computer system liked best.

HireVue offers only the most limited peek into its interview algorithms, both to protect its trade secrets and because the company doesn't always know how the system decides on who gets labeled a "future top performer."

The company has given only vague explanations when defining which words or behaviors offer the best results. For a call center job, the company says, "supportive" words might be encouraged, while "aggressive" ones might sink one's score.

HireVue said its board of expert advisers regularly reviews its algorithmic approach, but the company declined to make the system available for an independent audit. The company, Larsen said, is "exploring the use of an independent auditor right now, to see how that could work."

HireVue launched its AI assessment service in 2014 as an add-on to its video-interview software, which more than 700 companies have used for nearly 12 million interviews worldwide. The Utah-based company won't disclose its revenue, the cost for employers or a full list of clients.

The company said last month that the private-equity giant Carlyle Group would become its new majority investor, providing an undisclosed sum from an $18.5 billion fund. Patrick McCarter, a managing director at the investment firm—which uses HireVue's video interviews internally and said it "will look to deploy AI-driven candidate assessments over time"—said the money would help the company expand to more employers and more specialized job openings, both in the United States and around the world.

At the hotel giant Hilton International, thousands of applicants for reservation-booking, revenue management and call center positions have gone through HireVue's AI system, and executives credit the automated interviews with shrinking their average hiring time from six weeks to five days.

Sarah Smart, the company's vice president of global recruitment, said the system has radically redrawn Hilton's hiring rituals, allowing the company to churn through applicants at lightning speed. Hiring managers inundated with applicants can now just look at who the system ranked highly and filter out the rest: "It's rare for a recruiter to need to go out of that range," she said.

At the consumer goods conglomerate Unilever, HireVue is credited with helping save 100,000 hours of interviewing time and roughly $1 million in recruiting costs a year. Leena Nair, the company's chief human resource officer, said the system had also helped steer managers away from hiring only "mini-mes" who look and act just like them, boosting the company's "diversity hires," as she called them, by about 16 percent.

"The more digital we become, the more human we become," she added.

Dane E. Holmes, the global head of human-capital management at HireVue client Goldman Sachs, wrote in the Harvard Business Review this spring that the banking giant's roughly 50,000 video-interview recordings were "a treasure trove of data that will help us conduct insightful analyses."

The investment bank said it uses HireVue's video-interview system but not its computer-generated assessments. But Holmes said data from those videos could help the company figure out how candidates' skills and backgrounds might correspond to how well they would work or how long they would stay at the firm. The company, he added, is also "experimenting with résumé-reading algorithms" that would help decide new hires' departments and tasks.

"Can I imagine a future in which companies rely exclusively on machines and algorithms to rate résumés and interviews? Maybe, for some," he wrote. (The "human element" of recruiting, he pledged, would survive at Goldman Sachs.)

Is your pregnancy app sharing your intimate data with your boss?

HireVue's expansion has also helped it win business from smaller groups such as Re:work, a Chicago nonprofit organization that trains unemployed local job seekers for careers in the tech industry. Shelton Banks, the group's chief, said HireVue had proved to be an irreplaceable guide in assessing which candidates would be worth the effort.

The nonprofit organization once allowed almost anyone into its intensive eight-week training program, but many burned out early. Now, every candidate goes through the AI assessment first, which ranks them on problem-solving and negotiation skills and helps the group determine who might have the most motivation, curiosity and grit.

"Knowing where that person is at a starting place, when it comes to this person's life," Banks said, "can help us make more accurate assessments of the people we're saying yes or no to."

But Lisa Feldman Barrett, a neuroscientist who studies emotion, said she is "strongly skeptical" that the system can really comprehend what it's looking at. She recently led a team of four senior scientists, including an expert in "computer vision" systems, in assessing more than 1,000 published research papers studying whether the human face shows universal expressions of emotion and how well algorithms can understand them.

The systems, they found, have become quite perceptive at detecting facial movements—spotting the difference, say, between a smile and a frown. But they're still worryingly imprecise in understanding what those movements actually mean and woefully unprepared for the vast cultural and social distinctions in how people show emotion or personality.

Look at scowling, Barrett said: A computer might see a person's frown and furrowed brow and assume they're easily angered—a red flag for someone seeking a sales associate job. But people scowl all the time, she said, "when they're not angry: when they're concentrating really hard, when they're confused, when they have gas."

Luke Stark, a researcher at Microsoft's research lab in Montreal studying emotion and AI—who spoke as an individual, not as a Microsoft employee—was similarly skeptical of HireVue's ability to predict a worker's personality from their intonations and turns of phrase.

Systems like HireVue, he said, have become quite skilled at spitting out data points that seem convincing, even when they're not backed by science. And he finds this "charisma of numbers" really troubling because of the overconfidence employers might lend them while seeking to decide the path of applicants' careers.

The best AI systems today, he said, are notoriously prone to misunderstanding meaning and intent. But he worried that even their perceived success at divining a person's true worth could help perpetuate a "homogenous" corporate monoculture of automatons, each new hire modeled after the last.

The company, HireVue's Larsen said, audits its performance data to look for potentially discriminatory hiring practices, known as adverse impacts, using "world-class bias testing" techniques. The company's algorithms, he added, have been trained "using the most deep and diverse data set of facial action units available, which includes people from many countries and cultures."

HireVue's growth, however, is running into some regulatory snags. In August, Illinois Gov. J. B. Pritzker (D) signed a first-in-the-nation law that will force employers to tell job applicants how their AI hiring system works and get their consent before running them through the test. The measure, which HireVue said it supports, will take effect Jan. 1.

State Rep. Jaime Andrade Jr. (D), who co-sponsored the bill, said he pushed the transparency law after learning how many job applicants were rejected at the AI stage of a job interview. He worried that spoken accents or cultural differences could end up improperly warping the results, and that people who declined to sit for the assessment could be unfairly punished by not being considered for the job.

"What is the model employee? Is it a white guy? A white woman? Someone who smiles a lot?" he said. "What are the data points being used? There has to be some explanation, and there has to be consent."

HireVue cautions candidates that there is no way to trick, cheat or hack the system, because it assesses tens of thousands of factors to assess a "unique set of personal competencies." "Do what feels most natural to you," the company says in an online guide.

But roughly a dozen interviewees who have taken the AI test—including some who got the job—told *The Post* it felt alienating and dehumanizing to have to wow a computer before being deemed worthy of a company's time.

They questioned what would be done with the video afterward and said they felt uneasy about having to perform to unexplained AI demands. Several said they refused to do the interview outright because, in the words of one candidate, the idea "made my skin crawl."

Candidates said they have scrambled for ideas on how to maximize their worthiness before the algorithm's eye, turning to the hundreds of videos and online handbooks suggesting, for instance, that they sit in front of a clean white wall, lest the background clutter dock their grade. "Glue some googly eyes to your webcam. It'll make it easier to maintain eye contact," one user on the message board Reddit suggested.

Stark, the AI researcher, said these "folk theories of algorithms" were a natural response from people facing impenetrable AI systems with the power to decide their fate. The survival techniques could feel reassuring, he said, even if they were wrong: Pick the right words, use the right tone, put on a sufficiently happy face. "It's a way of trying to give people confronting an opaque system they don't understand some feeling of agency," he said.

But some HireVue interviewees questioned whether it was fair or even smart to judge a person's workplace performance or personal abilities based on half an hour spent looking into a webcam. They also worried that people's nerves about the odd nature of the exam might end up disqualifying them outright.

Emma Rasiel, an economics professor at Duke University who regularly advises students seeking jobs on Wall Street, said she has seen a growing number of students excessively unsettled about their upcoming HireVue test. The university's economics department now offers a guide to HireVue interviews on its student resources website, including typical questions ("What does integrity mean to you?") and behavioral tips ("Act natural, talk slowly!").

"It's such a new and untried way of communicating who they are that it adds to their anxiety," Rasiel said. "We've got an anxious generation, and now we're asking them to talk to a computer screen, answering questions to a camera … with no real guidelines on how to make themselves look better or worse."

The mysterious demands can also push people's angst into overdrive. When Sheikh Ahmed, a 25-year-old in Queens, applied for teller jobs at banks around New York, he said he received eight HireVue assessment offers, all scheduled for the same day.

He studied guides on how to talk and act but found the hardest part was figuring out the camera angle: Too high, he worried, and he would look domineering; too low, and he would look shrunken and weak.

Before his marathon of AI interviews, he put on a crisp dress shirt, a tie and pajama pants and went to his dad's soundproof music studio, away from the family's chirping society finch. He also turned off his air conditioning system, hoping the background noise wouldn't mess up his score.

He changed his answers slightly in each interview, in the hopes that the algorithm would find something it liked. But he found it exhausting and disheartening to boil down his life experience and worthiness into a computer-friendly sound bite.

By the end, his mouth was dry, he was covered in sweat and he was paranoid he hadn't made enough eye contact while worrying about the bird. A few weeks after the interviews, he said, he's still waiting to hear whether he got a job.

Excerpt from Managing for Stakeholders*

R. Edward Freeman

Managing for Stakeholders

The basic idea of "managing for stakeholders" is quite simple. Business can be understood as a set of relationships among groups which have a stake in the activities that make up the business. Business is about how customers, suppliers, employees, financiers (stockholders, bondholders, banks, etc.), communities, and managers interact and create value. To understand a business is to know how these relationships work. And, the executive's or entrepreneur's job is to manage and shape these relationships, hence the title, "managing for stakeholders."

Figure 5.3.1 depicts the idea of "managing for stakeholders" in a variation of the classic "wheel and spoke" diagram.[1] However, it is important to note that the stakeholder idea is perfectly general. Corporations are not the center of the universe, and there are many possible pictures. One might put customers in the center to signal that a company puts customers as the key priority. Another might put employees in the center and link them to customers and shareholders. We prefer the generic diagram because it suggests, pictorially, that "managing for stakeholders" is a theory about management and business; hence, managers and companies are in the center. But, there is no larger metaphysical claim here.

Stakeholders and Stakes

Owners or financiers (a better term) clearly have a financial stake in the business in the form of stocks, bonds, and so on, and they expect some kind of financial return from them. Of course, the stakes of financiers will differ by type of owner, preferences for money, moral preferences, and

* Freeman, Ed. "Managing for Stakeholders," In Beauchamp, Bowie, Arnold (eds) 2009. *The Purpose of the Corporation*. Pearson. Reprinted with permission. Note: This is an excerpt from the original so footnote and endnote numbering may be modified.

DOI: 10.1201/9781003278290-32

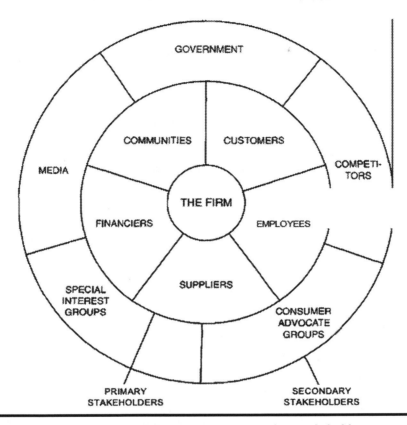

Figure 5.3.1 Stakeholder diagram with primary and secondary stakeholders.

so on, as well as by type of firm. The shareholders of Google may well want returns as well as be supportive of Google's articulated purpose of "Do No Evil." To the extent that it makes sense to talk about the financiers "owning the firm," they have a concomitant responsibility for the uses of their property.

Employees have their jobs and usually their livelihood at stake; they often have specialized skills for which there is usually no perfectly elastic market. In return for their labor, they expect security, wages, benefits, and meaningful work. Often, employees are expected to participate in the decision-making of the organization, and if the employees are management or senior executives, we see them as shouldering a great deal of responsibility for the conduct of the organization as a whole. And, employees are sometimes financiers as well, since many companies have stock ownership plans, and loyal employees who believe in the future of their companies often voluntarily invest. One way to think about the employee relationship is in terms of contracts.

Customers and suppliers exchange resources for the products and services of the firm and in return receive the benefits of the products and services. As with financiers and employees, the customer and supplier relationships are enmeshed in ethics. Companies make promises to customers via their advertising, and when products or services don't deliver on these promises, then management has a responsibility to rectify the situation. It is also important to have suppliers who are committed to making a company better. If suppliers find a better, faster, and cheaper way of making critical parts or services, then both supplier and company can win. Of course, some suppliers simply compete on price, but even so, there is a moral element of fairness and transparency to the supplier relationship.

Finally, the local community grants the firm the right to build facilities, and in turn, it benefits from the tax base and economic and social contributions of the firm. Companies have a real impact on communities, and being located in a welcoming community helps a company create value for its other stakeholders. In return for the provision of local services, companies are expected to be good citizens, as is any individual person. It should not expose the community to unreasonable hazards in the form of pollution, toxic waste, etc. It should keep whatever commitments it makes to the community, and operate in a transparent manner as far as possible. Of course, companies don't have perfect knowledge, but when management discovers some danger or runs afoul of new competition, it is expected to inform and work with local communities to mitigate any negative effects, as far as possible.

While any business must consist of financiers, customers, suppliers, employees, and communities, it is possible to think about other stakeholders as well. We can define "stakeholder" in a number of ways. First of all, we could define the term fairly narrowly to capture the idea that any business, large or small, is about creating value for "those groups without whose support, the business would cease to be viable." The inner circle of Figure 5.3.1 depicts this view. Almost every business is concerned at some level with relationships among financiers, customers, suppliers, employees, and communities. We might call these groups "primary" or "definitional." However, it should be noted that as a business starts up, sometimes one particular stakeholder is more important than another. In a new business startup, sometimes there are no suppliers, and paying lots of attention to one or two key customers, as well as to the venture capitalist (financier), is the right approach.

There is also a somewhat broader definition that captures the idea that if a group or individual can affect a business, then the executives must take that group into consideration in thinking about how to create value. Or, a stakeholder is any group or individual that can affect or be affected by the realization of an organization's purpose. At a minimum some groups affect primary stakeholders and we might see these as stakeholders in the outer ring of Figure 5.3.1 and call them "secondary" or "instrumental."

There are other definitions that have emerged during the last 30 years, some based on risks and rewards, some based on mutuality of interests. And, the debate over finding the one true definition of "stakeholder" is not likely to end. We prefer a more pragmatic approach of being clear of the purpose of using any of the proposed definitions. Business is a fascinating field of study. There are very few principles and definitions that apply to all businesses all over the world. Furthermore, there are many different ways to run a successful business, or if you like, many different flavors of "managing for stakeholders." We see limited usefulness in trying to define one model of business, either based on the shareholder or stakeholder view, that works for all businesses everywhere. We see much value to be gained in examining how the stakes work in the value creation process, and the role of the executive.

The Responsibility of the Executive in Managing for Stakeholders

Executives play a special role in the activity of the business enterprise. On the one hand, they have a stake like every other employee in terms of an actual or implied employment contract. And, that stake is linked to the stakes of financiers, customers, suppliers, communities, and other employees. In addition, executives are expected to look after the health of the overall enterprise, to keep the varied stakes moving in roughly the same direction, and to keep them in balance.[2]

No stakeholder stands alone in the process of value creation. The stakes of each stakeholder group are multifaceted, and inherently connected to each other. How could a bondholder recognize any returns without management's paying attention to the stakes of customers or employees? How could customers get the products and services they need without employees and suppliers? How could employees have a decent place to live without communities? Many thinkers see the dominant problem of "managing for stakeholders" as how to solve the priority problem, or "which stakeholders are more important," or "how do we make trade-offs among stakeholders." We see this as a secondary issue.

First and foremost, we need to see stakeholder interests as joint, as inherently tied together. Seeing stakeholder interests as "'joint" rather than "opposed" is difficult. It is not always easy to find a way to accommodate all stakeholder interests. It is easier to trade off one versus another. Why not delay spending on new products for customers in order to keep earnings a bit higher? Why not cut employee medical benefits in order to invest in a new inventory control system?

Managing for stakeholders suggests that executives try to reframe the questions. How can we invest in new products and create higher earnings? How can we be sure our employees are healthy and happy and are able to work creatively so that we can capture the benefits of new information technology such as inventory control systems? In a recent book reflecting on his experience as CEO of Medtronic, Bill George summarized the managing for stakeholders' mindset:[3]

> Serving all your stakeholders is the best way to produce long term results and create a growing, prosperous company ... Let me be very clear about this: there is no conflict between serving all your stakeholders and providing excellent returns for shareholders. In the long term it is impossible to have one without the other. However, serving all these stakeholder groups requires discipline, vision, and committed leadership.

The primary responsibility of the executive is to create as much value as possible for stakeholders.[4] Where stakeholder interests conflict, the executive must find a way to rethink the problems so that these interests can go together, so that even more value can be created for each. If trade-offs have to be made, as often happens in the real world, then the executive must figure out how to make the trade-offs, and immediately begin improving the trade-offs for all sides. Managing for stakeholders is about creating as much value as possible for stakeholders, without resorting to trade-offs. We believe that this task is more easily accomplished when a business has a sense of purpose. Furthermore, there are few limits on the kinds of purpose that can drive a business. WalMart may stand for "everyday low price." Merck can stand for "alleviating human suffering." The point is that if an entrepreneur or an executive can find a purpose that speaks to the hearts and minds of key stakeholders, it is more likely that there will be sustained success.

Purpose is complex and inspirational. The Grameen Bank wants to eliminate poverty. Fannie Mae wants to make housing affordable to every income level in society. Tastings (a local restaurant) wants to bring the taste of really good food and wine to lots of people in the community. And, all of these organizations have to generate profits, or else they cannot pursue their purposes. Capitalism works because we can pursue our purpose with others. When we coalesce around a big idea, or a joint purpose evolves from our day-to-day activities with each other, then great things can happen.

To create value for stakeholders, executives must understand that business is fully situated in the realm of humanity. Businesses are human institutions populated by real live complex human beings. Stakeholders have names and faces and children. They are not mere placeholders for social roles. As such, matters of ethics are routine when one takes a managing for stakeholders' approach.

Of course this should go without saying, but a part of the dominant story about business is that business people are only in it for their own narrowly defined self-interest. One main assumption of the managerial view with shareholders at the center is that shareholders only care about returns, and therefore their agents, managers, should only care about returns. However, this does not fit either our experiences or our aspirations. In the words of one CEO, "The only assets I man· age go up and down the elevators every day."

Most human beings are complicated. Most of us do what we do because we are self- interested and interested in others. Business works in part because of our urge to create things with others and for others. Working on a team, or creating a new product or delivery mechanism that makes customer's lives better or happier or more pleasurable, all can be contributing factors to why we go to work each day. And, this is not to deny the economic incentive of getting a pay check. The assumption of narrow self-interest is extremely limiting, and can be self-reinforcing-people can begin to act in a narrow self-interested way if they believe that is what is expected of them, as some of the scandals such as Enron, have shown. We need to be open to a more complex psychology—one any parent finds familiar as they have shepherded the growth and development of their children.

Notes

1. The spirit of this diagram is from R. Phillips, *Stakeholder Theory and Organizational Ethics* (San Francisco: Berret-Koehler Publishers, 2003).
2. In earlier versions of this essay in this volume we suggested that the notion of fiduciary duty to stockholders be extended to "fiduciary duty to stakeholders." We believe that such a move cannot be defended without doing damage to the notion of "fiduciary." The idea of having a special duty to either one or a few stakeholders is not helpful.
3. Bill George, *Authentic Leadership* (San Francisco: Jossey Bass, 2004).
4. This is at least as clear as the directive given by the dominant model: create as much value as possible for shareholders.

Chapter 5.4

Excerpt from The Problem of Corporate Purpose[*]

Lynn A. Stout

What is the purpose of the modern public corporation? Most people today would say corporations have but one proper purpose: maximizing their shareholders' wealth as measured by stock price. Other goals—serving customers, building great products, providing good jobs—are viewed as legitimate business ends only to the extent they increase "shareholder value."

This view prevails in large part because it's what is taught in our nation's classrooms. According to a recent Brookings study of the curricula of top law and business schools, professional school courses emphasize maximizing corporate profits and shareholder value as the proper purpose of business corporations. As a result, "students believe the primary purpose of the corporation is to maximize shareholder value, and they believe this is how current corporate leaders behave when they are making business decisions."[1]

In my book *The Shareholder Value Myth*, I demonstrate how this "shareholder primacy" theory can be hazardous to the health of investors, companies, and the public alike.[2] Shareholder value ideology in fact is a relatively new development in the business culture. It is not supported by the traditional rules of American corporate law; is not consistent with the real economic structure of business corporations; and is not supported by the bulk of the empirical evidence on what makes corporations and economies work.

Indeed, there is good reason to suspect that focusing on "shareholder value" may in fact be a mistake for most business firms. This is because there is no single shareholder value—different shareholders have different needs and interests depending on their investing time frame, degrees of diversification and interests in other assets, and perspectives on corporate ethics and social responsibility. Shareholder value ideology focuses on the interests of only a narrow subgroup of shareholders, those who are most short-sighted, opportunistic, willing to impose external costs, and indifferent to ethics and others' welfare. As a result, shareholder value thinking can lead

---

[*] Lynn A. Stout, "The Problem of Corporate Purpose," *Issues in Governance Studies* 48, no. 1 (2012): 1–14. Lynn A. Stout is the Distinguished Professor of Corporate and Business Law, the first endowed professorship in the Clarke Business Law Institute at Cornell School of Law. Reprinted with permission. Note: This is an excerpt from the original so footnote and endnote numbering may be modified.

DOI: 10.1201/9781003278290-33

managers to focus myopically on short-term earnings reports at the expense of long-term performance; discourage investment and innovation; harm employees, customers, and communities; and lure companies into reckless and socially irresponsible behaviors. This ultimately harms most shareholders themselves—along with employees, customers, and communities.

[…]

How Shareholder Value Thinking Gets the Law Wrong

One of the most striking symptoms of how shareholder primacy thinking dominates contemporary discussions of corporations is the way it has become routine for journalists, economists, and business experts to claim as undisputed fact that US corporate law requires directors of public companies to try to maximize shareholder wealth. As one editor of Business Ethics put it, "courts continue to insist that maximizing returns to shareholders is the sole aim of the corporation. And directors who fail to do so can be sued."[3]

This common and widespread perception lacks any solid basis in actual corporate law. The corporate code of Delaware, where the majority of Fortune 500 businesses are incorporated, states that corporations can be formed for any lawful purpose.[4] Similarly, the typical public company charter broadly defines the company's purpose as "anything lawful." (Although it is perfectly possible for a corporate charter to state that the company's purpose is to maximize shareholder value, virtually no public company charter does so.) This leaves advocates of shareholder primacy in something of a bind. Where, exactly, can the supposed legal requirement that directors maximize shareholder value be found?

When pressed, shareholder primacy advocates typically cite the nearly century-old case Dodge v. Ford, in which the Michigan Supreme Court famously observed that "a business corporation is organized and carried on primarily for the profit of the shareholders. The powers of the directors are to be employed for that end."[5] This remark, however, was what lawyers call "mere dicta," an offhand remark that was not needed for the court to reach its desired result in the case, and that does not create binding precedent. More importantly, modern courts—especially Delaware courts—simply do not follow this element of *Dodge v. Ford*. To the contrary, thanks to a vital legal doctrine known as the business judgment rule, directors of public companies enjoy virtually unfettered legal discretion to determine the corporation's goals.

In brief, the business judgment rule holds that so long as a board of directors is not tainted by personal conflicts of interest and makes a reasonable effort to become informed, courts will not second-guess the board's decisions about what is best for the company—even when those decisions predictably reduce profits or share price. Consider the recent Delaware case of *Air Products, Inc. v. Airgas, Inc.*[6] Air Products wanted to acquire Airgas, whose stock had been trading in the $40s and $50s, at a price of $70 per share. Airgas' board refused Air Products' amorous advances, even though many Airgas shareholders supported the sale as a way to make a quick profit. The Delaware Court supported the Airgas boards' decision to reject the offer, stating that the board "was not under any per se duty to maximize shareholder value in the short term."[7] As Airgas and many other cases show, disinterested and informed directors are free to reduce profits and share price today when they claim to believe this will help the corporation in "the long run." They are also free to decide what is in the corporation's "long run" interests.

How Shareholder Value Thinking Gets the Economics Wrong

Even if the law does not require directors to maximize shareholder value, it is of course still possible to argue it ought to. In other words, shareholder primacy can be defended not as a legal requirement, but as a superior philosophy for managing corporations to ensure they contribute the most to the economy and to our society. Many advocates of shareholder value maximization do indeed seem to believe this rule ensures corporations provide the maximum possible benefits to society: an increase in share price is viewed as tantamount to an increase in overall economic efficiency. This belief, in turn, seems based not on experience or hard evidence but on the seductive appeal of a theory, the principal-agent model of the corporation.

The principal-agent model is associated with a 1976 article published in the *Journal of Financial Economics* by business school dean William Meckling and finance theorist Michael Jensen.[8] This article, titled "The Theory of the Firm," explored in economic terms the problem that arises when the owner of a business (the so-called principal) hires an employee (the agent) to run the firm on the owner's behalf. Because the agent does all the work while the principal gets all the profit, we can expect the agent to shirk or even steal at the principal's expense. Thus undesirable "agency costs" are created when ownership is separated from control.

Jensen and Meckling's article—the most frequently-cited article in business academia today[9]—assumed without discussion the "principals" in public corporations were the shareholders, and directors were the shareholders' "agents." Yet Jensen and Meckling were economists, not lawyers, and this assumption (as we shall see below) fundamentally mistakes the real economic and legal relationships among shareholders, executives, creditors, and directors in public corporations. Nevertheless, the principal-agent model was eagerly embraced by a generation of academics in law, business, and economics as a simple way of understanding the complex reality of public corporations. Among other advantages, it gave a clear answer to the murky question of corporate purpose, because it taught that the best way to maximize the total value of the company was to focus on maximizing share price, which represented the shareholders' interest as the firm's supposed "residual claimant."

There is one serious problem with this analysis, however. Put bluntly, the principal-agent model is wrong. Not wrong in a normative sense; there's nothing objectionable about a principal hiring an agent. But it's clearly incorrect, as a descriptive matter, to say the principal-agent model captures the reality of modern public corporations with thousands of shareholders, scores of executives, and a dozen or more directors.

This becomes readily apparent if we consider the three factual claims that lie at the heart of the principal-agent model. The first incorrect factual claim is that shareholders "own" corporations. As a legal matter, shareholders do not own corporations. Corporations are independent legal entities that own themselves, holding property in their own names, entering their own contracts, and committing their own torts. What do shareholders own? The label "shareholder" gives the answer. Shareholders own shares of stock, and shares in turn are contracts between the shareholder and the corporation that give shareholders limited rights under limited circumstances. (Owning shares in Ford doesn't entitle you to help yourself to the car in the Ford showroom). In a legal sense, stockholders are no different from bondholders, suppliers, and employees. All have contractual relationships with the corporate entity. None "owns" the company itself.

The second mistaken factual claim underlying the principal-agent model is that shareholders are the sole residual claimants in corporations. Corporate "stakeholders" like employees, customers, and creditors are assumed to receive only the benefits their formal contracts and the law entitle them to (fixed salaries, interest, and so forth), while shareholders supposedly get all profits left over after the firm has met those fixed obligations. Again, this assumption is patently incorrect. The only time shareholders are treated anything like residual claimants is when a company falls into bankruptcy. In operating firms, shareholders only get money when the directors decide the shareholders should get money, which the board can arrange either by declaring a dividend (a decision entirely in the board's discretion) or by choosing to limit expenses so the company builds up accounting profits and "retained earnings." (If a company is minting cash, its directors have the option of allowing accounting profits to increase employee benefits, or make corporate charitable contributions.) The corporation is its own residual claimant, and its board of directors decides which groups get what share of the corporation's residual.

Finally, the third fundamental but mistaken belief associated with the principal-agent model is that shareholders and directors are just that—principals and agents. Again, this premise is wrong. The hallmark of an agency relationship is that the principal retains the right to control the agent's behavior. Yet one of the most fundamental rules of corporate law is that corporations are controlled by boards of directors, not by shareholders. Although in theory shareholders have the right to elect and remove directors, in practice the costs of mounting a proxy battle combined with dispersed shareholders' "rational apathy" raises near-insurmountable obstacles to organized shareholder action in most public firms.[10] Thanks to the business judgment rule, shareholders also can't successfully sue directors who place stakeholders' or society's interests above the shareholders' own. Finally, while the ability to sell her shareholdings sometimes can protect a disgruntled individual investor who wants to express her unhappiness with a board by "voting with her feet," when disappointed shareholders in public companies sell en masse, they drive down share price, making selling a Pyrrhic solution.

The economic structure of public corporations insulates boards of directors from dispersed shareholders' command and control in ways that make it impossible to fit the square peg of the public corporation into the round hole of the principal-agent model. Of course, one could always argue that shareholder powerlessness is exactly the problem that needs to be remedied, and that corporations would work better if shareholders acted more like principals and if directors acted more like shareholders' agents, Yet this argument leaves shareholder primacy dogma at its most vulnerable. If changing corporate governance rules to make boards more shareholder-oriented really improves corporate performance, we should see evidence of this in the business world. That evidence is notably missing.

How Shareholder Value Thinking Gets the Evidence Wrong

Over the past two decades, legal and economic scholars have generated dozens of empirical studies testing the statistical relationship between various measures of corporate performance and supposedly shareholder-friendly elements of corporate governance like director independence, a single share class, or the absence of staggered boards and poison pills. These tests have produced mostly confusion. For example, one recent paper surveyed the results of nearly a dozen empirical studies of what happens when companies use dual share classes to reduce or eliminate public shareholders' voting rights, a governance structure the principal-agent model predicts should harm corporate performance by increasing agency costs. The survey concluded that some studies found no effect on performance, some found a mild negative effect, and some a mild positive effect. At least one study found that dual share classes greatly improved performance—exactly the opposite of what shareholder primacy advocates would predict.[11]

This lack of empirical support for the supposed superiority of the shareholder-oriented model has captured at least some scholarly attention. (Roberta Romano of Yale Law School has famously called some shareholder-oriented governance reforms "quack corporate governance.")[12] But the evidence in support of shareholder primacy is even weaker than it appears. This is because most empirical studies focus only on how giving shareholders greater power effects economic performance at the level of the individual company, typically measured over a few days or at most a year or two. These studies may be looking in the wrong place, for the wrong time period. It is not only possible, but probable, that raising the share price of individual firms relative to the rest of the market in the short run reduces aggregate shareholder wealth over time.

To understand this counterintuitive idea, imagine trying to empirically test the best method for catching fish. On first inspection, one reasonable method would be to study the individual fishermen who fish in a particular lake, comparing their techniques with the amount of fish they catch. You might find that fishermen who use worms as bait get more fish than those who use minnows, and conclude fishing with worms is more efficient.

But what if some fishermen start using dynamite in the lake, and simply gather up all the dead fish that float to the surface after the blast? Your statistical test would show that individuals who fish with dynamite catch far more fish than those who use either worms or minnows, and also show that fishermen who switch from baited hooks to dynamite see an initial dramatic improvement in their fishing "performance." But as many real-world cases illustrate, communities that fish with dynamite see long-run declines in the size of the average haul, and eventually total collapse of the fish population.

Fishing with dynamite is a good strategy for an individual fisherman, for a while. But in the long run, it is very bad for fishermen collectively. There is reason to suspect the same can be said for shareholders, when corporations are driven to "maximize shareholder value."

There Is No Single "Shareholder Value"

To understand how encouraging corporate directors to maximize shareholder value can hurt shareholders themselves, we must begin by recognizing that "shareholder" is a fictional noun. The principal-agent model presumes shares in public companies are held by homogeneous entities that care only about the firm's share price. Yet no such homogenous entities exist.

When we think of shareholders, we are really thinking of human beings, who typically own shares either directly or through pension and mutual funds. Human beings inevitably have many different values and interests.[13] For example, some want to hold their shares for only a short time, and care only about tomorrow's stock price. Others may be investing for retirement or to pay a child's college tuition, and care about long-term returns. (The old "efficient markets" idea that stocks prices perfectly measure future returns has been discredited.)[14] Some want their firms to make informal commitments that build employee and customer loyalty that will pay off in the future; others who plan to sell soon want firms to opportunistically renege on such commitments. Some hold widely diversified portfolios and worry about how the corporation's behavior affects the value of their other assets and interests; others are relatively undiversified and unconcerned. Finally, some shareholders may care only about their own material wealth. But many and possibly most are "prosocial," and prefer their companies not earn profits by harming third parties or breaking the law.[15]

This means the idea of a single "shareholder value" is intellectually incoherent, because different shareholders value different things. It also means that business strategies designed to raise share price help some shareholders primarily by hurting others.

Suppose, for example, Anne and Betty each own shares in Apple corporation. Anne is an asocial hedge fund manager who seeks only to "buy low and sell high," who takes positions in only two or three companies at a time, and who churns her investment portfolio two or three times annually. Betty is a prosocial, diversified, buy-and-hold investor saving toward her retirement, who works as an elementary school teacher in California.

Anne wants her Apple investment to generate immediate profits in the form of dividends or quick stock appreciation. She has incentive to pressure Apple's board to pay out all its cash in the form of dividends instead of retaining earnings to reinvest in innovative future products that the stock market can't easily value today—even though retaining earnings might increase Betty's future returns. Anne also wants Apple to reduce its expenditures on customer support and product quality. In the long run, this will likely hurt employee and customer loyalty and Apple sales, but Anne expects to have sold her Apple shares and moved on to her next investment long before these long-run harms are reflected in Betty's stock price. Anne also wants Apple to outsource as many jobs as possible to areas of the world where labor is cheap and taxes are low, even though cutting Apple's employment rolls and tax payments in California may harm California's public education system (and Betty's job). Finally, Anne is happy when Apple violates labor laws to make a few more pennies of profit on each iPad it sells. Prosocial Betty is not.

Clearly, Anne's and Betty's interests and values are different. Unfortunately, the idea that Apple's directors should only focus on raising Apple's stock price resolves these differences and conflicts of interest by simply assuming -- without evidence or justification -- that Anne's interests must always trump Betty's. And Anne is perfectly happy to fish with dynamite, because she gets all the benefits of short-term strategies that (perhaps temporarily) bump up Apple's share price, while Betty bears the costs. Privileging Anne's interests over Betty's creates a kind of investing "Tragedy of the Commons." Individual investors do best by pursuing short-term, opportunistic, external-cost-generating corporate strategies, but investors as a group suffer over time when all pursue this strategy.

Revisiting the Idea of Corporate Purpose

To avoid the trap of shareholder value thinking, it is essential to recognize that even if shareholders are the only participants in corporations whom we care about, it is still unwise to reduce shareholders' interests to the single metric of today's share price. The idea that one can "maximize" shareholder value rests on an impossible abstraction of the shareholder as a Platonic entity that cares only about the market price of a single corporation's equity. This reduces shareholders to their lowest possible common human denominator: short-sighted, opportunistic and untrustworthy, happy to impose external costs that reduce the value of other assets, and psychopathically indifferent to the welfare of other people, future generations, and the planet. Such a single-dimensioned conception of the shareholder is not only unrealistic, but dysfunctional.

Advocates for shareholder value thinking sometimes argue that without a single, objective metric to judge how well directors and executives are running firms, these corporate "agents" will run amok.[16] This argument ignores the obvious human capacity to balance, albeit imperfectly, competing interests and responsibilities. Parents with more than one child routinely balance the interests of competing siblings (not to mention balancing their children's welfare against their own), just as judges routinely balance justice against judicial efficiency and professors balance teaching against research and scholarship. The fact that balancing interests is sometimes difficult does not mean it cannot be done. Indeed, decently satisfying several sometimes-competing objectives, rather than trying to "maximize" one, is the rule and not the exception in human affairs. Although we should not expect directors to do a perfect job of balancing the competing interests of different shareholders, there is no reason to think they can't do it well enough that shareholder interest-balancing is preferable to serving only the interests of the most short-sighted, opportunistic, undiversified, and unethical shareholders.

Accepting directors' obligation and authority to mediate between different shareholder interests, and abandoning the quixotic and ultimately self-defeating idea that corporate success can and should be measured by a single objective metric, allows us to understand a host of otherwise-puzzling realities of corporate law and practice. Perhaps the most obvious is how the US public corporation managed to thrive for most of the twentieth century. Thanks to dispersed shareholders' rational apathy and the business judgment rule, directors of public companies who avoided personal conflicts of interest enjoyed virtually unfettered discretion to set corporate policy, even over some shareholders' vocal objections. This undoubtably increased "agency costs," but it did not stop public corporations from producing excellent results for investors, employees, and communities. More recently, as shareholder value thinking has gained traction, boards have lost some of their ability to resist shareholder demands. Perhaps in consequence, aggregate shareholder returns have eroded and the numbers of public companies have been declining.

That possibility carries at least two important implications. The first is that policymakers and would-be reformers should stop reflexively responding to every business crisis or scandal by trying make managers pay more attention to "shareholder value." For over two decades, the Congress, the SEC, and various policy entrepreneurs have successfully pushed through a number of individually modest but collectively significant regulations designed to make managers focus more on increasing shareholder wealth as typically measured by stock price. These supposed reforms have done nothing to improve investor returns or shareholder satisfaction. Similarly, there is no reason to think that promoting "shareholder democracy" through rules like the SEC's controversial proxy access proposal[17] will serve shareholders' collective welfare. Such regulatory changes may provide an immediate windfall to certain types of shareholders (for example, undiversified hedge funds that want to pressure boards to do share repurchases or asset sales). But they may ultimately work against the interest of shareholders as a whole.

The second and more important lesson is that investors and business leaders need to liberate themselves from the tyranny of shareholder value thinking. While regulatory shifts have helped to move Corporate America closer to the shareholder value ideal, a far more important factor has been the business world's own intellectual embrace of shareholder primacy. In the interest of maximizing shareholder value, corporate directors have voluntarily de-staggered boards, adopted stock-based compensation schemes, outsourced jobs, and cut back on research and development to meet quarterly earnings estimates. In the interest of shareholder value, pension and mutual funds have joined with hedge funds to pressure boards to "unlock value" through repurchases and asset sales, while turning a blind eye to questions of corporate responsibility and ethics. This has happened not because of regulatory requirements, but because investors and managers alike have come to accept shareholder value thinking as a necessary evil in the world.

John Maynard Keynes famously said that

> … the ideas of economists and political philosophers, both when they are right and when they are wrong, are more powerful than is commonly understood. Indeed the world is ruled by little else. Practical men, who believe themselves to be quite exempt from any intellectual influence, are usually the slaves of some defunct economist.

Shareholder value ideology shows all the signs of a defunct economists' idea. It is inconsistent with corporate law; misstates the economic structure of public companies; and lacks persuasive empirical support. Not only does shareholder value ideology fail on inductive grounds, it is riddled with deductive flaws as well, especially its premise that the only shareholder whose values should count is the shareholder who is myopic, untrustworthy, self-destructive, and without a social conscience.

Nevertheless, as described in the Brookings study, shareholder primacy continues to be taught in our nation's law schools, business schools, and economics departments. Meanwhile, firms run according to the mantra of shareholder value cut safety corners (BP), outsource jobs and exploit workers (Apple), and indulge in criminal misbehavior (Walmart). If we want our corporations to perform better for investors and the rest of us as well, we need to re-visit the wisdom of shareholder value thinking.

Notes

1. Darrell West, The Purpose of the Corporation in Business and Law School Curricula (Brookings, July 18, 2011) www.brookings.edu/-
2. Lynn Stout, *The Shareholder Value Myth: How Putting Shareholders First Harms Investors, Corporations, and the Public* (San Francisco: Berrett-Koehler Publishers, 2012).
3. Marjorie Kelly, The Divine Right of Capital: Dethroning the Corporate Aristocracy (San Francisco: Berrett-Koehler Publishers, 2001, 2003) 54.
4. Delaware General Corporation Law, Section 102 (2011).
5. Dodge v. Ford Motor Co., 170 N.W. 668 (Mich. 1919).
6. Air Products and Chemicals, Inc. v. Airgas Inc., Civ. 5249-CC, 5256-CC (Del. Ch., Feb. 15, 2011).
7. Id. 92, citing Paramount Communications Inc. v. Time, Inc., 571 A.2d 1140, 1150 (Del. 1990).
8. Jensen and Meckling, supra.
9. Roger Martin, Fixing the Game: Bubbles, Crashes, and What Capitalism Can Learn from the NFL (Boston, Massachusetts: Harvard Business Review Press, 2011) 11.
10. Lucian A. Bebchuk, "The Myth of the Shareholder Franchise," 73 *Virginia Law Review* 675 (2007).
11. Renee Adams and Daniel Ferreira, "One Share-One Vote: The Empirical Evidence," 12 *Review of Finance* 51 (2008).
12. Roberta Romano, "The Sarbanes Oxley Act and the Makings of Quack Corporate Governance," Vol. 114 *Yale Law Journal* 114 (2005).
13. Iman Anabtawi, "Some Skepticism About Increasing Shareholder Power," 53 *University of California Los Angeles Law Review* 561 (2006).
14. Lynn A Stout, "The Mechanisms of Market Inefficiency: An Introduction to the New Finance," 23 *Journal of Corporation Law* 635 (2003); John Quiggen, *Zombie Economics: How Dead Ideas Still Walk Among Us* (Princeton, New Jersey and London: Princeton University, 2010).
15. Lynn Stout, Cultivating Conscience: How Good Laws Make Good People (Princeton and Oxford: Princeton University Press, 2011) 98.
16. Michael C. Jensen, "Value Maximization, Stakeholder Theory, and the Corporate Objective Function," Vol. 12 *Business Ethics Quarterly* (April, 2002) 238.
17. *Business Roundtable et al. v. Securities Exchange Commission*, No. 10-1305 (D.C. Cir., July 22, 2011).

Chapter 5.5

Recommending an Insurrection: Facebook and Recommendation Algorithms*

Kirsten Martin

A campaign to undermine the 2020 US Presidential Election grew on social media and culminated in an armed attack on the US Capital and Capital Police on January 6, 2021. Many of those involved had organized through social media sites. In the aftermath, these companies examined their approach to deciding not only what content to remove but also their ongoing decisions as to which content to promote and recommend to users. Facebook was no different in examining their role. But, Facebook, with over 1 billion users, was over 8 times larger than any other social network and faced the bulk of the criticism for their content moderation decisions.

Facebook faced two types of decisions. First, what content or accounts do you remove from your platform? In many ways, this was an easier yet more visible decision, where most platforms had guidelines as to the type of content allowed.

However, the second decision was more complicated: what content do you promote or amplify on your platform? Many groups posting hateful content and information on the insurrection were promoted on Facebook. This second type of decision impacted Facebook's topline metrics and how it judged itself to be successful: user engagement. While the takedown of a single account may make headlines, the subtle promotion and recommendation of content drove user engagement. And, as Facebook and other platforms found out, user engagement did not always correspond with the best content.

DOI: 10.1201/9781003278290-34

Section 230

Facebook, YouTube, Twitter, Yelp, eBay, etc. are all considered platforms in that the companies bring together third parties to interact, share content, and trade. Originally, platforms were held responsible for what happened between users on their platform. In 1995, Prodigy, an online communication platform, was sued for defamation for a user's post on their bulletin board. The court found Prodigy to be legally responsible for their user's posts because Prodigy had moderated some of the content on its sites. This moderation, according to the court, meant that Prodigy had become a publisher similar to a newspaper and would be held responsible for the defamatory content a user posted about someone else.

In response to that court decision, Section 230 of the Communications Decency Act was passed stating, "No provider or user of an interactive computer service shall be treated as the publisher or speaker of any information provided by another information content provider."[1] The law was meant "to indemnify Internet companies for exerting editorial control over the material that appeared on their sites."[2] Section 230 allows websites to host user videos, user reviews, classified ads, and user posts without being held legally responsible for third-party content[3] and was intended to give platforms an incentive to moderate their content and rid the Internet of offensive and illegal material.[4]

The law allows platforms to moderate unsavory or offensive content as well as remove illegal material, such as revenge porn, copyrighted material, harassment, cyberstalking, hate speech, calls for violence, etc. However, the line to draw as to content moderation is left to the platform, and each platform created their own rules, guidelines, and standards.[5]

Facebook (and others) have made progress is dealing with revenge porn or non-consensual intimate images as well as fraud. Not only is Facebook respecting requests to remove non-consensual intimate images, Facebook created a tool for users to preemptively upload photos of themselves so that Facebook can then proactively block anyone from uploading the same image in the future – an approach that experts believe is safe and effective.[6] In addition, Facebook has been aggressive in identifying and blocking fraud targeting their users through ads.[7] Rob Leathern, Facebook's director of product management, told BuzzFeed News "We don't want ads seeking to scam people out of money on Facebook—they aren't good for people, erode trust in our services and damage our business."[8]

Facebook's Philosophy of Content Moderation

Facebook's stated philosophy for content moderation is decentralization and majority rule: allow local communities to decide what is offensive and where their line is for content. CEO Mark Zuckerberg is quoted as describing this as a "large-scale democratic process to determine standards with AI to enforce them."[9]

> "The idea is to give everyone in the community options for how they would like to set the content policy for themselves. Where is your line on nudity? On violence? On graphic content? On profanity? What you decide will be your personal settings," he wrote. "For those who don't make a decision, the default will be whatever the majority of people in your region selected, like a referendum."[10]

Facebook's goal was more voices: "You can't impose tolerance top-down," Mark Zuckerberg said in a speech at Georgetown University. "It has to come from people opening up, sharing experiences, and developing a shared story for society that we all feel we're a part of. That's how we make progress together."[11] In balancing between giving users a voice and keeping the community safe, Facebook would draw a line at what they called "real harm": "The principles that we have on what we remove from the service are: If it's going to result in real harm, real physical harm, or if you're attacking individuals, then that content shouldn't be on the platform."[12]

As noted by Laura Murphy, a civil rights lawyer hired by Facebook to perform an independent audit of their practices in 2020, "When you put free expression on top of every other consideration, I think civil rights considerations take more of a back seat."[13]

Content moderation to make the platform more civil or less offensive was seen as "paternalistic," by executives within Facebook.[14] "We're explicitly not going to build products that attempt to change people's beliefs," a Facebook 2018 document states. "We're focused on products that increase empathy, understanding, and humanization of the 'other side."[15] Similarly, Facebook executives have stated that they are not in a position to stop conflict or prevent people from forming communities.[16]

Facebook and Content Removal

For content removal, Facebook's AI programs have been successful at identifying nudity and fraud for removal. However, the nuance of human language, cultural contexts, and widespread disagreements about what constitutes hate speech created a far more challenging problem to identify other content needing to be removed. The issue became clear in June 2009, when a paramilitary organization in Iran killed protester Neda Agha-Soltan, and a video of the murder went viral on Facebook. The company decided to leave it on the platform.[17] In 2009, Facebook had just 12 people moderating more than 120 million users worldwide and began formalizing rules as when to remove material.[18]

Facebook has long banned hate speech—defined as violent or dehumanizing speech—based on race, gender, sexuality and other protected characteristics. In 2018, Facebook's AI detected 38 percent of the hate speech-related posts it removed but was only effective in English and Portuguese due to a lack of training data.[19] In mid-2019, Facebook began allowing algorithms to take down hate speech content automatically, without being first sent to a human reviewer. This software was able to detect 65 percent of the comments that Facebook ultimately determined were hate speech and removed. As of 2020, the company reported the number is 95 percent (95% of the content that is eventually removed is detected through AI) and that 1 of every 1,000 comments seen on the platform are hate speech.[20]

Facebook faced pressure from users as to the content seen on the site. Black and Hispanic Facebook users were some of the most engaged groups on Facebook in terms of overall activity and the numbers of videos watched and uploaded. Yet, Black users also had been raising concerns about growing anti-Black speech on the platform since 2017 and complained that their accounts were being suspended for discussing discrimination and other content on the site.[21]

In the months after a white supremacist riot in Charlottesville, VA, where a woman was killed, Facebook re-examined its approach to removing hate speech.[22] Originally Facebook did not distinguish between different targets of hate speech – e.g., the target being those in power versus those who are traditionally marginalized. In doing so, "comments like *White people are stupid* were treated the same as anti-Semitic or racist slurs."[23] In 2020, Facebook began assigning a numerical score signifying the perceived harm of the hate speech.[24]

An exemplary content removal decision was around Alex Jones. After spreading conspiracy theories that the 2012 Sandy Hook elementary school massacre was a hoax and the 2018 Parkland shooting survivors were crisis actors, TV and radio personality Alex Jones crossed a line for Facebook in spreading hate against minority groups and marginalized people and qualified as a "dangerous individual or organization" per Facebook's own policies. Such a designation required Facebook to remove not only Jones' account but also content that expressed "praise or support" for him.[25] However, Mark Zuckerberg reportedly decided Alex Jones was not "a hate figure" and ordered the internal decision to be overturned: Jones would be banned, but support for him would be allowed to remain.[26] "At some point," Lenny Pozner, whose 6-year-old son Noah was a victim of the Sandy Hook shooting, "Zuckerberg has to be held responsible for his role in allowing his platform to be weaponized and for ensuring that the ludicrous and the dangerous are given equal importance as the factual." [27]

Facebook and Recommending Content

While Facebook promoted a hands-off approach to let users decide what content should be *removed*, Facebook took a more active approach when it came to the promotion and *recommendation* of content and in telling users what to read, watch, or join next.

Facebook's removal of an account or content was instantly public, subject to scrutiny, and even brought before their own oversight board. The thornier problem was how to design the program to promote or recommend content to their users. For example, in 2016, Facebook researchers found extremist content growing in a large portion of German political groups. The majority of the content was from a small group of very active users.[28] The content was concerning, but how the group grew was even more alarming: the majority of the extremist group growth was due to Facebook's own recommendation tools such as "Groups You Should Join." In other words, users were not finding the content on their own, Facebook was recommending and promoting the groups and content. In the 2016 presentation, Facebook researchers noted, "Our recommendation systems grow the problem."[29]

In 2016, Facebook was also at the center of an attempt to influence US elections by Russia.[30] However, efforts to discuss the ability of Russia to manipulate users on the Facebook platform was met with resistance internally, leading the exit of a high-profile executive in charge of security.[31]

The Girl Scout 'Super User' Problem. Then, in 2017, Facebook started Integrity Teams to analyze the way recommendation algorithms worked with the Newsfeed program and investigate how click bait, spam, and inauthentic users were handled. The team began pushing to diminish the impact of hyperactive users. As was found in the initial study on extremist groups in 2016, the Facebook algorithm prioritized hyperactive users or "super sharers" who like, share, or comment on 1,500 pieces of content, compared to regular users who engage with only 15 posts per day. These super sharers were also suspicious in being online over 20 hours a day and spamming the platform. One proposal was to reduce the importance of hyperactive users on the recommendation algorithm. These that also happened to be hyper partisan according to Facebook's research.[32] The internal researchers also believed the approach, to reduce the importance of hyperactive users in the recommendation algorithm, would help defend against spam and targeted manipulation, such as that performed by Russia in the lead-up to the 2016 election.[33]

However, combating seemingly 'bad' behavior, such as decreasing clickbait and fraud, would impact a disproportionate number of far right "super sharers," because the far right had a larger set of accounts and publishers producing this type of material compared to the far left. This raised concerns from the government policy department within Facebook who had been hearing complaints from far-right and conservative politicians about content.[34]

In addition, the team found that attempts to decrease polarization would have a negative effect on user engagement.[35] User engagement was the ultimate goal for Facebook, and decisions were measured based on whether the action would increase or decrease engagement. Karen Hao, of *MIT Technology Review*, reported that a key metric used was "called L6/7" or "the fraction of people who logged in to Facebook six of the previous seven days" in addition to measurements of engagement such as the number of posts, comments, likes, shares, etc.[36] Engagement was different from reach, which just measured the number of users who saw content. Engagement was important to Facebook because engaged users were more likely to stay on Facebook; and users had to be on Facebook to see ads; and selling ads was how Facebook earned revenue.

The engineers had approved of the modification to decrease the importance of superusers in the recommendation algorithm.[37] The program to merely stop promoting superusers, who were found to have disproportionate amount of problematic material, was then stopped by the government policy group with the stated concern that a very active Girl Scout troop could be sidelined if they were super users.[38]

While Girl Scouts were on Facebook, so were extremists. This decision left material that was close to being banned, e.g., far-right white supremacists' posts, then becoming recommended given the algorithm's approach to content moderation. The more outrageous material led to greater user engagement, which then led to "lawful but awful"[39] content being promoted by Facebook. Facebook even created a graph to describe the phenomenon and posted it publicly (Figure 5.5.1).

While Facebook acknowledged the relationship between 'lawful but awful' content and user engagement, the post does not mention the role of the recommendation algorithm to promote that material. As noted in a 2018 internal Facebook presentation, "Our algorithms exploit the human brain's attraction to divisiveness."[40] Within an internal Facebook effort to understand how the platform shaped users and the impact of their recommendations, employees put forth a number of suggestions.[41]

P(Bad for World). Facebook's P(Bad For World) was a study that Facebook researchers conducted where they surveyed users as to whether posts where "good for the world" or "bad for the world." The researchers found that high-reach posts seen by many users were more likely

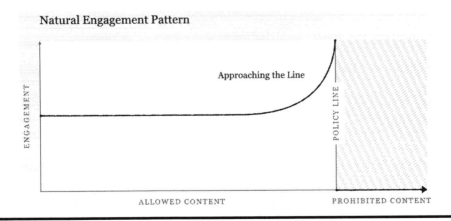

Natural Engagement Pattern

ENGAGEMENT

Approaching the Line

POLICY LINE

ALLOWED CONTENT   PROHIBITED CONTENT

Figure 5.5.1 Graph of obscenity of content to user engagement. As content came close to being prohibited (lawful but awful), the more Facebook found users engaged with the content. And the more awful the content, the more Facebook recommended the content. https://www .facebook.com/notes/mark-zuckerberg/a-blueprint-for-content-governance-and-enforcement /10156443129621634/

to be considered "bad for the world."[42] A finding that reportedly alarmed employees. The team used machine learning to predict posts that would be considered "bad for the world" and did not recommend them in news feeds (demoted them from where they would be 'normally' with Facebook's algorithm). The new algorithm reduced the visibility of "bad for the world" content, but also lowered the number of times users opened Facebook.[43]

A modified approach was tested where a larger amount of "bad for the world" content was recommended. More objectionable posts were seen, and users' sessions and time spent (engagement) remained the same as before the tests began. The modified approach was approved. [44]

The increase in user engagement for 'lawful but awful' material was partly due to the type of content that Facebook recommended and partly due to the type of people Facebook targeted. As Karen Hao reported:

> The [Facebook] researcher's team also found that users with a tendency to post or engage with melancholy content—a possible sign of depression—could easily spiral into consuming increasingly negative material that risked further worsening their mental health. The team proposed tweaking the content-ranking models for these users to stop maximizing engagement alone, so they would be shown less of the depressing stuff.

"The question for leadership was: Should we be optimizing for engagement if you find that somebody is in a vulnerable state of mind?" she remembers.[45]

Facebook in 2020. Both types of content problems – deciding what to remove and deciding what to promote– came to a head in 2020. The decision to make an exception for Jones previously in 2018 set a precedent for Facebook to not ban extremist militant organizations that were eventually involved in the Jan. 6 attempted insurrection at the US Capitol:

> "Once the Alex Jones thing had blown over, they froze designations, and that lasted for close to a year, and they were very rarely willing to push through anything. That impacted the lead-up to the election last year. Teams should have been reviewing the Oath Keepers and Three Percenters, and essentially these people weren't allowed to," said an policy employee.[46]

Facebook researchers told executives that "enthusiastic calls for violence every day" filled one 58,000-member Facebook Group, according to an internal presentation. Another top Group claimed it was set up by fans of Donald Trump but it was actually run by "financially motivated Albanians" directing a million views daily to fake news stories and other provocative content.[47] Roughly "70% of the top 100 most active US Civic Groups are considered non-recommendable for issues such as hate, misinfo, bullying and harassment," the presentation concluded. "We need to do something to stop these conversations from happening and growing as quickly as they do," the researchers wrote, suggesting measures to slow the growth of Groups at least long enough to give Facebook staffers time to address violations.[48] "Our existing integrity systems," they wrote, "aren't addressing these issues."[49] However, Facebook recommended and promoted groups for users – similar to the recommendation and promotion of posts in Newsfeed – and allowed new users to preview group material in an effort to have them join the recommended group.

In August 2020, in preparation for the 2020 US elections, Facebook's research team charged with protecting election integrity found that users were being polarized in political discussion groups. The team proposed only that Facebook stop recommending such groups to new users in a program Facebook called "Groups You Should Join."[50] In other words, the groups would remain on Facebook but not be promoted, recommended, and amplified by Facebook.

However, the policy team warned against stopping the process of Facebook recommending groups and accounts since it could "could reduce those pages' engagement and traffic, and possibly inspire complaints from publishers," according to an August post to Facebook's internal message board. [51]

> *"A noticeable drop in distribution for these producers (via traffic insights for recommendations) is likely to result in high-profile escalations that could include accusations of shadowbanning and/or FB bias against certain political entities during the US 2020 election cycle," the employee explained on the message board.*[52]

The policy team had also reportedly overruled misinformation strikes against right-wing figures such as Breitbart and Prager University. Such strikes were from third-party fact-checkers and can result in slowing down how the content can be shared, demoting the material, demonetizing the account, or removing the account.[53]

Eventually, Facebook paused recommending political group recommendations just before the November elections, then removed them permanently after the attempted US Capital insurrection on January 6. Employees pointed to Facebook's decision to ignore the integrity team's suggestion initially as illustrative of the type of considerations made to stop initiatives aimed at stopping misinformation and radicalization.[54]

After the election, Facebook also added more labels to new posts from Mr. Trump, checking his claims by noting that "as expected, election results will take longer this year."[55] However, unlike Twitter, Facebook did not restrict users from sharing or commenting on Mr. Trump's posts. But it was the first time Facebook had used such labels, part of the company's plan to add context to posts about the election.[56]

Facebook after the Attempted Insurrection

After the 2020 election and attempted insurrection, Facebook created a "playbook" to help its employees rebut criticism that the company's products fuel political polarization and social division.[57] The document was posted to Facebook's internal Workplace discussion forum by two executives.[58] While denying that Facebook meaningfully contributes to polarization, Pablo Barberá, a research scientist at the company, also suggested political polarization could be a good thing during an internal presentation:[59]

"If we look back at history, a lot of the major social movements and major transformations, for example, the extension of civil rights or voting rights in this country have been the result of increasing polarization," he told employees.[60]

When the webinar was opened up to questions from employees, one asked whether Facebook was like a tobacco company funding research to show its products were not a problem.[61]

At one point, Facebook executives appeared to acknowledge the issues created with recommending content. "We know we have a greater responsibility when we are amplifying or recommending content," Facebook's vice president of engineering, said in a post, "As behaviors evolve on our platform, though, we recognize we need to do more."[62]

In April 2021, an internal report at Facebook concluded that "Facebook failed to stop a highly influential movement from using its platform to delegitimize the election, encourage violence, and help incite the Capitol riot."[63] Facebook accounts promoted groups that glorified hate and incited violence leading up to the election and then leading up to the January 6 insurrection. Joan Donovan, research director of Harvard University's Shorenstein Center on Media, Politics, and Public Policy, said

> "For me, at the end of the day, it comes down to: Do you care? Do you care enough about democracy? Do you care enough about the fate of the nation to ensure that your product is not used to coordinate and overthrow the government?" …There is something about the way Facebook organizes groups that leads to massive public events. And when they're organized on the basis of misinformation, hate, incitement, and harassment, we get very violent outcomes."[64]

While Facebook attempted to remove individual accounts when the behavior reached a particular threshold, only after January 6 did Facebook realize that the movement had "normalized delegitimization and hate in a way that resulted in offline harm and harm to the norms underpinning democracy"[65] The report was made public one week after CEO Mark Zuckerberg testified to Congress and he said that Facebook was "inhospitable" to harmful content about the election.

The report found that super-inviter accounts within the groups invited 67% of the groups' members and worked in a coordinated fashion as to timing, disinformation, and evasion from Facebook detection. The groups with the fastest growth had high levels of hate, incitement of violence, and misinformation about the election. Within these groups, 47% contained violent comments, 29% contained hate, and 15% contained references to militias (compared to 0.8%, 2.9%, and 0.05% of all civic groups).[66] After the report became public, employees were prevented from accessing or reading the report.[67]

Facebook's Oversight Board, created to handle appeals to decision as to content *removal*, were tasked with deciding whether the removal of Donald Trump from the platform was correct. In gathering data on the case, the board asked Facebook to answer dozens of questions. However, questions around how Facebook's recommendations impacted the visibility of Mr. Trump's content and whether Facebook has plans to research the design of their newsfeed recommendation algorithm in relation to the events of January 6, 2021 were conspicuously not answered.[68]

Dissent in the Ranks

By 2020, an internal survey found employees felt less pride in the company compared to previous years.

About half felt that Facebook was having a positive impact on the world, down from roughly three-quarters earlier this year, according to a copy of the survey, known as Pulse, which was reviewed by The New York Times. *Employees' "intent to stay" also dropped, as did confidence in leadership.*[69]

Internally, complaints about the direction of the company were voiced on Facebook's internal Workplace network. After Facebook declined to remove then-president Trump's post "when the looting starts, the shooting starts," 1500 employees formed a new group "Take Action" for internal dissent and used a "Black Lives Matter" fist as their profile picture. Then in June, employees staged a virtual walk out.[70]

Employees had started to leave after the 2020 election citing Facebook's failure to stem misinformation and hate speech[71] and one stated they "could no longer stomach working for a company whose products they considered harmful."[72]

"Facebook salaries are among the highest in tech right now, and when you're walking home with a giant paycheck every two weeks, you have to tell yourself that it's for a good cause," said Gregor Hochmuth, a former engineer with Instagram, which Facebook owns, who left in 2014. "Otherwise, your job is truly no different from other industries that wreck the planet and pay their employees exorbitantly to help them forget." [73]

Employees began quitting in protest over the company's policies on hate speech.[74] In December 2020, a former employee wrote a letter on the political influences on content policy including removing penalties for misinformation from conservative pages, stopping attempts to increase the quality of news in Newsfeed.[75] Employees were upset at the outside influence of the company's policy team on content moderation decisions who were also influenced by political figures. One Facebook worker quit saying the company 'is on the wrong side of history':[76] "I'm quitting because I can no longer stomach contributing to an organization that is profiting off hate in the US and globally," Facebook software engineer Ashok Chandwaney.[77]

In July 2020, Facebook advertisers organized a boycott over civil rights issues and Facebook's treatment of marginalized groups. And Facebook's own independent auditors found Facebook's hate speech policies to be a "tremendous setback" when it came to protecting its users of color.[78]

The report criticized Facebook's choice to leave several posts by President Trump untouched, including three in May that the auditors said "clearly violated" the company's policies prohibiting voter suppression, hate speech and incitement of violence. The report also found that Facebook provides a forum for white supremacy and white nationalism.[79]

In May, 2021, Starbuck's began re-evaluating whether they should continue to have a presence on Facebook given the 'hateful comments' on the site.[80] Shortly before, the Premier League and all 20 soccer teams, boycotted Facebook to bring awareness to the racists abuse their players face on the platform. Previously, in 2020, advertisers, such as North Face, REI, and Patagonia, boycotted paying for advertising on Facebook due to hate speech on the platform.[81]

External Researchers

A number of researchers outside Facebook attempted to understand how the Facebook recommendation algorithm works and the type of content that was promoted. However, the findings have not always been well-received by Facebook.

For example, researchers at the Tech Transparency Project found more than half of the white supremacist organizations identified by the Anti-Defamation league and the Southern Poverty Law Center as hate groups had a page on Facebook; and many had pages generated by Facebook for the white supremacists when someone listed the organization as their employer. After the report, Facebook then removed 137 of the 153 white supremacist pages identified in the report.[82]

The *New York University*'s Ad Observatory ran an ongoing project where participants added a browser extension to capture data on their Facebook experience including what ads they see and what content they are recommended. In 2020, Laura Edelson at the Ad Observatory found that "[s]ources of news and information rated as far-right generate the highest average number of interactions per follower with their posts, followed by sources from the far-left, and then news sources closer to the center of the political spectrum." The research found that far-right sources designated as 'spreaders of misinformation' did better on engagement than far-right non-misinformation sources. However, center and left partisan categories incur a misinformation *penalty*. In other words, while right-leaning sources do better on engagement by spreading misinformation, center and left-leaning content does *worse* by spreading misinformation in Facebook's content recommendation algorithm.[83]

Facebook's response was to demand that the *New York University* research project stop collecting information on October 16, 2020. Laura Edelson, of the Ad Observatory project, said, "The only thing that would prompt us to stop doing this would be if Facebook would do it themselves, which we have called on them to do."[84]

Others have examined whether Facebook upheld their promises in regards to content moderation. In April 2021, The Tech Transparency Project found that Facebook continued to label people interested in militia for targeted advertising, even after promising to ban militia groups.[85] And, investigative journalists at The Markup run the Facebook Inspector that captures data from participants' Facebook feeds.[86] The Markup found that Facebook's pledge to remove misinformation about vaccines was unsuccessful. The Markup "shows that not only is COVID-19 misinformation still easy to find on Facebook, the company has also continued to recommend health groups to its users, including blatantly anti-vaccine groups and pages explicitly founded to propagate lies about the pandemic." [87]

Finally, Facebook-owned CrowdTangle was a transparency tool for users or anyone to analyze Facebook trends and measure post performance. However, the tool brought unwanted attention to Facebook when a reporter started the Twitter account @FacebooksTop10 which posted ten most-engaged Facebook posts daily. Researchers demonstrated that "right-wing commentators like Ben Shapiro and Dan Bongino were getting much more engagement on their Facebook pages than mainstream news outlets." Sometimes, that list was *only* 10 posts by Ben Shapiro and Dan Bongino.[88]

Facebook executives reportedly were worried that the tool would show that Facebook was amplifying harmful content and worked as a far-right echo chamber. Executives within Facebook wanted to shut down access to this information and curate their own reports.

In April 2021, Facebook decided to break up CrowdTangle and not offer the stand-alone service. Executives who had been arguing *for* transparency were also sidelined. [89]

Other Industries

Social networking sites and Facebook were not the first businesses to face a question as to whether the company should make money in a manner that may harm others. For years, Purdue Pharmaceutical made billions of dollars selling OxyContin – a trademarked opioid found to be highly addictive. The company had less addictive options, but those were not as lucrative. The company engaged in transactions that allowed consumers to make decisions as to which product, drug, or service they wanted and met the market's preferences, while also possibly harming communities.

Similarly, Juul, a Silicon Valley startup with 75% of the US e-cigarette market, was positioned as helping adult smokers quit tobacco.[90] But a team of researchers found that the company's marketing campaign between Juul's launch in 2015 and fall 2018 "was patently youth-oriented."[91] And a major national survey recently found that the number of high schoolers who used e-cigarettes in the past 30 days has increased by about 75 percent since 2017. [92]

Options Going Forward

As of 2021, Facebook had a number of ideas to improve the site.

1. *Correct the Record* was built on an existing product used to notify users who have shared COVID-19 misinformation. The proposal was to expand the product to false news and disinformation generally. However, policy executives decided it would disproportionately correct the record of right-wing accounts given Facebooks own research.
2. One project could identify and 'slow down' (not recommend) "hate bait" – "posts that don't strictly violate Facebook's hate speech rules, but that provoke a flood of hateful comments." The policy team determined that slowing down "hate bait" would affect right-wing accounts disproportionately given Facebooks own research.[93]
3. Facebook's *P(Bad For World)* was a proposal to predict posts that would be considered "bad for the world" and not recommend them in news feeds (demoted them from where they would be 'normally' with Facebook's algorithm). The new algorithm reduced the visibility of "bad for the world" content, but also user engagement.[94]
4. In reaction to a reported uptick in misinformation on Facebook's Newsfeed before and after the 2020 presidential election, employees recommended emphasizing a news source's "news ecosystem quality" score in the recommendation algorithm. The *N.E.Q*, was an internal ranking Facebook assigned to accounts based on the quality of their journalism.[95] N.E.Q. scores usually were not a major factor in recommending what appears in a user's Newsfeed. The program appeared to work: several days after the election, Mr. Zuckerberg agreed to increase the weight that Facebook's algorithm gave to N.E.Q.[96] The adjustment resulted in more recommendations for publishers such as CNN and NPR and made hyperpartisan accounts (e.g., Breitbart, Occupy Democrats) less visible.[97]

The question for Facebook was whether these design approaches would ever be implemented.

Notes

1. 47 USC 230. Communications Decency Act. https://uscode.house.gov/view.xhtml?req=(title:47%20 section:230%20edition:prelim)
2. Halpern, Sue. 2020. "How Joe Biden Could Help Internet Companies Moderate Harmful Content." *The New Yorker*. December 4, 2020. https://www.newyorker.com/tech/annals-of-technology/how-joe -biden-could-help-internet-companies-moderate-harmful-content
3. "CDA 230 The Most Important Law Protecting Internet Speech." *Electronic Frontier Foundation*. https://www.eff.org/issues/cda230
4. Halpern, Sue. 2020. "How Joe Biden Could Help Internet Companies Moderate Harmful Content."
5. "Twitter has "the Twitter Rules," Reddit has a "Content Policy," YouTube has "Community Guidelines," and Facebook has "Community Standards." Koebler, Jason and Joseph Cox. 2018. The Impossible Job: Inside Facebook's Struggle to Moderate Two Billion People Vice News https://www .vice.com/en/article/xwk9zd/how-facebook-content-moderation-works
6. "Danielle Citron, author of *Hate Crimes in Cyberspace* and a professor at the University of Maryland's law school, told Motherboard that Facebook's "oh shit" moment came in 2013, after a group called Women, Action, and the Media successfully pressured advertisers to stop working with Facebook because it allowed rape jokes and memes on its site" Koebler, Jason and Joseph Cox. 2018. The Impossible Job: Inside Facebook's Struggle to Moderate Two Billion People Vice News https://www .vice.com/en/article/xwk9zd/how-facebook-content-moderation-works

7. Ads Inc. Shut Down, But The Tools It Used To Trick People On Facebook Have Lived On https://www.buzzfeednews.com/article/craigsilverman/ads-inc-crypto-scams-facebook

8. Ads Inc. Shut Down, But The Tools It Used To Trick People On Facebook Have Lived On

9. Koebler, Jason and Joseph Cox. 2018.

10. Koebler, Jason and Joseph Cox. 2018.

11. Horwitz, J. and D. Seetharaman. 2020. Facebook Executives Shut Down Efforts to Make the Site Less Divisive. *Wall Street Journal.* https://www.wsj.com/articles/facebook-knows-it-encourages-division-top-executives-nixed-solutions-11590507499

12. For example, in an interview in 2018, Zuckerberg said did not think that Holocaust denials should be taken down. He has since reversed that position. https://www.vox.com/explainers/2018/7/20/17590694/mark-zuckerberg-facebook-holocaust-denial-recode

13. Dwoskin, Elizabeth and Cat Zakrzewski. 2020. "Facebook's Own Civil Rights Auditors Say Its Policy Decisions Are a 'Tremendous Setback'." *The Washington Post.* July 8, 2020. https://www.washingtonpost.com/technology/2020/07/08/facebook-civil-rights-audit/

14. Horwitz, J. and D. Seetharaman. 2020.

15. Horwitz, J. and D. Seetharaman. 2020.

16. Horwitz, J. and D. Seetharaman. 2020

17. Koebler, Jason and Joseph Cox. 2018.

18. "This is the difference between having 100 million people and a few billion people on your platform," Kate Klonick, an assistant professor at St. John's University Law School and the author of an extensive legal review of social media content moderation practices, told Motherboard. Koebler, Jason and Joseph Cox. 2018.

19. Facebook says its AI tools—many of which are trained with data from its human moderation team—detect nearly 100 percent of spam, and that 99.5 percent of terrorist-related removals, 98.5 percent of fake accounts, 96 percent of adult nudity and sexual activity, and 86 percent of graphic violence-related removals. This means that 100% of the spam content that is removed is identified via AI and not humans (not that 100% of spam is removed). Koebler, Jason and Joseph Cox. 2018. The Impossible Job: Inside Facebook's Struggle to Moderate Two Billion People Vice News https://www.vice.com/en/article/xwk9zd/how-facebook-content-moderation-works

20. 2020 Facebook to start policing anti-Black hate speech more aggressively than anti-White comments, documents show. *Washington Post.* https://www.washingtonpost.com/technology/2020/12/03/facebook-hate-speech/

21. 2020 Facebook to start policing anti-Black hate speech more aggressively than anti-White comments,

22. Cox, Joseph. 2018. "Leaked Documents Show Facebook's Post-Charlottesville Reckoning with American Nazis." *Vice Motherboard.* https://www.vice.com/en/article/mbkbbq/facebook-charlottesville-leaked-documents-american-nazis

23. 2020 Facebook to start policing anti-Black hate speech more aggressively than anti-White comments,

24. 2020 Facebook to start policing anti-Black hate speech more aggressively than anti-White comments, It turns out that removal from larger, more dominant platforms works to minimize disinformation and extreme speech. Alternative social media platforms are not an effective substitute. Rauchfleisch, Adrian and Kaiser, Jonas, Deplatforming the Far-right: An Analysis of YouTube and BitChute (June 15, 2021). Available at SSRN: https://ssrn.com/abstract=3867818 or http://dx.doi.org/10.2139/ssrn.3867818

25. Mac, Ryan and Craig Silverman. 2021. ""Mark Changed The Rules": How Facebook Went Easy On Alex Jones And Other Right-Wing Figures." *Buzzfeed News.* February 22, 2021. https://www.buzzfeednews.com/article/ryanmac/mark-zuckerberg-joel-kaplan-facebook-alex-jones

26. Mac, Ryan and Craig Silverman. 2021. "Mark Changed The Rules."

27. Mac, Ryan and Craig Silverman. 2021 "Mark Changed The Rules."

28. Horwitz, J. and D. Seetharaman. 2020.

29. Horwitz, J. and D. Seetharaman. 2020.

30. https://intelligence.house.gov/social-media-content/

31. https://www.nytimes.com/2018/03/19/technology/facebook-alex-stamos.html

32. Horwitz, J. and D. Seetharaman. 2020. Facebook Executives Shut Down Efforts to Make the Site Less Divisive.

33. Horwitz, J. and D. Seetharaman. 2020.

34. Horwitz, J. and D. Seetharaman. 2020. The Policy Group Reportedly Defined Fairness to Mean Any Action "Should Not Affect Conservatives More Than Liberals" Hao, K. 2021. How Facebook Got Addicted to Spreading Misinformation. *MIT Technology Review*. https://www.technologyreview.com /2021/03/11/1020600/facebook-responsible-ai-misinformation/

35. Horwitz, J. and D. Seetharaman. 2020.

36. Hao, K. 2021. How Facebook Got Addicted to Spreading Misinformation. *MIT Technology Review.* https://www.technologyreview.com/2021/03/11/1020600/facebook-responsible-ai -misinformation/

37. Horwitz, J. and D. Seetharaman. 2020.

38. Horwitz, J. and D. Seetharaman. 2020. An added difficulty was that to make the changes credible, Facebook would need to partner with academics and nonprofits. Given public controversies and statements, a Facebook presentation in 2018 succinctly stated "People don't trust us."

39. Elizabeth Reneiros has used this term in regards to content moderation as has Daphne Keller (https:// itif.org/podcast-how-section-230-shapes-content-moderation-daphne-keller).

40. The presentation continued, ""If left unchecked," … Facebook would feed users "more and more divisive content in an effort to gain user attention & increase time on the platform." Horwitz, J. and D. Seetharaman. 2020. Facebook Executives Shut Down Efforts to Make the Site Less Divisive.

41. Horwitz, J. and D. Seetharaman. 2020.

42. Roose, K. M. Isaac, F. Sheera. Facebook Struggles to Balance.

43. As reported by *The New York Times*, a Facebook summary concluded, "The results were good except that it led to a decrease in sessions, which motivated us to try a different approach." Roose, K. M. Isaac, F. Sheera. Facebook Struggles to Balance.

44. Roose, K. M. Isaac, F. Sheera. Facebook Struggles to Balance.

45. Hao, K. 2021. How Facebook Got Addicted to Spreading Misinformation. *MIT Technology Review*. https://www.technologyreview.com/2021/03/11/1020600/facebook-responsible-ai-misinformation/

46. Mac, Ryan and Craig Silverman. 2021 "Mark Changed The Rules."

47. Horwitz, Jeff. 2021. Facebook Knew Calls for Violence Plagued 'Groups,' Now Plans Overhaul *Wall Street Journal.* https://www.wsj.com/articles/facebook-knew-calls-for-violence-plagued-groups-now -plans-overhaul-11612131374

48. Horwitz, Jeff. 2021. Facebook Knew Calls for Violence Plagued 'Groups.

49. Horwitz, Jeff. 2021. Facebook Knew Calls for Violence Plagued 'Groups.

50. Mac, Ryan and Craig Silverman. 2021.

51. Mac, Ryan and Craig Silverman. 2021 "Mark Changed The Rules."

52. Mac, Ryan and Craig Silverman. 2021 "Mark Changed The Rules".

53. Silverman, Craig and Ryan Mac. 2020. "Facebook Fired An Employee Who Collected Evidence Of Right-Wing Pages Getting Preferential Treatment." *Buzzfeed News*. August 6, 2020. https://www .buzzfeednews.com/article/craigsilverman/facebook-zuckerberg-what-if-trump-disputes-election -results

54. Mac, Ryan and Craig Silverman. 2021 "Mark Changed The Rules."

55. Conger, Kate, Mike Isaac, and Daisuke Wakabayashi. 2020. "Social Media Companies Survived Election Day. More Tests Loom." *The New York Times*. https://www.nytimes.com/2020/11/04/tech-nology/social-media-companies-election-misinformation.html

56. Conger, Kate, Mike Isaac, and Daisuke Wakabayashi. 2020. "Social Media Companies Survived Election Day."

57. Mac, Ryan and Craig Silverman. 2021. Facebook Created An Employee "Playbook" To Respond To Accusations Of Polarization. *Buzzfeed News*. https://www.buzzfeednews.com/article/ryanmac/face-book-execs-polarization-playbook. March 12,2021.

58. Mac, Ryan and Craig Silverman. 2021. Facebook Created An Employee "Playbook"

59. Mac, Ryan and Craig Silverman. 2021. Facebook Created An Employee "Playbook"

60. "Cox contrasted the fragmented media environments of the US, one of the most polarized countries by Facebook's research, with places like the Philippines and Myanmar, where he said the "internet is incredibly important" in presenting views outside of state-controlled media. (Philippine President

Rodrigo Duterte relied on Facebook misinformation campaigns to win an election, while the United Nations found that the site's spread of hate speech abetted genocide against Rohingya Muslims in Myanmar.)" Mac, Ryan and Craig Silverman. 2021. Facebook Created An Employee "Playbook."

61. Mac, Ryan and Craig Silverman. 2021. Facebook Created An Employee "Playbook."
62. Mac, Ryan and Craig Silverman. 2021. Facebook Created An Employee "Playbook."
63. Silverman, Craig, Ryan Mac, and Jane Lytvnenko. 2021. Facebook Knows It Was Used To Help Incite The Capitol Insurrection *Buzzfeed News*. https://www.buzzfeednews.com/article/craigsilverman/facebook-failed-stop-the-steal-insurrection
64. Silverman, Craig, Ryan Mac, and Jane Lytvnenko. 2021. Facebook Knows It Was Used. *Buzzfeed News*.
65. Quoting the internal report. Silverman, Craig, Ryan Mac, and Jane Lytvnenko. 2021. Facebook Knows It Was Used. *Buzzfeed News*.
66. Silverman, Craig, Ryan Mac, and Jane Lytvnenko. 2021. Facebook Knows It Was Used. *Buzzfeed News*.
67. Silverman, Craig, Ryan Mac, and Jane Lytvnenko. 2021. Facebook Stopped Employees From Reading An Internal Report About Its Role In The Insurrection. You Can Read It Here. *Buzzfeed News*. https://www.buzzfeednews.com/article/ryanmac/full-facebook-stop-the-steal-internal-report
68. https://www.oversightboard.com/decision/FB-691QAMHJ
69. Roose, K. M. Isaac, F. Sheera. Facebook Struggles to Balance Civility and Growth. *New York Times*. November 24, 2020. https://www.nytimes.com/2020/11/24/technology/facebook-election-misinformation.html; Mac, Ryan and Craig Silverman. "Plunging Morale And Self-Congratulations: Inside Facebook The Day Before The Presidential Election." *BuzzFeed News* https://www.buzzfeednews.com/article/ryanmac/inside-facebook-24-hours-before-election-day
70. Roose, K. M. Isaac, F. Sheera. Facebook Struggles to Balance Civility and Growth. *New York Times*; 2020 Facebook to start policing anti-Black hate speech more aggressively than anti-White comments,
71. Mac, Ryan and Craig Silverman. 2021 "Mark Changed The Rules"
72. Roose, K. M. Isaac, F. Sheera. Facebook Struggles to Balance Civility and Growth. *New York Times*.
73. Roose, K. M. Isaac, F. Sheera. Facebook Struggles to Balance Civility and Growth. *New York Times*.
74. 2020 Facebook to start policing anti-Black hate speech more aggressively than anti-White comments,
75. Mac, Ryan and Craig Silverman. 2021 "Mark Changed The Rules":
76. Timberg, Craig and Elizabeth Dwoskin. 2020. "Another Facebook Worker Quits in Disgust, Saying the Company 'Is on the Wrong Side of History'." *The Washington Post*. September 9, 2020. https://www.washingtonpost.com/technology/2020/09/08/facebook-employee-quit-racism/
77. Chandwaney specifically cited the company's role in fueling genocide in Myanmar and, more recently, violence in Kenosha, Wis. Facebook did not remove a militia group's event encouraging people to bring guns to protests ahead of fatal shootings last month despite hundreds of complaints, in what Zuckerberg called an "operational mistake." 2020 Facebook to start policing anti-Black hate speech more aggressively than anti-White comments.
78. Dwoskin, Elizabeth and Cat Zakrzewski. 2020. "Facebook's Own Civil Rights Auditors."
79. Dwoskin, Elizabeth and Cat Zakrzewski. 2020. "Facebook's Own Civil Rights Auditors."
80. "In internal discussions seen by BuzzFeed News, Facebook employees who manage the social network's relationship with Starbucks wrote that the company has become so frustrated by the hate and intolerance on the platform that it may remove its Facebook page." https://www.buzzfeednews.com/article/ryanmac/facebooks-starbucks-leave-social-network-hate
81. Paul, Kari. 2020. "Facebook Faces Advertiser Revolt Over Failure to Address Hate Speech." *The Guardian*. June 22, 2020. https://www.theguardian.com/technology/2020/jun/22/facebook-hate-speech-advertisers-north-face
82. "White Supremacist Groups Are Thriving on Facebook." 2020. *Tech Transparency Project*. May 21, 2020. https://www.techtransparencyproject.org/articles/white-supremacist-groups-are-thriving-on-facebook
83. Laura Edelson, Minh-Kha Nguyen, Ian Goldstein, Oana Goga, Tobias Lauinger, and Damon McCoy. Mar 3 2020. Far-Right News Sources on Facebook More Engaging. https://medium.com/cybersecurity-for-democracy/far-right-news-sources-on-facebook-more-engaging-e04a01efae90

84. Horwitz, Jeff. Facebook Seeks Shutdown of NYU Research Project Into Political Ad Targeting. *Wall Street Journal*. October 23, 2020. https://www.wsj.com/articles/facebook-seeks-shutdown-of-nyu-research-project-into-political-ad-targeting-11603488533/

85. Mac, Ryan. Despite A Ban, Facebook Continued To Label People As Interested In Militias For Advertisers. *Buzzfeed News*. April 7, 2021. https://www.buzzfeednews.com/article/ryanmac/facebook-militia-interest-category-advertisers-ban

86. Mattu, Surya, Leon Yin, Angie Waller, and Jon Keegan. 2021 "How We Built a FacebookInspector." *The Markup*. January 5, 2021. https://themarkup.org/citizen-browser/2021/01/05/how-we-built-a-facebook-inspector

87. Mattu, Surya, Leon Yin, Angie Waller, and Jon Keegan. 2021 "How We Built a FacebookInspector.""

88. Rose, Kevin. 2021. *"Inside Facebook's Data Wars" The New York Times*. July 14, 2021. https://www.nytimes.com/2021/07/14/technology/facebook-data.html

89. Rose, Kevin. 2021. *"Inside Facebook's Data Wars" The New York Times.*

90. Belluz, Julia. 2019. The vape company Juul said it doesn't target teens. Its early ads tell a different story. *Vox*. https://www.vox.com/2019/1/25/18194953/vape-juul-e-cigarette-marketing

91. Belluz, Julia. 2019. "The Vape Company Juul Said It Doesn't Target Teens."

92. Belluz, Julia. 2019. "The Vape Company Juul Said It Doesn't Target Teens."

93. Roose, K. M. Isaac, F. Sheera. Facebook Struggles to Balance Civility and Growth. *New York Times*. November 24, 2020. https://www.nytimes.com/2020/11/24/technology/facebook-election-misinformation.html

94. Roose, K. M. Isaac, F. Sheera. Facebook Struggles to Balance.

95. Roose, K. M. Isaac, F. Sheera. Facebook Struggles to Balance Mac, Ryan and Craig Silverman. 2021 "Mark Changed The Rules."

96. Roose, K. M. Isaac, F. Sheera. Facebook Struggles to Balance Civility and Growth.

97. Roose, K. M. Isaac, F. Sheera. Facebook Struggles to Balance Civility and Growth.

Chapter 5.6

Excerpt from Can Socially Responsible Firms Survive in a Competitive Environment?*

Robert H. Frank

In his celebrated 1970 article, Milton Friedman that

> there is one and only one social responsibility of business - to use its resources and engage in activities designed to increase its profits so long as it stays within the rules of the game, which is to say, engages in open and free competition without deception of fraud.

(p. 126)

In Friedman's view, managers who pursue broader social goals - say, by adopting more stringent emission standards and required by law, or by donating corporate funds to charitable organizations - are simply spending other people's money. Firms run by these managers will have higher cost than those run by managers whose goal is to maximize shareholder wealth. According to the standard theory of competitive markets, the latter firms will attract more capital and eventually drive the former firms out of business.

Of course, as Friedman himself clearly recognized, there are many circumstances in which the firm's narrow interests coincide with those of the broader community. He noted, for example, that

> it may be well within the long-run interest of a corporation that is a major employer in a small community to devote resources to providing amenities to that community or to improving its government. That may make it easier to attract desirable employees,

---

* Robert H. Frank. "Can Socially Responsible Firms Survive in a Competitive Environment." In *What Price the Moral High Ground?* (Princeton, 2004). Reprinted with permission. Note: This is an excerpt from the original so footnote and endnote numbering may be modified.

DOI: 10.1201/9781003278290-35

it may reduce the wage bill or lessen losses from pilferage and sabotage or have other worthwhile effects.

(p. 124)

Friedman argued against using the term *social responsibility* to characterize those activities of a firm that, while serving the broader community, also augment the firm's profit. He believes that this language has great potential to mislead politicians and voters about the proper role of the corporation in society and will foster excessive regulation.

In the years since Friedman wrote this article, the development of the theory of repeated games has given us ever more sophisticated accounts of the forces that often align self-interest with the interests of others. For example, Robert Axelrod (1984) suggest that firms pay their suppliers not because they feel a moral obligation to do so but because they require future shipments from them.

Clearly, repeated in her actions often do give rise to behaviors that smack of social responsibility. Yet as Friedman suggested, it is erroneous - or at least misleading - to call these behaviors morally praiseworthy. After all, even a firm whose owners and managers had no concerned about the welfare of the broader community would have ample motive to engage in them. When material incentives favor cooperation, it is more descriptive to call the cooperating parties prudent than socially responsible.

It is also an error to assume that repeated interactions always provide ready solutions to social dilemmas and other collective action problems. Even among parties who deal with one another repeatedly, one shot dilemmas - opportunities for cheating and other opportunistic behavior - often arise. Even a long-standing client of a law firm, for example, has no way to verify that the firm has billed only the number of hours actually worked.

In many cases, the knowledge that opportunities to cheat will arise may preclude otherwise profitable business ventures. Consider a person whose mutual fund has just been taken over by new management. She wants advice about whether to stay with the fund under its new management or switch to a different fund. She considers seeking a consultation, for a fee, from a knowledgeable stockbroker - a mutually beneficial exchange. Yet the investor also knows that a broker's interest may differ from her own. Perhaps, for example, the broker will receive a large commission or finder's fee if the client switches to a new fund. Fearing the consequences of opportunistic behavior, the investor may refrain from seeking advice, in the process depriving both herself and an informed broker of the gains from trade.

When parties to a business transaction confront a one-shot dilemma, their profits will be higher if they defect - that is, if they cheat - than if they cooperate. Yet when each party defects, profits for each are lower than if both had cooperated. In this paper, I will refer to firms that cooperate in one shot-dilemmas as socially responsible firms.

The question I pose is whether such firms can survive in competitive environments. At first glance, it would appear that the answer must be no, for defecting were indeed a dominant strategy, then socially responsible firms would always have lower returns than pure profit maximizers. Evolutionary models pertaining to individuals have recently shown, however, the conditions often exist in which cooperation in one shot dilemmas is sustainable in competitive environments. I will review some of this work and suggest that many of its conclusions carry over to populations of competitive firms.

Evolutionary Models of One-shot Cooperation

One of the enduring questions and evolutionary biology is whether altruistic individuals can survive. In this framework, the design criterion for each component of human motivation is the same as for an arm or a leg or an eye: To what extent does it assist the individual in the struggle to acquire the resources required for survival and reproduction? If it works better than the available alternatives, selection pressure will favor it. Otherwise, selection pressure will work against in (see Dawkins 1976, especially Chapter 3).

At first glance, this theoretical structure appears to throw its weight squarely behind the self-interest conception of human motivation. Indeed, if natural selection favors the traits and behaviors that maximize individual reproductive fitness, and if we *define* behaviors that enhance personal fitness a selfish, then self-interest becomes the only viable human motive by definition. This tautology was the central message of much of the sociobiological literature of the 1970s and 1980s.

On closer look, however, the issues are not so simple. There are many situations in which individuals whose only goal is self-interest are likely to be especially bad at acquiring and holding resources. Thomas Shelling (1960) provided a vivid illustration with his account of a kidnapper who gets cold feet and wants to set his victim free but fears that if he does so, the victim will go to the police. The victim promises to remain silent. The problem, however, is that both he and the kidnapper know that it will not be in the victim's narrow self-interest to keep his promise once he is free. And so the kidnapper reluctantly concludes that he must kill his victim.

Suppose, however, that the victim were not a narrowly self-interested person but rather a person of Honor. If this fact could somehow be communicated to the kidnapper, their problem would be solved. The kidnapper would set the victim free, secure in the knowledge that even though it would been be in the victim's interest to go to the police, he would not want to do.

Schelling's kidnapper and victim face a *commitment problem*, a situation in which they have an incentive to commit themselves to behave in a way that will later seems contrary to self-interest. Such problems are a common feature of social life. Consider, for example, the farmer who is trying to deter a transient thief from stealing his ox. Suppose this farmer is known to be a narrowly self-interested rational person. If the thief knows that the farmer's cost of pursuing him exceeds the value of the ox, he can then steal the ox with impunity. But suppose that the farmer cares also about not being victimized, quite independently of the effect of the victimization on his wealth. If he holds this goal with sufficient force, and if the potential thief knows of the farmers commitment, the ox will no longer be such an inviting target.

In the one-shot prisoner's dilemma, if the two players cooperate, each does better than if both defect, and yet each individual gets a higher payoff by defecting no matter which strategy the other player chooses. Both players thus have a clear incentive to commit themselves to cooperate. Yet a mere promise issued by a narrowly self-interested person clearly will not suffice, for his partner knows he will have no incentive to keep his promise. If both players know one another to be honest, however, both could reap the gains of cooperation.

In both these examples, note that merely having the relevant motivations or goals is by itself insufficient to solve the problem. It is also necessary that the presence of these goals be discernible by others. Someone with a predisposition to cooperate in the one-shot prisoner's dilemma, for instance, is in fact at a disadvantage unless others can identify that predisposition in him and he can identify similar predispositions in others.

Can the moral sentiments and other psychological forces that often drive people to ignore narrow self-interest be reliably discerned by outsiders? In a recent study (Frank, Giovich, and Regan 1993) found that subjects were surprisingly accurate at predicting who would cooperate and who would defect in one-shot prisoner's dilemmas played with near strangers.

In our study, the base rate of cooperation was 73.7 percent, the base rate of defection only 26.3 percent. A random prediction of cooperation with us have been accurate 73.7 percent of the time, a random prediction of defection accurate only 26.3 percent of the time. The actual accuracy rates for these two kinds of predictions were 80.7 percent and 56.8 percent, respectively. The likelihood of such high accuracy rates occurring by chance is less than one in one thousand.

Subjects in this experiment were strangers at the outset and were able to interact with one another for only 30 minutes before making their predictions.[1] It is plausible to suppose that predictions would be considerably more accurate for people we have known for a long time. Word example, consider it a thought experiment based on the following scenario:

> An individual has a gallon jug of unwanted pesticide. To protect the environment, the law requires that unused pesticide be turned into government disposal facility located thirty minutes' drive from her home. She knows, however, that she could simply pour the pesticide down her basement drain with no chance of being caught and punished. She also knows that her 1 gallon of pesticide, by itself, will cause only negligible harm if disposed of in this fashion.

Now the thought experiment: can you think of anyone who you feel certain would dispose of the pesticide properly? Most people respond affirmatively, and usually they have in mind someone they have known for a long time. If you answer yes, then you, too, accept the central premise of the commitment model - namely, that it is possible to identify non-self-interested motives in at least some other people.

The presence of such motives, coupled with the ability of others to discern them, makes it possible to solve commitment problems of the sort that have been presented. Knowing that others could discern her motives, even a rational, self-interested individual would have every reason to choose preferences that were not narrowly self-interested. Of course, people do not choose their preferences in any literal sense. The point is that if moral sentiments can be reliably discerned by others, the complex interaction of genes and culture that yields human preferences can sustain preferences that lead people to subordinate narrow self-interest in the pursuit of other goals.

An Equilibrium Mix of Motives

It might seem that if moral sentiments help solve important commitment problems, then evolutionary forces would assure that everyone have a full measure of these sentiments. But a closer look at the interplay between self-interest and other-regarding motives suggest that this is unlikely (see Frank 1988, chapter 3, for an extended discussion of this point). Imagine, for example, an environment populated by two types of people, cooperators and defectors. And suppose that people earn their livelihood by interacting in pairs, where the commitment problem they confront is the one-shot prisoner's dilemma.

If cooperators and defectors were perfectly indistinguishable, interactions would occur on a random basis and the average payoffs would always be larger for the defectors (owing to the dominance of defection in all prisoner's dilemmas). In evolutionary models, the rule governing population dynamics is that each type reproduces in proportion to its material payoff relative to other types. This implies that if the two types are indistinguishable, the eventual result would be extinction for The cooperators. In highly simplified form, this is the Darwinian story that inclines many social scientist to believe that self-interest is the only important human motive.

But now suppose that cooperators are distinguishable at a glance from defectors. Then interaction would no longer take place on a random basis. Rather, the cooperators would pair off systematically with one another to reap the benefits of mutual cooperation. Defectors would be left to interact with one another, and would receive the lower payoff associated with these pairings. The eventual result this time is that the defectors would be driven to extinction.

Neither of these two polar cases seems descriptive of actual populations, which typically contain a mix of cooperators and defectors. Such a mixed population is precisely the result we get if we make one small modification to the original story. Again suppose that cooperators are observably different from defectors, but that some effort is required to make the distinction. If the population initially consisted almost entirely of cooperators, it would not pay to expand this effort because one would be overwhelmingly likely to achieve a high payoff merely by interacting at random with another person. In such an environment, cooperative would cease to be vigilant in their choice of trading partners. Defectors would then find a ready pool of victims, and the resulting higher payoff would cause their share of the total population to grow.

As defectors become more numerous, however, it would begin to pay cooperators to exercise greater vigilance in their choice of partners. With sufficient defectors in the population, cooperators would be vigilant in the extreme, and we would again see pairings among like types only. That, in turn, would cause the prevalence of cooperators to grow. At some point, a stable balance would be struck in which operators would be vigilant enough to prevent further encroachment by defectors. The average payoff of the two types would be the same, and their population shares would remain constant. There would be, in other words, a stable niche for each type.

Five Ways a Socially Responsible Firm Might Prosper

The commitment model just described shows how it is possible for cooperative individuals to survive in competitive environments. What does this model have to say about the possibilities for survival of socially responsible firms? Recall that the socially responsible firm's problem is that by cooperating in one-shot dilemmas, it receives a lower pay off then do firm that defect. In the sections that follow, I will describe five possible areas in which the socially responsible firm might compensate for that disadvantage. The first three involve the recognition of potential commitment problems that arise within firms and between firms and the outside world. The last two involve the fact that people value socially responsible action and are willing to pay for it in the marketplace, even when they do not benefit from it directly in a material sense.

By Solving Commitment Problems with Employees

Just as commitment problems arise when independent individuals, so too do they arise among owners, managers, and employees. Many of these problems, like those among independent individuals, hinge on perceptions of trustworthiness and fairness. Some examples:

Shirking and Opportunism. The owner of a business perceived an opportunity to open a branch in a distant city. He knows that if he can hire and honest manager, the branch will be highly profitable. He cannot monitor the manager, however, and if the manager cheats, the branch will be unprofitable. By cheating, the manager can earn three times as much as he could by being honest. This situation defines a commitment problem. If the owner lacks the ability to identify an honest manager, the venture cannot go forward to, but if he has that ability, he can pay the manager well and still earn an attractive return.

[...]

Other Implicit Contacts. A firm with a skilled legal department might be able to devise some formal contractual arrangement whereby a could commit itself not to fire older workers. But such a contract would entail a potentially costly loss of flexibility. No firm can be certain of the future demand for its product, and at the time may come when its survival may depend on its ability to reduce its workforce. Both the firm and its workers would pay a price if this flexibility were sacrificed.

[…]

By Solving Commitment Problems with Customers

A variety of commitment problems arise between firms and their customers, and at least some of these are amenable to solution along line similar to those just discussed. Quality assurance is a clear example.

George Akerlof's celebrated paper on lemons (1970) describes a commitment problem in which sellers and buyers alike would benefit if the seller could somehow commit to providing a product or service of high-quality. A variety of means have been suggested for solving this problem through reliance on material incentives. Firms can guarantee their products, for example, or they can develop public reputations for supplying high-quality (see Klein and Leffler 1981).

Many forms of the quality assurance problem, however, cannot be resolved by manipulating materials incentives. Consider a law firm that could provide the legal services a client wants at a price the client would be willing to pay. But suppose that the client has no way to evaluate the quality of his lawyer services. The outcome if his case by itself is not diagnostic. He might win despite having received shotty legal help, or he might lose despite having receive the best possible help. In such situations, clients are willing to pay premium fees to a firm run by someone they feel they can trust.

By Solving Commitment Problems with Other Firms

Commitment problems also arise in the context of business transactions between firms, and here too solutions that rely on character assessment often play a role.

The Subcontractor Holdup Problem. Consider the familiar example of the subcontractor that does most of its business with a single buyer. To serve this buyer at the lowest possible price, much of the subcontractor's human and physical capital has to be tailored to the buyer's specific needs. Have you made those investments, however, the subcontractor is vulnerable to the holdup problem; because the buyer knows that the subcontractors customized assets cost more than they would bring in the open market, it can pay its subcontractor a price that is above the subcontractor's marginal cost but lower than its average cost. Anticipating this problem, subcontractors will be willing to invest in the capital of that best serves their customers' needs only if they believe their customers can be trusted not to exploit them.

In a recent study, Edward Lawrence (1988) spells out why material incentives are inadequate to solve the commitment problems that arise between small French manufacturing firms and their subcontractors. He described in detail how parties shop for trustworthy partners. For example, all the respondents in his sample emphasized the heavy weight they placed on personal relationships in this process.

Quality Assurance. The problem of quality assurance arises not just between firms and consumers but also between one firm and another. Consider, for example, the relationship between a parent company and its franchisees. What a franchise owner provides high-quality service to the public he enhances not just his own reputation with consumers but also the reputations of other outlets. The parent firm would like him to take both of those benefits into account in setting his service levels, but his private incentives are to focus only on how good service affects his own customers. Accordingly, it is common for franchise agreements to call on franchisees to provide higher-quality service than would otherwise be in their interest to provide. Franchisers incur cost in the attempt to enforce these agreements, but their ability to monitor service at the local level is highly imperfect. The franchiser thus has a strong incentive to recruit franchisees who assign intrinsic value to living up to their service agreements. And prospective franchisees so identified are at a competitive advantage over those motivated by self-interest alone.

Maintaining Confidentiality. Many consulting firms provide services that require access to competitively sensitive information. Clearly no firm could succeed in this line of work if it acquired a reputation for making such information available to rivals. When employees leave these firms, however, their material incentives to maintain confidentiality fall considerably. In some cases, material incentives to maintain confidentiality are weakened by the fact that a number of people have had access to the sensitive information, so that it is much harder to trace the source of the leak. With these possibilities in mind a client would be much more willing to deal with a consulting firm that is able to identify and attract employees who assign intrinsic value to honoring confidentiality agreements.

In the examples just discussed firms compensate for the higher cost of socially responsible behavior by their ability to solve commitment problems. In addition, socially responsible firms benefit from a match with the moral values of socially responsible consumers and recruits.

By Reflecting Consumers' Moral Values

The standard free-rider model suggests that buyers will not be willing to pay a premium for products produced by socially responsible firms. For example, consumers may not like the fact that Acme Tire Corporation pollutes the air, but they are said to realize that their own purchase of Acme tires will have a virtually unmeasurable effect on air quality. Accordingly, the theory predicts, if Acme tires sell for even a little less than those produced by a rival with a cleaner technology, consumers will buy from Acme.

The commitment model challenges this account by showing that many people have come to develop a taste for socially responsible behavior. People with such a tasteful prefer dealing with socially responsible firms even when they realize that their own purchases are too small to affect the outcomes they care about. Conventional free-rider theory predicted that Star Kist Tuna sales and profits would fall when it raised its prices to cover the added cost of purchasing tuna only from suppliers who used dolphin-safe net. Star Kist sales and profits went up, however, not down. And consumers who stopped to ponder the matter would know that a single household tuna purchase would have no discernible impact on the fate of dolphins. Even so, it appears that many consumers are willing to pay higher prices in the name of a cause they cared about. There is also evidence that Ben & Jerry's sells more ice cream because of its preservation efforts on behalf of Amazon rainforest, that The Body Shop sells more cosmetics because of its environmentally friendly packaging, and that McDonald's sells more hamburgers because of its support for the parents of seriously ill children.

Experimental evidence from the "dictator game" provides additional evidence of consumers' willingness to incur cost on behalf of moral values. The dictator game is played by two players. The first is given a sum of money - say $20 - and is then asked to choose one of two ways of dividing it with the second player: either $10 each or $18 for the first player and $2 for the second player. One

Study (Kahneman, Knetsch, and Thaler, 1986) found that more than three-quarters of subjects chose the $10 - $10. The researchers then describe this experiment to a separate group of subjects, to whom they then gave a choice between splitting $10 with one of the subjects who had chosen the $10 - $10 split or splitting $12 with one of the subjects who had chosen the $18 - $2 split. More than 80% of these subjects chose the first option, which the authors of the study interpreted as a willingness to spend a dollar to punish an anonymous stranger who had behaved unfairly in the earlier experiment.

Taken together, the market data and experimental evidence appears to shift the burden of proof to proponents of the free-rider hypothesis.

By Reflecting Prospective Employees' Moral Values

A fifth and final benefit accrues to socially responsible firms is the relative advantage they enjoy in recruiting. Jobs differ in countless dimensions, one of which is the degree to which the worker contributes to the well-being of others. Consider two jobs identical along all dimensions except for this one. (For example, one job might involve writing advertising copy for a product known to cause serious health problems, while the other involves writing advertising copy for the United Way.) If people derive satisfaction from engaging an altruistic behavior, it follows that if the wages in these two jobs were the same, there would be an excess supply of applicants to the second job, a shortage of applicants to the first. In equilibrium, we would therefore expect a compensating wage premium for the less altruistic job. A job applicant who wants to occupy the moral high ground can do so only by accepting lower wages. And these lower wages, in turn, help balance the higher cost of socially responsible operations.

Conclusions

When a business confronts an ethical dilemma, it must incur higher costs if it takes the high road. For example, in the process of refusing to supply master automobile keys to mail order customers he believes to be car thieves, a locksmith sustains a penalty on the bottom line. Indeed, if the morally preferred action involved no such a penalty, there would be no moral dilemmas.

In this chapter, I have described five advantages that help a socially-responsible firm to compensate for the higher direct cost of his actions. Three of these involve the ability to avoid commitment problems and other one shot dilemmas. The socially responsible firm is better able than its opportunistic rivals to solve commitment problems that might arise with employees, with customers, and with other firms. A fourth advantage is that buyers are often willing to pay more for the products of socially responsible firms. And finally, the socially responsible firm enjoys an advantage when recruiting against its less responsible rivals. Taken together, these advantages often appear to be sufficient to offset the higher cost of socially responsible action.

This claim may invite the complaint that what I am calling socially responsible behavior is really just selfishness by another name. Consider this trenchant commentary by Albert Carr, and economic advisor to Harry Truman:

> The illusion that business can afford to be guided by ethics as conceived in private life is often fostered by speeches and articles containing such phrases as "it pays to be ethical" or, "sound ethics is good business." Actually this is not an ethical question at all; it is a self-serving calculation in disguise. The speaker is really saying that in the

long run a company can make money if it does not antagonize competitors, suppliers, employees, and customers by squeezing them too hard. He is saying that oversharp policies reduce ultimate gains. That is true, but it has nothing to do with ethics.

(Carr 1968, 148)

This line of reasoning applies that any business behavior consistent with survival is selfish by definition. Such a definition, however, is completely at odds with our everyday understanding of the concept. Cooperation in one shot dilemmas is costly in both the short run and the long run, and for that reason it is properly called unselfish. I have argued that because traits of character are discernible by others, the kind of people who cooperate in one shot dilemmas enjoy the advantages in other spheres, and these advantages may help them survive in competition with less scrupulous rivals. It simply invites confusion to call the cooperative behaviors themselves self-serving.

Note

1. In the version of the experiment reported here, subjects were permitted to discuss the PD game itself, and, if they chose, to make promises concerning their strategy choices.

References

Akerlof, G. 1970."The Market for Lemons", *Quarterly Journal of Economics* 84: 488–500.

Akerlof, R. 1984. *The Evolution of Cooperation*. New York: Basic Books.

Carr, A. 1968. "Is Business Bluffing Ethical?" In *Ethical Issues in Business*, 4th edition, Thomas Donaldson and Patricia Werhane (eds). (Englewood Cliffs, NJ: Prentice Hall).

Dawkins, R. 1976. *The Selfish Gene*. (New York: Oxford University Press).

Frank, R. H. 1993. *"What Price the Moral High Ground?"* Unpublished manuscript, Cornell University.

Frank, R. H., T. Gilovich, and D. Regan. 1993. "The Evolution of One-Shot Cooperation," *Ethology and Sociobiology* 14 (July): 247–256.

Frank, R. H. 1988. *Passions Within Reason: The Strategic Role of The Emotions* (New York: Norton).

Friedman, M. 1970. "The Social Responsibility of Businesses to Increase Its Profits." *The New York Times Magazine.* 33 (September 13): 116–129.

Kahneman, D., J. Knetsche, and R. Thaler. 1986. "Perceptions of Unfairness: Constraints on Wealth Seeking," *American Economic Review* 76 columns 728–741.

Klein, B., and K. Lefler. 1981."The Role of Market Forces in Assuring Contractual Performance." *Journal of Political Economy* 89: 615–641.

Lorenz, E. 1988. "Neither Friends nor Strangers: Informal Networks of Some Contracting in French Industry." In *Trust: The Making and Breaking a Cooperative Relations*, Diego Gambetta (ed.). (New York: Basil Blackwell).

Shelling, T. C. 1960. *Strategy and Conflict*. (Cambridge: Harvard University Press).

Studley, J. 1989. "Financial Sacrifice outside the Private Sector." *National Law Journal*, March 27th, 1989, 16.

FAIRNESS AND JUSTICE IN DATA ANALYTICS

6

"That's not fair" is a common refrain, whether complaining about a rule being enforced at work or that a sister got a larger ice cream cone. However, explaining *why* an act is not fair is quite nuanced. In the case of data analytics, how do we judge whether Lemonade Insurance's AI Jim is fair? When the number of claims awarded based on AI Jim is analyzed, should it be the same as when humans decide claims? The same across types of damages? Types of people? Does the outcome matter for fairness?

Justice scholars differentiate between distributive and procedural justice. Distributive justice focuses on the fairness of *outcomes* whereas procedural justice focuses on the fairness of the *rules and process* followed in making the decision. In other words, people can find an outcome fair even when not everyone receives the same amount, as long as the procedure followed is perceived as fair. A professor can be seen as fair even if not all students receive an "A," as long as their process is clear, organized, and rewards people on the merits. Organizational scholars also include *interactional* justice to encompass the perceived fairness of how someone was treated during the decision. To extend the example, a professor is seen as fair if they also treat students with respect and offer ways for students to rectify mistakes.

Definitions of justice and fairness are important for the ethics of data analytics because many times the programs are designed to allocate "things" or "goods," to use the term of justice scholars. We care how goods like admittance to college, health care, bonuses, sentences, and even ice cream, are allocated whether by the government or by a company or by our parents.

Within data analytics and computer science, the study of fairness has grown in recent years. However, some technical approaches to fairness can conflate questions of discrimination with questions of fairness, where the ideas behind discrimination law are equated to questions of fairness. However, decisions can be legal and nondiscriminatory and still be considered unfair to people. For example, giving jobs to friends just because they are friends is not illegal or even discriminatory, but it is unfair. In addition, these approaches can lack nuance since researchers and developers may define fairness in a way that is easily measured or for which they currently have a technical solution: e.g., equalized odds of being categorized given particular properties, equal opportunity of different classes of people being categorized a particular way, not using protected class data, achieving mistakes at an equal rate across groups, having the same prediction for someone when they are assigned a different class (demographic group) in a "counterfactual" world, similar mistakes for similar people, etc.[1] However, as summarized by Mitchell et al. in their overview,

DOI: 10.1201/9781003278290-36

defining fairness in a way that is "mathematically convenient" may not address the injustices we are seeking to solve.[2] For organizations using and developing data analytics, a discrimination/fairness test will not suffice—even if it is easier to implement.[3]

Here, we step back to explore three different approaches to fairness and justice in philosophy, where each has a different answer to *what does it mean to be fair and just?* We devote a separate chapter on discrimination and data.

Summary of Readings

Three very different approaches to fairness and justice are included. These apply to life in general and not only to algorithms and analytics. Importantly, data analysts and computer scientists may hear that their program is unfair from those that do not care about a technical definition of fairness that was designed into the program.

John Rawls develops his theory of justice, or the criteria to judge outcomes as just or not, starting behind a veil of ignorance. He suggests that anyone standing in an original position without knowledge of who they are or their station in life, would choose the principles he is about to propose. Rawls puts forward two principles. First, the equal liberty principle requires "equality in the assignment of basic rights and duties." This first principle is important because a violation of the liberty principle for Rawls, means the system is unjust. One cannot sacrifice the liberty of any for an efficient outcome. Second, the difference principle requires (a) that the position to which the inequality is attached is open to all and (b) that any differences work out to, at minimum, not further harm the least fortunate. Since data analytics is frequently distributing social goods, e.g., education, jobs, loans, opportunities, etc., Rawls's three-pronged test applies to the fairness of many analytics programs. In analyzing a data analytics program according to a Rawlsian approach, one would ask (a) is the opportunity to receive an outcome open to everyone *with the same background/criteria* (for AI Jim, are there types of customers more likely to be denied a claim irrespective of the merit of their claim); and (b) is the system of allocating the outcome (deciding whose claim is paid) not harming those least fortunate, where the least fortunate is defined before the system was implemented.

1. Are anyone's rights being diminished with this data analytics program? Does this pass the liberty test for Rawls?
2. Is the attainment of the opportunity (categorization, good being distributed, etc.) open to all?[4] If predicting or categorizing, are there groups of people more or less likely to be categorized?
3. Who is the least fortunate—are they systematically worse off with this program?

For Robert Nozick, on the other hand, inequalities are seen as a fact of life. Nozick questions interventions to change the status quo and fix inequalities. In this excerpt from *Anarchy, State, and Utopia,* Nozick lays out his approach to thinking about justice which centers on whether the holding (the thing of value) was acquired justly and whether the holding was then transferred justly. Nozick is not concerned with, what he calls, end-pattern inequalities. Nozick is concerned, first, whether the good was acquired by someone without deception, fraud, theft, manipulation, etc. And, second, Nozick is concerned whether that person transferred the good without deception, fraud, theft, manipulation. For data analytics, Nozick exemplifies an approach to justice which only asks if the organization has acquired something justly (a program, data, etc.) and whether that organization then transfers the holding justly to someone else. Data analytics could be involved in the acquisition (scraping pictures online) or the transfer (allocating healthcare or vaccines). For our cases, Nozick will focus on (a) if the acquisition of the program or data was without deception or fraud; and (b) if the program was used (transferred a good) without deception, fraud, manipulation, etc.

1. Is there any deception or fraud or manipulation in the acquisition of the data used in the program?
2. Is there deception or fraud or manipulation in the use of the data analytics program?

Michael Walzer's approach differs in that Walzer allows for more than one way to distribute goods. This pluralistic approach would allow valid distribution schemes in different "spheres" of life, e.g., politics, education, healthcare, etc. However, Walzer makes a case that the problem, what he calls tyranny, is when someone who dominates in one sphere is able to dominate in another sphere *merely because* they dominate in the first sphere. For example, winners in the education sphere should not be allocated health care merely because they were winners in the education sphere. So, if a healthcare allocation program was prioritizing patients based on their highest degree attained, Walzer would say that it is unfair. More than unfair, Walzer refers to such acts as tyrannical. As Walzer generalizes: "No social good x should be distributed to men and women who possess some other good y merely because they possess y and without regard to the meaning of x." Walzer then critiques alternative approaches—which could be valid in a specific sphere: free exchange (which sounds like Nozick), need, and dessert. He wisely notes that in a market approach, money can be a dominant good, which can unjustly dictate the distribution of other goods in other spheres of life (education, healthcare, etc.). *For data analytics, Walzer's approach is important because data from one sphere in a large data set could be used in the analytics applied to another sphere.* In our cases here, Walzer's framework of justice would highlight if data from one sphere is being used in an allocation decision that is measuring success or failure in another sphere of life. So, whether or not someone has a high GPA could reasonably impact their admittance into college, but the income of their parents (success in the commercial sphere by a family member) would be seen as unjust if used to decide admittance to college without regard to the merits. In applying Walzer to a data analytics program, one would ask (1) are winners in another sphere of life given preference in the allocation of opportunities in the data analytics program? Through proxies?

Related Cases

The *COMPAS case* brings to light the measurement of accuracy and the types of mistakes that a categorizing algorithm can make. The COMPAS program was designed as a risk assessment tool to inform decisions in criminal justice such as setting bond amounts or even sentencing and parole. A defendant's risk score is based on 137 measurements of their life which includes their childhood, the family life and friends, and their current crimes. The program proved unreliable as a predictor: only 20 percent of people predicted to commit violent crimes actually did so. However, even more problematic, the case highlights the importance of measuring accuracy including both false positive and false negatives. A false positive is when the algorithm or AI program labels an individual as within a category (here, High Risk), but the person is not. So, the defendant would receive a higher sentence or not be granted parole even though they would not go on to commit crimes. The authors found a racial disparity in the types of mistakes that were made with the COMPAS program. The case explores many ways the program could be considered unfair according to Rawls, Nozick, or Walzer.

For background, given the factors used for the algorithm, the United States has a history of discriminatory practices within criminal justice. For example, The Hamilton Project calculated that Black Americans were 6.5 times as likely as White Americans to be incarcerated for drug-related offenses. However, Black and White Americans sell/use drugs at similar rates.[5]

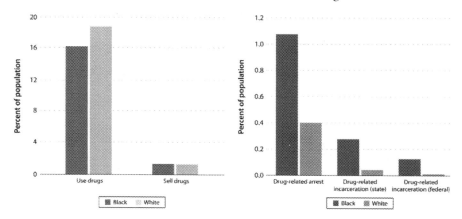

Racial disparities in criminal justice originate from differential drug laws and harsher sentences imposed on Black defendants, disparities in the initial point of contact with police by person or zip code, or prosecutorial charging decisions.[6] Even interactions with the police are found to be biased, such as "stop and frisk" policing. In precincts where Black and Hispanic citizens made up less than 10 percent of the population,

> … individuals identified as belonging to these racial groups nevertheless accounted for more than half of the total "stops" during the covered period. Blacks accounted for 30% of all persons "stopped" in these precincts; Hispanics accounted for 23.4% of all persons "stopped."[7]

In the second case, "Major Universities Are Using Race as a 'High Impact Predictor' of Student Success," outlines the use of a program used to predict student success. One of the factors included is race, and the program could be used to advise students to take easier majors and classes.

Notes

1. Ninareh Mehrabi et al., "A Survey on Bias and Fairness in Machine Learning," *ArXiv Preprint ArXiv:1908.09635*, 2019; Sahil Verma and Julia Rubin, "Fairness Definitions Explained" (2018 ieee/acm international workshop on software fairness (fairware), IEEE, 2018), 1–7.
2. Mitchell et al. provide an excellent overview focusing on testable definitions of fairness. Shira Mitchell et al., "Algorithmic Fairness: Choices, Assumptions, and Definitions," *Annual Review of Statistics and Its Application* 8 (2020): 49.
3. As noted by Hutchinson and Mitchell, such quantitative definitions of fairness have actually been around for decades and are strikingly similar to the questions around fairness and data analytics in the education and hiring area. Ben Hutchinson and Margaret Mitchell, "50 Years of Test (Un) Fairness: Lessons for Machine Learning," 2019, 49–58.

4. This idea of Rawls is similar to the idea of equal opportunity in Moritz Hardt, Eric Price, and Nathan Srebro, "Equality of Opportunity in Supervised Learning," *ArXiv Preprint ArXiv:1610.02413*, 2016. However, Rawls is not focused solely on discrimination and protected classes.

5. https://www.hamiltonproject.org/charts/rates_of_drug_use_and_sales_by_race_rates_of_drug _related_criminal_justice

6. https://www.sentencingproject.org/publications/color-of-justice-racial-and-ethnic-disparity-in-state -prisons/#IV.%20Drivers%20of%20Disparity

7. https://squareonejustice.org/wp-content/uploads/2019/10/roundtable-oct2018-Racial-History-of -Criminal-Justice-in-America-by-Heather-Ann-Thompson.pdf

Chapter 6.1

Machine Bias*

Julia Angwin, Jeff Larson, Surya Mattu, and Lauren Kirchner

There's software used across the country to predict future criminals. And it's biased against blacks.

ON A SPRING AFTERNOON IN 2014, Brisha Borden was running late to pick up her god-sister from school when she spotted an unlocked kid's blue Huffy bicycle and a silver Razor scooter. Borden and a friend grabbed the bike and scooter and tried to ride them down the street in the Fort Lauderdale suburb of Coral Springs.

Just as the 18-year-old girls were realizing they were too big for the tiny conveyances—which belonged to a 6-year-old boy—a woman came running after them saying, "That's my kid's stuff." Borden and her friend immediately dropped the bike and scooter and walked away.

But it was too late—a neighbor who witnessed the heist had already called the police. Borden and her friend were arrested and charged with burglary and petty theft for the items, which were valued at a total of $80.

Compare their crime with a similar one: The previous summer, 41-year-old Vernon Prater was picked up for shoplifting $86.35 worth of tools from a nearby Home Depot store (Figure 6.1.1).

Prater was the more seasoned criminal. He had already been convicted of armed robbery and attempted armed robbery, for which he served five years in prison, in addition to another armed robbery charge. Borden had a record, too, but it was for misdemeanors committed when she was a juvenile.

Yet something odd happened when Borden and Prater were booked into jail: A computer program spat out a score predicting the likelihood of each committing a future crime. Borden—who is black—was rated a high risk. Prater—who is white—was rated a low risk.

Two years later, we know the computer algorithm got it exactly backward. Borden has not been charged with any new crimes. Prater is serving an eight-year prison term for subsequently breaking into a warehouse and stealing thousands of dollars' worth of electronics.

Scores like this—known as risk assessments—are increasingly common in courtrooms across the nation. They are used to inform decisions about who can be set free at every stage of the criminal justice system, from assigning bond amounts—as is the case in Fort Lauderdale—to

---

* Julia Angwin, Jeff Larson, Surya Mattu, Lauren Kirchner, "Machine Bias," *ProPublica* (May 23, 2016). Reprinted with permission.

                           DOI: 10.1201/9781003278290-37

even more fundamental decisions about defendants' freedom. In Arizona, Colorado, Delaware, Kentucky, Louisiana, Oklahoma, Virginia, Washington and Wisconsin, the results of such assessments are given to judges during criminal sentencing.

Rating a defendant's risk of future crime is often done in conjunction with an evaluation of a defendant's rehabilitation needs. The Justice Department's National Institute of Corrections now encourages the use of such combined assessments at every stage of the criminal justice process. And a landmark sentencing reform bill currently pending in Congress would mandate the use of such assessments in federal prisons.

In 2014, then U.S. Attorney General Eric Holder warned that the risk scores might be injecting bias into the courts. He called for the U.S. Sentencing Commission to study their use. "Although these measures were crafted with the best of intentions, I am concerned that they inadvertently undermine our efforts to ensure individualized and equal justice," he said, adding, "they may exacerbate unwarranted and unjust disparities that are already far too common in our criminal justice system and in our society."

The sentencing commission did not, however, launch a study of risk scores. So ProPublica did, as part of a larger examination of the powerful, largely hidden effect of algorithms in American life.

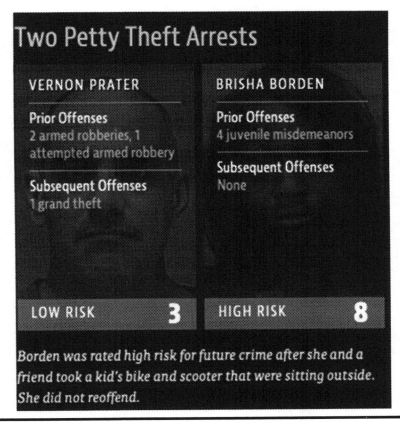

Figure 6.1.1   Comparison of risk scores for two petty theft arrests.

We obtained the risk scores assigned to more than 7,000 people arrested in Broward County, Florida, in 2013 and 2014 and checked to see how many were charged with new crimes over the next two years, the same benchmark used by the creators of the algorithm.

The score proved remarkably unreliable in forecasting violent crime: Only 20 percent of the people predicted to commit violent crimes actually went on to do so.

When a full range of crimes were taken into account—including misdemeanors such as driving with an expired license—the algorithm was somewhat more accurate than a coin flip. Of those deemed likely to re-offend, 61 percent were arrested for any subsequent crimes within two years.

We also turned up significant racial disparities, just as Holder feared. In forecasting who would re-offend, the algorithm made mistakes with black and white defendants at roughly the same rate but in very different ways (Figure 6.1.5).

- The formula was particularly likely to falsely flag black defendants as future criminals, wrongly labeling them this way at almost twice the rate as white defendants.
- White defendants were mislabeled as low risk more often than black defendants.

Could this disparity be explained by defendants' prior crimes or the type of crimes they were arrested for? No. We ran a statistical test that isolated the effect of race from criminal history and recidivism, as well as from defendants' age and gender. Black defendants were still 77 percent more likely to be pegged as at higher risk of committing a future violent crime and 45 percent more likely to be predicted to commit a future crime of any kind. (Read our analysis.)

The algorithm used to create the Florida risk scores is a product of a for-profit company, Northpointe. The company disputes our analysis.

In a letter, it criticized ProPublica's methodology and defended the accuracy of its test: "Northpointe does not agree that the results of your analysis, or the claims being made based upon that analysis, are correct or that they accurately reflect the outcomes from the application of the model."

Northpointe's software is among the most widely used assessment tools in the country. The company does not publicly disclose the calculations used to arrive at defendants' risk scores, so it is not possible for either defendants or the public to see what might be driving the disparity. (On Sunday, Northpointe gave ProPublica the basics of its future-crime formula — which includes factors such as education levels, and whether a defendant has a job. It did not share the specific calculations, which it said are proprietary.)

Northpointe's core product is a set of scores derived from 137 questions[1] that are either answered by defendants or pulled from criminal records. Race is not one of the questions. The survey asks defendants such things as: "Was one of your parents ever sent to jail or prison?" "How many of your friends/acquaintances are taking drugs illegally?" and "How often did you get in fights while at school?" The questionnaire also asks people to agree or disagree with statements such as "A hungry person has a right to steal" and "If people make me angry or lose my temper, I can be dangerous." (Figure 6.1.2).

The appeal of risk scores is obvious: The United States locks up far more people than any other country, a disproportionate number of them black. For more than two centuries, the key decisions in the legal process, from pretrial release to sentencing to parole, have been in the hands of human beings guided by their instincts and personal biases.

If computers could accurately predict which defendants were likely to commit new crimes, the criminal justice system could be fairer and more selective about who is incarcerated and for how long. The trick, of course, is to make sure the computer gets it right. If it's wrong in one direction,

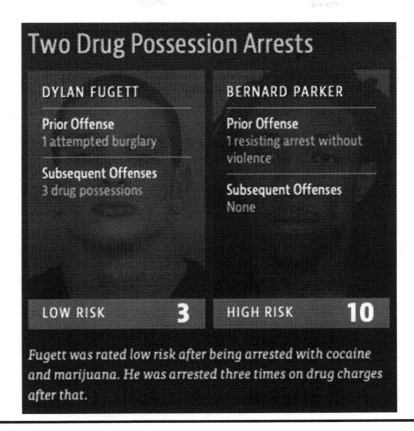

Figure 6.1.2   Comparison of risk scores for two drug possession arrests.

a dangerous criminal could go free. If it's wrong in another direction, it could result in someone unfairly receiving a harsher sentence or waiting longer for parole than is appropriate.

The first time Paul Zilly heard of his score—and realized how much was riding on it — was during his sentencing hearing on Feb. 15, 2013, in court in Barron County, Wisconsin. Zilly had been convicted of stealing a push lawnmower and some tools. The prosecutor recommended a year in county jail and follow-up supervision that could help Zilly with "staying on the right path." His lawyer agreed to a plea deal.

But Judge James Babler had seen Zilly's scores. Northpointe's software had rated Zilly as a high risk for future violent crime and a medium risk for general recidivism. "When I look at the risk assessment," Babler said in court, "it is about as bad as it could be."

Then Babler overturned the plea deal that had been agreed on by the prosecution and defense and imposed two years in state prison and three years of supervision.

CRIMINOLOGISTS HAVE LONG TRIED to predict which criminals are more dangerous before deciding whether they should be released. Race, nationality and skin color were often used in making such predictions until about the 1970s, when it became politically unacceptable, according to a survey of risk assessment tools by Columbia University law professor Bernard Harcourt.

In the 1980s, as a crime wave engulfed the nation, lawmakers made it much harder for judges and parole boards to exercise discretion in making such decisions. States and the federal government began instituting mandatory sentences and, in some cases, abolished parole, making it less important to evaluate individual offenders.

But as states struggle to pay for swelling prison and jail populations, forecasting criminal risk has made a comeback.

Dozens of risk assessments are being used across the nation—some created by for-profit companies such as Northpointe and others by nonprofit organizations. (One tool being used in states including Kentucky and Arizona, called the Public Safety Assessment, was developed by the Laura and John Arnold Foundation, which also is a funder of ProPublica.)

There have been few independent studies of these criminal risk assessments. In 2013, researchers Sarah Desmarais and Jay Singh examined 19 different risk methodologies used in the United States and found that "in most cases, validity had only been examined in one or two studies" and that "frequently, those investigations were completed by the same people who developed the instrument."

Their analysis of the research through 2012 found that the tools "were moderate at best in terms of predictive validity," Desmarais said in an interview. And she could not find any substantial set of studies conducted in the United States that examined whether risk scores were racially biased. "The data do not exist," she said.

Since then, there have been some attempts to explore racial disparities in risk scores. One 2016 study examined the validity of a risk assessment tool, not Northpointe's, used to make probation decisions for about 35,000 federal convicts. The researchers, Jennifer Skeem at University of California, Berkeley, and Christopher T. Lowenkamp from the Administrative Office of the U.S. Courts, found that blacks did get a higher average score but concluded the differences were not attributable to bias.

The increasing use of risk scores is controversial and has garnered media coverage, including articles by the Associated Press, and the Marshall Project and FiveThirtyEight last year.

Most modern risk tools were originally designed to provide judges with insight into the types of treatment that an individual might need—from drug treatment to mental health counseling.

"What it tells the judge is that if I put you on probation, I'm going to need to give you a lot of services or you're probably going to fail," said Edward Latessa, a University of Cincinnati professor who is the author of a risk assessment tool that is used in Ohio and several other states.

But being judged ineligible for alternative treatment—particularly during a sentencing hearing—can translate into incarceration. Defendants rarely have an opportunity to challenge their assessments. The results are usually shared with the defendant's attorney, but the calculations that transformed the underlying data into a score are rarely revealed.

"Risk assessments should be impermissible unless both parties get to see all the data that go into them," said Christopher Slobogin, director of the criminal justice program at Vanderbilt Law School. "It should be an open, full-court adversarial proceeding."

Proponents of risk scores argue they can be used to reduce the rate of incarceration. In 2002, Virginia became one of the first states to begin using a risk assessment tool in the sentencing of nonviolent felony offenders statewide. In 2014, Virginia judges using the tool sent nearly half of those defendants to alternatives to prison, according to a state sentencing commission report. Since 2005, the state's prison population growth has slowed to 5 percent from a rate of 31 percent the previous decade.

In some jurisdictions, such as Napa County, California, the probation department uses risk assessments to suggest to the judge an appropriate probation or treatment plan for individuals being sentenced. Napa County Superior Court Judge Mark Boessenecker said he finds the recommendations helpful. "We have a dearth of good treatment programs, so filling a slot in a program with someone who doesn't need it is foolish," he said.

However, Boessenecker, who trains other judges around the state in evidence-based sentencing, cautions his colleagues that the score doesn't necessarily reveal whether a person is dangerous or if they should go to prison.

"A guy who has molested a small child every day for a year could still come out as a low risk because he probably has a job," Boessenecker said. "Meanwhile, a drunk guy will look high risk because he's homeless. These risk factors don't tell you whether the guy ought to go to prison or not; the risk factors tell you more about what the probation conditions ought to be."

Sometimes, the scores make little sense even to defendants.

James Rivelli, a 54-year old Hollywood, Florida, man, was arrested two years ago for shoplifting seven boxes of Crest Whitestrips from a CVS drugstore. Despite a criminal record that included aggravated assault, multiple thefts and felony drug trafficking, the Northpointe algorithm classified him as being at a low risk of reoffending (Figure 6.1.6).

"I am surprised it is so low," Rivelli said when told by a reporter he had been rated a 3 out of a possible 10. "I spent five years in state prison in Massachusetts. But I guess they don't count that here in Broward County." In fact, criminal records from across the nation are supposed to be included in risk assessments.

Less than a year later, he was charged with two felony counts for shoplifting about $1,000 worth of tools from Home Depot. He said his crimes were fueled by drug addiction and that he is now sober.

NORTHPOINTE WAS FOUNDED in 1989 by Tim Brennan, then a professor of statistics at the University of Colorado, and Dave Wells, who was running a corrections program in Traverse City, Michigan.

Wells had built a prisoner classification system for his jail. "It was a beautiful piece of work," Brennan said in an interview conducted before ProPublica had completed its analysis. Brennan and Wells shared a love for what Brennan called "quantitative taxonomy"—the measurement of personality traits such as intelligence, extroversion and introversion. The two decided to build a risk assessment score for the corrections industry.

Brennan wanted to improve on a leading risk assessment score, the LSI, or Level of Service Inventory, which had been developed in Canada. "I found a fair amount of weakness in the LSI," Brennan said. He wanted a tool that addressed the major theories about the causes of crime.

Brennan and Wells named their product the Correctional Offender Management Profiling for Alternative Sanctions, or COMPAS. It assesses not just risk but also nearly two dozen so-called "criminogenic needs" that relate to the major theories of criminality, including "criminal personality," "social isolation," "substance abuse" and "residence/stability." Defendants are ranked low, medium or high risk in each category.

As often happens with risk assessment tools, many jurisdictions have adopted Northpointe's software before rigorously testing whether it works. New York State, for instance, started using the tool to assess people on probation in a pilot project in 2001 and rolled it out to the rest of the state's probation departments—except New York City—by 2010. The state didn't publish a comprehensive statistical evaluation of the tool until 2012. The study of more than 16,000 probationers found the tool was 71 percent accurate, but it did not evaluate racial differences.

A spokeswoman for the New York state division of criminal justice services said the study did not examine race because it only sought to test whether the tool had been properly calibrated to fit New York's probation population. She also said judges in nearly all New York counties are given defendants' Northpointe assessments during sentencing.

In 2009, Brennan and two colleagues published a validation study that found that Northpointe's risk of recidivism score had an accuracy rate of 68 percent in a sample of 2,328 people. Their study

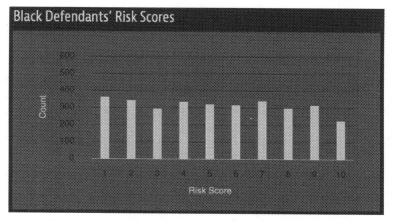

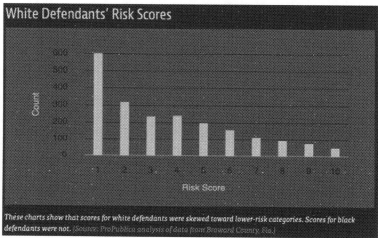

Figure 6.1.3 Distribution of White and Black defendants' risk scores.

also found that the score was slightly less predictive for black men than white men—67 percent versus 69 percent. It did not examine racial disparities beyond that, including whether some groups were more likely to be wrongly labeled higher risk (Figure 6.1.3).

Brennan said it is difficult to construct a score that doesn't include items that can be correlated with race—such as poverty, joblessness and social marginalization. "If those are omitted from your risk assessment, accuracy goes down," he said.

In 2011, Brennan and Wells sold Northpointe to Toronto-based conglomerate Constellation Software for an undisclosed sum.

Wisconsin has been among the most eager and expansive users of Northpointe's risk assessment tool in sentencing decisions. In 2012, the Wisconsin Department of Corrections launched the use of the software throughout the state. It is used at each step in the prison system, from sentencing to parole (Figure 6.1.4).

In a 2012 presentation, corrections official Jared Hoy described the system as a "giant correctional pinball machine" in which correctional officers could use the scores at every "decision point."

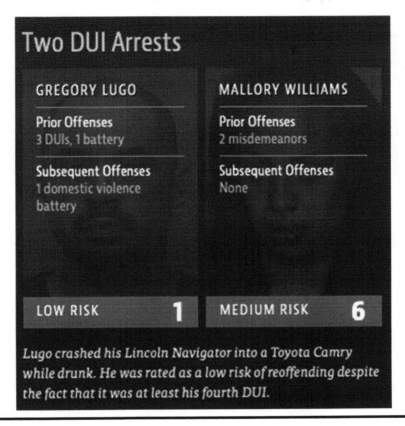

Figure 6.1.4 Comparison of risk scores for two DUI arrests.

Wisconsin has not yet completed a statistical validation study of the tool and has not said when one might be released. State corrections officials declined repeated requests to comment for this article.

Some Wisconsin counties use other risk assessment tools at arrest to determine if a defendant is too risky for pretrial release. Once a defendant is convicted of a felony anywhere in the state, the Department of Corrections attaches Northpointe's assessment to the confidential presentence report given to judges, according to Hoy's presentation.

In theory, judges are not supposed to give longer sentences to defendants with higher risk scores. Rather, they are supposed to use the tests primarily to determine which defendants are eligible for probation or treatment programs.

But judges have cited scores in their sentencing decisions. In August 2013, Judge Scott Horne in La Crosse County, Wisconsin, declared that defendant Eric Loomis had been "identified, through the COMPAS assessment, as an individual who is at high risk to the community." The judge then imposed a sentence of eight years and six months in prison.

Loomis, who was charged with driving a stolen vehicle and fleeing from police, is challenging the use of the score at sentencing as a violation of his due process rights. The state has defended Horne's use of the score with the argument that judges can consider the score in addition to other factors. It has also stopped including scores in presentencing reports until the state Supreme Court decides the case.

Prediction Fails Differently for Black Defendants	WHITE	AFRICAN AMERICAN
Labeled Higher Risk, But Didn't Re-Offend	23.5%	44.9%
Labeled Lower Risk, Yet Did Re-Offend	47.7%	28.0%

Overall, Northpointe's assessment tool correctly predicts recidivism 61 percent of the time. But blacks are almost twice as likely as whites to be labeled a higher risk but not actually re-offend. It makes the opposite mistake among whites: They are much more likely than blacks to be labeled lower risk but go on to commit other crimes. (Source: ProPublica analysis of data from Broward County, Fla.)

Figure 6.1.5   Percent of mistakes for White and Black defendants.

"The risk score alone should not determine the sentence of an offender," Wisconsin Assistant Attorney General Christine Remington said last month during state Supreme Court arguments in the Loomis case. "We don't want courts to say, this person in front of me is a 10 on COMPAS as far as risk, and therefore I'm going to give him the maximum sentence."

That is almost exactly what happened to Zilly, the 48-year-old construction worker sent to prison for stealing a push lawnmower and some tools he intended to sell for parts. Zilly has long struggled with a meth habit. In 2012, he had been working toward recovery with the help of a Christian pastor when he relapsed and committed the thefts.

After Zilly was scored as a high risk for violent recidivism and sent to prison, a public defender appealed the sentence and called the score's creator, Brennan, as a witness.

Brennan testified that he didn't design his software to be used in sentencing. "I wanted to stay away from the courts," Brennan said, explaining that his focus was on reducing crime rather than punishment. "But as time went on I started realizing that so many decisions are made, you know, in the courts. So I gradually softened on whether this could be used in the courts or not."

Still, Brennan testified, "I don't like the idea myself of COMPAS being the sole evidence that a decision would be based upon."

After Brennan's testimony, Judge Babler reduced Zilly's sentence, from two years in prison to 18 months. "Had I not had the COMPAS, I believe it would likely be that I would have given one year, six months," the judge said at an appeals hearing on Nov. 14, 2013.

Zilly said the score didn't take into account all the changes he was making in his life—his conversion to Christianity, his struggle to quit using drugs and his efforts to be more available for his son. "Not that I'm innocent, but I just believe people do change."

FLORIDA'S BROWARD COUNTY, where Brisha Borden stole the Huffy bike and was scored as high risk, does not use risk assessments in sentencing. "We don't think the [risk assessment] factors have any bearing on a sentence," said David Scharf, executive director of community programs for the Broward County Sheriff's Office in Fort Lauderdale.

Broward County has, however, adopted the score in pretrial hearings, in the hope of addressing jail overcrowding. A court-appointed monitor has overseen Broward County's jails since 1994 as a result of the settlement of a lawsuit brought by inmates in the 1970s. Even now, years later, the Broward County jail system is often more than 85 percent full, Scharf said.

In 2008, the sheriff's office decided that instead of building another jail, it would begin using Northpointe's risk scores to help identify which defendants were low risk enough to be released on bail pending trial. Since then, nearly everyone arrested in Broward has been scored soon after

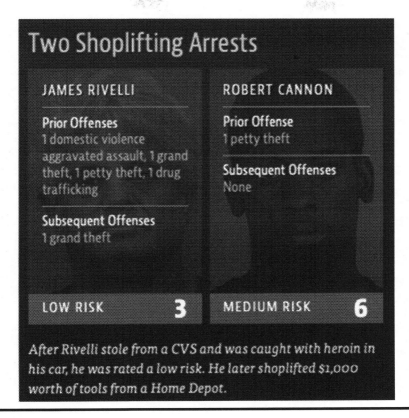

Two Shoplifting Arrests

JAMES RIVELLI	ROBERT CANNON
Prior Offenses 1 domestic violence aggravated assault, 1 grand theft, 1 petty theft, 1 drug trafficking	**Prior Offense** 1 petty theft
Subsequent Offenses 1 grand theft	**Subsequent Offenses** None
LOW RISK **3**	**MEDIUM RISK** **6**

After Rivelli stole from a CVS and was caught with heroin in his car, he was rated a low risk. He later shoplifted $1,000 worth of tools from a Home Depot.

Figure 6.1.6 **Comparison of risk scores for two shoplifting arrests.**

being booked. (People charged with murder and other capital crimes are not scored because they are not eligible for pretrial release.)

The scores are provided to the judges who decide which defendants can be released from jail. "My feeling is that if they don't need them to be in jail, let's get them out of there," Scharf said.

Scharf said the county chose Northpointe's software over other tools because it was easy to use and produced "simple yet effective charts and graphs for judicial review." He said the system costs about $22,000 a year.

In 2010, researchers at Florida State University examined the use of Northpointe's system in Broward County over a 12-month period and concluded that its predictive accuracy was "equivalent" in assessing defendants of different races. Like others, they did not examine whether different races were classified differently as low or high risk.

Scharf said the county would review ProPublica's findings. "We'll really look at them up close," he said.

Broward County Judge John Hurley, who oversees most of the pretrial release hearings, said the scores were helpful when he was a new judge, but now that he has experience he prefers to rely on his own judgment. "I haven't relied on COMPAS in a couple years," he said.

Hurley said he relies on factors including a person's prior criminal record, the type of crime committed, ties to the community, and their history of failing to appear at court proceedings.

ProPublica's analysis reveals that higher Northpointe scores are slightly correlated with longer pretrial incarceration in Broward County. But there are many reasons that could be true other than judges being swayed by the scores—people with higher risk scores may also be poorer and have difficulty paying bond, for example.

Most crimes are presented to the judge with a recommended bond amount, but he or she can adjust the amount. Hurley said he often releases first-time or low-level offenders without any bond at all.

However, in the case of Borden and her friend Sade Jones, the teenage girls who stole a kid's bike and scooter, Hurley raised the bond amount for each girl from the recommended $0 to $1,000 each.

Hurley said he has no recollection of the case and cannot recall if the scores influenced his decision.

The girls spent two nights in jail before being released on bond.

"We literally sat there and cried" the whole time they were in jail, Jones recalled. The girls were kept in the same cell. Otherwise, Jones said, "I would have gone crazy." Borden declined repeated requests to comment for this article.

Jones, who had never been arrested before, was rated a medium risk. She completed probation and got the felony burglary charge reduced to misdemeanor trespassing, but she has still struggled to find work.

"I went to McDonald's and a dollar store, and they all said no because of my background," she said. "It's all kind of difficult and unnecessary."

Note

1. https://www.documentcloud.org/documents/2702103-Sample-Risk-Assessment-COMPAS-CORE .html

Chapter 6.2

Bias in Criminal Risk Scores Is Mathematically Inevitable, Researchers Say[*]

Julia Angwin and Jeff Larson

> *ProPublica's analysis of bias against black defendants in criminal risk scores has prompted research showing that the disparity can be addressed—if the algorithms focus on the fairness of outcomes.*

The racial bias that ProPublica found in a formula used by courts and parole boards to forecast future criminal behavior arises inevitably from the test's design, according to new research.

The findings were described in scholarly papers published or circulated over the past several months. Taken together, they represent the most far-reaching critique to date of the fairness of algorithms that seek to provide an objective measure of the likelihood a defendant will commit further crimes.

Increasingly, criminal justice officials are using similar risk prediction equations to inform their decisions about bail, sentencing and early release.

The researchers found that the formula, and others like it, have been written in a way that guarantees black defendants will be inaccurately identified as future criminals more often than their white counterparts.

The studies, by four groups of scholars working independently, suggests the possibility that the widely used algorithms could be revised to reduce the number of blacks who were unfairly categorized without sacrificing the ability to predict future crimes.

The author of one of the papers said that her ongoing research suggests that this result could be achieved through a modest change in the working of the formula ProPublica studied, which is known as COMPAS.

---

[*] Julia Angwin and Jeff Larson. "Bias in Criminal Risk Scores Is Mathematically Inevitable, Researchers Say," *ProPublica* (December 30, 2016). https://www.propublica.org/article/bias-in-criminal-risk-scores-is-mathematically-inevitable-researchers-say. Reprinted with permission.

DOI: 10.1201/9781003278290-38

An article published earlier this year by ProPublica focused attention on possible racial biases in the COMPAS algorithm. We collected the COMPAS scores for more than 10,000 people arrested for crimes in Florida's Broward's County and checked to see how many were charged with further crimes within two years.

When we looked at the people who did not go on to be arrested for new crimes but were dubbed higher risk by the formula, we found a racial disparity. The data showed that black defendants were twice as likely to be incorrectly labeled as higher risk than white defendants. Conversely, white defendants labeled low risk were far more likely to end up being charged with new offenses than blacks with comparably low COMPAS risk scores.

Northpointe, the company that sells COMPAS, said in response that the test was racially neutral. To support that assertion, company officials pointed to another of our findings, which was that the rate of accuracy for COMPAS scores—about 60 percent—was the same for black and white defendants. The company said it had devised the algorithm to achieve this goal. A test that is correct in equal proportions for all groups cannot be biased, the company said.

This question of how an algorithm could simultaneously be fair and unfair intrigued some of the nation's top researchers at Stanford University, Cornell University, Harvard University, Carnegie Mellon University, University of Chicago and Google.

The scholars set out to address this question: Since blacks are re-arrested more often than whites, is it possible to create a formula that is equally predictive for all races without disparities in who suffers the harm of incorrect predictions?

Working separately and using different methodologies, four groups of scholars all reached the same conclusion. It's not.

Revealing their preliminary findings on a Washington Post blog, a group of Stanford researchers wrote: "It's actually impossible for a risk score to satisfy both fairness criteria at the same time."

The problem, several said in interviews, arises from the characteristic that criminologists have used as the cornerstone for creating fair algorithms, which is that formula must generate equally accurate forecasts for all racial groups.

The researchers found that an algorithm crafted to achieve that goal, known as "predictive parity," inevitably leads to disparities in what sorts of people are incorrectly classified as high risk when two groups have different arrest rates.

"'Predictive parity' actually corresponds to 'optimal discrimination,'" said Nathan Srebro, associate professor of computer science at the University of Chicago and the Toyota Technological Institute at Chicago. That's because predictive parity results in a higher proportion of black defendants being wrongly rated as high-risk.

Srebro's research paper, "Equality of Opportunity in Supervised Learning," was co-authored with Google research scientist Moritz Hardt and University of Texas at Austin computer science professor Eric Price in October. Their paper proposed a definition of "nondiscrimination" that requires the error rates between groups be equalized. Otherwise, Srebro said, one group ends up "paying the price for the uncertainty" of the algorithm.

The need to look at the harms that arise when a test is inaccurate arises frequently in statistics, particularly in fields like health care. When researchers weigh the merits of exams like mammograms, they want to know both how often they correctly detect breast cancer and how often they falsely indicate that patients have the disease.

False findings are significant in medicine because they can cause patients to unnecessarily undergo painful procedures like breast biopsies. It's entirely possible that a test could correctly identify most breast cancers, showing what's known as "positive predictive value," and yet make so many mistakes that it is viewed as unusable.

When he first heard about the COMPAS debate, Jon Kleinberg, a computer science professor at Cornell University, hoped he could figure out a way to reduce false findings while keeping the positive predictive value intact. "We thought, can we fix it?" he said.

But after he, his graduate student Manish Raghavan and Harvard economics professor Sendhil Mullainathan downloaded and crunched ProPublica's data, they realized that the problem was not resolvable. A risk score, they found, could either be equally predictive or equally wrong for all races—but not both.

The reason was the difference in the frequency with which blacks and whites were charged with new crimes. "If you have two populations that have unequal base rates," Kleinberg said, "then you can't satisfy both definitions of fairness at the same time."

Kleinberg and his colleagues went on to construct a mathematical proof that the two notions of fairness are incompatible. The paper, "Inherent Trade-Offs in the Fair Determination of Risk Scores" was posted online in September.

In the criminal justice context, false findings can have far-reaching effects on the lives of people charged with crimes. Judges, prosecutors and parole boards use the scores to help decide whether defendants can be sent to rehab programs instead of prison or be given shorter sentences.

Defendants inaccurately classed as "high risk" and deemed more likely to be arrested in the future may be treated more harshly than is just or necessary, said Alexandra Chouldechova, Assistant Professor of Statistics & Public Policy at Carnegie Mellon University, who also studied ProPublica's COMPAS findings.

Chouldechova said focusing on outcomes might be a better definition of fairness. To create equal outcomes, she said, "You would have to treat people differently." Chouldechova's paper, "Fair prediction with disparate impact: A study of bias in recidivism prediction instruments," was posted online in October.

Chouldechova is continuing to research ways to improve the likelihood of equal outcomes.

Using the Broward County data we made public, Chouldechova rearranged how the COMPAS scores are interpreted so that they were wrong equally often about black and white defendants.

This shift meant that the algorithm's predictions of future criminal behavior were no longer the same for all races. Chouldechova said her revised formula was unchanged for white defendants (59 percent correct) while its predictive accuracy rose from 63 to 69 percent for black defendants.

Northpointe, the company that sells the COMPAS tool, said it had no comment on the critiques. And officials in Broward County said they have made no changes in how they use the COMPAS scores in response to both ProPublica's initial findings and the research papers that followed.

Chapter 6.3

Major Universities Are Using Race as a "High Impact Predictor" of Student Success[*]

Todd Feathers

Students, professors, and education experts worry that that's pushing Black students in particular out of math and science

Major universities are using their students' race, among other variables, to predict how likely they are to drop out of school. Documents obtained by The Markup through public records requests show that some schools are using education research company EAB's Navigate advising software to incorporate students' race as what the company calls a "high-impact predictor" of student success—a practice experts worry could be pushing Black and other minority students into "easier" classes and majors.

The documents, called "predictive model reports," describe how each university's risk algorithm is tailored to fit the needs of its population. At least four out of seven schools from which The Markup obtained such documents incorporate race as a predictor, and two of those describe race as a "high impact predictor." Two schools did not disclose the variables fed into their models (Figure 6.3.1).

More than 500 universities across the country use Navigate's "risk" algorithms to evaluate their students. In addition to documents on how the models work, the Markup obtained aggregate student risk data from four large public universities—the University of Massachusetts Amherst, the University of Wisconsin–Milwaukee, the University of Houston, and Texas A&M University—for the fall 2020 semester. We found large disparities in how the software treats students of different races, and the disparity is particularly stark for Black students, who were deemed high risk at as much as quadruple the rate of their White peers.

At the University of Massachusetts Amherst, for example, Black women are 2.8 times as likely to be labeled high risk as White women, and Black men are 3.9 times as likely to be labeled high

[*] Todd Feathers. 2021. "Major Universities Are Using Race as a "High Impact Predictor" of Student Success," *The Markup* (March 2, 2021). https://themarkup.org/news/2021/03/02/major-universities-are-using-race-as-a-high-impact-predictor-of-student-success. Reprinted with permission.

DOI: 10.1201/9781003278290-39

Black students are regularly labeled a higher risk for failure than White students

Percentage of student body labeled as "high risk" to not graduate within their selected major

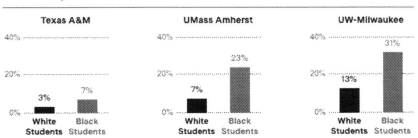

Figure 6.3.1 Comparison of Black and White students' risk scores across three universities. Sources: Texas A&M, University of Massachusetts Amherst, and University of Wisconsin–Milwaukee.

risk as White men. At the University of Wisconsin–Milwaukee, the algorithms label Black women high risk at 2.2 times the rate of White women, and Black men at 2.9 times the rate of White men. And at Texas A&M University, they label Black women high risk at 2.4 times the rate of White women, and Black men at 2.3 times the rate of White men.

Latinx students were also assigned high risk scores at substantially higher rates than their White peers at the schools The Markup examined, although not to the same degree as Black students. The algorithms labeled Asian students high risk at similar or lower rates than White students.

Put another way, Black students made up less than 5 percent of UMass Amherst's undergraduate student body, but they accounted for more than 14 percent of students deemed high risk for the fall 2020 semester.

"This opens the door to even more educational steering," said Ruha Benjamin, a professor of African American studies at Princeton and author of "Race After Technology," after reviewing EAB's documents. "College advisors tell Black, Latinx, and indigenous students not to aim for certain majors. But now these gatekeepers are armed with 'complex' math."

The scores, which are one of the first things a professor or administrator may see when pulling up a list of students, can leave advisers with an immediate and potentially life-changing impression of students and their prospects within a given major.

"You can easily find situations where there are two students who have similar low GPAs and different risk scores, and there's no obvious explanation for why that's the case," said Maryclare Griffin, a statistics professor at UMass Amherst. "I've looked at several examples of students in STEM that have a moderate risk score; they are underrepresented in their major, and the Major Explorer [a function within the software] is saying you should push them to another major where their risk score is lower."

Navigate's racially influenced risk scores "reflect the underlying equity disparities that are already present on these campuses and have been for a long time," Ed Venit, who manages student success research for EAB, wrote in an email. "What we are trying to do with our analytics is highlight these disparities and prod schools to take action to break the pattern." In an interview he added that EAB provides its clients with as much as 200 hours of training and consultation per year, some of it devoted to avoiding bias.

Students of color at the EAB client schools that The Markup examined say they were never told they were being judged by algorithms and that they don't see the company's altruistic depiction of the scores playing out.

"I don't think UMass gives enough resources for students of color regardless, and I absolutely don't think this score would help in that respect," said Fabiellie Mendoza, a senior at UMass Amherst, which has used EAB's software since 2013. "You should have a blank slate. If you're coming in and you already have a low score because of your background, your demographic, or where you're from, it's just very disheartening."

Aileen Flores, a junior at Texas A&M University, was also unnerved to learn she and her peers were being scored by algorithms. "We all work just as hard as each other," she said. "We all deserve to be respected and seen as one and not judged off of our risk score, or skin tone, or background."

The Sales Pitch

The rise of predictive analytics has coincided with significant cuts in government funding for public colleges and universities. In 2018, 41 states contributed less money to higher education—on average 13 percent less per student—than they did in 2008.

EAB has aggressively marketed its Navigate software as a potential solution. Boosting retention is "not just the right thing to do for students but (is) a financial imperative to preserve these investments," the company wrote in a presentation prepared for Kansas State University.

The proposed answer: Identify the high-risk students and target them with "high-touch support."

EAB representatives told The Markup that its tools should be used to identify big-picture solutions and create resources for groups of similarly situated students. But those kinds of changes can be expensive, and actually using the software to make institutional changes, rather than individual advising recommendations, seems to be the exception, not the rule at universities The Markup examined.

In its marketing literature, EAB's proof of concept is often Georgia State University. It was one of the earliest schools to partner with the company, beginning in 2012, and its success improving retention and graduation rates over the subsequent years is impressive. From the 2010–11 school year to the 2019–20 school year, Georgia State increased the number of degrees it awarded by 83 percent, and the groups that saw the largest improvement were Pell Grant recipients and Black and Latinx students. The school has also seen a 32 percent drop in students changing majors after their first year, according to Tim Renick, executive director of Georgia State's National Institute for Student Success.

But close examination reveals important differences between Georgia State's predictive models and retention efforts and those at other EAB schools. Perhaps most significant: Georgia State does not include race in its models, while almost all the schools from which The Markup obtained model documentation do. And many of them incorporate race as a "high-impact predictor."

High-impact predictors "are responsible for more than 5 percent of the variance in scores across all of the students" who have earned similar amounts of credits, according to the report EAB prepared for the University of Wisconsin–Milwaukee. "This may mean that the variable has a moderate impact on the scores of many students, or a high impact on the scores of just a few students."

Venit, from EAB, said it's up to each school to decide which variables to use.

Predictive algorithms that are explicitly influenced by a student's race are particularly concerning to experts.

"Using race for any kind of system, even if it's in a very narrow context of trying to end racial disparities in higher education … you can go into that with the best of intentions and then it takes very, very few steps to get you in place where you're doing further harm," said Hannah Quay-de la Vallee, a senior technologist who studies algorithms in education at the Center for Democracy and Technology.

In Georgia State's case, Renick said, race, ethnicity, and income level are not factors the school considers valuable for incorporation into a risk score.

"If somebody is at risk because they're … from a racial background, that's of no use to the academic adviser" because the adviser can't change it, Renick said.

Something that is potentially fixable, like a student's financial struggles, will come up during conversations with advisers, he said, which is where another key difference between Georgia State and other EAB schools comes into play. The school spent $318,000 on its EAB subscription for 2020, but it has also invested heavily elsewhere in order to gain its reputation as a national role model for student retention, spending millions of dollars each year on additional resources like tutors and micro-loans, and about $3 million since 2012 hiring more student advisers, Renick said.

Georgia State now has a student-to-adviser ratio of about 350 to 1. Compare that to the University of Wisconsin–Milwaukee, a similarly sized public institution that also has large minority and low-income student populations and accepts nearly every student who applies. UW-Milwaukee, which does use race as a high-impact predictor, has used Navigate since 2014 and has expressly said it aims to replicate Georgia State's successes. Its student-to-adviser ratio is as high as 700 to 1, according to Jeremy Page, the assistant dean for student services in the school of education, who oversees the partnership with EAB.

Intention vs. Reality

The Markup reviewed documents describing the predictive models used at five EAB client schools. Four of them—UW-Milwaukee, Texas A&M, Texas Tech University, and South Dakota State University—included race as a risk factor. Only Kansas State University did not.

Texas Tech and South Dakota State did not respond by press time to questions about why they chose to incorporate race as a variable.

UMass Amherst and the University of Houston, two of the schools from which The Markup obtained aggregate data showing racial disparities in students' risk scores, either rejected public records requests for their predictive model summaries or heavily redacted their response.

Administrators at some EAB client schools said they were not aware of the disproportionate rates at which EAB's algorithms label students of color high risk or that race was even a factor in how the scores are calculated.

"I certainly haven't had a lot of information from behind the proprietary algorithms," Carolyn Bassett, associate provost for student success at UMass Amherst told The Markup.

"What I learned from EAB, over and over, about the process was that the algorithm to determine risk was proprietary and protected," Tim Scott, associate provost for academic affairs and student success at Texas A&M, told The Markup. Advisers at the university do view the risk scores but "Quite frankly, we have wondered and thought about whether we should turn it off completely." Texas A&M's contract with EAB runs through 2022.

Page said he was aware that UW-Milwaukee's model incorporates race but not how heavily it is weighed. The Navigate dashboard, which also includes information like a student's GPA, is designed to give overworked advisers a 30-second snapshot of a student's progress, he said, but "there are other times when the model score might feel off, and that's just the nature of working with predictive models."

EAB's algorithms also use other information to predict student success, such as SAT or ACT scores, high school percentile, credits attempted versus completed, and "estimated skills." Notably among the schools The Markup reviewed, only Kansas State University's model, which doesn't include race, considers any factors related to a student's financial stability, despite the cost of college being one of the primary reasons students drop out.

The company's models are also trained on historic student data, anywhere from two to 10 or more years of student outcomes from each individual client school, another aspect of the software experts find problematic.

"When you use old data and base decisions you make on that now, you're necessarily encoding lots of racist and discriminatory practices that go uninvestigated," said Chris Gilliard, a Harvard Shorenstein Center research fellow who studies digital redlining in education.

Once the software produces a risk score, it's generally up to the schools themselves to decide what to do with them, but professors who serve as student advisers say they're given little guidance on how to use the risk scores.

"At no point in required training did they really explain what this [risk score] really is," Griffin, from UMass Amherst, said.

Others worry that seeing a student labeled "high risk" may improperly influence a teacher in guiding his or her students.

"Are we behaving in a certain way right off the bat because we're looking at the risk factor?" Carol Barr, senior vice provost for academic affairs for UMass Amherst, said. "We'll be talking about that."

Particularly, experts worry, professors may guide their students towards less "risky" majors, from which they're considered more likely to stay enrolled and graduate.

One aspect of the Navigate software's design in particular seems to encourage this: the Major Explorer function, which shows a student's predicted risk score in a variety of majors. In a document prepared for Rutgers University, EAB says that advisers should not tell all high risk students to switch to a major in which they would immediately become low risk.

But they should "explain to students their risk score to create a sense of urgency for resistant students" to "explore major options" and which courses to take.

"While it may be intended to be a supportive move, we know that labels can be stigmatizing," said Roxana Marachi, a professor at San José State University who studies big data and predictive analytics in education. "The challenging part is that it's marketed to be an indicator to provide resources and supports, but it can also be weaponized and used against students."

LaToya White, a senior director at EAB, said that the company has been trying to move away from using phrases like "high risk" in training sessions because of how they can be misinterpreted. "There are human biases that we all have and we all bring to any situation," she said. "Something that we have been introducing is that you need to be talking about these biases."

There is scant research into the efficacy of these tools, but some research suggests that the more one interacts with students, the less valuable predictive risk scoring appears. A 2018 study by the Community College Resource Center at Columbia University found that school administrators thought about tools like EAB's Navigate positively, while "the more closely participants were involved with using predictive analytics on the ground with students, and the more advanced the associated institution was with its implementation, the more critical the participants were." The primary concerns raised by advisers and faculty: They didn't believe in the validity of the risk scores, they thought the scores depersonalized their interactions with students, and they didn't understand how the scores were calculated.

Setting the Precedent

None of the universities The Markup contacted for this article are currently using EAB's risk scoring algorithms in their admission process, although they do assign students risk scores before they've ever taken a class. But the financial pressure on public universities from years of state austerity and the declining rate at which high schoolers are choosing to go to college has some educators worried that predictive analytics will soon become prescriptive analytics—the deciding factor in who does or doesn't get accepted.

There are already indications that some schools are looking to these kinds of metrics to streamline their student bodies. In 2015, the president of Mount St. Mary's University, Simon Newman, proposed using student data to cull a portion of the incoming class deemed unlikely to succeed. Speaking to a group of faculty and administrators, he reportedly said, "You think of the students as cuddly bunnies, but you can't. You just have to drown the bunnies ... put a Glock to their heads." Newman resigned shortly after the student newspaper published his comments.

Chapter 6.4

Excerpt from Distributive Justice[*]

Robert Nozick

The minimal state is the most extensive state that can be justified. Any state more extensive violates people's rights. Yet many persons have put forth reasons purporting to justify a more extensive state. It is impossible within the compass of this book to examine all the reasons that have been put forth. Therefore, I shall focus upon those generally acknowledged to be most weighty and influential, to see precisely wherein they fail. In this chapter we consider the claim that a more extensive state is justified, because necessary (or the best instrument) to achieve distributive justice; in the next chapter we shall take up diverse other claims.

The term "distributive justice" is not a neutral one. Hearing the term "distribution," most people presume that some thing or mechanism uses some principle or criterion to give out a supply of things. Into this process of distributing shares some error may have crept. So it is an open question, at least, whether redistribution should take place; whether we should do again what has already been done once, though poorly. However, we are not in the position of children who have been given portions of pie by someone who now makes last minute adjustments to rectify careless cutting. There is no *central* distribution, no person or group entitled to control all the resources, jointly deciding how they are to be doled out. What each person gets, he gets from others who give to him in exchange for something, or as a gift. In a free society, diverse persons control different resources, and new holdings arise out of the voluntary exchanges and actions of persons. There is no more a distributing or distribution of shares than there is a distributing of mates in a society in which persons choose whom they shall marry. The total result is the product of many individual decisions which the different individuals involved are entitled to make. Some uses of the term "distribution," it is true, do not imply a previous distributing appropriately judged by some criterion (for example, "probability distribution"); nevertheless, despite the title of this chapter, it would be best to use a terminology that clearly is neutral. We shall speak of people's holdings; a principle of justice in holdings describes (part of) what justice tells us (requires) about holdings. I shall state

DOI: 10.1201/9781003278290-40

first what I take to be the correct view about justice in holdings, and then turn to the discussion of alternate views.[1]

Section 1

The Entitlement Theory

The subject of justice in holdings consists of three major topics. The first is the *original acquisition of holdings*, the appropriation of unheld things. This includes the issues of how unheld things may come to be held, the process, or processes, by which unheld things may come to be held, the things that may come to be held by these processes, the extent of what comes to be held by a particular process, and so on. We shall refer to the complicated truth about this topic, which we shall not formulate here, as the principle of justice in acquisition. The second topic concerns the *transfer of holdings* from one person to another. By what processes may a person transfer holdings to another? How may a person acquire a holding from another who holds it? Under this topic come general descriptions of voluntary exchange, and gift and (on the other hand) fraud, as well as reference to particular conventional details fixed upon in a given society. The complicated truth about this subject (with placeholders for conventional details) we shall call the principle of justice in transfer. (And we shall suppose it also includes principles governing how a person may divest himself of a holding, passing it into an unheld state.)

If the world were wholly just, the following inductive definition would exhaustively cover the subject of justice in holdings.

1. A person who acquires a holding in accordance with the principle of justice in acquisition is entitled to that holding.
2. A person who acquires a holding in accordance with the principle of justice in transfer, from someone else entitled to the holding, is entitled to the holding.
3. No one is entitled to a holding except by (repeated) applications of 1 and 2.

The complete principle of distributive justice would say simply that a distribution is just if everyone is entitled to the holdings they possess under the distribution.

A distribution is just if it arises from another just distribution by legitimate means. The legitimate means of moving from one distribution to another are specified by the principle of justice in transfer. The legitimate first "moves" are specified by the principle of justice in acquisition. Whatever arises from a just situation by just steps is itself just. The means of change specified by the principle of justice in transfer preserve justice. As correct rules of inference are truth-preserving, and any conclusion deduced via repeated application of such rules from only true premises is itself true, so the means of transition from one situation to another specified by the principle of justice in transfer are justice-preserving, and any situation actually arising from repeated transitions in accordance with the principle from a just situation is itself just. The parallel between justice-preserving transformations and truth-preserving transformations illuminates where it fails as well as where it holds. That a conclusion could have been deduced by truth-preserving means from premises that are true suffices to show its truth. That from a just situation a situation could have arisen via justice-preserving means does not suffice to show its justice. The fact that a thief's victims voluntarily could have presented him with gifts does not entitle the thief to his ill-gotten gains. Justice in holdings is historical; it depends upon what actually has happened. We shall return to this point later.

Not all actual situations are generated in accordance with the two principles of justice in holdings: the principle of justice in acquisition and the principle of justice in transfer. Some people steal from others, or defraud them, or enslave them, seizing their product and preventing them from living as they choose, or forcibly exclude others from competing in exchanges. None of these are permissible modes of transition from one situation to another. And some persons acquire holdings by means not sanctioned by the principle of justice in acquisition. The existence of past injustice (previous violations of the first two principles of justice in holdings) raises the third major topic under justice in holdings: the rectification of injustice in holdings. If past injustice has shaped present holdings in various ways, some identifiable and some not, what now, if anything, ought to be done to rectify these injustices? What obligations do the performers of injustice have toward those whose position is worse than it would have been had the injustice not been done? Or, than it would have been had compensation been paid promptly? How, if at all, do things change if the beneficiaries and those made worse off are not the direct parties in the act of injustice, but, for example, their descendants? Is an injustice done to someone whose holding was itself based upon an unrectified injustice? How far back must one go in wiping clean the historical slate of injustices? What may victims of injustice permissibly do in order to rectify the injustices being done to them, including the many injustices done by persons acting through their government? I do not know of a thorough or theoretically sophisticated treatment of such issues.[2]

Idealizing greatly, let us suppose theoretical investigation will produce a principle of rectification. This principle uses historical information about previous situations and injustices done in them (as defined by the first two principles of justice and rights against interference), and information about the actual course of events that flowed from these injustices, until the present, and it yields a description (or descriptions) of holdings in the society. The principle of rectification presumably will make use of its best estimate of subjunctive information about what would have occurred (or a probability distribution over what might have occurred, using the expected value) if the injustice had not taken place. If the actual description of holdings turns out not to be one of the descriptions yielded by the principle, then one of the descriptions yielded must be realized.[3]

The general outlines of the theory of justice in holdings are that the holdings of a person are just if he is entitled to them by the principles of justice in acquisition and transfer, or by the principle of rectification of injustice (as specified by the first two principles). If each person's holdings are just, then the total set (distribution) of holdings is just. To turn these general outlines into a specific theory we would have to specify the details of each of the three principles of justice in holdings: the principle of acquisition of holdings, the principle of transfer of holdings, and the principle of rectification of violations of the first two principles. I shall not attempt that task here (Locke's principle of justice in acquisition is discussed below.).

[...]

Notes

1. The reader who has looked ahead and seen that the second part of this chapter discusses Rawls' theory mistakenly may think that every remark or argument in this first part against alternative theories of justice is meant to apply to, or anticipate, a criticism of Rawls' theory. That is not so; there are other theories worth criticizing.
2. See, however, the useful book by Boris Bittker, *The Case for Black Reparations* (New York: Random House, 1973).
3. If the principle of rectification of violations of the first two principles yields more than one description of holdings, then some choice must be made as to which of these is to be realized. Perhaps the sort of considerations about distributive justice and equality that I argue against play a legitimate role in *this* subsidiary choice. Similarly, there may be room for such considerations in deciding which otherwise arbitrary features a statute will embody, when such features are unavoidable because other considerations do not specify a precise line; yet a line must be drawn.

Chapter 6.5

Excerpt from Justice as Fairness[*]

John Rawls

The Main Idea of the Theory of Justice

My aim is to present a conception of justice which generalizes and carries to a higher level of abstraction the familiar theory of the social contract as found, say, in Locke, Rousseau, and Kant. In order to do this we are not to think of the original contract as one to enter a particular society or to set up a particular form of government. Rather, the guiding idea is that the principles of justice for the basic structure of society are the object of the original agreement. They are the principles that free and rational persons concerned to further their own interests would accept in an initial position of equality as defining the fundamental terms of their association. These principles are to regulate all further agreements; they specify the kinds of social cooperation that can be entered into and the forms of government that can be established. This way of regarding the principles of justice I shall call justice as fairness.

Thus we are to imagine that those who engage in social cooperation choose together, in one joint act, the principles which are to assign basic rights and duties and to determine the division of social benefits. Men are to decide in advance how they are to regulate their claims against one another and what is to be the foundation charter of their society. Just as each person must decide by rational reflection what constitutes his good, that is, the system of ends which it is rational for him to pursue, so a group of persons must decide once and for all what is to count among them as just and unjust. The choice which rational men would make in this hypothetical situation of equal liberty, assuming for the present that this choice problem has a solution, determines the principles of justice.

In justice as fairness the original position of equality corresponds to the state of nature in the traditional theory of the social contract. This original position is not, of course, thought

* A THEORY OF JUSTICE by John Rawls, Cambridge, Mass.: The Belknap Press of Harvard University Press, Copyright © 1971 by the President and Fellows of Harvard College. Reprinted with permission. Note: This is an excerpt from the original so footnote and endnote numbering may be modified.

of as an actual historical state of affairs, much less as a primitive condition of culture. It is understood as a purely hypothetical situation characterized so as to lead to a certain conception of justice? Among the essential features of this situation is that no one knows his place in society, his class position or social status, nor does anyone know his fortune in the distribution of natural assets and abilities, his intelligence, strength, and the like. I shall even assume that the parties do not know their conceptions of the good or their special psychological propensities. The principles of justice are chosen behind a veil of ignorance. This ensures that no one is advantaged or disadvantaged in the choice of principles by the outcome of natural chance or the contingency of social circumstances. Since all are similarly situated and no one is able to design principles to favor his particular condition, the principles of justice are the result of a fair agreement or bargain. For given the circumstances of the original position, the symmetry of everyone's relation to each other, this initial situation is fair between individuals as moral persons, that is, as rational beings with their own ends and capable, I shall assume, of a sense of justice. The original position is, one might say, the appropriate initial status quo, and the fundamental agreements reached in it are fair. This explains the propriety of the name "justice as fairness": it conveys the idea that the principles of justice are agreed to in an initial situation that is fair. The name does not mean that the concepts of justice and fairness are the same, any more that the phrase "poetry as metaphor" means that the concepts of poetry and metaphor are the same.

Justice as fairness begins, as I have said, with one of the most general of all choices which persons might make together, namely, with the choice of the first principles of a conception of justice which is to regulate all subsequent criticism and reform of institutions. Then, having chosen a conception of justice, we can suppose that they are to choose a constitution and a legislature to enact laws, and so on, all in accordance with the principles of justice initially agreed upon. Our social situation is just if it is such that by this sequence of hypothetical agreements we would have contracted into the general system of rules which defines it. Moreover, assuming that the original position does determine a set of principles (that is, that a particular conception of justice would be chosen), it will then be true that whenever social institutions satisfy these principles those engaged in them can say to one another that they are cooperating on terms to which they would agree if they were free and equal persons whose relations with respect to one another were fair. They could all view their arrangements as meeting the stipulations which they would acknowledge in an initial situation that embodies widely accepted and reasonable constraints on the choice of principles. The general recognition of this fact would provide the basis for a public acceptance of the corresponding principles of justice. No society can, of course, be a scheme of cooperation which men enter voluntarily in a literal sense; each person finds himself placed at birth in some particular position in some particular society, and the nature of this position materially affects his life prospects. Yet a society satisfying the principles of justice as fairness comes as close as a society can to being a voluntary scheme, for it meets the principles which free and equal persons would assent to under circumstances that are fair. In this sense its members are autonomous and the obligations they recognize self-imposed.

One feature of justice as fairness is to think of the parties in the initial situation as rational and mutually disinterested. This does not mean that the parties are egoists, that is, individuals with only certain kinds of interests, say in wealth, prestige, and domination. But they are conceived as not taking an interest in one another's interests. They are to presume that even their spiritual aims may be opposed, in the way that the aims of those of different religions maybe opposed. Moreover, the concept of rationality must be interpreted as far as possible in the narrow sense, standard in economic theory, of taking the most effective means to given ends. I shall modify this concept to some extent, as explained later, but one must try to avoid introducing into it any controversial ethical elements. The initial situation must be characterized by stipulations that are widely accepted.

In working out the conception of justice as fairness one main task clearly is to determine which principles of justice would be chosen in the original position. To do this we must describe this situation in some detail and formulate with care the problem of choice which it presents. These matters I shall take up in the immediately succeeding chapters. It may be observed, however, that once the principles of justice are thought of as arising from an original agreement in a situation of equality, it is an open question whether the principle of utility would be acknowledged. Offhand it hardly seems likely that persons who view themselves as equals, entitled to press their claims upon one another, would agree to a principle which may require lesser life prospects for some simply for the sake of a greater sum of advantages enjoyed by others. Since each desires to protect his interests, his capacity to advance his conception of the good, no one has a reason to acquiesce in an enduring loss for himself in order to bring about a greater net balance of satisfaction. In the absence of strong and lasting benevolent impulses, a rational man would not accept a basic structure merely because it maximized the algebraic sum of advantages irrespective of its permanent effects on his own basic rights and interests. Thus it seems that the principle of utility is incompatible with the conception of social cooperation among equals for mutual advantage. It appears to be inconsistent with the idea or reciprocity implicit in the notion of a well-ordered society. Or, at any rate, so I shall argue.

I shall maintain instead that the persons in the initial situation would choose two rather different principles: the first requires equality in the assignment of basic rights and duties, while the second holds that social and economic inequalities, for example inequalities of wealth and authority, are just only if they result in compensating benefits for everyone, and in particular for the least advantaged members of society.

These principles rule out justifying institutions on the grounds that the hardships of some are offset by a greater good in the aggregate. It may be expedient but it is not just that some should have less in order that others may prosper. But there is no injustice in the greater benefits earned by a few provided that the situation of persons not so fortunate is thereby improved. The intuitive idea is that since everyone's well-being depends upon a scheme of cooperation without which no one could have a satisfactory life, the division of advantages should be such as to draw forth the willing cooperation of everyone taking part in it, including those less well situated. Yet this can be expected only if reasonable terms are proposed. The two principles mentioned seem to be a fair agreement on the basis of which those better endowed, or more fortunate in their social position, neither of which we can be said to deserve, could expect the willing cooperation of others when some workable scheme is a necessary condition of the welfare of all. Once we decide to look for a conception of justice that nullifies the accidents of natural endowment and the contingencies of social circumstance as counters in quest for political and economic advantage, we are led to these principles. They express the result of leaving aside those aspects of the social world that seem arbitrary from a moral point of view.

[….]

Two Principles of Justice

I shall now state in a provisional form the two principles of justice that I believe would be chosen in the original position. In this section I wish to make only the most general comments, and therefore the first formulation of these principles is tentative. As we go on I shall run through several formulations and approximate step by step the final statement to be given much later. I believe that doing this allows the exposition to proceed in a natural way.

The first statement of the two principles read as follows:

> First: each person is to have an equal right to the most extensive basic liberty compatible with similar liberty for others.
>
> Second: social and economic inequalities are to be arranged so that they are both (a) reasonably expected to be to everyone's advantage, and (b) attached to positions and offices open to all....

By way of general comment, these principles primarily apply, as I have said, to the basic structure of society. They are to govern the assignment of rights and duties and to regulate the distribution of social and economic advantages. As their formulation suggests, these principles presuppose that the social structure can be divided into two more or less distinct parts, the first principle applying to the one, the second to the other. They distinguish between those aspects of the social system that define and secure the equal liberties of citizenship and those that specify and establish social and economic inequalities. The basic liberties of citizens are, roughly speaking, political liberty (the right to vote and to be eligible for public office) together with freedom of speech and assembly; liberty of conscience and freedom of thought; freedom of the person along with the right to hold (personal) property; and freedom from arbitrary arrest and seizure as defined by the concept of the rule of law. These liberties are all required to be equal by the first principle, since citizens of a just society are to have the same basic rights.

The second principle applies, in the first approximation, to the distribution of income and wealth and to the design of organizations that make use of differences in authority and responsibility, or chains of command. While the distribution of wealth and income need not be equal, it must be to everyone's advantage, and at the same time, positions of authority and offices of command must be accessible to all. One applies the second principle by holding positions open, and then, subject to this constraint, arranges social and economic inequalities so that everyone benefits.

These principles are to be arranged in a serial order with the first principle prior to the second. This ordering means that a departure from the institutions of equal liberty required by the first principle cannot be justified by, or compensated for, by greater social and economic advantages. The distribution of wealth and income, and the hierarchies of authority, must be consistent with both the liberties of equal citizenship and equality of opportunity.

It is clear that these principles are rather specific in their content, and their acceptance rests on certain assumptions that I must eventually try to explain and justify. A theory of justice depends upon a theory of society in ways that will become evident as we proceed. For the present, it should be observed that the two principles (and this holds for all formulations) are a special case of a more general conception of justice that can be expressed as follows:

All social values – liberty and opportunity, income and wealth, and the bases of self-respect – are to be distributed equally unless an unequal distribution of any, or all, of these values is to everyone's advantage.

Injustice, then, is simply inequalities that are not to the benefit of all. Of course, this conception is extremely vague and requires interpretation.

As a first step, suppose that the basic structure of society distributes certain primary goods, that is, things that every rational man is presumed to want. ... For simplicity, assume that the chief primary goods at the disposition of society are rights and liberties, powers and opportunities, income and wealth. (… the primary good of self-respect has a central place.) These are the social primary goods. Other primary goods such as health and vigor, intelligence and imagination, are natural goods; although their possession is influenced by the basic structure, they are not so directly under its control. Imagine, then, a hypothetical initial arrangement in which all the social primary goods are equally distributed: everyone has similar rights and duties, and income and wealth are evenly shared. This state of affairs provides a benchmark for judging improvements. If certain inequalities of wealth and organizational powers would make everyone better off than in this hypothetical starting situation, then they accord with the general conception.

Now it is possible, at least theoretically, that by giving up some of their fundamental liberties men are sufficiently compensated by the resulting social and economic gains. The general conception of justice imposes no restrictions on what sort of inequalities are permissible; it only requires that everyone's position be improved. We need not suppose anything so drastic as consenting to a condition of slavery. Imagine instead that men forego certain political rights when the economic returns are significant and their capacity to influence the course of policy by the exercise of these rights would be marginal in any case. It is this kind of exchange which the two principles as stated rule out; being arranged in serial order they do not permit exchanges between basic liberties and economic and social gains. The serial ordering of principles expresses an underlying preference among primary social goods. When this preference is rational so likewise is the choice of these principles in this order.

Chapter 6.6

Excerpt from Tyranny and Complex Equality[*]

Michael Walzer

I want to argue that we should focus on the reduction of dominance – not, or not primarily, on the break-up or the constraint of monopoly. We should consider what it might mean to narrow the range within which particular goods are convertible and to vindicate the autonomy of distributive spheres. But this line of argument, though it is not uncommon historically, has never fully emerged in philosophical writing. Philosophers have tended to criticize (or to justify) existing or emerging monopolies of wealth, power, and education. Or, they have criticized (or justified) particular conversions – of wealth into education or of office into wealth. And all this, most often, in the name of some radically simplified distributive system. The critique of dominance will suggest instead a way of reshaping and then living with the actual complexity of distributions.

Imagine now a society in which different social goods are monopolistically held – as they are in fact and always will be, barring continual state intervention – but in which no particular good is generally convertible. As I go along, I shall try to define the precise limits on convertibility, but for now the general description will suffice. This is a complex egalitarian society. Though there will be many small inequalities, inequality will not be multiplied through the conversion process. Nor will it be summed across different goods, because the autonomy of distributions will tend to produce a variety of local monopolies, held by different groups of men and women. I don't want to claim that complex equality would necessarily be more stable than simple equality, but I am inclined to think that it would open the way for more diffused and particularized forms of social conflict. And the resistance to convertibility would be maintained, in large degree, by ordinary men and women within their own spheres of competence and control, without large-scale state action.

This is, I think, an attractive picture, but I have not yet explained just why it is attractive. The argument for complex equality begins from our understanding – I mean, our actual, concrete, positive, and particular understanding – of the various social goods. And then it moves on to an account of the way we relate to one another through those goods. Simple equality is a simple

* From *Spheres of Justice* by Michael Walzer, copyright © 1983. Reprinted by permission of Basic Books, an imprint of Hachette Book Group, Inc. Note: This is an excerpt from the original so footnote and endnote numbering may be modified.

DOI: 10.1201/9781003278290-42

distributive condition, so that if I have fourteen hats and you have fourteen hats, we are equal. And it is all to the good if hats are dominant, for then our equality is extended through all the spheres of social life. On the view that I shall take here, however, we simply have the same number of hats, and it is unlikely that hats will be dominant for long. Equality is a complex relation of persons, mediated by the goods we make, share, and divide among ourselves; it is not an identity of possessions. It requires then, a diversity of distributive criteria that mirrors the diversity of social goods.

The argument for complex equality has been beautifully put by Pascal in one of his *Pensées*.

The nature of tyranny is to desire power over the whole world and outside its own sphere.

There are different companies – the strong, the handsome, the intelligent, the devout – and each man reigns in his own, not elsewhere. But sometimes they meet, and the strong and the handsome fight for mastery – foolishly, for their mastery is of different kinds. They misunderstand one another, and make the mistake of each aiming at universal dominion. Nothing can win this, not even strength, for it is powerless in the kingdom of the wise.

Tyranny. The following statements, therefore, are false and tyrannical: "Because I am handsome, so I should command respect." "I am strong, therefore men should love me." "I am et cetera."

Tyranny is the wish to obtain by one means what can only be had by another. We owe different duties to different qualities: love is the proper response to charm, fear to strength, and belief to learning.[1]

Marx made a similar argument in his early manuscripts; perhaps he had this *pensée* in mind:

> Let us assume man to be man, and his relation to the world to be a human one. Then love can only be exchanged for love, trust for trust, etc. If you wish to enjoy art you must be an artistically cultivated person; if you wish to influence other people, you must be a person who really has a stimulating and encouraging effect upon others If you love without evoking love in return, i.e., if you are not able, by the manifestation of yourself as a loving person, to make yourself a beloved person – then your love is impotent and a misfortune.[2]

These are not easy arguments, and most of my book is simply an exposition of their meaning. But here I shall attempt something more simple and schematic: a translation of the arguments into the terms I have already been using.

The first claim of Pascal and Marx is that personal qualities and social goods have their own spheres of operation, where they work their effects freely, spontaneously, and legitimately. There are ready or natural conversions that follow from, and are intuitively plausible because of, the social meaning of particular goods. The appeal is to our ordinary understanding and, at the same time, against our common acquiescence in illegitimate conversion patterns. Or, it is an appeal from our acquiescence to our resentment. There is something wrong, Pascal suggests, with the conversion of strength into belief. In political terms, Pascal means that no ruler can rightly command my opinions merely because of the power he wields. Nor can he, Marx adds, rightly claim to influence my actions: if a ruler wants to do that, he must be persuasive, helpful, encouraging, and so on. These arguments depend for their force on some shared understanding of knowledge, influence, and power. Social goods have social meanings, and we find our way to distributive justice through an interpretation of those meanings. We search for principles internal to each distributive sphere.

The second claim is that the disregard of these principles is tyranny. To convert one good into another, when there is no intrinsic connection between the two, is to invade the sphere where another company of men and women properly rules. Monopoly is not inappropriate within the spheres. There is nothing wrong, for example, with the grip that persuasive and helpful men and women (politicians) establish on political power. But the use of political power to gain access to other goods is a tyrannical use. Thus, an old description of tyranny is generalized: princes become tyrants, according to medieval writers, when they seize the property or invade the family of their subjects.[3] In political life – but more widely, too – the dominance of goods makes for the domination of people.

The regime of complex equality is the opposite of tyranny. It establishes a set of relationships such that domination is impossible. In formal terms, complex equality means that no citizen's standing in one sphere or with regard to one social good can be undercut by his standing in some other sphere, with regard to some other good. Thus, citizen X may be chosen over citizen Y for political office, and then the two of them will be unequal in the sphere of politics. But they will not be unequal generally so long as X's office gives him no advantages over Y in any other sphere – superior medical care, access to better schools for his children, entrepreneurial opportunities, and so on. So long as office is not a dominant good, is not generally convertible, office holders will stand, or at least can stand, in a relation of equality to the men and women they govern.

But what if dominance were eliminated, the autonomy of the spheres established – and the same people were successful in one sphere after another, triumphant in every company, piling up goods without the need for illegitimate conversions? This would certainly make for an inegalitarian society, but it would also suggest in the strongest way that a society of equals was not a lively possibility. I doubt that any egalitarian argument could survive in the face of such evidence. Here is a person whom we have freely chosen (without reference to his family ties or personal wealth) as our political representative. He is also a bold and inventive entrepreneur. When he was younger, he studied science, scored amazingly high grades in every exam, and made important discoveries. In war, he is surpassingly brave and wins the highest honors. Himself compassionate and compelling, he is loved by all who know him. Are there such people? Maybe so, but I have my doubts. We tell stories like the one I have just told, but the stories are fictions, the conversion of power or money or academic talent into legendary fame. In any case, there aren't enough such people to constitute a ruling class and dominate the rest of us. Nor can they be successful in every distributive sphere, for there are some spheres to which the idea of success doesn't pertain. Nor are their children likely, under conditions of complex equality, to inherit their success. By and large, the most accomplished politicians, entrepreneurs, scientists, soldiers, and lovers will be different people; and so long as the goods they possess don't bring other goods in train, we have no reason to fear their accomplishments.

The critique of dominance and domination points toward an open-ended distributive principle. *No social good* x *should be distributed to men and women who possess some other good* y *merely because they possess* y *and without regard to the meaning of* x. This is a principle that has probably been reiterated, at one time or another, for every y that has ever been dominant. But it has not often been stated in general terms. Pascal and Marx have suggested the application of the principle against all possible y's, and I shall attempt to work out that application. I shall be looking, then, not at the members of Pascal's companies – the strong or the weak, the handsome or the plain – but at the goods they share and divide. The purpose of the principle is to focus our attention; it doesn't determine the shares or the division. The principle directs us to study the meaning of social goods, to examine the different distributive spheres from the inside.

Three Distributive Principles

The theory that results is unlikely to be elegant. No account of the meaning of a social good, or of the boundaries of the sphere within which it legitimately operates, will be uncontroversial. Nor is there any neat procedure for generating or testing different accounts. At best, the arguments will be rough, reflecting the diverse and conflict-ridden character of the social life that we seek simultaneously to understand and to regulate – but not to regulate until we understand. I shall set aside, then, all claims made on behalf of any single distributive criterion, for no such criterion can possibly match the diversity of social goods. Three criteria, however, appear to meet the requirements of the open-ended principle and have often been defended as the beginning and end of distributive justice, so I must say something about each of them. Free exchange, desert, and need: all three have real force, but none of them has force across the range of distributions. They are part of the story, not the whole of it.

Free Exchange

Free exchange is obviously open-ended; it guarantees no particular distributive outcome. At no point in any exchange process plausibly called "free" will it be possible to predict the particular division of social goods that will obtain at some later point.[4] (It may be possible, however, to predict the general structure of the division.) In theory at least, free exchange creates a market within which all goods are convertible into all other goods through the neutral medium of money.

There are no dominant goods and no monopolies. Hence the successive divisions that obtain will directly reflect the social meanings of the goods that are divided. For each bargain, trade, sale, and purchase will have been agreed to voluntarily by men and women who know what that meaning is, who are indeed its makers. Every exchange is a revelation of social meaning. By definition, then, no *x* will ever fall into the hands of someone who possesses *y*, merely because he possesses *y* and without regard to what *x* actually means to some other member of society. The market is radically pluralistic in its operations and its outcomes, infinitely sensitive to the meanings that individuals attach to goods. What possible restraints can be imposed on free exchange, then, in the name of pluralism?

But everyday life in the market, the actual experience of free exchange, is very different from what the theory suggests. Money, supposedly the neutral medium, is in practice a dominant good, and it is monopolized by people who possess a special talent for bargaining and trading – the green thumb of bourgeois society. Then other people demand a redistribution of money and the establishment of the regime of simple equality, and the search begins for some way to sustain that regime. But even if we focus on the first untroubled moment of simple equality – free exchange on the basis of equal shares – we will still need to set limits on what can be exchanged for what. For free exchange leaves distributions entirely in the hands of individuals, and social meanings are not subject, or are not always subject, to the interpretative decisions of individual men and women.

Consider an easy example, the case of political power. We can conceive of political power as a set of goods of varying value, votes, influence, offices, and so on. Any of these can be traded on the market and accumulated by individuals willing to sacrifice other goods. Even if the sacrifices are real, however, the result is a form of tyranny – petty tyranny, given the conditions of simple equality. Because I am willing to do without my hat, I shall vote twice; and you who value the vote less than you value my hat, will not vote at all. I suspect that the result is tyrannical even with regard to the two of us, who have reached a voluntary agreement. It is certainly tyrannical with regard to all the other citizens who must now submit to my disproportionate power. It is not the case that votes can't be bargained for; on one interpretation, that's what democratic politics is all about. And democratic politicians have certainly been known to buy votes, or to try to buy them, by promising public expenditures that benefit particular groups of voters. But this is done in public, with public funds, and subject to public approval. Private trading is ruled out by virtue of what politics, or democratic politics, is – that is, by virtue of what we did when we constituted the political community and of what we still think about what we did.

Free exchange is not a general criterion, but we will be able to specify the boundaries within which it operates only through a careful analysis of particular social goods. And having worked through such an analysis, we will come up at best with a philosophically authoritative set of boundaries and not necessarily with the set that ought to be politically authoritative. For money seeps across all boundaries – this is the primary form of illegal immigration; and just where one ought to try to stop it is a question of expediency as well as of principle. Failure to stop it at some reasonable point has consequences throughout the range of distributions, but consideration of these belongs in a later chapter.

Desert

Like free exchange, desert seems both open-ended and pluralistic. One might imagine a single neutral agency dispensing rewards and punishments, infinitely sensitive to all the forms of individual desert. Then the distributive process would indeed be centralized, but the results would still be unpredictable and various. There would be no dominant good. No *x* would ever be distributed without regard to its social meaning; for, without attention to what *x* is, it is conceptually impossible to say that *x* is deserved. All the different companies of men and women would receive their appropriate reward. How this would work in practice, however, is not easy to figure out. It might make sense to say of this charming man, for example, that he deserves to be loved. It makes no sense to say that he deserves to be loved by this (or any) particular woman. If he loves her while she remains impervious to his (real) charms, that is his misfortune. I doubt that we would want the situation corrected by some outside agency. The love of particular men and women, on our understanding of it, can only be distributed by themselves, and they are rarely guided in these matters by considerations of desert.

The case is exactly the same with influence. Here, let's say, is a woman widely thought to be stimulating and encouraging to others. Perhaps she deserves to be an influential member of our community. But she doesn't deserve that I be influenced by her or that I follow her lead. Nor would we want my followership, as it were, assigned to her by any agency capable of making such assignments. She may go to great lengths to stimulate and encourage me, and do all the things that are commonly called stimulating or encouraging. But if I (perversely) refuse to be stimulated or encouraged, I am not denying her anything that she deserves. The same argument holds by extension for politicians and ordinary citizens. Citizens can't trade their votes for hats; they can't individually decide to cross the boundary that separates the sphere of politics from the marketplace. But within the sphere of politics, they do make individual decisions; and they are rarely guided, again, by considerations of desert. It's not clear that offices can be deserved – another issue that I must postpone; but even if they can be, it would violate our understanding of democratic politics were they simply distributed to deserving men and women by some central agency.

Similarly, however we draw the boundaries of the sphere within which free exchange operates, desert will play no role within those boundaries. I am skillful at bargaining and trading, let's say, and so accumulate a large number of beautiful pictures. If we assume, as painters mostly do, that pictures are appropriately traded in the market, then there is nothing wrong with my having the pictures. My title is legitimate. But it would be odd to say that I deserve to have them simply because I am good at bargaining and trading. Desert seems to require an especially close connection between particular goods and particular persons, whereas justice only sometimes requires a connection of that sort. Still, we might insist that only artistically cultivated people, who deserve to have pictures, should actually have them. It's not difficult to imagine a distributive mechanism. The state could buy all the pictures that were offered for sale (but artists would have to be licensed, so that there wouldn't be an endless number of pictures), evaluate them, and then distribute them to artistically cultivated men and women, the better pictures to the more cultivated. The state does something like this, sometimes, with regard to things that people need – medical care, for example – but not with regard to things that people deserve. There are practical difficulties here, but I suspect a deeper reason for this difference. Desert does not have the urgency of need, and it does not involve having (owning and consuming) in the same way. Hence, we are willing to tolerate the separation of owners of paintings and artistically cultivated people, or we are unwilling to require the kinds of interference in the market that would be necessary to end the separation. Of course, public provision is always possible alongside the market, and so we might argue that artistically cultivated people deserve not pictures but museums. Perhaps they do, but they don't deserve that the rest of us contribute money or appropriate public funds for the purchase of pictures and the construction of buildings. They will have to persuade us that art is worth the money; they will have to stimulate and encourage our own artistic cultivation. And if they fail to do that, their own love of art may well turn out to be "impotent and a misfortune."

Even if we were to assign the distribution of love, influence, offices, works of art, and so on, to some omnipotent arbiters of desert, how would we select them? How could anyone deserve such a position? Only God, who knows what secrets lurk in the hearts of men, would be able to make the necessary distributions. If human beings had to do the work, the distributive mechanism would be seized early on by some band of aristocrats (so they would call themselves) with a fixed conception of what is best and most deserving, and insensitive to the diverse excellences of their fellow citizens. And then desert would cease to be a pluralist criterion; we would find ourselves face to face with a new set (of an old sort) of tyrants. We do, of course, choose people as arbiters of desert – to serve on juries, for example, or to award prizes; it will be worth considering later what the prerogatives of a juror are. But it is important to stress here that he operates within a narrow range. Desert is a strong claim, but it calls for difficult judgments; and only under very special conditions does it yield specific distributions.

Need

Finally, the criterion of need. "To each according to his needs" is generally taken as the distributive half of Marx's famous maxim: we are to distribute the wealth of the community so as to meet the necessities of its members.[5] A plausible proposal, but a radically incomplete one. In fact, the first half of the maxim is also a distributive proposal, and it doesn't fit the rule of the second half. "From each according to his ability" suggests that jobs should be distributed (or that men and women should be conscripted to work) on the basis of individual qualifications. But individuals don't in any obvious sense need the jobs for which they are qualified. Perhaps such jobs are scarce, and there are a large number of qualified candidates: which candidates need them most? If their material needs are already taken care of, perhaps they don't need to work at all. Or if, in some non-material sense, they all need to work, then that need won't distinguish among them, at least not to the naked eye. It would in any case be odd to ask a search committee looking, say, for a hospital director to make its choice on the basis of the needs of the candidates rather than on those of the staff and the patients of the hospital. But the latter set of needs, even if it isn't the subject of political disagreement, won't yield a single distributive decision.

Nor will need work for many other goods. Marx's maxim doesn't help at all with regard to the distribution of political power, honor and fame, sailboats, rare books, beautiful objects of every sort. These are not things that anyone, strictly speaking, needs. Even if we take a loose view and define the verb to *need* the way children do, as the strongest form of the verb *to want*, we still won't have an adequate distributive criterion. The sorts of things that I have listed cannot be distributed equally to those with equal wants because some of them are generally, and some of them are necessarily, scarce, and some of them can't be possessed at all unless other people, for reasons of their own, agree on who is to possess them.

Need generates a particular distributive sphere, within which it is itself the appropriate distributive principle. In a poor society, a high proportion of social wealth will be drawn into this sphere. But given the great variety of goods that arises out of any common life, even when it is lived at a very low material level, other distributive criteria will always be operating alongside of need, and it will always be necessary to worry about the boundaries that mark them off from one another.

Within its sphere, certainly, need meets the general distributive rule about x and y. Needed goods distributed to needy people in proportion to their neediness are obviously not dominated by any other goods. It's not having y, but only lacking x that is relevant. But we can now see,

I think, that every criterion that has any force at all meets the general rule within its own sphere, and not elsewhere. This is the effect of the rule: different goods to different companies of men and women for different reasons and in accordance with different procedures. And to get all this right, or to get it roughly right, is to map out the entire social world.

Hierarchies and Caste Societies

Or, rather, it is to map out a particular social world. For the analysis that I propose is imminent and phenomenological in character. It will yield not an ideal map or a master plan but, rather, a map and a plan appropriate to the people for whom it is drawn, whose common life it reflects. The goal, of course, is a reflection of a special kind, which picks up those deeper understandings of social goods which are not necessarily mirrored in the everyday practice of dominance and monopoly. But what if there are no such understandings? I have been assuming all along that social meanings call for the autonomy, or the relative autonomy, of distributive spheres; and so they do much of the time. But it's not impossible to imagine a society where dominance and monopoly are not violations but enactments of meaning, where social goods are conceived in hierarchical terms. In feudal Europe, for example, clothing was not a commodity (as it is today) but a badge of rank. Rank dominated dress. The meaning of clothing was shaped in the image of the feudal order. Dressing in finery to which one wasn't entitled was a kind of lie; it made a false statement about who one was. When a king or a prime minister dressed as a commoner in order to learn something about the opinions of his subjects, this was a kind of politic deceit. On the other hand, the difficulties of enforcing the clothing code (the sumptuary laws) suggests that there was all along an alternative sense of what clothing meant. At some point, at least, one can begin to recognize the boundaries of a distinct sphere within which people dress in accordance with what they can afford or what they are willing to spend or how they want to look. The sumptuary laws may still be enforced, but now one can make – and ordinary men and women do, in fact, make – egalitarian arguments against them.

Can we imagine a society in which all goods are hierarchically conceived? Perhaps the caste system of ancient India had this form (though that is a far-reaching claim, and it would be prudent to doubt its truth: for one thing, political power seems always to have escaped the laws of caste). We think of castes as rigidly segregated groups, of the caste system as a "plural society," a world of boundaries.[6] But the system is constituted by an extraordinary integration of meanings. Prestige, wealth, knowledge, office, occupation, food, clothing, even the social good of conversation: all are subject to the intellectual as well as to the physical discipline of hierarchy. And the hierarchy is itself determined by the single value of ritual purity. A certain kind of collective mobility is possible, for castes or subcastes can cultivate the outward marks of purity and (within severe limits) raise their position in the social scale. And the system as a whole rests upon a religious doctrine that promises equality of opportunity, not in this life but across the lives of the soul. The individual's status here and now "is the result of his conduct in his last incarnation … and if unsatisfactory can be remedied by acquiring merit in his present life which will raise his status in the next."[7] We should not assume that men and women are ever entirely content with radical inequality. Nevertheless, distributions here and now are part of a single system, largely unchallenged, in which purity is dominant over other goods – and birth and blood are dominant over purity. Social meanings overlap and cohere.

The more perfect the coherence, the less possible it is even to think about complex equality. All goods are like crowns and thrones in a hereditary monarchy. There is no room, and there are no criteria, for autonomous distributions. In fact, however, even hereditary monarchies are rarely so simply constructed. The social understanding of royal power commonly involves some notion of divine grace, or magical gift, or human insight; and these criteria for office holding are potentially independent of birth and blood. So it is for most social goods: they are only imperfectly integrated into larger systems; they are understood, at least sometimes, in their own terms. The theory of goods explicates understandings of this sort (where they exist), and the theory of complex equality exploits them. We say, for example, that it is tyrannical for a man without grace or gift or insight to sit upon the throne. And this is only the first and most obvious kind of tyranny. We can search for many other kinds.

Tyranny is always specific in character: a particular boundary crossing, a particular violation of social meaning. Complex equality requires the defense of boundaries; it works by differentiating goods just as hierarchy works by differentiating people. But we can only talk of a *regime* of complex equality when there are many boundaries to defend; and what the right number is cannot be specified. There is no right number. Simple equality is easier: one dominant good widely distributed makes an egalitarian society. But complexity is hard: how many goods must be autonomously conceived before the relations they mediate can become the relations of equal men and women? There is no certain answer and hence no ideal regime. But as soon as we start to distinguish meanings and mark out distributive spheres, we are launched on an egalitarian enterprise.

Notes

1. Blaise Pascal, *The Pensees,* trans. J.M. Cohen (Harmondsworth, England, 1961), p. 96 (no 244).
2. Karl Marx, *Economic and Philosophical Manuscript,* in *Early Writings,* ed. T.B. Bortomore (London, 1963),pp. 193-94. It is interesting to note an earlier echo of Pascal's argument in Adam Smith's *Theory of Moral Sentiments* (Edinburgh, 1813), vol I, pp. 378-79; but Smith seems to have believed that distributions in his own society actually conformed to this view of appropriateness – a mistake that Pascal nor Marx ever made

3. See the summary account in Jean Bodin, *Six Books of a Commonweale,* ed. Kenneth Douglas McRae (Cambridge, Mass, 1962), pp. 210–18.

4. Cf. Nozick on "patterning," *Anarchy, State, and Utopia* [2], pp. 155ff.

5. Marx, "Gotha Program", (above) p. 23.

6. J.H Hutton, *Caste in India: Its Nature, Function, and Origins* (4th ed., Bombay, 1963), pp. 127-28. I have also drawn on Celestin Bougle, *Essays on the Caste System,* trans. D.F. Pocock (Cambridge, England, 1971), esp. Part III, chaps. 3 and 4; and Louis Dumont, *Homo Hierarchus: The Caste System and Its Implications* (revised English ed., Chicago, 1980).

7. Hutton, *Caste in India,* (above) p. 125.

DISCRIMINATION AND DATA ANALYTICS

7

When data analytics programs are used to augment business decisions, laws still apply to the decisions. So, when Facebook was limiting who could see ads for rental properties and employment to particular races, ages, and genders in 2016, Facebook was potentially in violation of the Fair Housing Act of 1968 and the Civil Rights Act of 1964. Both laws have provisions prohibiting discrimination based on protected classes of individuals. Facebook was taken to court,[1] but settled and agreed to remove targeting options for discriminatory advertising specifically in employment, housing, or credit.[2]

Data analytics programs are frequently used in decisions governed by the concepts of disparate treatment and disparate impact. *Disparate treatment* is the US legal term for differentially treating a protected class (e.g., gender, race, ethnicity, religion, national origin, etc.) and requires proof of not only the disparate treatment but also the intent to treat a class of individuals differently based on their status. Allowing advertisers to specifically target only men in housing advertising is an example of disparate treatment. *Disparate impact* is the legal term for discriminatory effects even when applying facially neutral rules.[3] For example, stating you will only hire people over six feet tall would have a disparate impact on at least one protected class (women) if their average height is significantly lower. Disparate impact does not require intent.

Consider the example of job search sites. Job search sites, such as LinkedIn or ZipRecruiter, bring together businesses advertising for jobs with a labor market looking for work. Most matching algorithms optimize on generating applications for the businesses posting jobs and use three types of user information to "suggest" jobs: information provided by the user, information assigned to the user by the platform (based on "similar" users), and user behavioral data based on their interactions and responses on the site.[4] However, such an approach has led to issues around disparate impact:

> …while men are more likely to apply for jobs that require work experience beyond their qualifications, women tend to only go for jobs in which their qualifications match the position's requirements. The algorithm interprets this variation in behavior and [then] adjusts its recommendations in a way that inadvertently disadvantages women.[5]

In other words, similarly qualified people were not exposed to the same opportunities; and women were not receiving ads for employment that they are qualified for on the job search site. However, the program was not designed to target men with an explicit coding "Men Only." Instead, based on a facially neutral rule, men were disproportionately offered more opportunities. Facebook faces

DOI: 10.1201/9781003278290-43

a similar problem: even after Facebook removed the option for companies to specifically target based on race, outside researchers found "significant skew in delivery along gender and racial lines for "real" ads for employment and housing opportunities despite neutral targeting parameters."[6] Facebook was running into the disparate impact problem.[7]

It turns out, humans are not great at hiring, credit, and employment decisions either.[8] And a number of relevant laws govern decisions made by humans (and those augmented by data analytics) include the concepts of disparate treatment and disparate impact as measurements for discrimination: Fair Housing Act of 1968, Americans with Disabilities Act, the Age Discrimination in Employment Act, Equal Credit Opportunity Act, and the Civil Rights Act of 1964.

For some, discrimination is how fairness is defined in data analytics, AI, and machine learning. However, here we distinguish between the study of discrimination from the study of fairness and justice in data analytics with a separate chapter on fairness (Chapter 6). Given the proliferation of data analytics programs to categorize people, understanding legal discrimination concepts of disparate treatment and disparate impact is critical to the ethics of data and analytics.

Discrimination analysis is particularly important to the ethics of data analytics because automation has been paradoxically offered as a mechanism to *combat* discrimination.[9] Professor Ifeoma Ajunwa notes that removing humans from decision-making is believed to eliminate bias and discrimination. However, and as we read below, data analytics and machine learning can still have a disparate impact on protected classes while these new hiring tools *also* make it difficult to detect bias.[10] Whether combing through resumes or recording applicants during an interview, data analytics programs can discriminate when classifying employees and potential employees.[11]

In addition, computer scientists and data analysts are continually working on ways to test for the discriminatory implications of programs (such as those in our cases here). Barocas, Hardt, and Narayanan offer formal methods to characterize these problems and computational methods to address them in design and development.[12] How a data analytics program is designed and developed will impact whether the use of the program will violate discrimination law. As Barocas, Hardt, and Narayanan summarize,

> Our historical examples of the relevant outcomes will almost always reflect historical prejudices against certain social groups, prevailing cultural stereotypes, and existing demographic inequalities. And finding patterns in these data will often mean replicating these very same dynamics.[13]

Summary of Readings

We turn to two articles on discrimination in analytics. In "Big Data's Disparate Impact,"[14] Professors Solon Barocas and Andrew Selbst outline the many ways data analytics, specifically data mining, can discriminate in the design of a program. This includes defining the outcome of interest or the phenomenon the program will attempt to optimize. Barocas and Selbst identify how disparate impact or treatment in the past can manifest in the training data. Separately, in a paper on fairness in machine learning, Mitchell et al. offer a related figure illustrating how bias can cause a program to be discriminatory (Figure 7.1):

Data, seen this way, is a "social mirror"[15] which reflects the discriminatory acts of the past. Therefore, even the training data includes value judgments that can introduce discrimination and

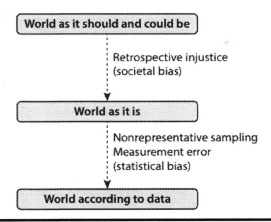

Figure 7.1   A schematic showing two components of biased data: societal bias and statistical bias. (From Shira Mitchell et al., "Algorithmic Fairness: Choices, Assumptions, and Definitions," *Annual Review of Statistics and Its Application* 8 (2020)).

fairness issues, such as choosing the data set (as in Figure 7.1), labeling the data, selecting features, including proxies for protected classes, etc. Discrimination can manifest in odd ways.

Sometimes features that are very important, for example, experience with a particular programming language, may not have enough feature variance in the training data set thereby forcing the AI program to pick up on other features that do differ across protected classes. So, if everyone has coding experience, the model may focus on factors that did differ (such as gender). Barocas and Selbst make a clear connection between the work of data analysts and law around disparate impact and treatment. In examining a data analytics program according to Barocas and Selbst, one would examine whether the program has a discriminatory disparate impact through defining the target variable and labels, training data, feature selection, proxies, or masking.

Professor Anna Lauren Hoffman's essay "Where Fairness Fails: Data, Algorithms and the Limits of Antidiscrimination Discourse" highlights the limitations of only discussing discrimination in regards to algorithms. These limits include an overemphasis on bad actors, a tendency toward single-axis thinking, and a focus on a narrow set of goods (rights, opportunities, and resources). Instead, Professor Hoffman offers nuanced shifts in the way we talk about discrimination and algorithms. First Hoffman suggests allowing for structural inequalities that can infect our systems and produce unfair outcomes and treatment rather than an attempt to find the bad actor who discriminated. The previous chapter, on fairness and justice, exemplifies how discrimination does not even cover all the fairness concerns, let alone issues of power and marginalization. Second, we should examine intersectionality rather than allow individuals to fall along a single axis. For example, "Black women are vulnerable to discrimination not merely by virtue of being Black women, but because the law's single-axis thinking explicitly produces vulnerabilities for those who, like Black women, are multiply-oppressed." Finally, Professor Hoffman shifts from the mere distribution of goods to the degree of access some have to supposedly accessible goods. Professor Hoffman's article reminds us of how fairness and justice ideas can carry assumptions that miss the morally important context.

Related Cases

Two cases offer an opportunity to apply the ideas of disparate treatment and impact. In the first, Amazon designed an algorithm to read resumes with the goal of hiring a more diverse labor force.[16] The model was trained on the previous ten years of hiring at Amazon in order to cull through thousands of resumes automatically. The program ended up penalizing applicants with the word "women's" included (e.g., "women's chess club"). The case offers an opportunity to discuss whether and how Amazon's program was discriminatory and who is at fault (if it is). In addition, what could have been done differently to improve the program?

In the second article, software used by banks favor wealthier white applicants.[17] The question would be, what can banks do to improve their programs? Is it their fault if the outcome is biased? For both cases, we can examine how the programs discriminate and what changes would you make to improve the data analytics program?

Notes

1. Julia Angwin and Terry Parris Jr, "Facebook Lets Advertisers Exclude Users by Race," *ProPublica*, October 28, 2016, https://www.propublica.org/article/facebook-lets-advertisers-exclude-users-by-race

2. Colin Lecher. 2019. "Facebook Drops Targeting Options for Housing, Job, and Credit Ads after Controversy." *The Verge*. March 19, 2019. https://www.theverge.com/2019/3/19/18273018/facebook-housing-ads-jobs-discrimination-settlement

3. Solon Barocas and Andrew D. Selbst, "Big Data's Disparate Impact." *California Law Review* 104 (2016).

4. Sheridan Wall and Hilke Schellmann. 2021. "LinkedIn's Job-Matching AI was Biased. The Company's Solution? More AI." *MIT Technology Review*. https://www.technologyreview.com/2021/06/23/1026825/linkedin-ai-bias-ziprecruiter-monster-artificial-intelligence/

5. Sheridan Wall and Hilke Schellmann, "LinkedIn's Job-Matching AI was Biased. The Company's Solution? More AI," *MIT Technology Review* (2021). https://www.technologyreview.com/2021/06/23/1026825/linkedin-ai-bias-ziprecruiter-monster-artificial-intelligence/

6. Muhammad Ali et al., "Discrimination through Optimization: How Facebook's Ad Delivery Can Lead to Biased Outcomes," *Proceedings of the ACM on Human-Computer Interaction* 3, no. CSCW (2019): 1.

7. The issue of automated hiring is an area where companies should be required to audit their programs used to choose candidates as we cover in Chapter 10 on transparency and accountability. Ajunwa, Ifeoma, The Auditing Imperative for Automated Hiring (March 15, 2019). 34 *Harv. J.L. & Tech.*(forthcoming 2021). Available at SSRN: https://ssrn.com/abstract=3437631 or http://dx.doi.org/10.2139/ssrn.3437631

8. Humans make bad decisions about housing and mortgages as well as discriminatory decisions in hiring. Vanessa Gail Perry, "A Loan at Last? Race and Racism in Mortgage Lending," in *Race in the Marketplace* (Springer, 2019), 173–92; Corinne A Moss-Racusin et al., "Science Faculty's Subtle Gender Biases Favor Male Students," *Proceedings of the National Academy of Sciences* 109, no. 41 (2012): 16474–16479; Natasha Quadlin "The Mark of a Woman's Record: Gender and Academic Performance in Hiring," *American Sociological Review* 83, no. 2 (2018): 331–360; (In asking human's to assess resumes, Quadlin found "high-achieving men are called back significantly more often than high-achieving women—at a rate of nearly 2-to-1 … Employers value competence and commitment among men applicants, but instead privilege women applicants who are perceived as likeable."). Judd B. Kessler, Corinne Low, and Colin D. Sullivan, "Incentivized Resume Rating: Eliciting Employer Preferences without Deception," *American Economic Review* 109, no. 11 (2019): 3713–44. (Kessler et al found "employers hiring in STEM fields penalized résumés with minority or female names. The

effect was big: These candidates were penalized by the equivalent of 0.25 GPA points, based solely on the name at the top of the résumé. That meant such a candidate needed a 4.0 GPA to get the same rating as a white male with a 3.75." https://www.latimes.com/opinion/story/2020-07-24/employment-hiring-bias-racism-resumes?_amp=true

9. For example, Frida Polli, who is the CEO of a job matching platform, wrote an article that we should be "Using AI to Eliminate Bias from Hiring," *Harvard Business Review.* 2019.

10. Ifeoma Ajunwa, "The Paradox of Automation as Anti-Bias Intervention," *Cardozo L. Rev.* 41 (2020): 1671–1741.

11. Pauline T. Kim, "Data-Driven Discrimination at Work," *Wm. & Mary L. Rev.* 58 (2016): 857.

12. Solon Barocas, Moritz Hardt, and Arvind Narayanan, "Fairness and Machine Learning: Limitations and Opportunities." 2018.

13. Barocas, Hardt, and Narayanan.

14. Barocas and Selbst, "Big Data's Disparate Impact."

15. Moritz Hardt (2014). "How Big Data is Unfair." *Medium.* https://medium.com/@mrtz/how-big-data-is-unfair-9aa544d739de

16. https://www.reuters.com/article/us-amazon-com-jobs-automation-insight-idUSKCN1MK08G

17. https://www.technologyreview.com/2021/06/17/1026519/racial-bias-noisy-data-credit-scores-mortgage-loans-fairness-machine-learning/

Chapter 7.1

Amazon Scraps Secret AI Recruiting Tool that Showed Bias against Women[*]

Jeffrey Dastin

SAN FRANCISCO (Reuters) - Amazon.com Inc's AMZN.O machine-learning specialists uncovered a big problem: their new recruiting engine did not like women.

The team had been building computer programs since 2014 to review job applicants' resumes with the aim of mechanizing the search for top talent, five people familiar with the effort told Reuters.

Automation has been key to Amazon's e-commerce dominance, be it inside warehouses or driving pricing decisions. The company's experimental hiring tool used artificial intelligence to give job candidates scores ranging from one to five stars - much like shoppers rate products on Amazon, some of the people said.

"Everyone wanted this holy grail," one of the people said. "They literally wanted it to be an engine where I'm going to give you 100 resumes, it will spit out the top five, and we'll hire those."

But by 2015, the company realized its new system was not rating candidates for software developer jobs and other technical posts in a gender-neutral way.

That is because Amazon's computer models were trained to vet applicants by observing patterns in resumes submitted to the company over a 10-year period. Most came from men, a reflection of male dominance across the tech industry (Figure 7.1.1).

In effect, Amazon's system taught itself that male candidates were preferable. It penalized resumes that included the word "women's," as in "women's chess club captain." And it downgraded graduates of two all-women's colleges, according to people familiar with the matter. They did not specify the names of the schools.

[*] Dastin, Jeffrey. 2019. "Amazon scraps secret AI recruiting tool that showed bias against women" *Reuters.* https://www.reuters.com/article/us-amazon-com-jobs-automation-insight-idUSKCN1MK08G Reprinted with permission.

DOI: 10.1201/9781003278290-44

Dominated by men

Top U.S. tech companies have yet to close the gender gap in hiring, a disparity most pronounced among technical staff such as software developers where men far outnumber women. Amazon's experimental recruiting engine followed the same pattern, learning to penalize resumes including the word "women's" until the company discovered the problem.

GLOBAL HEADCOUNT

▪ Male ▪ Female

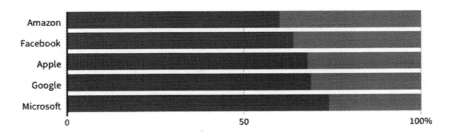

EMPLOYEES IN TECHNICAL ROLES

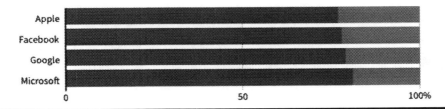

Figure 7.1.1 Employee distribution by gender for big tech companies.

Amazon edited the programs to make them neutral to these particular terms. But that was no guarantee that the machines would not devise other ways of sorting candidates that could prove discriminatory, the people said.

The Seattle company ultimately disbanded the team by the start of last year because executives lost hope for the project, according to the people, who spoke on condition of anonymity. Amazon's recruiters looked at the recommendations generated by the tool when searching for new hires, but never relied solely on those rankings, they said.

Amazon declined to comment on the technology's challenges, but said the tool "was never used by Amazon recruiters to evaluate candidates." The company did not elaborate further. It did not dispute that recruiters looked at the recommendations generated by the recruiting engine.

The company's experiment, which Reuters is first to report, offers a case study in the limitations of machine learning. It also serves as a lesson to the growing list of large companies including Hilton Worldwide Holdings Inc HLT.N and Goldman Sachs Group Inc GS.N that are looking to automate portions of the hiring process.

Some 55 percent of U.S. human resources managers said artificial intelligence, or AI, would be a regular part of their work within the next five years, according to a 2017 survey by talent software firm CareerBuilder.

Employers have long dreamed of harnessing technology to widen the hiring net and reduce reliance on subjective opinions of human recruiters. But computer scientists such as Nihar Shah, who teaches machine learning at Carnegie Mellon University, say there is still much work to do.

"How to ensure that the algorithm is fair, how to make sure the algorithm is really interpretable and explainable - that's still quite far off," he said.

Masculine Language

Amazon's experiment began at a pivotal moment for the world's largest online retailer. Machine learning was gaining traction in the technology world, thanks to a surge in low-cost computing power. And Amazon's Human Resources department was about to embark on a hiring spree: Since June 2015, the company's global headcount has more than tripled to 575,700 workers, regulatory filings show.

So it set up a team in Amazon's Edinburgh engineering hub that grew to around a dozen people. Their goal was to develop AI that could rapidly crawl the web and spot candidates worth recruiting, the people familiar with the matter said.

The group created 500 computer models focused on specific job functions and locations. They taught each to recognize some 50,000 terms that showed up on past candidates' resumes. The algorithms learned to assign little significance to skills that were common across IT applicants, such as the ability to write various computer codes, the people said.

Instead, the technology favored candidates who described themselves using verbs more commonly found on male engineers' resumes, such as "executed" and "captured," one person said.

Gender bias was not the only issue. Problems with the data that underpinned the models' judgments meant that unqualified candidates were often recommended for all manner of jobs, the people said. With the technology returning results almost at random, Amazon shut down the project, they said.

The Problem, or the Cure?

Other companies are forging ahead, underscoring the eagerness of employers to harness AI for hiring.

Kevin Parker, chief executive of HireVue, a startup near Salt Lake City, said automation is helping firms look beyond the same recruiting networks upon which they have long relied. His firm analyzes candidates' speech and facial expressions in video interviews to reduce reliance on resumes.

"You weren't going back to the same old places; you weren't going back to just Ivy League schools," Parker said. His company's customers include Unilever PLC ULVR.L and Hilton.

Goldman Sachs has created its own resume analysis tool that tries to match candidates with the division where they would be the "best fit," the company said.

Microsoft Corp's MSFT.O LinkedIn, the world's largest professional network, has gone further. It offers employers algorithmic rankings of candidates based on their fit for job postings on its site.

Still, John Jersin, vice president of LinkedIn Talent Solutions, said the service is not a replacement for traditional recruiters.

"I certainly would not trust any AI system today to make a hiring decision on its own," he said. "The technology is just not ready yet."

Some activists say they are concerned about transparency in AI. The American Civil Liberties Union is currently challenging a law that allows criminal prosecution of researchers and journalists who test hiring websites' algorithms for discrimination.

"We are increasingly focusing on algorithmic fairness as an issue," said Rachel Goodman, a staff attorney with the Racial Justice Program at the ACLU.

Still, Goodman and other critics of AI acknowledged it could be exceedingly difficult to sue an employer over automated hiring: Job candidates might never know it was being used.

As for Amazon, the company managed to salvage some of what it learned from its failed AI experiment. It now uses a "much-watered down version" of the recruiting engine to help with some rudimentary chores, including culling duplicate candidate profiles from databases, one of the people familiar with the project said.

Another said a new team in Edinburgh has been formed to give automated employment screening another try, this time with a focus on diversity.

Chapter 7.2

Bias Isn't the Only Problem with Credit Scores—and No, AI Can't Help[*]

Will Douglas Heaven

The biggest-ever study of real people's mortgage data shows that predictive tools used to approve or reject loans are less accurate for minorities.

We already knew that biased data and biased algorithms skew automated decision-making in a way that disadvantages low-income and minority groups. For example, software used by banks to predict whether or not someone will pay back credit-card debt typically favors wealthier white applicants. Many researchers and a slew of start-ups are trying to fix the problem by making these algorithms fairer.

But in the biggest ever study of real-world mortgage data, economists Laura Blattner at Stanford University and Scott Nelson at the University of Chicago show that differences in mortgage approval between minority and majority groups is not just down to bias, but to the fact that minority and low-income groups have less data in their credit histories.

This means that when this data is used to calculate a credit score and this credit score used to make a prediction on loan default, then that prediction will be less precise. It is this lack of precision that leads to inequality, not just bias.

The implications are stark: fairer algorithms won't fix the problem.

"It's a really striking result," says Ashesh Rambachan, who studies machine learning and economics at Harvard University, but was not involved in the study. Bias and patchy credit records have been hot issues for some time, but this is the first large-scale experiment that looks at loan applications of millions of real people.

Credit scores squeeze a range of socio-economic data, such as employment history, financial records, and purchasing habits, into a single number. As well as deciding loan applications, credit

[*] Heaven, Will Douglas. 2021. Bias isn't the only problem with credit scores—and no, AI can't help. *MIT Technology Review.* https://www.technologyreview.com/2021/06/17/1026519/racial-bias-noisy-data-credit -scores-mortgage-loans-fairness-machine-learning/ Reprinted with permission.

DOI: 10.1201/9781003278290-45

scores are now used to make many life-changing decisions, including decisions about insurance, hiring, and housing.

To work out why minority and majority groups were treated differently by mortgage lenders, Blattner and Nelson collected credit reports for 50 million anonymized US consumers, and tied each of those consumers to their socio-economic details taken from a marketing dataset, their property deeds and mortgage transactions, and data about the mortgage lenders who provided them with loans.

One reason this is the first study of its kind is that these datasets are often proprietary and not publicly available to researchers. "We went to a credit bureau and basically had to pay them a lot of money to do this," says Blattner.

Noisy Data

They then experimented with different predictive algorithms to show that credit scores were not simply biased but "noisy," a statistical term for data that can't be used to make accurate predictions. Take a minority applicant with a credit score of 620. In a biased system, we might expect this score to always overstate the risk of that applicant and that a more accurate score would be 625, for example. In theory, this bias could then be accounted for via some form of algorithmic affirmative action, such as lowering the threshold for approval for minority applications.

Ripple effects of automation in credit scoring extend beyond finances

But Blattner and Nelson show that adjusting for bias had no effect. They found that a minority applicant's score of 620 was indeed a poor proxy for her creditworthiness but that this was because the error could go both ways: a 620 might be 625, or it might be 615.

This difference may seem subtle, but it matters. Because the inaccuracy comes from noise in the data rather than bias in the way that data is used, it cannot be fixed by making better algorithms.

"It's a self-perpetuating cycle," says Blattner. "We give the wrong people loans and a chunk of the population never gets the chance to build up the data needed to give them a loan in the future."

Blattner and Nelson then tried to measure how big the problem was. They built their own simulation of a mortgage lender's prediction tool and estimated what would have happened if borderline applicants who had been accepted or rejected because of inaccurate scores had their decisions reversed. To do this they used a variety of techniques, such as comparing rejected applicants to similar ones who had been accepted, or looking at other lines of credit that rejected applicants had received, such as auto loans.

Putting all of this together, they plugged these hypothetical "accurate" loan decisions into their simulation and measured the difference between groups again. They found that when decisions about minority and low-income applicants were assumed to be as accurate as those for wealthier, white ones the disparity between groups dropped by 50%. For minority applicants, nearly half of this gain came from removing errors where the applicant should have been approved but wasn't. Low income applicants saw a smaller gain because it was offset by removing errors that went the other way: applicants who should have been rejected but weren't.

Blattner points out that addressing this inaccuracy would benefit lenders as well as underserved applicants. "The economic approach allows us to quantify the costs of the noisy algorithms in a meaningful way," she says. "We can estimate how much credit misallocation occurs because of it."

Righting Wrongs

But fixing the problem won't be easy. There are many reasons that minority groups have noisy credit data, says Rashida Richardson, a lawyer and researcher who studies technology and race at Northeastern University. "There are compounded social consequences where certain communities may not seek traditional credit because of distrust of banking institutions," she says. Any fix will have to deal with the underlying causes. Reversing generations of harm will require myriad solutions, including new banking regulations and investment in minority communities: "The solutions are not simple because they must address so many different bad policies and practices."

Lack of transparency and biased training data mean these tools are not fit for purpose. If we can't fix them, we should ditch them.

One option in the short term may be for the government simply to push lenders to accept the risk of issuing loans to minority applicants who are rejected by their algorithms. This would allow lenders to start collecting accurate data about these groups for the first time, which would benefit both applicants and lenders in the long run.

A few smaller lenders are starting to do this already, says Blattner: "If the existing data doesn't tell you a lot, go out and make a bunch of loans and learn about people." Rambachan and Richardson also see this as a necessary first step. But Rambachan thinks it will take a cultural shift for larger lenders. The idea makes a lot of sense to the data science crowd, he says. Yet when he talks to those teams inside banks they admit it's not a mainstream view. "They'll sigh and say there's no way they can explain it to the business team," he says. "And I'm not sure what the solution to that is."

Blattner also thinks that credit scores should be supplemented with other data about applicants, such as bank transactions. She welcomes the recent announcement from a handful of banks, including JPMorgan Chase, that they will start sharing data about their customers' bank accounts as an additional source of information for individuals with poor credit histories. But more research will be needed to see what difference this will make in practice. And watchdogs will need to ensure that greater access to credit does not go hand in hand with predatory lending behavior, says Richardson.

Many people are now aware of the problems with biased algorithms, says Blattner. She wants people to start talking about noisy algorithms too. The focus on bias—and the belief that it has a technical fix—means that researchers may be overlooking the wider problem.

Richardson worries that policymakers will be persuaded that tech has the answers when it doesn't. "Incomplete data is troubling because detecting it will require researchers to have a fairly nuanced understanding of societal inequities," she says. "If we want to live in an equitable society where everyone feels like they belong and are treated with dignity and respect, then we need to start being realistic about the gravity and scope of issues we face."

Chapter 7.3

Excerpt from Big Data's Disparate Impact[*]

Solon Barocas and Andrew D. Selbst

Advocates of algorithmic techniques like data mining argue that these techniques eliminate human biases from the decision-making process. But an algorithm is only as good as the data it works with. Data is frequently imperfect in ways that allow these algorithms to inherit the prejudices of prior decision makers. In other cases, data may simply reflect the widespread biases that persist in society at large. In still others, data mining can discover surprisingly useful regularities that are really just preexisting patterns of exclusion and inequality. Unthinking reliance on data mining can deny historically disadvantaged and vulnerable groups full participation in society. Worse still, because the resulting discrimination is almost always an unintentional emergent property of the algorithm's use rather than a conscious choice by its programmers, it can be unusually hard to identify the source of the problem or to explain it to a court.

This Essay examines these concerns through the lens of American antidiscrimination law—more particularly, through Title VII's prohibition of discrimination in employment. In the absence of a demonstrable intent to discriminate, the best doctrinal hope for data mining's victims would seem to lie in disparate impact doctrine. Case law and the Equal Employment Opportunity Commission's Uniform Guidelines, though, hold that a practice can be justified as a business necessity when its outcomes are predictive of future employment outcomes, and data mining is specifically designed to find such statistical correlations. Unless there is a reasonably practical way to demonstrate that these discoveries are spurious, Title VII would appear to bless its use, even though the correlations it discovers will often reflect historic patterns of prejudice, others' discrimination against members of protected groups, or flaws in the underlying data.

Addressing the sources of this unintentional discrimination and remedying the corresponding deficiencies in the law will be difficult technically, difficult legally, and difficult politically. There are a number of practical limits to what can be accomplished computationally. For example, when discrimination occurs because the data being mined is itself a result of past intentional

[*] Solon Barocas and Andrew D Selbst, "Big Data's Disparate Impact," *California Law Review* 104 (2016). Reprinted with permission. Note: This is an excerpt from the original so footnote and endnote numbering may be modified.

discrimination, there is frequently no obvious method to adjust historical data to rid it of this taint. Corrective measures that alter the results of the data mining after it is complete would tread on legally and politically disputed terrain. These challenges for reform throw into stark relief the tension between the two major theories underlying antidiscrimination law: anticlassification and antisubordination. Finding a solution to big data's disparate impact will require more than best efforts to stamp out prejudice and bias; it will require a wholesale reexamination of the meanings of "discrimination" and "fairness."

[…]

I. How Data Mining Discriminates

Although commentators have ascribed myriad forms of discrimination to data mining,[1] there remains significant confusion over the precise mechanisms that render data mining discriminatory. This Part develops a taxonomy that isolates and explicates the specific technical issues that can give rise to models whose use in decision making may have a disproportionately adverse impact on protected classes. By definition, data mining is always a form of statistical (and therefore seemingly rational) discrimination. Indeed, the very point of data mining is to provide a rational basis upon which to distinguish between individuals and to reliably confer to the individual the qualities possessed by those who seem statistically similar. Nevertheless, data mining holds the potential to unduly discount members of legally protected classes and to place them at systematic relative disadvantage. Unlike more subjective forms of decision making, data mining's ill effects are often not traceable to human bias, conscious or unconscious. This Part describes five mechanisms by which these disproportionately adverse outcomes might occur, walking through a sequence of key steps in the overall data mining process.

A. Defining the "Target Variable" and "Class Labels"

In contrast to those traditional forms of data analysis that simply return records or summary statistics in response to a specific query, data mining attempts to locate statistical relationships in a dataset.[2] In particular, it automates the process of discovering useful patterns, revealing regularities upon which subsequent decision making can rely. The accumulated set of discovered relationships is commonly called a "model," and these models can be employed to automate the process of classifying entities or activities of interest, estimating the value of unobserved variables, or predicting future outcomes.[3] Familiar examples of such applications include spam or fraud detection, credit scoring, and insurance pricing. These examples all involve attempts to determine the status or likely outcome of cases under consideration based solely on access to correlated data.[4] Data mining helps identify cases of spam and fraud and anticipate default and poor health by treating these states and outcomes as a function of some other set of observed characteristics.[5] In particular, by exposing so-called "machine learning" algorithms to examples of the cases of interest (previously identified instances of fraud, spam, default, and poor health), the algorithm "learns" which related attributes or activities can serve as potential proxies for those qualities or outcomes of interest.[6]

Two concepts from the machine learning and data mining literature are important here: "target variables" and "class labels." The outcomes of interest discussed above are known as target variables.[7] While the target variable defines what data miners are looking for, "class labels" divide all possible values of the target variable into mutually exclusive categories.

The proper specification of the target variable is frequently not obvious, and the data miner's task is to define it. To start, data miners must translate some amorphous problem into a question that can be expressed in more formal terms that computers can parse. In particular, data miners must determine how to solve the problem at hand by translating it into a question about the value of some target variable. The open-endedness that characterizes this part of the process is often described as the "art" of data mining. This initial step requires a data miner to "understand the project objectives and requirements from a business perspective [and] then convert this knowledge into a data mining problem definition."[8] Through this necessarily subjective process of translation, data miners may unintentionally parse the problem in such a way that happens to systematically disadvantage protected classes.

Problem specification is not a wholly arbitrary process, however. Data mining can only address problems that lend themselves to formalization as questions about the state or value of the target variable. Data mining works exceedingly well for dealing with fraud and spam because these cases rely on extant, binary categories. A given instance either is or is not fraud or spam, and the definitions of fraud or spam are, for the most part, uncontroversial.[9] A computer can then flag or refuse transactions or redirect emails according to well-understood distinctions.[10] In these cases, data miners can simply rely on these simple, preexisting categories to define the class labels.

Sometimes, though, defining the target variable involves the creation of new classes. Consider credit scoring, for instance. Although now taken for granted, the predicted likelihood of missing a certain number of loan repayments is not a self-evident answer to the question of how to successfully extend credit to consumers.[11] Unlike fraud or spam, "creditworthiness" is an artifact of the problem definition itself. There is no way to directly measure creditworthiness because the very notion of creditworthiness is a function of the particular way the credit industry has constructed the credit issuing and repayment system. That is, an individual's ability to repay some minimum amount of an outstanding debt on a monthly basis is taken to be a nonarbitrary standard by which to determine in advance and all-at-once whether he is worthy of credit.[12]

Data mining has many uses beyond spam detection, fraud detection, credit scoring, and insurance pricing. As discussed in the introduction, this Essay will focus on the use of data mining in employment decisions. Extending this discussion to employment, then, where employers turn to data mining to develop ways of improving and automating their search for good employees, they face a number of crucial choices.

Like creditworthiness, the definition of a good employee is not a given. "Good" must be defined in ways that correspond to measurable outcomes: relatively higher sales, shorter production time, or longer tenure, for example. When employers mine data for good employees, they are, in fact, looking for employees whose observable characteristics suggest that they would meet or exceed some monthly sales threshold, perform some task in less than a certain amount of time, or remain in their positions for more than a set number of weeks or months. Rather than drawing categorical distinctions along these lines, data mining could also estimate or predict the specific numerical value of sales, production time, or tenure period, enabling employers to rank rather than simply sort employees.

These may seem like eminently reasonable things for employers to want to predict, but they are, by necessity, only part of an array of possible definitions of "good." An employer may instead attempt to define the target variable in a more holistic way—by, for example, relying on the grades that prior employees have received in annual reviews, which are supposed to reflect an overall assessment of performance. These target variable definitions simply inherit the formalizations involved in preexisting assessment mechanisms, which in the case of human-graded performance reviews, may be far less consistent.[13]

Thus, the definition of the target variable and its associated class labels will determine what data mining happens to find. While critics of data mining have tended to focus on inaccurate classifications (false positives and false negatives),[14] as much—if not more—danger resides in the definition of the class label itself and the subsequent labeling of examples from which rules are inferred.[15] While different choices for the target variable and class labels can seem more or less reasonable, valid concerns with discrimination enter at this stage because the different choices may have a greater or lesser adverse impact on protected classes. For example, as later parts will explain in detail, hiring decisions made on the basis of predicted tenure are much more likely to have a disparate impact on certain protected classes than hiring decisions that turn on some estimate of worker productivity. If the turnover rate happens to be systematically higher among members of certain protected classes, hiring decisions based on predicted length of employment will result in fewer job opportunities for members of these groups, even if they would have performed as well as or better than the other applicants the company chooses to hire.

B. Training Data

As described above, data mining learns by example. Accordingly, what a model learns depends on the examples to which it has been exposed. The data that function as examples are known as "training data"—quite literally, the data that train the model to behave in a certain way. The character of the training data can have meaningful consequences for the lessons that data mining happens to learn. As computer science scholars explain, biased training data leads to discriminatory models.[16] This can mean two rather different things, though: (1) if data mining treats cases in which prejudice has played some role as valid examples to learn from, that rule may simply reproduce the prejudice involved in these earlier cases; or (2) if data mining draws inferences from a biased sample of the population, any decision that rests on these inferences may systematically disadvantage those who are under- or overrepresented in the dataset. Both can affect the training data in ways that lead to discrimination, but the mechanisms—improper labeling of examples and biased data collections—are sufficiently distinct that they warrant separate treatment.

1. Labeling Examples

Labeling examples is the process by which the training data is manually assigned class labels. In cases of fraud or spam, the data miners draw from examples that come prelabeled: when individual customers report fraudulent charges or mark a message as spam, they are actually labeling transactions and email for the providers of credit and webmail. Likewise, an employer using grades previously given at performance reviews is also using prelabeled examples.

In certain cases, however, there may not be any labeled data and data miners may have to figure out a way to label examples themselves. This can be a laborious process, and it is frequently fraught with peril.[17] Often the best labels for different classifications will be open to debate. On which side of the creditworthy line does someone who has missed four credit card payments fall, for example?[18] The answer is not obvious. Even where the class labels are uncontested or uncontroversial, they may present a problem because analysts will often face difficult choices in deciding which of the available labels best applies to a particular example. Certain cases may present some, but not all, criteria for inclusion in a particular class.[19] The situation might also work in reverse, where the class labels are insufficiently precise to capture meaningful differences between cases. Such imperfect matches will demand that data miners exercise judgment.

The unavoidably subjective labeling of examples will skew the resulting findings such that any decisions taken on the basis of those findings will characterize all future cases along the same lines. This is true even if such characterizations would seem plainly erroneous to analysts who looked more closely at the individual cases. For all their potential problems, though, the labels applied to the training data must serve as ground truth.[20] Thus, decisions based on discoveries that rest on haphazardly labeled data or data labeled in a systematically, though unintentionally, biased manner will seem valid according to the customary validation methods employed by data miners. So long as prior decisions affected by some form of prejudice serve as examples of correctly rendered determinations, data mining will necessarily infer rules that exhibit the same prejudice.

Consider a real-world example from a different context as to how biased data labeling can skew results. St. George's Hospital, in the United Kingdom, developed a computer program to help sort medical school applicants based on its previous admissions decisions.[21] Those admissions decisions, it turns out, had systematically disfavored racial minorities and women with credentials otherwise equal to other applicants'.[22] In drawing rules from biased prior decisions, St. George's Hospital unknowingly devised an automated process that possessed these very same prejudices. As editors at the British Medical Journal noted at the time, "[T]he program was not introducing new bias but merely reflecting that already in the system."[23] Were an employer to undertake a similar plan to automate its hiring decisions by inferring a rule from past decisions swayed by prejudice, the employer would likewise arrive at a decision procedure that simply reproduces the prejudice of prior decision makers. Indeed, automating the process in this way would turn the conscious prejudice or implicit bias of individuals involved in previous decision making into a formalized rule that would systematically alter the prospects of all future applicants. For example, the computer may learn to discriminate against certain female or black applicants if trained on prior hiring decisions in which an employer has consistently rejected jobseekers with degrees from women's or historically black colleges.

Not only can data mining inherit prior prejudice through the mislabeling of examples, it can also reflect current prejudice through the ongoing behavior of users taken as inputs to data mining. This is what Professor Latanya Sweeney discovered in a study that found that Google queries for black-sounding names were more likely to return contextual (i.e., keyword triggered) advertisements for arrest records than those for white-sounding names.[24] Sweeney confirmed that the companies paying for these advertisements had not set out to focus on black-sounding names; rather, the fact that black-sounding names were more likely to trigger such advertisements seemed to be an artifact of the algorithmic process that Google employs to determine which advertisements to display alongside certain queries.[25] Although it is not fully known how Google computes the so-called "quality score" according to which it ranks advertisers' bids, one important factor is the predicted likelihood, based on historical trends, that users will click on an advertisement.[26] As Sweeney points out, the process "learns over time which [advertisement] text gets the most clicks from viewers [of the advertisement]" and promotes that advertisement in its rankings accordingly.[27] Sweeney posits that this aspect of the process could result in the differential delivery of advertisements that reflect the kinds of prejudice held by those exposed to the advertisements.[28] In attempting to cater to users' preferences, Google will unintentionally reproduce the existing prejudices that inform users' choices.

A similar situation could conceivably arise on websites that recommend potential employees to employers, as LinkedIn does through its Talent Match feature.[29] If LinkedIn determines which candidates to recommend based on the demonstrated interest of employers in certain types of candidates, Talent Match will offer recommendations that reflect whatever biases employers happen to exhibit. In particular, if LinkedIn's algorithm observes that employers disfavor certain candidates who are members of a protected class, Talent Match may decrease the rate at which it recommends these candidates to employers. The recommendation engine would learn to cater to the prejudicial preferences of employers.

There is an old adage in computer science: "garbage in, garbage out." Because data mining relies on training data as ground truth, when those inputs are themselves skewed by bias or inattention, the resulting system will produce results that are at best unreliable and at worst discriminatory.

2. Data Collection

Decisions that depend on conclusions drawn from incorrect, partial, or nonrepresentative data may discriminate against protected classes. The individual records that a company maintains about a person might have serious mistakes,[30] the records of the entire protected class of which this person is a member might also have similar mistakes at a higher rate than other groups, and the entire set of records may fail to reflect members of protected classes in accurate proportion to others.[31] In other words, the quality and representativeness of records might vary in ways that correlate with class membership (e.g., institutions might maintain systematically less accurate, precise, timely, and complete records for certain classes of people). Even a dataset with individual records of consistently high quality can suffer from statistical biases that fail to represent different groups in accurate proportions. Much attention has focused on the harms that might befall individuals whose records in various commercial databases are error ridden.[32] Far less consideration, however, has been paid to the systematic disadvantage that members of protected classes may suffer from being miscounted and, as a result, misrepresented in the evidence base.

Recent scholarship has begun to stress this point. Jonas Lerman, for example, worries about "the nonrandom, systemic omission of people who live on big data's margins, whether due to poverty, geography, or lifestyle, and whose lives are less 'datafied' than the general population's."[33] Professor Kate Crawford has likewise warned that "[b]ecause not all data is created or even collected equally, there are 'signal problems' in big-data sets—dark zones or shadows where some citizens and communities are overlooked or underrepresented."[34] Errors of this sort may befall historically disadvantaged groups at higher rates because they are less involved in the formal economy and its data-generating activities, have unequal access to and relatively less fluency in the technology necessary to engage online, or are less profitable customers or important constituents and therefore less interesting as targets of observation.[35] Not only will the quality of individual records of members of these groups be poorer as a consequence, but these groups as a whole will also be less well represented in datasets, skewing conclusions that may be drawn from an analysis of the data.

As an illustrative example, Crawford points to Street Bump, an application for Boston residents that takes advantage of accelerometers built into smart phones to detect when drivers ride over potholes.[36] While Crawford praises the cleverness and cost-effectiveness of this passive approach to reporting road problems, she rightly warns that whatever information the city receives from Street Bump will be biased by the uneven distribution of smartphones across populations in different parts of the city.[37] In particular, systematic differences in smartphone ownership will very likely result in the underreporting of road problems in the poorer communities where protected groups disproportionately congregate.[38] If the city were to rely on this data to determine where it should direct its resources, it would only further underserve these communities. Indeed, the city would discriminate against those who lack the capability to report problems as effectively as wealthier residents with smartphones.[39]

A similar dynamic could easily apply in an employment context if members of protected classes are unable to report their interest in and qualification for jobs listed online as easily or effectively as others due to systematic differences in Internet access. The EEOC has established a program called "Eradicating Racism & Colorism from Employment" (E-RACE) that aims, at least in part, to prevent this sort of discrimination from occurring due to an employer's desire for high-tech hiring, such as video résumés.[40] E-RACE not only attempts to lower the barriers that would disproportionately burden applicants who belong to a protected class, but also ensures that employers do not develop an inaccurate impression of the incidence of qualified and interested candidates from these communities. If employers were to rely on tallies of high-tech candidates to direct their recruiting efforts, for example, any count affected by a reporting bias could have adverse consequences for specific populations systematically underrepresented in the dataset. Employers would deny equal attention to those who reside in areas incorrectly pegged as having a relatively lower concentration of qualified candidates.

Additional and even more severe risks may reside in the systematic omission of members of protected classes from such datasets. The Street Bump and Internet job application examples only discuss decisions that depend on raw tallies, rather than datasets from which decision makers want to draw generalizations and generate predictions. But data mining is especially sensitive to statistical bias because data mining helps to discover patterns that organizations tend to treat as generalizable findings even though the analyzed data only includes a partial sample from a circumscribed period. To ensure that data mining reveals patterns that hold true for more than the particular sample under analysis, the sample must be proportionally representative of the entire population, even though the sample, by definition, does not include every case.[41]

If a sample includes a disproportionate representation of a particular class (more or less than its actual incidence in the overall population), the results of an analysis of that sample may skew in favor of or against the over- or underrepresented class. While the representativeness of the data is often simply assumed, this assumption is rarely justified and is "perhaps more often incorrect than correct."[42] Data gathered for routine business purposes tend to lack the rigor of social scientific data collection.[43] As Lerman points out, "Businesses may ignore or undervalue the preferences and behaviors of consumers who do not shop in ways that big data tools can easily capture, aggregate, and analyze."[44]

In the employment context, even where a company performs an analysis of the data from its entire population of employees—avoiding the apparent problem of even having to select a sample—the organization must assume that its future applicant pool will have the same degree of variance as its current employee base. An organization's tendency, however, to perform such analyses in order to change the composition of their employee base should put the validity of this assumption into immediate doubt. The potential effect of this assumption is the future mistreatment of individuals predicted to behave in accordance with the skewed findings derived from the biased sample. Worse, these results may lead to decision procedures that limit the future contact an organization will have with specific groups, skewing still further the sample upon which subsequent analyses will be performed.[45] Limiting contact with specific populations on the basis of unsound generalizations may deny members of these populations the opportunity to prove that they buck the apparent trend.

Overrepresentation in a dataset can also lead to disproportionately high adverse outcomes for members of protected classes. Consider an example from the workplace: managers may devote disproportionate attention to monitoring the activities of employees who belong to a protected class and consequently observe mistakes and transgressions at systematically higher rates than others, in part because these managers fail to subject others who behave similarly to the same degree of scrutiny. Not only does this provide managers with justification for their prejudicial suspicions, but it also generates evidence that overstates the relative incidence of offenses by members of these groups. Where subsequent managers who hold no such prejudicial suspicions cannot observe everyone equally, they may rely on this evidence to make predictions about where to focus their attention in the future and thus further increase the disproportionate scrutiny that they place on protected classes.

The efficacy of data mining is fundamentally dependent on the quality of the data from which it attempts to draw useful lessons. If these data capture the prejudicial or biased behavior of prior decision makers, data mining will learn from the bad example that these decisions set. If the data fail to serve as a good sample of a protected group, data mining will draw faulty lessons that could serve as a discriminatory basis for future decision making.

C. Feature Selection

Through a process called "feature selection," organizations—and the data miners that work for them—make choices about what attributes they observe and subsequently fold into their analyses.[46] These decisions can also have serious implications for the treatment of protected classes if those factors that better account for pertinent statistical variation among members of a protected class are not well represented in the set of selected features.[47] Members of protected classes may find that they are subject to systematically less accurate classifications or predictions because the details necessary to achieve equally accurate determinations reside at a level of granularity and coverage that the selected features fail to achieve.

This problem arises because data are necessarily reductive representations of an infinitely more specific real-world object or phenomenon.[48] These representations may fail to capture enough detail to allow for the discovery of crucial points of contrast. Increasing the resolution and range of the analysis may still fail to capture the mechanisms that account for different outcomes because such mechanisms may not lend themselves to exhaustive or effective representation in the data, if such representations even exist. As Professors Toon Calders and Indrė Žliobaitė explain, "[I] t is often impossible to collect all the attributes of a subject or take all the environmental factors into account with a model."[49] While these limitations lend credence to the argument that a dataset can never fully encompass the full complexity of the individuals it seeks to represent, they do not reveal the inherent inadequacy of representation as such.

At issue, really, are the coarseness and comprehensiveness of the criteria that permit statistical discrimination and the uneven rates at which different groups happen to be subject to erroneous determinations. Crucially, these erroneous and potentially adverse outcomes are artifacts of statistical reasoning rather than prejudice on the part of decision makers or bias in the composition of the dataset. As Professor Frederick Schauer explains, decision makers that rely on statistically sound but nonuniversal generalizations "are being simultaneously rational and unfair" because certain individuals are "actuarially saddled" by statistically sound inferences that are nevertheless inaccurate.[50] Obtaining information that is sufficiently rich to permit precise distinctions can be expensive. Even marginal improvements in accuracy may come at significant practical costs and may justify a less granular and encompassing analysis.[51]

To take an obvious example from the employment context, hiring decisions that consider academic credentials tend to assign enormous weight to the reputation of the college or university from which an applicant has graduated, even though such reputations may communicate very little about the applicant's job-related skills and competencies.[52] If equally competent members of protected classes happen to graduate from these colleges or universities at disproportionately low rates, decisions that turn on the credentials conferred by these schools, rather than some set of more specific qualities that more accurately sort individuals, will incorrectly and systematically discount these individuals. Even if employers have a rational incentive to look beyond credentials and focus on criteria that allow for more precise and more accurate determinations, they may continue to favor credentials because they communicate pertinent information at no cost to the employer.[53]

Similar dynamics seem to account for the practice known as "redlining,"[54] in which financial institutions employ especially general criteria to draw distinctions between subpopulations (i.e., the neighborhood in which individuals happen to reside), despite the fact that such distinctions fail to capture significant variation within each subpopulation that would result in a different assessment for certain members of these groups. While redlining in America is well known to have had its basis in racial animus and prejudice,[55] decision makers operating in this manner may attempt to justify their behavior by pointing to the cost efficiency of relying on easily accessible information. In other words, decision makers can argue that they are willing to tolerate higher rates of erroneous determinations for certain groups because the benefits derived from more granular data—and thus better accuracy—do not justify the costs. Of course, it may be no coincidence that such cost-benefit analyses seem to justify treating groups composed disproportionately of members of protected classes to systematically less accurate determinations.[56] Redlining is illegal because it can systematically discount entire areas composed primarily of members of a protected class, despite the presence of some qualified candidates.[57]

Cases of so-called rational racism are really just a special instance of this more general phenomenon—one in which race happens to be taken into consideration explicitly. In such cases, decision makers take membership in a protected class into account, even if they hold no prejudicial views, because such membership seems to communicate relevant information that would be difficult or impossible to obtain otherwise. Accordingly, the persistence of distasteful forms of discrimination may be the result of a lack of information, rather than a continued taste for discrimination.[58] Professor Lior Strahilevitz has argued, for instance, that when employers lack access to criminal records, they may consider race in assessing an applicant's likelihood of having a criminal record because there are statistical differences in the rates at which members of different racial groups have been convicted of crimes.[59] In other words, employers fall back on more immediately available and coarse features when they cannot access more specific or verified information.[60] Of course, as Strahilevitz points out, race is a highly imperfect basis upon which to predict an individual's criminal record, despite whatever differences may exist in the rates at which members of different racial groups have been convicted of crimes, because it is too coarse as an indicator.[61]

D. Proxies

Cases of decision making that do not artificially introduce discriminatory effects into the data mining process may nevertheless result in systematically less favorable determinations for members of protected classes. This is possible when the criteria that are genuinely relevant in making rational and well-informed decisions also happen to serve as reliable proxies for class membership. In other words, the very same criteria that correctly sort individuals according to their predicted likelihood of excelling at a job—as formalized in some fashion—may also sort individuals according to class membership.

In certain cases, there may be an obvious reason for this. Just as "mining from historical data may … discover traditional prejudices that are endemic in reality (i.e., taste-based discrimination)," so, too, may data mining "discover patterns of lower performances, skills or capacities of protected-by-law groups."[62] These discoveries not only reveal the simple fact of inequality, but they also reveal that these are inequalities in which members of protected classes are frequently in the relatively less favorable position. This has rather obvious implications: if features held at a lower rate by members of protected groups nevertheless possess relevance in rendering legitimate decisions, such decisions will necessarily result in systematically less favorable determinations for these individuals. For example, by conferring greater attention and opportunities to employees that they predict will prove most competent at some task, employers may find that they subject members of protected groups to consistently disadvantageous treatment because the criteria that determine the attractiveness of employees happen to be held at systematically lower rates by members of these groups.[63]

Decision makers do not necessarily intend this disparate impact because they hold prejudicial beliefs; rather, their reasonable priorities as profit seekers unintentionally recapitulate the inequality that happens to exist in society. Furthermore, this may occur even if proscribed criteria have been removed from the dataset, the data are free from latent prejudice or bias, the features are especially granular and diverse, and the only goal is to maximize classificatory or predictive accuracy. The problem stems from what researchers call "redundant encodings," cases in which membership in a protected class happens to be encoded in other data.[64] This occurs when a particular piece of data or certain values for that piece of data are highly correlated with membership in specific protected classes. Data's significant statistical relevance to the decision at hand helps explain why data mining can result in seemingly discriminatory models even when its only objective is to ensure the greatest possible accuracy for its determinations. If there is a disparate distribution of an attribute, a more precise form of data mining will be more likely to capture that distribution. Better data and more features will simply come closer to exposing the exact extent of inequality.

E. Masking

Data mining could also breathe new life into traditional forms of intentional discrimination because decision makers with prejudicial views can mask their intentions by exploiting each of the mechanisms enumerated above. Stated simply, any form of discrimination that happens unintentionally can also be orchestrated intentionally. For instance, decision makers could knowingly and purposefully bias the collection of data to ensure that mining suggests rules that are less favorable to members of protected classes.[65] They could likewise attempt to preserve the known effects of prejudice in prior decision making by insisting that such decisions constitute a reliable and impartial set of examples from which to induce a decision-making rule. And decision makers could intentionally rely on features that only permit coarse-grained distinction making—distinctions that result in avoidably higher rates of erroneous determinations for members of a protected class. In denying themselves finer-grained detail, decision makers would be able to justify writing off entire groups composed disproportionately of members of protected classes. A form of digital redlining, this decision masks efforts to engage in intentional discrimination by abstracting to a level of analysis that fails to capture lower level variations. As a result, certain members of protected classes might not be seen as attractive candidates. Here, prejudice rather than some legitimate business reason (such as cost) motivates decision makers to intentionally restrict the particularity of their decision making to a level that can only paint in avoidably broad strokes. This condemns entire groups, composed disproportionately of members of protected classes, to systematically less favorable treatment.

Because data mining holds the potential to infer otherwise unseen attributes, including those traditionally deemed sensitive,[66] it can indirectly determine individuals' membership in protected classes and unduly discount, penalize, or exclude such people accordingly. In other words, data mining could grant decision makers the ability to distinguish and disadvantage members of protected classes even if those decision makers do not have access to explicit information about individuals' class membership. Data mining could instead help to pinpoint reliable proxies for such membership and thus place institutions in the position to automatically sort individuals into their respective class without ever having to learn these facts directly.[67] The most immediate implication is that institutions could employ data mining to circumvent the barriers, both practical and legal, that have helped to withhold individuals' protected class membership from consideration.

Additionally, data mining could provide cover for intentional discrimination of this sort because the process conceals the fact that decision makers determined and considered the individual's class membership. The worry, then, is not simply that data mining introduces novel ways for decision makers to satisfy their taste for illegal discrimination; rather, the worry is that it may mask actual cases of such discrimination.[68] Although scholars, policy makers, and lawyers have long been aware of the dangers of masking,[69] data mining significantly enhances the ability to conceal acts of intentional discrimination by finding ever more remote and complex proxies for proscribed criteria.[70]

Intentional discrimination and its masking have so far garnered disproportionate attention in discussions of data mining,[71] often to the exclusion of issues arising from the many forms of unintentional discrimination described above. While data mining certainly introduces novel ways to discriminate intentionally and to conceal those intentions, most cases of employment discrimination are already sufficiently difficult to prove; employers motivated by conscious prejudice would have little to gain by pursuing these complex and costly mechanisms to further mask their intentions.[72] When it comes to data mining, unintentional discrimination is the more pressing concern because it is likely to be far more common and easier to overlook.

II. Title VII Liability for Discriminatory Data Mining

Current antidiscrimination law is not well equipped to address the cases of discrimination stemming from the problems described in part I. This Part considers how Title VII might apply to these cases. Other antidiscrimination laws, such as the Americans with Disabilities Act, will exhibit differences in specific operation, but the main thrust of antidiscrimination law is fairly consistent across regimes, and Title VII serves as an illustrative example.[73]

An employer sued under Title VII may be found liable for employment discrimination under one of two theories of liability: disparate treatment and disparate impact.[74] Disparate treatment comprises two different strains of discrimination: (1) formal disparate treatment of similarly situated people and (2) intent to discriminate.[75] Disparate impact refers to policies or practices that are facially neutral but have a disproportionately adverse impact on protected classes.[76] Disparate impact is not concerned with the intent or motive for a policy; where it applies, the doctrine first asks whether there is a disparate impact on members of a protected class, then whether there is some business justification for that impact, and finally, whether there were less discriminatory means of achieving the same result.[77]

Liability under Title VII for discriminatory data mining will depend on the particular mechanism by which the inequitable outcomes are generated. This Part explores the disparate treatment and disparate impact doctrines and analyzes which mechanisms could generate liability under each theory.

Notes

1. Solon Barocas, Data Mining and the Discourse on Discrimination, PROC. DATA ETHICS WORKSHOP (2014), https://dataethics.github.io/proceedings/DataMiningandtheDiscourseOn Discrimination.pdf [https://perma.cc/D3LT-GS2X].

2. See generally Usama Fayyad, The Digital Physics of Data Mining, 44 COMM. ACM, Mar. 2001, at 62.

3. More formally, classification deals with discrete outcomes, estimation deals with continuous variables, and prediction deals with both discrete outcomes and continuous variables, but specifically for states or values in the future. Michael J. A. Berry & Gordon S. Linoff, Data Mining Techniques: for Marketing, Sales, and Customer Relationship Management 8–11 (2004).

4. Pedro Domingos, A Few Useful Things to Know About Machine Learning, COMM. ACM, Oct. 2012, at 78–80.

5. Id.

6. Id.

7. Comm. on the Analysis of Massive Data et al., Frontiers in Massive Data Analysis 101 (2013), http:// www.nap.edu/catalog.php??record_id=18374 [https://perma.cc/5DNQ-UFE4]. The machine learning community refers to classification, estimation, and prediction—the techniques that we discuss in this Essay—as "supervised" learning because analysts must actively specify a target variable of interest. Id. at 104. Other techniques known as "unsupervised" learning do not require any such target variables and instead search for general structures in the dataset, rather than patterns specifically related to some state or outcome. Id. at 102. Clustering is the most common example of "unsupervised" learning, in that clustering algorithms simply reveal apparent hot spots when plotting the data in some fashion. Id. We limit the discussion to supervised learning because we are primarily concerned with the sorting, ranking, and predictions enabled by data mining.

8. Pete Chapman et al., CRISP-DM 1.0: Step-by-Step Data Mining Guide 10 (2000).

9. See David J. Hand, Classifier Technology and the Illusion of Progress, 21 STAT. SCI. 1, 10 (2006).

10. Though described as a matter of detection, this is really a classification task, where any given transaction or email can belong to one of two possible classes, respectively: fraud or not fraud, or spam or not spam.

11. See generally Martha Ann Poon, What Lenders See—A History of the Fair Isaac Scorecard, (2013) (unpublished Ph.D. dissertation, University of California, San Diego), http://search.proquest.com/ docview/1520318884 [https://perma.cc/YD3S-B9N7]

12. Hand, supra note 26, at 10.

13. Joseph M. Stauffer & M. Ronald Buckley, The Existence and Nature of Racial Bias in Supervisory Ratings, 90 *J. Applied Psychol.* 586, 588–89 (2005) (showing evidence of racial bias in performance evaluations). Nevertheless, devising new target variables can have the salutary effect of forcing decision makers to think much more concretely about the outcomes that justifiably determine whether someone is a "good" employee. The explicit enumeration demanded of data mining thus also presents an opportunity to make decision making more consistent, more accountable, and fairer overall. This, however, requires conscious effort and careful thinking, and is not a natural consequence of adopting data mining.

14. Bruce Schneier, Data Mining for Terrorists, Schneier on Security (Mar. 9, 2006), https://www.schneier .com/blog/archives/2006/03/data_mining_for.html [https://perma.cc/ZW44- N2KR]; Oscar H. Gandy Jr., Engaging Rational Discrimination: Exploring Reasons for Placing Regulatory Constraints on Decision Support Systems, 12 ETHICS & INFO. TECH. 29, 39–40 (2010); Mireille Hildebrandt & Bert-Jaap Koops, The Challenges of Ambient Law and Legal Protection in the Profiling Era, 73 MOD. L. REV. 428, 433–35(2010).

15. See infra Part I.B.

16. Bart Custers, Data Dilemmas in the Information Society: Introduction and Overview, in *Discrimination and Privacy in the Information Society* 3, 20 (Bart Custers et al. eds., 2013).

17. Hand, supra note 26, at 10–11.

18. Id. at 10 ("The classical supervised classification paradigm also takes as fundamental the fact that the classes are well defined. That is, that there is some fixed clear external criterion, which is used to produce the class labels. In many situations, however, this is not the case. In particular, when the classes are defined by thresholding a continuous variable, there is always the possibility that the defining threshold might be changed. Once again, this situation arises in consumer credit, where it is common to define a customer as 'defaulting' if they fall three months in arrears with repayments.

This definition, however, is not a qualitative one (contrast has a tumor/does not have a tumor) but is very much a quantitative one. It is entirely reasonable that alternative definitions (e.g., four months in arrears) might be more useful if economic conditions were to change.").

19. Id. at 11.

20. Id. at 12. Even when evaluating a model, the kinds of subtle mischaracterizations that happen during training will be impossible to detect because most "evaluation data" is just a small subset of the training data that has been withheld during the learning process. Any problems with the training data will be present in the evaluation data.

21. Stella Lowry & Gordon Macpherson, A Blot on the Profession, 296 BRIT. MED. J. 657, 657 (1988).

22. *Id.* at 657.

23. *Id.*

24. Latanya Sweeney, Discrimination in Online Ad Delivery, COMM. ACM, May 2013, at 44, 47 (2013).

25. Id. at 48, 52.

26. Check and Understand Quality Score, Google, https://support.google.com/adwords/answer/2454010 ?hl=en [https://perma.cc/A88T-GF8X] (last visited July 26, 2014).

27. Sweeney, supra note 41, at 52.

28. The fact that black people may be convicted of crimes at a higher rate than nonblack people does not explain why those who search for black-sounding names would be any more likely to click on advertisements that mention an arrest record than those who see the same exact advertisement when they search for white-sounding names. If the advertisement implies, in both cases, that a person of that particular name has an arrest record, as Sweeney shows, the only reason the advertisements keyed to black-sounding names should receive greater attention is if searchers confer greater significance to the fact of prior arrests when the person happens to be black. Id. at 53.

29. Dan Woods, LinkedIn's Monica Rogati on "What Is a Data Scientist?," FORBES (Nov. 27, 2011), http://www.forbes.com/sites/danwoods/2011/11/27/linkedins-monica-rogati-on-what-is-a-data- scientist [https://perma.cc/N9HT-BXU3].

30. Data quality is a topic of lively practical and philosophical debate. See, e.g., Luciano Floridi, Information Quality, 26 PHIL. & TECH. 1 (2013); Richard Y. Wang & Diane M. Strong, Beyond Accuracy: What Data Quality Means to Data Consumers, 12 *J. Mgmt. Info. Sys.* 5 (1996). The components of data quality have been thought to include accuracy, precision, completeness, consistency, validity, and timeliness, though this catalog of features is far from settled. See generally Larry P. English, Information Quality Applied (2009).

31. Cf. Zeynep Tufekci, Big Questions for Social Media Big Data: Representativeness, Validity and Other Methodological Pitfalls, *Eighth Int'l AAAI Conf. Weblogs & Soc. Media* (2014), http://www.aaai.org/ ocs/index.php/ICWSM/ICWSM14/paper/viewFile/8062/8151 [https://perma.cc/G4G7-2VZ8].

32. See, e.g., FED. TRADE COMM'N, REPORT TO CONGRESS UNDER SECTION 319 OF THE FAIR AND ACCURATE CREDIT TRANSACTIONS ACT OF 2003 A-4 (2012) (finding that nearly 20 percent of consumers had an error in one or more of their three credit reports and that 5.4 percent of consumers had errors that could result in less favorable loan terms).

33. Jonas Lerman, Big Data and Its Exclusions, 66 Stan. L. Rev. Online 55, 57 (2013).

34. Kate Crawford, Think Again: Big Data, *Foreign Pol'y* (May 10, 2013), http://www.foreignpolicy.com /articles/2013/05/09/think_again_big_data [https://perma.cc/S9ZAXEXH].

35. See id.; Lerman, supra note 50, at 57.

36. Crawford, supra note 51 (explaining that a sudden movement suggesting a broken road will automatically prompt the phone to report the location to the city).

37. Id.

38. See id.

39. This is, of course, a more general problem with representative democracy. For a host of reasons, the views and interests of the poor are relatively less well represented in the political process. See, e.g., Larry M. Bartels, Economic Inequality and Political Representation, in The Unsustainable American State 167 (Lawrence Jacobs & Desmond King eds., 2009); Martin Gilens, Affluence and Influence:

Economic Inequality and Political Power in America (2012). The worry here, as expressed by Crawford, is that, for all its apparent promise, data mining may further obfuscate or legitimize these dynamics rather than overcome them.

40. Why Do We Need E-RACE?, EQUAL EMPLOY. OPPORTUNITY COMM'N, http://www1.eeoc .gov/eeoc/initiatives/e-race/why_e-race.cfm [https://perma.cc/S3GY-2MD6] (last visited Mar. 1, 2013). Due to the so-called "digital divide," communities underserved by residential Internet access rely heavily on mobile phones for connectivity and thus often have trouble even uploading and updating traditional résumés. Kathryn Zickuhr & Aaron Smith, Digital Differences, PEW RES. CTR. (Apr. 13, 2012), http://www.pewinternet.org/2012/04/13/digital-differences [https://perma.cc/S545 -42GY] ("Among smartphone owners, young adults, minorities, those with no college experience, and those with lower household income levels are more likely than other groups to say that their phone is their main source of internet access.").

41. Data mining scholars have devised ways to address this known problem, but applying these techniques is far from trivial. See Sinno Jialin Pan & Qiang Yang, A Survey on Transfer Learning, 22 *IEEE Transactions on Knowledge & Data Eng'g* 1345, 1354–56 (2010).

42. Hand, supra note 26, at 7.

43. David Lazer, Big Data and Cloning Headless Frogs, Complexity & Soc. Networks Blog (Feb. 16, 2014), https://web.archive.org/web/20140711164511/http://blogs.iq.harvard.edu/ netgov/2014/02/ big_data_and_cloning_headless.html [https://perma.cc/TQ9A-TP2Z].

44. Lerman, supra note 50, at 59.

45. Practitioners, particularly those involved in credit scoring, are well aware that they do not know how the person purposefully passed over would have behaved if he had been given the opportunity. Practitioners have developed methods to correct for this bias (which, in the case of credit scoring, they refer to as reject inference). See, e.g., Jonathan Crook & John Banasik, Does Reject Inference Really Improve the Performance of Application Scoring Models?, 28 *J. Banking & Fin.* 857 (2004).

46. *Feature Extraction, Construction and Selection* 71–72 (Huan Liu & Hiroshi Motoda eds., 1998).

47. Toon Calders & Indrė Žliobaitė, Why Unbiased Computational Processes Can Lead to Discriminative Decision Procedures, in *Discrimination and Privacy in the Information Society*, supra note 33, at 43, 46 ("[T]he selection of attributes by which people are described in [a] database may be incomplete.").

48. Annamarie Carusi, Data as Representation: Beyond Anonymity in E-Research Ethics, 1 Int'l J. Internet Res. Ethics 37, 48–61 (2008).

49. Calders & Žliobaitė, supra note 64, at 47.

50. Frederick Schauer, *Profiles, Probabilities, and Stereotypes* 3–7 (2006). Insurance offers the most obvious example of this: the rate that a person pays for car insurance, for instance, is determined by the way other people with similar characteristics happen to drive, even if the person is a better driver than those who resemble him on the statistically pertinent dimensions.

51. Kasper Lippert-Rasmussen, "We Are All Different": Statistical Discrimination and the Right to Be Treated as an Individual, 15 *J. Ethics* 47, 54 (2011) ("[O]btaining information is costly, so it is morally justified, all things considered, to treat people on the basis of statistical generalizations even though one knows that, in effect, this will mean that one will treat some people in ways, for better or worse, that they do not deserve to be treated."); see also Brian Dalessandro, Claudia Perlich & Troy Raeder, Bigger Is Better, but at What Cost?: Estimating the Economic Value of Incremental Data Assets, 2 *Big Data* 87 (2014).

52. See Matt Richtel, How Big Data Is Playing Recruiter for Specialized Workers, *N.Y. Times* (Apr. 28, 2013), http://www.nytimes.com/2013/04/28/technology/how-big-data-is-playing-recruiter- for-specialized-workers.html [https://perma.cc/DC7A-W2B5].

53. As one commentator has put it in contemplating data-driven hiring, "Big Data has its own bias. . . . You measure what you can measure." Id.

54. See generally David M. P. Freund, Colored Property: State Policy and White Racial Politics in Suburban America.

55. Id.

56. While animus was likely the main motivating factor for redlining, the stated rationales were economic and about housing value. See Douglas S. Massey & Nancy A. Denton, *American Apartheid: Segregation and the Making of THE Underclass* 51–52 (1993). Redlining persists today and may actually be motivated by profit, but it has the same deleterious effects. See Rachel L. Swarns, Biased Lending Evolves, and Blacks Face Trouble Getting Mortgages, *N.Y. Times* (Oct. 30 2015), http://www.nytimes.com/2015/10/31/nyregion/hudson-city-bank- settlement.html [https://perma.cc/P4YX-NTT9].

57. See *Nationwide Mut. Ins. Co. v. Cisneros*, 52 F.3d 1351, 1359 (6th Cir. 1995) (holding that the Fair Housing Act prohibited redlining in order "to eliminate the discriminatory business practices which might prevent a person economically able to do so from purchasing a house regardless of his race"); *NAACP v. Am. Family Mut. Ins. Co.*, 978 F.2d 287, 300 (7th Cir. 1992).

58. See generally Andrea Romei & Salvatore Ruggieri, Discrimination Data Analysis: A Multi-Disciplinary Bibliography, in *Discrimination and Privacy in the Information Society*, supra note 33, at 109, 120.

59. Lior Jacob Strahilevitz, Privacy Versus Antidiscrimination, 75 *U. Chi. L. Rev.* 363, 364 (2008).

60. Id. This argument assumes that criminal records are relevant to employment, which is often not true. See infra text accompanying note 175.

61. Strahilevitz, supra note 76, at 364; see also infra Part II.A. The law holds that decision makers should refrain from considering membership in a protected class even if statistical evidence seems to support certain inferences on that basis. The prohibition does not depend on whether decision makers can gain (easy or cheap) access to alternative criteria that hold greater predictive value. See *Grutter v. Bollinger*, 539 U.S. 306, 326 (2003).

62. Romei & Ruggieri, supra note 75, at 121.

63. Faisal Kamiran, Toon Calders & Mykola Pechenizkiy, Techniques for Discrimination-Free Predictive Models, in Discrimination and Privacy in the Information Society, supra note 33, at 223–24.

64. Cynthia Dwork et al., Fairness through Awareness, 3 *Proc. Innovations Theoretical Computer Sci. Conf.* 214 app. at 226 (2012) ("Catalog of Evils").

65. See id. (discussing the "[s]elf-fulfilling prophecy").

66. See Solon Barocas, Leaps and Bounds: Toward a Normative Theory of Inferential Privacy 9 (Nov. 11, 2015) (in-progress and unpublished manuscript) (on file with authors).

67. Id. At 9–13.

68. Data miners who wish to discriminate can do so using relevant or irrelevant criteria. Either way the intent would make the action "masking." If an employer masked using highly relevant data, litigation arising from it likely would be tried under a "mixed-motive" framework, which asks whether the same action would have been taken without the intent to discriminate. See infra Part II.A.

69. See, e.g., Custers, supra note 33, at 9–10.

70. See Barocas, supra note 83.

71. See, e.g., Alistair Croll, Big Data Is Our Generation's Civil Rights Issue, and We Don't Know It, Solve for Interesting (July 31, 2012, 12:40 PM), http://solveforinteresting.com/big-data- is-our-generations-civil-rights-issue-and-we-dont-know-it [https://perma.cc/BS8S-6T7S]. This post generated significant online chatter immediately upon publication and has become one of the canonical texts in the current debate. It has also prompted a number of responses from scholars. See, e.g., Anders Sandberg, Asking the Right Questions: Big Data and Civil Rights, PRAC. ETHICS (Aug. 16, 2012), http://blog.practicalethics.ox.ac.uk/2012/08/asking-the-right-questions-big-data-and-civil-   rights [https://perma.cc/NC36-NBZN].

72. See Linda Hamilton Krieger, The Content of Our Categories: A Cognitive Bias Approach to Discrimination and Equal Employment Opportunity, 47 Stan. L. Rev. 1161, 1177 (1995).

73. The biggest difference between the Americans with Disabilities Act and Title VII is the requirement that an employer make "reasonable accommodations" for disabilities. 42 U.S.C. § 12112(b) (5) (2012). But some scholars have argued that even this difference is illusory and that accommodations law is functionally similar to Title VII, though worded differently. See Samuel R. Bagenstos, "Rational Discrimination," Accommodation, and the Politics of (Disability) Civil Rights, 89 VA. L.

REV. 825, 833 & n.15 (2003) (comparing accommodations law to disparate treatment); Christine Jolls, Antidiscrimination and Accommodation, 115 HARV. L. REV. 642, 652 (2001) (comparing accommodations law to disparate impact).

74. See 42 U.S.C. § 2000e; Ricci v. DeStefano, 557 U.S. 557, 577 (2009).

75. Richard A. Primus, The Future of Disparate Impact, 108 MICH. L. REV. 1341, 1351 n.56 (2010) (explaining that, for historical reasons, disparate treatment became essentially "not-disparate-impact" and now we rarely notice the two different embedded theories).

76. See *Griggs v. Duke Power Co.*, 401 U.S. 424, 430 (1971).

77. 42 U.S.C. § 2000e-2(k).

Chapter 7.4

Excerpt from Where Fairness Fails: Data, Algorithms, and the Limits of Antidiscrimination Discourse[*]

Anna Lauren Hoffman

Engaging The Limits of Fairness and Antidiscrimination Discourse

Today, it is widely recognized that data and algorithms risk reproducing biases against historically disadvantaged populations in ways that, as Barocas and Selbst (2016) put it, 'look a lot like discrimination' (p. 673). In the United States, this risk – and efforts to mitigate it – have in many ways echoed liberal antidiscrimination discourses in the law, which have historically sought to address injustices in the distribution and exercise of important rights, opportunities, and resources in domains like voting, housing, and employment. But the degree to which the law has succeeded in these efforts is an open and ongoing question. In particular, certain well documented tendencies in the way courts have interpreted ideals like fairness and antidiscrimination have arguably hindered its effectiveness. These tendencies point toward (perhaps fatal) limits of antidiscrimination discourse for realizing social justice in any broad or meaningful way – limits that extant work on data and discrimination risk inheriting.

Below, I briefly sketch three of these tendencies – 1) an emphasis on discrete 'bad actors,' 2) single-axis thinking and the centering of disadvantage, and 3) inordinate focus on a limited set of goods – paying particular attention to their sources, motivations, and consequences. I then demonstrate parallel limits in attempts to address problems of unfairness and bias and data-based

[*] Anna Lauren Hoffmann, "Where Fairness Fails: Data, Algorithms, and the Limits of Antidiscrimination Discourse," *Information, Communication & Society* 22, no. 7 (2019): 900–915. Reprinted with permission. Note: This is an excerpt from the original so footnote and endnote numbering may be modified.

DOI: 10.1201/9781003278290-47

discrimination, especially those centered on mitigating the prejudices of imperfect humans behind the machine or developing computational solutions to problems of bias and unfairness. It is worth noting one limitation of the following discussion: its focus is exclusively on distinctly US-based discourses of fairness and anti-discrimination. However, my aim here is not a full accounting of these critiques and the bodies of work that have grown up around them; rather, I simply mean to draw out some salient features of these discussions that shed light on similar tendencies in efforts to combat data and discrimination.

From 'Bad Actors' to 'Bad Algorithms'

The first tendency centers on the law's concern with neutralizing inappropriate conduct on the part of individual perpetrators — what I call the 'bad actor' frame. In his pathbreaking article 'Legitimizing Racial Discrimination Through Antidiscrimination Law,' Alan David Freeman (1978) showed United States Supreme Court doctrine was hindered by limited interpretations of 'fault' and 'causation' that tilted antidiscrimination law away from its broader aims of social emancipation and towards a kind of narrow, mechanistic reasoning. Instead of addressing pernicious social and systemic injustices, the notion of 'fault' had, according to Freeman (1978), morphed into a requirement to identify and near-surgically separate from the sum total of possible sources of discrimination only 'those blameworthy individuals … violating an otherwise shared norm' (pp. 1053–1054). Similarly, the idea of 'causation' bracketed broad social or systemic issues, instead allowing only claims that could be demonstrated in narrow cause-and-effect terms (Freeman, 1978, p. 1056). Working in tandem, these requirements placed on victims the onerous and often impossible burden of isolating only those conditions mechanically linked to discrete and 'blameworthy' perpetrators, 'regardless of whether other conditions … would have to be remedied for the outcome of the case to make any difference at all' (Freeman, 1978, p. 1056).

For Freeman (1978), this model generated at least two unsatisfactory outcomes. First, the reliance on a narrow cause-and-effect conception of discrimination stripped discriminatory events of their broader social or cultural context, positing discrimination not as a social phenomenon 'but merely as the misguided conduct of particular actors' (Freeman, 1978, p. 1054). Or, as Neil Gotanda (1991) describes it, 'despite the fact that personal racial prejudices have social origins, racism is considered an individual and personal trait' (p. 44). As a consequence, important social and contextual issues were left 'beyond' the law's reach, including discriminatory conduct that may be unintentional or prejudicial actions that could not be easily traced to a discrete discriminatory effect (Freeman, 1978, p. 1056). Second, the model positions the problem of discrimination not as something that will not be solved until all contributing conditions have been eliminated, but, rather, as a matter of neutralizing inappropriate conduct on the part of individual perpetrators (Freeman, 1978, p. 1053).

Similarly, combatting discrimination in the context of data and algorithmic systems means identifying specific data sources, technical features, or human biases at the root of particular unfair outcomes. Sometimes this means looking at the decisions of specific designers or the demographic composition of engineering or data science teams to identify their social 'blindspots' (Snow, 2018). The idea here is that, as one New York Times article put it, 'software is not free of human influence' because 'algorithms are written and maintained by people' (Miller, 2015, n.p.). But just as the search for bad actors' places structural issues beyond the law's reach, appealing to the 'blindspots' of particular designers or teams ignores the structuring role of technology, instead reducing a system's shortcomings to the biases of its imperfect human designers.

Of course, not all work in this area reduces discrimination entirely to some set of 'blamewor-thy' humans behind the machine. Many discussions make clear that algorithmic discrimination can happen in ways that are unintentional or difficult to account for, for example when upstream social biases are reflected in training data in ways that may be difficult to predict. In these cases, biases are said to 'sneak in' (University of Bath, 2017), 'whether on purpose or by accident' (Barocas & Selbst, 2016, p. 674), or in ways that only emerge over time (Friedman & Nissenbaum, 1996). As one White House report put it, there is an acute risk of 'unintentional perpetuation and promo-tion of historical biases,' especially in cases 'where a feedback loop causes bias in inputs or results of the past to replicate itself in the outputs of an algorithmic system' (Muñoz et al., 2016, p. 8). But de-emphasizing intentionality does not automatically move us beyond a discrete source mentality, as it still emphasizes a kind of technical causation that simply replaces 'bad actors' with 'bad data' or 'bad algorithms.' It still permits ignorance of the ways humans and technology co-conspire to not just passively reproduce but actively uphold and reproduce discriminatory social structures, especially in the case of negative externalities 'learned' by, for example, machine learning systems based on subsequent user interaction (Overdorf, Kulynych, Balsa, Troncoso, & Gürses, 2018). But for most 'fair' solutions, sources of discrimination that cannot be traced to discrete bad mecha-nisms are bracketed, dismissed as someone else's problem or, worse, couched as untouchable facts of history—mere accidents that are 'caused,' if at all, by biases that 'sneak in' to the system.

It is important to note that, despite these limitations, our understanding of structural and other conditions that contribute to discrimination has improved greatly in recent decades, in part a result of what Samuel Bagenstos (2006) calls 'the structural turn' in antidiscrimination scholar-ship (p. 2). For example, social psychological research into the nature and pervasiveness of 'uncon-scious' or implicit bias has inspired legal scholars to better account for unintentional forms of discrimination – that is, prejudicial associations between particular attributes and particular social groups that are not apparent or even consciously available to individuals (e.g., Krieger, 1995). Obviously, the existence of unconscious bias calls into question the 'bad actor' frame's depen-dency on narrow causal links and 'blameworthy' perpetrators. In the context of the law, however, Bagenstos (2006) notes that these efforts, rather than liberating antidiscrimination law from its former constraints, are instead further evidence of the law's limits. In a technology context, engi-neers and technology firms have started to gesture towards unconscious bias as that intangible something else we ought to address. Here, bias is externalized and transformed into something that, as Linda Hamilton Krieger (1995) once put it, 'sneak[s] up on' us from the outside (p. 1188), as opposed to something that is variously, but systematically cultivated and maintained. The idea that our biases are somehow apart from us yet can infect our decision-making converts them into something akin to what Freeman (1978) sarcastically called our 'ancestral demons' – that is, a pos-session or invasion for which we are not at fault but which we should nonetheless seek to purge. In this space, unconscious bias training programs pick up where technical fixes leave off: rather than take responsibility for the ways we are daily and actively complicit in reifying culturally-situated violences, we externalize bias and – after a few all-day seminars – count our demons exorcized.

Taking Intersectionality Seriously

The second limit is a tendency of antidiscrimination discourse towards single-axis thinking cen-tered on disadvantage. This insight is central to Kimberlé Crenshaw's influential notion of 'inter-sectionality' (1989, 1988, 1991) and the law's role in producing the very social categories through which we come to understand and adjudicate discrimination. Crenshaw's (1989) foundational work showed that the propensity of courts to focus on one axis of discrimination at a time – for example, race or gender – made vulnerable those whose experiences were not reducible to one axis or another. In her paradigmatic example, Crenshaw found that Black women in employment discrimination cases were unsuccessful, in part, because courts compared their claims against the experiences of similarly situated Black men (for racial discrimination cases) or white women (for gender discrimination) – both groups that, unlike Black women, enjoy systematic advantages along at least one historically-contingent dimension (gender, for Black men; race, for white women).

Despite broader debates about the possibilities and limits of intersectionality as a theoretical lens (e.g., Mutua, 2006; Nash, 2017), Crenshaw's basic insight remains indispensable:

Black women are vulnerable to discrimination not merely by virtue of being Black women, but because the law's single-axis thinking explicitly produces vulnerabilities for those who, like Black women, are multiply-oppressed. Accordingly, thinking intersectionally is not – as it is sometimes couched – simply a matter of 'stacking' or counting oppressions and arriving at a sum total of disadvantages; nor does it mean adopting a quasi-positivist stance that regards identity categories as static or pre-given (Carastathis, 2016, p. 4). Rather, recalling Crenshaw's often-overlooked metaphor of the basement, intersectionality is concerned with both the production and hierarchical ordering of identity categories, as in the above example where the law's single-axis thinking promotes the interests of some and relegates others to the 'basement' of the social hierarchy (Carastathis, 2016). Accordingly, intersectionality does not seek some 'flat geography' (McKittrick, 2006) of identity categories, but aims to map the contingencies of particular institutional or social arrangements.

Single-axis thinking also tends to focus on relative disadvantage at the expense of attention to the production of systematic benefits or privileges. Factors like race or sex tend to only become salient when they explicitly disadvantage victims, while the privileging of, for example, whiteness or maleness itself is not made explicit (Crenshaw, 1989, p. 151). As Barbara Flagg (1993) describes with regard to race, there is a 'tendency of whites not to think about whiteness, or about norms, behaviors, experiences, or perspectives that are white-specific' (p. 957). Moreover, the tendency to associate disadvantage with particular (pre-given) groups represents, as Vivian May (2015) argues, a kind of '"special case" closed logic' that foregrounds comparison across groups at the expense of attention to relevant intragroup differences (p. 26). Black womanhood, for example, is 'neither singular nor monolithic,' but the focus on disadvantage works to reproduce homogenizing stereotypes (May, 2015, p. 26). Instead of treating as morally abhorrent those structural processes that unjustly advantage certain groups, the focus on disadvantage forces us into a kind of benevolent – or, worse, patronizing – stance that flattens our understanding of those already relegated to the 'basement' of the social hierarchy.

As with the law, work on data and discrimination has been slow to fully absorb the lessons of intersectionality. Single-axis thinking is pervasive in efforts to isolate and identify discriminatory biases in data-intensive systems. As Kearns et al. (2017) point out, for example, work on fairness in machine learning tends to focus only on small sets of predefined protected attributes (like race or gender). Against this, they propose methods for identifying various combinations of protected attributes and certifying fairness across 'exponentially many' subgroups (p. 1). But this move, while an improvement, still falls short as an 'intersectional' approach. Intersectionality is not a matter of randomly combining infinite variables to see what 'disadvantages' fall out; rather, it is about mapping the production and contingency of social categories. As Buolamwini and Gebru (2018) have shown in their work on facial recognition systems, problematic distinctions between groups are not limited to pre-existing categories but may be produced through interactions between labels in a system (as with labels for race and gender). Despite claims that both works are 'intersectional' in the sense employed by Crenshaw (Mitchell, Potash, & Barocas, 2018), only Buolamwini and Gebru (2018) begin to gesture toward the social contingency of difference with which intersectionality is concerned. However, both fall short in terms of addressing the institutionalization of (and liberation from) social hierarchy. For example, Buolamwini and Gebru's (2018) stated aim of 'increasing phenotypic and demographic representation in face datasets and algorithmic evaluation' (p. 12) does not address justice issues that arise from the institutional contexts within which facial recognition is employed – a limitation Buolamwini (2018) and Gebru (AI Now Institute, 2018) have emphasized elsewhere.

Further, computational solutions to problems of fairness almost exclusively focus on disadvantage. Zafar, Valera, Gomez Rodriguez, and Gummadi (2017), for example, seek to mitigate problems of misclassification across groups (i.e., making sure that women are not misclassified more often than men) in order to ensure that no one group is 'mistreated' or put 'at an unfair disadvantage', a result of their assumption that there is a 'ground truth' of static and pre-given – rather than contingent and constructed – social categories (p. 1). The seductiveness of disadvantage as a focus is also evident in foundational work. For example, the opening illustration in Friedman and Nissenbaum's (1996) germinal 'Bias in Computer Systems' features airline reservation software criticized for systematically benefiting one airline at the expense of others, while the reminder of the article addresses systematic disadvantage. The shift is subtle, but consequential: by centering disadvantage, we fail to question the normative conditions that produce – and promote the qualities or interests of – advantaged subjects.

In other cases, discrimination is recast in painfully neutral terms – i.e., 'non-discrimination.' For Hardt, Price, and Srebro (2016), for example, 'non-discrimination' is conceived as rough parity in false negative and false positive rates across protected groups. But while this may appear to move us beyond mere disadvantage, it does little to address the different real-world consequences false results might have for different groups. A person of relative socioeconomic advantage is more likely to have the time or resources necessary to contest an unfair decision – an imbalance that persists regardless of the fact that differently-situated groups stood an equal chance of being falsely flagged within the system. Instead of grappling with the processes that generate patterns of advantage and disadvantage within and across groups, both disadvantage-focused and 'nondiscrimination' approaches limit us to solutions that are, at best, reactive and superficial. Or, as Virginia Eubanks (2018) summarizes, 'when automated decision-making tools are not built to explicitly dismantle structural inequalities, their increased speed and vast scale intensify them dramatically' (Paragraph 17).

Data-Based Discrimination beyond Distributions

The last limitation centers on the tendency of antidiscrimination discourses to focus on disadvantage relative to a narrow set of goods, namely rights, opportunities, and resources. As critics of distributive justice have long shown, near exclusive focus on these goods cannot account for justice issues related the design of social, economic, and physical institutions that structure decision-making power and shape normative standards of identity and behavior (Young, 2006). Disabilities scholars, for example, have shown how normative standards of ability shape our world in ways that are biased, as when buildings without wheelchair access impose a normative standard of mobility that excludes many otherwise capable persons. Mere focus on distributions of goods, then, fails to account for the way background features of the world – like the built environment – structure the ability to use goods in the first place. Further, as Shew (2017) points out, disability hinges not only on the distribution of assistive technologies or accommodating designs, but also on their maintenance and the social meanings attached to them (see also Bell, 2010; Garland-Thomson, 2006). Social attitudes, for example, play a significant role in shaping persons' well-being in ways that are relevant to the realization of justice, but addressing them is not wholly reducible to matters of redistribution.

Of course, these critiques would ring hollow if centering rights, opportunities, and material wealth had resulted in appreciable and unequivocal gains for those most vulnerable to discrimination or violence. It is far from clear, however, that this is the case. Contrary to the cherry-picked arguments of liberal humanists like Steven Pinker, the tools of conventional liberalism have not straightforwardly or evenly improved people's life chances, even in affluent countries. As John Gray (2011) notes, these arguments tend to downplay features of contemporary social life – like the persistence and resilience of racism and xenophobia – which suggest that 'outside of some fairly narrowly defined areas of scientific investigation, progress is at best fitful and elusive' (n.p.). Indeed, one of the most obvious arguments against centering rights, opportunities, and resources is that – for those groups that continue to be relegated to Crenshaw's 'basement' – doing so has not worked. Liberalism's promises of equal rights and freedom from domination continue – as Charles Mills (2017) describes – to allude many, especially people of color. In the United States, violence against people of color persists (especially in the form of mass incarceration, e.g., Alexander, 2012) and racial wealth gaps continue to grow (Spade, 2015, p. 81). This is not to say that a focus on these goods can never produce positive outcomes for oppressed people, nor that they should not be components of future solutions. Rather, it is only to point out that, on their own, they have not proven absolute forces for progress.

A cursory survey of work on data and discrimination reveals focus areas firmly rooted in the liberal rubric of rights, opportunities, and material resources. They include, but are not limited to: freedom of expression, especially automated moderation of online content (e.g., Gillespie, 2012, 2017); criminal justice, especially in policing and sentencing (e.g., Harcourt, 2006; Rosenblat, Randhava, Boyd, Gangadharan, & Yu, 2014a); employment, especially hiring and surveillance (e.g., Ajunwa, 2019; Barocas & Selbst, 2016; Levy, 2015); consumer protection, especially privacy and consumer choice (Calo, 2013; Rosenblat et al., 2014b): education, especially admissions and evaluation (Fontaine, 2016); and finance, notably credit risk and market manipulation (Pasquale, 2016). The focus on discrimination only as it relates to particular distributive outcomes is also evident in Friedman and Nissenbaum's (1996) argument that 'systematic discrimination does not establish bias unless it is joined with an unfair outcome' (p. 333). But an outsized focus on these goods obscures dimensions of justice not easily reconciled with a rubric of rights, opportunities, and wealth. In particular, emphasis on distributions of these goods fails to appropriately attend to the legitimating, discursive, or dignitary dimensions of data and information in its social and political context (Dencik, Jansen, & Metcalfe, 2018; Hoffmann, 2016, 2017). Moreover, representational or intimate harms are not easily or intuitively remedied, as made clear by Safiya Noble (2018) and her account of Google search's explicit and degrading results for the query 'black girls.' Money lost can be replaced and rights violated can be restored, but corporate apologies, subtle tweaks to a system, or even financial compensation ring hollow in the face of attacks on one's dignity.

Finally, conversations that center rights, opportunities, and resources also often implicitly position data and algorithms as primarily instrumental in nature. This implicit assumption, as Nick Seaver (2017) notes, recognizes that data and algorithms both shape and are shaped by cultural context, but it casts them as akin to a rock in a stream: 'the rock is not part of the stream, though the stream may jostle and erode it and the rock may produce ripples and eddies in the stream' (p. 4). On this model, addressing discrimination requires a clear distinction between 'the algorithm' or 'the data' and all other sources of discrimination and connecting 'the algorithm' or 'the data' to a discrete effect or 'ripple in the stream.' Doing so is, of course, exceedingly difficult, as algorithms operating in networked information environments are, in Mike Ananny's (2016) words, 'moving targets' (p. 108). They incorporate real-time feedback from various sources and optimize over variables that are constantly changing, sometimes in unpredictable ways (Overdorf et al., 2018). Accordingly, algorithmic or automated systems do not only issue decisions, they are also intertwined in the production of social and cultural meaning. As André Brock (2018) argues, cultural artifacts like race are not pre-given variables that are simply plugged in to online platforms or technical systems – rather, they are actively mediated by the system's 'computational, network, and semantic qualities' (p. 1025).

In this way, data and algorithms do not merely shape distributive outcomes, but they are also intimately bound up in the production of particular kinds of meaning, reinforcing certain discursive frames over others (e.g., Bivens & Hoque, 2018; Sweeney, 2016; Willson, 2017). For example, as Julie Cohen (2018) has demonstrated, extant framings of personal data as both available and potentially valuable sets up a particular kind of relationship between people and those entities that seek to capitalize on people's data, namely one 'supports the reorganization of sociotechnical activity in ways directed toward extraction and appropriation' (p. 214). But this normative frame is not an additional 'good' to set alongside rights, opportunities, and wealth –rather, it informs the very backdrop against which we understand those goods and ideals of their fair distribution.

[…]

References

AI Now Institute. (2018, November 25). AI Now 2018 Symposium [Video recording]. Retrieved from https://www.youtube.com/watch?v=NmdAtfcmTNg&feature=youtu.be&t=2219

Ajunwa, I. (2019). Algorithms at work: Productivity monitoring platforms and wearable technology as the new data-centric research agenda for employment and labor law. *St. Louis University Law Journal*, 63(47), 1–47.

Ananny, M. (2016). Toward an ethics of algorithms: Convening, observation, Probability, and Timeliness. *Science, Technology, & Human Values*, 41(1), 93–117.

Bagenstos, S. R. (2006). The structural turn and the limits of antidiscrimination law. *California Law Review*, 94(1), 1–47.

Barocas, S., & Selbst, A. D. (2016). Big data's disparate impact. *California Law Review*, 104, 671–732.

Bell, C. (2010). Is disability studies actually white disability studies? In L. J. Davis (Ed.), *The disability studies Reader* (3rd ed., pp. 266–273). New York, NY: Routledge.

Bivens, R., & Hoque, A. S. (2018). Programming sex, gender, and sexuality: Infrastructural failures in the "feminist" dating app Bumble. *Canadian Journal of Communication*, 43(3), 441–459.

Buolamwini, J., & Gebru, T. (2018). Gender shades: Intersectional accuracy disparities in commercial gender classification. *Proceedings of Machine Learning Research*, 81, 77–91.

Calders, T., & Verwer, S. (2010). Three naive Bayes approaches for discrimination-free classification. *Data Mining and Knowledge Discovery*, 21(2), 277–292.

Calo, R. (2013). Consumer subject review boards: A thought experiment. *Stanford Law Review*, 66, 97–102.

Carastathis, A. (2016). *Intersectionality: Origins, contestations, horizons*. Lincoln, NE: University of Nebraska Press.

Cohen, J. E. (2018). The biopolitical public domain: The legal construction of the surveillance economy. *Philosophy & Technology*, 31(2), 213–233.

Crenshaw, K. (1988). Race, reform, and retrenchment: Transformation and legitimation in antidiscrimination law. *Harvard Law Review*, 101(7), 1331–1387.

Crenshaw, K. (1989). Demarginalizing the intersection of race and sex: A Black feminist critique of antidiscrimination doctrine, feminist theory and antiracist politics. *University of Chicago Legal Forum*, 1(8), 139–167.

Crenshaw, K. (1991). Mapping the margins: Intersectionality, identity politics, and violence against Women of Color. *Stanford Law Review*, 43(6), 1241–1299.

Dencik, L., Jansen, F., & Metcalfe, P. (2018, August 30). A conceptual framework for approaching social justice in an age of datafication. *DATAJUSTICE project*. Retrieved from https:// datajusticeproject .net/2018/08/30/a-conceptual-framework-for-approaching-social-justice-in- an-age-of-datafication/

Eubanks, V. (2018, January). The digital poorhouse. Harper's Magazine. Retrieved from https:// harpers.or g/archive/2018/01/the-digital-poorhouse/

Flagg, B. J. (1993). "Was blind, but now I see": White race consciousness and the requirement of discriminatory intent. *Michigan Law Review*, 91(5), 953–1017.

Freeman, A. D. (1978). Legitimizing racial discrimination through antidiscrimination law: A critical review of Supreme Court doctrine. *Minnesota Law Review*, 62, 1049–1120.

Friedman, B., & Nissenbaum, H. (1996). Bias in computer systems. *ACM Transactions on Information Systems (TOIS)*, 14(3), 330–347.

Garland-Thomson, R. (2006). Ways of staring. *Journal of Visual Culture*, 5(2), 173–192.

Gotanda, N. (1991). A critique of "Our Constitution Is color-Blind". *Stanford Law Review*, 44(1), 1–68.

Gray, J. (2011, September 21). Delusions of peace. *Prospect Magazine*. Retrieved from https://www.prospect-magazine.co.uk/magazine/john-gray-steven-pinker-violence-review

Harcourt, B. E. (2006). *Against prediction: Profiling, policing, and punishing in an actuarial age* (Reprint ed.). Chicago: University of Chicago Press.

Hardt, M., Price, E., & Srebro, N. (2016, December). *Equality of opportunity in supervised learning.* Paper presented at the 30th Conference on Neural information processing systems (NIPS 2016), Barcelona, Spain.

Hoffmann, A. L. (2016). Google books, libraries, and self-respect: Information justice beyond distributions. *The Library Quarterly*, 86(1), 76–92.

Hoffmann, A. L. (2017). Beyond distributions and primary goods: Assessing applications of Rawls in information science and technology literature since 1990. *Journal of the Association for Information Science and Technology*, 68(7), 1601–1618.

Kearns, M., Neel, S., Roth, A., & Wu, Z. S. (2017). Preventing fairness gerrymandering: Auditing and learning for subgroup fairness. ArXiv:1711.05144 [Cs.LG]. Retrieved from http://arxiv.org/abs/ 1711.05144

Krieger, L. H. (1995). The content of our categories: A cognitive bias approach to discrimination and equal employment opportunity. *Stanford Law Review*, 47(6), 1161–1248.

Levy, K. E. C. (2015). The contexts of control: Information, power, and truck-driving work. *The Information Society*, 31(2), 160–174.

May, V. M. (2015). *Pursuing intersectionality, unsettling dominant imaginaries.* New York: Routledge.

McKittrick, K. (2006). *Demonic grounds: Black women and the cartographies of struggle.* Minneapolis, MN: University of Minnesota Press.

Miller, C. C. (2015, July 9). When algorithms discriminate. *The New York Times.* Retrieved from https:// www.nytimes.com/2015/07/10/upshot/when-algorithms-discriminate.html

Mills, C. W. (2017). *Black rights/white wrongs: The critique of racial liberalism.* Oxford, UK: Oxford University Press.

Mitchell, S., Potash, E., & Barocas, S. (2018). Prediction-based decisions and fairness: A catalogue of choices, assumptions, and definitions. ArXiv:1811.07867 [stat.AP]. Retrieved from http://arxiv.org /abs/1711.05144

Muñoz, C., Smith, M., & Patil, D. J. (2016). *Big data: A report on algorithmic systems, opportunity, and civil rights.* Washington, D.C.: Executive Osffice of the President.

Mutua, A. D. (2006). The rise, development and future directions of critical race theory and related scholarship. *Denver University Law Review*, 84, 329–394.

Nash, J. C. (2017). Intersectionality and its discontents. *American Quarterly*, 69(1), 117–129.

Noble, S. U. (2016). A future for intersectional Black feminist technology studies. *The Scholar & Feminist Online*, 13.3–14.1. Retrieved from http://sfonline.barnard.edu/traversing-technologies/safiya-umoja-noble-a-futurefor-

Noble, S. U. (2018). *Algorithms of oppression: How search engines reinforce racism*. New York, NY: New York University Press.

Overdorf, R., Kulynych, B., Balsa, E., Troncoso, C., & Gürses, S. (2018, December). Questioning the assumptions behind fairness solutions. Paper presented at the 32nd Conference on Neural information processing systems (NIPS 2018), Montreal, Canada.

Pasquale, F. (2016). *The black box society: The secret algorithms that control money and information* (Reprint ed.). Cambridge, MA: Harvard University Press.

Rosenblat, A., Randhava, R., Boyd, D., Gangadharan, S. P., & Yu, C. (2014a). *Data & civil rights: Consumer finance primer* [Report]. Data & Society Research Institute. Retrieved from http:// www.datacivil-rights.org/pubs/2014-1030/Finance.pdf

Seaver, N. (2017). Algorithms as culture: Some tactics for the ethnography of algorithmic systems. *Big Data & Society*, 4(2), 1–12.

Shew, A. (2017, November 11). Technoableism, cyborg bodies, and Mars *[Blog post]*. Retrieved from https://techanddisability.com/2017/11/11/technoableism-cyborg-bodies-and-mars/

Snow, J. (2018, February 14). "We're in a diversity crisis": Cofounder of Black in AI on what's poisoning algorithms in our lives. *MIT Technology Review*. Retrieved from https://www.technologyreview.com/s/610192/were-in-a-diversity-crisis-black-in-ais-founder-on-whats- poisoning-the-algorithms-in-our/

Spade, D. (2015). *Normal life: Administrative violence, critical trans politics, and the limits of law* (Revised and expanded ed.). Durham, NC: Duke University Press.

Sweeney, M. E. (2016). The intersectional interface. In S. U. Noble & B. M. Tynes (Eds.), *The intersectional internet: Race, sex, class, and culture online* (pp. 215–228). Switzerland: Peter Lang International Academic Publishers. University of Bath. (2017, April 13). Biased bots: Human prejudices sneak into AI systems [Press release]. Retrieved from http://www.bath.ac.uk/research/news/2017/04/13/biased-bots-artificialintelligence/

Young, I. M. (2006). Taking the basic structure seriously. *Perspectives on Politics*, 4(1), 91–97.

Zafar, M. B., Valera, I., Gomez Rodriguez, M., & Gummadi, K. P. (2017). In *Proceedings of the 26th International Conference on World Wide Web* (pp. 1171–1180). Perth, Australia: ACM Press.

CREATING OUTCOMES AND ACCURACY IN DATA ANALYTICS 8

When judging if a data analytics program works or not, we tend to focus on accuracy. In this book, we have broadened what we consider in adding questions around fairness, harms, rights, privacy, surveillance, etc. We turn now to identify the ethical issues in *accuracy* including choosing the outcome variable, measuring accuracy, and the problem of creating accuracy.

Choosing Outcomes. A facial recognition program analyzing a patient's face during a therapy session is predicting *something*. In other words, we have a problem in the world we are trying to solve, such as identifying individuals who need therapy. That phenomenon of interest then needs to be translated into an outcome variable such as "words per minute" to capture a frantic feeling of the patient or the outcome may be "shifting eyes" to capture someone feeling uncomfortable. The first step of any program is to create an outcome variable that measures something you are interested in—but the outcome is actually constructed based on the phenomenon of interest (what we are worried about or interested in the world) as well as what is easily measured and labeled by a program.[1]

The creation of the outcome variable is important to the ethics of data and analytics. The outcome variable chosen has implications as to what the organization thinks is important and whose interests are prioritized in the design of the data analytics program. For job search platforms, such as ZipRecruiter or LinkedIn, optimizing the number of applicants to any given job advertisement prioritizes the business placing ads and not the users looking for a job. The business placing ads benefits from more applicants, those looking for work benefit from better matches. Also, the outcome variable may or may not adequately represent the phenomenon of interest. In designing a distribution plan for the COVID-19 vaccine, Stanford created a score to estimate "does this person need a vaccine." The score may have been reliably and consistently predicted, but the score did not represent whether someone needed a vaccine. In other words, the score may measure whether a department had an outbreak of COVID-19, but the outbreak may not have anything to do with the risk of their job and more to do with the behavior of the employees while not at work (e.g., younger people getting a higher score). Finally, the outcome variable may adequately capture the phenomenon of interest for some people—but not all.

DOI: 10.1201/9781003278290-48

Measuring Accuracy. Accuracy is often used as the measure of a working data analytics program, where accuracy is how well the program predicts or categorizes people. When measuring a program's accuracy, companies often report the number of true positives: such as how many fraudulent claims are caught by AI Jim, or how many of those who cheat are caught by a cheating detection program. In this book, we have learned to be worried about the proportion of false positives and false negatives. The types of errors—false positives versus false negatives—are often *not* morally equivalent. For a given context, what types of mistakes are important? Which types are more morally fraught? For example, a false positive in the criminal justice system (falsely finding someone guilty) is more morally problematic than a false negative because we have a presumption of innocence in the United States. However, which type of error is preferred is based on the context of the decision.

In addition, the meaning of *inaccuracy* can vary from project to project. Attempting parity across types of mistakes or in reporting confidence intervals, where all types of mistakes are reported as similarly important, could mislead someone as to the ethical implications of the data analytics program. Accuracy for the majority (even if meaningful) does not mean a program is accurate for all groups. Programs may be more accurate or have a particular type of mistake for some groups (e.g., facial recognition and White men) and not others (e.g., facial recognition and Black women).

For some programs, however, the question as to the outcome of interest and how to measure if the program *works* is more ethically salient. For example, in predictive policing, law enforcement uses a program to predict if a crime is likely to occur in a particular neighborhood. Police can then deploy officers to that area. A popular predictive policing program, PredPol, focuses specifically on petty crimes and misdemeanors in the hopes that arrest for petty crimes may reduce felony crimes. However, the program predicts crimes based on training data of where people have been arrested in the past. A common complaint is that these programs are based on biased data and therefore predict in a biased manner.[2]

Predictive policing also exemplifies the ethical questions about creating outcomes and measuring accuracy. While petty crimes are the outcome of interest for PredPol, focusing on misdemeanors is not always the way to decrease crime; petty crime does, however, provide more data points and would therefore show more impact if one is to be found. Second, in measuring mistakes in this situation, what is the preferred or morally problematic type of mistake? Mistakenly over-policing an area with low crime or under-policing an area with high crime? And which mistake is the program more likely to create?

Third, how would one measure if such a program is "accurate" or "works"? When the prediction leads immediately to action (officers deployed), measuring accuracy becomes tricky. We will call this *creating accuracy*.

Creating Accuracy. We face the challenge in predictive data analytics in creating accuracy, where individuals with a particular outcome variable *are treated differently* than those with a different predictive score—making measuring accuracy very messy. In other words, when we measure and compare the end state of those labeled and those not labeled, is the comparison comparing similarly treated conditions? Figure 8.1 illustrates the problem.

Predictive analytics runs into the possible problem of *creating accuracy* in categorizing someone with an outcome variable (promotable, hirable, trustworthy, high likelihood of recidivism, etc.) which pushes the individual into a course of treatment that then creates the outcome predicted by the program.[3]

The case of predictive policing is perhaps the quintessential example of *creating accuracy*. Identifying a particular neighborhood as possibly being more likely to have petty crimes (the

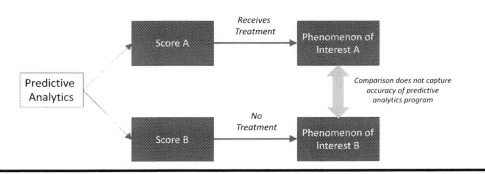

Figure 8.1   Measuring accuracy and treatment effects.

prediction) leads to more officers being sent to look for crimes in that neighborhood (the treatment). A larger number of officers find more crimes and arrest more people. This is the standard argument as to how predictive analytics can feed into creating a new reality and create the perception of being "accurate."

The case of Chicago's predictive policing program is an even more stark example of creating accuracy. Robert McDaniel was visited by Chicago police and told

> an algorithm built by the Chicago Police Department predicted—based on his proximity to and relationships with known shooters and shooting casualties—that McDaniel would be involved in a shooting. That he would be a "party to violence," but it wasn't clear what side of the barrel he might be on. He could be the shooter, he might get shot. They didn't know. But the data said he was at risk either way.[4]

McDaniel was also told that the police would be watching him. And while McDaniel had no violent history, he was suddenly under constant surveillance by the police. The data analytics program made a prediction, the police department was the immediate treatment. However, this increased attention and visits by the police looked suspicious to those in his neighborhood who thought he was working *with* the police. McDaniel was then shot—twice—by those in his neighborhood who believed he was a snitch given the amount of police attention he was receiving.[5] In this case, the program appears quite accurate since the prediction was that McDaniel would be involved in a shooting, and he was shot—twice.

This problem occurs frequently in predictive data analytics. At a parole hearing, courts may label a prisoner with a higher recidivism score predicting they are likely to commit more crimes (e.g., COMPAS). The courts then place additional requirements on those paroled prisoners (where they can live, drug tests, how frequently they need to check in, who they can live with, etc.) which make them more likely to commit a parole violation, which counts as a crime. The program created accuracy.

The issue is similar to measuring the treatment effect in medical research, only in medical research we are actually interested in how effective the treatment is, so there is an incentive to measure its effect. Here, for some companies developing a data analytics program, measuring the treatment effect means acknowledging that the data analytics program is, perhaps, not as accurate as once thought. In other words, firms selling data analytics programs may not want research into the idea of creating accuracy and measuring treatment effects to isolate whether their data analytics program actually "works." The more impact a treatment has—e.g., sending more police to a given area—the less the data analytics program actually works.

Treating People as Individuals. Finally, data analytics predictions that require a particular treatment—e.g., predicted likely to succeed and given additional help, predicted likely to be shot and given additional scrutiny, etc.—can undermine the individualization of the subjects and can harm the dignity of not being "seen" as an individual. The "deindividualization of the person" is the tendency to judge and treat people on the basis of group characteristics instead of on their own individual characteristics and merits.[6] In other words, the prediction and immediate treatment of someone as a cheater, fraud, criminal, not-hirable, etc., based on the possible characteristics they share with others, is seen as undermining their dignity as a human and the idea that, in some circumstances, people have a right to be treated as an individual.[7] Virginia Eubanks refers to this phenomenon as "flattening" the individual to a set of data points.

Is there an area where we should not make decisions because people like you "are never successful" or "will get into trouble"? Programs that attempt to predict people, with all their contextual and ever-changing attributes, attempt to "automate ambiguity," which Professor Birhane defines as when automation pretends to "impose order, equilibrium, and stability to the active, fluid, messy, and unpredictable nature of human behaviour and the social world at large."[8]

The problem of individualization is particularly salient when the prediction is "sticky" in that the label has a semi-permanent consequence for the individual. For example, when the categorization does not change over time or has consequences for someone over a long period of time, the prediction is sticky. Sticky predictions are morally important when the individual is at a transitional stage (e.g., entering into college, taking on a new job), or the impact is for pivotal decisions (getting a mortgage), or when the person will change (younger subjects).

Therefore, the ethical examination of data analytics programs would need to question the creation of the outcome variable, the measurement of accuracy (including the types of mistakes and which are preferred), and the possibility of creating accuracy through the program.

Summary of Readings

The readings in this section circle the issue of accuracy—how we measure accuracy and what accuracy, as measured, actually *means*. Rachel Thomas and David Uminsky focus on the measurement problem in "The Problem with Metrics Is a Fundamental Problem for AI."[9] They quote Goodhart's Law that *"When a measure becomes a target, it ceases to be a good measure."* The authors note that we often cannot measure the things that matter the most: e.g., trustworthiness of a person as an employee or consumer. As such, the outcome variables and metrics we choose are proxies for "what you really care about." In analyzing a data analytics program, one would examine whether the program fell into one of these traps:

- Any metric is just a proxy for what you really care about
- Metrics can, and will, be gamed
- Metrics tend to overemphasize short-term concerns
- Many online metrics are gathered in highly addictive environments

Thomas and Uminsky recommend a framework for a better use of metrics (and a more ethical data analytics program for us):

- Use a slate of metrics to get a fuller picture
- Combine metrics with qualitative accounts
- Involve a range of stakeholders, including those who will be most impacted

In "Designing Ethical Algorithms," I argue developers and data analysts should ensure algorithms support good decisions—including managing mistakes. This requires data analysts to *expect* mistakes to occur and designing data analytics programs should include planning the ability to identify, judge, and correct mistakes. While mistakes may be unintentional, ignoring, or even fostering mistakes is unethical. And, by creating inscrutable algorithms, which are difficult to understand or govern in use, developers are precluding users from being responsible for any mistakes. Ethical data analytics programs, plan for the identification, judgment, and correction of mistakes. Unethical programs allow mistakes to go unnoticed and perpetuate mistakes. In analyzing a data analytics program according to this reading, one would examine if the program (a) created mistakes and if the type of mistakes was appropriate for the decision context; and (b) allows for the identification, judgment, and correction of mistakes.

Related Cases

A number of the cases in this book touch upon the issues of creating outcomes and creating accuracy through data analytics: COMPAS, Medical triage algorithm, wrongfully accused, HireVue, and (in the next chapter) the cheating detection program for students. Here we focus on a Florida school's program with the local police to label their students as possible future criminals. The labeling of middle- and high-school students as pre-criminals has different consequences for a false positive versus a false negative. The case illustrates the ethical implications of creating outcomes and accuracy in data analytics and when there may be slippage between the outcome variable and the phenomenon of interest in the real world.

Notes

1. Often in class, when someone says that a measurement is objective, we will translate that to "that which is easily quantified and measured" to reinforce the idea that numbers do not mean "objective."
2. https://www.vice.com/en/article/d3m7jq/dozens-of-cities-have-secretly-experimented-with-predictive-policing-software. Predictive policing is "driven by what seems to be objective historical data that itself reflects longstanding and pervasive bias," [Shahid] Buttar [of the Electronic Frontier Foundation] said. "If you overpolice certain communities, and only detect crime within those communities, and then try to provide a heat map of predictions, any AI will predict that crimes will occur in the places that they've happened before." In addition, researchers have found that *dirty* data was included in the training data for many cities. Richardson, Rashida and Schultz, Jason and Crawford, Kate, "Dirty Data, Bad Predictions: How Civil Rights Violations Impact Police Data, Predictive Policing Systems, and Justice" (February 13, 2019). 94 *N.Y.U. L. REV. ONLINE*, 192 (2019), Available at SSRN: https://ssrn.com/abstract=3333423
3. Perdomo et al. refers to this phenomenon as "performative prediction" when predictions support decisions and also influence the outcome they aim to predict. Juan Perdomo et al., "Performative Prediction" (International Conference on Machine Learning, PMLR, 2020), 7599–7609. For example, when assessing someone as a credit risk, a bank may then immediately assign a higher interest rate, therefore making someone a higher credit risk by increasing their default risk. One way to identify this problem is when the distribution over data points begins to shift since the outcome of the data analytics program is impacting the outcome being measured.
4. Matt Stroud. 2021. "Heat Listed." *The Verge*. https://www.theverge.com/22444020/chicago-pd-predictive-policing-heat-list
5. Matt Stroud. 2021. "Heat Listed."

6. Anton Vedder. "KDD: The Challenge to Individualism," *Ethics and Information Technology.*

7. Kasper Lippert-Rasmussen, "'We Are All Different': Statistical Discrimination and the Right to Be Treated as an Individual," *The Journal of Ethics* 15, no. 1–2 (2011): 47–59.

8. Abeba Birhane, "The Impossibility of Automating Ambiguity," *Artificial Life*, 27, no. 1 (2021): 44–61.

9. Rachel Thomas and David Uminsky, "The Problem with Metrics Is a Fundamental Problem for Ai," *ArXiv Preprint ArXiv:2002.08512*, 2020.

Chapter 8.1

Pasco's Sheriff Uses Grades and Abuse Histories to Label Schoolchildren Potential Criminals: The Kids and Their Parents Don't Know*

Neil Bedi and Kathleen McGory

The Pasco Sheriff's Office keeps a secret list of kids it thinks could "fall into a life of crime" based on factors like whether they've been abused or gotten a D or an F in school, according to the agency's internal intelligence manual.

The Sheriff's Office assembles the list by combining the rosters for most middle and high schools in the county with records so sensitive, they're protected by state and federal law.

School district data shows which children are struggling academically, miss too many classes or are sent to the office for discipline. Records from the state Department of Children and Families flag kids who have witnessed household violence or experienced it themselves.

According to the manual, any one of those factors makes a child more likely to become a criminal.

Four hundred and twenty kids are on the list, the Sheriff's Office said.

The process largely plays out in secret. The Sheriff's Office doesn't tell the kids or their parents about the designation. In an interview, schools superintendent Kurt Browning said he was unaware the Sheriff's Office was using school data to identify kids who might become criminals. So were the principals of two high schools.

* Bedi, Neil and Kathleen McGory. 2020. "Pasco's Sheriff Uses Grades and Abuse Histories to Label Schoolchildren Potential Criminals. The kids and their parents don't know." *Tampa Bay Times*. November 19, 2020. https://projects.tampabay.com/projects/2020/investigations/police-pasco-sheriff-targeted/school-data/ Reprinted with permission.

DOI: 10.1201/9781003278290-49

The Department of Children and Families didn't answer when asked if it knew its data was being fed into such a system.

Sheriff Chris Nocco declined requests to be interviewed, and his agency did not make anyone from its intelligence-led policing or school resource divisions available for comment.

In a series of written statements, the Sheriff's Office said the list is used only to help the deputies assigned to middle and high schools offer "mentorship" and "resources" to students.

Asked for specifics, it pointed to one program where school resource officers take children fishing and another where they give clothes to kids in need.

Ten experts in law enforcement and student privacy questioned the justification for combing through thousands of students' education and child-welfare records.

They called the program highly unusual. Many said it was a clear misuse of children's confidential information that stretched the limits of the law.

"Can you imagine having your kid in that county and they might be on a list that says they may become a criminal?" said Linnette Attai, a consultant who helps companies and schools comply with student privacy laws.

"And you have no way of finding out if they are on that list?"

The Sheriff's Office said its data sharing practices with the school district date back 20 years and are crucial to keeping campuses safe.

It added that only a juvenile intelligence analyst and the school resource officers have access to the list and the underlying data.

The agency also objected to the characterization of the list as potential future criminals, saying it was also designed to identify students at risk for victimization, truancy, self-harm and substance abuse.

But the intelligence manual—an 82-page document[1] that school resource officers and other deputies are required to read (Figure 8.1.1)—doesn't mention those other risks. Instead, in five separate places, it describes efforts to pinpoint kids who are likely to become criminals.

The office could not provide any documents instructing school resource officers to interpret the list another way.

The list of school kids isn't the agency's only effort to identify and target people it considers likely to commit crimes. In September, a *Tampa Bay Times* investigation revealed that the department's intelligence arm also uses people's criminal histories and social networks to predict if they will break the law.

The Sheriff's Office pursues those people even when there's no evidence of a new crime. Former deputies told the *Times* they were ordered to harass people on the target list by visiting their homes repeatedly and looking for reasons to write tickets and make arrests. One in 10 of the people targeted have been teenagers.

The ways the agency has extended its intelligence effort into mining education and child-welfare records have not previously been reported.

Because the children themselves don't know if they've been flagged, it is difficult to say how it affects interactions between students and school resource officers or other deputies. The Sheriff's Office declined to release a copy of its list of students to the *Times*.

When a reporter described the effort to Browning, he said he did not find it concerning.

"We have an agreement with the Sheriff's Office," the superintendent said. "The agreement requires them to use (the data) for official law enforcement purposes. I have to assume that's exactly what they are using it for."

Later, in a written statement, he added: "If there is any need to revisit any aspect of our relationship, we will do so in a thoughtful manner with the goal of keeping our students and staff safe."

Two members of the Pasco School Board, Megan Harding and Alison Crumbley, described the district's relationship with the Sheriff's Office as strong and referenced safeguards to protect

EXCERPTS: **How the manual defines at-risk youth**

The following are some of the passages from the Pasco Sheriff's Office's intelligence-led policing manual that describe at-risk students as potential criminals and offenders.

Identifying at-risk youth who are destined to a life of crime and engaging them to prevent them from developing into prolific offenders also has significant crime prevention potential. Accurate identification and intervention of at-risk youth can set them on the right path. In Ratcliffe's book, he writes:

> David Farrington has pointed out that our knowledge of offending patterns is such that 'potential offenders can be identified at an early age with a reasonable degree of accuracy' (1990: 105-106). He estimated that the best predictors in 10-year-olds of having a criminal conviction later in life are socio-economic deprivation, antisocial parents and siblings, poor parental supervision and child rearing, coming from broken homes, low intelligence and a poor school record. However, many of these variables are unlikely to be available to police departments, so this information has little value from an intelligence-led policing perspective. (Ratcliffe, 2016: 44)

Often SROs will hear about past, present or future crimes well before others in the law enforcement community. In addition to scanning for information that may assist with active investigations, it is critical that SROs also look to identify students who are at-risk of developing into prolific offenders and engaging those students in an effort to get them back on the right track.

Figure 8.1.1 Excerpt from the manual for schools on what defines at-risk youth.

students' privacy. The agreement between the two institutions says the Sheriff's Office must keep the records confidential and use them in legal ways.

The three other School Board members did not return calls or declined to comment.

Experts said having school resource officers single out children could be harmful, especially if the kids were struggling at home or in school, or if they didn't trust police.

They also said the effort was based on flawed science and likely biased against children of color and children with disabilities.

"It is a recipe for violating people's rights and civil liberties," said Harold Jordan, a senior policy advocate for the American Civil Liberties Union of Pennsylvania.

Elsewhere in the country, scandals have erupted when law enforcement agencies were found to have access to children's private data, said Andrew Guthrie Ferguson, a law professor at American University and national expert in predictive policing.

Sensitive information about kids, Ferguson said, should remain "in the hands of people who can offer help."

"Police are not in the business of offering help to juveniles," he said. "They are in the business of policing."

Bad Grades and Childhood Trauma

In its intelligence manual, the Pasco Sheriff's Office says most police departments have no way of knowing if kids have "low intelligence" or come from "broken homes"—factors that can predict whether they'll break the law.

"Fortunately," it continues, "these records are available to us."

The manual says the Sheriff's Office has access to the information through partnerships with the Pasco school district and the state Department of Children and Families.

The district pays the sheriff $2.3 million annually to place 32 deputies in middle and high schools. It also provides access to its Early Warning System, which tracks all students' grades, attendance and behavior.

Separately, the Department of Children and Families allows law enforcement agencies across Florida to use to its child welfare database so they can investigate child abuse and find missing children. The database, known as the Florida Safe Families Network, contains detailed case notes and kids' abuse histories.

The Sheriff's Office has its own records, too, which indicate if children have been the subject of custody disputes, have run away from home, have violated the county's curfew for young people or have been caught with drugs or alcohol. The office also keeps track of who is friends with whom.

It feeds information from all three datasets into a system that scores kids in 16 different categories.[2] In each, children are assigned one of four labels: on track, at risk, off track or critical.

It doesn't take much to be designated "at risk."

Getting a D on your report card is enough, the manual says (Figure 8.1.2). So is missing school three or more times in a quarter.

Kids are also labeled "at risk" if they've experienced a childhood trauma. That includes witnessing household violence, being the victim of abuse or neglect, or having a parent go to prison.

Internal emails show the list was last updated in October for the new school year.

The agency said it only looks at data in schools where it provides school resource officers—the vast majority of the district's middle and high schools. In total, those schools have more than 30,000 students.

Elementary schools have armed security guards and are not included, the agency said.

The Sheriff's Office has been identifying and monitoring at-risk children as part of its intelligence operation since at least 2011, when Nocco first became sheriff.

That summer, school resource officers made hundreds of home visits to at-risk kids, according to news reports. They offered support to the children and their families, they told reporters at the time. But they also questioned them about local crimes and arrested kids who violated probation or curfew orders.

In one of its statements to the *Times*, the Sheriff's Office said it looks for alternatives to arrest "when possible" and that supporting struggling kids is an important part of any school resource officer's job.

Internal documents, however, show that those officers do more than mentor.

The intelligence manual encourages them to work their relationships with students to find "the seeds of criminal activity" and to collect information that can help with investigations.

"Often SROs will hear about past, present or future crimes well before others in the law enforcement community," the manual says.

One school resource officer's annual performance review, obtained by the *Times* through a public records request, noted he contributed to intelligence briefings. It also praised him for filing nearly two dozen "field interview reports" based on interactions with at-risk kids.

A 'Circular Effect'

Law enforcement and privacy experts found many aspects of the Sheriff's Office's formula for identifying kids alarming.

GRAPHIC: **FACTORS THAT CAN PUT YOUR CHILD ON THE AT-RISK LIST**

The Pasco Sheriff's Office uses data from the school district and the state Department of Children and Families, as well as its own records, to identify children it considers at risk of becoming criminals.

The Sheriff's Office analyzes the data for more than 30,000 students in most of the middle and high schools in the county. (Pasco Middle School, Pasco High School, Gulf Middle School, Gulf High School and Harry Schwettman Education Center have school resource officers from other law enforcement agencies, so their students' data is not included.)

The system flags kids who meet the "at-risk" criteria in 16 different categories.

Children who are deemed "on track" in all categories are removed from the list before it is distributed. The final version removes the underlying student data by using shaded labels to represent the child's risk level in each category. The color codes are: on-track (green), at-risk (yellow), off-track (pink) or critical (red).

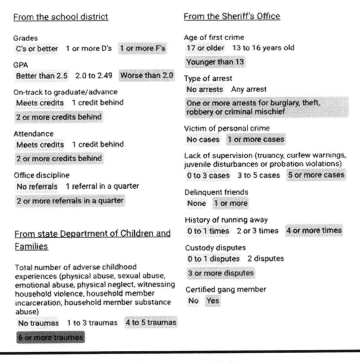

From the school district

Grades
C's or better   1 or more D's   1 or more F's

GPA
Better than 2.5   2.0 to 2.49   Worse than 2.0

On-track to graduate/advance
Meets credits   1 credit behind
2 or more credits behind

Attendance
Meets credits   1 credit behind
2 or more credits behind

Office discipline
No referrals   1 referral in a quarter
2 or more referrals in a quarter

From state Department of Children and Families

Total number of adverse childhood experiences (physical abuse, sexual abuse, emotional abuse, physical neglect, witnessing household violence, household member incarceration, household member substance abuse)
No traumas   1 to 3 traumas   4 to 5 traumas
6 or more traumas

From the Sheriff's Office

Age of first crime
17 or older   13 to 16 years old
Younger than 13

Type of arrest
No arrests   Any arrest
One or more arrests for burglary, theft, robbery or criminal mischief

Victim of personal crime
No cases   1 or more cases

Lack of supervision (truancy, curfew warnings, juvenile disturbances or probation violations)
0 to 3 cases   3 to 5 cases   5 or more cases

Delinquent friends
None   1 or more

History of running away
0 to 1 times   2 or 3 times   4 or more times

Custody disputes
0 to 1 disputes   2 disputes
3 or more disputes

Certified gang member
No   Yes

Figure 8.1.2   Factors that can put a child on the at-risk list.

Some metrics, they said, were completely outside of kids' control. Others were likely biased. Take school discipline.

In Pasco County, Black students and students with disabilities are twice as likely to be suspended or referred to law enforcement, according to federal data.

Bacardi Jackson, a senior supervising attorney for children's rights for the Southern Poverty Law Center, said designating those kids as potential criminals could have a "circular effect." They would likely receive even more attention from school resource officers and as a result, face additional discipline.

Leah Plunkett, an expert in digital privacy law and lecturer at Harvard Law School, said the program also appeared to be discriminatory.

Singling out kids based on whether they had been involved in custody disputes, for example, could be considered differential treatment based on family status, she said.

The Sheriff's Office says its program is based on research. It points to a 2015 study that found young people who had experienced multiple childhood traumas were at a higher risk of becoming serious, violent criminals than those who hadn't.

But David Kennedy, a renowned criminologist and professor at the John Jay College of Criminal Justice whose research is referenced in Pasco's manual, said the associations between childhood trauma and criminal behavior are "extremely weak." He said using them to make predictions about individuals "flies in the face of the science."

The methodology used by the Sheriff's Office, he added, was likely to generate a large pool of children, the vast majority of whom would never get in serious trouble.

"There's nothing—absolutely nothing—that can be fed into even the most sophisticated algorithm or risk-assessment tool based on information available when someone is a child that can say this person is going to be a criminal later on, much less a serious prolific criminal," he said.

Legal Concerns

After the *Times* started asking questions about the use of data to target young people, the Sheriff's Office seems to have started revamping elements of its program.

Emails show the agency has been drafting a policy for how school resource officers should interact with at-risk students that focuses more on offering support and building positive relationships.

Even with those changes, experts questioned whether using student data this way was legal.

Under federal law, education records can only be released to outside parties in certain circumstances.

Law enforcement agencies can use the information to help thwart school shootings and offer support to students who are in the juvenile justice system. But in cases like those, experts said, they can only look at records relating to a specific student or situation.

"You can't just give every student's record out," said LeRoy Rooker, who led the federal Department of Education's oversight of student privacy for more than two decades.

The law does say school resource officers can access education records because they can be considered "school officials." But under most circumstances, they can't share the records with the rest of the department, said Amelia Vance, a member of the Maryland Department of Education's Student Data Privacy Council who works for the nonprofit Future of Privacy Forum.

And they can't use them in a law enforcement investigation without permission from a parent, unless there is a court order or a health and safety emergency, Vance said.

In its statement, the Sheriff's Office said it had access to the data "lawfully" and noted that school resource officers receive annual training on the federal student privacy law.

The school district has recently been criticized for lax privacy practices. Last year, a state audit found that too many district employees had access to current and former students' sensitive data, including social security numbers. The district later revoked privileges for 570 employees.

Attai, the student privacy consultant, said the school district should take action in this case, too, and reconsider its arrangement with the Sheriff's Office.

"This is a district that is sending millions of dollars to the sheriff of Pasco County to target its students as criminals," she said.

Full rubric is online[3]**

Notes

1. https://www.documentcloud.org/documents/20412738-ilp_manual012918
2. https://www.documentcloud.org/documents/20412738-ilp_manual012918#document/p71 Educational risk factors include course performance (1 D), credits (1 behind), attendance (3-4 absences in a quarter), office discipline referrals (1 in a quarter), can make one at-risk. Next level is 'off track' then 'critical.'
3. ** https://www.documentcloud.org/documents/20412738-ilp_manual012918#document/p71

Chapter 8.2

Excerpt from Reliance on Metrics is a Fundamental Challenge for AI[*]

Rachel L. Thomas and David Uminsky

Introduction

Metrics can play a central role in decision making across data driven organizations and their advantages and disadvantages have been widely studied (Likierman 2009, Kaplan and Norton 1992). Metrics play an even more central role in AI algorithms and as such their risks and disadvantages are heightened. Some of the most alarming instances of AI algorithms run amok, such as recommendation algorithms contributing to radicalization (Ribeiro et al. 2019), teachers described as "creative and motivating" being fired by an algorithm (Tuque 2012), or essay grading software that rewards sophisticated garbage (Ramineni and Williamson 2018) all result from over-emphasizing metrics. We have to understand this dynamic in order to understand the urgent risks we are facing due to misuse of AI.

At their heart, what most current AI approaches do is to optimize metrics. The practice of optimizing metrics is not new nor unique to AI, yet AI can be particularly efficient (even too efficient!) at doing so. This unreasonable effectiveness at optimizing metrics results in one of the grand challenges in AI design and ethics: the metric optimization central to AI often leads to manipulation, gaming, a focus on short-term quantities (at the expense of longer-term concerns), and other undesirable consequences, particularly when done in an environment designed to exploit people's impulses and weaknesses. Moreover, this challenge also yields, in

[*] Thomas, Rachel and David Uminsky. 2020. The Problem with Metrics is a Fundamental Problem for AI. EDSC (Ethics of Data Science Conference) 2020. Reprinted with permission of the authors. Note: This is an excerpt from the original so footnote and endnote numbering may be modified.

DOI: 10.1201/9781003278290-50

parallel, an equally grand contradiction in AI development: optimizing metrics results in far from optimal outcomes.

Some of the issues with metrics are captured by Goodhart's Law, "When a measure becomes a target, it ceases to be a good measure" (Goodhart 2015 and Strathern 1997). We examine in this paper, through a review of a series of real-world case studies, how Goodhart's Law as well as additional consequences of AI's reliance on optimizing metrics is already having an impact in society. We find from this review the following well supported principles:

- Any metric is just a proxy for what you really care about
- Metrics can, and will, be gamed
- Metrics tend to overemphasize short-term concerns
- Many online metrics are gathered in highly addictive environments

Given the harms of over-emphasizing metrics, it is important to work to mitigate these issues which will remain in most use cases of AI. We conclude by proposing a framework for the healthier use of metrics that includes:

- Use a slate of metrics to get a fuller picture
- Combine metrics with qualitative accounts
- Involve a range of stakeholders, including those who will be most impacted

[…]

We Can't Measure the Things that Matter Most

Metrics are typically just a proxy for what we really care about. Mullainathan and Obermeyer (2017), cover an interesting example: the researchers investigate which factors in someone's electronic medical record are most predictive of a future stroke and find that several of the most predictive factors (such as accidental injury, a benign breast lump, or colonoscopy) don't make sense as risk factors for stroke. It turned out that the model was simply identifying people who utilize health care a lot. They didn't actually have data of who had a stroke (a physiological event in which regions of the brain are denied new oxygen); they had data about who had access to medical care, chose to go to a doctor, were given the needed tests, and had this billing code added to their chart. But a number of factors influence this process: who has health insurance or can afford their co-pay, who can take time off of work or find childcare, gender and racial biases that impact who gets accurate diagnoses, cultural factors, and more. As a result, the model was largely picking out people who utilized healthcare versus who did not.

This is an example of the common phenomenon of having to use proxies: You want to know what content users like, so you measure what they click on. You want to know which teachers are most effective, so you measure their students' test scores. You want to know about crime, so you measure arrests. These things are not the same. Many things we do care about cannot be measured. Metrics can be helpful, but we can't forget that they are just proxies.

As another example, Google used hours spent watching YouTube as a proxy for how happy users were with the content, writing on the Google blog that "If viewers are watching more YouTube, it signals to us that they're happier with the content they've found" (Meyerson 2012). Guillaume Chaslot, founder of independent watch group AlgoTransparency and an AI engineer who formerly worked at Google/YouTube, shares how this had the side effect of incentivizing conspiracy theories, since convincing users that the rest of the media is lying kept them watching more YouTube (Chaslot 2018).

Metrics Can, and Will, Be Gamed

It is almost inevitable that metrics will be gamed, particularly when they are given too much power. A detailed case study about "a system of governance of public services that combined targets with an element of terror" developed for England's health care system in the 2000s covers many ways that gaming can occur (Bevan and Hood 2006). The authors identify three well-documented forms of gaming from Soviet era production targets: (1) ratchet effects: 'a wise director fulfils the plan 105%, but never 125%', (2) threshold effects: crowd distribution towards target, (3) output distortions: achieve targets at the cost of significant but unmeasured aspects of performance. They then detail many specific examples of how gaming manifested in the English healthcare system. For example, targets around emergency department wait times led some hospitals to cancel scheduled operations in order to draft extra staff to the emergency room, to require patients to wait in queues of ambulances, and to turn stretchers into "beds" by putting them in hallways. There were also significant discrepancies in numbers reported by hospitals versus those reported by patients; for instance, around wait times, according to official numbers 90% of patients were seen in less than 4 hours, but only 69% of patients said they were seen in less than 4 hours when surveyed (Bevan and Hood 2006).

As education policy in the United States began over-emphasizing student test scores as the primary way to evaluate teachers, there have been widespread scandals of teachers and principals cheating by altering students' scores, in Georgia, Indiana, Massachusetts, Nevada, Virginia, Texas, and elsewhere (Gabriel 2010). One consequence of this is that teachers who don't cheat may be penalized or even fired, when it appears student test scores have dropped to more average levels under their instruction (Turque 2012). When metrics are given undue importance, attempts to game those metrics become common.

A modern AI case study can be drawn from recommendation systems, which are widely used across many platforms to rank and promote content for users. Platforms are rife with attempts to game their algorithms, to show up higher in search results or recommended content, through fake clicks, fake reviews, fake followers, and more (Tufekci 2019). There are entire marketplaces for purchasing fake reviews and fake followers, etc.

During one week in April 2019, Chaslot collected 84,695 videos from YouTube and analyzed the number of views and the number of channels from which they were recommended (Harwell and Timberg 2019). The state-owned media outlet Russia Today, abbreviated RT, was an extreme outlier in how much YouTube's algorithm had selected it to be recommended by a wide variety of other YouTube channels. According to Harwell (2019):

> Chaslot said in an interview that while the RT video ultimately did not get massive viewership—only about 55,000 views—the numbers of recommendations suggest that Russians have grown adept at manipulating YouTube's algorithm, which uses machine-learning software to surface videos it expects viewers will want to see. The result, Chaslot said, could be a gradual, subtle elevation of Russian views online because such videos result in more recommendations and, ultimately, more views that can generate more advertising revenue and reach.

Automatic essay grading software currently used in at least 22 USA states focuses primarily on metrics like sentence length, vocabulary, spelling, and subject-verb agreement, but is unable to evaluate aspects of writing that are hard to quantify, such as creativity. As a result, gibberish essays randomly generated by computer programs to contain lots of sophisticated words score well. Essays from students in mainland China, which do well on essay length and sophisticated word choice, received higher scores from the algorithms than from expert human graders, suggesting that these students may be using chunks of pre-memorized text (Ramineni and Williamson, 2018).

Metrics Overemphasize Short-Term Concerns

It is much easier to measure short-term quantities: click through rates, month-over-month churn, quarterly earnings. Many long-term trends have a complex mix of factors and are tougher to quantify. While short-term incentives have led YouTube's algorithm to promote pedophilia (Fisher and Taub 2019), white supremacy (Ribeiro et al. 2019), and flat-earth theories (Landrum 2018), the long-term impact on user trust will not be positive. Similarly, Facebook has been the subject of years worth of privacy scandals, political manipulation, and facilitating genocide (Vaidhyanathan 2018), which is now having a longer-term negative impact on Facebook's ability to recruit new engineers (Bowles 2018).

Simply measuring what users click on is a short-term concern, and does not take into account factors like the potential long-term impact of a long-form investigative article which may have taken months to research and which could help shape a reader's understanding of a complex issue and even lead to significant societal changes.

The Wells Fargo account fraud scandal provides a case study of how letting metrics replace strategy can harm a business (Harris and Tayler 2019). After identifying cross-selling as a measure of long-term customer relationships, Wells Fargo went overboard emphasizing the cross-selling metric: intense pressure on employees combined with an unethical sales culture led to 3.5 million fraudulent deposit and credit card accounts being opened without customers' consent. The metric of cross-selling is a much more short-term concern compared to the loftier goal of nurturing long-term customer relationships. Overemphasizing metrics removes our focus from long-term concerns such as our values, trust and reputation, and our impact on society and the environment, and myopically focuses on the short-term.

Many Metrics Gather Data of What We Do in Highly Addictive Environments

It matters which metrics we gather and in what environment we do so. Metrics such as what users click on, how much time they spend on sites, and "engagement" are heavily relied on by tech companies as proxies for user preference, and are used to drive important business decisions. Unfortunately, these metrics are gathered in environments engineered to be highly addictive, laden with dark patterns, and where financial and design decisions have already greatly circumscribed the range of options.

While this is not a characteristic inherent to metrics, it is a current reality of many of the metrics used by tech companies today. A large-scale study analyzing approximately 11K shopping websites found 1,818 dark patterns present on 1,254 websites, 11.1% of the total sites (Mathur et al.

2019). These dark patterns included obstruction, misdirection, and misrepresenting user actions. The study found that more popular websites were more likely to feature these dark patterns.

Zeynep Tufekci compares recommendation algorithms (such as YouTube choosing which videos to auto-play for you and Facebook deciding what to put at the top of your newsfeed) to a cafeteria shoving junk food into children's faces (Lewis 2018):

> This is a bit like an autopilot cafeteria in a school that has figured out children have sweet-teeth, and also like fatty and salty foods. So you make a line offering such food, automatically loading the next plate as soon as the bag of chips or candy in front of the young person has been consumed.

As those selections get normalized, the output becomes ever more extreme: "So the food gets higher and higher in sugar, fat and salt – natural human cravings – while the videos recommended and auto-played by YouTube get more and more bizarre or hateful."

Too many of our online environments are like this, with metrics capturing that we love sugar, fat, and salt, not taking into account that we are in the digital equivalent of a food desert and that companies haven't been required to put nutrition labels on what they are offering. Such metrics are not indicative of what we would prefer in a healthier or more empowering environment.

A Framework for a Healthier Use of Metrics

All this is not to say that we should throw metrics out altogether. Data can be valuable in helping us understand the world, test hypotheses, and move beyond gut instincts or hunches. Metrics can be useful when they are in their proper context and place. We propose a few mechanisms for addressing these issues:

- Use a slate of metrics to get a fuller picture
- Combine with qualitative accounts
- Involve a range of stakeholders, including those who will be most impacted

Use a Slate of Metrics to Get a Fuller Picture and Reduce Gaming

One way to keep metrics in their place is to consider a slate of many metrics for a fuller picture (and resist the temptation to try to boil these down to a single score). For instance, knowing the rates at which tech companies hire people from under-indexed groups is a very limited data point. For evaluating diversity and inclusion at tech companies, we need to know comparative promotion rates, cap table ownership, retention rates (many tech companies are revolving doors driving people from under-indexed groups away with their toxic cultures), number of harassment victims silenced by NDAs, rates of under-leveling, and more. Even then, all this data should still be combined with listening to first-person experiences of those working at these companies.

Likierman wrote in Harvard Business Review (2009) that using a diverse slate of metrics is one strategy to avoid gaming:

> It helps to diversify your metrics, because it's a lot harder to game several of them at once. [International law firm] Clifford Chance replaced its single metric of billable

hours with seven criteria on which to base bonuses: respect and mentoring, quality of work, excellence in client service, integrity, contribution to the community, commitment to diversity, and contribution to the firm as an institution.

Likierman (2009) also cites the example of Japanese telecommunications company SoftBank using performance metrics defined for three distinct time horizons to make them harder to game.

Combine with Qualitative Accounts

Columbia professor and New York Times Chief Data Scientist Chris Wiggins wrote that quantitative measures should always be combined with qualitative information,

> "Since we cannot know in advance every phenomenon users will experience, we cannot know in advance what metrics will quantify these phenomena. To that end, data scientists and machine learning engineers must partner with or learn the skills of user experience research, giving users a voice."
>
> **(Wiggins 2018)**

Proposals such as Model Cards for Model Reporting (Mitchell et al. 2019) and Datasheets for Datasets (Gebru et al. 2018) can be viewed in line with this thinking. These works acknowledge that the metrics typically accompanying models, such as performance on a particular dataset, are insufficient to cover the many complex interactions that can occur in real-world use, as the model is applied to different populations and in different use cases, and as the use potentially veers away from the initial intent. Mitchell et al. (2019) and Gebru et al. (2018) propose documenting much richer and more comprehensive details about a given model or dataset, including more qualitative aspects, such as intended use cases, ethical considerations, underlying assumptions, caveats, and more.

Involve a Range of Stakeholders, Including Those Who Will Be Most Impacted

Another key to keeping metrics in their proper place is to keep domain experts and those who will be most impacted closely involved in their development and use. Empowering a diverse group of stakeholders to understand the implications and underlying assumptions of AI models is one of the goals of Model Cards for Model Reporting (Mitchell et al. 2018). We suggest going even further and including these stakeholders in the initial development process of these metrics in the first place.

Tool 3 in the Markkula Center's Ethical Toolkit for Engineering/Design Practice (Vallor, Green, and Raicu 2018) is to "expand the ethical circle" to include the input of all stakeholders. They suggest a number of questions to ask about this topic, including:

■ Whose interests, desires, skills, experiences and values have we simply assumed, rather than actually consulted? Why have we done this, and with what justification?

- Who are all the stakeholders who will be directly affected by our product? How have their interests been protected? How do we know what their interests really are—have we asked?
- Who/which groups and individuals will be indirectly affected in significant ways? How have their interests been protected? How do we know what their interests really are—have we asked?

While their focus is on tech policy, the Diverse Voices paper (Young, Magassa, and Friedman 2019) provides a detailed methodology on how to elicit the expertise and feedback of underrepresented populations that would be useful in improving the design and implementation of metrics.

An additional argument for the importance of including a range of stakeholders comes from the fragile and elastic nature of deep learning algorithms combined with the incompatible incentives the owners of these algorithms have to address this fragility (Slee 2019). Specifically:

> …if subjects follow their incentives then the algorithm ceases to function as designed. To sustain their accuracy, algorithms need external rules to limit permissible responses. These rules form a set of guardrails which implement value judgments, keeping algorithms functioning by constraining the actions of subjects.

Slee proposes that external guardrails on how users are allowed to engage with the algorithms are a necessary corrective measure for the associated gaming and abuses cited above, but that the algorithm owners themselves are incentivized to create guardrails that don't align with their algorithms, an act of regulatory arbitrage. Given that guardrails are *a restriction on the user*, transparent and just corrective measures will depend on how effective the ethical circle has been expanded in the design and creation of the guardrails. Slee gives the example of the incompatible incentives Facebook faces in addressing ethical issues with its News Feed Algorithm, and suggests that journalists not tempted by the financial incentives driving Facebook would be better equipped to address this.

While it is impossible to simply oppose metrics, the harms caused when metrics are overemphasized include manipulation, gaming, a focus on short-term outcomes to the detriment of longer-term values, and other harmful consequences, particularly when done in an environment designed to exploit people's impulses and weaknesses, such as most of our online ecosystem. The unreasonable effectiveness of metric optimization in current AI approaches is a fundamental challenge to the field, and yields an inherent contradiction: solely optimizing metrics leads to far from optimal outcomes. However, we provide evidence in this paper that healthier use of metrics can be created by: (1) using a slate of metrics to get a fuller and more nuanced picture, (2) combining metrics with qualitative accounts, and (3) involving a range of stakeholders, including those who will be most impacted. This framework may help address the core paradox of metric optimization within AI, and not solely relying on metric optimization may lead to a more optimal use of AI.

References

Bowles, N. 2018. 'I Don't Really Want to Work for Facebook.' So Say Some Computer Science Students. *The New York Times*. Nov. 15, 2018.

Chaslot, G. 2018. How Algorithms Can Learn to Discredit the Media. *Medium*. Feb1, 2018. https://medium.com/@guillaumechaslot/how-algorithms-can-learn-to-discredit-the-media-d1360157c4fa

Fisher, M. and Taub, A. On YouTube's Digital Playground, an Open Gate for Pedophiles. *The New York Times*. June 3, 2019.

Gabriel, T. 2010. Under Pressure, Teachers Tamper With Tests. *The New York Times*. June 10, 2010.

Gebru, T.; Morgenstern, J.; Vecchione, B.; Vaughan, J.; Wallach, H.; Daumeé, H.; and Crawford, K. 2018. *Datasheets for Datasets*.

Goodhart, C. 2015. Goodhart's Law. In *The Encyclopedia of Central Banking*, ed. Rochon, L. and Rossi, S. 227–228. Cheltenham, UK: Edward Elgar Publishing.

Harris, M. and Tayler, B. 2019. Don't Let Metrics Undermine Your Business. *Harvard Business Review*, Sept-Oct 2019.

Harwell, D. and Timberg, C. 2019. YouTube recommended a Russian media site thousands of times for analysis of Mueller's report, a watchdog group says. *The Washington Post*, April 26, 2019.

Kaplan, R. and Norton D. 1992. The balanced scorecard: measures that drive performance. *Harvard Business Review*, 70 (1), 71–79, 1992.

Lewis, P. 2018. 'Fiction is outperforming reality': how YouTube's algorithm distorts truth, *The Guardian*, Feb 2, 2018.

Likierman, A. 2009. The Five Traps of Performance Measurement. *Harvard Business Review*. October2009. 87(10):96–101, 141.

Mathur, A.; Acar, G.; Friedman, M.; Lucherini, E.; Mayer, J.; Chetty, M.; and Narayanan, A. 2019. Dark Patterns at Scale: Findings from a Crawl of 11K Shopping Websites. *Proc. ACM Hum.-Comput. Interact.* November 2019. 3, CSCW, Article 81, 32 pages. https://doi.org/10.1145/3359183

Mitchell, M.; Wu, S.; Zaldivar, A.; Barnes, P.; Vasserman, L.; Hutchinson, B.; Spitzer, E.; Raji, I. D.; and Gebru, T. 2019. Model Cards for Model Reporting. In *Proceedings of the Conference on Fairness, Accountability, and Transparency (FAT* '19)*. ACM, New York, NY, USA, 220–229.

Mullainathan, S. and Obermeyer, Z. 2017. Does Machine Learning Automate Moral Hazard and Error? *Am Econ Rev.* 107(5): 476–480.

Ramineni, C. and Williamson, D. 2018. Understanding Mean Score Differences Between the e-rater® Automated Scoring Engine and Humans for Demographically Based Groups in the GRE® General Test. *ETS Research Report Series*, Volume 2018, Issue 1.

Ribeiro, M. H.; Ottoni, R.; West, R.; Almeida, V. A. F.; and Meira Jr., W. Auditing Radicalization Pathways on YouTube. ArXiv abs/1908.08313 (2019): 1–18.

Strathern, M. 1997. 'Improving ratings': audit in the British University System. *European Review*. Volume 5, Issue 03, pp 305–321.

Tufekci, Z. 2019. The Imperfect Truth About Finding Facts in a World of Fakes. *Wired*, March 2019.

Turque, B. 2012. 'Creative … motivating' and fired. *The Washington Post*. March 6, 2012.

Vaidhyanathan, S. 2018. *Antisocial Media: How Facebook Disconnects Us and Undermines Democracy*. New York: Oxford University Press.

Vallor, S.; Green, B.; and Raicu, I. 2018. Ethics in Technology Practice. *The Markkula Center for Applied Ethics at Santa Clara University. https://www.scu.edu/ethics/*

Young, M.; Magassa, L.; and Friedman, B. 2019. Toward inclusive tech policy design: a method for under-represented voices to strengthen tech policy documents. *Ethics and Information Technology*, https://doi .org/10.1007/s10676-019- 09497-z

Chapter 8.3

Excerpt from Designing Ethical Algorithms[*]

Kirsten Martin

[...]

Algorithmic Decisions Make Mistakes

Framing algorithms as taking on a role within a decision changes how we think about designing algorithms, because an important task in decisions concerns mistakes. All decisions contain the possibility of mistakes, and better decisions contain a vehicle to identify, judge, and fix mistakes. In manufacturing, the decision to ship final inventory includes a check to identify flaws, judge if the flaws are within an error range, and (if needed) assign someone to fix the mistake. Alternatively, a machine could be designed to ship inventory without allowing for any of these steps, thereby precluding humans from identifying, judging, and correcting mistakes. For example, the shipping label could be glued on the final product and shipped directly from the machine.

In general, managers, firms, and management researchers persistently seek to understand bad business decisions and avoid mistakes. Decisions can be unethical, unfair, bad for the long-term value creation for stakeholders, or just self-defeating. Firms and managers make bad decisions due to bad inputs (myopic, limited sources), bad reasoning (maximizing on a single objective function) and bad execution (sloppiness, laziness, lack of courage). In doing so, managers regularly do things they should not such as promote the wrong person, and not do things they should, such as pass over a good hire. Management scholars research how to minimize and manage these bad decisions. The goal is to support good decisions, that create value and minimize mistakes.

Algorithmic decisions are no different. Algorithms, whether as merely augmenting or automating human decisions, are used in important organizational decisions such as who is hired, who is fired, whether someone is deemed a terrorist, the terms offered for financing, whether an insurance company negotiates over a claim, and even how someone is sentenced.[1] In other words, we need

[*] Kirsten Martin, "Designing Ethical Algorithms.," *MIS Quarterly Executive* 18, no. 2 (2019). Reprinted with permission. Note: This is an excerpt from the original so footnote and endnote numbering may be modified.

DOI: 10.1201/9781003278290-51

to ask whether and how algorithmic decisions produce biased "answers" or mistakes, to categorize the mistakes and discuss who should be responsible for managing the mistakes. These mistakes destroy value, lead to bad decisions, and end up on the front page of the newspaper.

Mistakes—an action or judgment that is misguided or wrong—need not necessarily be unethical or unfair. Mistakes occur all the time in business and in life due to mistaken information or reasoning. However, ungoverned decisions, where mistakes are unaddressed, nurtured, or even exacerbated, are unethical. Ungoverned decisions show a certain casual disregard as to the (perhaps) unintended harms of the decisions; for important decisions, this could mean issues of unfairness or diminished rights. Further, some algorithmic decisions learn from previous decisions and can therefore quickly cause mistakes to impact thousands if not millions of decisions. In other words, while mistakes may be inadvertent, governance decisions are not. A lack of intentionality may be a fair excuse for a mistake but not a valid excuse for not governing mistakes.

Below I explain how algorithms may be designed to preclude individuals from identifying, judging and correcting mistakes and, therefore, take on the responsibility for those mistakes.

Identifying Mistakes in Algorithmic Decisions

The Algorithmic decision mistakes fall into two classes—category mistakes and process mistakes.

Category Mistakes. Algorithms that categorize and prioritize individuals, such as individuals who need an ad, prefer a search result, are employable, are a terrorist, have cancer, etc., scan large datasets to label individuals. These algorithmic decisions are vulnerable to two types of classic mistakes, which I call category mistakes (Figure 8.3.1). First, false positives, or Type I errors, are the incorrect assignment of a label. For example, when someone is labeled as a terrorist when they are not, when someone is categorized as having cancer when they do not, or when someone is labeled as a future criminal when they are not. False positives are when the algorithmic decision (or human-centric decision) scans the universe of individuals and mistakenly labels the individual as within the preferred category.

Alternatively, false negatives, or Type II errors, incorrectly exclude someone from a category; false negatives encompass letting someone slip away by not labeling them. For example, identifying someone as not a terrorist when they are, categorizing someone as not employable when

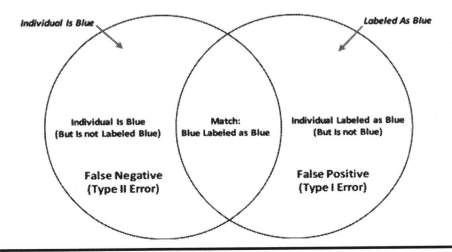

Figure 8.3.1 Venn diagram of types of mistakes.

they are, or labeling someone as not a future criminal when they are. False negatives entail the algorithmic decision scanning the universe of individuals and not labeling them as the preferred category when the label may actual fit. Figure 2 illustrates the types of mistakes decisions.

Importantly, all decisions, both human-centric and algorithmic, contain a probability for each type of mistake. And, the likelihood of each type of mistake is not necessarily symmetrical, in general or across specific groups of individuals, as depicted in Figure 2. The mistake could be more frequently found in one group of individuals, making the mistake itself biased. For example, recent work in facial recognition illustrates that the distribution of category mistakes is not consistent across races and ethnicities: facial recognition algorithms are good at identifying white males and regularly misidentify black females.[2]

Process Mistakes. In addition to categorizing incorrectly, algorithms can make mistakes in the process of making the decision. Whereas category mistakes show up in the outcome of the algorithm, process mistakes occur when an algorithm makes a mistake in how the decision was made, regardless of the outcome. Table 1 compares these types of mistakes for different decision contexts such as education, public policy, health care, banking etc. Each context has norms as to the type of factors that should be considered in making a decision. When a doctor is making a diagnosis and treatment plan, using your friends' high school GPA[3] would be inappropriate and outside the norm of the decision. Similarly, when being approved for public housing or food stamps, considering the applicant's father's undergraduate degree would be inappropriate. Particularly with machine learning or neural networks (i.e., algorithms that "learn" what factors are important from existing data), the resulting decision may inadvertently use inappropriate factors in the decision—even when not designed to do so. Previous work has highlighted how algorithms must abide by procedural norms, including considerations of due process, disparate treatment and impact, and norms of justice.[4] These types of process mistakes may be by design or learned by the algorithm from biased training data.

Judging Mistakes

Within a given context, certain types of mistakes are preferred, and not all mistakes are a cause for concern. For a medical decision, the preference may be to mistakenly identify someone as having cancer rather than letting cancer go undetected. The medical community tends to avoid false negatives, whereby a patient is not labeled as sick when the individual is actually sick or hurt. The justice system tends to avoid false positives for convictions and has a slight preference to not mistakenly find someone guilty who is actually innocent. However, the COMPAS algorithm is an interesting example: black defendants were more likely to be mistakenly labeled "likely to re-offend" (when they were not), compared to white defendants.

Even within a type of decision, mistake preferences are not necessarily consistent. Firms may find nothing worse than hiring the wrong person or categorizing someone as a "good hire" (when they are not), thereby avoiding a false positive. However, earlier in the hiring process, greater diversity can be achieved by being overly inclusive in who is brought in for an interview. The preference earlier in the hiring process is to label someone as possibly good even if they are not, thereby preferring a false positive. Even within hiring, the preferred type of mistake may shift. Importantly, the appropriateness of a mistake, the risk tolerance and error ranges for mistakes, and the preference for a type of mistake is contingent upon the decision context and would need to be considered in the design and use of the algorithm. Mistakes occur in all decisions, and certain types of mistakes are preferred depending on the context of the decision.

Correcting Mistakes

Finally, algorithmic decisions need an ability to correct mistakes by adjusting the algorithm's outcome in the larger decision—particularly when the outcome feeds back into the dataset used to train or test the algorithm. Machine learning algorithms learn from existing data what factors are important for a given result. If uncorrected, the mistakes can feed into a cycle whereby the mistake becomes a part of the dataset the algorithm depends upon. And, when an algorithm creates mistakes with increasing frequency, the technology appears to learn from current mistakes, create "answers" that are mistakes, and contribute to a new data set that is riddled with mistakes from which future algorithms will learn—thus creating a biased cycle of discrimination with little human intervention required.[5]

Algorithms and Ethical Decision-Making

Mistakes Go Unnoticed in the Current Algorithmic Decision Model

Mistakes can easily be missed due to the current model of algorithmic decision-making that presumes a rational decision model with linear processing and a goal of "efficiency." Mistakes can be missed because of an algorithm's artificially inflated role within a decision, where the algorithm is framed as a powerful yet inscrutable entity that does not make mistakes. Algorithms can wrongly be presumed to be clean or not biased and viewed with a veneer of objectivity, where individuals defer to the perceived power of the very notion of an algorithm. In addition, algorithms are a less visible part of the decision and often less accessible to question—even being held secret. The current approach to algorithmic decision-making runs the danger of treating the algorithmic process and output as both inevitable and final, where the algorithmic outcome cannot be questioned or changed, and mistakes are left ungoverned. Fortunately, decision-making scholarship offers solutions to both of these objectivity problems.

Adding Social Embeddedness Helps to Identify and Judge Mistakes

The problem of viewing a decision as inevitable can be countered by acknowledging the context, or social embeddedness,[6] of the algorithmic decision-making process (Figure 8.3.2): how

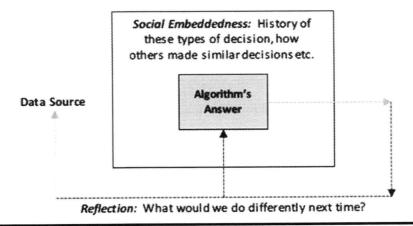

Figure 8.3.2   Adding social embeddedness and reflection to improve decisions.

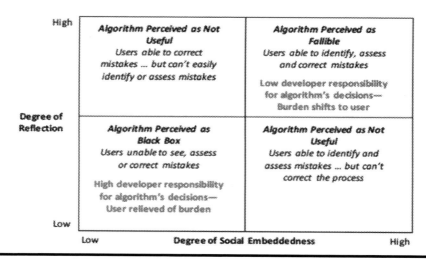

Figure 8.3.3 How social embeddedness and reflection can shift the responsibility of the decision from the developer to the user.

the algorithmic process and output could have been done differently and produced a different outcome. In more human-centric decision-making, social anchoring helps put the decision into context and perspective by checking in with others. Similarly, philosopher Richard Rorty calls for greater contingency to put quandaries into perspective.[7] For algorithmic decisions, algorithm developers could add visualization to show how the output such as a defendant's risk assessment score, compares to others committing the same crime or to those from the same state, illustrates how sensitive the outcome is based on the assumptions made, allows the user of the algorithm to change some of the input variables to see how the answer changes, or provides sensitivity tests. Such a contingent approach would be part of the design and development of the algorithm. Importantly, mistakes can only be identified if the output is placed into the perspective of similar decisions, the larger context, and historical decisions as depicted in Figure 3 (Figure 8.3.3). The historical perspective may not necessarily be better or more desirable, but it does offer a way to measure progress in striving for a better decision.

Adding Reflection Helps to Correct Mistakes

Second, the issue of viewing algorithmic decisions with a degree of finality suggests users do not question changes for the future, as if the algorithm and the surrounding decision-making assemblage offer the best we have to offer without mistakes. In human-centric decision-making, reflection in decisions calls for the ability to go back to revisit, challenge and question the outcome and process; in pragmatic terms, Richard Rorty calls on us to not treat the decision like a final vocabulary but rather with an ironic view of the decision.[8] For algorithmic decision-making, designers would need to inscribe[9] the ability to go back to question algorithmic output with due process and reflection. For example, in using algorithms for worker evaluations, such as analyzing technology workers for idea generation or sifting through potential employees for a job, a weakness in judging the effectiveness of the algorithm is the difficulty of finding false negatives—i.e., people the algorithm falsely labels as "bad." The company does not know what happened to the good applicant that got away and therefore how ineffective the algorithm might be. However, such examinations are possible. As noted by Cathy O'Neil, the author of *Weapons of Math Destruction*, Amazon goes to great lengths to make sure the "right" decision is made, in terms of customer retention and marketing techniques, and is able to find the false negatives and correct the algorithm, illustrating that reflection is possible if designed into the algorithm. Algorithmic decision-making can incorporate the ability to revisit the answers to ensure that the classification is working as desired and not creating mistakes.

Notes

1. See: (1) Angwin, J., Kirchner, L., Larson, J. and Mattu, S. "Machine Bias: There's Software Used Across the Country to Predict Future Criminals. And it's biased against blacks," *ProPublica*, May 23, 2016, available at https://www.propublica.org/article/machine-bias-risk-assessments-in-criminal-sentencing; (2) Brown, K. When Facebook decides who's a terrorist, *Splinter*, October 11, 2016, available at http://fusion.net/story/356354/facebook-kashmir-terrorism/; and (3) O'Neil, C. *Weapons of Math Destruction: How Big Data Increases Inequality and Threatens Democracy*, Crown Publishing Group, 2016.
2. Buolamwini, J. and Gebru, G. "Gender Shades: Intersectional Accuracy Disparities in Commercial Gender Classification," *Proceedings of the 1st Conference on Fairness, Accountability and Transparency* (81), 2018, pp. 77–91.
3. Grade point average—a number representing the average value of the accumulated final grades earned in courses over time.
4. For more information, see: (1) O'Neil, C., op. cit., 2016; (2) Citron, D. K. "Technological Due Process," *Washington University Law Review* (85:6), 2008, pp. 1249-; and (3) Barocas, S. and Selbst, A. D. "Big Data's Disparate Impact," *California Law Review* (104:3), June 2016, pp. 671–732.
5. Cathy O'Neil refers to these types of exacerbating impacts—where the algorithm produces biased mistakes, impacts the less fortunate and does so at the velocity associated with big data initiatives—as weapons of math destruction. See O'Neil, C., op. cit., 2016.
6. Martin, K. E. and Parmar, L. P. "Assumptions in Decision Making Scholarship: Implications for Business Ethics Research," *Journal of Business Ethics* (105:3), May 2012, pp. 289–306.
7. Rorty, R. "Contingency, Irony, and Solidarity," *Cambridge University Press*, 1989; see also Sonenshein, "The Role of Construction, Intuition, and Justification in Responding to Ethical Issues at Work: The Sensemaking-Intuition Model," *Academy of Management Review* (32:4), October 2007, 1022–1040.
8. Rorty, R. op cit., 1989.
9. Madeleine Akrich argues that "… a large part of the work of innovators is that of 'inscribing' this vision of (or prediction about) the world in the technical content of the new object." Designers of technology—including algorithms—make assumptions about what the world will do and inscribe during design how their technology will fit into that world. See Akrich, M. "The De-Scription of Technological Objects," in *Shaping Technology/Building Society: Studies in Sociotechnical Change*, W. Bijkerand J. Law (eds.), MIT Press, 1992, pp. 205–224.

GAMIFICATION, MANIPULATION, AND DATA ANALYTICS

9

Organizations increasingly use analytics to nudge, influence, or possibly undermine the decision-making of individuals. For example, Amazon uses a program that creates games for its warehouse employees to improve efficiency.[1] The games allow workers to win prizes for reaching certain targets:

> The games can register the completion of the task, which is tracked by scanning devices, and can pit individuals, teams or entire floors in a race to pick or stow Lego sets, cellphone cases or dish soap, for instance. Game-playing employees are rewarded with points, virtual badges and other goodies throughout a shift.[2]

Managers can increase productivity goals and the games would hide the higher goals by subtly changing the employee's target. So, rewards for handling 20 customers can be shifted to 22 or 25 customers without the worker noticing (the algorithm is kept secret).

This type of gamification is a part of a suite of data analytics tactics designed to influence decision-making, which includes the use of dark patterns, manipulative advertising, and deepfakes. All four seek to influence an individual—their beliefs, their behaviors, their decisions—in a manner that is not obvious to the target. The attempt by companies to exploit the cognitive limitations of consumers is not novel, as noted by Ryan Calo, Professor of Law at the University of Washington.[3] Professor Calo links the idea back to early attempts to influence or undermine consumer decision-making through marketing. Technology now allows companies to "design every aspect of the interaction with the consumer" thereby giving companies more opportunities to change consumer decisions. These tactics of data analytics become problematic when they undermine the autonomy of the individuals or cause the target harm.

Dark Patterns. Nudges are techniques, like default settings or ordering of choices, that subtly guide people to a decision that the designer has in mind.[4] Dark patterns are user interface design choices that lead, deceive, or manipulate users into making decisions they might not otherwise make.[5] Narayanan et al. see dark patterns as a combination of nudges with manipulative practices.

DOI: 10.1201/9781003278290-52

One insidious use of dark patterns is to manipulate users into disclosing more data.[6] This can be through linking the sharing of information to in-app benefits, hiding data protection options behind layers of interfaces, or changing the default setting and making the "accept" buttons more obvious than "do not accept."[7]

Manipulative Advertising. Through the tracking of consumers online, data brokers have access to many of our concerns, preferences, and vulnerabilities: e.g., whether someone is in financial distress, having a health crisis, or battling an addiction. And these vulnerabilities are valuable to marketers in order to silently steer consumers' decisions toward the manipulator's interests. *Targeted manipulation is the covert leveraging of a specific target's vulnerabilities to steer their decisions to the manipulator's interests.* The hiddenness differentiates manipulation from mere persuasion. Persuasion works because the tactic is known by the target, whereas manipulation works only if the tactics are hidden. In fact, manipulation is necessary when direct, open appeals to the preferences of the target do not work. One can attempt to persuade a child to put on clothes or a consumer to buy a soft drink by openly engaging with the target with cogent (or not so cogent) arguments. In this way, manipulation starts where persuasion ends—where the manipulator ceases to engage openly with the target in a way that the target could counter. Defenders of manipulation broaden the definition to include persuasion and advertising, thereby rendering the definition of manipulation so broad as to include legitimate acts—and making the act impossible to regulate.[8] Here we focus on manipulation as being covert in steering the target's interests.

Gamification. Gamification is the use of game design elements in non-game contexts and has been used on employees and users.[9] Businesses use alternative incentives, such as digital points, badges, and friendly competitions in the workplace to motivate particular behaviors of employees. Target is a good example of the use of gamification: Target has a check-out game where cashiers saw a signal as to whether their scan was fast enough (G for fast enough and R for too slow). Cashiers did get faster and reported higher work satisfaction.[10] The question for companies is when does gamification cross a line to becoming exploitive of users or employees by not only getting them to do something the company wants, but getting them to do something *they did not want to do or if it is against their interests.*

Deepfakes. AI-generated fake videos, or deepfake videos, gained traction in 2017 through a Reddit account (named Deepfakes) that posted nonconsensual pornography created with AI face-swapping technology. In that same year, researchers at the University of Washington created technology to modify a video to make it appear the speakers said something they did not.[11] Now the term *deepfake* is used for AI-generated, highly realistic impersonating videos.[12] This technology can be used in education and art; however, the harms from the proliferation of deepfake videos span from harming individuals to exploitation and sabotage.[13] For example, the majority of deepfake videos are nonconsensual pornography and the majority of the victims of deepfake pornography are women.[14] Deepfake technology has also been used in disinformation campaigns in elections and, as we read in this chapter, the technology can be used for advertising. In fact, a growing industry is in deepfake detection in order to identify and takedown harmful deepfakes.

When employed in their best possible use, these tactics act for the betterment of the individual (the target) and society. For example, gamification has been used to increase job satisfaction; manipulation has been used to get a child to put on clothes in the winter; deepfakes can be used in education to offer a video in other languages; dark patterns can lead people to become organ donors or save for retirement. However, when employed in alternative uses, these data analytics tactics can be exploitive and undermine individuals' decision-making.

These tactics—manipulation, deepfakes, nudges, and gamification—can undermine the target's ability to make their own decisions. In doing so, these tactics can not only diminish individual welfare but also diminish the autonomy of the individual. Autonomy is considered an end worth protecting not in terms of optimizing a decision or in service of some larger good but because maintaining autonomy allows an individual to be the author of her own decisions.[15] Someone who is autonomous is able to evaluate options, assess plans, and decide what is best.

Summary of Readings

In this excerpt from "More than Just a Game: Ethical Issues in Gamification,"[16] Professors Tae Wan Kim and Kevin Werbach develop a framework to address the major ethical considerations associated with gamification. Importantly, the authors do not see gamification as inherently wrong and note valid uses of the technique. In analyzing a data analytics program using this framework, one would ask if the use of gamification practices: (1) take unfair advantage of workers (e.g., exploitation); (2) infringe any involved workers' or customers' autonomy (e.g., manipulation); (3) intentionally or unintentionally harm workers and other involved parties; or (4) have a negative effect on the moral character of involved parties.

In this excerpt from "Manipulation, Choice, and Privacy,"[17] I focus on manipulation and the collection of intimate data about individuals. Data traffickers gather information about individuals, "to predict if someone is depressed, anorexic, addicted to drugs or alcohol, or has a medical condition." Online-marketing companies pay top dollar for consumers in financial and emotional difficulty "to promote gambling, cures, rehab, and payday loans and to more effectively target vulnerable consumers generally."[18] Note, that the most money is not spent targeting people *who have disposable money to spend*. Instead, online advertising is able to predict vulnerabilities and those vulnerabilities are what is valuable to advertisers.

Importantly, these potential weaknesses, e.g., whether someone is in financial distress, having a health crisis, or battling an addiction, are valuable to marketers and ad networks in order to silently steer consumers' market actions toward the manipulator's interests. I define targeted manipulation as the covert leveraging of a specific target's vulnerabilities to steer their decisions to the manipulator's interests. One examining a data analytics program according to this excerpt would look for (1) the use of a target's vulnerabilities, (2) to steer their decisions to the manipulator's interests, and (3) in a manner that is covert. While the paper is focused on manipulative advertising and targeted marketing online, the idea of manipulation could apply to data analytics programs that generally seek to influence individuals' behavior such as those included in this introduction.

In this excerpt from "Ethics of the Attention Economy: The Problem of Social Media Addiction," Professors Vikram Bhargava and Manuel Velasquez explore how the design of user interfaces could create social media addiction.[19] Internet addiction has garnered substantial attention in research and practice. Investors in Facebook and Apple have spoken out about the problem of teenagers becoming addicted to technologies and internet addiction has received government attention in some countries including the establishment of clinics devoted to treating internet addiction.

The authors characterize the kind of wrong involved when social media companies addict their users. Addicting users to social media is wrong because it unjustifiably harms users and undermines autonomy and does so in a way that is both demeaning and objectionably exploitative. The authors argue that the way in which social media companies addict their users is demeaning because of how social media platforms get users to provide the very data that will be used to addict them.

Related Cases

Two cases are included that highlight the issues around manipulation and autonomy. First, the use of deepfakes in advertising is explored in "How Deepfakes Could Change Fashion Advertising." The combination of a better deepfake technology and the ability to hyper-targeted ads created for an individual allows marketing companies to create a visually appealing ad *based on the attributes of the consumer*. In fact, technology is available to *place* the consumer in the ad. This is desirable because marketers know that "When consumers see products as extensions of themselves, they are willing to buy more, pay a higher price and advocate to friends."[20] So, placing people in ads, or creating people in ads that *look* like the targeted individual, is known to make people subconsciously want to pay more for the product.

Note how consumers are framed as approving this tactic: the proof used is that individuals were willing to use a free deepfake app that allowed them to see themselves dancing by just uploading a picture. Uploading the picture to a game is framed as providing consent for deepfake advertising later. However, we know from Chapter 3 that individuals share information in a context (game that allows you to see yourself dancing) while having expectations of how the data is used (not being manipulated by deepfake ads).

Second, Uber uses gamification and nudges in order to get their drivers to work more hours.[21] This includes letting drivers know when they are close to a target and automatically showing drivers the next ride opportunity without any effort from the driver. For each, the readings offer boundary conditions as to when data analytics programs cross a line and unethically undermine the autonomy of the individual.

Notes

1. Paris Martineau and Mark Di Stefano. 2021. "Amazon Expands Effort to 'Gamify' Warehouse Work." *The Information*, March 15, 2021. https://www.theinformation.com/articles/amazon-expands -effort-to-gamify-warehouse-work
2. Greg Bensinger. 2019. "'MissionRacer': How Amazon Turned the Tedium of Warehouse Work into a Game." *The Washington Post.* May 21, 2019. https://www.washingtonpost.com/technology/2019/05 /21/missionracer-how-amazon-turned-tedium-warehouse-work-into-game/
3. Ryan Calo, "Digital Market Manipulation," *George Washington Law Review* 82, no. 4 (2014).
4. Nudges, or any part of a choice architecture that alters people's behavior, became famous with a book: Richard Thaler and Cass Sunstein. 2009. *Nudge: Improving Decisions About Health, Wealth, and Happiness.* Penguin Books.
5. Arvind Narayanan et al., "Dark Patterns: Past, Present, and Future," *Queue* 18, no. 2 (2020): 67–92.
6. Alessandro Acquisti et al., "Nudges for Privacy and Security: Understanding and Assisting Users' Choices Online," *ACM Computing Surveys (CSUR)* 50, no. 3 (2017): 1–41.
7. Ari Ezra Waldman, "Cognitive Biases, Dark Patterns, and the 'Privacy Paradox,'" *Current Opinion in Psychology* 31 (2020): 105–109.
8. In fact, conflating manipulation with persuasion makes manipulation harmless and omnipresent. Sunstein defines manipulation as a form of persuasion and then summarizes, "the problem is that as defined here, manipulation can plausibly be said to be pervasive. It can be found on television, on the Internet, in every political campaign, in countless markets, in friendships, and in family life." Sunstein, "Fifty Shades of Manipulation." 8.
9. Sebastian Deterding et al., "From Game Design Elements to Gamefulness: Defining Gamification," 2011, 9–15.
10. Tae Wan Kim, "Gamification of Labor and the Charge of Exploitation," *Journal of Business Ethics*, 152, no. 1 (2018): 27–39.

11. James Vincent, "New AI Research Makes It Easier to Create Fake Footage of Someone Speaking," *VERGE* (July 12, 2017), https://www.theverge.com/2017/7/12/15957844/ai-fake-video-audio-speech-obama

12. Siwei Lyu. 2020. "Deepfakes and the New AI-Generated Fake Media Creation-Detection Arms Race" *Scientific American*. July 20, 2020. https://www.scientificamerican.com/article/detecting-deepfakes1/

13. Bobby Chesney and Danielle Citron, "Deep Fakes: A Looming Challenge for Privacy, Democracy, and National Security," *Calif. L. Rev.* 107 (2019): 1753. In addition, Chesney and Citron introduce the concept of the Liar's Dividend: "Deep fakes will make it easier for liars to deny the truth in distinct ways …. some will try to escape accountability for their actions by denouncing authentic video and audio as deep fakes." (p. 1785). The proliferation of deep fakes pose a threat to institutional trust (we don't know what to trust and what is fake) as well as making it easier for liars to deny the truth.

14. Mary Anne Franks and Ari Ezra Waldman, "Sex, Lies, and Videotape: Deep Fakes and Free Speech Delusions," *Md. L. Rev.* 78 (2018): 892.

15. Daniel Susser, Beate Roessler, and Helen Nissenbaum, "Technology, Autonomy, and Manipulation," *Internet Policy Review*, 8, no. 2 (2019).

16. Tae Wan Kim and Kevin Werbach, "More than Just a Game: Ethical Issues in Gamification," *Ethics and Information Technology*, 18, no. 2 (2016): 157–73.

17. Kirsten E. Martin, "Manipulation, Choice, and Privacy," *Albany Law Review*, 2021, https://doi.org/10.2139/ssrn.3491696

18. https://www.wordstream.com/blog/ws/2017/06/27/most-expensive-keywords Examples of keywords related to urgent problems were ranked by how much marketers were willing to pay for them and included: "Bail bonds" at #2 "Lawyer" at #4 "Cash services & payday loans" at #7 "Rehab" at #11 "Plumber" at #18 "Termites" at #19 "Pest control" at #20.

19. Vikram R. Bhargava and Manuel Velasquez, "Ethics of the Attention Economy: The Problem of Social Media Addiction," *Business Ethics Quarterly*, 2020, 1–39.

20. Kati Chitrakorn. 2021. "How Deepfakes Could Change Fashion Advertising." *VogueBusiness*, https://www.voguebusiness.com/companies/how-deepfakes-could-change-fashion-advertising-influencer-marketing

21. Noam Schieber. 2017. "How Uber Uses Psychological Tricks to Push Its Drivers' Buttons." *The New York Times*. April 2, 2017. https://www.nytimes.com/interactive/2017/04/02/technology/uber-drivers-psychological-tricks.html

Chapter 9.1

How Uber Uses Psychological Tricks to Push Its Drivers' Buttons*

Noam Scheiber

The company has undertaken an extraordinary experiment in behavioral science to subtly entice an independent work force to maximize its growth.

The secretive ride-hailing giant Uber rarely discusses internal matters in public. But in March, facing crises on multiple fronts, top officials convened a call for reporters to insist that Uber was changing its culture and would no longer tolerate "brilliant jerks."

Notably, the company also announced that it would fix its troubled relationship with drivers, who have complained for years about falling pay and arbitrary treatment.

"We've underinvested in the driver experience," a senior official said. "We are now re-examining everything we do in order to rebuild that love."

And yet even as Uber talks up its determination to treat drivers more humanely, it is engaged in an extraordinary behind-the-scenes experiment in behavioral science to manipulate them in the service of its corporate growth—an effort whose dimensions became evident in interviews with several dozen current and former Uber officials, drivers and social scientists, as well as a review of behavioral research.

Uber's innovations reflect the changing ways companies are managing workers amid the rise of the freelance-based "gig economy." Its drivers are officially independent business owners rather than traditional employees with set schedules. This allows Uber to minimize labor costs, but means it cannot compel drivers to show up at a specific place and time. And this lack of control can wreak havoc on a service whose goal is to seamlessly transport passengers whenever and wherever they want.

Uber helps solve this fundamental problem by using psychological inducements and other techniques unearthed by social science to influence when, where and how long drivers work. It's

---

* Scheiber, Noam. 2017. "How Uber Uses Psychological Tricks to Push Its Drivers' Buttons." *The New York Times*. April 2, 2017. Reprinted with permission.

DOI: 10.1201/9781003278290-53

a quest for a perfectly efficient system: a balance between rider demand and driver supply at the lowest cost to passengers and the company.

Employing hundreds of social scientists and data scientists, Uber has experimented with video game techniques, graphics and noncash rewards of little value that can prod drivers into working longer and harder—and sometimes at hours and locations that are less lucrative for them.

To keep drivers on the road, the company has exploited some people's tendency to set earnings goals—alerting them that they are ever so close to hitting a precious target when they try to log off. It has even concocted an algorithm similar to a Netflix feature that automatically loads the next program, which many experts believe encourages binge-watching. In Uber's case, this means sending drivers their next fare opportunity before their current ride is even over.

And most of this happens without giving off a whiff of coercion.

"We show drivers areas of high demand or incentivize them to drive more," said Michael Amodeo, an Uber spokesman. "But any driver can stop work literally at the tap of a button—the decision whether or not to drive is 100 percent theirs."

Uber's recent emphasis on drivers is no accident. As problems have mounted at the company, from an allegation of sexual harassment in its offices to revelations that it created a tool to deliberately evade regulatory scrutiny, Uber has made softening its posture toward drivers a litmus test of its ability to become a better corporate citizen. The tension was particularly evident after its chief executive, Travis Kalanick, engaged in a heated argument with a driver that was captured in a viral video obtained by Bloomberg and that prompted an abject apology.

But an examination by The New York Times found that Uber is continuing apace in its struggle to wield the upper hand with drivers. And as so-called platform-mediated work like driving for Uber increasingly becomes the way people make a living, the company's example illustrates that pulling psychological levers may eventually become the reigning approach to managing the American worker.

While Uber is arguably the biggest and most sophisticated player in inducing workers to serve its corporate goals, other "gig economy" platforms are also involved. Uber's main competitor, Lyft, and popular delivery services like Postmates rely on similar approaches. So do companies and individuals posting assignments on crowdsourcing sites like Amazon Mechanical Turk, where hundreds of thousands of workers earn piece-rate wages by completing discrete tasks.

Of course, many companies try to nudge consumers into buying their products and services using psychological tricks. But extending these efforts to the work force is potentially transformative.

Though employers have long borrowed insights from social science to get more out of their workers—tech companies like Google have calculated that employees interact more with unfamiliar colleagues when they can graze together at snack bars—they are constrained in doing so. A large body of law and custom in the United States holds that because employers have far more power over their employees than businesses do over their customers, they must provide them with far greater protections—not least, a minimum wage and overtime pay.

Uber exists in a kind of legal and ethical purgatory, however. Because its drivers are independent contractors, they lack most of the protections associated with employment. By mastering their workers' mental circuitry, Uber and the like may be taking the economy back toward a pre-New Deal era when businesses had enormous power over workers and few checks on their ability to exploit it.

"We're talking about this kind of manipulation that literally affects people's income," said Ryan Calo, a law professor at the University of Washington who with Alex Rosenblat has written a paper on the way companies use data and algorithms to exploit psychological weaknesses. Uber officials, he said, are "using what they know about drivers, their control over the interface and the terms of transaction to channel the behavior of the driver in the direction they want it to go."

An Empathy Question

In early 2016, a group of roughly 100 Uber employees responsible for signing up drivers and getting them to drive more voted to change its name—from "supply growth" to "driver growth."

The vote was not unprompted. For much of the previous year, Uber executives had agonized over how to lower the rate at which drivers were deserting the platform.

Alongside Uber's already daunting targets for expanding its pool of drivers to meet mounting demand, the high turnover threatened to cap the company's growth and throw it into crisis.

Uber conducted interviews and focus groups while executives peppered employees with questions like, "What are we doing to have more empathy for the driver side of the equation?"

Underlying the tension was the fact that Uber's interests and those of drivers are at odds on some level. Drivers, who typically keep what's left of their gross fare after Uber takes a roughly 25 percent commission, prefer some scarcity in their ranks to keep them busier and push up earnings. For its part, Uber is desperate to avoid shortages, seeking instead to serve every customer quickly, ideally in five minutes or less.

This is particularly true of shortages so pronounced as to create a "surge"—that is, a higher fare than normal. While surges do mitigate shortages, they do so in part by repelling passengers, something directly at odds with Uber's long-term goal of dominating the industry. "For us, it's better not to surge," said Daniel Graf, Uber's vice president of product. "If we don't surge, we can produce more rides."

As a result, much of Uber's communication with drivers over the years has aimed at combating shortages by advising drivers to move to areas where they exist, or where they might arise. Uber encouraged its local managers to experiment with ways of achieving this.

"It was all day long, every day—texts, emails, pop-ups: 'Hey, the morning rush has started. Get to this area, that's where demand is biggest,'" said Ed Frantzen, a veteran Uber driver in the Chicago area. "It was always, constantly, trying to get you into a certain direction."

Some local managers who were men went so far as to adopt a female persona for texting drivers, having found that the uptake was higher when they did.

"'Laura' would tell drivers: 'Hey, the concert's about to let out. You should head over there,'" said John P. Parker, a manager in Uber's Dallas office in 2014 and 2015, referring to one of the personas. "We have an overwhelmingly male driver population."

Uber acknowledged that it had experimented with female personas to increase engagement with drivers.

The friction over meeting demand was compounded by complaints about arrangements like aggressive car leases that required many drivers to work upward of 50 or 60 hours each week to eke out a profit. Uber officials began to worry that a driver backlash was putting them at a strategic disadvantage in their competition with Lyft, which had cultivated a reputation for being more driver-friendly.

Uber had long been a reflection of Mr. Kalanick, its charismatic and hard-charging chief, who has often involved himself in corporate minutiae. According to an article in The Information, Mr. Kalanick had complained to subordinates that he was not informed sooner about a glitch with the company's push notifications and had personally weighed in on the time at which employees could receive free dinner.

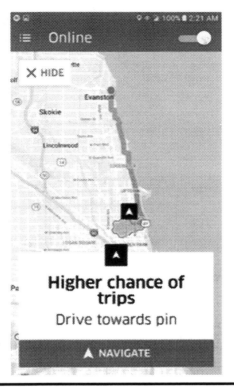

Figure 9.1.1 A screengrab of a prompt that Eli Solomon, an Uber driver in the Chicago area, received on his app.

Now Uber began a process of, in effect, becoming a little less like Mr. Kalanick, and a little more like Lyft.

It rethought a lease program, softened the hectoring tone of its messages and limited their volume. At times it became positively cheery.

During roughly the same period, Uber was increasingly concerned that many new drivers were leaving the platform before completing the 25 rides that would earn them a signing bonus. To stem that tide, Uber officials in some cities began experimenting with simple encouragement: You're almost halfway there, congratulations!

While the experiment seemed warm and innocuous, it had in fact been exquisitely calibrated. The company's data scientists had previously discovered that once drivers reached the 25-ride threshold, their rate of attrition fell sharply.

And psychologists and video game designers have long known that encouragement toward a concrete goal can motivate people to complete a task.

"It's getting you to internalize the company's goals," said Chelsea Howe, a prominent video game designer who has spoken out against coercive psychological techniques deployed in games. "Internalized motivation is the most powerful kind."

Mr. Amodeo, the Uber spokesman, defended the practice. "We try to make the early experience as good as possible, but also as realistic as possible," he said. "We want people to decide for themselves if driving is right for them."

That making drivers feel good could be compatible with treating them as lab subjects was no surprise. None other than Lyft itself had shown as much several years earlier.

In 2013, the company hired a consulting firm to figure out how to encourage more driving during the platform's busiest hours.

At the time, Lyft drivers could voluntarily sign up in advance for shifts. The consultants devised an experiment in which the company showed one group of inexperienced drivers how much more they would make by moving from a slow period like Tuesday morning to a busy time like Friday night—about $15 more per hour.

For another group, Lyft reversed the calculation, displaying how much drivers were losing by sticking with Tuesdays.

The latter had a more significant effect on increasing the hours drivers scheduled during busy periods.

Kristen Berman, one of the consultants, explained at a presentation in 2014 that the experiment had roots in the field of behavioral economics, which studies the cognitive hang-ups that frequently skew decision-making. Its central finding derived from a concept known as loss aversion, which holds that people "dislike losing more than they like gaining," Ms. Berman said.

Still, Ms. Berman disclosed in an interview, Lyft eventually decided against using the loss-aversion approach, suggesting that the company has drawn brighter lines when it comes to potential manipulation.

Almost There

As he tried to log off at 7:13 a.m. on New Year's Day last year, Josh Streeter, then an Uber driver in the Tampa, Fla., area, received a message on the company's driver app with the headline "Make it to $330." The text then explained: "You're $10 away from making $330 in net earnings. Are you sure you want to go offline?" Below were two prompts: "Go offline" and "Keep driving." The latter was already highlighted.

"I've got screen shots with dozens of these messages," said Mr. Streeter, who began driving full time for Lyft and then Uber in 2014 but quit last year to invest in real estate.

Mr. Streeter was not alone. For months, when drivers tried to log out, the app would frequently tell them they were only a certain amount away from making a seemingly arbitrary sum for the day, or from matching their earnings from that point one week earlier.

The messages were intended to exploit another relatively widespread behavioral tic—people's preoccupation with goals—to nudge them into driving longer.

Over the past 20 years, behavioral economists have found evidence for a phenomenon known as income targeting, in which workers who can decide how long to work each day, like cab drivers, do so with a goal in mind—say, $100—much the way marathon runners try to get their time below four hours or three hours.

While there is debate among economists as to how widespread the practice is and how strictly cabdrivers follow such targets, top officials at Uber and Lyft have certainly concluded that many of their drivers set income goals. "Others are motivated by an income target for sure," said Brian Hsu, the Lyft vice president in charge of supply. "You hear stories about people who want to buy that next thing." He added, "We've started to allow drivers to set up those goals as well in the app."

Uber even published a study last year, using its vast pile of data on drivers' rides and hours, finding that a "substantial, although not most, fraction of partners" practice an extreme form of income targeting when they start on the platform, though they abandon it as they gain more experience. Strict income targeting is highly inefficient because it leads drivers to work long hours on days when business is slow and their hourly take is low, and to knock off early on days when business is brisk.

The beauty of the messages that Uber sent Mr. Streeter and his fellow drivers is that the drivers need not have even had a specific income goal in mind in order for the messages to work. Some of the most addictive games ever made, like the 1980s and '90s hit Tetris, rely on a feeling of progress toward a goal that is always just beyond the player's grasp. As the psychologist Adam Alter writes in his book "Irresistible," this mental state has a name: the "ludic loop." (The term was coined by the anthropologist and slot machine expert Natasha Schüll.)

Uber, for its part, appears to be aware of the ludic loop. In its messages to drivers, it included a graphic of an engine gauge with a needle that came tantalizingly close to, but was still short of, a dollar sign.

And the ludic loop is far from the only video game feature that Uber has adapted as a way of keeping drivers on the road.

At any moment, the app shows drivers how many trips they have taken in the current week, how much money they have made, how much time they have spent logged on and what their overall rating from passengers is. All of these metrics can stimulate the competitive juices that drive compulsive game-playing.

"The whole thing is like a video game," said Eli Solomon, a veteran Uber and Lyft driver in the Chicago area, who said he sometimes had to fight the urge to work more after glancing at his data (Figure 9.1.1).

Figure 9.1.2   One of the messages Uber has sent its drivers to encourage them to stay on the road.

Sometimes the so-called gamification is quite literal (Figure 9.1.2). Like players on video game platforms such as Xbox, PlayStation and Pogo, Uber drivers can earn badges for achievements like Above and Beyond (denoted on the app by a cartoon of a rocket blasting off), Excellent Service (marked by a picture of a sparkling diamond) and Entertaining Drive (a pair of Groucho Marx glasses with nose and eyebrows).

Of course, managers have been borrowing from the logic of games for generations, as when they set up contests and competition among workers. More overt forms of gamification have proliferated during the past decade. For example, Microsoft has used the approach to entice workers to perform the otherwise sleep-inducing task of software debugging.

But Uber can go much further. Because it mediates its drivers' entire work experience through an app, there are few limits to the elements it can gamify. Uber collects staggering amounts of data that allow it to discard game features that do not work and refine those that do. And because its workers are contractors, the gamification strategies are not hemmed in by employment law.

Kevin Werbach, a business professor who has written extensively on the subject, said that while gamification could be a force for good in the gig economy—for example, by creating bonds among workers who do not share a physical space—there was a danger of abuse. "If what you're doing is basically saying, 'We've found a cheap way to get you to do work without paying you for it, we'll pay you in badges that don't cost anything,' that's a manipulative way to go about it," he said.

For some drivers, that is precisely the effect. Scott Weber said he drove full time most weeks last year, picking up passengers in the Tampa area for both Uber and Lyft, yet made less than $20,000 before expenses like gas and maintenance. "I was a business that had a loss," said Mr. Weber, who is looking for another job. "I'm using payday loans."

Still, when asked about the badges he earns while driving for Uber, Mr. Weber practically gushed. "I've got currently 12 excellent-service and nine great-conversation badges," he said in an interview in early March. "It tells me where I'm at."

'Constantly Busy'

When asked whether Uber's product managers and data scientists were akin to developers at a social gaming company like Zynga, Jonathan Hall, Uber's head of economic and policy research, accepted the analogy but rejected the implication.

"I think there's something to that, but ultimately Zynga should worry mostly about how fun its games are rather than trying to get you to play a little bit more by some trick," he said. He argued that exploiting people's psychological tics was unlikely to have more than a marginal effect on how long they played Zynga's games or drove for Uber. It is "icing on the cake," he said.

Mr. Hall is clearly right about the effects of certain techniques, like those pitched at drivers' tendency to set income targets or to focus more on losses than gains. On the other hand, even features that produce relatively small changes in driving patterns can become quite important to a company like Uber.

According to Mr. Parker, the former Uber manager in Dallas, increasing the number of drivers on the road by 20 percent at certain hours of the day, or in a busy part of town, can rein in a large fare surge.

More important, some of the psychological levers that Uber pulls to increase the supply of drivers have quite powerful effects.

Consider an algorithm called forward dispatch—Lyft has a similar one—that dispatches a new ride to a driver before the current one ends. Forward dispatch shortens waiting times for passengers, who may no longer have to wait for a driver 10 minutes away when a second driver is dropping off a passenger two minutes away.

Perhaps no less important, forward dispatch causes drivers to stay on the road substantially longer during busy periods—a key goal for both companies.

Uber and Lyft explain this in essentially the same way. "Drivers keep telling us the worst thing is when they're idle for a long time," said Kevin Fan, the director of product at Lyft. "If it's slow, they're going to go sign off. We want to make sure they're constantly busy."

While this is unquestionably true, there is another way to think of the logic of forward dispatch: It overrides self-control.

Perhaps the most prominent example is that such automatic queuing appears to have fostered the rise of binge-watching on Netflix. "When one program is nearing the end of its running time, Netflix will automatically cue up the next episode in that series for you," wrote the scholars Matthew Pittman and Kim Sheehan in a 2015 study of the phenomenon. "It requires very little effort to binge on Netflix; in fact, it takes more effort to stop than to keep going."

As with viewers and binge-watching, many drivers appear to enjoy the forward-dispatch feature, which can increase earnings by keeping them busier. But it can also work against their interests by increasing the number of drivers on the road and defusing fare surges. And whether they enjoy it is separate from the question of agency—whether they have it, or whether the company does.

Uber officials say the feature initially produced so many rides at times that drivers began to experience a chronic Netflix ailment—the inability to stop for a bathroom break. Amid the uproar, Uber introduced a pause button.

"Drivers were saying: 'I can never go offline. I'm on just continuous trips. This is a problem.' So we redesigned it," said Maya Choksi, a senior Uber official in charge of building products that help drivers. "In the middle of the trip, you can say, 'Stop giving me requests.' So you can have more control over when you want to stop driving."

It is true that drivers can pause the services' automatic queuing feature if they need to refill their tanks, or empty them, as the case may be. Yet once they log back in and accept their next ride, the feature kicks in again. To disable it, they would have to pause it every time they picked up a new passenger. By contrast, even Netflix allows users to permanently turn off its automatic queuing feature, known as Post-Play.

This pre-emptive hard-wiring can have a huge influence on behavior, said David Laibson, the chairman of the economics department at Harvard and a leading behavioral economist. Perhaps most notably, as Ms. Rosenblat and Luke Stark observed in an influential paper on these practices, Uber's app does not let drivers see where a passenger is going before accepting the ride, making it hard to judge how profitable a trip will be.

Sometimes all that is necessary is the mere setting of a so-called default. Because humans tend to be governed by inertia, automatically enrolling them in retirement savings plans and then allowing them to opt out results in far higher participation than letting them opt in. Making Post-Play the default can have the same effect.

"If done right, these things can be socially beneficial," Mr. Laibson said. "But you can think of all sorts of choice architecture that are quite contrary to human well-being."

Even Mr. Hall, the Uber research director who downplayed the importance of behavioral economics to the company, did make at least one concession. "The optimal default we set is that we want you to do as much work as there is to do," he said of the company's app. "You're not required to by any means. But that's the default."

Imagining the Future

There are aspects of the platforms that genuinely do increase drivers' control over their work lives, as Uber frequently points out. Unlike most workers, an Uber driver can put in a few hours each day between dropping children off at school and picking them up in the afternoon.

Uber is even in the process of developing a feature that allows drivers to tell the app in advance that they need to arrive at a given location at a given time. "If you need to pick up your kids at soccer practice at 6 p.m.," said Nundu Janakiram, the Uber official in charge of products that improve drivers' experiences, "it will start to give you trips to take you in the general direction to get to a specific place in time."

There is also the possibility that as the online gig economy matures, companies like Uber may adopt a set of norms that limit their ability to manipulate workers through cleverly designed apps.

Kelly Peters, chief executive of BEworks, a management consulting firm specializing in behavioral science, argued that the same data that makes it easier for Uber to nudge drivers into working an additional 30 or 60 minutes also makes it hard to escape the obligation to look after them.

For example, the company has access to a variety of metrics, like braking and acceleration speed, that indicate whether someone is driving erratically and may need to rest. "The next step may be individualized targeting and nudging in the moment," Ms. Peters said. "'Hey, you just got three passengers in a row who said they felt unsafe. Go home.'" Uber has already rolled out efforts in this vein in numerous cities.

That moment of maturity does not appear to have arrived yet, however. Consider a prompt that Uber rolled out this year, inviting drivers to press a large box if they want the app to navigate them to an area where they have a "higher chance" of finding passengers. The accompanying graphic resembles the one that indicates that an area's fares are "surging," except in this case fares are not necessarily higher.

Some drivers believe that the intent is to trick them into driving where Uber wants them to go, rather than where driving would be most profitable, by implying that they will find a surge there. "They're trying to move people where they want them," said Mr. Weber, the Tampa-area driver. "But you get there and it's nothing. It happens all the time." Mr. Weber noted that the design of the graphic makes the prompt much easier to accept than decline, which requires pressing a small rectangle in the top left corner.

Uber said that the feature was an experiment intended primarily to help new drivers who frequently say they do not know where to find passengers, and that it could be changed if drivers were dissatisfied.

Individual features aside, the broader question of how much Uber seeks to influence drivers through behavioral science may come down to how much its business model requires it.

While the company has made no secret of its investment in self-driving cars, it could be a decade or more before they completely replace human drivers. In the meantime, as long as Uber continues to set growth and passenger volume as critical goals, it will have an incentive to make wringing more hours out of drivers a higher priority than the drivers' bottom line whenever it faces a close call between the two.

It will also have an incentive to obtain these hours as cheaply as possible. And there is simply no cheaper way than hiring contractors and nudging them to drive when and where they are needed. Industry insiders estimate that relying on independent contractors rather than employees can lower direct costs by roughly 25 percent.

Moreover, the contractor model itself provides a strong impetus for companies like Uber to grow. Many companies in the gig economy simply do not have enough workers, or rich enough data about their workers' behavior, to navigate busy periods using nudges and the like. To avoid chronic understaffing, they have switched to an employee model that allows them to compel workers to log in when the companies most need them.

Once companies achieve a certain scale, on the other hand, they enter a virtuous cycle: The risk of understaffing drops with a big enough pool of workers, and the cost savings of using contractors begins to outweigh the inefficiencies. This in turn frees up money to enter new markets and acquire new customers, which makes the contractor model still more efficient, and throws off still more savings.

It is, as a result, not too hard to imagine a future in which massive digital platforms like Uber have an appetite for tens of millions of workers—not only for ferrying people, but also for delivering food and retail goods. Nor is it hard to imagine workers' obliging them, perhaps because their skills do not match the needs of more traditional employers, or because they need to supplement their wages.

In such an economy, experts say, using big data and algorithms to manage workers will not simply be a niche phenomenon. It may become one of the most common ways of managing the American labor force.

> "You have all these players entering into this space, and the assumption is they'll do it through vast armies of underemployed people looking for extra hours, and we can control every nuance about what they do but not have to pay them,"

said David Weil, the top wage-and-hour official under President Barack Obama.

When you stop to consider the enormous cost advantages, Mr. Weil said, "it says to me this is an area that will grow fast."

Chapter 9.2

How Deepfakes Could Change Fashion Advertising*

Kati Chitrakorn

Deepfakes are moving out of the darker corners of the internet. Tech experts predict positive applications for fashion.

A 2018 Zalando campaign featuring model Cara Delevingne across 290,000 localised ads was achieved using deepfake technology to produce a range of alternative shots and voice fonts. Now, as the algorithms for manipulating and synthesising media become more powerful, the fashion sector is beginning to take notice.

In the tech world, deepfakes specifically refer to media produced by artificial intelligence technology called generative adversarial networks. Deepfakes are video or audio that has been modified, such as by changing a face, the words spoken or the language used. The term was first coined on the internet in 2017 by combining "deep-learning" and "fakes".

Zalando's campaign ran on Facebook across 12 countries, gaining 180 million impressions across social media, according to Infinitizer, the micro-targeting specialist agency that worked on the campaign.

Advances in technology have made it harder to distinguish between real and fabricated media. Deepfakes have had a bad reputation, not least because the majority are fake pornography. Critics also point out the dangers of political deepfakes that might generate convincing fake news. "Any digital window to the real world is one that can be duped and faked sometimes," acknowledges Sunny Dhillon, a VC who has invested in a deepfake marketing company.

Like a rising number of marketers and investors, Dhillon emphasises the "absolutely positive" applications of the technology. As COVID-19 lockdowns restrict in-person activities, and advertisers explore digital technologies, deepfakes have significant potential for experiential marketing. Face-swapping technology, which once took weeks to execute, can now be completed in minutes with a result that is "Hollywood quality", according to Reface co-founder Dima Shvets.

---

* Chitrakorn, Kati. 2021. "How Deepfakes Could Change Fashion Advertising." *Vogue Business*. Reprinted with permission. https://www.voguebusiness.com/companies/how-deepfakes-could-change-fashion-advertising -influencer-marketing

                                                  DOI: 10.1201/9781003278290-54

Experiential marketing tends to be associated with the physical environment, like pop-up stores, but deepfake technology can bring experiential marketing online, directly to consumers, says Dhillon. Examples might include interactive fashion weeks or gaming experiences, he says.

Dynamic Influencer Marketing

Dynamic campaigns—the term for micro-targeted ads at scale—are becoming a key tool in a marketer's arsenal. Deepfakes have the potential to help brands reach customers with highly targeted and personalised messaging. For influencers and celebrities, deepfakes help them to easily broaden their reach by agreeing to front a fashion ad campaign and model clothes without even turning up for a photo shoot. Millions of different deepfake ads can instantly run across platforms like Facebook, while up to 100 different influencer ads targeted at various audiences could run, says Simon Lejeune, a growth marketing consultant.

It's not a giant leap in a world where digital identities such as gaming avatars are already overlapping with real-life identities, while CGI models are mixing with real-life influencers. Imagine a new kind of deal, where an influencer provides a brand with a sample of 15 minutes of audio content and a few video shots. Using deepfake technology, a brand can transform that content into thousands of hyper-targeted ads. "Influencers might start licensing their faces and voices to brands," says Lejeune. "A computer can take their faces and voices and reproduce them in 16 different languages or poses, and select the most persuasive one."

Over the past year, brands have pivoted towards acquiring licensing and usage rights to influencer-produced content and using the content as ads from their brand channels, rather than paying influencers to post on their own feeds, says Emily Hall, campaign director at marketing agency Goat, which has offices in London, New York and Singapore. By acquiring usage rights, brands can decide on captions that better match their tone of voice or produce different cuts and edits of the content to post on whichever social media they consider most effective, with metrics available. "It gives brands an element of control," says Hall.

Organic influencer content typically costs 5 per cent more, but acquiring usage rights could cost 20 to 30 per cent more than the original fee. "It's still very good value for money," says Hall. "The influencers are still creating content and doing the heavy lifting for the brands."

Dynamic voiceover and deepfake videos offer huge potential for marketers in many sectors. A 2019 malaria awareness ad featuring David Beckham speaking nine languages showed how deepfakes can broaden the reach of a public message, receiving 400 million impressions globally within two months.

Deepfakes can also support influencers and content creators who are asked to create more live content but may not be exceptional performers in all media, says Dhillon. Hall agrees: "You're taking away that risk of a human element, while still retaining a human touch."

Hyper-Personalized Advertising

Chinese tech companies are further along in using deepfakes in marketing. In a July 2020 white paper about its plans for AI, Chinese tech giant Tencent emphasises that deepfakes are "not just about 'faking' and 'deceiving', but a highly creative and groundbreaking technology". The company urged regulators to avoid clamping down on this nascent tech trend. For fashion, Tencent cited how deepfakes can show outfits on a broader variety of models with different skin tones, heights and weights. When consumers see products as extensions of themselves, they are willing to buy more, pay a higher price and advocate to friends, *Harvard Business Review* found.

Deepfakes can provide a route to "very quick understanding" for customers viewing new collections from a brand, says Matthew Drinkwater, head of the Fashion Innovation Agency (FIA) at London College of Fashion. He first started running deepfake experiments in 2019, when Microsoft sponsored a project that enabled his team to insert consumers in ads. "This isn't about fit. It's about giving you a first impression of how something might look."

This month, Gucci has partnered with software firm Niantic to release a new collaboration with The North Face in a game of Pokémon Go. "Imagine if Gucci could take it one step further and send its top 50 clients personalised videos of themselves wearing the new collection," Shvets of Reface AI says. In 2020, Reface AI enabled users to virtually try on Gucci clothes as part of a trial with Kering, resulting in one million swaps in a single day.

Retailers can also hyper-personalise service using a deepfaked assistant to help with online enquiries who is a customer's exact demographic and speaks their language. Rather than talk to a faceless bot, shoppers could talk to a "real" face, which could enhance trust, says Drinkwater. "All of the indications are that if you're able to personalise content, consumers are more likely to engage, so there's a real practical application for the industry to start using this more widely."

Some form of regulation is likely, notes marketer Lejeune. Potential discretion could include labels clarifying that deepfakes are not real people, he says. Dhillon adds that blockchain has potential as a future means of tracking authenticity.

Consumer data protection is another hot subject. Supporters of deepfakes say that the success of existing face-swap apps shows that consumers are comfortable with sharing their data. In 2019, AI photo editor FaceApp, which enables users to change their facial expressions, looks and age, was a viral hit. In 2020, Sway, an AI-powered app that enables users to visualise themselves dancing, became the third most downloaded app in the US during Super Bowl weekend.

The ethical implications of deepfakes have yet to be fully explored, suggests FIA's Drinkwater. But he is convinced deepfakes are here to stay.

> "The technologies that surround artificial intelligence and machine learning are already critical to how brands can manage different aspects of their business, from their supply chain to marketing and communications. [Adoption] is not so much a pivot but a deepening commitment to technology and deep learning."

Chapter 9.3

Excerpt from Ethics of Gamification[*]

Tae Wan Kim and Kevin Werbach

3. Framing the Ethical Issues

As gamification becomes a more common business practice, a growing number of practitioners and scholars are highlighting normative concerns. Accounts in the popular press describe worries about the manipulative or exploitative potential of gamification (e.g., Bréville and Rimbert 2014; Fleming 2012; Knowledge@Wharton 2011b). Surveying gamification experts and stakeholders, Shari et al. (2014) found diverse areas of ethical concern.

This awareness has not, however, led to the development of a robust code of conduct for gamification designers. The Engagement Alliance, a non-profit association for gamification practitioners, released a "proposed ethics statement" for public comment in December 2012 (Zichermann 2012). The first element is to "help individuals, organizations, and societies achieve their true potential"; the second is to "not obfuscate the use of game mechanics with intent to deceive." As a standard for ethically responsible gamification, this statement is woefully wanting. It is not clear why these commitments were chosen, or how they provide useful guidance to practitioners. "True potential" is exceedingly vague. The third and final provision in the proposed statement, to "share what I've learned about motivating behavior with the community" does not even concern gamification practices themselves. Not surprisingly, no provider appears to have endorsed the statement. The absence of thorough ethical analysis is in striking contrast to the rapid adoption of gamification in the marketplace.

[…]

As noted earlier, gamification ethics is under-theorized, at least in part, because the technological novelty and rapid adoption of the practice have outstripped careful consideration. Both proponents and detractors, therefore, tend to generalize too rapidly from particular examples. What is needed,

---

[*] Kim, Tae Wan, and Kevin Werbach. "More than just a game: ethical issues in gamification." *Ethics and Information Technology* 18, no. 2 (2016): 157-173. Reprinted with permission. Note: This is an excerpt from the original so footnote and endnote numbering may be modified.

DOI: 10.1201/9781003278290-55

thus, is a conceptual map of the terrain. Such an endeavor will by necessity be abstracted and incomplete: it cannot address all possible scenarios in detail, nor can it encompass all possible factors of moral salience. However, it should be more than a mere taxonomy. An ethical map of gamification can offer normative guidance to both scholars and practitioners if it identifies deep structures that tie together seemingly disparate phenomena and anchors the topic in established scholarly literature. Our starting point is that we need to take a context-relative stance—that is, gamification may or may not be ethically or socially acceptable in specific cases. The proper question is "What forms of gamification are unacceptable in which contexts, and which moral norms are primarily relevant to which contexts?" We propose that the ethical status of a practice of gamification, primarily, but not exhaustively, is determined by the extent to which the practice (1) takes unfair advantage of workers (e.g., exploitation); (2) infringes any involved workers' or customers' autonomy (e.g., manipulation); (3) intentionally or unintentionally harms workers and involved parties in various ways; or (4) has a socially unacceptable degree of negative effect on the character of involved parties. In the discussions below, we expand on the four categories of ethical difficulties that may arise. Each encapsulates a cluster of related concerns. For example, manipulation also brings to bear questions of autonomy, transparency, consent, and self-reflection, while exploitation highlights issues of voluntariness and fairness.

3.1 Exploitation

Game designer and critic Ian Bogost (2011a, 2015) dubs gamification "exploitationware." He writes:

> "…gamification proposes to replace real incentives with fictional ones … Organizations ask for loyalty, but they reciprocate that loyalty with shames, counterfeit incentives that neither provide value nor require investment. When seen in this light, 'gamification' is a misnomer. A better name for this practice is 'exploitationware'"

(2011a)

Sociologist P. J. Rey (2012) supports Bogost's claim by calling gamification a menacingly exploitative form of "play-bor" (Kücklich 2005). However, neither Bogost nor Rey fully develops the normative argument to support his claims. In this section, we consider whether their charge of exploitation can be further developed or justified.

Alan Wertheimer's (1996) work is probably the most influential normative account of exploitation, according to which Transaction *x* is exploitative when Person *A* takes unfair advantage of Person *B*. Consider a standard example, *The Port Caledonia and the Anna*, in which the master of a ship *A* in danger asked for help from a nearby ship and the master of the nearby ship *B* offered £1,000 or no rescue. In this case, *A* voluntarily agreed to pay £1,000. Wertheimer explains that the transaction was voluntary, but it was exploitative because *B* was in a unique position to take advantage of *A*'s vulnerabilities, which made the transaction unfair.[1] Wertheimer argues that the transaction would not be unfair if a reasonable amount of competing ships were nearby, in which case *A* would not have unique vulnerabilities. That is, if there were some more competing ships, the price would probably be way less than £1,000. Hence, Wertheimer proposes that, in general, Transaction *x* is fair if it is an option that would be chosen by Parties *A* and *B* in a hypothetically imagined competitive market.

According to Wertheimer's fairness-based account, most consumer-facing gamified products would not be exploitative with customers, because the real market is already a competitive market.

For instance, Nike+ is a mobile app that makes running a game-like experience, and competing apps or other products exist in the market. If a user chooses to adopt Nike+, we can assume the arrangement is fair, and, therefore, not exploitative.

One might say that Wertheimer's fairness account does not give us a clear view of gamified workplaces. First, it is not easy to hypothetically construct a competitive market for gamified workplaces. A company that provides gamification is already in a situation in which it hires employees. One might also say that the hired employees are not completely out of the labor market because they can always quit and change workplaces. In addition, because many competing companies already provide different systems of gameful environments, the real labor market is already like a hypothetically competitive market. It follows that most gamified workplaces are, therefore, not exploitative.

But this approach is not always appropriate. First of all, gamified environments are not always clearly included in job advertisings. Furthermore, quitting a job in order to avoid a certain practice of gamification that employees participate in during spare time—as in the case of Microsoft's Language Quality Game (Werbach and Hunter, 2012), for instance—seems an unreasonable burden to employees. Third, and most fundamental, it is not clear whether or not workers are well informed about their situations and options regarding gamification. If the player is not reasonably informed about her most-preferred option, and voluntarily chooses virtual rewards in gamification, she may still enter into an unfair transaction.

One might say that in games, players sometimes endure seemingly unfair activities to achieve certain long-term objectives, even if they do not find an activity itself rewarding. A good example is "grinding," a common feature in massively multiplayer online games (MMOGs) such as World of Warcraft, in which players must spend long periods doing repetitive tasks as a condition for something they desire. Grinding achieves several purposes in these games, such as increasing the perceived value of the desired objective. In this specific case, the long-term benefit can probably justify the uselessness of the short-term rewards. Then, what long-term benefits, if any, do exist to justify the uselessness of virtual rewards such as points or badges at the gamified labor? For instance, gamification can probably lead to positive trickle-down effects to employees. If gamification promotes workplace productivity, which in turn enhances corporate financial performance, then it can potentially also enhance employee benefits such as increased salaries, bonuses, or longer employment. But as G. A. Cohen (1992, 1996) points out, unless corporate leaders have an egalitarian ethos, such a trickle down effect, in theory, does not necessarily occur. Even if it occurs, ordinary workers often cannot clearly see the trickle-down effect, so cannot take it into account when assessing their own welfare, unless the provider clearly explains it to them.

So far, we have discussed a micro account of the fairness view that focuses on individuals' discrete transactions (Snyder 2010). By contrast, macro fairness accounts of exploitation (e.g., Sample 2003) hold that transactions that can be viewed as innocuous from micro perspectives can nevertheless be unfair if they are based upon questionably unfair macro structures that have been historically created through global economic orders. The macro fairness account is not itself relevant to our purposes, because most gamification providers are U.S.- or developed country-based companies. Yet, the underlying idea that workers can be structurally exploited can, nonetheless, be relevant and is worth pursuing.

A simple sociological mechanism underneath gamification is that workers in the contemporary world find their jobs more or less boring, monotonous, and sometimes meaningless, whereas gamification can offer fun and excitement. In fact, many popular books or lectures about gamification begin by emphasizing how unsatisfactory, not fun, and stressful most modern workplaces are (e.g., Burke 2014; Herger 2014; Paharia 2013; Zicherman and Linder 2013). If it can be argued that the monotonous and meaningless working condition is a structural issue of modern capitalist society that makes modern workers vulnerable to those who have capabilities or power they can leverage through gamification, then a society in which gamification is marketable and preferred by workers is itself a clue that we need to be concerned about the fundamental economic paradigm in which workers cannot but choose gamification to find meaning and fun.[2]

3.2 Manipulation

[...]

Whichever psychological approach one adopts, gamification can be viewed as a means of shaping actions without conscious rational consideration. This alone does not clearly make it manipulative. There must be some factor that *inhibits* rational self-reflection, and, thus, unjustifiably undermines autonomy. Otherwise, every teacher who used the extrinsic reward of a good grade to motivate students to study, and every manager who convinced employees of the inherent joy of succeeding in a challenging assignment would be guilty of wrongful manipulation.

Below we discuss two examples of specific inhibitors of rational self-reflection that can potentially arise in gamification: addiction and distraction.[3]

One of the defining features of addiction is an "impairment of self-control" or "compulsion" (Levy 2013: 1). It is possible that in a game, players are so engaged, addicted, and compulsive that they have difficulty stopping. Concerned about such effects, the Chinese government even passed a law requiring online game operators to install software that discourages players under 18 from playing more than three hours per day (People's Daily Online 2007). Game developers can argue that addiction is an unintended outcome, but they can be responsible for such unintended outcomes if they should have been aware of them (Sher 2009). In addition, in other cases such as that of the casino slot machine, enticing uncontrolled play is a primary design goal (Schüll 2012). The same mechanics of seduction and variable rewards that are the basis for slot machines can also be found in gamification systems (Carr 2011; Thompson 2015). Virtual reward structures that promote obsessive behavior deserve ethical scrutiny.

Players bear significant responsibility for their actions, but so do those who take advantage of psychological vulnerabilities to neutralize players' rational capabilities. Moreover, casino patrons and game players know they are entering a seductive game space, even if they don't appreciate the strength of its pull. As discussed in the manipulation context, those subject to gamification may be unaware of that fact.

We realize that it is in part an empirical matter whether addictive gamification is a concern in practice. Gameful systems lack the complex, immersive environment that may suck some players into massively multiplayer online games (MMOGs) to the exclusion of all else. If only complex games can get people to be addicted, then it is less likely that gamification gets people to be addicted. But one might also say that people are often more vulnerable to simple and repeated game environments such as points and badges. Simple social video games such as Farmville or Candy Crush Saga in fact target intensive players and rely on obsessive "whales" spending heavily for virtual goods (Johnson 2014). Of course, not all people can become easily addicted to simple games, but that does not justify behavior that targets vulnerable customers or workers. If a gamification system deliberately or negligently applies techniques to promote compulsive behavior, or fails to take corrective action when some players display such behavior, it falls short of ethical duties regarding manipulation.

Another gamification factor that can hinder rational self-reflection is the possibility of excessive distraction. Distraction is typically less compulsive than addiction, but it can still prevent a person from attending to a rational assessment of how his decision-making and behaviors affect his interests and welfare. There are opportunity costs to the time and energy players put into gameful activities. To the extent that these are voluntary choices by players, they reflect the natural variation in preference functions: one person's waste of time is another's worthwhile pursuit. At some point, though, the costs of a gameful experience can decisively outweigh the hedonic benefits. In contrast to full-blown games, which can create rich, immersive experiences, gamification tends towards shallower game-like activity. Such "cheap fun" is, as mentioned above, sometimes difficult to justify. Typically, a rational self-reflector would not prefer such an option. However, gamification can often easily distract players to make irrational choices.

Bogost's Cow Clicker, created to illustrate the perils of gamification, is an extreme version of this distraction scenario (Tanz 2012). Cow Clicker was a casual social game that invited players to click repeatedly on virtual cows every eight hours for no purpose other than earning virtual rewards. It attracted over 50,000 players, one of whom clicked a cow over 100,000 times. Cow Clicker is not itself an example of gamification; it is a stand-alone game. However, if the mechanics of Cow Clicker are emblematic of gamification, as Bogost apparently intended to suggest, an ethical challenge arises. The danger is similar to what media scholar Neil Postman described, in connection with television, as "amusing ourselves to death" (Postman 1985).

As with the addictive forms of manipulation, the line between ethical and unethical distraction is partly an empirical question. Thus, a rigorous normative investigation cannot be complete until enough empirical research about the distracting or addictive nature of gamification is conducted. Until then, we suggest the following as a rule of thumb: when a player would, upon rational reflection, conclude the time participating in a gamified activity would have been better spent otherwise, there is good *prima facie* reason to believe the line has been crossed.

3.3 Harms

We can safely assume that gamification providers do not intend to cause physical or psychological harm. Their goal, as discussed at the outset, is to achieve some organizational objective using a motivational technique. What if harms do in fact arise in connection with gamified actions? We consider the ethical implications of such scenarios in this section. The risks of physical harm due to gamification primarily involve injury to others outside the gamified system, while the risks of psychological harms generally involve the players themselves.

Physical harms[...]

Gamification can also unintentionally, recklessly, negligently, or inadvertently encourage players to cause harms to involved parties. For instance, Lazzaro (2012), a noted game designer, observed the San Francisco Bay Bridge, where variable-rate tolls exist and where large screens display the current rate of cars crossing the bridge. This is a kind of gamification: a feedback loop with rewards for meeting the challenge of avoiding rush hour. Some drivers approaching the bridge near the cutoff time for the lower toll swerve off the road to wait before entering the toll plaza or stop in an active lane, creating a serious safety hazard. Sometimes the players themselves may suffer the harms. Several users of Strava, a gamified tool for cyclists, have suffered fatal crashes because, allegedly, they were too focused on the game rather than safety (Hill 2012).

Unlike cases of manipulation, these examples do not involve subverting the players' goals to those of the providers. In the case of the Bay Bridge, the results are even contrary to the provider's interest in offering safe transportation. The primary ethical responsibility may, therefore, remain with the player. Nonetheless, a responsible gamification designer should consider not just the direct harm for players, but potential indirect harm as well. If it is reasonably foreseeable that players may respond to gamification incentives in ways that harm themselves or others, the provider accordingly bears some responsibility.

A lesson from game design that carries over to gamification is that players are apt to "game the system" and sometimes act in ways the designer never anticipated (Werbach and Hunter 2012). Players might seek to absolve themselves from responsibility on the grounds that gamification numbed them to the serious implications of their actions,[4] but this claim will be difficult to sustain when players are clearly acting outside the expressed frame of the gameful system. Both providers and players, therefore, have duties to avoid situations that contribute significantly to the risk of harm or unethical conduct.

Psychological harms: A video screen leaderboard system for the housekeeping staff at Disneyland hotels in Anaheim, California generated significant anxiety, embarrassment, and shame among workers, who labeled it "the electronic whip" (Lopez 2011). Seeing their performance ranked against that of coworkers on a large screen often caused some workers to skip bathroom breaks[5] and others to become panicked about losing their jobs.

Many gamification systems involve competition and ranking. For example, digital leaderboards showing the relative performances of players are a popular game element to adapt to the workplace. If contextually taken as a stick rather than a carrot, such features can sometimes produce "expressive harms" (Anderson and Pildes 2000). The Disneyland hotels' "electronic whip," mentioned above, is an obvious example. Plausibly, each of us generally has a negative duty not to gratuitously insult, offend, or humiliate others (Feinberg 1985; Kim and Strudler 2012) or a "duty of decency" (Kim 2014), which may be violated in such social contexts. Expressive harm is oftentimes not a trivial matter. As Margalit (1998: 9) argues, "humiliation," including insult, offense, embarrassment, or disrespectfulness, "constitutes a sound reason for a person to consider his or her *self-respect* injured," and self-respect is an important condition for a person to preserve her dignity (Dilon 1997; Hill Jr. 1973; Stark 2012). Thus, psychological harms, if incurred through gamification, can sometimes be an experience that strips workers of a certain dignity.[6]

In this context, transparency and voluntariness are not fundamental solutions. First of all, gameful activities can harm not only voluntary players, but also any other indirectly involved parties. Second, and more fundamental, one can wrongfully harm a person even if she consents to and prefers to receive such treatment, e.g., slavery or sweatshop labor (Meyers 2004). Both morality and law recognize that while people are autonomous actors capable of assuming certain risks, they cannot consent *ex ante* to all injuries. Murder is an obvious example, and more commonly, harms that the reasonable person cannot be expected to evaluate fully and rationally. In fact, in the context of Disneyland, the more information workers have about their relative performance, the more humiliated they will feel. A gamification provider clearly should not mislead workers into thinking a gamified comparison system will be part of the performance review process when it is not. But if the gamification system is actually intended to identify poor performers, disclosing that fact will not alleviate the potential humiliation. If it is not intended in this way, players will appropriately wonder why the organization is going to the trouble.

In such social contexts, the normative concern centers on the socially interpreted messages to individuals in the real world. The player's actions within the game—in the Disney case, performing existing job functions—are not themselves problematic. Or at least, those actions are no more problematic than they were before the introduction of gamification. The potential for expressive harm arises from the socially interpreted impact on the workers' real-world job status. Yet the essence of the mental pain is not that the employer benefits unfairly, as with exploitation, but that the workers are pushed to feel diminished in relation to their co-workers or other individuals. The moral failing lies in ignoring the possibility that a competitive hierarchy that is innocuous within a game can be expressively pernicious in some social contexts. To avoid such expressive harms, gamification designers should anticipate and pay enough attention to the expressive dimensions of gamification and social norms governing public interpretations of given contexts (Anderson 1993; Hellman 2000; Nissenbaum 2004, 2010).

3.4 Character

As Grant (2012) explains, incentives can sometimes have a negative effect upon people's character traits. A standard example is that parents often hesitate to use candy as a reward to change their child's behavior, not just for health-related reasons, but for its negative impact upon important social character traits like autonomy, self-governance, etc. Moral character is a complex concept (see e.g., Adams 2006; Hursthouse 2001) and we do not aim to fully cover how gamification can impact different aspects of character. We discuss how gamification in some limited social contexts can motivate people to cultivate and display a socially inappropriate degree of moral indifference—a building block of bad character or vice (Arpaly 2003; Arpaly and Schroeder 2014)[7]— to fundamental human values such as the sanctity of life (Dworkin 1993). Let us quickly move on to real cases.

In 2012, the Israel Defense Force (IDF) launched a blog and social media effort to rally support for its military action against the group Hamas. The campaign raised eyebrows when it incorporated gameful badges and levels to reward readers who searched for information on the blog and shared content through social media connections. John Mitchell, a writer for a popular technology blog, was flabbergasted:

> "This is a WAR. Israel is trying to enlist the people of the world in its campaign with military ranks, badges and points. Innocent people are dying on all sides, and the IDF wants to reward people for tweeting about it." (Emphasis in original.)

(Mitchell 2012)

Mitchell's objection has intuitive appeal, but is difficult to justify on deeper investigation. From the IDF's perspective, the gameful war blog was a fully transparent effort to engage and motivate supporters. What, then, was the ethical problem? Unlike full-fledged video games or serious games, gamification involves not just simulating reality but influencing it. The IDF blog was actually part of the war effort. Specifically, it was a propaganda tool. The real concern implicit in Mitchell's moral reservation might be that participants would come to see the Israeli campaign in a positive light. The game-like environment might contribute by de-emphasizing the brutality of combat, but so would a stirring speech about the rightness of the cause. If this is the source of Mitchell's concern, one could certainly conclude that the IDF blog was in poor taste, but to declare it ethically suspect is a contestable conclusion about the IDF's campaign against Hamas, rather than about gamification.

Furthermore, it is unclear whether the problem is that war should never be associated with games. War games, both physical and virtual, are a widespread and essential military planning tool. Nor is there an inherent ethical problem with digital games related to war. Although concerns are sometimes raised about the dangers of violent video games, it is unclear whether there was something uniquely violent displayed in the IDF's social media campaign. It was about a war, but participating in it was not actually like fighting in a war. The IDF blog is more akin to strategy games, such as the well-regarded Civilization series, which show battles as a stylized, bloodless movement of armies. Even critics of violent video games rarely attack such titles.

Nonetheless, a moral remainder could still exist. There is more than one way to address Mitchell's suspicion, but one interpretation of his quote is that the wartime context is inherently serious because it inevitably involves serious injuries, including killing innocent people, but that gamification in this context is used to motivate people to cultivate and display a certain moral indifference to fundamental human values like the sanctity of life, an indifference that one can find morally and socially unacceptable. Suppose that two men are playing a video game that involves physically saving a drowning child. They compete for the sake of fun, points, and badges, but not for the sake of the sanctity of life. Of course, their act itself—saving children in danger—is a right thing to do. Thus, their act is not itself blameworthy. But their desire to save the child, encouraged by the game, can be interpreted as inappropriate because it expresses moral indifference to a certain fundamental human value that deserves serious consideration. If the players were repeatedly or habitually exposed to such motivating influences, it could have a serious impact upon the players' moral character.

As in the case of the other moral concerns we have discussed, each case must be contextually examined. If some incentives for morally good actions, such as tax deductions for charitable giving, do not have a socially unacceptable degree of negative impact upon tax payers' civic character, such incentives would not be interpreted as cultivating a socially unacceptable form of moral indifference to values like beneficence or generosity. In the case of wartime, however, gamification can more likely, depending upon contexts, encourage people to cultivate and express unjustifiable moral indifference to fundamental human values like the sanctity of innocent life. Wartime businesses and other business activities that involve fundamental human values should be extremely careful of using gamification. Another example that tests the boundaries of what can be gamified, with respect to fundamental human values, involves a U.S. military base in Griesheim, Germany that was involved in tapping email and other electronic communications in connection with the global effort to fight terrorism. As part of training, operatives were challenged to earn "skilz points" and unlock achievements based on their success at finding promising information (Poitras, Rosenbauch, and Stark, 2013). Here again, some observers would intuit that something was inappropriate about the use of gamification, but it is difficult to divorce that sense from one's contextual perspective about the underlying activity. Imagine a social context in which gamification had been used by the British team at Bletchley Park that cracked the Nazi Enigma code during World War II. One might believe, then, that any motivational approach that improved those scientists' performance would be viewed favorably. But the moral reality is not that clear. In the saving-the-drowning-child game, the players' act was not itself wrong, but displayed a certain moral indifference—and the gaming encouraged them to do so. It is possible that the gameful system can have a negative impact upon the British team's moral character, by repeatedly or habitually encouraging them to have a certain moral indifference to fundamental human values. Ethical gamification designers should pay attention to this unintended moral trade-off and should try to minimize players' moral cost, especially given the dominant role of working life in the contemporary world and its strong spillover impact on other aspects of our lives and our character traits.

Of course, because gamification obfuscates the norms of two different spheres, where to draw the line is not always clear. If motivational techniques derived from games should not always be employed in "serious" environments, that would apply to services such as Free Rice, an online quiz game created by the United Nations World Food Programme that educates players about world hunger, or Half the Sky, a social game on Facebook that raises awareness about the mistreatment of women around the world. Rather than providing definite answers here, we propose a basic guideline: carefully examine whether or not gamification repeatedly encourages players to be indifferent to fundamental human values.

Notes

1. Matt Zwolinski (2007, 2008, 2009, 2012) claims in his libertarian account of exploitation that voluntarily chosen transactions are justified or tolerated. Thus, Zwolinski would not believe that the transaction in *The Port Caledonia* was a wrongful form of exploitation. Along the same logic, Zwolinski also believes that most practices of sweatshops and price gouging are not exploitative or that even if they are exploitative they are justified forms of exploitation. In this article, we do not discuss the libertarian view. First, for the sake of consistency within the fairness account, we opt to primarily rely on Wertheimer's view (1996). Second, we disagree with Zwolinski, mainly because we do not believe that voluntariness is the most important moral consideration. For a more detailed discussion about this issue, see Michael Kate's (2015) recent criticism of Zwolinski's view.

2. There are important accounts of exploitation that we do not explore in this section. For example, we do not discuss the Kantian account of exploitation as using workers as a mere means (Arnold 2003, 2010; Arnold and Bowie 2003, 2007), which typically, requires, in the context of organizational life, meeting minimum or reasonable safety standards and providing a minimum or living wage. We do not explore Robert Goodin's (1986, 1988) vulnerability-based account or Mikhail Valdman's (2009) excessive benefit based account. In theory, these other, unexplored accounts of exploitation can potentially address gamification as exploitative.

3. Sicart (2015), a games scholar and philosopher of technology, argues that gamification inherently diminishes self-reflection, even when employed entirely at the user's choosing. From his neo-Aristotelian viewpoint, gamification interferes with human flourishing by introducing an artificial set of motivators that substitute for personal reflection on the goals and content of the experience. Because we discuss an impermissible and wrongful form of manipulation, to our perspective, the important question is whether the player's autonomy has been unjustifiably compromised. If not, the player is entitled to choose the stimuli through which she achieves her goals, although the choice can be bad in an Aristotelian sense. Nonetheless, we agree with Sicart that workers have a good reason to avoid bad choices.

4. It is a controversial issue whether or not addiction or manipulation can absolve responsibility or blameworthiness. In this article, we only assume the widely acceptable principle that a person is responsible or blameworthy for a wrongdoing to the extent that she has a relevant capability to avoid it. For more detailed discussions, see Levy (2013), Poland and Graham (2011), and Sher (2009).

5. Causing employees to skip bathroom breaks can potentially involve issues of freedom. For a philosophical analysis about freedom, dignity, and use of the bathroom, see Waldron (1991).

6. In this manner, Margalit (1996: 149) says, "if there is no concept of human dignity, then there is no concept of humiliation either."

7. A reverse moral indifference or goodwill is a building block of good moral character. See Arpaly and Schroeder (2014).

References

Adams, R. M. (2006). *A theory of virtue: Excellence in being for the good*. New York: Oxford University Press.

Anderson, E. (1993). *Values in ethics and economics*. Cambridge, MA: Harvard University Press.

Anderson, E., & Pildes, R. (2000). Expressive theories of law: A general restatement. *University of Pennsylvania Law Review* 148: 1503–1575.

Arpaly, N. (2003). *Unprincipled virtue: An inquiry into moral agency*. New York: Oxford University Press.

Arpaly, N., & Schroeder, T. (2014). *In praise of desire*. New York: Oxford University Press.

Bogost, I. (2011a). Gamification is bullshit. *Bogost.com*. August 8. http://www.bogost.com/blog/gamification_is_bullshit.shtml.

Bogost, I. (2015). Why gamification is bullshit. In S. P. Walz and S. Deterding (Eds.), *The gameful world: Approaches, issues, applications*. Cambridge: MIT Press.

Bréville, B. & Rimbert, P. (2014). Life is just a game: Using games to motivate behavior is a growing means of social control. *Pittsburgh Post-Gazette*, January 19.

Burke, B. (2014). *Gamify: How gamification motivates people to do extraordinary things*. Brookline, MA: Biblomotion.

Carr, D. (2011). Gamification: 75% psychology, 25% technology, *Information Week Government*, October 6.

Cohen, G. A. (1992). Incentives, inequality, and community In Peterson, G. (ed.), *The Tanner lectures on human values*, Salt Lake City: University of Utah Press.

Cohen, G. A. (1996). Where the action is: On the site of distributive justice, *Philosophy and Public Affairs* 26: 3–30.

Dilon, Robin S. (1997). Self-respect: Moral, emotional, political. *Ethics* 107(2): 226–249.

Dworkin, R. (1993). *Life's dominion*. New York: Vintage Books.

Feinberg, J. (1985). *Offense to others*. New York: Oxford University Press.

Fleming, Nic. (2012). Gamification: Is it game over? *BBC.com*. December 5. http://www.bbc.com/future/story/20121204-can-gaming-transform-your-life.

Grant, R. W. (2012). *Strings attached: Untangling the ethics of incentives*. Princeton, NJ: Princeton University Press.

Hellman, D. (2000). The expressive dimension of equal protection. *Minnesota Law Review* 85: 1–70.

Herger, M. (2014). *Enterprise gamification: Engaging people by letting them have fun*. EGC Media.

Hill, K. (2012). A quantified self fatality? Family says cyclist's death is fault of ride-tracking company Strava. *Forbes.com*. June 20. http://www.forbes.com/sites/kashmirhill/2012/06/20/a-quantified-self-fatality-family- says-cyclists-death-is-fault-of-ride-tracking-company-strava/

Hill Jr., T.E. (1973). Servility and self-respect. *Monist* 57(1): 87–104.

Hursthouse, R. (1999). *On virtue ethics*. New York: Oxford University Press.

Johnson, E. (2014). A long tail of whales: Half of mobile games money comes from 0.15 percent of players, *Re/Code*, February 26.

Kim, T. W. (2014). Decent termination: A moral case for severance pay. *Business Ethics Quarterly* 24(2): 203–227.

Kim, T. W., & Strudler, A. (2012). Workplace civility: A Confucian approach. *Business Ethics Quarterly* 22 (3): 557–578.

Knowledge@Wharton. (2011b). The dangerous side of online gaming. August 17. http://knowledge.wharton.upenn.edu/article/the-dangerous-side-of-online-gaming/.

Kücklich, J. (2005). Precarious playbour: Modders and the digital games industry. *Fibreculture*

Lazzaro, N. (2012). Nicole Lazzaro: Real world gamification can kill. *Fora.tv*. February 1. http://www.dailymotion.com/video/xgsnf2_nicole-lazzaro-real-world-gamification-can- kill_news

Levy, N. (2013). *Addiction and self-control: Perspectives from philosophy, psychology, and neuroscience*. New York: Oxford University Press.

Lopez, S. (2011). Disney hotel workers try to stay ahead of the "electronic whip." *Los Angeles Times*, October 19.

Margalit, A. (1998). *The decent society*. Translated by Naomi Goldblum. Cambridge: Harvard University Press.

Meyers, C. (2004). Wrongful beneficence: Exploitation and third world sweatshops. *Journal of Social Philosophy* 35(3): 319–333.

Nissenbaum, H. (2004). Privacy as contextual integrity. *Washington Law Review* 79: 119–158.

Nissenbaum, H. (2010) *Privacy in context: Technology, policy, and the integrity of social life.*Palo Alto, CA: Stanford University Press.

Paharia, R. (2013). *Loyalty 3.0: How to revolutionize customer and employee engagement with big data and gamification*. New York: McGraw Hill.

People's Daily Online. (2007). The more they play, the more they lose. April 10. http://english.people.com.cn/200704/10/eng20070410_364977.html

Poitras, L., Rosenbach, M., & Stark, H. (2013). Ally and target: US intelligence watches Germany closely, *Spiegel Online International*, August 12. http://www.spiegel.de/international/world/germany-is-a-both-a-partner-to-and-a-target- of-nsa-surveillance-a-916029.html.

Postman, N. (1985). *Amusing ourselves to death: Public discourse in the age of show business*. New York: Penguin.

Rey, P.J. (2012). Gamification, playbor & exploitation, *Cyborgology*. October 15. http://thesocietypages.org /cyborgology/2012/10/15/gamification-playbor-exploitation-2/.

Sample, R. (2003). *Exploitation: What it is and why it's wrong.* Lanham, ML: Rowman & Littlefield.

Schüll, N. D. (2012). *Addiction by design: Machine gambling in Las Vegas.* Princeton University Press.

Shahri, A., Hosseini, M., Phalp, K., Taylor, J., & Ali, R. (2014). Toward a code of ethics for gamification at enterprise. In *The practice of enterprise modeling*: 235–245. Heidelberg: Springer.

Sher, G. (2009). *Who knew?" Responsibility without awareness.* New York: Oxford University Press.

Snyder, J. (2010). Exploitation and sweatshop: Perspectives and issues. *Business Ethics Quarterly* 20(2): 187–213.

Stark, C. A. (2012). Rawlsian self-respect. In *Oxford studies in normative ethics*, by Mark Timmons (Ed.), 238–261. New York: Oxford University Press.

Tanz, J. (2012). The curse of cow clicker. *Wired* 20.1.

Thompson, A. (2015). Engineers of addiction: Slot machines perfected addictive gaming. Now, tech wants their tricks. *The Verge*, May 6. www.theverge.com/2015/5/6/8544303/casino-slot-machine-gambling -addiction-psychology-mobile-games.

Werbach, K, & Hunter, D. (2012). *For the win: How game thinking can revolutionize your business.* Philadelphia: Wharton Digital Press.

Wertheimer, A. (1996). *Exploitation.* Princeton, NJ: Princeton University Press.

Zichermann, G. (2012). The code of gamification ethics. December 10. http://www.gamification.co/2012 /12/10/code-of-gamification-ethics/.

Zichermann, G., and Linder, J. (2013). *The gamification revolution: How leaders leverage game mechanics to crush the competition.* McGraw-Hill.

Chapter 9.4

Excerpt from Manipulation, Privacy, and Choice[*]

Kirsten Martin

As individuals navigate their lives on websites and apps, their movements, searches, and actions are silently tracked. Streams of consumer data are then pooled by data aggregators and mined to identify potential vulnerabilities of consumers. These potential weaknesses, e.g., whether someone is in financial distress, having a health crisis, or battling an addiction, are valuable to marketers and ad networks to silently steer consumers' market actions towards the manipulator's interests. While identified early on as problematic within the economics of information broadly, the use of hyper-targeting to manipulate consumers is underappreciated as a threat to not only the autonomy of individuals but also the efficiency and legitimacy of markets. This article examines targeted manipulation as the covert leveraging of a specific target's vulnerabilities to steer their decisions to the manipulator's interests. This article positions online targeted manipulation as undermining the core economic assumptions of authentic choice in the market. It then explores how important choice is to markets and economics, how firms gained positions of power to exploit vulnerabilities and weaknesses of individuals without the requisite safeguards in place, and how to govern firms in the position to manipulate. The power to manipulate is the power to undermine choice in the market. As such, firms in the position to manipulate threaten the autonomy of individuals, diminish the efficiency of transactions, and undermine the legitimacy of markets.

This article argues that *firms merely in the position* to manipulate, with knowledge of individual's weaknesses and access to their decision making, should be regulated to ensure those firms' interests are aligned with the target. The economic oddity is not that firms have data that render another market actor vulnerable, rather the oddity is that so many firms have data to covertly manipulate others without safeguards in place. Market actors regularly share information about their concerns, preferences, weaknesses, and strengths within contracts or joint ventures or within a relationship with professional duties.

The point of manipulation is to covertly steer a target's decision towards the manipulator's interests and away from the target's; as such, manipulation impedes a market actor's ability to enact

[*] Martin, Kirsten. 2022. "Manipulation, Privacy, and Choice." *North Carolina Journal of Law and Technology.* Reprinted with permission. Note: This is an excerpt from the original so footnote and endnote numbering may be modified.

DOI: 10.1201/9781003278290-56

preferences through choice. This undermining of choice – rather than harms to the consumer – is the basis for additional safeguards on those in the position to manipulate. Governing targeted manipulation online will require additional safeguards on those firms in the position manipulate rather than attempting to identify each instance of targeted manipulation. First, additional safeguards are needed limiting data aggregators and ad networks – specifically any data trafficker without any relationship with consumers – to ensure the use of information is in the interests of the consumer. Second, customer facing websites and apps act as gatekeepers by luring consumers in to have their data tracked by third parties and later to be targeted with manipulative content. In so doing, consumer facing companies should be responsible to ensure all third parties that access their users – either for data collection or for targeting content – abide by standards of care that are audited. Where scholarship has focused on identifying instances of manipulation to regulate, this article argues that *firms merely in the position* to manipulate, with knowledge of the individual and access to their decision making, should be regulated to ensure their interests are aligned with the target.

I. Introduction

> *One should hardly have to tell academicians that information is a valuable resource: knowledge is power.*[1]

> *Data broker Acxiom provides up to 3,000 attributes and scores on 700 million people including purchases, net worth, likelihood someone is having a baby or adopting a child, and their health interests.*[2]

Data brokers proudly collect information on millions of individuals with thousands of data points on each target.[3] These companies collect this information from, among other sources, browsing history, shopping, location tracking, and public records and can use this mundane information to predict if someone is depressed, anorexic, addicted to drugs or alcohol, or has a medical condition.[4] Ad networks and advertisers are willing to pay top dollar to identify those in financial and emotional difficulty to promote gambling, cures, rehab, and payday loans and to more effectively target vulnerable consumers generally.[5] Paul Ohm succinctly summarizes, "[companies] hoard this data for future, undefined uses; redistribute it to countless third parties; and repurpose it in ways their customers never imagined."[6]

Advances in hyper-targeted marketing allow firms to generate leads, tailor search results, place content, and develop advertising based on a detailed picture of their target.[7] This article calls such tactics "targeted manipulation," which is the covert leveraging about a specific target's vulnerabilities to steer their decision to the manipulator's interest. As Ryan Calo predicted in one of the first papers on manipulation of consumers online, hyper-targeting, combined with the data collected on individuals, could allow firms to predict moods, personality, stress levels, health issues, etc., and potentially use that information to undermine the decisions of consumers.[8] In fact, Facebook offered advertisers the ability to target teens that are "psychologically vulnerable."[9] Data aggregators, data brokers, ad networks and other types of "data traffickers"[10] can not only predict what consumers want and how badly they need it, but can also leverage knowledge about individuals' vulnerabilities to steer their decisions in the interest of the firm.[11]

Recent examinations of online consumer manipulation have defined manipulation broadly as to include standard persuasion and advertising tactics,[12] or have focused on the use of human psychology to prime market decisions across consumers (e.g., nudging or dark patterns).[13] Folding targeted manipulation within persuasion or nudging allows manipulation—which operates closer to fraud or coercion in undermining choice in the market—to hide within more innocuous or difficult-to-regulate tactics that are deployed broadly across a group of users.

The phenomenon of interest is the ability of firms to covertly leverage a target's vulnerabilities to steer their decision to the manipulator's interests. In doing so, this article moves away from broader interpretations of manipulation centered on irrational decisions, nudges, and persuasion, which render manipulation so pervasive as to be un-governable. Instead, this article focuses on a stricter conceptualization—well known within law, philosophy, and economics—that focuses on the hidden nature of the tactic to exploit a specific target's vulnerabilities in order to hijack their decisions to the manipulator's ends.[14] Targeted manipulation defined here has three important factors: 1) the exploitation of an individual's vulnerabilities; 2) the covertness of tactic; and, 3) the divergence of interests between manipulator and target.

More specifically, this conceptualization focuses on manipulation as undermining an individual's ability to enact their preferences through choice. We generally seek to preserve choice in the market, where consumer choice is meaningful and indicative of consent to the transaction. Preserving choice-as-an-indicator-of-consent is not only critical for autonomy and a robust political society, but also a fundamental assumption in economics and business as to the efficiency of transactions and the legitimacy of markets. As such, this article positions manipulation as a close cousin to coercion and fraud in undermining an individual's choice in the market. Positioning targeted manipulation as akin to coercion and fraud changes the conversation about governance and brings in new parallel examples offline where consumer choice is protected.

The goal of this paper is to argue that *firms merely in the position* to manipulate, with knowledge of the individual and access to their decision-making, should be regulated to ensure their interests are aligned with the target. In other areas, when someone is in a position to manipulate—in a position to exploit the relative vulnerabilities or weaknesses of a target in order to usurp their decision-making—safeguards force their interests to be aligned and punishes acts that are seen as out of alignment of the target. Given this odd economic situation, where data traffickers have the knowledge and proximity of an intimate relationship without the governance and trust inherent to such relationships in the market, this article then asks: *how did firms gain positions of power to exploit vulnerabilities and weaknesses of individuals without the requisite safeguards in place?* This article argues that this current market problem—where firms, whose interests do not align with consumers, have the knowledge and position to manipulate consumers—is due to the incorrect framing of privacy as relinquished upon disclosure in economics and law.[15]

Governing targeted manipulation online will require placing responsibility on those in the position manipulate rather than attempting to identify each instance of targeted manipulation. This article advances two solutions in the last section. First, external auditing of data aggregators and ad networks in the position to manipulate, with the individualized data to identify weaknesses and vulnerabilities of consumers, would ensure that the use of information is not used to manipulate consumers. This external auditing will entail data integrity principles that are enforced through auditing by third parties. Importantly, these obligations of care do not rely on any harm to be quantified, an established consumer relationship, or enforcement by consumers. Instead, this article posits that data traffickers – companies that collect, store, process, individualized data – would be subject to annual audits similar to other industries requiring public trust but not regulated by the market (e.g., banks, accounting in firms, environmental impact for manufacturing).

Second, this article also argues that consumer-facing companies should be responsible for the third parties that access their users – either for the collection of data or for the targeting of content – and ensure that these third parties abide by standards of care and are audited. Consumer-facing websites and apps that lure consumers, so that their data is collected and later used against them, should be held responsible for the third parties that they invite to track and target their users. Current solutions place a duty of care or loyalty on consumer-facing firms, which can create pressure for these firms to then outsource bad privacy practices to third parties.[16] This article offers a complementary solution to those arguing for duties of loyalty and care to be imposed on consumer-facing firms by (1) extending the duties of consumer-facing firms to include a responsibility for the third parties they invite to track and target their users, and (2) by placing additional safeguards (an audit) on data traffickers in a position to manipulate consumers, but outside the reach of current regulations and proposed legal solutions, as well as outside any market pressures.

[…]

In sum, this article starts with the economic abnormality of firms in the position to leverage knowledge of individuals' vulnerabilities to manipulate consumers and then explores how firms gained the power and knowledge to manipulate indiscriminately without regulatory or market oversight. Firms being in a position to leverage aggregated consumer data is a symptom of the mistaken framing of privacy-as-concealment in law, economics, and public policy. Where scholarship has focused on identifying instances of manipulation to regulate, this article argues that firms merely in the position to manipulate, with the knowledge of the individual's vulnerabilities and access to their decision making, should be regulated to ensure their interests are aligned with the target. Governing targeted manipulation online will require additional safeguards on those firms in the position manipulate rather than attempting to identify each instance of targeted manipulation. First, additional safeguards are needed limiting data aggregators and ad networks—specifically any data trafficker without any relationship with consumers—to ensure the use of information is in the interests of the consumer. Second, customer-facing websites and apps act as gatekeepers by luring in consumers to have their data tracked by third parties and later to be targeted with manipulative content. In so doing, consumer-facing companies should be responsible for ensuring all third parties that access their users—either for data collection or for targeting content—abide by standards of care that are audited.

Notes

1. George J. Stigler, *The Economics of Information*, 69 J. Pol. Econ. 213, 213 (1961).
2. Sherman, Justin. 2021. Data Brokers and Sensitive Data on U.S. Individuals. 2021. https://sites.sanford.duke.edu/techpolicy/wp-content/uploads/sites/17/2021/08/Data-Brokers-and-Sensitive-Data-on-US-Individuals-Sherman-2021.pdf Steve Melendez & Alex Pasternack, *Here are the data brokers quietly buying and selling your personal information*, FAST COMPANY (Mar. 2, 2019) https://www.fastcompany.com/90310803/here-are-the-data-brokers-quietly-buying-and-selling-your-personal-information.
3. Melendez, Steven and Alex Pasternack. 2019. "Here are the data brokers quietly buying and selling your personal information". *Fast Company*. March 2, 2019. https://www.fastcompany.com/90310803/here-are-the-data-brokers-quietly-buying-and-selling-your-personal-information.
4. Martin, Kirsten, and Helen Nissenbaum. "What is it about location?." *Berkeley Tech. LJ* 35 (2020): 251.; Martin, Kirsten, and Helen Nissenbaum. "Privacy interests in public records: An empirical investigation." *Harv. JL & Tech.* 31 (2017): 111. Hill, Kashmir, "Data Broker Was Selling Lists Of Rape Victims, Alcoholics, and 'Erectile Dysfunction Sufferer", *Forbes* (Dec 19, 2013). https://www.forbes.com/sites/kashmirhill/2013/12/19/data-broker-was-selling-lists-of-rape-alcoholism-and-erectile-dysfunction-sufferers/?sh=3d72b8861d53 Committee on Commerce, Science, and Transportation US Senate. Dec 18, 2013. https://www.govinfo.gov/content/pkg/CHRG-113shrg95838/pdf/CHRG-113shrg95838.pdf WHAT INFORMATION DO DATA BROKERS HAVE ON CONSUMERS, AND HOW DO THEY USE IT?. https://www.govinfo.gov/content/pkg/CHRG-113shrg95838/pdf/CHRG-113shrg95838.pdf
5. Elisa Gabbert, *The 25 Most Expensive Keywords in Google Ads*, WORDSTREAM (June 27, 2017) https://www.wordstream.com/blog/ws/2017/06/27/most-expensive-keywords.

   Examples of keywords related to urgent problems were ranked by how much marketers were willing to pay for them and included: "Bail bonds" at #2, "Lawyer" at #4, "Cash services & payday loans" at #7, "Rehab" at #11, "Plumber" at #18, "Termites" at #19, and "Pest control" at #20.
6. Paul Ohm, *Sensitive Information*, 88 So. CAL. L. REV. 1125, 1128 (2015). https://southerncalifornialawreview.com/wp-content/uploads/2018/01/88_1125.pdf.

7. As an example, companies can morph a target's face with a model for advertising. Such face-morphs are thought to be more trusting that a stranger, however initial experiments have not shown this to impact behavior. Sonam Samat, Eyal Peer & Alessandro Acquisti, *Can Digital Face-Morphs Influence Attitudes and Online Behaviors?*, Proc. Fourteenth Symp. 117, 117 (2018). "Thus, self-morphs may be used online as covert forms of targeted marketing – for instance, using consumers' pictures from social media streams to create self-morphs, and inserting the resulting self-morphs in promotional campaigns targeted at those consumers." https://www.usenix.org/system/files/conference/soups2018/soups2018-peer.pdf.

8. Ryan Calo, *Digital Market Manipulation*, 82 George Wash. L. Rev. 995, 996 (2014). https://digitalcommons.law.uw.edu/faculty-articles/25/ Tal Zarsky was one of the first to identify manipulation online as problematic. *Tal Z. Zarsky, Online Privacy, Tailoring, and Persuasion*, Privacy and Technologies of Identity 209, 209 (2006). https://link.springer.com/chapter/10.1007/0-387-28222-X_12.

9. Nitasha Tiku, *Get Ready for the Next Big Privacy Backlash Against Facebook*, WIRED (May 21, 2017, 7:00 AM) https://www.wired.com/2017/05/welcome-next-phase-facebook-backlash/.

10. Professor Lauren Scholz uses the term 'data traffickers' to include companies who traffic in consumer data behind the scenes and without the knowledge of the consumer Lauren Henry Scholz, "Privacy Remedies," *Indiana Law Journal*, 2019, https://papers.ssrn.com/sol3/papers.cfm?abstract_id=3159746.. I use this term throughout to mean any company with individualized data without a relationship with users or customers. These companies make their money trafficking consumer data.

11. Ryan Calo, *Digital Market Manipulation*, 82 George Wash. L. Rev. 995, 996 (2014). https://digitalcommons.law.uw.edu/faculty-articles/25/ *Tal Z. Zarsky, Online Privacy, Tailoring, and Persuasion*, Privacy and Technologies of Identity 209, 209 (2006). https://link.springer.com/chapter/10.1007/0-387-28222-X_12.

12. Cass R. Sunstein, *Fifty Shades of Manipulation*, 1 J. Mktg. Behav. 213, 213 (2016). https://papers.ssrn.com/sol3/papers.cfm?abstract_id=2565892.

13. *See* Shmuel I. Becher & Yuval Feldman, *Manipulating, Fast and Slow: The Law of Non-Verbal Market Manipulations*, 38 Cardozo L. Rev. 459, 459 (2016) https://papers.ssrn.com/sol3/papers.cfm?abstract_id=2639862; T. Martin Wilkinson, *Nudging and Manipulation*, 61 Pol. Stud. 341, 341 (2013) https://onlinelibrary.wiley.com/doi/abs/10.1111/j.1467-9248.2012.00974.x; Anne Barnhill, *I'd like to Teach the World to Think: Commercial Advertising and Manipulation*, 1 J. Mktg. Behav. 307, X (2016) https://www.nowpublishers.com/article/Details/JMB-0020; Arvind Narayanan *et al.*, *Dark Patterns: Past, Present, and Future*, 18 Queue 67, 67 (2020) https://queue.acm.org/detail.cfm?id=3400901; Ari Ezra Waldman, *Cognitive Biases, Dark Patterns, and the 'Privacy Paradox'*, 31 Current Op. Psych. 105, 105 (2020) https://core.ac.uk/download/pdf/287298052.pdf. Acquisti *et al.* summarize the research on nudges regarding privacy in Alessandro Acquisti *et al.*, *Nudges for Privacy and Security: Understanding and Assisting Users' Choices Online*, 50 ACM Computing Surv. (CSUR) 1, 1 (2017) https://dl.acm.org/doi/pdf/10.1145/3054926.

14. Daniel Susser, Beate Roessler & and Helen Nissenbaum, *Online Manipulation: Hidden Influences in a Digital World*, 4 Geo. L. Tech. Rev. 1, 3 (2019) https://georgetownlawtechreview.org/wp-content/uploads/2020/01/4.1-p1-45-Susser.pdf; Joseph Raz, The Morality of Freedom 378 (1988); Eric A. Posner, *The Law, Economics, and Psychology of Manipulation*, 1 J. Mktg. Behav. 267, 267 (2016).

15. This article does not cover the harm from the individual being surveilled. That is not meant to diminish the ethical implications of surveillance, only to narrow the scope of the article. For example, respondents find being surveilled while forming preferences to undermine their autonomy. Yonat Zwebner & Rom Y. Schrift, *On My Own: The Aversion to Being Observed During the Preference-Construction Stage*, 47 J. Consumer Rsch. 475, 475 (2020); Julie E. Cohen, *Privacy, Visibility, Transparency, and Exposure*, U. Chi. L. Rev. 181, 181 (2008); Julie E. Cohen, *Examined Lives: Informational Privacy and the Subject as Object*, 52 Stan. L. Rev. 1373, 1373 (2000); Julie E. Cohen, *Turning Privacy inside Out*, 20 Theoretical Inquiries L. 1, 1 (2019). Professor Neil Richards defends intellectual privacy as the ability to develop ideas and beliefs away from an unwanted gaze.

16. Ian R. Kerr, *The Legal Relationship between Online Service Providers and Users*, 35 Can. Bus. L.J. 419, 419 (2019); Jack M. Balkin, *Information Fiduciaries and the First Amendment*, 49 U.C.D.L. Rev. 1183, 1183 (2015); Ariel Dobkin, *Information Fiduciaries in Practice: Data Privacy and User Expectations*, 33 Berkeley Tech. L.J. 33 1, 1 (2018); Neil M. Richards & Woodrow Hartzog, *Taking Trust Seriously in Privacy Law*, 19 Stan. Tech. L. Rev. 431, 431 (2016); Neil M. Richards & Woodrow Hartzog, *A Duty of Loyalty for Privacy Law*, 99 Wash. U. L. Rev. (forthcoming 2021) (available at https://papers.ssrn.com/sol3/papers.cfm?abstract_id=3642217).

Chapter 9.5

Excerpt from Ethics of the Attention Economy: The Problem of Social Media Addiction[*]

Vikram R. Bhargava and Manuel Velasquez

[…]

2. The Impermissibility of Making Social Media Addictive

The research and related literatures on internet addiction, on balance, then, would seem to suggest that there is a substantial social media addiction problem, and one that gives rise to various harms. We turn now to making three distinct, but related, moral arguments about this problem. First, we argue that in light of the kinds of harms associated with internet addictions, it is wrong to use social media platforms to addict users, and these harms are not justified by the benefits those technologies produce. Second, we argue that users of social media platforms are injured in a way that is demeaning, thereby adding insult to the injury. Third, we argue that addicting users to social media constitutes a particularly objectionable form of exploitation. These arguments, we believe, show not only that it is wrong to design social media platforms that addict users but also why it is wrong.

[*] Bhargava, Vikram R., and Manuel Velasquez. "Ethics of the Attention Economy: The Problem of Social Media Addiction." *Business Ethics Quarterly* (2021): 31:3 pp. 321–359. DOI:10.1017/beq.2020.32 . Reprinted with permission. Note: This is an excerpt from the original so footnote and endnote numbering may be modified.

DOI: 10.1201/9781003278290-57

2.1 The Harm Argument

Much of the literature on internet addiction has examined the harmful effects of both general internet addiction and addiction to social media, and several studies have confirmed their association with a wide range of harmful effects. Generalized internet addiction has been associated with poor performance at school because the addicted student fails to devote enough time to his or her studies (Fitzpatrick, Burkhalter, & Asbridge, 2019). It has also been associated with poor work performance because the addicted worker spends excessive amounts of time surfing the internet at work (Beard, 2002). A study focused on addiction to social media by Shakya and Christakis (2017) found that the more time young people spent on social media, particularly Facebook, the unhappier they were. Another study found that the more time adolescents spent on social media, the more depressed they became (Raudsepp & Kais, 2019). Kross et al. (2013) found that the longer people remained on Facebook, the more negative a mood they later reported.

It is significant that many of the harms associated with both general and specific internet addictions have a shared source: the time the addict spends on the technology. As the addicted person devotes more time to social media, the individual will necessarily have less time to devote to school, work, sleeping, caring for himself or herself, interacting with family, and face-to-face socializing with friends. As a result, the person's school, work, health, and social life often suffer. The individual's familial and other face-to-face social relationships will atrophy, leading one to become more isolated. In addition, as the empirical studies reviewed earlier show, the greater the amount of time the addicted person spends on the internet, the more that person will feel anxious and depressed. Moreover, even when the addicted person is not on social media, the addiction continues to put demands on their time. An individual who is addicted to social media, for example, finds themself repeatedly throughout the day shifting attention away from other activities to check social media feeds. Each time the person returns to their other activities, the individual not only needs additional time to refocus attention on those other activities but is able to give only limited attention to those other activities (Ward, Duke, Gneezy, & Bos, 2017). This repetitive fracturing of attention, then, decreases the time and attention the addict can devote to school, work, or socializing.

These harms are not negligible, and they are morally significant. To understand their moral significance, it will help if we set them against a plausible view of what human dignity requires. Toward that end, we here adopt the capabilities approach developed by Nussbaum (1997, 2000a, 2001, 2003, 2011b, 2011a) and Sen (1985, 1992, 1999). The capabilities approach has, of course, been subjected to criticisms (Giri, 2000; Menon, 2002; Pogge, 2010, 2002)—a number of which are addressed by Nussbaum (2000b, 2007, 2019)—and there are critical differences between Nussbaum and Sen, the two major proponents of the view (Nussbaum, 2003). However, we here adopt the approach as articulated by Nussbaum, not only because the approach remains plausible to us despite her critics, but because it has also been endorsed by a large number of philosophers and has become part of the theoretical foundations of contemporary international development policies, including the United Nation's Human Development Index (Stanton, 2007).[1]

Nussbaum (2003: 40) proposes ten "human capabilities" that, she argues, are required by "the dignity of the human being and ... a life worthy of that dignity." Among these are the following seven: 1) life; 2) bodily health; 3) senses, imagination, and thought (being able to sense, imagine, think, and reason in a "human" way informed by education); 4) emotions (being able to experience love, grief, longing, gratitude; not having one's emotional development blighted by fear and anxiety); 5) practical reason (the ability to form a conception of the good and engage in reflection about the course of one's life); 6) affiliation (being able to live with others, show concern for them, engage in social interaction with them); and 7) play (being able to laugh and enjoy recreational activities).[2] Nussbaum argues that these capabilities are "entitlements" of every person and that if we use the "language of rights," we can say that every individual has a "human right" to these capabilities (Nussbaum, 2011b: 36).

The harms that social media addiction—and internet addictions in general—inflict on the addict offend against these seven human capabilities that, according to Nussbaum, are required by human dignity and to which every person has a right.[3]

[…]

The harms associated with social media addictions, then, are substantial moral injuries inflicted on the users they encumber. If we accept Nussbaum's (2003: 40) argument—as we do—they are harms that strike at the "central requirements of a life with dignity." To use Nussbaum's language, inflicting such harms are violations of the addicted person's rights (Nussbaum, 2011a). Inflicting such harms, then, is, prima facie at least, morally wrong.

An objection might be raised to our argument at this point. We argue that internet addiction (particularly social media addiction) imposes serious harms on users. To support our argument, we have cited a number of studies, many of which are correlational studies, that show that addiction to social media is associated with certain detrimental conditions, such as depression and anxiety. It may be objected, however, that although correlational studies may show that addiction to social media is associated with these detrimental conditions, they do not show that the addiction to social media (or, more generally, to the internet) causes those harmful conditions. Recent critical reviews of the research on social media have, in fact, pointed out that the correlational studies do not adequately distinguish cause from effect (Odgers & Jensen, 2020; Orben & Przybylski, 2019). Moreover, it is possible that the causality is bidirectional (Zink, Belcher, Kechter, Stone, & Leventhal, 2019). Indeed, some studies have found evidence that depression and anxiety lead some people to become addicted to the use of social media, while the addiction to social media leads others to fall prey to depression and anxiety (Gamez, 2014; Li et al., 2018).

[…]

It may also be objected that just because an act harms, or imposes risks of harms, does not necessarily render it morally impermissible; after all, many surgeries, medicines, and so on, cause harms, but we nevertheless deem the harms justified because of the compensating benefits the act produces. One might argue that the aggregate benefits produced by websites like Facebook greatly outweigh (and may justify) the aggregate harms due to addiction. Facebook and other social media websites, for example, have allowed billions of people to communicate and interact in ways that have been of enormous benefit. They have allowed many people to go online and build new relationships or recover old relationships with distant family and friends, to share their expertise and knowledge with others, to educate themselves about what is happening in the world, to communicate in times of crisis, and to organize entire social movements. In other words, social media also produces benefits, particularly by enhancing communication. Such benefits are not negligible, and the benefits Facebook and other such websites have produced may very well outweigh the harms they produce.

But this objection fails to consider the fact that the immense benefits associated with the internet in general, and social media in particular, do not require the use of the mechanisms that have given these websites their addictive character. Much of the communicative and social interaction benefits social media websites deliver can be produced even if social media companies did not introduce the addictive mechanisms that they have designed into their websites, such as the intermittent variable rewards, social validation rewards, and elimination of natural stopping cues that we discussed earlier. These addictive mechanisms are not necessary to provide the communicative, relationship-building, educative, and organizational benefits social media has provided. The internet companies that build social media websites, then, build mechanisms into their websites that end up harming their users by addicting them, though they could provide similar valuable forms of social communication without those mechanisms.[4] Social media addiction is not a necessary part of delivering the benefits these products provide.

We conclude that it is morally wrong, then, to inflict on users the kinds of addictions that afflict many users as a result of the way social media companies construct their platforms and that the benefits produced by those platforms cannot justify the assaults on human dignity that result from the harms associated with those addictions.

2.2 The Adding Insult to Injury Argument

Not only are social media websites designed in ways that harm their users by addicting them but they add insult to the injury in a way that demeans and thus disrespects their users. To bring out this point, it will help first to briefly touch on a key feature of the design of social media platforms: adaptive algorithms.

Social media companies use so-called adaptive algorithms that continuously refine their platforms such that they can become more addictive for each user. The algorithms embedded in social media adjust the content they feed each particular user such that each user will remain engaged with the platform for ever longer periods of time (Lanier, 2018; Rader & Gray, 2015).[5] The algorithms do this by monitoring the amount of time particular kinds of content keep the particular user engaged with the platform, and they use that data to continuously adjust the content so that the particular user remains engaged with the platform for ever lengthening periods of time (Lee, Hosanagar, & Nair, 2018). The user's engagement with social media, then, produces an addictive feedback loop: the more one uses the platform, the more data the platform's algorithm has about what keeps that particular user engaged, and the more the algorithm feeds that particular user precisely the content that will keep them engaged even longer, and so the more addictive the platform becomes for that particular individual (Chessen, 2018; Schou & Farkas, 2016).

Of course, employing user data to influence content and presentation decisions is not new. Television has used Nielsen ratings to make both content and presentation decisions. What is new, however, is the level of granularity with which the adaptive algorithms are able to tailor their platforms to specific individuals and to do so continuously, automatically, and in real time. As Wharton professor Jonah Berger puts it, "social media is like a drug, but what makes it particularly addictive is that it is adaptive. It adjusts based on your preferences and behaviors" (Knowledge@ Wharton, 2019).

One might object that all addictions are characterized by tolerance, so that the more a person consumes an addictive substance, the more addicted that individual becomes. That is, the more a vulnerable person consumes alcohol, smokes cigarettes, or snorts cocaine, typically, the more addicted the person becomes to each of these things. So how is the rise in the addictive potential of social media different? While addictive substances change the addicted person by increasing the person's desire or craving for the substance, the adaptive algorithms of addictive social media websites change the website itself to increase its own addictive potential for each particular user. In other words, the more a person uses a social media platform, the more addictive the platform itself becomes (and in turn, the greater the propensity and likelihood of addicting the user or making the user more addicted). Cigarettes do not change themselves to become more addictive for each particular smoker; however, the more a person uses a social media website, the more addictive the website itself becomes for that particular individual.

Crucially, then, there is an added insult in the way the social media platform's addictive potential is increased: the social media companies involve the individual in the very process that makes the platform more addictive to that individual. Not only are social media companies inflicting the harms associated with the addiction but they get the user to contribute to their ability to do this. The user is being used against oneself, given that by using the social media platform, the user provides the data that make the platform itself more addictive for that individual. This adds a demeaning insult to the harms that accompany social media addictions and makes social media companies' act of addicting their users particularly perverse.[6]

To highlight the nature of the demeaning insult, it will help to consider insults in a different context: paternalistic policies. Shiffrin (2000: 207) argues that paternalistic policies "convey a special, generally impermissible, insult to autonomous agents." This sort of insult has been characterized as "effectively telling citizens that they are too stupid to run their lives, so Big Brother will have to tell them what to do" (Anderson, 1999: 301).[7] More simply, the thought such paternalistic policies and interventions express is the insulting thought that "you do not know best with regard to your own matters" (Cornell, 2015: 1316) and that "we know better than you what's good for you" (1317).

Now the insult in getting a person to contribute to making addictive the very thing to which that person becomes addicted expresses something worse than the insult involved in paternalism.[8] The insult involved when a social media website uses the person to harm themself is not the insult that a person does not know what is best for them (the insult expressed in some acts of paternalism); rather, it expresses the demeaning idea that the person's interests do not matter at all—a paradigmatic instance of disrespect. The insult involved in some cases of paternalism might be preferable, given that in such cases, at least what's best for you is a consideration in the decision calculus, even if it is condescending. But the insult involved in the case of social media is one that disrespects users through expressing the demeaning thought that the companies do not care whether it is better or worse for the user because the user does not matter; the user's interests do not figure into the social media company's decision-making.

The demeaning insult involved in the way social media companies addict users—by getting them to provide the data they will use to addict them—is a further reason why addicting users to social media is morally wrong. We will next turn to building on the argument in this and the previous sections to advance our final argument—that addicting users to social media constitutes a wrongful form of exploitation.

2.3 The Exploitation Argument

[...]

Wood (1995, 2016) has provided an important account of exploitation that has had influence in a diverse range of contexts (e.g., Arnold & Valentin, 2013; Healy, 2010; Miller, 2010; O'Neill, 2013; Rogers, Mackenzie, & Dodds, 2012). Wood (1995) holds that exploitation involves taking advantage of a person's vulnerability to advance one's own ends. He notes, "To exploit someone or something is to make use of him, her, or it for your own ends by playing on some weakness or vulnerability in the object of your exploitation" (Wood, 2005).

But not all acts of taking advantage of another's weakness or vulnerability for one's own ends are morally objectionable—that is, not all acts of exploitation are morally objectionable. For example, it is not wrong in basketball to exploit a defender's lapse in attention to pass the ball to a teammate for an easy layup, nor is it objectionable for an attorney to exploit a weakness in the opposition's argument (Wood, 1995: 152). So, what makes an act of exploitation morally objectionable? For an act of exploitation to be a wrongful kind, it must involve disrespect toward the object of exploitation (Arnold, 2010; Wood, 1995).

We will build on the argument in the previous subsection and argue that addicting users to social media involves a wrongful form of exploitation. We can characterize the components of the morally objectionable form of exploitation in which we are interested as follows: exploiting X involves 1) taking advantage of X's vulnerability to 2) advance one's own ends 3) in a way that disrespects X.[9] In section 2.2, we already discussed the demeaning insult that disrespects the user when social media companies design their websites in ways that addict their users. So now, we will focus on 1) and 2): how social media companies advance their own ends through taking advantage of their users' vulnerability.

According to Wood (1995), then, an act is exploitative only if the exploiter advances his or her ends (even if the exploiter does not benefit all things considered) through the interaction with the object of exploitation. This is clearly satisfied in the interaction between social media companies and their users. Social media companies, in fact, are among the most lucrative of all businesses, and given that their profitability stems largely from advertisements directed at users (PwC, 2018), it is clear that social media companies are advancing their own ends when they get users to engage and remain engaged with their social media platforms. This point is uncontroversial, and we will not say more about how social media companies benefit themselves through their interactions with their users.

However, for the interaction between social media companies and users to be exploitative, the companies must advance their ends in a certain way: they must do so by taking advantage of the vulnerability of the users. So, we now turn our attention to how social media companies take advantage of the vulnerability of social media users to advance their own ends.

There are two sources of vulnerability in social media users. The first source of vulnerability is seen in the garden-variety type of exploitation that exists between drug dealers and their addicted buyers. This vulnerability is based on the addicted person's powerful and sometimes desperate craving for the addictive object that is the usual outcome of becoming addicted to the object. Wood (1995: 143) notes that "an addict's need or desire for drugs, for example, is clearly a vulnerability which pushers may [exploit]."[10] Similarly, social media companies exploit the desire or craving to use their platforms that is the result of becoming addicted to those platforms, and the companies profit when this craving leads their users to engage with the platforms.

The second source of vulnerability is rooted in the pervasiveness and importance of the internet in our lives. Even if a user were to overcome the first source of vulnerability (i.e., were to overcome his or her addiction), the user must continue to contend with this second source. The second source of vulnerability is based on the fact that the same powerful desires or cravings that are the result of becoming addicted to an object in the first place can be reignited by environmental cues even after the addict has managed to overcome the addiction (Lu et al., 2002; Niaura, Rohsenow, Binkoff, Monti, Pedraza, & Abrams, 1988). Several studies have shown that objects or situations that are associated in the addict's memory with the object of his or her addiction will arouse the desires and cravings that originally accompanied the addiction, even years after the addict was presumed to have overcome the addiction (Conklin, 2006; Siegel, 1999). A former drug addict, for example, may begin to experience such cravings when seeing drug paraphernalia or watching a movie with scenes of people using drugs (University of Guelph, 2019; Wolter, Huff, Speigel, Winters, & Leri, 2019). In a similar way, people who have recovered from an addiction to social media (or some other form of internet addiction) may again experience a craving to engage with social media when they see others using a computer or smartphone or when they themselves use a computer or smartphone for some purpose unrelated to social media (Ko et al., 2013). Unfortunately, because of the pervasiveness of the internet and its unavoidability in our lives, this second source of vulnerability is inescapable in contemporary life.

In other words, the pervasiveness and importance of the internet in our lives create an inescapable vulnerability to exploitation that makes addicting users to social media especially invidious. Addictions to many other activities and goods—for example, gambling, heroin, marijuana, television, and, to a lesser extent, alcohol—are such that one can get through life without having to be in situations where one is exposed to the environmental cues that can reignite craving for the addictive object. One can maintain a productive life even if one, for example, avoids going to casinos, removes oneself from the environment in which heroin use was common, or gets rid of the television. But it is virtually impossible in today's world to avoid use of the internet. While one can get on with a fairly productive life with little or no exposure to heroin, television, or gambling, it is extremely difficult to get by in contemporary society without exposure to the internet.

Moreover, it is not just that the internet is pervasive; it also plays a legitimate and essential role in many of our lives (Jackson, 2011). Many professional jobs require one to use email. Students at universities rely on the internet, as universities use online portals for grades and assignments, email communications, and entire courses. Health care professionals often convey test results through the internet. One report indicates that a majority of employers are less likely to hire a person without an active online presence (Harris Poll, 2017). Some employers strongly encourage employees to be active on social media and to post their experience as employees so that they can serve as brand ambassadors (Cervellon & Lirio, 2017). Many university social groups rely heavily on social media. Alerts and active shooting warnings are often disseminated through social media platforms by local governments, university security departments, and regional police departments; in some cases, changes to national and foreign policy are announced through the social media accounts of government officials. In other words, the internet's reach into our lives is much deeper and wider than the reach of other addictive substances and that constant exposure provides the cues that produce the cravings of social media addiction. This gives social media businesses innumerable opportunities not only to addict but to also readdict users.

The pervasiveness feature is perhaps most worrying in the context of children and teens.[11] Unlike many addictive substances and activities that are illegal for minors, the internet is entirely licit. A fifth grader cannot go to a store to purchase cigarettes or alcohol. Similarly, teenagers and children are not permitted to gamble in casinos. Yet there are few barriers to a child's internet use, and in fact, children face a significant cost to not using the internet.[12] Children and teens, then, are exposed to the internet at a time when they lack full moral agency and are most susceptible to addiction (Chambers, Taylor, & Potenza, 2003; Jordan & Andersen, 2017).

In addition, some individuals, adults as well as children, have characteristics that make them particularly vulnerable to becoming addicted to the internet. Some studies have shown, for example, that users with low self-control (Li, Dang, Zhang, Zhang, & Guo, 2014; Özdemir, Kuzucu, & Ak, 2014) and neuroticism (Kuss, Griffiths, & Binder, 2013) are particularly vulnerable to internet addiction. The pervasiveness feature of the internet means that individuals with such vulnerabilities will find it particularly difficult to avoid becoming addicted.

Addicting users, given our current context, then, constitutes a form of morally objectionable exploitation. Social media companies exploit the vulnerabilities of potential targets who are vulnerable not because of deviant preferences but because our society now relies heavily on the internet. Internet companies have a vast number of potential addicts who cannot simply follow Nancy Reagan's infamous mantra to "just say no."

To conclude, given how pervasive the internet is in our lives, and how difficult it is for most of us to forgo the internet, addicting users to social media involves an especially invidious sort of exploitation. By inflicting its users with addiction, social media businesses engage in a form of morally objectionable exploitation.

2.4 Summary

In this section, we argued that addicting users to social media is impermissible because it involves unjustifiably harming them in a way that is demeaning and objectionably exploitative. We argued that addicting users to social media harms them in ways that violate their rights and that these harms are not justified given that whatever benefits social media may provide, they can be realized without addiction. Second, the way in which social media companies have users contribute to making the platforms themselves more addictive, we argued, is particularly perverse because it involves a demeaning insult. Furthermore, addicting users is a morally objectionable form of exploitation that is especially troubling because the pervasiveness and legitimate role the internet plays in our lives create for some users an inescapable vulnerability to such exploitation.

In what follows, we will discuss the nature of the business model used by social media companies and how it incentivizes this wrongful kind of behavior.

3. A Business that Incentivizes Wrongdoing

Many kinds of businesses (both technology and nontechnology businesses) provide products that addict their users. But addiction is merely a contingent feature of the business model of most of them. For example, a cigarette company would not object if a customer bought its product and threw it in the garbage, used the cigarettes to build model bridges, transformed them into modern art, or used the product in any other way apart from smoking, so long as the customer continued to purchase the product.[13] In other words, the cigarette company would be indifferent to whether a customer ever actually smoked its cigarettes, as long as its revenues continued to flow at the same or an increased rate.[14]

Something similar is true even for some addictive technology products that do not have an attention—economy business model. For example, consider subscription-based digital streaming services (e.g., Netflix): the contemporary popularity of the term binge-watching is perhaps in large part due to such services. But so long as their customers purchase or renew their memberships, it is immaterial to these subscription streaming services whether or not they binge-watch a given television series. This is not to say that these subscription-based streaming services do not employ mechanisms that render their platforms addictive: automatically rolling over into the next episode is a feature designed to keep users on the platform by eliminating natural stopping cues (e.g., having to end an episode and click into a new one). But the point is that it is not a necessary feature of the business model of companies with subscription-based streaming services that customers continue to watch the companies' shows. As long as customers renew or purchase their memberships, their failure to binge-watch is not a significant problem for these companies. Perhaps it is even beneficial to subscription-based streaming services; assuming a company pays royalties on a per-use basis, the company could lower its costs, and it would perhaps even be able to narrow its bandwidth infrastructure costs. To be clear, we are not saying that all of its customers would continue to buy and renew their subscriptions to these streaming services if they did not find the content addictive; rather, we are pointing out that making a platform addictive is not an essential feature of the subscription-based streaming service business model.

But attention-economy businesses—of which social media businesses are the paradigmatic example and our primary focus—have a business model that exhibits an important difference: it hinges on keeping users active on a platform for prolonged periods of time. The longer a user is active and engaged on a social media platform, the more profitable it is for the social media company. This is because the longer the user remains engaged with the platform, the more likely it is that this user will be exposed to, influenced by, and engaged with advertisements, and so the more the social media company can charge its advertisers (Lanier, 2018; McNamee, 2019; Price, 2018). Users of social media, unlike users of cigarettes, alcohol, or junk food, are not the source of the companies' revenues. The revenues of social media companies come from advertisers, not users. As the familiar slogan goes, with social media, you are not the customer, you are the product.[15] Thus built into the business model of social media is a strong incentive to keep users online for prolonged periods of time, even though this means that many of them will go on to develop addictions (Alter, 2017; Price, 2018). And, as we have argued, the significant harms of social media addiction have a temporal dimension: they are primarily related to the amount of time the person who becomes addicted spends on social media.[16] Given the arguments from the previous section—that addicting users to social media is impermissible because it inflicts unjustified harms in a way that is demeaning and objectionably exploitative—social media businesses have a strong incentive to engage in wrongdoing.

[...]

Notes

1. Beyond human development and human rights, the broader capability approach has had far-reaching influence on a number of fields, including welfare economics, environmental policy, gender studies, and global public health (Robeyns, 2016).
2. In addition to these seven, Nussbaum includes three other capabilities that are not directly relevant to our argument; these three are bodily integrity (freedom to move from place to place, security from violence, and choice in matters of reproduction), other species (being able to live with concern for and in relation to animals, plants, and the world of nature), and control over one's political and material environment.
3. We are not claiming, of course, that internet addiction assaults Nussbaum's capabilities more than other kinds of addictions.
4. We are not here claiming that social media companies are intentionally harming their users. Rather, we are saying that social media companies make decisions that—regardless of their intentions—end up addicting users and thereby end up inflicting morally significant harms on users. Whether the social media firms intend to perform the action under that description (of intending to harm) is an issue on which we here take no position. For an overview of philosophical theories of intention, see Setiya (2018).
5. Our point is not that spending lots of time on a social media platform is equivalent to addiction. As noted in section 1, one must satisfy additional conditions to be addicted. However, excessive time spent on social media is a particularly salient observable feature that does not rely on user reports about his or her mental state and is defeasible evidence of addiction.
6. The demeaning insult is analytically distinct from the harm because the harm can be realized without doing so in an insulting way (as is the case with other businesses that sell harmful products). Given this, the two are not one and the same, even if the insult and the harm are contingently linked. We thank an anonymous reviewer for asking us to clarify this point.
7. Citation due to de Marneffe's (2006: 80).
8. See Caulfield (2019) for an account of the value of assessing various problems in business ethics through an expressive lens.
9. Since Wood's (1995) article on exploitation, there have been numerous accounts of exploitation. The debate surrounding the concept of exploitation is an active area of research. For some overviews of the state of the debate on exploitation, along with some worries with Wood's account, see Vrousalis's (2018) and Zwolinski and Wertheimer's (2017). That said, Wood's key insight that exploitation involves taking advantage of another's vulnerability for one's benefit strikes us as capturing a critical

aspect of exploitation. Moreover, it has been a particularly important account in the realm of business ethics (Arnold [2010] calls it "perhaps the most compelling empirical account of exploitation"). So, while acknowledging that there are a variety of accounts of exploitation available, we think it plausible that Wood's account captures a key component of exploitation, even if his account ultimately falls short of offering an exhaustive set of individually necessary and jointly sufficient conditions for the concept of exploitation.

10. See also Mayer (2007: 137): "It is usually thought to be wrong to exploit another person's attributes, for example when a pusher takes advantage of an addict's craving and sells her more drugs."

11. The Royal College of Psychiatrists recently released a report calling on the British government to require social media companies to provide data so researchers can further study the mental health effects of social media on children (Dubicka & Theodosiou, 2020). We thank an anonymous reviewer for bringing this to our attention.

12. Of course, some social media companies might note that a child needs to be of a certain age to sign up, but this has been almost entirely ineffective given the ease with which one can input a different age when signing up (Coughlan, 2016).

13. There is, of course, the possibility that cigarette companies would want you to smoke them for the purpose of getting other people to think it is trendy. But insofar as you are able to make it look like you are smoking, it would be irrelevant to them whether you in fact smoked.

14. None of this is intended by way of apologetics for the many serious ethical worries that arise due to cigarette businesses. We acknowledge the innumerous public health consequences of cigarettes and the cigarette companies' efforts to thwart democratic processes through troubling lobbying efforts and their attempts to influence the research agendas of universities.

15. The fact that user data are also sold is another point that supports the notion that users' attention is the product.

16. The content of what users are exposed to also is plausibly linked to the harms. For example, exposure to content involving self-harm is linked to higher rates of suicidal ideation (Arendt, Scherr, & Romer, 2019). We thank an anonymous reviewer for raising this point about the relevance of the content that users encounter.

References

Alter, A. 2017. *Irresistible: The rise of addictive technology and the business of keeping us hooked*. New York: Penguin Press.

Arnold, D. G., & Valentin, A. 2013. Corporate social responsibility at the base of the pyramid. *Journal of Business Research*, 66: 1904–14.

Beard, K. W. 2002. Internet addiction: Current status and implications for employees. *Journal of Employment Counseling*, 39(1): 2–11.

Caulfield, M. 2019. Expressive business ethics. In J. Weber & D. M. Wasieleski (Eds.), *Business ethics*, vol. 3: 123–53. Bingley, UK: Emerald.

Cervellon, M. C., & Lirio, P. 2017. When employees don't "like" their employers on social media. *MIT Sloan Management Review*, 58(2): 63–70.

Chambers, R. A., Taylor, J. R., & Potenza, M. N. 2003. Developmental neurocircuitry of motivation in adolescence: A critical period of addiction vulnerability. *American Journal of Psychiatry*, 160: 1041–52.

Chessen, M. 2018. The MADCOM future. In R. V. Yampolskiy (Ed.), *Artificial intelligence safety and security*, 1st ed.: 127–44. New York: Chapman and Hall/CRC.

Conklin, C. A. 2006. Environments as cues to smoke: Implications for human extinction- based research and treatment. *Experimental and Clinical Psychopharmacology*, 14 (1): 12–19.

Cornell, N. 2015. A third theory of paternalism. *Michigan Law Review*, 113: 1295–1336.

Coughlan, S. 2016. Safer Internet Day: Young ignore "social media age limit." *BBC News*, February 09. https://www.bbc.com/news/education-35524429.

Dubicka, B., & Theodosiou, L. 2020. *Technology use and the mental health of children and young people*, CR225 ed. London: Royal College of Psychiatrists.

Fitzpatrick, C., Burkhalter, R., & Asbridge, M. 2019. Adolescent media use and its associ- ation to wellbeing in a Canadian national sample. *Preventive Medicine Reports*, 14: 1–6.

Gamez, M. 2014. Depressive symptoms and problematic internet use among adolescents: An analysis of the longitudinal relationships from the cognitive-behavioral model. *Cyberpsychology, Behavior, and Social Networking*, 11: 714–19.

Giri, A. K. 2000. Rethinking human well-being: A dialogue with Amartya Sen. *Journal of International Development*, 12: 1003–18.

Harris Poll. 2017. *Number of employers using social media to screen candidates at all-time high, finds latest CareerBuilder study*. CareerBuilder, June 15. http://press.careerbuilder.com/2017-06-15-Number-of-Employers-Using -Social-Media-to-Screen- Candidates-at-All-Time-High-Finds-Latest-CareerBuilder-Study.

Healy, K. 2010. *Last best gifts: Altruism and the market for human blood and organs*. Chicago: University of Chicago Press.

Jackson, N. 2011. United Nations declares internet access a basic human right. *Atlantic*, June 3. https:// www.theatlantic.com/technology/archive/2011/06/united-nations-declares- internet-access-a-basic-h uman-right/239911/.

Jordan, C. J., & Andersen, S. L. 2017. Sensitive periods of substance abuse: Early risk for the transition to dependence. *Developmental Cognitive Neuroscience*, 25: 29–44.

Knowledge@Wharton. 2019. *The impact of social media: Is it irreplaceable?* https:// knowledge.wharton.up enn.edu/article/impact-of-social-media/.

Kross, E., Verduyn, P., Demiralp, E., Park, J., Lee, D. S., Lin, N., et al. 2013. Facebook use predicts declines in subjective well-being in young adults. *PLoS ONE*, 8(8): e69841.

Kuss, D. J., Griffiths, M. D., & Binder, J. F. 2013. Internet addiction in students: Prevalence and risk factors. *Computers in Human Behavior*, 29: 959–66.

Lanier, J. 2018. *Ten arguments for deleting your social media accounts*. New York: Henry Holt.

Lee, D., Hosanagar, K., & Nair, H. S. 2018. Advertising content and consumer engagement on social media: Evidence from Facebook. *Management Science*, 64: 5105–31.

Li, C., Dang, J., Zhang, X., Zhang, Q., & Guo, J. 2014. Internet addiction among Chinese adolescents: The effect of parental behavior and self-control. *Computers in Human Behavior*, 41: 1–7.

Li, J., Mo, P., Lau, J., Su, X., Zhang, X., Anise, M. S., et al. 2018. Online social networking addiction and depression: The results from a large-scale prospective cohort study in Chinese adolescents. *Journal of Behavioral Addictions*, 7: 686–96.

Lu, L., Xu, N.-J., Ge, X., Yue, W., Su, W.-J., Pei, G., et al. 2002. Reactivation of morphine conditioned place preference by drug priming: Role of environmental cues and sensitization. *Psychopharmacology*, 159: 125–32.

Mayer, R. 2007. What's wrong with exploitation? *Journal of Applied Philosophy*, 24: 137–50.

McNamee, R. 2019. *Zucked*. New York: Penguin Press.

Menon, N. 2002. Universalism without foundations? *Economy and Society*, 31: 152–69.

Miller, R. W. 2010. *Globalizing justice: The ethics of poverty and power*. Oxford: Oxford University Press.

Niaura, R. S., Rohsenow, D. J., Binkoff, J. A., Monti, P. M., Pedraza, M., & Abrams, D. B. 1988. Relevance of cue reactivity to understanding alcohol and smoking relapse. *Journal of Abnormal Psychology*, 97: 133–52.

Nussbaum, M. C. 1997. Capabilities and human rights. *Fordham Law Review*, 6: 273–300.

Nussbaum, M. C. 2000a. *Women and human development: The capabilities approach*. Cambridge: Cambridge University Press.

Nussbaum, M. C. 2000b. Aristotle, politics, and human capabilities: A response to Antony, Arneson, Charlesworth, and Mulgan. *Ethics*, 111: 102–40.

Nussbaum, M. C. 2001. Disabled lives: Who cares? *New York Review of Books*, 34–37.

Nussbaum, M. C. 2003. Capabilities as fundamental entitlements: Sen and social justice. *Feminist Economics*, 9(2–3): 33–59.

Nussbaum, M. C. 2007. *Frontiers of justice: Disability, nationality, species membership*. Cambridge, MA: Harvard University Press.

Nussbaum, M. C. 2011a. *Creating capabilities: The human development approach.* Cambridge, MA: Harvard University Press.

Nussbaum, M. C. 2011b. Capabilities, entitlements, rights: Supplementation and critique. *Journal of Human Development and Capabilities* 12(1): 23–37.

Nussbaum, M. C. 2019. *The cosmopolitan tradition: A noble but flawed ideal.* Cambridge, MA: Belknap Press of Harvard University Press.

Odgers, C. L., & Jensen, M. R. 2020. Annual research review: Adolescent mental health in the digital age—facts, fears, and future directions. *Journal of Child Psychology and Psychiatry,* 61: 336–48.

O'Neill, J. 2013. *Markets, deliberation and environment.* New York: Routledge.

Orben, A., & Przybylski, A. K. 2019. The association between adolescent well-being and digital technology use. *Nature Human Behavior,* 3: 173–82.

Özdemir, Y., Kuzucu, Y., & Ak, S. 2014. Depression, loneliness, and Internet addiction: How important is low self-control? *Computers in Human Behavior,* 34: 284–90.

Pogge, T. W. 2002. Can the capability approach be justified? *Philosophical Topics,* 302: 167–228.

Pogge, T. 2010. A critique of the capability approach. In H. Brighouse & I. Robeyns (Eds.), *Measuring justice: Primary goods and capabilities*: 17–60. Cambridge: Cambridge University Press.

Price, C. 2018. The secret ways social media is built to be addictive (and what you can do to fight back). *BBC Science Focus Magazine,* October 29. https://www.sciencefocus.com/future-technology/trapped -the-secret-ways-social-media-is-built-to-be-addic tive-and-what-you-can-do-to-fight-back/.

PwC. 2018. *IAB internet advertising revenue report.* Corporate report.

Rader, E., & Gray, R. 2015. Understanding user beliefs about algorithmic curation in the Facebook news feed. In Proceedings of the 33rd annual ACM Conference on Human Factors in Computing Systems: 173–82. New York: Association for Computing Machinery.

Raudsepp, L., & Kais, K. 2019. Longitudinal associations between problematic social media use and depressive symptoms in adolescent girls. *Preventive Medicine Reports,* 15: 1–5.

Rogers, W., Mackenzie, C., & Dodds, S. 2012. Why bioethics needs a concept of vulnerability. *IJFAB: International Journal of Feminist Approaches to Bioethics,* 5(2): 11–38.

Schou, J., & Farkas, J. 2016. Algorithms, interfaces, and the circulation of information: Interrogating the epistemological challenges of Facebook. *KOME: An International Journal of Pure Communication Inquiry,* 4(1): 36–49.

Sen, A. 1985. *Commodities and capabilities.* Amsterdam: North-Holland.

Sen, A. 1992. *Inequality reexamined.* Oxford: Oxford University Press.

Sen, A. 1999. *Development as freedom.* Oxford: Oxford University Press.

Shakya, H. B., & Christakis, N. A. 2017. Association of Facebook use with compromised well-being: A longitudinal study. *American Journal of Epidemiology,* 185: 203–11.

Shiffrin, S. V. 2000. Paternalism, unconscionability doctrine, and accommodation. *Philosophy and Public Affairs,* 29: 205–50.

Siegel, S. 1999. Drug anticipation and drug addiction. The 1998 H. David Archibald lecture. *Addiction,* 94: 1113–24.

Stanton, E. A. 2007. *The human development index: A history.* PERI Working Paper no. 85.

University of Guelph. 2019. Why environmental cues make drug addiction extra hard to beat. *Science Daily.* https://www.sciencedaily.com/releases/2019/02/190227124848.htm.

Ward, A. F., Duke, K., Gneezy, A., & Bos, M. W. 2017. Brain drain: The mere presence of one's own smartphone reduces available cognitive capacity. *Journal of the Association for Consumer Research,* 2: 140–54.

Wolter, M., Huff, E., Speigel, T., Winters, B. D., & Leri, F. 2019. Cocaine, nicotine, and their conditioned contexts enhance consolidation of object memory in rats. *Learning and Memory,* 26(2): 46–55.

Wood, A. 1995. Exploitation. *Social Philosophy and Policy,* 12: 136–58.

Wood, A. 2005. Exploitation. In T. Honderich (Ed.), *The Oxford companion to philosophy,* 2nd ed.: 283–84. Oxford: Oxford University Press.

Wood, A. 2016. Unjust exploitation. *Southern Journal of Philosophy,* S1(54): 92–108.

Zink, J., Belcher, B., Kechter, A., Stone, M., & Leventhal, A. 2019. Reciprocal associations between screen time and emotional disorder symptoms during adolescence. *Preven- tive Medicine Reports,* 13: 281–88.

TRANSPARENCY AND ACCOUNTABILITY IN DATA ANALYTICS

10

When Lemonade Insurance uses AI Jim to determine if a claim should be paid, part of the problem is that their customers do not *know* a program is being used to judge them. This "not knowing" is a lack of transparency and the focus of many articles and criticisms of data analytics. COMPAS, the data analytics program used in sentencing defendants in court, came under scrutiny initially because the program to set parole and sentencing decisions was hidden from defendants. Even when the use of the program became known, the company would not share how it worked and claimed it was proprietary. Frank Pasquale coined the term the "Black Box Society" to capture the growing trend of companies to create data analytics programs that are not explained or transparent.[1] Here we are going to explore transparency in service of an *explanation*, for *accountability*, and for *contestability*.

Transparency, for data analytics, means providing enough information so that others can understand the performance of the program.[2] However, the information required to understand the program differs based not only on the person receiving the information (my favorite lawyer compared to my favorite computer scientist), but also based on *why* the person needs the information. Professor Zachery Lipton shows that the idea of interpretability and transparency of data analytics programs can be perceived to be difficult to implement because transparency or interpretability *is proposed for different end goals*. Lipton notes that we may desire to understand the causality of the decision. Or, we may desire transferability or the ability to use the program in a different situation and know it will work. And, how we offer interpretability of the data analytics program—visualizations, text explanations, etc.—would need to change based on the goal.[3]

Here, we examine three goals for transparency. First, transparency can offer stakeholders a right to an explanation of algorithmic decision-making similar to the idea of informed consent. In other words, subjects must consent to be the subject of algorithmic decision-making, and transparency is required for that informed consent and for subjects to *trust* the model.[4] Companies may argue that the algorithm is proprietary (this is common) or too complex technically.[5] The common argument against general transparency from data analysts and computer scientists is that *they* do not even understand how or why a program works.

DOI: 10.1201/9781003278290-58

It turns out, we do know a lot about how or why a program works. In an essay, "The Fallacy of Inscrutability," Joshua Kroll argues that the common argument that data analytics programs are inscrutable or black boxes is a fallacy. In fact, Professor Kroll argues that "inscrutability is not a result of technical complexity but rather of power dynamics in the choice of how to use those tools." This puts the responsibility on the designer of the data analytics program in creating a system that is a black box to users.[6]

A company may want to claim a program is inscrutable even if it is not. The company may want to protect a program they believe is a competitive advantage: this could be because it *is* a competitive advantage or due to sheer inertia (they always like to say things are a competitive advantage). The organization also may not like the answer they would need to provide, or the people asked may not know enough to answer. Recall the Stanford vaccine algorithm which had a clear answer but those being asked either did not understand how decisions were made or did not want to give the answer. Importantly, Professor Kroll argues that not understanding a system is just bad practice. As Kroll summarizes: "rather than discounting systems which cause bad outcomes as fundamentally inscrutable and therefore uncontrollable, we should simply label the application of inadequate technology what it is: malpractice, committed by a system's controller" (p. 5).

In addition, transparency as a right to an explanation does not ameliorate all our problems with AI and machine learning.[7] Many data analytics programs are used to distribute goods, such as jobs, government assistance, education, healthcare, etc., which have expectations of due process rights. For example, Amazon uses a prediction program to decide if their delivery drivers are doing a good job and then fires the drivers via an email. The drivers do not know the bases for their termination, however.[8] Therefore, we need to know enough about the way the program is making decisions to support their rights to due process.[9]

Second, transparency may be stated as required in order to *hold someone accountable or responsible* for the outcomes of the data analytics program. Nickolas Diakopoulos perhaps says this best:

> If the end goal is accountability, then transparency must serve to help locate the various positions of human agency and responsibility in these large and complex sociotechnical assemblages. Ultimately, it is people who must be held accountable for the behavior of algorithmic systems.[10]

In other words, transparency may be in service of monitoring performance as well as to make sure there is a human accountable for the outcomes.[11]

The issue of how to allocate accountability between technology and individuals is not new.[12] When designing autopilots for aircraft, we purposefully delegate roles and responsibilities to humans (and not to machines) to create what are referred to as "moral crumple zones" where the human bears the brunt of the moral penalties when the overall system fails—not because the human is required but because the decision is too important to let the computer program decide autonomously.[13] Similarly, the goal of military development of technology has moved away from increasing automation to more of a focus on "robots supporting human decision-making."[14]

How much the human should be in the loop is actually a design choice. One possibility is assessing the appropriate role and associated responsibility attributed to an algorithm as contingent upon the type of decision being made: the appropriate role of the algorithm versus human in a decision may be based on the relative importance of the decision in society. Not all decisions warrant equal scrutiny, with some having minimal importance and others being pivotal in the lives of individuals and society, e.g., getting into college, being fired, securing a loan, etc. The more important the decision, the more we expect a human agent to take responsibility within the decision

Another possibility is offered by Reuben Binns,[15] who outlines the many reasons why humans are said to be needed in algorithmic decision-making. Humans maintain oversight, creativity, and societal legitimacy and accountability in a decision; he suggests humans also are able to generate ground truth and avoid moral atrophy by being involved in an algorithmic-enhanced decision. Binns argues that humans are needed in algorithmic decision-making when *individual justice* is required: when "each case needs to be assessed on its own merits, without comparison to, or generalization from, previous cases." In other words, when "individual justice is required, algorithmic decision-making systems cannot (entirely) replace human judgment."[16]

So far, we have two related ideas. First, transparency may be in service of *explaining* the data analytics program. This idea is usually countered with a claim that the program is difficult if not impossible to explain—but we also know that's not exactly correct. Second, transparency is needed in service of *accountability* to understand the role of a human to be responsible for the outcomes. This brings us to the third reason we request transparency—to ask questions. And our readings cover the idea of *contestability* as an ethical design principle.

Summary of Readings

Karen Hao's "When algorithms mess up, the nearest human gets the blame"[17] focuses on who is held responsible for the outcomes of automated decisions. Hao uses a plane and Tesla crash as examples of how society purposely injects humans in computer-assisted decision systems and creates "moral crumple zones" which protect the integrity of the technological system, at the expense of the nearest human operator" (Elish, 2019). The concept of a moral crumple zone introduces the problem of designing liability into a data analytics program. When analyzing a data analytics program according to this reading, one would ask, who is in position to take responsibility for the outcomes of the program and who *should* be in the position to take responsibility?

In "Contestability as a Means to Promote Responsible Algorithmic Decision Making in the Professions,"[18] Mulligan, Kluttz, and Kohli offer "contestability" as the ultimate goal of the many discussions around transparency and accountability: our goal should be systems that "maintain human engagement." The authors explicitly link the calls for transparency and accountability to a fear of technological determinism (from Chapter 1): "A fear of being shaped and controlled by tools, rather than autonomously wielding them, lies at the heart of current concerns with machine learning and artificial intelligence systems (ML/AI systems)." This is made worse by terms such as "inscrutable" which frame AI systems as impossible to explain. The authors position contestability, the ability to contest decisions, as an alternative design goal to transparency and explainability—both popular approaches to governing AI systems. Where transparency merely grants openness or access, with the goal of being more informed about the system, contestability fosters critical engagement with the AI system. For those analyzing a data analytics program, one would examine (1) how this program should be transparent (to whom, in what way); (2) how is someone accountable for the program; and (3) how should this program be designed to be contestable?

Related Cases

While many of our cases touch upon the issues of transparency, accountability, and contestability (e.g., COMPAS, Stanford Vaccine case, Recommending an Insurrection case, etc.), two cases offer examples of data analytics programs where the questions about transparency, accountability, and contestability are more morally salient. First, the article on the Houston teachers outlines a court case where teachers sued the school district to be more transparent as to the program used to promote and fire teachers based on their performance. In reading the article, we can analyze not only *why are the teachers upset* about the program (using theory from this chapter) but also *how could the school district improve the program?*

Second, the article on cheating software used on students provides a case that touches upon most of the theories we have covered thus far. The students feel pressure not only to perform on the test but also to perform correctly for the cheating-detection software. The case touches upon issues of bias, fairness, surveillance, privacy, discrimination, and the ethical theories we have covered. In addition, the amount that students are expected to know about the program shows the negatives of transparency in overloading the student to understand.

Notes

1. Frank Pasquale, *The Black Box Society: The Secret Algorithms That Control Money and Information* (Cambridge, MA: Harvard University Press, 2015).
2. Nicholas Diakopoulos, "Transparency," in *The Oxford Handbook of Ethics of AI.*, 2020. Here, I am paraphrasing Diakopoulos who uses transparency as the availability of information required "to monitor the workings or performance ...." p. 198.
3. Zachary C. Lipton, "The Mythos of Model Interpretability: In Machine Learning, the Concept of Interpretability Is Both Important and Slippery," *Queue* 16, no. 3 (2018): 31–57.
4. Tae Wan Kim and Bryan R. Routledge, "Why a Right to an Explanation of Algorithmic Decision-Making Should Exist: A Trust-Based Approach," *Business Ethics Quarterly*, 2020, 1–28.
5. Jenna Burrell, "How the Machine 'Thinks': Understanding Opacity in Machine Learning Algorithms," *Big Data & Society* 3, no. 1 (2016).
6. Joshua A. Kroll, "The Fallacy of Inscrutability," *Philosophical Transactions of the Royal Society A: Mathematical, Physical and Engineering Sciences* 376, no. 2133 (2018): 20180084.
7. Lilian Edwards and Michael Veale, "Slave to the Algorithm: Why a Right to an Explanation Is Probably Not the Remedy You Are Looking For," *Duke L. & Tech. Rev.* 16 (2017): 18.
8. Soper, Spencer. 2021. "Fired by Bot at Amazon: 'It's You Against the Machine'. Bloomberg. June 28, 2021. https://www.bloomberg.com/news/features/2021-06-28/fired-by-bot-amazon-turns-to-machine-managers-and-workers-are-losing-out
9. Danielle Keats Citron, "Technological Due Process," *Washington University Law Review* 85 (2007): 1249; Danielle Keats Citron and Frank Pasquale, "The Scored Society: Due Process for Automated Predictions," *Washington & Lee Law Review* 89 (2014).
10. Diakopoulos, "Transparency."
11. Joanna Bryson summarizes this with "robots should be slaves:" "Robots are fully owned by us. We determine their goals and behaviour, either directly or indirectly through specifying their intelligence or how their intelligence is acquired." Joanna J Bryson, "Robots Should Be Slaves," *Close Engagements with Artificial Companions: Key Social, Psychological, Ethical and Design Issues* 8 (2010): 63–74.
12. Kirsten Martin, "Designing Ethical Algorithms.," *MIS Quarterly Executive* 18, no. 2 (2019).
13. Madeleine Clare Elish, "Moral Crumple Zones: Cautionary Tales in Human-Robot Interaction (Pre-Print)," *Engaging Science, Technology, and Society* (Pre-print), 2019.
14. Deborah G Johnson, "Technology with No Human Responsibility?," *Journal of Business Ethics* 127, no. 4 (2015): 707.
15. Reuben Binns, "Human Judgment in Algorithmic Loops: Individual Justice and Automated Decision-Making," *Regulation & Governance*, 2019.
16. Binns, 2.

17. Hao, Karen. 2019. When algorithms mess up, the nearest human gets the blame. *MIT Technology Review.*
18. Deirdre K. Mulligan, Daniel Kluttz, and Nitin Kohli, "Shaping Our Tools: Contestability as a Means to Promote Responsible Algorithmic Decision Making in the Professions," in *After the Digital Tornado*, ed. Kevin Werbach (Cambridge University Press, 2020).

Chapter 10.1

Houston Teachers to Pursue Lawsuit over Secret Evaluation System*

Shelby Webb

A federal judge ruled that the Houston ISD's use of a secret algorithm to evaluate teacher performance denied employees the right to challenge their terminations - giving teachers the green light to continue their lawsuit against the nation's seventh largest school district.

The algorithm used students' standardized testing data to compute a score that, among other factors, was used by district officials to determine which teachers were evaluated, fired and given bonuses between 2011 and 2015. It is no longer used by the district.

Louis Malfaro, president of the Texas American Federation of Teachers, said the judge's ruling means the case will likely be scheduled for a trial in coming months.

"We're going to proceed with this lawsuit, and based on what the judge wrote, we're winning the argument," Malfaro said.

> At the end of the day, educators care about education and want to see how they're doing and how to get better. It's time to take teacher evaluations back to what it should be - not another misuse of standardized testing data but a real opportunity for people to not only look at their own work and evaluate it, but also to have the opportunity to improve their practice.

But U.S. Magistrate Judge Stephen Wm. Smith stopped short of supporting all of the teachers' arguments, including that the standardized-testing-based algorithms failed to advance the district's goal of employing effective teachers and that the system did not show teachers how they could improve their scores.

---

* Webb, Shelby. 2017. "Houston Teachers to Pursue Lawsuit over Secret Evaluation System."*Houston Chronicle.* May 11, 2017. https://www.houstonchronicle.com/news/houston-texas/houston/article/Houston-teachers-to -pursue-lawsuit-over-secret-11139692.php Reprinted with permission.

DOI: 10.1201/9781003278290-59

"Of course, an employer's impulse to quantify employee performance is neither new nor inherently objectionable," Smith wrote last week.

The difficulty with this case, Smith added, was balancing the "understandable" secrecy of the algorithm with teachers' right to due process.

Trade Secret

The algorithm HISD used was part of the Educational Value Added Assessment System, or EVAAS, that was created by the private technology firm SAS.

The company viewed the algorithm and its teacher-evaluating software as a trade secret and never divulged details.

Because not even HISD administrators knew how the algorithm worked, teachers argued the district could not provide enough detail about terminations, leaving the teachers unable to defend against possible errors in the calculations.

A district website stated no teacher's score could be recalculated because that would force HISD to redo the analysis of every teacher, which would be "very costly for the district." A change to one teacher's report could force changes to all the others, it noted.

"The remarkable thing about this passage is not simply that cost considerations trump accuracy in teacher evaluations, troubling as that might be," Smith wrote. "Of greater concern is the house-of-cards fragility of the EVAAS system, where the wrong score of a single teacher could alter the scores of every other teacher in the district."

While teachers and unions further argued that EVAAS also was biased against teachers who educate economically disadvantaged students and English-language learners who typically struggle on standardized tests, the judge ruled that value-added models are a legitimate tool to measure teacher performance.

Watershed Moment

One of the teachers' experts admitted that there is evidence that a teacher's EVAAS score is correlated with that teacher's impact on student learning growth as measured by standardized test scores.

Union officials painted the ruling as a watershed moment in the fight against attaching high stakes to standardized tests, while district officials said the judgement has little bearing on its ability to use value-added models to evaluate teachers.

"The language used by the judge makes it pretty clear that the district doesn't have a leg to stand on in defending the defective evaluation system," said Houston Federation of Teachers' President Zeph Capo.

But district officials said the only change that must be made as a result of Smith's ruling is that teachers must be able to independently verify their performance scores.

"Should HISD ever again decide to use EVAAS or value-added scores, the Court's ruling leaves intact the District's ability to do so," the district said in a statement.

> The Court's ruling only requires that the score be verifiable by the teacher in the limited circumstance of contract dismissal decisions during the term of the contract. End-of-year dismissals for probationary and term contract teachers are not impacted by this ruling.

Chapter 10.2

Cheating-Detection Companies Made Millions During the Pandemic. Now Students Are Fighting back*

Drew Harwell

With remote proctors watching them take tests, some worry that even leaving for the bathroom will brand them as cheats.

When North Carolina A&T State University junior Arielle G. Brown took her International Marketing exam in September, a cheating-detection program analyzed her behavior through a computer webcam the entire time. After the test, her associate professor fired off a furious email ripping into her class for some "negative behavior" the software had flagged (Figure 10.2.1).

"A STUDENT IN 6 MINUTES HAD 776 HEAD AND EYE MOVEMENTS," she wrote, adding later, "I would hate to have to write you up."

But Brown and her classmates weren't about to take the shaky accusations of cheating lying down. They quickly lit up a group chat—"How the hell are we [supposed] to control our eyes," one student wrote—and Brown shared the email in a tweet that quickly got administrators' attention, as well as more than 100,000 "likes."

"It just felt so aggressive," she said in an interview. "Stuff that people wouldn't think twice about in a real classroom was being used against us." (The instructor and school officials did not respond to requests for comment.)

"Online proctoring" companies saw in coronavirus shutdowns a chance to capitalize on a major reshaping of education, selling schools a high-tech blend of webcam-watching workers and eye-tracking software designed to catch students cheating on their exams.

---

* Harwell, Drew. 2020. "Cheating-Detection Companies Made Millions during the Pandemic. Now Students are Fighting Back." *The Washington Post.* November 12, 2020. Reprinted with permission. https://www.washingtonpost.com/technology/2020/11/12/test-monitoring-student-revolt/

DOI: 10.1201/9781003278290-60

They've taken in millions of dollars, some of it public money, from thousands of colleges in recent months. But they've also sparked a nationwide school-surveillance revolt, with students staging protests and adopting creative tactics to push campus administrators to reconsider the deals.

Students argue that the testing systems have made them afraid to click too much or rest their eyes for fear they'll be branded as cheats. Some students also said they've wept with stress or urinated at their desks because they were forbidden from leaving their screens.

One system, Proctorio, uses gaze-detection, face-detection and computer-monitoring software to flag students for any "abnormal" head movement, mouse movement, eye wandering, computer window resizing, tab opening, scrolling, clicking, typing, and copies and pastes. A student can be flagged for finishing the test too quickly, or too slowly, clicking too much, or not enough.

If the camera sees someone else in the background, a student can be flagged for having "multiple faces detected." If someone else takes the test on the same network—say, in a dorm building—it's potential "exam collusion." Room too noisy, Internet too spotty, camera on the fritz? Flag, flag, flag.

As an unusually disrupted fall semester churns toward finals, this student rebellion has erupted into online war, with lawsuits, takedowns and viral brawls further shaking the anxiety-inducing backdrop of college exams. Some students have even tried to take the software down from the inside, digging through the code for details on how it monitors millions of high-stakes exams.

The tension has sparked deeper debates about America's breakneck shift toward education online. Is stopping a few cheaters worth the price of treating every student like a fraud? And how important are any of these tests, really, given the extra stress on students whose lives have already been turned inside out?

Jesse Stommel, a 20-year teacher and founder of an academic journal, Hybrid Pedagogy, that publicly sparred with Proctorio's chief this summer, said he's been flooded with emotional messages from students "talking about the pain, the anxiety, the fear, the worry the students are experiencing around this."

Most of them have gone from traditional tests to high-pressure video exams in which their every move is scrutinized. It's no wonder, he said, that they're fighting back. At the software's core, he said, "the most clear value conveyed to students is 'We don't trust you.'"

"Somebody Was Watching Me Just Lose My Mind"

The companies, with names like ProctorU, Respondus and Honorlock, advertise a wide range of cheater-nabbing tech that can lock down students' Web browsers, track their computer activity or connect their microphones and webcams to large call centers of "proctors" paid to watch the students take their tests. Some companies also offer artificial-intelligence software for spotting potentially suspect behavior, including face scanners to verify a test-taker's identity and eye sensors to flag if they're looking too long off-screen.

The companies say their systems can sniff out many of the inventive ways students game tests, such as looking at wall-mounted notes, copying from other websites or listening to a friend say the answers out loud. With Proctorio, any of these "behavior flags"—or anything a student does differently from the rest of the class, known as an "abnormality"—can raise a student's "suspicion level," which the students aren't allowed to see.

In interviews with 14 students, many of them said the systems also flagged them for lots of harmless little movements, such as when they jot down notes or read the questions aloud or look

Kc   **Testing Protocol**

All of you but 1 student violated a major testing protocol. Every one except 1 student resize their browser which means that you went to another website. If that happens again, you will get a 0 on the next assignment.

YOU have to have well lit room. You cannot take the test in the dark. SIT up. IF I only see your eyes then that is a violation of the testing protocol. YOU HAVE to video record. **It clearly states in the syllabus, no video, you get a 0.**

NO HEAD COVERING FOR BOTH MALES AND FEMALES. THIS MEANS NO WHAT I CALL SKULL CAPS AND REGULAR CAPS.

A LOT OF HEAD AND EYE MOVEMENTS FOR A SHORT TIME PERIOD. A STUDENT IN 6 MINUTES HAD 776 HEAD AND EYE MOVEMENTS. ANOTHER STUDENT HAD 624 EYE AND HEAD MOVEMENTS WITHIN 8 MINUTES.

THAT IS AN INDICATION OF EYES MOVING AWAY FROM THE SCREEN.

NOW IF THE PRETORIO BEHAVIOR DOES NOT IMPROVE ON CONNECT QUIZ 3, THEN YOU WILL HAVE TO BUY THE $15 VERSION OF PROCTORIO.

I TALKED TO Mc-GRAW-HILL AND THEY SAID THAT A LOT OF NEGATIVE BEHAVIOR WAS TAKING PLACE.

I would hate to have to write you up for online cheating which gets filed in the Dean's office.

Figure 10.2.1   Tweet of a student who forwarded the Testing Protocol with "… in the middle of a pandemic … school is a joke rn.. #ncat."

away to think. Though professors can change which student behaviors are monitored and ignore the systems' findings, nothing is guaranteed. And to defend their integrity, the students may have to prove the high-tech cheating detective somehow got it wrong.

Some students said the experience of having strangers and algorithms silently judge their movements was deeply unnerving, and many worried that even being accused of cheating could endanger their chances at good grades, scholarships, internships and post-graduation careers.

Several students said they had hoped for freeing, friend-filled college years but were now resigned to hours of monitored video exams in their childhood bedrooms, with no clear end in sight.

"You know how in high school, when you'd be doing a test and a teacher would walk around and peer over your shoulder?" said one student, who, like others, spoke on the condition of anonymity to avoid academic repercussions. "That anxiety you feel for those 10 seconds? … That's how basically all of us feel" all the time.

Said another: It felt like "somebody was watching me just lose my mind."

Company executives say a semester without proctors would turn online testing into a lawless wasteland. Scott McFarland, the chief executive of ProctorU, which works with more than 1,200 schools worldwide, pointed to company data from over the past year saying the system had caught "unpermitted resources" or triggered an "active intervention," with a proctor jumping in to address potential cheating in real time, in more than a million monitored tests. The system, he added, had flagged 247,000 "confirmed breaches of integrity"—or about 6 percent of their 3.9 million proctored exams.

Mike Olsen, the chief executive of Proctorio, which has charged some schools roughly $500,000 for a year of service, expects to monitor more than 25 million exams across more than 1,000 schools this year. He said that without anti-cheating measures in place during the pandemic, students' college accomplishments would be forever tarnished—a "corona diploma," as he called it, that future employers might find "not as credible."

But the systems' technical demands have made just taking the tests almost comically complicated. One student at Wilfrid Laurier University in Ontario shared the instructions for his online Introduction to Linear Algebra midterm: five pages, totaling more than 2,000 words, requiring students to use a special activity-monitoring Web browser and keep their face, hands and desk in view of their camera at all times.

To start, students must conduct an "environmental scan" by holding up everything they might use for their test, including their calculator and any scrap paper, in front of the webcam for three seconds each. They must also position a mirror to reflect back at the webcam to prove nothing is attached to the screen; the mirror itself must also be scanned.

Any student wanting to go to the bathroom must first "shout into the microphone: 'I need to go to the washroom and will come back quickly,'" the guide states. Students who break the rules or face technical difficulties can be investigated for academic misconduct.

"The instructions," the student said, "are giving me more anxiety than the test itself."

'The Most Important Exam of My Life'

Fear of setting off the systems' alarms has led students to contort themselves in unsettling ways. Students with dark skin have shined bright lights at their face, worrying the systems wouldn't recognize them. Other students have resorted to throwing up in trash cans.

Some law students who took New York's first online bar exam last month, a 90-minute test proctored by the company ExamSoft, said they had urinated in their chairs because they weren't allowed to leave their computers, according to a survey by two New York state lawmakers pushing to change the rules for licensing new attorneys during the pandemic.

One respondent who said they had used a metal pot wrote,

> I informed the recording by speaking aloud that I had to pee … I had to keep eye contact with my camera in order to not violate the rules. It was extremely embarrassing and humiliating. Now some faceless [proctor] has video of me peeing while taking the exam.

The lawmakers, State Sen. Brad Hoylman and Assembly member Jo Anne Simon, decried the test's "profound lack of decency" and said hundreds of others faced technical glitches. ExamSoft spokeswoman Nici Sandberg said that, while stepping away from the camera could have constituted an "integrity breach," all test-takers had been told of "the format and parameters of the exams well ahead of time."

Some students said they fear they could be labeled suspect for movements or needs beyond their control. In a survey this summer by the National Disabled Law Students Association, hundreds said they worried they would be punished for their disability during what one called "the most important exam of my life."

"If we get flagged as cheaters," one respondent said, "we might as well kiss our licenses goodbye."

Others said they worried these systems would deepen the digital divide, because only students with a flawless Internet connection, secluded workspace and the right tech gadgets can pass the system's integrity tests.

Sarah Seyk, a nursing student at Sacramento City College, tried her best earlier this year to prepare for a competitive Proctorio-monitored exam. Between shifts in a COVID-19 unit at a nursing home, she commandeered the quietest room in the house, her little sister's, and walked around holding up her laptop camera to prove the space was clean and cheating-free.

Once the test started, though, she was kicked out three times, which she partially blames on her tendency of looking off-screen when lost in thought. Each time, she had to reverify her identity and the sanctity of her surroundings, burning vital time.

Proctorio's Olsen said the exam only terminates if a student's Internet access drops for more than 2 minutes or if they try to open an unauthorized program. The company, he added, recommends administrators show "increased empathy" for students during the pandemic.

"I didn't want to move my eyes too much. I didn't want to be writing too much. I was just full-on hysterically sobbing," Seyk said. "My poor little sister kept trying to come in the room, but you're not allowed to let anyone in."

'A Fight for the Future'

Students have increasingly turned to the Web to spotlight their anger at testing under constant watch, recording tearful TikTok videos and cataloguing their horror stories on Twitter accounts like "Procteario" and "ProcterrorU." They've also commiserated online over the creepy risks of letting virtual strangers into their home, voicing concerns over whether their proctors might track them down on social media after the test. (One student said her proctor kept calling her "sweetheart.")

But they've also sought to dig deeper into the technology itself. In September, Erik Johnson, an 18-year-old engineering student at Miami University in Ohio, said he poked around the files Proctorio saves to users' computers because he wanted to understand how the company kept students' data secure (Figure 10.2.2).

He shared his findings—which questioned the system's depth of monitoring and access to students' computers—in a series of tweets, tagging the university's leadership. "Change isn't going to happen if the universities and your professors don't know about these things," he wrote.

He was surprised to see how quickly the company fought back, pushing Twitter and other sites to remove Johnson's posts. Proctorio, he added, also blocked his Internet-protocol address,

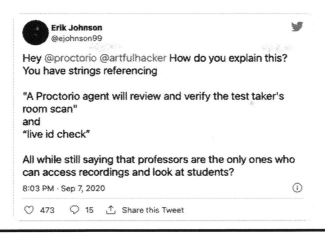

Figure 10.2.2   Email from Erik Johnson showing that Proctorio has others looking at students' rooms and recordings.

potentially preventing him from using it for future exams in what he called an "absurd" act of retribution.

Proctorio's Olsen said Johnson made false assumptions about the system and violated the company's rules and copyrights. Olsen said he offered to revoke the ban, which he said the software triggered automatically, if Johnson or the university specified Johnson's IP address. School officials did not respond to requests for comment.

It wasn't the first time Proctorio had responded forcefully to its critics. In June, Olsen waged an unusually blunt attack on a University of British Columbia student, posting customer-support chat logs to a college Reddit thread that he said had contradicted the student's complaint: "If you're gonna lie bro … don't do it when the company clearly has an entire transcript of your conversation," he wrote.

But the most bitter skirmish could be decided in court. In August, Ian Linkletter, a UBC learning technology specialist, tweeted links to Proctorio training videos that showed faculty how to watch students' webcam footage—clear proof, he said, of the "emotional harm you are doing to students by using this technology." The YouTube videos were visible only to people with the link, but Linkletter's tweets essentially opened them to public view.

Proctorio quickly deactivated the links, calling the videos "confidential and proprietary," and a week later filed a lawsuit against Linkletter seeking damages for copyright infringement and a "breach of confidence."

Linkletter's attorneys have argued it's not illegal to share links to videos already available on the Internet. But the suit's underlying message, Linkletter said, is an attempt to intimidate other critics from speaking up.

"All of us have the right to discuss whether this academic-surveillance software is ethical," he said in an interview. In a fundraiser for his legal defense, Linkletter called it "a fight for the future" and said, "Can you imagine being sued for 8 tweets?"

Olsen said the videos were embedded in a password-protected faculty help center, and he argues that the court filing is meant to defend the company's intellectual property, not silence criticism. "We're not interested in his money," Olsen said. "If we wanted to go after his job, we would have just gone to the university."

'Is It Okay If I Cry?'

The proctoring companies have argued they're a champion for student success and privacy, but many students aren't convinced. Thousands of college students have signed petitions to cancel online-proctor deals in California, Colorado, Florida, Massachusetts, New York, Ohio, Texas, Wisconsin and Washington state. Others have organized letter-writing campaigns to administrators, arguing the technology is too invasive to support.

Students also have pointed to the companies' troves of personal video data as a major vulnerability for cyberattack. In July, hackers published more than 400,000 records taken from ProctorU, including names, passwords and home addresses. ProctorU said it has since enabled new security measures.

Last month, the parent company of Proctortrack, which advertises "the world's most advanced remote online proctoring solution" and says it verifies students' identities through face or "knuckle scan," took the service offline for eight days after hackers leaked its source code and sent offensive emails that appeared to come from official accounts.

The company, Verificient Technologies, apologized and said no personal data had been accessed. (Students at the Massachusetts Institute of Technology had raised concerns in a petition two months prior about the system's exposure to attack.)

Several students said they expect these systems will shape the college experience long after the shutdowns end. Nearly 60 percent of the higher-education institutions polled in April by the non-profit group Educause said they were using or considering "passive video surveillance of students" during exams.

But some corners of American schooling have voiced unease over the system's potential risks. A few schools, including the University of California at Berkeley, have already banned online proctoring due to privacy and accessibility concerns.

The College Board, which runs the SAT college-admissions exam, originally had planned to shift to an online-proctored test but stopped for fear of what it would require: three hours of uninterrupted, streaming-video-quality Internet, which many students can't guarantee, a College Board official told The Washington Post. Officials also worried about introducing a huge new burden for students not exactly lacking in outside stress.

Proctorio's Olsen defends the company as an early-warning system for academic-dishonesty violations, saying it's up to the instructor to review the flags and punish or respond in an appropriate way. He did, however, say that "a lot of faculty are overreacting these days," requiring students, for instance, to take tests only in highly controlled areas even though the pandemic has upended their life.

He has also criticized the student backlash as misguided—saying in June that "it's hilarious, students pretending to care where their data goes"—and based largely on "regurgitated" criticism of how the service works. Most students, he said, just need to get used to it: "College is stressful. … It's always been stressful."

Students like Ohio State University senior Madison Tracy, who has taken 18 Proctorio-monitored exams, argue the companies' surveillance-or-chaos argument is a false choice. The problem, she said, isn't the cheating; it's the tests. Instead of the closed-book, easily Googled memorization drills proctoring software is built for, classes could offer exams with more original prompts, creative improvisation and critical thinking—no webcam oversight required.

Some of Tracy's professors have already gone that route, using tests she said leave her feeling just as challenged and far less overwhelmed. But for now, Tracy, who has attention-deficit/hyperactivity disorder, said she has to remind herself before every proctored test that the little techniques she typically does to refocus—such as stretching her arms or looking away—could be flagged as potentially toxic behaviors.

"Half of my brain is so concentrated on not messing up or doing anything wrong or making the wrong move ... and the other half is trying to actually work on the exam," Tracy said. "I've seen so many memes of students saying, 'Is it okay if I cry in front of the camera?' How far is this going to go?"

Chapter 10.3

When Algorithms Mess Up, the Nearest Human Gets the Blame[*]

Karen Hao

A look at historical case studies shows us how we handle the liability of automated systems.

Earlier this month, Bloomberg published an article about an unfolding lawsuit over investments lost by an algorithm. A Hong Kong tycoon lost more than $20 million after entrusting part of his fortune to an automated platform. Without a legal framework to sue the technology, he placed the blame on the nearest human: the man who sold it to him.

It's the first known case over automated investment losses, but not the first involving the liability of algorithms. In March of 2018, a self-driving Uber struck and killed a pedestrian in Tempe, Arizona, sending another case to court. A year later, Uber was exonerated of all criminal liability, but the safety driver could face charges of vehicular manslaughter instead.

Both cases tackle one of the central questions we face as automated systems trickle into every aspect of society: Who or what deserves the blame when an algorithm causes harm? Who or what actually gets the blame is a different yet equally important question.

Madeleine Clare Elish, a researcher at Data & Society and a cultural anthropologist by training, has spent the last few years studying the latter question to see how it can help answer the former. To do so, she has looked back at historical case studies. While modern AI systems haven't been around for long, the questions surrounding their liability are not new.

The self-driving Uber crash parallels the 2009 crash of Air France flight 447, for example, and a look at how we treated liability then offers clues for what we might do now. In that tragic accident, the plane crashed into the Atlantic Ocean en route from Brazil to France, killing all 228 people on board. The plane's automated system was designed to be a completely "foolproof," capable of handling nearly all scenarios except for the rare edge cases when it needed a human

[*] Hao, Karen. 2019. "When Algorithms Mess Up, the Nearest Human Gets the Blame." *MIT Technology Review.* May 28, 2019. *https://www.technologyreview.com/2019/05/28/65748/ai-algorithms-liability-human-blame/* Reprinted with permission.

pilot to take over. In that sense, the pilots were much like today's safety drivers for self-driving cars—meant to passively monitor the flight the vast majority of the time but leap into action during extreme scenarios.

What happened the night of the crash is, at this point, a well-known story. About an hour and a half into the flight, the plane's air speed sensors stopped working because of ice formation. After the autopilot system transferred control back to the pilots, confusion and miscommunication led the plane to stall. While one of the pilots attempted to reverse the stall by pointing the plane's nose down, the other, likely in a panic, raised the nose to continue climbing. The system was designed for one pilot to be in control at all times, however, and didn't provide any signals or haptic feedback to indicate which one was actually in control and what the other was doing. Ultimately, the plane climbed to an angle so steep that the system deemed it invalid and stopped providing feedback entirely. The pilots, flying completely blind, continued to fumble until the plane plunged into the sea.

In a recent paper, Elish examined the aftermath of the tragedy and identified an important pattern in the way the public came to understand what happened. While a federal investigation of the incident concluded that a mix of poor systems design and insufficient pilot training had caused the catastrophic failure, the public quickly latched onto a narrative that placed the sole blame on the latter. Media portrayals, in particular, perpetuated the belief that the sophisticated autopilot system bore no fault in the matter despite significant human-factors research demonstrating that humans have always been rather inept at leaping into emergency situations at the last minute with a level head and clear mind.

Humans Act Like a "Liability Sponge"

In other case studies, Elish found the same pattern to hold true: even in a highly automated system where humans have limited control of its behavior, they still bear most of the blame for its failures. Elish calls this phenomenon a "moral crumple zone." "While the crumple zone in a car is meant to protect the human driver," she writes in her paper, "the moral crumple zone protects the integrity of the technological system, at the expense of the nearest human operator." Humans act like a "liability sponge," she says, absorbing all legal and moral responsibility in algorithmic accidents no matter how little or unintentionally they are involved.

This pattern offers important insight into the troubling way we speak about the liability of modern AI systems. In the immediate aftermath of the Uber accident, headlines pointed fingers at Uber, but less than a few days later, the narrative shifted to focus on the distraction of the driver.

"We need to start asking who bears the risk of [tech companies'] technological experiments," says Elish. Safety drivers and other human operators often have little power or influence over the design of the technology platforms they interact with. Yet in the current regulatory vacuum, they will continue to pay the steepest cost.

Regulators should also have more nuanced conversations about what kind of framework would help distribute liability fairly. "They need to think carefully about regulating sociotechnical systems and not just algorithmic black boxes," Elish says. In other words, they should consider whether the system's design works within the context it's operating in and whether it sets up human operators along the way for failure or success. Self-driving cars, for example, should be regulated in a way that factors in whether the role safety drivers are being asked to play is reasonable.

"At stake in the concept of the moral crumple zone is not only how accountability may be distributed in any robotic or autonomous system," she writes, "but also how the value and potential of humans may be allowed to develop in the context of human-machine teams."

Chapter 10.4

Shaping Our Tools: Contestability as a Means to Promote Responsible Algorithmic Decision Making in the Professions[*]

Daniel N. Kluttz, Nitin Kohli, and Deirdre K. Mulligan

Abstract

The standard response to concerns about "black box" algorithms is to make those algorithms transparent or explainable. Such approaches, however, involve significant limitations, especially in professional contexts such as medicine, law, or financial advice. Instead, systems should be designed to be contestable, meaning that those subject to algorithmic decisions can engage with and challenge them. Both laws and norms can encourage contestability of automated decisions, but systems designers still must take explicit steps to promote effective questioning and challenges.

[...]

Transparency: Perspectives and Limitations

Due to the challenges described above, algorithmic handoffs have been met with calls for greater transparency.[1] At a fundamental level, transparency refers to some notion of openness or access,

---

[*] Kluttz, Daniel N., Nitin Kohli, and Deirdre K. Mulligan. "Shaping Our Tools: Contestability as a Means to Promote Responsible Algorithmic Decision Making in the Professions." *After the Digital Tornado: Networks, Algorithms, Humanity* (2020). Reprinted with permission. Note: This is an excerpt from the original so footnote and endnote numbering may be modified.

DOI: 10.1201/9781003278290-62

with the goal of becoming informed about the system. However, the word "transparency" lends itself to the question: *What* is being made transparent?

Given the growing role that algorithmically driven systems are poised to play across government and the private sector, we should exercise care in choosing policy objectives for transparency. A trio of federal laws – two adopted in the 1970s due to fears that the federal government was amassing data about citizens – exemplify three policy approaches to transparency relevant to algorithmic systems. Together, the laws aim to ensure citizens "know what their Government is up to,"[2] that "all federal data banks be fully and accurately reported to the Congress and the American people,"[3] that individuals have access to information about themselves held in such data banks, and that privacy considerations inform the adoption of new technologies that manage personal information. These approaches can be summarized as relating to (1) scope of a system, (2) the decision rules of a process, and (3) the outputs.

The Privacy Act of 1974,[4] which requires notices to be published in the Federal Register prior to the creation of a new federal record-keeping system, and section 208 of the E-Government Act of 2002,[5] which requires the completion of privacy impact assessments, exemplify the scope perspective. These laws provide notice about the existence and purpose of data-collection systems and the technology that supports them. For example, the Privacy Act of 1974 requires public notice that a system is being created and additional information about the system, including its name and location, the categories of individual and record maintained in the system, the use and purpose of records in the system, agency procedures regarding storage, retrieval, and disposal of the records, etc.[6] The first tenet of the Code of Fair Information Practices, first set out in a 1973 HEW (Health, Education, Welfare) Report[7] and represented in the Privacy Act of 1974 and data-protection laws the world over, stipulates in part that "there must be no personal-data record-keeping systems whose very existence is secret."[8] With the Privacy Act of 1974, the transparency theory is one of public notice and scope. Returning to our previous question of "what is being made transparent," in this approach to transparency, it is precisely the existence and scope being made available.

Unlike the scope aspect of transparency, the decision-rules aspect is not concerned with whether or not such a system exists. Rather, this view of transparency refers to tools to extract information about how these systems function. As an example, consider the Freedom of Information Act (FOIA), a law that grants individuals the ability to access information and documents controlled by the federal government.[9] The transparency theory here is that the public has a vested interest in accessing such information. But instead of disclosing the information upfront, it sets up a mechanism to meet the public's demand for it. As such, FOIA allows for individuals to gain access to the decisional rules of these systems and processes. Similarly, the privacy impact assessment requirement of the E-Government Act of 2002 provides transparency around agencies' consideration of new technologies, as well as their ultimate design choices.

Last, several privacy laws allow individuals to examine the inputs and outputs of systems that make decisions about them. Under this perspective, transparency is not the end goal itself. Rather, transparency supports the twin goals of ensuring fair inputs and understanding the rationale for the outputs by way of pertinent information about the inputs and reasoning. The laws all entitle individuals to access information used about them and to correct or amend data. Some of the privacy laws in this area also entitle individuals to receive information about the reasons behind negative outcomes.[10] For example, under the Equal Credit Opportunity Act, if a candidate's credit application is rejected, the credit bureau must provide the key reasons for the decision.[11] Thus, this type of transparency refers to notice of how a particular decision was reached. These forms of transparency are aimed at individual, rather than collective, understanding; they provide, to a limited extent, insight into the data and the reasoning – or functioning – of systems.

Within the computer science literature, transparency is similar to the functional and outputs perspective presented in law. That is, transparency often refers to some notion of openness around either the internals of a model or system, or around the outputs. Typically, less focus is given to disclosing the subjective choices that were invoked during the system design and engineering process or to system inputs.

The social sciences and statistics, however, take a more comprehensive perspective on transparency. Transparency in these disciplines not only captures the ideas from law and computer science, but also means disclosures about how the data was gathered, how it was cleaned and normalized, the methods used in the analysis, the choice of hyperparameters and other thresholds, etc., often in line with the goals of reproducibility.[12] The sweep of transparency reflects an understanding that these choices contribute to the methodological design and analysis. This more holistic approach to transparency acknowledges the effect that humans have in this process (reflected in decisions about data, as well as behaviors captured in the data), which is particularly pertinent for predictive algorithms.

Current policy debates, and scientific research, center around explainability and interpretability. Transparency is being reframed, particularly in the computer science research agenda, as an instrumental rather than final objective of regulation and system design. The goal is not to lay bare the workings of the machine, but rather to ensure that users understand how the machines are making decisions – whether those decisions be offering predictions to inform human action or acting independently. This reflects both growing recognition of the inability of humans to understand how some algorithms work even with full access to code and data, but also an emphasis on the overall system – rather than solely the *algorithm* – as the artifact to be known.

Explainability: Perspectives and Limitations

Explainability is an additional design goal for machine-learning systems. Driven in part by growing recognition of the limits of transparency to foster human understanding of algorithmic systems, and in part by pursuit of other goals such as safety and human compatibility, researchers and regulators are shifting their focus to techniques and incentives to produce machine-learning systems that can explain themselves to their human users. Such desires are well-founded in the abstract. For the purposes of decision making or collaboration, explanations can act as an interface between an end-user and the computer system, with the purpose of keeping a human in the loop for safety and discretion. Hence, explanations invite questioning of AI models and systems to understand limits, build trust, and prevent harm. As with transparency, different disciplines have responded to this call to action by operationalizing both explanations and explainability in differing ways.

One notable use of explanations and explainability comes from the social sciences. Miller[13] performed a comprehensive literature review of over 200 articles from the social sciences and found that explanations are causal, contrastive, selective, and social. What is pertinent from this categorization is how well the paradigms invoked in predictive algorithms (machine learning, artificial intelligence, etc.) fall within social understandings of explanations. Machine learning raises difficulties for all four of Miller's attributes of explanations.

For concreteness and clarity, imagine we have a predictive algorithm that classifies a patient's risk for breast cancer as either low risk, medium risk, or high risk. In this scenario, a causal explanation would answer the question: "Why was the patient classified as high risk?" Alternatively, a contrastive explanation would answer questions of the form, "Why was the patient classified as high risk as opposed to low risk or medium risk?" As such, explanations of the causal type require singular scope on the outcome, whereas contrastive explanations examine not only the predicted outcome, but other candidate alternatives as well.

With respect to machine learning, this distinction is important and suggestive. Machine learning is itself a correlation box. As such, the *output itself should not be interpreted as causal*. However, when individuals ask for *causal explanations* of predictive algorithms, they are not necessarily assuming that the underlying data mechanism is causal. Rather, the notion of causality is seeking to understand what caused the algorithm to decide that the patient was high risk, not what caused the patient to be high risk in actuality. Thus, causal explanations can be given of a model built on correlation. However, the fact that they can be produced doesn't mean that causal explanations further meaningful understanding of the system.

Contrastive explanations are a better fit for machine learning. The very paradigm of machine learning – classification models – are built in a contrastive manner. These models are trained to learn to pick the "best" output given a set of inputs – or equivalently stated, the model is taught to discern an answer to a series of input questions based on the fixed set of alternatives available. Combining these insights, it follows that requiring causal explanations for classification models is inappropriate for determining why a model predicted the value it did. Contrastive explanations, which provide insight into the counterfactual alternatives that the model rejected as viable, transfer more knowledge about the system, than causal ones.

Regardless of whether the type of explanation is causal or contrastive, Miller argued that explanations in the social sciences were selective. That is, explanations tend to highlight a few key justifications rather than being completely exhaustive. Consider the case of a doctor performing a breast cancer-screening test in the absence of a predictive algorithm. When relaying the rationale of their diagnosis to a patient, a doctor would provide sufficient reasons for their decision to justify their answer. Now, consider the state of the world where a hand-off has been made to the predictive model. Suppose the model being used relies on 500 features. When explaining why the model predicted the outcome it did, it is indeed unreasonable to assume that providing information about all 500 features would practically relay any information about why the model made the choice it did. As such, requiring explanations of predictive models requires honing into the relevant features of a decision problem, which may differ from patient to patient and may vary over time.

On the aspect of explanations being social, Miller noted that explanations are meant to transfer knowledge from one individual to another. In the example above, where the doctor performs the breast cancer-screening test, this was the point of having the doctor justify their diagnosis to the patients – to inform the patient about their breast cancer-risk level. When applied to technical systems, the goal is to transfer knowledge about the internal logic of how the system reached its conclusion to some individual (or class of individuals). In the case of our breast cancer-risk prediction, this would manifest itself as a way to justify why the algorithm predicted high risk as opposed to low risk. It is worth noting that for predictive algorithms, it is often difficult to truly achieve the social goal of explanations. Certain qualities of algorithms – such as their functional form (e.g., nonlinear, containing interaction terms), their input data, and other characteristics – make it particularly difficult to assess the internal logic of the algorithm itself, or for the system to even explain what it is doing. It is therefore difficult for these machine systems to transfer knowledge to individuals in the form of an explanation that is either causal or contrastive. To the extent that explanations are aimed at improving human understanding of the logic of algorithms, the qualities of some algorithms may be incompatible with this means of transferring knowledge. It may be that the knowledge transfer must come the other way around, from the human to the machine, which is then bound to particular way or ways of knowing.[14]

Thus, there are tensions between the paradigms of predictive algorithms and those characteristics laid out by Miller. As such, the discussion above suggests that our target is off. That is, to actually fully and critically engage with predictive algorithms, this suggests that we require something stronger than transparency and explainability. Enter *contestability* – the ability to challenge machine predictions.

Toward Contestability as a Feature of Expert Decision-Support Systems

Contestability fosters engagement rather than passivity, questioning rather than acquiescence. As such, contestability is a particularly important system quality where the goal is for predictive algorithms to enhance and support human reasoning, such as decision-support systems. Contestability is one way "to enable responsibility in knowing"[15] as the production of knowledge is spread across humans and machines. Contestability can support critical, generative, and responsible engagement between users and algorithms, users and system designers, and ideally between users and those subject to decisions (when they are not the users), as well as the public.

Efforts to make algorithmic systems knowable respond to the individual need to understand the tools one uses, as well as the social need to ensure that new tools are fit for purpose. Contestability is a design intervention that can contribute to both.[16] However, our focus here is on its potential contribution to the creation of governance models that "support epistemically responsible behavior"[17] and support shared reasoning about the appropriateness of algorithmic systems behavior.[18]

Contestability, the ability to contest decisions, is at the heart of legal rights that afford individuals access to personal data and insight into the decision-making processes used to classify them,[19] and it is one of the interests that transparency serves. Contestability as a design goal, however, is more ambitious and far-reaching. A system designed for contestability would protect the ability to contest a specific outcome, consistent with privacy and consumer protection law. It would also facilitate generative engagement between humans and algorithms throughout the use of the machine-learning system and support the interests and rights of a broader range of stakeholders – users, designers, as well as decision subjects – in shaping its performance.

Hirsch et al. set out contestability as a design objective to address myriad ethical risks posed by the potential reworking of relationships and redistribution of power caused by the introduction of machine-learning systems.[20] Based on their experience designing a machine-learning system for psychotherapy, Hirsch et al. offer three lower-level design principles to support contestability: (1) improving accuracy through phased and iterative deployment with expert users in environments that encourage feedback; (2) heightening legibility through mechanisms that "unpack aggregate measures" and "trac[e] system predictions all the way down" so that "users can follow, and if necessary, contest the reasoning behind each prediction"; and relatedly, in an effort to identify and vigilantly prevent system misuse and implicit bias, (3) identifying "aggregate effects" that may imperil vulnerable users through mechanisms that allow "users to ask questions and record disagreements with system behavior" and engage the system in self-monitoring.[21] Together, these design principles can drive active, critical, real-time engagement with the reasoning of machine-learning system inputs, outputs, and models.

This sort of deep engagement and ongoing challenge and recalibration of the reasoning of algorithms is essential to yield the benefits of humans and machines reasoning together. Concerns that engineers will stealthily usurp or undermine the decision-making logics and processes of other domains have been an ongoing and legitimate complaint about decision support and other computer systems.[22] Encouraging human users to engage and reflect on algorithmic processes can reduce the risk of stealthy displacement of professional and organizational logics by the logics of software developers and their employers. Where an approach based on explanations imagines questioning and challenging as out-of-band activities – exception handling, appeals processes, etc. – contestable systems are designed to foster critical engagement within the system. Such systems use that engagement to iteratively identify and embed domain knowledge and contextual values, as decision making becomes a collaborative effort within a sociotechnical system.

In the context of decision-support systems, increasing system explainability and interpretability is viewed as a strategy to address errors that stem from automation bias and to improve trust.[23] Researchers have examined the impact of various forms of explanatory material, including confidence scores, and comprehensive and selective lists of important inputs, on the accuracy of decisions, deviation from system recommendations, and trust.[24] The relationship between explanations and correct decision making is not conclusive.[25]

Policy debates, like the majority of research on interpretable systems, envision explanations as static.[26] Yet, the responsive and dynamic tailoring at which machine learning and AI systems excel could allow explanations to respond to the expertise and other context-specific needs of the user, yielding decisions that leverage, and iteratively learn from, the situated knowledge and professional expertise of users.

The human engagement contestable systems invite would align well with regulatory and liability rules that seek to keep humans in the loop. For example, the Food and Drug Administration is directed to exclude from the definition of "device" those clinical decision support systems whose software function is intended for the purpose of:

> … supporting or providing recommendations to a health care professional about prevention, diagnosis, or treatment of a disease or condition; and enabling [providers] to independently review the basis for such recommendations … so that it is not the intent that such [provider] rely primarily on any of such recommendations to make a clinical diagnosis or treatment decision regarding an individual patient.[27]

By excluding systems that prioritize human discretion from onerous medical-device approval processes, Congress shows its preference for human expert reasoning. Similarly, where courts have found professionals exhibiting overreliance on tools, they have structured liability to foster professional engagement and responsibility.[28] Systems designed for contestability invite engagement rather than delegation of responsibility. They can do so through both the provision of different kinds of information and an interactive design that encourages exploration and querying.

Professionals appropriate technologies differently, employing them in everyday work practice, as informed by routines, habits, norms, values and ideas and obligations of professional identity. Drawing attention to the structures that shape the adoption of technological systems opens up new opportunities for intervention. Appropriate handoffs to, and collaborations with, decision-support systems demand that they reflect professional logics and provide users with the ability to understand, contest, and oversee decision making. Professionals are a potential source of governance for such systems, and policy should seek to exploit and empower them, as they are well-positioned to ensure ongoing attention to values in handoffs and collaborations with machine-learning systems.

Regulatory approaches should seek to put professionals and decision support systems in conversation, not position professionals as passive recipients of system wisdom who must rely on out-of-system mechanisms to challenge them. For these reasons, calls for explainability fall short and should be replaced by regulatory approaches that drive contestable design. This requires attention to both the *information* demands of professionals – what they need to know such as training data, inputs, decisional rules, etc. – and *processes* of interaction that elicit professional expertise and allow professionals to learn about and shape machine decision making.

Notes

1. Brauneis, Robert, and Ellen P. Goodman. 2018. "Algorithmic Transparency for the Smart City." *Yale Journal of Law & Technology* 20: 103–76, p. 108.
2. *US Dept. of Justice v. Reporters Committee*, 489 *U.S.* 749, 773 (1989).
3. Ware, W. H., 1973. Records, Computers and the Rights of Citizens (No. P-5077). Santa Monica, CA: RAND Corporation.
4. 5 U.S.C. § 552a (2014).
5. Pub. L. No. 107–347, § 208, 116 Stat. 2899 (Dec. 17, 2002).
6. 5 U.S.C. § 552a(e)(4); *see also* United States Department of Health, Education, and Welfare. 1973. "Report of the Secretary's Advisory Committee on Automated Personal Data Systems, Records, Computers, and the Rights of Citizens." MIT Press (discussing purpose and provisions of Privacy Act).[22] US Department of Health, Education, and Welfare. "Report of the Secretary's Advisory Committee on Automated Personal Data Systems: Records, Computers and the Rights of Citizens," 1973, at § III. Safeguards for Privacy
7. US Department of Health, Education, and Welfare. "Report of the Secretary's Advisory Committee on Automated Personal Data Systems: Records, Computers and the Rights of Citizens," 1973, at § III. Safeguards for Privacy
8. The full Code of Fair Information Practices can be found at https://epic.org/privacy/consumer/code_fair_info.html
9. 5 U.S.C. § 553 (2016).
10. See, e.g., The Equal Credit Opportunity Act (ECOA), 15 U.S.C. § 1691 et seq., as implemented by Regulation B, 12 C.F.R. §1002.9. *See also* The Fair Credit Reporting Act (FCRA), 15 U.S.C. § 1681 et seq.
11. 15 U.S.C. § 1691(d).
12. Miguel, Edward, Colin Camerer, Katherine Casey, Joshua, Cohen, Kevin M. Esterling, Alan Gerber, Rachel Glennerster, et al. 2014. "Promoting Transparency in Social Science Research." *Science* 343(6166): 30–31.
13. Miller, Tim. 2017. "Explanation in Artificial Intelligence: Insights from the Social Sciences." *ArXiv:1706.07269 [Cs]*, June. http://arxiv.org/abs/1706.07269 (https://arxiv.org/abs/1706.07269).
14. Kroll, Joshua A., Joanna Huey, Solon Barocas, Edward W. Felten, Joel R. Reidenberg, David G. Robinson, and Harlan Yu. 2017. "Accountable Algorithms." *University of Pennsylvania Law Review* 165 (3): 633–705.
15. Simon, Judith. 2015. "Distributed Epistemic Responsibility in a Hyperconnected Era." *The Onlife Manifesto*, pp. 145–59. Cham, CH: Springer International Publishing, at p. 146 (separating out two aspects of "epistemic responsibility": 1) the individualistic perspective, which asks, "what does it mean to be responsible in knowing?"; and 2) the governance perspective with asks, "what does it take to enable responsibility in knowing?").
16. For insights on how contestable systems advance individual understanding, see, e.g., Eslami, Motahhare, and Karrie Karahalios. 2017. "Understanding and Designing around Users' Interaction with Hidden Algorithms in Sociotechnical Systems." *CSCW Companion* (describing several studies finding that seamful designs, which expose algorithmic reasoning to users, facilitated understanding, improved user engagement, and in some instances altered user behavior); Eslami, Motahhare

et al. 2015. "I Always Assumed that I Wasn't Really That Close to [Her]: Reasoning about Invisible Algorithms in News Feeds." *Proceedings of the 33rd Annual ACM Conference on Human Factors in Computing Systems* (describing the lasting effects on how users engage with Facebook to influence the News Feed algorithm after an experimental design intervention that visualized its curatorial voice); Jung, Malte F., David Sirkin, and Martin Steinert. 2015. "Displayed Uncertainty Improves Driving Experience and Behavior: The Case of Range Anxiety in an Electric Car." *Proceedings of the 33rd Annual ACM Conference on Human Factors in Computing Systems* (CHI '15) (gradient plot that reveals uncertainty reduced anxiety over single point estimate of remaining range of electric vehicle); Joslyn, Susan, and Jared LeClerc. 2013. "Decisions with Uncertainty: The Glass Half Full." *Current Directions in Psychological Science* 22 (4): 308–15 (displaying uncertainty in weather predictions can lead to more optimal decision making and trust in a forecast: transparency about probabilistic nature of prediction engenders trust even when predictions are wrong); Stumpf, Simone, et al. 2007. "Toward Harnessing User Feedback for Machine Learning." *Proceedings of the 12th International Conference on Intelligent User Interfaces*; Stumpf, Simone, et al. 2009. "Interacting Meaningfully with Machine-Learning Systems: Three Experiments." *International Journal of Human-Computer Studies* 67 (8): 639–62 (explainable systems can improve user understanding and use of system and enable users to provide deep and useful feedback to improve algorithms); Moor, Travis, et al. 2009. "End-User Debugging of Machine-Learned Programs: Toward Principles for Baring the Logic" (salient explanations helped users adjust their mental models); Amershi, Saleema, et al. 2014. "Power to the People: The Role of Humans in Interactive Machine Learning." *AI Magazine* 35 (4): 105–20 (providing an overview of interactive machine learning research, with case studies, and discussing value of interactive machine learning approaches for machine learning community as well as users).

17. Simon, Judith. 2015. "Distributed Epistemic Responsibility in a Hyperconnected Era." In *The Onlife Manifesto: Being Human in a Hyperconnected Era*, edited by Luciano Floridi, pp. 145–59. Cham, CH: Springer International Publishing, at p. 158.

18. Reuben Binns argues that "*public reason*—roughly, the idea that rules, institutions and decisions need to be justifiable by common principles, rather than hinging on controversial propositions which citizens might reasonably reject—is an answer to the problem of reasonable pluralism in the context of algorithmic decision making," and requires transparency. Binns, Reuben. 2017. "Algorithmic Accountability and Public Reason." *Philosophy & Technology*, May.

19. See, e.g., regulations under the notification provisions of the Equal Credit Opportunity Act 15 U.S.C. § 1691 et seq. that require those denied credit to be provided specific, principal reasons for the denial ECOA 12 C.F.R. § 1002.1, et seq. at §1002.9; Hildebrandt, M. 2016. "The New Imbroglio. Living with Machine Algorithms." In *The Art of Ethics in the Information Society*, edited by L. Janssens, 55–60. Amsterdam: Amsterdam University Press, p. 59 (arguing that the EU General Data Protection Regulation requires "[Algorithmic] decisions that seriously affect individuals' capabilities must be constructed in ways that are comprehensible as well as contestable. If that is not possible, or, as long as this is not possible, such decisions are unlawful.") However, in reality, what the GDPR requires may be much more limited. See also Wachter, Sandra, Brent Mittelstadt, and Luciano Floridi. 2017. "Why a Right to Explanation of Automated Decision-Making Does Not Exist in the General Data Protection Regulation." *International Data Privacy Law* 7 (2): 76–99, p. 93 (arguing that a fairer reading of the GDPR provisions and recitals, and member states implementation of the EU Data Protection Directive it replaces, would require "limited disclosures of the 'logic involved' in automated decision making, primarily concerning system functionality rather than the rationale and circumstances of specific decisions").

20. Hirsch, Tad, Kritzia Merced, Shrikanth Narayanan, Zac E. Imel, and David C. Atkins. 2017. "Designing Contestability: Interaction Design, Machine Learning, and Mental Health." *DIS. Designing Interactive Systems (Conference)* 2017 (June): 95–99 (describing the way an automated assessment and training tool for psychotherapists could be used as a "blunt assessment tool" of management to the detriment of therapists and patients) at p. 98.

21. Id. at p. 98.

22. See Citron, Danielle Keats. 2008. "Technological Due Process." *Washington University Law Review* 85 (6): 1249–313 (identifying the slippage and displacement of case worker values by engineering rules embedded in an expert system); Moor, James H. 1985. "What Is Computer Ethics?" *Metaphilosophy* 16 (4): 266–75 (identifying three ways invisible values manifest in technical systems – to hide immoral behavior, gap-filling during engineering that invisibly embeds coders' value choices, and through complex calculations that defy values analysis); Burrell, Jenna. 2016. "How the Machine 'Thinks': Understanding Opacity in Machine Learning Algorithms." *Big Data & Society* 3 (1): 1–13 (describing three forms of opacity in corporate or state secrecy, technical illiteracy, and complexity and scale of machine-learning algorithms).

23. Nunes, Ingrid, and Dietmar Jannach. 2017. "A Systematic Review and Taxonomy of Explanations in Decision Support and Recommender Systems." *User Modeling and User-Adapted Interaction* 27 (3–5): 393–444 (reviewing approaches to explanations in "advice-giving systems"); Bussone, A., S. Stumpf, and D. O'Sullivan. 2015. "The Role of Explanations on Trust and Reliance in Clinical Decision Support Systems." In *2015 International Conference on Healthcare Informatics*, 160–69.

24. Bussone et al. 2015, supra note 38.

25. Id. at 161 (describing different research finding explanations leading to better and worse decisions).

26. Abdul, Ashraf, Jo Vermeulen, Danding Wang, Brian Y. Lim, and Mohan Kankanhalli. 2018. "Trends and Trajectories for Explainable, Accountable and Intelligible Systems: An HCI Research Agenda." In *Proceedings of the International Conference on Human Factors in Computing Systems*, 1–18 CHI '18 (research review concluding that the explainable AI research community generally produces static explanations focused on conveying a single message and recommending that research explore interactive explanations that allow users to more dynamically explore and interact with algorithmic decision-making systems); but see also Nunes, Ingrid, and Dietmar Jannach. 2017. "A Systematic Review and Taxonomy of Explanations in Decision Support and Recommender Systems." *User Modeling and User-Adapted Interaction* 27 (3–5): 393–444, p. 408 (describing research on interactive explanations that engage users by providing a starting point and allow them to probe systems through "(i) *what-if* (what the output would be if alternative input data were provided); (ii) *why* (why the system is asking for a particular input); and (iii) *why-not* (why the system has not provided a given output)" approaches).

27. 21 U.S.C. § 360j(o)(1)(E)(ii)-(iii) (2016); the term "device" is defined in 21 U.S.C. § 321(h).

28. *Aetna Cas. and Sur. Co. v. Jeppesen & Co.*, 642 F.2d 339, 343 (9th Cir. 1981) (rejecting district court finding that pilots who relied on map that was defectively designed (showing topographical and elevation in distinct scales) were not negligent, because it would endorse a standard of care that would consider "pilot reliance on the graphics of the chart and complete disregard of the words and figures accompanying them" "as reasonable attention to duty by a pilot of a passenger plane" and opting instead to apportion fault).

ETHICS, AI, RESEARCH, AND CORPORATIONS

11

While this book has covered many of the moral implications of data analytics and AI, it is actually openly debated as to *who* should be considering and evaluating the ethics of data and analytics. Computer science, as a discipline, is not of one mind as to whether their job includes identifying the social impact of their work[1] or thinking through the ethics of programming.[2] Companies have not figured out whether and how they are responsible for the ethical implications of AI and machine learning programs they develop, use, or sell.

Here we take the approach that the design and development of data analytics programs is value-laden; therefore, computer scientists and data analysts need to be considering the ethics of data and analytics in the design, development, and deployment of their work. At a broad level, Professor Michael Zimmer rightly identifies the many research ethics questions that data scientists deal with in designing projects such as subject consent, privacy, and the ethical dimensions of big data research: whether rights and welfare of the subjects are protected, anonymity, etc.[3] The fundamental argument is that computer scientists make value judgments *as they are designing a project* and not just in implementation.

Data analysts' value-laden decisions include how the program is designed, tested, and reported, both internally in an organization and externally through publications. For example, in a summary of the current problems with machine learning work, Lipton and Steinhardt argue machine learning researchers (and practitioners) frequently do not identify the source of performance gains: researchers and programmers overfit their model to the training data thereby reducing the robustness of the model to be used across contexts in the wild while also showing high "accuracy" in the study for a particular data set.[4] This makes programs *appear* efficient or accurate and hides the lack of robustness in how well the program will work on different, not controlled data sets. Also problematic, researchers and practitioners can focus on technical explanations to obfuscate the findings. These research decisions by data analysts and computer scientists are important to the ethics of data and analytics because "[f]lawed scholarship threatens to mislead the public and stymie future research by compromising ML's intellectual foundations."[5] In addition, claiming a program is accurate or works (e.g., facial recognition programs or large language models) when in practice the program violates laws, causes harms, or undermines the autonomy and dignity of individuals is unethical.

Finally, Lipton and Steinhart note that practitioners and researchers fail to differentiate between explanation and speculation which leads to little ability to understand *why* a given technique

DOI: 10.1201/9781003278290-63

worked and, therefore, when it would work again. In other words, data analysts and computer scientists *guess* and *guess* until they find a model that "works." This is similar to the call for greater scientific methods (e.g., hypotheses to be developed and tested) to be applied in machine learning in order to not only understand effect but to also understand cause of the performance.[6]

This type of work is important to the ethics of data and analytics since understanding the *limitations* of research is critical to avoid the unethical application of that same research. If we use pharmaceutical research as an example, it's important to know *why* a drug works (is it healing the wound or hiding the pain) to not only know the conditions the drug will work in the future but also when the drug would cause harm if applied.[7] Misleading the public or even just upper management as to the usefulness or robustness of data analytics programs has moral implications for marginalized communities who were not considered in the design as we have seen throughout this book.

Relatedly, computer scientists and data analysts make moral decisions in their choice of what questions to ask, how to answer those questions, who is important to consider in the research, and their criteria for success. For example, Birhane et al. examine 100 highly cited machine learning papers at two major conferences and labeled value decisions made in the design of each including how researchers justified their choice of project and considered negative consequences.[8]

Abebe et al. examine how computing—computer science, data analytics, data science, etc.—takes on a role in social change.[9] In other words, how technical approaches, including data analytics, can be a part of the solution of social problems. Abebe et al. frame computer scientists and data analysts work as performing these roles in society:

> Computing research can serve as a *diagnostic*, helping us to understand and measure social problems with precision and clarity. As a *formalizer*, computing shapes how social problems are explicitly defined—changing how those problems, and possible responses to them, are understood. Computing serves as *rebuttal* when it illuminates the boundaries of what is possible through technical means. And computing acts as *synecdoche* when it makes long-standing social problems newly salient in the public eye.[10]

Developers are taking on many of these roles without being conscious of their decisions. For example, by not explaining clearly their choice of assumptions about the training data or about the world, a developer is perpetuating the current status as if that is justified. For AI Jim, what assumptions did the developer make about the type of clients or their tendency to commit fraud? How did the developer explain the limitations of the program and what questions still need to be answered?

There is also a case that data analysts have a duty to be more conscientious, ethical, and deliberate as to their value judgments in design. Data analysts and computer scientists are in a unique position with special knowledge and in a position to effect change. Data analytics programs are easy to change in design and development and harder to change when in use. Companies that develop AI and data analytics become members of the decision context into which they are selling their products. Similar to engineers needing to understand the best manufacturing practices when designing robots for a car plant, data analysts and computer scientists need to understand the norms of the algorithm in use as well as the best practices of ethical decision-making. In making the decision to sell an algorithm to scan people filing insurance claims or visually read patients receiving therapy, developers willingly enter into that community as a member of the decision system. And as a member of the community, that firm now has an obligation to understand the norms of the decision (therapy, insurance) and not violate those norms in the use of the algorithm.[11]

Pushing the ethical evaluation of the design and development of AI and data analytics generally to people outside the corporation has implications as to how corporations critically evaluate their technology: who can ask questions, what questions can be asked, and how any critical, ethical evaluation is performed. And these are the types of issues being debated in corporations and in academic research right now around computer science and data analytics.[12] Whether corporations should be responsible to critically evaluate their own technology is not established and some in computer science debate whether researchers should have to include ethics statements in their work. Corporations have pushed back against being responsible for the moral implications of their data analytics programs by limiting the type of research conducted in the organization[13] or by outside researchers.[14] We tackle this hard-to-square position—to not critically examine their own work but also not allow others access to examine their products—through a particular case at Google Research and readings by Rudner.

Summary of Readings

In "The Scientist qua Scientist Makes Value Judgments,"[15] Philosopher Richard Rudner (famously) argues that scientists in their jobs as scientists make value judgments. The job of the scientist includes proactively acknowledging and managing those value-laden decisions, such as which problems to solve, what is important to consider, what is a good result, etc. For computer scientists and data analysts, the argument is to similarly broaden what it means to be a good algorithm developer or computer scientist. The job of a developer includes making value-laden decisions. The very job of developing a good algorithm and the criteria of judging a good algorithm would include governance questions, such as design decisions about bias, fairness, marginalization, power, surveillance, privacy, rights, consequences, harms, discrimination, manipulation, etc.

If one was to take seriously the idea that data analysts and computer scientists are making value judgments, organizations would have computer scientists and data analysts trained in the ethics of data and analytics and protected, like pharmaceutical researchers or manufacturing engineers, when they identify problems. This would be similar to manufacturing and design engineers being responsible for the safety, quality and environmental decision they make in care manufacturing.

In this excerpt from "*Ethical Implications and Accountability of Algorithms*," I identify how firms that develop algorithms are responsible for the ethical implications of algorithms in use. I broaden the scope of this responsibility to include not only how AI may diminish rights, reinforce power, and violate rules or norms, but also how the design of data analytics programs influences the delegation of roles and responsibilities between the program and the users within an ethical decision. In other words, in addition to the design of value-laden algorithms, developers make a moral choice as to the delegation of who-does-what between algorithms and individuals within the decision. Importantly, this has implications for the (supposed) "defense" of data analytics and AI programs being "inscrutable" (from Chapter 10):

> Firms can be held accountable for the ethical implications of the inscrutable algorithms they develop. "It's complicated" or "I do not know how it works" turns out to be an unsatisfying response to "who is responsible for this algorithm's value-laden biases?"

… I find creating inscrutable algorithms may, in fact, necessitate *greater* accountability afforded to the algorithm and the developer rather than less.[16]

Related Cases

The case on Google Research offers an opportunity to examine the role of the ethical examination of data analytics and AI within a corporation. The case centers on a particular researcher being told she had to leave over research that highlighted the ethical issues of large language models (models which are critical to Google's search business). The case, however, is emblematic of this larger question of who should be asking and answering questions about the ethical implications of data analytics programs and what role corporations should have in deciding what questions can be asked in regards to their technologies.

Notes

1. For example, Taylor Soper. 2020. "Retired UW Computer Science Professor Embroiled in Twitter Spat Over AI Ethics and 'Cancel Culture.'" *GeekWire*. https://www.geekwire.com/2020/retired-uw -computer-science-professor-embroiled-twitter-spat-ai-ethics-cancel-culture/
2. Davide Castelvecchi. 2020. "Prestigious AI Meeting Takes Steps to Improve Ethics of Research". *Nature*. https://www.nature.com/articles/d41586-020-03611-8
3. Michael Zimmer. "Addressing Conceptual Gaps in Big Data Research Ethics: An Application of Contextual Integrity," *Social Media+ Society* 4, no. 2 (2018): 2056305118768300.
4. Zachary C. Lipton and Jacob Steinhardt, "Troubling Trends in Machine Learning Scholarship," *ArXiv Preprint ArXiv:1807.03341,* 2018, 2.
5. Ibid.
6. Jessica Zosa Forde and Michela Paganini, "The Scientific Method in the Science of Machine Learning," *ArXiv Preprint ArXiv:1904.10922,* 2019.
7. I am thankful to Connor Martin (UCLA) for making this connection to pharmaceuticals.
8. Abeba Birhane et al., "The Values Encoded in Machine Learning Research," 2021, https://arxiv.org/ abs/2106.15590. The authors also find increasing influence of tech companies on published work via authorship.
9. Rediet Abebe et al., "Roles for Computing in Social Change," 2020, 252–260.
10. Abebe et al.
11. Kirsten Martin, "Ethical Issues in the Big Data Industry," *MIS Quarterly Executive* 14, no. 2 (2015): 67–85. This is a social contract argument where the firm developing and selling the algorithm (and the actual computer scientists as members of that organization) take on the obligation of being good members of the community they willingly enter.
12. As an example, I was asked to be on a project using facial recognition technology. When I asked why there was no mention of the problems with FR programs in the overview, I was told that they were going for corporate funding and did not want to include any negative comments about current FR technology.
13. Karen Hao. 2020. "We Read the Paper That Forced Timnit Gebru out of Google. Here's What It Says." *MIT Technology Review*. https://www.technologyreview.com/2020/12/04/1013294/google-ai-ethics -research-paper-forced-out-timnit-gebru/
14. Jeff Horwitz. 2020. "Facebook Seeks Shutdown of NYU Research Project into Political Ad Targeting." *The Wall Street Journal*. https://www.wsj.com/articles/facebook-seeks-shutdown-of-nyu-research -project-into-political-ad-targeting-11603488533/

15. Richard Rudner, "The Scientist qua Scientist Makes Value Judgments," *Philosophy of Science* 20, no. 1 (1953): 1–6.
16. Kirsten Martin, "Ethical Implications and Accountability of Algorithms," *Journal of Business Ethics* 160, no. 4 (2019): 835–50.

Chapter 11.1

Google Research: Who Is Responsible for Ethics of AI?*

Kirsten Martin

Google Research: Who is Responsible for Ethics of AI?*

Kirsten Martin

Timnit Gebru 🔵
@timnitGebru

Is there anyone working on regulation protecting Ethical AI researchers, similar to whistleblower protection? Because with the amount of censorship & intimidation that goes on towards people in specific groups, how does anyone trust any real research in this area can take place?

10:24 PM · Nov 30, 2020 · Twitter Web App

Timnit Gebru 🔵
@timnitGebru

Apparently my manager's manager sent an email my direct reports saying she accepted my resignation. I hadn't resigned—I had asked for simple conditions first and said I would respond when I'm back from vacation. But I guess she decided for me :) that's the lawyer speak.

10:41 PM · Dec 2, 2020 · Twitter Web App

Figure 11.1.1 Two tweets sent by Dr. Gebru two days apart. The first asking about whistle-blower protections and the second announcing she had been told she no longer works for Google by her direct report.

DOI: 10.1201/9781003278290-64

Technology companies direct the research into the bias, fairness, and ethics of their own products and services. In fact, companies in Big Tech had a separate research division with their own researchers to critically examine their technologies – and where academics had part time positions or their students could intern during their studies. Corporate research would be presented along with academic research at conferences, and many papers had coauthors from both Big Tech and academia.

Dr. Gebru was one such researchers in Google's division devoted to research. Dr. Gebru was a coauthor on a paper that critically examined the large data sets used for language processing models. Google, however, demanded the paper be retracted or that authors affiliated with Google be removed from the paper. Dr. Gebru, at the time, was the co-lead of their Ethics of AI group and pushed back for an explanation. Her employment at Google was then terminated via an email to her subordinates at Google Research in December 2020.

What unfolded after Dr. Gebru's forced exit was a renewed spotlight on Big Tech's odd relationship with research on AI, data analytics, and machine learning. The ensuing months exposed the fault lines in the design of leaving technology companies to decide when and how their products and services would be examined.

The Firing

Dr. Timnit Gebru, the co-lead of Google's ethical AI team, announced on December 2, 2020 that Google had forced her out (Figure 11.1.1).[1] The exit was over a paper Dr. Gerbu had co-authored with three other Google employees and two researchers from academia.[2]

Before being published, the paper went through Google's internal PubApprove process, used to ensure no sensitive or confidential material would be released. Initially, the paper received a general approval from a subject matter expert and Dr. Gebru's immediate supervisor, Samy Bengio. In parallel, the authors asked for peer feedback from over two dozen colleagues from inside and outside Google. The author team also let the public relations department know about the paper on September 18 and included public relations as reviewers in the PubApprove system on October 7.[3]

On October 8, Dr. Gebru et al.'s paper received approval for publication through PubApprove internally, the same day as the deadline for the conference where they submitted the draft paper (FAccT).[4] On November 18, the Google authors were invited to a meeting and told to retract the paper or remove their names.[5] No written feedback was provided and the authors were not given an opportunity to make revisions based on the feedback before the final version would be due to the conference. On November 27, Dr. Gebru was provided anonymous feedback in a meeting with her immediate manager, Samy Bengio, who was told to only read the list to Dr. Gebru. The criticisms were that the paper was too casual about the downsides and that Google's use of such models were "engineered to avoid" any of the problems with large language models identified in the paper.[6]

Dr. Gebru responded with an email saying she would remove herself from the paper if Google provided who was involved in the feedback and an "understanding the parameters of what would be acceptable research at Google."[7] If those conditions were not met, Gebru wrote, she would leave once she could ensure her team would not be too destabilized.[8]

Five days later on December 2, while Dr. Gebru was on vacation, executives skipped her manager, Samy Bengio, and directly emailed Dr. Gebru's subordinates to tell them her resignation had been accepted. The subordinates then let Dr. Gebru know what they had been told.[9] In her personal email account, Gebru found an email from an executive rejecting Gebru's offer and stating "The end of your employment should happen faster than your email reflects."[10]

By the end of December, the paper was accepted to the Conference on Fairness, Accountability and Transparency (FaccT), as part of its anonymous review process.[11]

The Paper

The paper in question, "On the Dangers of Stochastic Parrots: Can Language Models Be Too Big?," is on the risks and downsides of language models based on large test data sets. These models are used to automatically read, understand, and write text. These models can read emails for content in order to provide relevant ads for Google users or read through text in posts and group chats on a social network platform to identify hate speech and disinformation. The language models provide automatic replies, write news articles, pretend to be people in emails, scan for content, etc.

The "Stochastic Parrots" paper provides a history of such natural language processing models (NLP) and identifies types of risks in the models. Larger data sets are more likely (1) to have environmental and financial costs, (2) to create models that appear inscrutable, (3) to include hate speech as well as sexist and racist language, and (4) to be used for disinformation campaigns by appearing authentic.

One of the co-authors, Professor Bender from the University of Washington, said

> "We are working at a scale where the people building the things can't actually get their arms around the data," …. "And because the upsides are so obvious, it's particularly important to step back and ask ourselves, what are the possible downsides? … How do we get the benefits of this while mitigating the risk?"

Because Google depends on large language models, both Gebru and her coworker (and coauthor) Margaret Mitchell included public relations and policy for the review.

Dr. Timnit Gebru

Dr. Timnit Gebru received her PhD from the Stanford Artificial Intelligence Lab and did her postdoctoral research at Microsoft Research as part of a group focused on accountability and ethics in AI.[12] While at Microsoft Research, Dr. Gebru and Joy Buolamwini, then a student at MIT Media Lab, published a seminal study on bias in AI and facial recognition that found facial recognition tools were 99% accurate at identifying White males but only 35 % effective with Black women.[13] In 2018, Dr. Gebru joined Google's Ethical A.I. team. [14]

In October 2020, two months before the blow up with the "Stochastic Parrots" paper, Dr. Gebru received a strong annual review and was promoted to co-lead of a group focused on ethical artificial intelligence.[15] In an interview with the Washington Post, Dr. Gebru said,

"I can't imagine anybody else who would be safer than me...I was super visible. I'm well known in the research community, but also the regulatory space. I have a lot of grass-roots support — and this is what happened." [16]

AI Research Reaction

As of December 15, 2020, over 2,600 Google employees and 4,300 others in academia, industry, and civil society had signed a petition denouncing the dismissal of Dr. Gebru, calling it "unprecedented research censorship" and "an act of retaliation."[17] Articles in the *The New York Times, Washington Post, MIT Technology Review, Wired,* and *Reuters* made the dismissal a national story.

The ACM Conference for Fairness, Accountability, and Transparency (FAccT) suspended its sponsorship relationship with Google stating

> The Executive Committee made the decision that having Google as a sponsor for the 2021 conference would not be in the best interests of the community and impede the Strategic Plan. We will be revising the sponsorship policy for next year's conference. [18]

Luke Stark, a professor at the University of Western Ontario, turned down a $60,000 grant from Google in protest of its treatment of Dr. Gebru.[19]

Google's Response

After the public reaction to the removal of Dr. Gebru, Google responded with a series of emails and meetings to address the concerns. First, Jeff Dean, the executive in charge of Google AI, wrote an email that the paper "didn't meet our bar for publication" because the paper "ignored too much relevant research."[20] Dean wrote that "our aim is to rival peer-reviewed journals in terms of the rigor and thoughtfulness in how we review research before publication."[21] Dean then published his internal email publicly online.[22] However, peers noted the paper's long citation list, with 128 references, thorough informal review to 28 colleagues, and the acceptance at a top conference as undermining Dean's claims.[23] In addition, a fellow Google AI researcher, Nicolas Le Roux, tweeted, "My submissions were always checked for disclosure of sensitive material, never for the quality of the literature review." [24]

In the email, Jeff Dean reportedly said that the authors did not give the internal process enough time to complete the review and stated that two weeks are required. However, coworkers at Google said that "an internal analysis shows that just under half of the papers submitted to PubApprove are done so with *a day or less* notice to approvers."[25]

Finally, Google mistakenly claimed the authors were being demanding to know the names of the anonymous reviewers in the peer review process. But anonymous peer review does not exist within Google. Manas Tungare (Dec 13, 2020) tweeted:

> Can confirm. I've reviewed papers at Google and the process is not designed to be anonymous. There's a proper web app that handles incoming reviews tied to Googlers' internal usernames & identities. We review fully knowing that the authors (will) know our identities.

Online harassers picked up on Google's claims – made public by posting the email – that (a) the research had not met the bar for publication and (b) the authors had been demanding. Online harassers made personal attacks so extreme that their accounts were removed from Twitter.[26] Google remained silent even when the executives were tagged in the harassing tweets.

Google claimed on its public-facing website that its scientists have "substantial" freedom.[27] In fact, Google implemented a new sensitive topics review where researchers could be requested to not discuss their technology in a negative manner and states that researchers should work with legal, policy and public relations teams when working with "sensitive topics."[28] The new process was in addition to Google's standard review of papers for corporate trade secrets.[29] For example, Google officials asked researchers to take a "positive tone" in a paper on content recommendation technology.[30]

Previous Issues at Google

In contrast to the fate of Dr. Gebru, Google's response to two other very public employee issues appear to have favored the employee in question. Google received complaints that their executive in charge of the AI arm, DeepMind, was bullying staff. Google hired an outside law firm to conduct an independent probe. The executive was given professional development training to address the areas of concern and was removed from managing large teams. Google kept the executive on but moved him to a different team at Google and made a public, supportive statement that "he makes valued contributions on AI policy and regulation."[31]

In a second very public example, a different executive was accused of sexual misconduct. Google investigated and found the claim credible. "Google could have fired Mr. Rubin and paid him little to nothing on the way out. Instead, the company handed him a $90 million exit package, paid in installments of about $2 million a month for four years...."[32] Neither employee had an internal email written about their performance nor was one posted online.

AI Ethics Research

Google was typical of Big Tech in both having a separate research division and in supporting research on the ethics of AI in academia. Through writing joint papers, funding of conferences, providing grants, hiring doctoral students, and hiring professors, Big Tech had influence on the content and direction of AI ethics research.[33]

Many saw the influence of Big Tech on academic research start with the move of two famous computer science professors in 2012, Professors Geoffrey Hinton and Yann LeCun, from tenured faculty in academia to Google and Facebook respectively. This began a wave of expertise moving from universities to Big Tech.[34] The rest of Big Tech followed hiring academics and publishing co-authored papers in conferences.[35]

The industry realized that companies could only recruit top researchers with the promise that these PhDs could still publish their work and share ideas. At the time, the field believed that sharing ideas was critical to the industry getting better. Facebook's AI lead, Yann LeCun, told a Wired reporter in 2016, "When you do research in secret, you fall behind."[36] In fact, in 2016, OpenAI, started by Elon Musk and Sam Altman, quickly hired some of the best researchers in the field from academia by promising that all research would be freely shared.[37] The goal was to provide the academic freedom at universities in the setting of industry – researchers would be free to publish whatever they found in their investigations without being controlled by the company.

Hiring academics to conduct research within the Big Tech umbrella was one avenue to direct the research. Big Tech also provided significant funding for AI research at universities and was able to heavily influence research priorities.[38] Two researchers examined the CVs of computer science faculty at four top universities and found that 58% received funding from Big Tech.[39]

In 2020, the US government committed only $1 billion to non-defense-related AI research,[40] and corporations have filled the gap to fund the research they believe is needed.[41] However, even government funding has corporate's touch: Amazon funded a joint grant with the National Science Foundation.[42]

Conferences provided corporations a pathway to influence through the direct funding of the AI conferences as well as an avenue to publish the research Big Tech has decided to pursue. ACM's Conference on Fairness, Accountability, and Transparency (FAcct) is funded by Google, Facebook, IBM, and Microsoft.[43] NeurIPS, a prestigious machine learning conference, has been sponsored by Big Tech companies since 2015. Researchers found that at NeurIPS, "When considering workshops relating to ethics or fairness, all but one have at least one organizer who is affiliated or was recently affiliated with Big Tech."[44] In sponsoring conferences and workshops, Big Tech is influencing the type of research on data analytics, AI, and machine learning and has antagonized a group of academic researchers in the process. An associate professor from the University of California, Berkeley, wore a T-Shirt that read "Corporate conferences still suck" when accepting an award at NeurIPS.[45]

One criticism is that Big tech prefers supporting research focused on engineered fixes to problems rather than critically examining how AI models shift power, exacerbate inequalities, or diminish rights.[46] Big Tech, in relying on their current capabilities for solutions, only provide problems with fixes they already have or are possible.

A second criticism is that the type of research pursued by Big Tech is often only possible in Big Tech – so the data required and the computing power required for the research can only be done with corporate assets. For example, the large language models proposed by Big Tech researchers are also only possible at Big Tech.

Repeat of the Past: Big Tech and Big Tobacco

According to two researchers, Abdalla and Abdalla, Big Tech's approach to research is similar to the strategy of Big Tobacco many decades ago. Specifically, Big Tech's focus on only identifying fixes that do not interrogate underlying problems is reminiscent of how Big Tobacco would fund cancer research in general but not research that investigated the link between tobacco and cancer.[47] In addition, Big Tobacco funded academics whose research was sympathetic to their cause; this funding allowed the companies to cite studies that undermined the link between tobacco and lung cancer, "such as research exploring if it was the keeping of birds as pets, as opposed smoking that increased the risk of lung disease."[48] Big Tobacco also paid researchers to testify at legislative hearings in support of their cause. The authors of the study linking Big Tech to Big Tobacco's research strategy explicitly link the Big Tobacco approach to Google:

> ...Google was noted to "[groom] academic standard-bearers, prominent academics who will drive younger peers in a direction that is more favorable to the company" [27]. In an article published by The Intercept, we discover that Eric Schmidt, previously of

Google, was advised on which "academic AI ethicists Schmidt's private foundation should fund" [49]. This is not a one-time occurrence either. Schmidt also inquired to Joichi Ito (formerly of MIT's Media Lab) if he "should fund a certain professor who, like Ito, later served as an "expert consultant" to the Pentagon's innovation board" [47]. … Or consider the case where Schmidt cited a Google-funded paper when writing to congress without mentioning that the paper had been funded by Google [14].[49]

Push Back against the Type of Research that Corporations Fund

A few conferences enacted new policies to push back on the influence of Big Tech and the type of research they funded. Some conferences requested authors share their code with their research paper submission in order for outsiders to better estimate the rigor of the submission and generalizability of the findings. At one conference, ICML 2019, nearly 70% of authors submitted code with their papers: 90% of researchers who submitted code came from academia with 27% including an author from industry. However, nearly 84% of authors overall came from industry.[50] A second machine learning conference, NeurIPS, made submitting code the official policy in 2020.[51]

Conferences also asked authors to include an impact statement of their papers and declare financial conflicts of interest.[52] NeurIPS instituted two changes. First, a set of reviewers were available as ethical advisors to give feedback on controversial papers. Second, every author was required to include an impact statement to discuss the positive and negative future impacts of their research. Impact statements are not novel and are a common requirement in other academic areas of research "but this change didn't go over well with everyone."[53] Other conferences followed.

In particular, ICLR, a conference on AI and deep learning, has a code that states, "Researchers have an additional obligation to report any signs of system risks that might result in harm." As Margaret Mitchell noted, "On the ICLR ethics board, realizing that the presumable changes @ JeffDean and others wanted on The Paper with @timnitGebru and @emilybender would not meet ICLR ethics bar on how to report system harms."[54]

Alternative Models to Research

Big Tech's approach to research on their own products and services differs from other industries who also have a general impact on society. For example, the pharmaceutical industry not only works within the confines of the FDA for drug development, the industry also has the Federal Drug and Cosmetics Act (FD&C) where researchers have protections for "objecting to or refusing to participate in any activity that he or she reasonably believes to be in violation of the FD&C."[55] Further, pharmaceutical companies have stated research ethics standards as to how research can be conducted and how conflicts of interest must be reported.[56] This does not mean that pharmaceutical companies do not run into trouble for violating these principles, however the industry has guidelines to give researchers room to critically evaluate the products they develop.

Similarly, the automobile industry works within the NTSB for safety research and their employees have stated protections from retaliation for whistleblowing under OSHA.[57] And, when AI falls under the scope of the NTSB, as with self-driving cars, the engineers have whistleblower protections.[58] These companies are not unique, industries are required to proactively research and identify harms caused by their products and whistleblowers are offered protections in dozens of industries.[59]

Across industries, technical projects such as constructing a building, bridge, car, plane etc requires a professional engineer to oversee the project and sign off on the design and testing of the safety and quality of the project. These engineers have obligations to both the company who hires them as well as their professional obligations that are independent of their current employer. In other words, if a civil engineer allows a project to go forward that cuts corners or does not mitigate harms, their professional license is at stake.[60] These engineers have protections from retaliations similar to the whistleblower protection regulations in specific industries.

Conducting AI Research

Along these lines, a number of suggestions have emerged to improve research in AI.

Protecting Whistleblowers. Whistleblower protections have been recommended for tech workers. Sonia Katyal, professor of law at UC Berkeley, analyzed whistleblower protection laws in the context of AI and called them "totally insufficient."[61] Colleagues at Google Research also recommended legislatures strengthen whistleblower protections to protect workers who report harmful technology.[62] These calls are echoed in a recommendation sent by the National Security Commission on AI that government agencies should establish a policy to give workers an avenue to raise concerns. However, those recommendations were for *government* workers and not private industry.[63] Others have called for worker protection through collective action or tech worker unionization.[64]

Separating Corporate and Academic Research. A number of recommendations had been made to better distinguish corporate research from academic research. One solution suggested was to have separate tracks for corporate research and academic research at the prominent conferences as other disciplines have done.[65] Also, conferences could require all submissions to include the 'publication approval policies' associated with the paper. While for academics, there are no "approval policies," corporations can have strict approval policies that would influence the type of content in the papers submitted.[66] The goal would be to better differentiate between research conducted for the purpose of benefiting a company and research conducted for the purpose of expanding knowledge. Computer science researchers recently argued that papers in the field did little to interrogate their own limitations and do not develop generalizable findings that could be used in different contexts.[67]

Adding Internal Checks. The Algorithmic Accountability Act, introduced in 2019, would require all companies to analyze the impact of automated decision-making systems.[68]

In other areas, companies perform audits on large engineering projects to identify safety or environmental impacts. Requiring audits could create an industry for auditing algorithms, similar to accounting firms auditing company financials. However, the question remained how to create a demand for algorithmic audits and where in the company should audits be performed? Within the product line or as a separate research group?

Allowing Outside Examinations. Outside examinations of AI systems in a private company can take a few forms. First, bias bounties would provide money (a bounty) for outsiders who discover bias and safety issues within an AI system.[69] The idea is patterned on bug bounties which reward outsiders identifying security violations.[70] Companies could also be more open to outside researchers examining the quality, robustness, and biases of their AI systems. For example, after NYU's Ad Observatory conducted research to capture data on user's Facebook experience (with consent) and found bias in the type of information recommended, Facebook's response was to demand that the New York University research project stop collecting information.[71] Alternatively, companies could be welcoming of outsiders to test their systems or identify possible problems with the aim of fixing the AI program with the new information.

Providing Alternative Funding. Finally, alternative funding for academic research would reduce the reliance on corporate funding and reduce the need to design research programs to meet corporate needs within academia. For example, the federal government could improve funding for general research for computer science faculty (e.g., NSF). More PhD students could be funded by universities by having them TA courses rather than rely on corporate funding; opportunities could be provided so that PhD students do not design research projects in order to be funded over the summer.

Moving Forward

In the aftermath,

- Sam Bengio, Gebru's manager and supporter, resigned in April 2021 and went to Apple to lead a new AI research unit.[72] Nicolas Le Roux, who defended Timnit Gebru and corrected Jeff Dean's public statements, left Google in May 2021.[73]
- Also in May 2021, at a developer's conference, Google outlined their plans around leveraging advanced language AI using large language models – the same type of large language model critiqued as harmful in the "Stochastic Parrots" paper. Google's goal was to use such large language models in order to have a new kind of search where users would have conversations with computers and be given a more direct answer rather than a list of possible sites. The announcement mentioned none of the dangers and downsides of such models.[74]
- Google's parent company, Alphabet, asked shareholders to vote down a proposal that called for a third-party review of the effectiveness of Google's whistleblower policies, specifically citing the exit of Timnit Gebru.[75]
- Timnit Gebru was named one of the World's 50 Greatest Leaders by Fortune,[76] which included the Prime Minister of New Zealand, Football quarterback Tom Brady, Senator Tim Scott, and the CEO of Costco.

Big Tech has grown due to the academic power of elite research universities and relies on academia to not only develop new PhDs in computer science but also to develop new technologies to use. The question going forward would be how would Big Tech supports the same general research that both powers its innovation and critically examines its products and services.

The question remained – who is responsible for the critical evaluation of the products and services developed by Big Tech? If not the industry, who has access to the models and data to test their products? If the industry is expected to self-regulate, how are employees protected if they raise concerns? *What is the responsibility of a company to critically evaluate their own technology?*

Notes

1. Hao, K. 2020. "We Read The Paper That Forced Timnit Gebru Out Of Google. Here's What It Says." *MIT Technology Review.* https://www.technologyreview.com/2020/12/04/1013294/google-ai-ethics-research-paper-forced-out-timnit-gebru/
2. The paper has six coauthors, four from Google. Professor Emily Bender was interviewed about the paper as a coauthor from outside Google, but asked to not disclose the others' names. Professor Bender, a tenured professor at the University of Washington, noted, "I think this is underscoring the value of academic freedom."

3. Google Walkout For Real Change. 2020. "Setting the Record Straight." *Medium*. December 7, 2020. https://googlewalkout.medium.com/setting-the-record-straight-isupporttimnit-believeblackwomen -5d7bbfe4ed90

4. Google Walkout For Real Change. 2020. "Setting the Record Straight."

5. Google Walkout For Real Change. 2020. "Setting the Record Straight." Simonite, Tom. 2020. "A Prominent AI Ethics Researcher Says Google Fired Her." *Wired*. December 3, 2020. https://www .wired.com/story/prominent-ai-ethics-researcher-says-google-fired-her/

6. Simonite, Tom. 2021. "What Really Happened When Google Ousted Timnit Gebru" *Wired*. July/ August 2021. https://www.wired.com/story/google-timnit-gebru-ai-what-really-happened/; Setting the record straight. Medium. https://googlewalkout.medium.com/setting-the-record-straight-isup-porttimnit-believeblackwomen-5d7bbfe4ed90

7. Google Walkout For Real Change. 2020. "Setting the record straight."

8. Simonite, Tom. 2021. "What Really Happened When Google Ousted Timnit Gebru"

9. Another co-author at Google was Margaret Mitchell. A version online included an author named "Shmargaret Shmitchell" without any affiliation. (bit.ly/3kmXwKW) Dastin, Jeffrey and Paresh Dave. 2021. "Exclusive: Google pledges changes to research oversight after internal revolt." *Reuters* https://www.reuters.com/article/us-alphabet-google-research-exclusive-idUSKBN2AP1AC. Mitchell was also fired a few months later.

10. Simonite, Tom. 2021. "What Really Happened When Google Ousted Timnit Gebru"

11. Tiku, Nitasha. 2020. "Google hired Timnit Gebru to be an outspoken critic of unethical AI. Then she was fired for it." *The Washington Post*. December 23, 2020 https://www.washingtonpost.com/technol-ogy/2020/12/23/google-timnit-gebru-ai-ethics/

12. Tiku, Nitasha. 2020. "Google Hired Timnit Gebru To Be An Outspoken Critic Of Unethical AI."

13. Tiku, Nitasha. 2020. "Google hired Timnit Gebru to be an outspoken critic of unethical AI."

14. Metz, Cade and Daisuke Wakabayashi. 2020. **"Google Researcher Says She Was Fired Over Paper Highlighting Bias in A.I."** *The New York Times*. December 3, 2020. https://www.nytimes.com/2020 /12/03/technology/google-researcher-timnit-gebru.html

15. Tiku, Nitasha. 2020. "Google Hired Timnit Gebru To Be An Outspoken Critic Of Unethical AI."

16. Tiku, Nitasha. 2020. "Google Hired Timnit Gebru To Be An Outspoken Critic Of Unethical AI."

17. Hao, K. 2020. "I Started Crying": Inside Timnit Gebru's Last Days At Google—And What Happens Next." *MIT Technology Review*. https://www.technologyreview.com/2020/12/16/1014634/google-ai -ethics-lead-timnit-gebru-tells-story/

18. Johnson, Khari. 2021. "AI Ethics Research Conference Suspends Google Sponsorship." *Venture Beat* March 2, 2021. https://venturebeat.com/2021/03/02/ai-ethics-research-conference-suspends-google -sponsorship/

19. Simonite, Tom. 2021. "What Really Happened When Google Ousted Timnit Gebru"

20. Hao, K. 2020. "We Read The Paper That Forced Timnit Gebru Out Of Google. Here's What It Says."

21. Hao, K. 2020. "We Read The Paper That Forced Timnit Gebru Out Of Google. Here's What It Says."

22. https://twitter.com/JeffDean/status/1334953632719011840

23. Hao, K. 2020. "We Read The Paper That Forced Timnit Gebru Out Of Google. Here's What It Says."

24. Tweet: Nicolas Le Roux "Now might be a good time to remind everyone that the easiest way to dis-criminate is to make stringent rules, then to decide when and for whom to enforce them. My submis-sions were always checked for disclosure of sensitive material, never for the quality of the literature review." (Dec. 3, 2020). Hao, K. 2020. "We Read The Paper That Forced Timnit Gebru Out Of Google. Here's What It says."

25. Setting the record straight. Medium. https://googlewalkout.medium.com/setting-the-record-straight -isupporttimnit-believeblackwomen-5d7bbfe4ed90

26. Schiffer, Zoe. "Timnit Gebru Was Fired From Google — Then The Harassers Arrived." *The Verge* https://www.theverge.com/22309962/timnit-gebru-google-harassment-campaign-jeff-dean

27. Dave, Paresh and Jeffrey Dastin. 2021. "Google Told Its Scientists To 'Strike A Positive Tone' In AI Research - Documents." *Reuters*. Dec 23, 2020. https://www.reuters.com/article/us-alphabet-google -research-focus-idUSKBN28X1CB

28. Dastin, Jeffrey and Paresh Dave. 2021. "Exclusive: Google Pledges Changes To Research Oversight After Internal Revolt."; Dave, Paresh and Jeffrey Dastin. 2021. "Google Told Its Scientists To 'Strike A Positive Tone' In AI Research - Documents."

29. Dave, Paresh and Jeffrey Dastin. 2021. "Google Told Its Scientists To 'Strike A Positive Tone' In AI Research - Documents."

30. Dave, Paresh and Jeffrey Dastin. 2021. "Google told Its Scientists To 'Strike A Positive Tone' In AI Research - Documents."

31. Copeland, Rob and Parmy Olson. 2021. "Artificial Intelligence Will Define Google's Future. For Now, It's a Management Challenge." *The Wall Street Journal.* January 26, 2021. https://www.wsj .com/articles/artificial-intelligence-will-define-googles-future-for-now-its-a-management-challenge -11611676945

32. Wakabayashi, Daisuke and Katie Benner. 2018. "How Google Protected Andy Rubin, the 'Father of Android'." *The New York Times.* October 25, 2018. https://www.nytimes.com/2018/10/25/technology /google-sexual-harassment-andy-rubin.html

33. Simonite, T. 2020. The Dark Side of Big Tech's Funding for AI Research. https://www.wired.com/ story/dark-side-big-tech-funding-ai-research/

34. Simonite, Tom. 2017. "Google's AI Wizard Unveils a New Twist on Neural Networks." *Wired.* https:// www.wired.com/story/googles-ai-wizard-unveils-a-new-twist-on-neural-networks/

35. Simonite, Tom. 2020. "The Dark Side of Big Tech's Funding for AI Research." *Wired.*

36. Metz, Cade. 2016. "Artificial Intelligence Just Broke Steve Jobs' Wall of Secrecy." *Wired.* https://www .wired.com/2016/12/artificial-intelligence-just-broke-steve-jobs-wall-secrecy/

37. Metz, Cade. 2016. "Artificial Intelligence Just Broke Steve Jobs' Wall of Secrecy."

38. Hao, Karen. 2021. "Inside the Fight To Reclaim AI From Big Tech's Control" *MIT Technology Review.* June 14, 2021. https://www.technologyreview.com/2021/06/14/1026148/ai-big-tech-timnit -gebru-paper-ethics/

39. Abdalla, Mohamed and Moustafa Abdalla. 2021. "The Grey Hoodie Project: Big Tobacco, Big Tech, and the threat on academic integrity." *AIES-21 Conference Proceedings.* https://arxiv.org/abs/2009 .13676

40. To put it in perspective, Google spent more than $27 billion on research and design generally in 2020. McCormick, John. 2021. AI Ethics Teams Bulk Up in Size, Influence at Tech Firms *The Wall Street Journal.* May 27, 2021. https://www.wsj.com/articles/ai-ethics-teams-bulk-up-in-size-influence -at-tech-firms-11622113202?redirect=amp#click=https://t.co/rChd8XQUXA

41. The Biden administration is now asking Congress to invest an additional $180 billion in emerging technologies, with AI as a top priority. Hao, Karen. 2021. "Inside the Fight To Reclaim AI From Big Tech's Control" *MIT Technology Review.* June 14, 2021. https://www.technologyreview.com/2021/06 /14/1026148/ai-big-tech-timnit-gebru-paper-ethics/

42. Schwab, Katherine. 2021. "This Is Bigger Than Just Timnit': How Google Tried To Silence A Critic And Ignited A Movement." *Fast Company.* February 26, 2021. https://www.fastcompany.com /90608471/timnit-gebru-google-ai-ethics-equitable-tech-movement

43. FAcct forbids sponsors to influence content. Schwab, Katherine. 2021. "This Is Bigger Than Just Timnit': How Google Tried To Silence A Critic And Ignited A Movement."

44. Mohamed Abdalla of the University of Toronto and Moustafa Abdalla of Harvard Medical School. Schwab, Katherine. 2021. "This Is Bigger Than Just Timnit': How Google Tried To Silence A Critic And Ignited A Movement."

45. Simonite, T. 2020. The Dark Side of Big Tech's Funding for AI Research. https://www.wired.com/ story/dark-side-big-tech-funding-ai-research/

46. Tech companies "throw their weight behind engineered solutions to what are social problems," says Ali Alkhatib, a research fellow at the Center for Applied Data Ethics at the University of San Francisco. Schwab, Katherine. 2021. "This Is Bigger Than Just Timnit': How Google Tried To Silence A Critic And Ignited A Movement."

47. Abdalla, Mohamed and Moustafa Abdalla. 2021. "The Grey Hoodie Project:

48. Abdalla, Mohamed and Moustafa Abdalla. 2021. "The Grey Hoodie Project:

49. Joichi Ito had to step down in 2020 after it was revealed that he took money from a convicted sex offender.

50. Johnson, Khari. 2020. "From Whistleblower Laws To Unions: How Google's AI Ethics Meltdown Could Shape Policy." *Venture Beat.* December 16, 2020. https://venturebeat.com/2020/12/16/from -whistleblower-laws-to-unions-how-googles-ai-ethics-meltdown-could-shape-policy/

51. "NeurIPS 2020 Code Submission Policy." 2020. NeurIPS. https://nips.cc/Conferences/2020/ PaperInformation/CodeSubmissionPolicy

52. Johnson, Khari. 2020. "From whistleblower laws to unions:

53. Lazzaro, Sage. 2021. "DeepMind Scientist Calls For Ethical AI As Google Faces Ongoing Backlash" *Venture Beat.* June 22, 2021. https://venturebeat.com/2021/06/22/deepmind-scientist-calls-for-ethi cal-ai-as-google-faces-ongoing-backlash/

54. References code of ethics: https://iclr.cc/public/CodeOfEthics

55. OSHA Fact Sheet. https://www.osha.gov/sites/default/files/publications/OSHA3714.pdf

56. E.g.,Research Ethics. *Lilly.* https://www.lilly.com/science/discovery/research-ethics

57. OSHA. 2016. "OSHA Issues Final Rule Establishing Procedures For Handling Retaliation Complaints From Workers In The Automotive Industry." https://www.osha.gov/news/newsreleases/ trade/12142016

58. Purtell, Daniell. 2017. "NTSB Details Tesla's Role in First Self-Driving Car Fatality." https://www .mceldrewyoung.com/ntsb-tesla-fatality-fault/

59. "Whistleblowers." *OSHA.* https://www.osha.gov/publications/bytopic/whistleblowers

60. "Ethics." *American Society of Civil Engineers.* https://www.asce.org/ethics/

61. https://venturebeat.com/2020/12/16/from-whistleblower-laws-to-unions-how-googles-ai-ethics -meltdown-could-shape-policy/

62. The Future Must Be Ethical: #MakeAIEthical | by Google Walkout For Real Change | Mar, 2021 | Medium https://googlewalkout.medium.com/the-future-must-be-ethical-makeaiethical-9eb3edd7cf3c

63. https://venturebeat.com/2021/03/01/national-security-commission-on-artificial-intelligence-issues -report-on-how-to-maintain-u-s-dominance/

64. https://venturebeat.com/2020/12/16/from-whistleblower-laws-to-unions-how-googles-ai-ethics -meltdown-could-shape-policy/

65. Simonite, T. 2020. The Dark Side of Big Tech's Funding for AI Research. https://www.wired.com/ story/dark-side-big-tech-funding-ai-research/

66. The Future Must Be Ethical: #MakeAIEthical | by Google Walkout For Real Change | Mar, 2021 | Medium https://googlewalkout.medium.com/the-future-must-be-ethical-makeaiethical-9eb3edd7cf3c

67. Zachary C. Lipton and Jacob Steinhardt, "Troubling Trends in Machine Learning Scholarship," *ArXiv Preprint ArXiv:1807.03341*, 2018.

68. https://www.fastcompany.com/90608471/timnit-gebru-google-ai-ethics-equitable-tech-movement

69. https://venturebeat.com/2020/04/17/ai-researchers-propose-bias-bounties-to-put-ethics-principles -into-practice/

70. Miles Brundage et al., "Toward Trustworthy AI Development: Mechanisms for Supporting Verifiable Claims," *ArXiv Preprint ArXiv:2004.07213*, 2020.

71. *Laura Edelson, Minh-Kha Nguyen, Ian Goldstein, Oana Goga, Tobias Lauinger, and Damon McCoy.* Mar 3 2020. Far-right news sources on Facebook more engaging https://medium.com/cybersecurity -for-democracy/far-right-news-sources-on-facebook-more-engaging-e04a01efae90

72. Nellis, Stephen and Paresh Dave. 2021. Apple Hires Ex-Google AI Scientist Who Resigned After Colleagues' Firings. Reuters. https://www.reuters.com/technology/apple-hires-ex-google-ai-scientist -who-resigned-after-colleagues-firing-2021-05-03/

73. https://twitter.com/le_roux_nicolas/status/1399812601392009225?s=11 He also noted "Also, now that I know more about how resignation at Google works, let's be absolutely clear about one thing: @ timnitGebru did not resign." June 1, 2021.

74. Vincent, James. May 19, 2021. Google Made AI Language The Centerpiece Of I/O While Ignoring Its Troubled Past At The Company *The Verge.* https://www.theverge.com/2021/5/19/22443441/ google-ai-language-models-dangers-risk-io-timnit-gebru-margaret-mitchell-firing

75. Sumagaysay, Levi. 2021. Amid Labor Strife, Google Opposes Shareholder Call For Whistleblower-Policy Review. *MarketWatch*. https://www.marketwatch.com/story/amid-labor-strife-google-opposes-shareholder-call-for-whistleblower-policy-review-11619483210

76. Fortunate Top 50. 2021. *Fortune*. https://fortune.com/worlds-greatest-leaders/2021/timnit-gebru/

Chapter 11.2

The Scientist *Qua* Scientist Makes Value Judgments[*]

Richard Rudner

The question of the relationship of the making of value judgments in a typically ethical sense to the methods and procedures of science has been discussed in the literature at least to that point which e. e. cummings somewhere refers to as "The Mystical Moment of Dullness." Nevertheless, albeit with some trepidation, I feel that something more may fruitfully be said on the subject.

In particular the problem has once more been raised in an interesting and poignant fashion by recently published discussions between Carnap (1) and Quine (3) on the question of the ontological commitments which one may make in the choosing of language systems.

I shall refer to this discussion in more detail in the sequel; for the present, however, let us briefly examine the current status of what is somewhat loosely called the "fact-value dichotomy."

I have not found the arguments which are usually offered, by those who believe that scientists do essentially make value judgments, satisfactory. On the other hand the rebuttals of some of those with opposing viewpoints seem to have had at least a *prima facie* cogency although they too may in the final analysis prove to have been subtly perverse.

Those who contend that scientists do essentially make value judgments generally support their contentions by either

A. pointing to the fact that our having a science at all somehow "involves" a value judgment, or
B. by pointing out that in order to select, say among alternative problems, the scientist must make a value judgment; or (perhaps most frequently)
C. by pointing to the fact that the scientist cannot escape his quite human self - he is a "mass of predilections" and these predilections must inevitably influence all of his activities not excepting his scientific ones.

To such arguments, a great many empirically oriented philosophers and scientists have responded that the value judgments involved in our decisions to have a science, or to select

[*] Rudner, Richard. "The scientist qua scientist makes value judgments." *Philosophy of Science* 20, no. 1 (1953): 1-6. Reprinted with permission. Note: This is an excerpt from the original so footnote and endnote numbering may be modified.

DOI: 10.1201/9781003278290-65

problem A for attention rather than problem B are, *of course*, extra-scientific. If (they say) it is necessary to make a decision to have a science before we can have one, then this decision is literally pre-scientific and the act has thereby certainly not been shown to be any part of the *procedure* of science. Similarly the decision to focus attention on one problem rather than another is extra-problematic and forms no part of the procedures involved in dealing with the problem *decided* upon. Since it is *these* procedures which constitute the method of science, value judgments, so they respond, have not been shown to be involved in the scientific method as such. Again, with respect to the inevitable presence of our predilections in the laboratory, most empirically oriented philosophers and scientists agree that this is "unfortunately" the case; but, they hasten to add, if science is to progress toward objectivity the influence of our personal feelings or biases on experimental results must be minimized. We must try not to let our personal idiosyncrasies affect our scientific work. The perfect scientist - the scientist *qua* scientist does not allow this kind of value judgment to influence his work. However much he may find doing so unavoidable *qua* father, *qua* lover, *qua* member of society, *qua* grouch, *when* he does so he is not behaving *qua* scientist.

As I indicated at the outset, the arguments of neither of the protagonists in this issue appear quite satisfactory to me. The empiricists' rebuttals, telling prima facie as they may against the specific arguments that evoke them, nonetheless do not appear ultimately to stand up, but perhaps even more importantly, *the original arguments* seem utterly too frail.

I believe that a much stronger case may be made for the contention that value judgments are essentially involved in the procedures of science. And what I now propose to show is that scientists as scientists *do* make value judgments.

Now I take it that no analysis of what constitutes the method of science would be satisfactory unless it comprised some assertion to the effect that the scientist as scientist accepts or rejects hypotheses.

But if this is so then clearly the scientist as scientist does make value judgments. For, since no scientific hypothesis is ever completely verified, in accepting a hypothesis the scientist must make the decision that the evidence is *sufficiently* strong or that the probability is *sufficiently* high to warrant the acceptance of the hypothesis. Obviously our decision regarding the evidence and respecting how strong is "strong enough", is going to be a function of the *importance,* in the typically ethical sense, of making a mistake in accepting or rejecting the hypothesis. Thus, to take a crude but easily manageable example, if the hypothesis under consideration were to the effect that a toxic ingredient of a drug was not present in lethal quantity, we would require a relatively high degree of confirmation or confidence before accepting the hypothesis - for the consequences of making a mistake here are exceedingly grave by our moral standards. On the other hand, if say, our hypothesis stated that, on the basis of a sample, a certain lot of machine stamped belt buckles was not defective, the degree of confidence we should require would be relatively not so high. *How sure we need to be before we accept a hypothesis will depend on how serious a mistake would be.*

The examples I have chosen are from scientific inferences in industrial quality control. But the point is clearly quite general in application. It would be interesting and instructive, for example, to know just how high a degree of probability the Manhattan Project scientists demanded for the hypothesis that no uncontrollable pervasive chain reaction would occur, before they proceeded with the first atomic bomb detonation or first activated the Chicago pile above a critical level. It would be equally interesting and instructive to know why they decided that *that* probability value (if one was decided upon) was high enough rather than one which was higher; and perhaps most interesting of all to learn whether the problem in this form was brought to consciousness at all.

In general then, before we can accept any hypothesis, the value decision must be made in the light of the seriousness of a mistake, that the probability is *high enough* or that, the evidence is *strong enough,* to warrant its acceptance.

Before going further, it will perhaps be well to clear up two points which might otherwise prove troublesome below. First I have obviously used the term "probability" up to this point in a quite loose and pre-analytic sense. But my point can be given a more rigorous formulation in terms of a description of the process of making statistical inference and of the acceptance or rejection of hypotheses in statistics. As is well known, the acceptance or rejection of such a hypothesis presupposes that a certain level of significance or level of confidence or critical region be selected.[1]

It is with respect at least to the *necessary* selection of a confidence level or interval that the necessary value judgment in the inquiry occurs. For, "the size of the critical region (one selects) is related to *the risk one wants to accept* in testing a statistical hypothesis" (4: 435).

And clearly how great a risk one is willing to take of being wrong in accepting or rejecting the hypothesis will depend upon how seriously in the typically ethical sense one views the consequences of making a mistake.

I believe, of course, that an adequate rational reconstruction of the procedures of science would show that every scientific inference is properly construable as a statistical inference (i.e. as an inference from a set of characteristics of a sample of a population to a set of characteristics of the total population) and that such an inference would be scientifically in control only in so far as it is statistically in control. But it is not necessary to argue this point, for even if one believes that what is involved in some scientific inferences is not statistical probability but rather a concept like strength of evidence or degree of confirmation, one would still be concerned with making the decision that the evidence was *strong enough* or the degree of confirmation *high enough* to warrant acceptance of the hypothesis. Now, many empiricists who reflect on the foregoing considerations agree that acceptances or rejections of hypotheses do essentially involve value judgments, but they are nonetheless loathe to accept the conclusion. And one objection which has been raised against this line of argument by those of them who are suspicious of the intrusion of value questions into the "objective realm of science," is that actually the scientist's task is only to *determine* the degree of confirmation or the strength of the evidence which *exists* for an hypothesis. In short, they object that while it may be a function of the scientist *qua member of society* to decide whether a degree of probability associated with the hypothesis is high enough to warrant its acceptance, *still* the task of the scientist *qua* scientist is *just the determination* of the degree of probability or the strength of the evidence for a hypothesis and not the acceptance or rejection of that hypothesis.

But a little reflection will show that the plausibility of this objection is apparent merely. For the determination that the degree of confirmation is say, *p*, or that the strength of evidence is such and such, which is on this view being held to be the indispensable task of the scientist *qua* scientist, is clearly nothing more than *the acceptance by the scientist of the hypothesis that the degree of confidence is p or that the strength of the evidence is such and such;* and as these men have conceded, acceptance of hypotheses does require value decisions. The second point which it may be well to consider before finally turning our attention to the Quine-Carnap discussion has to do with the nature of the suggestions which have thus far been made in this essay. In this connection, it is important to point out that the preceeding remarks do *not* have as their import that an empirical description of every present day scientist ostensibly going about his business would include the statement that he made a value judgment at such and such a juncture. This is no doubt the case; but it is a hypothesis which can only be confirmed by a discipline which cannot be said to have gotten extremely far along as yet; namely, the Sociology and Psychology of Science, whether such an empirical description is warranted, cannot be settled from the armchair.

My remarks have, rather, amounted to this: any adequate analysis or (if I may use the term) rational reconstruction of the method of science must comprise the statement that the scientist *qua* scientist accepts or rejects hypotheses; and further that an analysis of that statement would reveal it to entail that the scientist *qua* scientist makes value judgments.

I think that it is in the light of the foregoing arguments, the substance of which has, in one form or another, been alluded to in past years by a number of inquirers (notably C. W. Churchman, R. L. Ackoff, and A. Wald) that the Quine-Carnap discussion takes on heightened interest. For, if I understand that discussion and its outcome correctly, although it apparently begins a good distance away from any consideration of the fact-value dichotomy, and although all the way through it both men touch on the matter in a way which indicates that they believe that questions concerning that dichotomy are, if anything, merely tangential to their main issue, yet it eventuates with Quine by an independent argument apparently in agreement with at least the conclusion here reached and also apparently having forced Carnap to that conclusion. (Carnap, however, is expected to reply to Quine's article and I may be too sanguine here.)

The issue of ontological commitment between Carnap and Quine has been one of relatively long standing. In this recent article (1), Carnap maintains that we are concerned with two kinds of questions of existence relative to a given language system. One is what *kinds* of entities it would be permissable to speak about as existing when that language system is used; i.e. what kind of *framework* for speaking of entities should our system comprise. This, according to Carnap, is an *external* question. It is the *practical* question of what sort of linguistic system we want to choose. Such questions as "are there abstract entities?," or "are there physical entities?" thus are held to belong to the category of external questions. On the other hand, having made the decision regarding which linguistic framework to adopt, we can then raise questions like "are there any black swans?" "What are the factors of 544?" etc. Such questions are *internal* questions.

For our present purposes, the important thing about all of this is that while for Carnap *internal* questions are theoretical ones, i.e., ones whose answers have cognitive content, external questions are not theoretical at all. They are *practical questions-they* concern our decisions to employ one language structure or another. They are of the kind that face us when for example we have to decide whether we ought to have a Democratic or a Republican administration for the next four years. In short, though neither Carnap nor Quine employ the epithet, they are *value questions*.

Now if this dichotomy of existence questions is accepted Carnap can still deny the essential involvement of the making of value judgments in the procedures of science by insisting that concern with *external* questions, admittedly necessary and admittedly axiological, is nevertheless in some sense a pre-scientific concern. But most interestingly, what Quine then proceeds to do is to show that the dichotomy, as Carnap holds it is untenable. This is not the appropriate place to repeat Quine's arguments which are brilliantly presented in the article referred to. They are in line with the views he has expressed in his "Two Dogma's of Empiricism" essay and especially with his introduction to his recent book, *Methods of Logic*. Nonetheless the final paragraph of the Quine article I'm presently considering sums up his conclusions neatly:

> Within natural science there is a continuum of gradations, from the statements which report observations to those which reflect basic features say of quantum theory or the theory of relativity. The view which I end up with, in the paper last cited, is that statements of ontology or even of mathematics and logic form a continuation of this continuum, a continuation which is perhaps yet more remote from observation than

are the central principles of quantum theory or relativity. The differences here are in my view differences only in degree and not in kind. Science is a unified structure, and in principle it is the structure as a whole, and not its component statements one by one, that experience confirms or shows to be imperfect. Carnap maintains that ontological questions, and likewise questions of logical or mathematical principle, are questions not of fact but of choosing a convenient conceptual scheme or frame work for science; and with this I agree only if the same be conceded for every scientific hypothesis.

(3: 71–72)

In the light of all of this I think that the statement that *Scientists qua Scientists* make value judgments, is also a consequence of Quine's position.

Now, if the major point I have here undertaken to establish is correct, then clearly we are confronted with a first order crisis in science & methodology. The positive horror which most scientists and philosophers of science have of the intrusion of value considerations into science is wholly understandable. Memories of the (now diminished but to a certain extent still continuing) conflict between science and, e.g., the dominant religions over the intrusion of religious value considerations into the domain of scientific inquiry, are strong in many reflective scientists. The traditional search for objectivity exemplifies science's pursuit of one of its most precious ideals. But for the scientist to close his eyes to the fact that scientific method *intrinsically* requires the making of value decisions, for him to push out of his consciousness the fact that he does make them, can in no way bring him closer to the ideal of objectivity. To refuse to pay attention to the value decisions which *must* be made, to make them intuitively, unconsciously, haphazardly, is to leave an essential aspect of scientific method scientifically out of control.

What seems called for (and here no more than the sketchiest indications of the problem can be given) is nothing less than a radical reworking of the ideal of scientific objectivity. The slightly juvenile conception of the coldblooded, emotionless, impersonal, passive scientist mirroring the world perfectly in the highly polished lenses of his steel rimmed glasses - this stereotype is no longer, if it ever was, adequate.

What is being proposed here is that objectivity for science lies at least in becoming precise about what value judgments are being and might have been made in a given inquiry - and even, to put it in its most challenging form, what value decisions ought to be made; in short that a science of ethics is a necessary requirement if science's progress toward objectivity is to be continuous.

Of course the establishment of such a science of ethics is a task of stupendous magnitude and it will probably not even be well launched for many generations. But a first step is surely comprised of the reflective self awareness of the scientist in making the value judgments he must make.

Note

1. "In practice three levels are commonly used: 1 per cent, 5 per cent and 0.3 of one per cent. There is nothing sacred about these three values; *they have become established in practice without any rigid theoretical justification*." (my italics) (4: 435). To establish significance at the 5 per cent level means that one is willing to take the risk of accepting a hypothesis as true when one will be thus making a mistake, one time in twenty. Or in other words, that one will be wrong, (over the long run) once every twenty times if one employed an.05 level of significance. See also (2: ch. V) for such statements as "which of these two errors is most *important* to avoid (it being necessary to make such a decision in order to accept or reject the given hypothesis) is a *subjective matter* ..." (p. 262) (my italics).

References

Carnap, R., "Empiricism, Semantics, and Ontology," *Revue Internationale de Philosophie*, XI, 1950, p. 20–40.

Neyman, J., *First Course in Probability and Statistics*, New York: Henry Holt & Co.,1950.

Quine, W. V., "On Carnap's Views on Ontology," *Philosophical Studies*, II, No. 5, 1951.

Rosander, A. C., *Elementary Principles of Statistics*. New York: D. Van Nostrand Co.,1951.

Chapter 11.3

Excerpt from Ethical Implications and Accountability of Algorithms[*]

Kirsten Martin

Algorithms silently structure our lives. Algorithms can determine whether someone is hired, promoted, offered a loan, or provided housing as well as determine which political ads and news articles consumers see. Yet, the responsibility for algorithms in these important decisions is not clear. This article identifies whether developers have a responsibility for their algorithms later in use, what those firms are responsible for, and the normative grounding for that responsibility. I conceptualize algorithms as value-laden, rather than neutral, in that algorithms create moral consequences, reinforce or undercut ethical principles, and enable or diminish stakeholder rights and dignity. In addition, algorithms are an important actor in ethical decisions and influence the delegation of roles and responsibilities within these decisions. As such, firms should be responsible for not only the value-laden-ness of an algorithm but also for designing who-does-what within the algorithmic decision. As such, firms developing algorithms are accountable for designing how large a role individuals will be permitted to take in the subsequent algorithmic decision. Counter to current arguments, I find that if an algorithm is designed to preclude individuals from taking responsibility within a decision, then the designer of the algorithm should be held accountable for the ethical implications of the algorithm in use.

[...]

II. Algorithms as Value-Laden Actors within Decisions

The ethical implications of algorithms outlined above are important to acknowledge not only because we should ensure biases are just and appropriate to the norms of the decision context,

---

[*] Martin, K. Ethical implications and accountability of algorithms. Journal of Business Ethics 160, no. 4 (2019): 835-850. Reprinted with permission. Note: This is an excerpt from the original so footnote and endnote numbering may be modified.

but also, as I turn to next, because value-laden algorithms become an important actor of a larger decision – an actor that determines the roles and responsibilities of individuals in the decision. To claim that technology takes on roles and responsibilities within a system of actors is not without controversy. Algorithms have been referred to as actants (Tufekci 2015) as has technology more generally (Johnson and Noorman 2014), where material artifacts are designed to act within a system of material and non-material (i.e. human) actors that seeks to achieve a goal. Below, I leverage two scholars – Madeleine Akrich and Bruno Latour – to frame how algorithms impact the role and responsibilities of individuals and algorithms within a decision.

1. *Role of Algorithms in Decisions*

According to socio-technical studies (STS) scholar Madeleine Akrich, the design of technology is a projection of how the technology will work within a network of material and non-material actors. A car is designed with assumptions about the type of driver, how the roads are constructed, the number of passengers and how they will behave, the size of other cars on the road, etc. Cars have particular size openings (doors) and are designed at a width and height to both fit within the roads and keep individuals safe from other cars. While a plane may require a copilot, cars do not make such an assumption about what passengers will do. The safety of the passengers is designed into the car with airbags, seatbelts, anti-lock brakes, collapsible front-ends, etc as well as how the individuals and technologies will work together. As Akrich notes,

> A large part of the work of innovators is that of '*inscribing*' this vision of (or prediction about) the world in the technical content of the new object. I will call the end product of this work a 'script' or a 'scenario'.

(Akrich 1992, 208)

Designers of technological artifacts make assumptions about what the world will do and, relatedly, inscribe how their technology will fit into that world.

In terms of algorithms, Akrich's 'script' is actually *less* obscure since the design is embodied in code that resembles language. Where the script behind a car or iPhone or toaster may require some imagination as to what the designer is saying, the algorithm comes in a form familiar to many—some even with comments throughout to explain the design. Algorithms are designed with assumptions about what is important, the type of data that will be available, how clean the data will be, the role of the actor imputing the data, and who will use the output and for what purpose. The sentencing algorithm assumes the data is in a certain form and, in effect, states that those data required for the algorithm to make a decision are most important.

Technologies as scripts survive outside the hands of the designer. Scripts are durable, and the technology's script becomes independent of the innovator once in use. Akrich uses the example of the two-handled Angolan hoe as made for women carrying children on their backs. (Akrich 1992, 208). The hoe exists with this biased script – giving preference to women carrying children – decades later. In the sentencing algorithm case above, the factors taken into consideration, such as COMPAS algorithm's 137 questions, exist after the algorithm is put into use. Changing the hoe's, the algorithm's, or a car's design after production is difficult. Importantly, while technology and algorithms are constructed by humans, technology's scripts endure to influence the behavior, acts, and beliefs of individuals.[1]

These technologies survive to have biases that are value laden (Friedman and Nissenbaum 1996; Johnson 2004) or have politics (Winner 1980). The design of the car to fit within roads and survive most crashes is value-laden: the script acknowledges the validity of the current road design and preferences certain types of people (by size, weight, gender) to survive a crash.[2] The quintessential example within technology studies is Langdon Winner's analysis of bridges on the road to Jones Beach. These bridges were designed at a height that would preclude public buses (and people who took public buses) from accessing Jones Beach, thus prioritizing those with cars and excluding those who rely on public transportation. The technology's script answers who matters, which group is important, who counts, which race/ethnicity is included and delineated. In the sentencing example, the algorithm states that a defendant's paternal criminal history is important but the defendant's own recovery from addiction is not. The algorithm-as-script makes assumptions as to the accuracy of the data and how the output will be used. Akrich suggests the following thought experiment which is of particular importance for algorithms:

> How can the prescriptions encoded in the mechanism be brought out in words? By replacing them by strings of sentences (often in the imperative) that are uttered (silently and continuously) by the mechanisms for the benefit of those who are mechanized: do this, do that, behave this way, don't go that way, you may do so, be allowed to go there. Such sentences look very much like a programming language.

2. Algorithm's Delegation of Roles and Responsibilities in Decisions

Technologies, such as algorithms, influence a group of actors assembled to perform a task. Algorithmic biases not only impact the achievement of the task as well as whether and how ethical norms are respected, but also the function and role of the other actors in the decision. Latour uses the combination of a door and a door groomer to illustrate how tasks may be delegated between material and non-material actors. The door hinge allows us to gain access to a room without tearing down walls and rebuilding them.[3] The combination of the door, the hinge, and the doorman creates the opportunity to walk through a wall without leaving a gaping hole in the wall. Similarly, a system of airbags, seatbelt, driver, and an annoying chime combine to secure the driver in the event of a crash (Latour 1992). In the case of the sentencing algorithm, COMPAS works within a system of actors in the court to adjudicate the sentence including the judge, probation officer, defense attorney, defendant, prosecutor, clerks, etc.

At a minimum, technologies alleviate the need for others to do a task. In the case of Latour's seatbelt, making the seat belt automatic – attaching the seatbelt to the door so that it is in place automatically – alleviates the driver from the responsibility to ensure the seatbelt is used. In the case of doors, hydraulic door hinges ensure the door is closed gently without the need of a human door groomer. In the case of sentencing algorithms, COMPAS makes sense of the defendants' profile and predicts their risk assessment, thereby alleviating the need of the probation officer or judge from making that judgment. As Latour rightly summarizes, "every time you want to know what a nonhuman does, simply imagine what other humans or other nonhumans would have to do were this character not present" (p. 155). This delegation of tasks is a choice, and this delegation is constructed and constantly up for deliberation. The divvying up of tasks between material and nonmaterial actors (i.e. algorithms and individuals) within a safety system, sentencing system, or go-through-the-wall system appears as a *fait accompli* when the system works. However, this delegation as to who-does-what deserves careful consideration.

Importantly, the substitution of technology for human is not a perfect substitution: As Latour notes, "springs do the job of replacing grooms, but they play the role of a very rude, uneducated, and dumb porter who obviously prefers the wall version of the door to its hole version. They simply slam the door shut" (p. 157). Also, due to their prescriptions, these door springs have biases and "*discriminate* against very little and very old persons" (p. 159, italics in original). Sentencing algorithms in sentencing illustrate a similar problem with unjust biases perpetuating human discrimination. Similarly, an algorithm for university admittance could be as discriminatory by design or the algorithm could be trained on data with historical biases.[4] Replacing the discriminatory human with a biased technology does not erase the discrimination.

Technologies, such as algorithms, are designed to perform a task with a particular moral delegation in mind. This moral delegation by designers impacts the moral behavior of other actors. In the case of the doors, designers decide "either to discipline the people or to substitute for the unreliable humans a delegated nonhuman character whose only function is to open and close the door. This is called a door-closer or a groom" (Latour 1992, 157). The hydraulic door groom takes on the responsibility to close the door.

Here, I suggest that computer scientists perform the same delegation of tasks in designing an algorithm. Just as there is a distribution of competences between technology and individuals, there is also a distribution of associated responsibility. Latour suggests thinking about the morality in extreme cases: where the design of the car stipulates that the seatbelt must be fastened before the car could start versus where the car is designed without any nudges for the driver.

> "Worse yet – the design where 'a seat belt that politely makes way for me when I open the door and then straps me as politely but very tightly when I close the door'…The program of action "IF a car is moving, THEN the driver has a seat belt" is enforced…I cannot be bad anymore. I, plus the car, plus the dozens of patented engineers, plus the police are making me be moral"
>
> **(p. 152)**

In delegating the task of driver safety to the technology the designer alleviates the individual from having to take on that responsibility.

Delegating a task to a technology – such as a seatbelt or an algorithm – does not remove the associated responsibility for that task. Latour uses physicists looking for 'missing mass' in the universe as a metaphor for sociologists or ethicists looking for missing responsibility in a system of technologies and individuals. Latour suggests we start looking in material actors for the missing masses "who make up our morality" (Latour 1992, 152–53). Figure 11.3.1 makes explicit (some of) the missing masses in algorithmic decision making. By adding back the questions we are silently asking and perhaps delegating to algorithms in design, Latour's missing masses crowd out the role of the algorithm in Figure 11.3.1.

3. *Designing an Algorithm Prescribes the Delegation of Responsibilities in Decisions*

This delegation of roles and responsibilities of the decision and the value-laden-ness of algorithms are important ethical decisions we continually make in design and development – whether firms acknowledge the decisions or not. Each box in Figure 11.2 can be answered by an algorithm or a human, and designers decide the delegation of roles and responsibilities between humans and algorithms when creating an algorithm. This decision of how roles and responsibilities are allocated to human and algorithm is performed by the engineer. For Latour

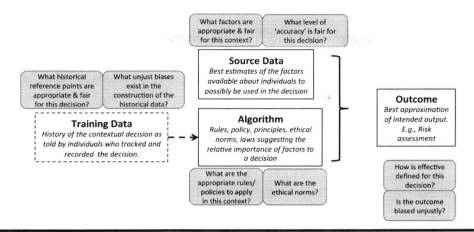

Figure 11.3.1   Adding back missing masses to algorithmic decision process.

> It is the complete chain that makes up the missing masses, not either of its extremities. The paradox of technology is that it is thought to be at one of the extremes, whereas it is the ability of the engineer to travel easily along the whole gradient and substitute one type of delegation for another that is inherent to the job.
>
> **(1992, 166)**

Ignoring the moral delegation of roles, responsibilities, and the missing masses does not make them disappear or become less important. As noted by Richard Rudner in regards to the value-laden decision throughout the scientific process, "To refuse to pay attention to the value decisions which must be made, to make them intuitively, unconsciously, haphazardly, is to leave an essential aspect of scientific method scientifically out of control" (1953, 6). The decisions about biases, roles, and responsibilities should be brought into the foreground for designers as in Figure 11.3.1. When algorithmic decision-making is anemically framed as in Figure 11.3.1, Latour's 'masses that make up our morality' go missing, and the delegation of responsibility appears to be inevitable and taken-for-granted.[5] No one is accountable for the decision as to who can and should answer the questions in Figure 11.3.1. However, the argument here is that the moral delegation of roles and responsibilities is still occurring in the scripts of the algorithm as inscribed in design.

In other words, in addition to the design of value-laden biases, firms make a moral choice as to the delegation of tasks and responsibilities between algorithms and individuals in design. This choice, if ignored, will not only be out of control as noted by Rudner, but the construction of biases and the delegations of roles, responsibilities, and missing masses will continue unquestioned.

[…]

III. Accountability for Algorithmic Decision-Making

In this article, I have conceptualized how algorithms are value-laden rather than neutral, where algorithms are inscribed with a preferred set of outcomes with ethical implications. The value-laden biases are important to acknowledge not only because we should ensure algorithms are just, conform to principles and norms of the decision, and enable rather than diminish rights (Section

I), but also because algorithms are an important part of a larger decision and influence the delegation of roles and responsibilities within ethical decisions (Section II). I now turn to explore why firms have a unique obligation in the development of algorithms around the ethical implications and roles of an algorithm in an ethical decision.

1. *Accountability and Inscrutable Algorithms*

Previous approaches to algorithmic accountability amount to a dichotomous choice. At one extreme, algorithms are value-neutral and determined by their use, with accountability falling exclusively on the users or even 'society' (Kraemer, Van Overveld, and Peterson 2011). At the other end of the spectrum is a more deterministic argument, whereby algorithms are controlling yet obscure, powerful yet inscrutable (Neyland 2016; Ziewitz 2016) and veer towards algorithms as beyond our control and the primary actors. For example, Desai and Kroll (2017) argue

Some may believe algorithms should be constructed to provide moral guidance or enforce a given morality. Others claim that moral choices are vested with a system's users and that the system itself should be neutral, allowing all types of use and with moral valences originating with the user. In either case, ... the author's deference to algorithms is a type of "worship" that reverses the skepticism of the Enlightenment. Asking algorithms "to enforce morality" is not only a type of idolatry, it also presumes we know whose morality they enforce and can define what moral outcomes are sought. [Underlining added].

Desai and Kroll rightly identify the challenge we face in identifying the moral norms an algorithm either supports or undercuts. However, algorithms are currently enforcing morality by preferencing outcomes and the roles of others in the decision, whether or not we acknowledge that enforcement and seek to govern the design decisions. The question is, who is responsible for the ethical implications rather than whether or not the algorithm provides moral guidance.

When developers design the algorithm to be used in a decision, they also design how accountability is delegated within the decision.[6] Sometimes algorithms *are designed* to absorb the work and associated responsibility of the individuals in the decision by precluding users from taking on roles and responsibilities within the decision system – e.g., inscrutable algorithms designed to be more autonomous and with less human intervention (Barocas, Hood, and Ziewitz 2013; Desai and Kroll 2017; Introna 2016; Ziewitz 2016). For example, the COMPAS algorithm was designed to preclude individuals from understanding how it works or from taking any responsibility for how it is implemented. Importantly, this is a design choice because other risk assessment algorithms are designed to be more open, thereby delegating more responsibility for the decision to individuals (Kramer 2017).

Importantly, firms can be held accountable for inscrutable systems. Inscrutable algorithms that are designed to minimize the role of individuals in the decision take on more accountability for the decision. In fact, one should be suspect of the Inscrutable Defense: when systems have been called inscrutable in order to avoid being effectively governed such as Enron's accounting, banks' credit-default swaps, or a teenager's reasons behind a bad grade. The Inscrutable Defense ("It's too complicated to explain") does not absolve a firm from responsibility, otherwise firms would have an incentive to create complicated systems to avoid accountability. Firms and individuals are held accountable for decisions and products that are difficult to explain. Some cars are designed to be maintained by anyone including the owner; others are designed to require a professional license where the manufacturer takes on responsibility to ensure the car is working properly. Importantly, firms develop products *knowing* they are going to be held accountable.

According to the argument herein, inscrutable algorithms – designed to be difficult to under-stand and argued to be hard to explain – may force greater accountability on the designer to own the algorithmic decision since their design of the algorithm has precluded anyone else from taking on a larger role in the decision when in use. Previous arguments against algorithmic transparency have centered on pitting fairness against accuracy or as being inefficient or just difficult to accom-plish (Ananny and Crawford 2016; Jones 2017; Kroll et al. 2017). Creating inscrutable algorithms precludes users from taking responsibility for the ethical implications identified above and places the responsibility of the ethical implications on the firm who developed the algorithm. The design of the algorithm not only scripts what users can do but also the reasonable expectations of users to take responsibility for the use of the algorithm.

2. *Why Firms Are Responsible for the Algorithms They Develop*

Within the arguments of this article, the onus now shifts to the developer of the algorithm to take responsibility for not only the ethical implications of the algorithm in use but also how roles will be delegated in making a decision. Alternatively, developers can design the algorithm to allow users to take responsibility for algorithmic decisions. However, the responsibility for such design decisions is on the knowledgeable and uniquely positioned developers. This obligation is based on two arguments. First, a firm's obligation for the ethical implications of an algorithm is created because the firm is knowledgeable as to the design decisions and is in a unique position to inscribe the algorithm with the value-laden biases as well as roles and responsibilities of the algorithmic decision. Developers are those most capable of enacting change in the design and are sometimes the *only* individuals in a position to change the algorithm. In other words, by willingly creating an algorithm that works in a value-laden and particular manner, firms voluntarily become a party to the decision system and take on the responsibility of the decision to include the harms created, principles violated, and rights diminished by the decision system. How much responsibility and for what acts depends on how the algorithm is designed. In fact, as is argued here, the more the algorithm is constructed as inscrutable and autonomous, the *more* accountability attributed to the algorithm and the firm that designed the algorithm.

Second, an obligation is created when the firm developing the algorithm willingly enters into the decision context by selling the algorithm for a specific purpose. Selling an algorithm to the courts to be a risk assessment tool creates an obligation for the firm as a member of the criminal justice community. In social contract terms, firms that develop algorithms are members of the community to which they sell the algorithm – e.g., criminal justice, medicine, education, human resources, military, etc – and create an obligation to respect the norms of the community as a member (Donaldson and Dunfee 1994). If a company does not wish to abide by the norms of the decision (e.g., being transparent for due process rights of defendants) or be accountable for the moral consequences and rights impacted by a pivotal decision in society, then the firm should not be in that business and not sell the algorithm into that particular context. By entering the market, the firm voluntarily takes on the rules of that market including the norms of the decisions it is facilitating.

For example, the decision to manufacture drones for the military created an obligation for defense contractors to understand the rules of engagement for our military using the drones. For a company developing manufacturing equipment, the designer must understand how the plant worker can be expected to work given not only the laws governing safety but also the norms of the industry (this is normally called human factors engineering). Algorithms are no different: when companies decide to develop and sell algorithms within a decision context, the organization willingly takes on the obligation to understand the values of the decision to ensure the algorithms' ethical implications is congruent with the context.

Notes

1. Latour, Akrich, this article, and others (Martin and Freeman 2004) remain outside the technological determinism versus social constructivism divide. As Akrich notes: "technological determinism pays no attention to what is brought together, and ultimately replaced, by the structural effects of a network. By contrast social constructivism denies the obduracy of objects and assumes that only people can have the status of actors" (p. 206). Martin and Freeman rightly separate the idea of technology's value-laden-ness and social control as independent attributes: a technology can have a value-laden bias while also being influenced by society in general and by individuals.
2. A recent example concerning crash tests and female crash-test dummies confirms this longstanding issue (Shaver 2012). Cars were only designed and tested for the safety of men until 2011.
3. As Latour notes, "we have delegated….to the hinge the work of reversibly solving the wall-hole dilemma" (Latour 1992, 155).
4. In this way, Latour notes that technology – including algorithms – is anthropomorphic: "first, it has been made by humans; second, it substitutes for the actions of people and is a delegate that permanently occupies the position of a human; and third, it shapes human action by prescribing back" what humans should do (p. 160).
5. As Ackrich notes, "two vital questions start to come into focus. The first has to do with the extent to which the composition of a technical object constrains acants in the way they relate to both the object and to one another. The second concerns the character of these actants and their links, the extent to which they are able to reshape the object, and the various ways in which the object may be used. Once considered in this way, the boundary between the inside and the outside of an object comes to be seen as a *consequence* of such interaction rather than something that determines it." (Akrich 1992).
6. Interesting challenges arise for algorithms with learning capacities, as they defy the traditional conception of designer responsibility–programmers see themselves as less involved in the final product since the algorithm 'learns' from the data rather than being 100% coded directly by the programmer. See also Mittelstadt et al (2016).

References

Akrich, Madeleine. 1992. "The De-Scription of Technological Objects." In *Shaping Technology/Building Society: Studies in Sociotechnical Change*, edited by Wiebe Bijker and John Law, 205–24. Cambridge, MA: MIT Press.

Ananny, Mike, and Kate Crawford. 2016. "Seeing without Knowing: Limitations of the Transparency Ideal and Its Application to Algorithmic Accountability." *New Media & Society*, 1461444816676645. https://doi.org/10.1177/1461444816676645.

Barocas, Solon, Sophie Hood, and Malte Ziewitz. 2013. "Governing Algorithms: A Provocation Piece." http://dx.doi.org/10.2139/ssrn.2245322.

Desai, Deven R, and Joshua A Kroll. 2017. "Trust But Verify: A Guide to Algorithms and the Law." *Harvard Journal of Law and Technology*. https://papers.ssrn.com/sol3/papers.cfm?abstract_id=2959472.

Donaldson, Thomas, and Thomas W Dunfee. 1994. "Toward a Unified Conception of Business Ethics: Integrative Social Contracts Theory." *Academy of Management Review* 19 (2): 252–84.

Friedman, Batya, and Helen Nissenbaum. 1996. "Bias in Computer Systems." *ACM Transactions on Information Systems (TOIS)* 14 (3): 330–47.

Introna, Lucas D. 2016. "Algorithms, Governance, and Governmentality: On Governing Academic Writing." *Science, Technology, & Human Values* 41 (1): 17–49.

Johnson, Deborah G. 2004. "Is the Global Information Infrastructure a Democratic Technology?" *Readings in Cyberethics* 18: 121.

Johnson, Deborah G, and Merel Noorman. 2014. "Artefactual Agency and Artefactual Moral Agency." In *The Moral Status of Technical Artefacts*, 143–58. Springer.

Jones, Meg Leta. 2017. "A Right to a Human in the Loop: Legal Constructions of Computer Automation & Personhood from Data Banks to Algorithms." *Social Studies of Science* 47 (2): 216–39.

Kraemer, Felicitas, Kees Van Overveld, and Martin Peterson. 2011. "Is There an Ethics of Algorithms?" *Ethics and Information Technology* 13 (3): 251–60.

Kramer, Sarah. 2017. "An Algorithm Is Replacing Bail Hearings in New Jersey." Motherboard. February 23, 2017. https://motherboard.vice.com/en_us/article/an-algorithm-is-replacing-bail-hearings-in-new-jersey.

Kroll, Joshua A, Joanna Huey, Solon Barocas, Edward W Felten, Joel R Reidenberg, David G Robinson, and Harlan Yu. 2017. "Accountable Algorithms." *University of Pennsylvania Law Review* 165. https://papers.ssrn.com/sol3/papers.cfm?abstract_id=2765268.

Latour, Bruno. 1992. "Where Are the Missing Masses? The Sociology of a Few Mundane Artifacts." In *Shaping Technology/Building Society: Studies in Sociotechnical Change*, edited by Wiebe Bijker and John Law, 225–58. Cambridge, MA: MIT Press.

Martin, Kirsten, and R Edward Freeman. 2004. "The Separation of Technology and Ethics in Business Ethics." *Journal of Business Ethics* 53 (4): 353–64.

Mittelstadt, Brent Daniel, Patrick Allo, Mariarosaria Taddeo, Sandra Wachter, and Luciano Floridi. 2016. "The Ethics of Algorithms: Mapping the Debate." *Big Data & Society* 3 (2): 1–21.

Neyland, Daniel. 2016. "Bearing Account-Able Witness to the Ethical Algorithmic System." *Science, Technology & Human Values* 41 (1): 50–76.

Rudner, Richard. 1953. "The Scientist qua Scientist Makes Value Judgments." *Philosophy of Science* 20 (1): 1–6.

Shaver, Katherine. 2012. "Female Dummy Makes Her Mark on Male-Dominated Crash Tests." Washington Post. March 25, 2012. https://www.washingtonpost.com/local/trafficandcommuting/female-dummy-makes-her-mark-on-male-dominated-crash-tests/2012/03/07/gIQANBLjaS_story.html

Tufekci, Zeynep. 2015. "Algorithmic Harms beyond Facebook and Google: Emergent Challenges of Computational Agency." *J. on Telecomm. & High Tech. L.* 13: 203.

Winner, Langdon. 1980. "Do Artifacts Have Politics?" *Daedalus* 109 (1): 121–36.

Ziewitz, Malte. 2016. "Governing Algorithms Myth, Mess, and Methods." *Science, Technology & Human Values* 41 (1): 3–16.

Index